D1514725

Gabay's Copywriters' Compendium

The definitive professional writer's guide

J. Jonathan Gabay

ELSEVIER
BUTTERWORTH
HEINEMANN

AMSTERDAM · BOSTON · HEIDELBERG · LONDON · NEW YORK · OXFORD
PARIS · SAN DIEGO · SAN FRANCISCO · SINGAPORE · SYDNEY · TOKYO

Elsevier Butterworth-Heinemann
Linacre House, Jordan Hill, Oxford OX2 8DP
30 Corporate Drive, Burlington, MA 01803

First published 2005
Reprinted 2006

British Library Cataloguing in Publication Data
A catalogue record for this book is available from the British Library

Library of Congress Cataloguing in Publication Data
A catalogue record for this book is available from the Library of Congress

ISBN 0 7506 6402 9

For information on all Elsevier Butterworth-Heinemann
publications visit our website at www.books.elsevier.com

Working together to grow
libraries in developing countries

www.elsevier.com | www.bookaid.org | www.sabre.org

ELSEVIER   BOOK AID International   Sabre Foundation

Printed and bound in Great Britain

*This book is dedicated to my
wonderful sister Brenda
who passed away whilst I wrote it.
Her love of life and for her family,
was far deeper than
any words could ever describe.*

May she at last find peace.

With thanks to Nicki Sneath and Tim Goodfellow for
believing in this project, the brilliant Simon Brewster and
Jacqueline Palmer of Grand Union Design, John Haslam for
his witty illustrations, Sarel Jansen for cover photography,
Helen and Greig for their editorial support and Maurice
Benzimra for his guidance and ingenuity.

Contents

Introduction   page 6

1   The creative briefing process   page 11
Write and deliver the perfect creative brief.

2   Mind your Ps and Qs   page 21
Tell people exactly where to stick their apostrophes,
as well as every other punctuation mark.

3   Why use ten words when one will do?   page 57
Choose the appropriate word for the right occasion.

4   Is it 'its' or 'it's'?   page 75
The bare necessities to sort out your 'bear' from
your 'bare'.

5   Spell well   page 153
An 'A' to 'Z' of words which would otherwise drive
you to your nearest dictionary.

6   Consonants divided by continents.   page 167
UK v US language.

7   Do you speak marketese?   page 191
Draw the 'line', 'above' or 'below',
on marketing gobbledegook.

8   Idioms make the heart grow fonder...   page 225
From meanings you can't grasp to
headlines you'll want to grab.

9   Clichés   page 257
Fresh thinking on old ideas.

10   Metaphors   page 275
Painting a thousand pictures with just a few words.

11   Similes   page 325
As useful as you make them.

12   Would you rather be cuddly or plump?   page 393
     It's all in the euphemism.
     (How to say what you dare not utter.)

13   Portmanteaus   page 407
     Proof that two words are better in one.

14   All together now   page 423
     What do you call a group of ...?

15   Rhyme time   page 433
     Rhyme and its reason.

16   Tongue twisters   page 461
     Keep your copy straight and your tongue in a twist.

17   Words from the wise   page 471
     Quotations that inspire.

18   The business of quotes   page 529
     Shrewd words mean better business.

19   Is it a bird? Is it a plane? No, it's a sloganeer   page 575
     Writing compelling slogans.

20   Today's the day...   page 605
     Link your special occasion with other notable
     dates in history.

21   A world of facts   page 649
     An overview of useful facts for your next
     creative project.

22   Top tips   page 671
     Additional trade secrets.

     Useful contacts   page 694

     Index   page 697

Introduction

The other day I was looking through some files and came across a definition of a copywriter which I wrote for the Chartered Institute of Marketing. Although I scribbled it some years ago, I still firmly believe that the explanation holds true today.

Copywriting does not just concern writing: it is about reaching into the hearts and minds of a marketplace through building bridges between what you market and what the consumer needs.

Each rivet of the bridge is reinforced with powerful propositions demonstrating how your product or service enhances a market's individuality and aspirations.

Once the bridge is built, existing customers and new clients can feel in touch, empowered and energised to take full advantage of the choices you offer and their rights to enjoy them.

As you refer to Gabay's Copywriters' Compendium, keep my definition in mind. Follow its principle and I guarantee that your chosen words will find the audience they were always intended to capture.

Good luck

Have genius, will travel – far

Do you want to drive your copywriting ambitions further? Whether you're a marketing student or work in advertising, public relations, journalism, design or business generally, you've come to the right place.

Over the last three decades, I've culled some of the greatest, surefire, 'inside the business' secrets on writing clear and compelling copy. Much of what I've learned has come from working at some of the biggest award-winning advertising agencies in the world, for many of the most demanding clients who insist on great copy and creative thinking.

Most recently as a member of the Faculty at the Chartered Institute of Marketing, and working in collaboration with other pan-European training bodies, I have taught copywriting and creative thinking techniques to many hundreds of Europe's most successful marketing professionals. In return many have shared their own tips, based on real-life scenarios, in just about every industry sector. Now I aim to show you the most fundamental lessons.

Rather than letting this compendium gather dust as a textbook on your book shelves, I suggest that you keep it to hand like a useful dictionary. In no time it should be a dog-eared mainstay of your work space, ready to be dipped into and flicked through as and when you fancy.

For example, if you happen to be writing a press release and need some quick help with grammar, simply dip into the 'Mind your Ps and Qs section' (Chapter 2) which offers a handy, at-a-glance overview of grammar and punctuation.

Or, for example, if you should come across a question concerning that bane of all conscientious writers – dreaded spelling – just look up the infuriating word in the 'Spell well' section (Chapter 5) where you can confirm your gut feelings – or worst fears!

The broad range of subjects covered in this book has been carefully chosen based on the feedback that I have had from professionals and students – as well as of course from my own experience. In addition to the core subjects, I'll be offering you 'quick lessons' aimed at helping you put your knowledge into practice. And for wannabe copywriters there will be attainable skills to help you take the next step up that soaring career ladder.

When the pressure is really on, you can turn to my 'Top tips' throughout the book under the heading of 'Gabay at a glance' as well as more in-depth tips in chapter 22.

General tips throughout the books include:

Top tips for great awareness ads

Top tips for brainstorming

Top tips to sell innovative copy

Top tips for writing reports

Top tips for thinking creatively

Top tips for great web copy

Top tips for great direct mail letters

Top tips for viral copy

Top tips for radio ads

Top tips for press release writing

Top tips for response advertising

Top tips for packaging copy

Top tips for point-of-sale copy

Top tips for great brochure copy

Top tips for poster copy

Top tips for multi-media copy

Top tips for video scripting.

Phew!

Sound good? Then if you're ready to super-charge your copy, please turn the page and we'll start at one of the most crucial of all copywriting skills – the ability to write and interpret a brief.

1. The creative briefing process

There's a famous quotation that often 'does the rounds' at marketing agencies. It comes from Abraham Lincoln, who said, 'If I had nine hours to chop down a tree I would spend the first three hours sharpening my axe.'

Briefs help you to sort out actual facts from personal opinions (let's face it, everyone who gets involved in writing copy has heard lots of those!).

It is essential that you agree a brief with whoever commissioned you, even down to 'signing it off'. This is because a brief should be treated with respect, as if it was a written contract.

In fact, even if the only person commissioning anyone is yourself, you should still write a brief because it helps you to focus completely on the task at hand.

Need more help?
www.gabaywords.com

The creative briefing process

Briefs help you to focus. Many argue that they are only useful for external agencies. On the contrary, I believe that briefs really come into their own for small to medium sized businesses juggling lots of tasks.

Overall, briefs help to separate personal opinion from facts. Here are some of the best:

Briefing form for direct mail letter writing

The full letter brief

1   Describe your audience (age, sector, job titles, etc).

2   What's the key benefit making your offer distinctive:
    The Unique Selling Point?

3   Has the audience heard from you before?
    If so, when and how often? (provide examples)

4   What is the featured offer, as opposed to the distinctive benefit?
    For example, are you offering price cuts or tie-in discounts
    with partner companies?

5   Explain the product's or service's:

    • strengths
    • weaknesses
    • opportunities
    • threats

    (See **SWOT**)

6   How do you want people to feel about your brand? (have you
    conducted any research to show how they currently feel?)

7   List the three most common customer descriptions that come
    to mind when people discuss dealing with your company.

8   Is your product or service a daily essential or does the
    concept need a detailed description?

9   Can you discuss your service's/product's associated benefits?
    (rank them from sixth to first place)

Loquacious language:

illatration – the act of barking at someone or something.

10 Name your top three competitors.

11 Provide recent examples of their work.

12 Are you testing elements of the letter? (this could include special offers, geographic distribution tests, response device tests or specific recipient type tests – e.g. job titles).

13 What action (such as dialing a telephone number) do you want the reader to take?

14 Are there any size/length restrictions?

15 When are you going to post your letter and to whom?

16 Are there any restrictions to take into consideration? (such as legal requirements).

17 When do you expect to see the letter copy?

18 Do you expect a first draft or completed letter?

19 Who will approve the final text?

The shorter letter brief

Give me five

1 What's in it for the reader?

2 Why is this service/product so different from any other on the market?

3 How will it improve the reader's life/work/education/finances/health...?

4 Why can't the competition match it?

5 What do you want the reader to do next?

The classic S W O T

Describe your product's or service's: **S**trengths *and* **W**eaknesses

Highlight any market: **O**pportunities

Pinpoint possible: **T**hreats

Etymology:

drama (c. 1515) – prior to this date most English plays were about religious issues. Following the introduction of plays based on ancient classical Greek themes, words such as 'drama', 'chorus', 'tragedy', 'orchestra', 'irony' and 'critic' were introduced to help describe the new content.

The S O S T A C method

S   Situation
    Describe where you are at the moment.

O   Objectives
    Describe where you want to be.

S   Strategy
    *Describe your overall thinking and how you will
    reach your goals.*

T   Tactics or Targets
    *Describe specific methods to reach your goals –
    for example, direct mail.*

A   Actions
    What do you want to see next?

C   Control
    How will you measure effectiveness?

The seven steps to understanding (research brief)

1   Consider your objectives. Unless in the case of exploratory
    research, restrict yourself to questions which are directly
    connected to your objectives.

2   Which creative research best reveals the answers you need?
    (be prepared for conditional conclusions)

3   Ensure that you and/or your researcher are fully briefed as to the
    kind and depth of information sought.

4   Understand the complete purpose of the research, including the
    commercial and creative implications of alternative findings.

5   Compare findings against previous research studies.

6   Interpret your findings creatively from a copywriting perspective
    rather than purely methodically.

7   Act upon your research.

    Once you have completed each of the seven stages, plan periodic
    reviews by exploring changes in the market, and then consider
    how your copy can adapt accordingly.

Writers' words:

'You write *from* what you know, but you write *in* what you *don't* know.' (Grace Paley)

Doors towards greater creativity

Design agencies often refer to the 'House of Creativity'. The house (which could be based on actual locations) has four rooms. Each represents an inspirational approach towards answering a creative brief.

The room of great works, such as an art gallery, contains outstanding examples of design from a variety of sources.

The room of reason, such as a research establishment, contains hard facts and figures relating to the project at hand.

The room of precedent contains previous examples of work by your company and/or competitors.

Once you have entered (either metaphorically – or literally) every other room, this empty room, **The room of the unknown,** offers infinite space to be as imaginative as you wish.

The straightforward copy brief

- What's the big message?
  (for example, you may be selling insurance, but the big message is – 'gain peace of mind')
- What's needed?
  - A press advertisement
  - Leaflet
  - Brochure
  - etc.

  (for each of the above, describe dimensions and print restrictions)
- What's on sale?
- What is the Unique Selling Point? (or Point of Difference).
- What's the Emotional Selling Point? (aspect that people personally identify with).
- Who wants it?
- What do you want the readers to do?
- What do they get out of it?
- When and where will the communication appear?

Medieval words:

beyond the pale – a social reject who must remain outside the paling fences, therefore is unprotected by the community.

- How much can you afford on creativity?
- What's the format?
- What's the background?
- What's next and when?

Website copy brief

For the front page (homepage)

The 'elevator test': write a description of what your website contains, what your company offers and who the website is aimed at (including why), all of which could be read in 40 seconds (approx. 120 words).

Gabay at a glance:

When writing copy for a service similar to one offered by your competitor, put yourself in your readers' shoes.

Consider their:

Position

Aim
- the connotation of that aim, in term of specific requirements.

Specific requirements - the advantage of being associated with your brand.

Benefits - of a long-term commercial partnership.

For individual sections of the site

Divide your website according the types of surfers who will view each section.

Then complete the following:

This section of my website needs to…

- … convince _____
- … to _____
- … because _____
- Evidence: _____
- Must include: _____

For example:

This section of my website needs to…

> … **convince** Dave, the student from Manchester
>
> … **to** surf my football site instead of *footballfans.com*
>
> … **because** it has all the sports news and views.
>
> **Evidence:** Editorial is direct from 150 colleges – by students for students.
>
> **Must include:** All the latest football fixtures

Then follow the same principles throughout the site.

Metaphors:

Power is poison. – Henry Adams, *The Education of Henry Adams*

Branding positioning copy brief

Identify your audience's:

- behaviour
- attitudes
- demographics
- psychographics.

Psychographics example

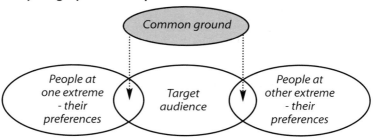

1   Problem or need being addressed

2   How does the competition address this?

3   Target benefits (ranked)

    1
    2
    3

4   How can those benefits be supported?

5   Describe your brand's personality, for example:

    - warm and friendly
    - smart and modern
    - traditional and cautious
    - other.

6   If the brand could be personified by a well know celebrity, who would it be and why?

7   Positioning statement, for example:

    My brand is for these types of people _____
    Aiming at achieving _____
    Given a choice of competitors, my brand is outstanding because _____
    I can support this claim because _____

Loquacious language:

iotacist – a person who makes excessive use of the letter 'I'.

Leaflet and brochure copy platform brief

- Purpose – my company's real motives
- My reader's real motive
- Key issue: if the reader only remembers one thing, what will it be?
- Audience
  - Who is my primary reader?
  - What does my reader need to know about the subject?
  - What's in it for my reader?
  - What's the angle? Technical? Lifestyle? etc
  - What's my reader's attitude towards the topic?

Last, but not least, take heed of Rudyard Kipling who wrote:

"I keep six honest serving-men
(They taught me all I knew);
Their names are What and Why and When
And How and Where and Who."

(from *'Elephant's Child'*, *Just So Stories*, Rudyard Kipling, 1902)

These lines have inspired many copy briefs, including the 'copy triangle' brief, appealing to copywriters who prefer to plan out briefs diagrammatically:

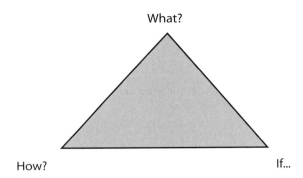

What?

How?   If...

Here's the 'copy triangle' in action. Imagine you were writing about a new Internet property finding service called HomE, aimed at first time homebuyers.

'What does ...' questions would deal with the service offerings.

For example:

- *What does HomE offer in terms of finding a new home?*
  It finds homes based on price, location, and type.

- *What does HomE offer in terms of securing a mortgage?*
  It offers the latest mortgage prices from the country's leading and most competitive mortgage lenders.

- *What does HomE offer in terms of legal moving property costs?*
  It offers an all-in-one property moving service – at the click of a button.

Then, it's a matter of demonstrating **'how can'** individual features be upgraded into reader benefits – from the reader's viewpoint. Perhaps:

- *How can you (the reader) access HomE?*
- *How can you book an appointment to view a property?*
- *How can you be sure that you are getting the best value mortgage?*

The final part of your creative triangle is **'what if'**:

- *What if a buyer could search, view and complete a property purchase project all in one place?*
- *What if a seller could market a property throughout the country, offering viewings twenty-four hours a day?*

The more **'what if'** questions, the greater your ability to stretch your imagination, fuelled with answers driven by your product's or service's features and benefits.

One final point to remember about briefs: think of them as legal contracts that must be approved in writing by the person who asks you to complete the task.

Loquacious language:

jactance – boasting

Brains, pen, action!

1   Write a brief to relaunch the toothpaste you used this morning – as a version for pets.

2   Read a piece of copy from one of your competitors. Now write a brief for it.

3   Read the briefs in this chapter, then amalgamate the parts which you like best to form your own briefing form.

Questions?
answers@gabaywords.com

Etymology:

utopia (c. 1516) – from Thomas More's book of the same title, which tells of an idealistic society.

2. Mind your Ps and Qs

Whenever I talk to students about grammar, faces fall and interest wanes. So what's the big deal with punctuation? As you will see in this chapter, grammar really is all about common sense. Rather like learning your alphabet, once you've got it, you'll never stop using it!

Hopefully these pages will help turn that look on your face to pure delight.

Enjoy!

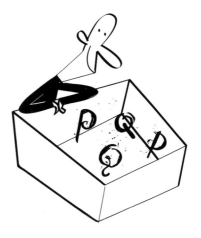

Need more help?
www.gabaywords.com

Mind your Ps and Qs

A guide to English grammar

There are lots of books about English grammar – enough to fill several libraries. Many linguists disagree on the basic rules. There are also differences in the classification and terminology used.

Hopefully this chapter will help to settle some old questions, but it may also raise a few new ones. The chapter provides a straightforward examination of the basic principles of English grammar, as well as looking at important issues of style – encompassing texts, numbers and dates – and punctuation.

The parts of speech

We'll start with the smallest parts and work our way up to the largest parts: sentences and paragraphs.

Vowels and consonants

There are five vowels: *a, e, i, o* and *u*. The remaining letters are called consonants. The problems of English spelling are due to the fact that the letter 'a', for example, can be long or short depending on which word it is in, what letters appear either side of it and what accent you speak with. Likewise the letter 'g' can be hard or soft. Compare the two letter 'gs' in the word engaged. (See chapter 5 Spell well for a guide to some common spelling errors and what you can do to avoid these.)

Words

Words are made up of letters representing the vowel and consonant sounds. Words make up phrases and clauses, which together form sentences. Words can be classified as verbs, nouns, prepositions, pronouns, conjunctions, adjectives and adverbs. Let's look at each of these in turn.

Verbs

In simple terms, verbs can be described as 'action words' or 'doing words', for example: *to be; to think; to run; to hold*. Every sentence should have a verb; without one, it wouldn't make sense.

Chiasmus:

'The tank was originally invented to clear a way for the infantry in the teeth of machine-gun fire. Now it is the infantry who will have to clear a way for the tanks.' Winston Churchill

Transitive and intransitive verbs

There are two kinds of verb usage: transitive and intransitive. Your choice of usage is mainly dependent on what other elements are to be used within the sentence.

Verbs that can be used without objects, such as *'appear', 'go', 'fall'* and *'rise'*, are called intransitive verbs.

> *I'm leaving.*
> *He is cooking.*
> *She died.*
> *We usually walk.*

Transitive verbs must have an object, as in:

> *I'm leaving my car here.*
> *He is cooking a meal.*
> *I need help.*
> *I use my computer.*

As you can see, many verbs can be used either transitively or intransitively.

The tense of a verb shows when the action takes place: present, past or future.

Present and past participles

Verbs with the ending *'...ed'* and *'...en'* are known as past participles, and those ending in *'...ing'* are know as present participles. (the *'...ing'* form is also known as a gerund). These verbs are used, as shown here, with the auxiliary verbs *'to be'* and *'to have'*:

> *I have **eaten** my dinner.*
> *I have **washed** my hair.*
> *I am **walking**.*
> *I have **been** camping.*

The participle does not change its form; it is the auxiliary verb that changes tense to show when the action takes place.

Just to confuse matters, these gerunds can become nouns, depending on the function of the word in the sentence, for example:

> ***Walking** is good exercise.*

'Walking' is the noun and *'is'* is the verb.

Loquacious language:

jape – a practical joke

Present tense

This deals with current happenings, for example:

*I **love** my teddy bear.*
*I **play** football with my friends.*

The present tense can also show what is currently occurring and continues to occur. The present tense of the verb *'to be'* (I am, you are, she/he/it is, we are, they are) is used along with the present participle '…ing'.

*The policemen are **inspecting** the grounds of the country house.*

Past tense

This is used when the action has already occurred, and is formed by adding '…ed' to the stem of the verb.

*I **loved** my teddy bear.*
*I **played** football with my friends.*

The past tense can also show what has finished happening. Moreover, the present tense of the verb *'to have'* (I have, you have, she/he/it has, we have, they have) is used along with the past participle '…ed' or '…en'.

*The policemen **have inspected** the grounds of the country house.*

Future tense

This relates to future actions. To form this tense *will* or *shall* is placed before the verb. Technically, you should use the following in formal writing:

I shall
you will
he/she/it will
we shall
you will
they will

…but in spoken form this is being lost.

To add emphasis, the sequence is reversed.

I will
you shall
he/she/it shall
we will
you shall
they shall

Etymology:

start-up (c. 1517) – originally a boot worn by peasants. Later used to describe a gaiter or legging (from the phrase 'start up', as in 'a shoe that starts up to the middle of the leg').

For example:

> I **shall** drown and no-one **will** save me (a cry for help)
> I **will** drown and no-one **shall** save me (defiant last words
> of someone about to commit suicide)

A related aspect of the future tense, known as the 'conditional tense', is formed by putting *should* or *would* before the verb. This indicates a future action which relies on something else. Its follows the same rules as shall and will.

> I **should** like to see you after the meeting.
> They **should** report the incident to the police.
> I **would** like to join the party.
> I **should** respect the court's decision.

The conditional tense can also be used to mean 'ought to'.

> You **ought** to behave yourself.

Irregular verbs

Some verbs do not follow the standard rules just mentioned. Here is a selection of such verbs.

Function	Past tense	Past participle
to see	saw	(have) seen
to eat	ate	(have) eaten

Nouns

At school you might have learnt that nouns are 'things' or 'names of things'. *The Oxford English Dictionary (OED)* offers a more concise description: 'a word (other than a pronoun) used to identify any of a class of people, places, or things (**common noun**) or to name a particular one of these (**proper noun**).'

Nouns are classified in different and contrasting ways:

Common nouns Names of ordinary things, e.g. boy, boat, dog.

Proper nouns Names of places, people and specific things, e.g. Heinz™, Moscow, New York.

Abstract nouns Intangible things, e.g. sadness, justice, colour, happiness.

Concrete nouns Tangible things, e.g. table, chair, door.

Countable nouns Nouns that can be made plural, i.e. you can place a number before them, e.g. ten apples, three children.

Uncountable nouns
  Nouns that are always singular, e.g. milk, information.

Loquacious language:

jejune – something which is short on interesting content

This distinction is important when deciding whether the verb that goes with the noun takes the plural form or the singular form. Compare, for example:

>*Ham **is** nice.*
>*Apples **are** nice.*
>*None of the apples **are** rotten.*
>*None of the ham **is** off.*

For collective nouns see Chapter 14 'All together now'. The basic rule is that a collective noun is always regarded as a single item. For example:

*The **fleet** was anchored outside Portsmouth.*
*The **management** is in charge.*

Articles

definite article (*the*)
>This is a specific item.

indefinite article ('*a*' or '*an*')
>These are not specific items.
>Use '*a*' before a word that starts with a consonant, e.g. *a boat, a bat, a dog.*

>Use '*an*' before a word that starts with a vowel (e.g. *an animal, an apple*) or a silent *h* (e.g. *an heir, an honour*).

Pronouns

Personal pronouns

These replace common or proper nouns so that you don't have to repeat the noun each time the person or thing is mentioned.

>***Maurice met Sarah. He spoke to her gently.***

Personal pronouns come in pairs: *I/me, you/you, he/him, she/her, it/it, we/us, they/them.*

Things can get a little baffling when you refer to more than one person in a sentence. Which of these is correct?

>*My friend and me like steak.*
>*My friend and I like steak.*

Chiasmus:

'Cultivated people harmonize without imitating. Immature people imitate without harmonizing.'
Confucius Analects--13.23

To find the right version all you have to do is split the two people like this:

> My **friend** likes steak. **I** also like steak.
> My friend and I like steak. ✔

But what about this?

> You have upset your father and I deeply. ✘
> You have upset your father and me deeply. ✔

Initially you would think that '*I*' is grammatically correct, but because it is the object of the verb rather than the subject, '*me*' is the in fact correct.

Between you and I?

Here is another common copywriting error to watch out for: Is it '*between you and I*' or '*between you and me*'? The way to settle this one is to think of the pronouns as a pair. So, *you and I* means *we* and *you and me* means *us*. So, you may conclude that *between you and I* really means *between we*. However that doesn't make sense! So the correct answer has to be *between you and me*.

Another slip to watch for is the use of the pronoun *myself*. The following is correct:

> I ate by myself.

Myself never replaces *me* or *I*.

> Myself and my friend went on holiday. ✘
> My friend and I went on holiday. ✔

Likewise, *ourselves* should never be used in replacement of *we* or *us*.

> There was a meeting between ourselves and the management. ✘
> There was a meeting between the management and us. ✔

Demonstrative pronouns

These are *this* and *that*, and *these* and *those*. Demonstrative pronouns represent the verb's subject.

> This is a good shop.
> That was a good game.
> These are good times.
> Those were good times.

Note: *this* and *these* relate to the present tense.

Etymology:

---

torpedo (c. 1520) – a fish with a cigar-shaped body and tapered tail and the ability to emits electric shocks

Interrogative pronouns

Who and *whom* are used in questions. Contrary to popular belief, they are not interchangeable. *Who* is the subject of a sentence that asks a question. *Whom* is the objective of a verb within the question.

To help you sort out your *who* from your *whom*, work out a likely answer. If it embraces 'I', 'he', 'she', 'we' or 'they', treat it like this:

> **Q:** *Who went to the fair?*
> **A:** *They went to the fair.*

If instead the answer is likely to be 'me', 'him', 'her', 'us' or 'them', use *whom*.

> **Q:** *To whom did you show the copy?*
> **A:** *I showed the copy to her.*

Gabay at a Glance

In practice, whom is hardly used in spoken English. On the other hand, when it comes to copy for reports or brochures, many companies insist on whom being accurately used.

More on pronouns

Possessive	my, mine, your, yours
Example:	Here is your watch.
Reflexive	myself, himself, yourself, herself
Example:	I appealed to the client himself.
Reciprocal	each other, one another
Example:	My sister and I share one another's clothes.
Relative	which, who, that
Example:	Who is your favourite movie star?
Indefinite (and numerical)	some, both
Examples:	He has some friends. You can have both books.

Adjectives

These are words which describe nouns in terms of shape, colour, size, and so on.

> *The red car.*
> *The large boat.*
> *The small kitten.*

Brand origins:

Sony – originally the company was named 'Tokyo Tsushin Kogo'. However the founder Akio Morita felt the name didn't really 'roll off the tongue'. Combining the Latin word for sound 'sonus' and the cheerful word 'sunny', he produced the portmanteau 'Sony' (see portmanteau on p407).

Compound adjectives

When two adjectives are linked by a hyphen (see Punctuation on p.33) the resulting word is called a compound adjective.

> *The red-stained carpet.*
> *The blue-eyed baby.*

Without the hyphen, the meaning of these examples would be completely different. *The red, stained carpet* is not the same as *the red-stained carpet.*

Comparative and superlative adjectives

To form the comparative and superlative features of an adjective, apply the following rules:

- For adjectives with one syllable just add '*-er*' to make them comparative. To make them superlative, simply add, '*-est*'.
  cool, cooler, coolest
- Where there is a single vowel before the last consonant, the last letter is doubled before adding '*-er*' or '*-est*'.
  big, bigger, biggest
- There are some exceptions. When the last consonant is '*w*' or '*g*" it should be a single letter.
  low, lower, lowest
- When the adjective has two syllables and ends in '*y*', the '*y*' is changed into '*i*' and then '*-er*' or '*-est*' is added.
  happy, happier, happiest
- In some cases – adjectives with two syllables and in all cases with three or more syllables – write '*more*' or '*most*'.
  beautiful, more beautiful, most beautiful

In instances where the comparison relates to two similar or identical things, you should apply comparative adjectives.

> *Mine is bigger than yours!*

When the comparison relates to three or more identical things, you should use the superlative adjective.

> *This is the finest china in the store.*

Then there are the completely irregular ones, but don't get flustered!

> *bad, worse, worst*
> *good, better, best*

Chiasmus:

'Life imitates art far more than art imitates life.' Oscar Wilde

Adjectival suffixes

A suffix is an ending added to a word that produces another word. Here are some suffixes that can be added to nouns to make adjectives:

-able, -ible   *audible, suitable, fashionable.*

-ous, -eous, -ious   *spacious, gaseous, virtuous.*

-y   *handy, wealthy, healthy, lucky.*

The suffix '-ed' forms adjectives from noun phrases.

open-minded, long-haired.

Adverbs

These mostly refer to verbs and are used to describe the detail of the actions.

The storm was blowing strongly.
The train was travelling slowly.

Note: there are instances when the same word can be used as both an adverb and an adjective.

Adverb: *He ran **fast**.*
Adjective: *He ran past a **fast** squirrel.*

Adverbs can further be used to qualify adjectives. However, make sure you position them in the correct place to ensure the intended meaning. If you don't position the adverb in the right place, the meaning can be completely different.

*The car needs servicing **badly**. (This implies that the service should be bad.)*
*The car **badly** needs servicing. (This states that the car requires a service, urgently.)*

Adverbial suffixes

The suffix '-ly' is added to adjectives to make adverbs.

fearfully, madly, quietly

If the adjective ends in '-ic' the suffix is '-ically'.

heroically, economically

The suffix -'wise' is added to nouns to make adverbs.

moneywise, clockwise.

Loquacious language:

karmadharaya – a compound word in which the first section of the word describes the second section, for example 'steamboat'

Prepositions

These usually go before nouns and pronouns showing their link to the rest of the sentence. There are three kinds of preposition:

1. Simple: *to, over, inside, under, up, between, in, on, with.*

Examples:

> *The girl gave chocolates to her friend.*
> *The ball went over the wall.*

2. Complex, containing two words: *ahead of, near to, due to, except for.*

Examples:

> *The spread of the disease was due to poor hygiene.*
> *All was well except for the agency's attitude.*
> *The winning horse was ahead of the rest.*

3. Complex, containing three words: *in accordance with, in addition to, on behalf of.*

Examples:

> *The group met in accordance with instructions.*
> *The celebrations were in addition to the victory parade.*
> *The chancellor spoke on behalf of the prime minister.*

Most of the important prepositions started their lives as adverbs – this explains why adverbs and prepositions are so closely related.

Examples:

Preposition	Adverb
*He stood **behind** her*	*Please walk **behind***
*He walked **around** the garden*	*The soldiers stood **around***
*He waited **inside** the house*	*He is **inside***

It is important that you use the right kind of preposition to ensure your reader understands your message.

> *similar **to***
> *lacking **in***
> *different **from***
> *comply **with***
> *opposite **to***

In other words:

I-pod – a bed designed for a single person

Conjunctions

These join words, phrases and sentences, helping to establish the general logic of a sentence. There are two classes of conjunctions: *co-ordinating* or *co-ordinators* and *subordinating* or *subordinators*. The central co-ordinators are 'and', 'or', and 'but'. They are used to link units of equal status.

> I can **and** will play in the team.
> She may pay by credit card **or** cheque.
> He was sorry, **but** refused to pay.

Subordinators, which include 'although', 'as', 'because', 'since', 'until' and 'when', introduce something called a subordinate clause.

> The battle stopped **because** both sides called for a ceasefire.

According to the Campaign for Plain English you can start a sentence with *and* or *but*. However, the idea of such a notion drives most copywriters potty! The established fact is that it is best not to use either *and* or *but* at the beginning of a sentence, especially if writing formally. (So 'ya boo sucks to you', government quangos!) Rather than starting a sentence with *but* I recommend *however* or *yet*. For example:

> *However, the workers would still not co-operate with the management.*

Note: In many versions of the Bible, the Old Testament starts:

> *'And in the beginning God created the Heavens and the Earth...'*

(Hmmm, maybe that quango had some kind of divine guidance after all!)

The sentence

Now that words are out of the way, let's deal with the largest sequential unit of words that is described in grammar as a sentence. The sentence is just about the most common of all grammatical units (you could think of it as the equivalent of 'Smith' in the phone book). As you know, we generally speak and write in sentences. Each sentence generally represents a complete thought.

The functions of a sentence are straightforward:

- to make statements
- to ask questions
- to express emotion
- to request action.

Etymology:

shampoo – the term meaning soap for the hair, comes from the days when early traders to India discovered that Sultans and Nabobs had servants who massaged their bodies after relaxing baths. The description of this practice was 'champoo' meaning 'to press'.

A clause is a complete statement that includes a verb and is part of a larger sentence. A phrase is a group of words which conveys an idea. This concept is often written as a short pithy expression. A sentence is a complete statement which includes a verb and stands on its own. Put all these factors together and – voila! – you have part of a paragraph. A paragraph comprises a number of sentences about the same topic, pulling together the different 'thoughts' of the sentences.

That seems simple enough, but it's how you put all this together that is the tricky part.

The 'anatomy' of a sentence

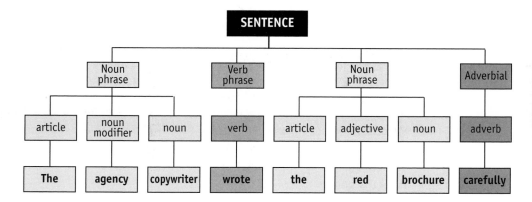

Punctuation

Whereas in spoken English all sorts of meanings are automatically taken care of, when it comes to written English, punctuation becomes an essential part of grammar. It ensures that sentences and their meanings are clear and precise.

The word 'punctuation' comes from the mid-seventeenth century, originally from the French *pointilleux*. Punctilious (noun *punctiliousness*) means showing great attention to detail or correct behaviour: *He was punctilious in providing every amenity for his guests.* Early biblical scholars, such as Talmudists, used punctuation to ensure clarity of meaning when interpreting the Bible. Ancient Greek actors used punctuation to add emphasis to texts. George Bernard Shaw often used punctuation in scripts of his plays to show actors where to add stress to key words of speech.

Without punctuation, and often even spaces between words, early manuscripts were virtually impossible to read.

Brand origins:

Some examples of medieval punctuation marks

Capitulum

Derived from the Latin for 'head', it led to what you know as a chapter (the beginning or head of a new section). In addition to indicating the end of a chapter, the 'C' with a vertical stroke showed paragraph divisions (equivalent to the paragraphus) and occasionally sentence divisions (like the current practice of capitalising the beginning of a sentence).

Littera notabilior

An enlarged letter was used to mark the beginning of a new section (chapter, paragraph, sentence, stanza or line of verse, etc.), like our capital letter.

Punctus (. or •)

The position (which could be at the baseline, in the middle or at the headline) was according to a system elaborated by Isidore of Seville. When placed at the baseline it indicated a pause in the middle of a sentence (like a comma). It was placed in the middle for a longer pause between clauses (like a semicolon) and at the headline for a long pause at the end of a sentence. The punctus is the ancestor of the current full stop.

Punctus versus

This small '7' shape over a full stop looked a bit like a semicolon. It was usually used to signify the end of a sentence (equivalent to a punctus).

Punctus elevatus

This looked like an inverted semicolon, with the tail going up and to the left. It indicated a key, medial pause (like a modern comma or semicolon).

Punctus flexus

This looked like a tilde or a small 'u' over a full stop. A tenth-century invention, it never really caught the public imagination. It marked a minor medial pause where the sense is not complete (corresponding to a comma when sorting out phrases within a clause).

Punctus interrogativus

This looked like a squiggle above a full stop. It showed the end of a question (denoting rising intonation). First appearing in the eighth century, it was not commonly used. The modern version is a seventeenth-century invention.

Chiasmus:

'Some men change their party for the sake of their principles; others their principles for the sake of their party.'
Winston Churchill

Virgula suspensiva (/)

Very much the rage between the thirteenth and seventeenth centuries, it indicated short pauses. Occasionally it stepped in for the punctus. Over time the virgula fell to the bottom of the line and curved, leading to the modern comma, which was a sixteenth-century development (the first known use in England was in a book printed in 1521).

Some you already know

Colon (:)

This first appeared in the late-fourteenth century and was used to indicate a full or medial pause.

Hyphen (-)

This first made its mark in the eleventh century (in England in the late-thirteenth century). Its only common medieval use was to point out words broken at the ends of lines.

Parentheses or brackets

This fifteenth-century invention was used to mark parenthetical material. They were curved in the opposite direction from modern parentheses and were usually accompanied by the underlining of the words between the parentheses:)here are some medieval brackets(.

Underlining

Underlining was used in medieval manuscripts to mark quotations, direct speech or parenthetical material. It was also commonly used to highlight proper names as well as being a form of expunction (to mark a word or words for deletion).

Exclamation mark (!)

Introduced in the seventeenth century.

Apostrophe (')

The modern apostrophe that you have grown to love (or should that be *hate*?) heralds from a medieval mark of abbreviation. It was a suspension mark indicating that some letters were missing.

Quotation marks (" ")

These can be found in eighteenth-century manuscripts. Underlining was sometimes used to indicate direct speech or quotations – especially for biblical quotations – but on the whole, quotations were indicated by rhetorical rather than graphic approaches.

Dash (–)

An eighteenth-century device.

Loquacious language:

limaranc – the first feelings of falling in love

What a difference a dot makes…

Here's a neat way to appreciate the difference a simple addition of punctuation can make to where you place the emphasis in a sentence. Consider the following variations:

- *What is this thing called? Love?*
- *What is this thing called 'love'?*
- *What is this thing called? Love!*
- *What! Is this thing called love?*
- *What! Is this thing called 'love'?*
- *'What is this thing?' called Love.*
- *'What is this, Thing?' called Love.*
- *'What is this thing called, Love?'*
- *What is this? Thing called 'Love!'*
- *What is this? 'Thing!' called Love.*

Back in Victorian days, pupils were taught punctuation in many novel ways, one of which even included a history lesson:

King Charles spoke half-an-hour after his head was cut off.
Or to be more historically accurate:
King Charles spoke. Half an hour after, his head was cut off.

Another was in verse:

Sentences start with a capital letter,
so as to make your writing better.
Use a full stop to mark the end.
It closes every sentence penned.
Insert a comma for short pauses and breaks,
And also for lists the writer makes.
Dashes - like these - are for thoughts.
They provide additional information (so do brackets, of course).
These two dots are colons: they pause to compare.
They also do this: list, explain and prepare.
The semicolon makes a break; followed by a pause.
It does the job of words that link; it's also a short pause.
An apostrophe shows the owner of anyone's things,
It's quite useful for shortenings.
I'm glad! He's mad! Don't walk on the grass!
To show strong feelings use an exclamation mark!

Brand origins:

Cheerios – General Mills, the cereal producer, originally called the cereal Cheery Oats. Their rivals Quaker Oats kicked up a fuss over the name, claiming that no other cereal producer had the rights to use 'Oats'. So the name was altered to Cheerios.

A question mark follows Where? When? Why? What? and How?
Can I? Do you? Shall We? Tell us now!
'Quotation marks' enclose what is said.
Which is why they are often called 'speech marks' instead.

Then there was story of the English professor who wrote the words *'A woman without her man is nothing'* on the blackboard and asked the students to punctuate it the sentence correctly.

The men wrote:	*A woman, without her man, is nothing.*
The women wrote:	*A woman: without her, man is nothing.*

The main components of modern punctuation

Full stop (or full point)

Always use a full stop to separate statements between which there is no continuity of thought. It is the most used of all the punctuation marks. However, in some cases the full stop has been erased from the copybooks altogether, such as when lists are shown in columns, as well as in abbreviations.

7 a.m.	➜	*7 am*
U.K.	➜	*UK*
R.S.P.C.A	➜	*RSPCA*

Commas

Whilst the full stop may be the most common of all punctuation marks, the comma remains the 'king of versatility'. It is the shortest pause in a sentence.

Commas are used for many different reasons. Here are some of them:

Bracketing (or isolating) commas

This is the most frequently used type of comma. A 'pair' of bracketing commas is used to mark off a 'weak interruption' in a sentence.

The managing director, in a sombre tone, paid tribute to the late chairman.

You could remove the bracketing comma and still the sentence would make sense.

The managing director paid tribute to the late chairman.

Sometimes a 'weak interruption' belongs at the beginning of a sentence.

> *Taking the results of the campaign into account, the team was satisfied with the outcome of the advertising.*
>
> *A year after the invasion of Iraq, the Spanish contingent withdrew.*

Some 'weak interruptions' appear at the beginning or end of a sentence, such as *after, although, even though, because, before, if, since, when, whenever.*

> *Although the Yankies beat The Red Sox, the crowd hissed at the New York players as they left the field.*
>
> *My accountant charged me an extra £100, even though he had no just cause.*

Gabay at a glance:

A cat has claws at the end of it's paws.

A comma has a pause at the end of it's clause.

Listing commas

The listing comma occurs in two different circumstances.

Firstly, it is used to separate items in a list, replacing the word *and* or *or*. In general, there is no comma after the penultimate item in a list. However, if a comma clarifies the meaning – as is often the case if the items in the list are clauses or phrases – by all means go ahead and place the comma.

All of these are correct:

> *French is spoken in France, Belgium, Germany and parts of the Channel Islands.*
>
> *You can travel to Manchester by train, coach or car.*
>
> *My favourite designers are Jean Paul Gaultier, Dolce and Gabbana, and Red or Dead.*
>
> *My all-time favourite sports celebrities are Beckham, Owen, and the Williams sisters.*

In the third example, I have used a comma after the penultimate item in a list to clarify that 'Dolce and Gabbana' and 'Red or Dead' are two separate items. In the final example, I have used the comma before *and* to clearly show that the Williams sisters are associated with another type of sport.

Secondly, a listing comma is used between words that modify the same object.

> *His long, black, glossy hair attracted her.*

The comma is only necessary here if the two (or more) adjectives are of the same type. For example, the comma is not necessary here:

A broken stained-glass window

Joining commas

A joining comma is used to connect two complete sentences, making them into a single sentence. It should only be used if it follows a suitable connecting word. Typical connecting words (conjunctions) are: *and, or, but, while* and *yet.* Examples include:

I need a cup of tea, and you can make it for me.
The teacher reprimanded the class, while the Headmaster looked on.

However, the comma is not necessary if the sentences to be joined are short and closely linked.

He arrived and she left.
He asked her to marry him but she declined.

Gapping commas

These show that one or more words (in this case the pronoun 'they') have been left out. Compare the following:

Some sports celebrities are uniting for the 2012 Olympics, considering such a step to be a valuable use of their Lottery subsidised training.
Some sports celebrities are uniting for the 2012 Olympics. They consider such a step to be a valuable use of their Lottery subsidised training.

Both are correct, but the first flows better. If a sentence appears clearer without the gapping comma, don't use it.

Common questions about commas

Q: Should you place a comma before direct speech?

A: Some copywriters use colons in order to offer the reader a long 'mental in-take of breath'. I suggest less drama; a simple comma will suffice.

The director asked, 'Did the client like the presentation?'

Q: Should you insert commas in a list of adjectives?

A: Go ahead, as long as the comma is replacing an *and* and all the words relating to the subject are of equal weight.

She was a slim, tanned woman.

Chiasmus:

'In both our lands, it is the people who control the Government, not the Government the people.'

(She was a slim and tanned woman.)

Q: Can I use a comma instead of a colon to join two sentences?

A: Providing one of the following words fall after the comma: *and, but,* or, *while, yet.*

Q: Should commas appear as pairs?

A: Commas often act as brackets. Just as you would close the bracket, so you close the thought or added information appearing in between the two commas with the second comma. If, *on the whole*, a sentence makes sense despite removing the section between the two commas, you are on the right track.

A closing comma isn't necessary if the comma is acting as a gapping, joining or listing device.

Gabay at a glance

Gabay's at-a-glance guide to commas

Commas separate items in a list.

Her favourite foods are chocolate, fish, oranges, peanut butter, wholemeal bread and marmalade.

- Commas indicate a break between clauses, where this increases clarity.

  Although I don't like coffee, milk shakes are one of my favourite drinks.

- Commas enclose sections of a sentence. This often shows that the enclosed section adds non-essential information.

  Basil Brush, for many years a marketing executive, is now our man in Havana.

- A comma should not appear between a subject and a verb unless the subject is a long complex clause.

  A long sentence with a clause which has many words, may sometimes need a comma before the verb.

The colon (:)

A colon shows that what follows is an explanation, elaboration, exemplification, restatement or interpretation of what came before. It is invariably preceded by a complete sentence, though what follows may not necessarily be a complete sentence. A colon can also replace 'as follows', 'namely' and 'that is'. A colon is not normally followed by a capital letter.

He was sure of one thing: he would never kiss such an ugly girl.

Medieval words:

Gabay at a glance

Gabay's at-a-glance guide to colons

- A colon introduces a list.

  It revealed a treasure trove of unlikely items: toys, telephones, fruit, books.

- A colon introduces a piece of speech or a quotation.

  At last Bush spoke: 'This is a defining moment for the coalition.'

- A colon introduces another section of text that the preceding words have led up to (i.e. it point forwards).

  If I have learned one thing in life, it is this: never trust someone who says 'Trust me'.

The semicolon (;)

This really only has one major use: joining two complete sentences into a single sentence, providing that the two sentences are closely related and are of equal samples. Examples include:

> *It was a great film; everyone laughed.*
> *I know this book like the back of my hand; I wrote it.*

The semicolon must be preceded by a complete sentence and followed by a complete sentence.

> *Moses led the Israelites to Sinai; they followed obediently.*

A semicolon may be used instead of a comma preceding a conjunction, where the emphasis is on the first sentence.

> *Truth ennobles the man; and learning adorns him.*

Gabay at a glance

Gabay's at-a-glance guide to the semicolon

- A semicolon is mid-way between a full stop and a comma in strength.

- It is used to separate two clauses that are related.

  Sometimes it is right to forgive; sometimes it is wrong to forget.

- It can separate a clause and a related phrase.

  To err is human; to forgive divine.

- It can separate items in a list, when these are either clauses (a sequence of words that normally includes a subject and a verb) or extended phrases.

  There were several reasons why the campaign failed: an unrealistic budget; unwillingness of the sales department to get involved; and a general lack of brand confidence.

Etymology:

to put someone on the spot – the phrase, which means placing someone in an awkward position, comes from the 1920s era of US gangsters. Someone 'on the spot' was marked for execution, as they were unfortunate enough to have been a witness at the spot where 'da bad guy woz rubbed out'.

The apostrophe (')

There are several instances when you would use an apostrophe. First, it is applied in contractions: shortened forms of words from which one or more letters have been left out.

it's	*it is* or *it has*
we'll	*we will* or *we shall*
aren't	*are not*
won't	*will not*

In each case, the apostrophe appears precisely in the position of the missing letters.

can't	*cannot*

Some words are still written with apostrophes even though they are rarely used in their full form.

o'clock	*of the clock*
will-o'-the-wisp	*will of the wisp*
Hallowe'en	*Halloweven*

Greengrocers in particular have a bad reputation for sticking their apostrophes where they clearly shouldn't be inserted, i.e. to indicate a plural. Does this look familiar?

Strawberry's £4

Grape's £2

This is why these kinds of mistakes are referred to as 'greengrocer apostrophes'.

Be careful not to confuse *contractions* with *abbreviations*. For example, the following do not require a comma to show that a letter is missing:

Mr for Mister, lb for pound, kg for kilogram

The following 'possessive determiners' and 'possessive pronouns' do not need an apostrophe:

Possessive pronouns	Possessive determiners
mine	*my*
ours	*our*
yours	*yours*
his	*his*
hers	*her*
theirs	*their*
its	*its*

Also note that *who's* = *who is* or *who has*: it is not a contraction of *whose*.

The possessive apostrophe

The rule is that to indicate possession you add 's to the end of the word.

> *my mother's sister, the woman's shoes, a year's work*

Note also this common mistake made on in-store promotional material:

> **Manager's Special** not **Managers Special**

When a noun is plural, the second 's' is not required.

> *Gabay's Copywriters' Compendium*
> *three weeks' time*

However, be careful with words that are plural but do not have an 's' at the end.

> **children's** not **childrens'**
> **people's** not **peoples'**
> **women's** not **womens'**

Singular nouns ending in an *s* sound can cause problems. When deciding whether to add an 's or just an apostrophe, consider how it would be pronounced, for example:

> **James's** torch but **Mr Burns'** dog
> **Charles's** book but **the scissors'** handle
> **Louis's** hands but **BA Baracus'** fear of flying

Sometimes it is better to change the word order to avoid the problem altogether. Compare, for example:

> *The scissors' handle was broken.*
> *The handle of the scissors was broken.*

With words ending in a silent *s*, the apostrophe and the possessive s are both required. This is quite common in French names, for example:

> *Alexandra Dumas's first novel*

An apostrophe isn't needed when making an acronym plural, as in *I have two CDs*, but it is required to show possession, as in *I like the CD's packaging*.

Chiasmus:

'I made art a philosophy and philosophy an art.' Oscar Wilde

Double possessives

Here's one that gets copywriters confused: do you write *a friend of my cousin* or *a friend of my cousin's*? This sticky problem is known as the double possessive, which can be described as 'post-genitive' or 'of followed by a possessive case or an absolute possessive pronoun' (*Oxford English Dictionary*).

The double can actually be quite helpful. For example, it can help to distinguish between *a picture of my son* (the dear boy in the picture) and *a picture of my son's* (which, knowing my son's admiration for Arsenal football club, I wouldn't want to see anyway – I support Manchester United). When writing copy for foreign readers, it can be more comprehensible to write *he's a fan of her's* than *he's a fan of her*.

With this in mind, all you have to remember is this: if what follows the of in a double possessive is definite and human, you can write, for example, *a friend of my aunt's*. On the other hand, if you write copy for, say, a charity fund-raiser on behalf of the local church, you wouldn't write *a friend of the church's*; you would write *a friend of the church*.

Two further exceptions:

1   The possessive word *its* never takes an apostrophe (a common copywriting mistake).
     The bear lowered its head (not it's head)

2   British usage does not use an apostrophe when pluralising dates.
     This ad dates back to the 1990s.

     However, US usage recommends placing an apostrophe here:
     This ad dates back to the 1990's.

Gabay at a glance

Gabay's at-a-glance guide to apostrophes

- Use it to show the omission of letters.

it is	*it's*
did not	*didn't*
shall not	*shan't (not sha'n't)*

  (Note: only use one apostrophe, between the *n* and the *t*.)

- Use *it* to show the omission of numbers in dates.
  the Rave of '06

- Use it to show possession of a singular noun.
  Harry's hat

Etymology:

on the nose – this phrase meaning 'on time' or 'precise', originates from early radio broadcasting when producers used hand signals to communicate with performers. A finger on the nose signified that a performance was on schedule.

- For plurals that end in *s*, just add the apostrophe after the *s*.
  her parents' advice

- When the noun is plural but doesn't already end in an *s*, add *'s*.
  men's sense of humour
  women's sense of obligation

- With words that end with an *s* sound, multiple *s* sounds, or a silent *s*, base your decision on what sounds best.

The en dash (–)

Don't get this confused with the hyphen, which is a shorter dash. Its purpose is to show an interruption to the flow of thought.

> *Team, if we win this business – and I don't doubt we will – we will celebrate as we have never celebrated before.*

The *en dash* has four other uses:

- To show a sudden turn away from the original thought of the sentence.
  Here are my two children, Asher and David – hey, Asher is not here!

- To show hesitation or missing letters.
  Er – um – oooh – I'm lost!
  P – ss off!

- In place of the word *to* in ranges of numbers and dates (except if the word *from* precedes the first date).
  2005–2006 (but from 2005 to 2006)
  Jan–Feb
  Friday–Monday
  50–60%

Note that there are no spaces either side of the dash here.

- To replace *and* or *to* where words linked together are of equal status and can be reversed without altering the meaning.
  the London–Edinburgh Express
  a mother–daughter relationship

In other words:

yellow – a cry of pain

The hyphen (-)

This is used to join two or more words or a prefix and a word to form a single unit. It links together words that cannot stand alone and/or cannot be swapped around without altering the meaning.

mother-in-law

twenty-five

one-third of participants

re-enact

sub-plot

non-specific

If in doubt as to whether it should be, say, *online* or *on-line*, the best thing to do is to look it up in a good dictionary.

For new words coined with the prefix *e* denoting electronic, you should only use the hyphen when you have a strained connection or when the expression hasn't already been established.

e-art, e-book, e-tailer

Once the expression has been accepted in common usage, you can drop the hyphen and close up the space. That is why email evolved as follows: electronic mail, e-mail, email.

A hyphen can also be used when a word has to split over two lines. When you break a word at the end of a line, you must ensure that the separation is coherent and sensible. This is why you should never to use a hyphen unless it is necessary. Compare the following:

it was a con-	*it is incon-*	*I have a die-*
sequence of ✔	*venient* ✔	*sel car* ✘

It is important to hyphenate compound modifiers which act as adjectives.

Mum gave her baby a good-night kiss.

Without the hyphen, this would mean: mum gave her baby a *good night* kiss.

Other common adjectival forms to watch out for:

common-sense approach

half-arsed attempt

part-time job

Anagrams:

from POINT to ON TIP

short-term plan
blue-eyed boy

(See the section on adjectives p29 combining words to form adjectives.)

Inverted commas: single ('...') and double ("...")

These can be used to enclose direct speech or quoted material.

> *I'm not sure what is meant when the contract refers to 'other persons'.*
> *The president announced, 'We are at war!'*
> *Mrs Jones of Smethwick was pleased with her Wash-o-matic: 'It has changed my life!'*

Note that when quoting direct speech, the closing punctuation mark goes within the quotes.

It's entirely up to you whether you use single quotes or double quotes: it may depend on your company house style.

Different publishers, particularly newspapers, differ in their preferences. For example, *the Sunday Times, The Times, The Independent* and *The Sun* go for pairs; *The Observer* and the *Daily Mail* opt for single quotes. Oxford University Press also prefers single quotes. Today, most people go for whatever is simpler.

Compare the following:

> *Penny asked, 'What did Liz mean when she said "You look as rough as I feel"?'*
> *Penny asked, "What did Liz mean when she said 'You look as rough as I feel'?"*

Both are acceptable. The main thing is to use them consistently, i.e. double quotes within single quotes or single quotes within double quotes.

Inverted commas (single or double, according to whichever style is your preference) are used to indicate titles of short poems, articles, chapter titles, song titles, titles of TV and radio programmes, such as 'Big Brother'. Note that titles of books, films, magazines, periodicals, long poems, albums, plays and TV series should not be in quotes but should be italic, and titles of holy books, such as the Bible and the Koran, should be in plain Roman text.

Etymology:

Jewish – from the tribe of Judah. Judah was one of Leah's sons.

Keep in mind that quotation marks (single or double) need to be placed around the direct word(s) of a quotation. Quotation marks separate the writer from a word of phrase and show that the writer is using that word or phrase with a different meaning.

Brackets

Parentheses (round brackets)

Round brackets enclose comments or explanations that are an aside or a digression from the main topic of the sentence. Their contents should be so secondary to the main statement that if you were to remove them you would be left with no gap in either sense or punctuation.

> *The account director (whose PA was sitting next to him) declared his devotion to his wife.*

Parentheses must always be in pairs. If a pair of parentheses is embedded within a sentence (as is the above example) there should be no capital letter and no closing punctuation (with the exception of exclamation marks and question marks!) within the parentheses. If a sentence appears entirely in parentheses the closing punctuation should appear within the parentheses.

> *The account director (did he know he had been found out?) declared his devotion to his wife. (Silence followed.)*

Square brackets

Square brackets are used to indicate that matter within a quotation has been added by the author or editor.

> *'Mr Black said, [no, Mr White] he may need to clarify who or what the quotation is about.'*

The question mark

This is self-explanatory, isn't it? It is used as closing punctuation for sentences that ask a question. When you use it, you shouldn't also use a full stop (the same is true when you are writing exclamation marks – see below).

> *Are you going to the club on Friday?*

For expressing incredulity or complete confusion you can use a double (??) or (?!), but use these sparingly: they lose their impact if used too often.

Writers' words:

48 'I don't wait for moods. You accomplish nothing if you do that. Your mind must know it has got to get down to work.'
Pearl S Buck

You can place a question mark in brackets after a word or phrase in a sentence that seems to you questionable.

> *He said he was delighted (?) that you were on the course.*

A question mark (unless followed by some other punctuation, such as closing quotation mark or bracket) should always be followed by a capital letter.

The exclamation mark

> Every exclamation ought to be put so as to be smooth and easy for the ear. *'Rejoice, thou flower of heavenly growth!'* comes in the hymn to Nikolay the Wonder-worker. It's not simply *'heavenly flower,'* but *'flower of heavenly growth.'* It's smoother so and sweet to the ear. That was just as Nikolay wrote it! Exactly like that! I can't tell you how he used to write!'

(From 'Easter Eve' by Anton Chekhov)

An exclamation mark (exclamation point in the US) conveys a strong emphasis.

> *You must be mad to want to join this company!*
> *Your creative brief is a lot of nonsense!*
> *You sexy creature!*
> *Go to hell!*

Gabay at a glance

Gabay's at-a-glance guide to exclamation marks

- Use them where the sentence is exclamatory. Use it to dramatise.
  'Get out of my way!' she shouted.
  'Oooer my luver! What's that in your 'and you're 'olding then?'

- It draws the reader's attention towards a specific product or service.
  You must be Kenco® not to try our coffee!

- It shows your esteem for something.
  What delicate toes you have!
  What big teeth you have!

- It can be used when writing direct speech to show mood and tone.
  'Cor blimey! What a mess!'

- It does the same in minor (verbless) sentences.
  Danger! Keep out!

Loquacious language:

loganamnosis – an obsession for trying to remember ['er, um, ... ah yes!'] forgotten words.

- It can be placed in brackets after a word or phrase in a sentence that seems to you amusing or ridiculous.

  He said that he was delighted (!) that you were on the course.

- It always appears at the end of a sentence!

Asterisks (*)

These are used in two instances:

- When you don't want to offend the reader by showing a word in full and so likely to cause offence

  *You f***ing idiot, why don't you just shut your *****y mouth!*

- When you want to point out that supplementary information is available elsewhere in the document.

Bullet points

Nowadays, just about every copywriter likes to condense sales messages into bullet points. The reasons speak for themselves:

- It is the most direct way to summarise product benefits or features.
- It highlights the 'must know' aspects of a service.
- It helps the reader 'scan' copy.

Keep in mind that bullet points should always be supported by some kind of substantiation, either in the preceding paragraph or within the bulleted sentence itself, and should be preceded by a colon.

A list of sentence fragments needs no other punctuation than a closing full point. This is relevant, for example, where the elements are:

- clauses
- phrases
- single words.

However, if one or more of the points is a complete sentence, each bullet point should start with a capital letter and end with a full stop (as shown in the first bullet list in this section).

Where there is a mixture of complete sentences and sentence fragments, each bullet point should start with a capital letter and end with a full point, rather than mixing punctuation systems.

A list should always have a line space or half line space above and below it.

Brand origins:

The famous Marlboro man was 'invented' in the 1960s. Originally, the company was British with a shop in Bond Street, London. The name 'Marlborough' was aristocratic. In the beginning, the cigarette – then with a red tip – was targeted at ladies.

The slash (/)

This oblique mark is also known as virgule (also see virgula suspensiva p.35), the stroke, the solidus or the shilling mark. It has limited uses.

- To indicate options

  An author may sometimes use male and female pronouns in the combination he/she to avoid upsetting his/her audience.

- To separate lines of verses when they are run on in the text rather than being set of different lines

  Mary, Mary quite contrary/how does your garden grow?/With silver bells…

- To abbreviate certain words

  A/C means account.

- In place of the word 'per' in measures

  Km/h means kilometres per hour.

- To show a 'year' that does not run from 1 Jan to 31 Dec

  For example, the 2003/04 football season.

A space should not be left between the slash and the words either side of it.

The ellipsis (…)

This is also called *suspension* or *omission marks*. It has three uses:

- It shows that some material has been left out of a direct quotation.

  In court, the account director went on and on… explaining that is was, in fact, his wife who couldn't be trusted.

- It is used to show that the sentence is unfinished.

  The best movie I have ever seen was… I can't remember now.

- It can be used to show that a series of, say, dates continues following the established pattern.

  Regular payments at two-month intervals as follows: January, March, May…

Do not use the ellipses mark and 'etc.': they both perform the same function, i.e. to show that the list is incomplete. Likewise, never use 'for example' in conjunction with 'etc.'

Chiasmus:

'Those who can win a war well can rarely make a good peace, and those who could make a good peace would never have won the war.' Winston Churchill

Style points

The following do not fall under the topic of punctuation, but are important in terms of keeping your meaning clear and your style consistent.

Italics, bold and underline

These are components for separating, highlighting and stressing words.

Italics

- Italics are mostly used for emphasis or contrast.

  On the contrary, he said he *was* coming to the party.
- A further use of italics is to cite titles of books, films, magazines, periodicals, long poems, albums, plays and TV series.

  ***Gulliver's Travels* by Jonathan Swift.**

  (See page 47 on inverted commas for titles that should not be italic.)

- A third use is to recognise foreign words when referring to them.

  When her divorce papers came through, the account director's wife was full of *joie de vivre.*

Bold

Bold type can be used for section titles, sub-headings and callouts. You can also use them for captions, such as captions under pictures in a brochure or a website. Some copywriters use bold type to introduce important new terms or keywords. If you must use it for emphasis in this way, use it sparingly and consistently.

Underline

Try to avoid using underlining as a form of emphasis; it looks awkward and is not particularly easy on the eye. It is sometimes useful to differentiate between two types of emphasis.

> *Gulliver's Travels by Jonathan Swift is <u>way</u> better than Around the World in 80 Days by Jules Verne.*

Be careful not to feature too many styles of emphasis on your page; whilst they can enliven text, they can also give the appearance of simply trying too hard to highlight a sales message.

Capitals

Use an initial capital for the first word of a sentence, a paragraph or a heading.

In other words:

legend – a foot

You may use capitals for each word in a heading (with the exception of prepositions – see page 31 – and the articles *a* and *the*) as long as you do so consistently. For example, the first level of heading may have initial capitals whilst the second level may have only the first word capitalised.

You should capitalise proper nouns (see page 25), for example recognised names of people, brands, places and organisations.

> *Chief Rabbi, Dr John Sacks, Oxfordshire, Heinz, Ford*

In some cases a word can be both a noun (see page 25) – such as revolution, government, police – and a proper noun – as in the Industrial Revolution, the Republican Government of 2000–2008, the Metropolitan Police. Job titles are commonly capitalised, although they need not be.

> *Tony Blair, the prime minister, said…*
> *Prime Minister Tony Blair said…*
> *The prime minister said…*

If the name comes first, the job title does not have initial capitals. If the job title comes first it has initial capitals. If a job title appears on its own it is lower case.

It is tempting to use capitals for emphasis, but it is grammatically incorrect.

> *Our new Refrigerator is the best on the market.* ✗
> *Our new refrigerator is the best on the market.* ✔

Numbers

Although opinion on the subject is divided, a good rule of thumb is to use words for numbers up to and including ten and numerals for numbers over ten, for example 11, 12, and so on. If, however you have a mixture of these in one sentence it is best to use numerals.

> *My lottery numbers are two, four, 11, 22, 28 and 39.* ✗
> *My lottery numbers are 2, 4, 11, 22, 28 and 39.* ✔

I recommend avoiding starting a sentence with a numeral, even if the number is 11 or higher; instead write the number in words or change the sentence around so that the number does not appear at the beginning.

Ordinal numbers, such as third, fourth, fifth, should be words rather than the shortened forms 3rd, 4th, 5th, etc.

Etymology:

pound (English) – called after its weight in Sterlings. This was a unit of currency from medieval England.

Remember to add a hyphen in between tens and units: twenty-five, forty-four, etc. Similarly, hyphenate simple fractions such as one-third and three-quarters. For mixed fractions it is recommended that you use numerals (e.g. 2 2/3), leaving a space between the whole number and the fraction.

Percentages

When writing running text, use the words *per cent* rather than the % symbol. Use the % symbol only in tables, lists, graphs, and so on. Remember that you don't always have to express figures as percentages; you could use fractions instead. You could express 50 per cent as half, 25 per cent as a quarter and 75 per cent as three-quarters.

Dates and times

Use 'o'clock' only with whole hours expressed in words (e.g. three o'clock). Use a.m. and p.m. only with numerals (e.g. 3 p.m.). Do not use a.m. and p.m. with the twenty-four hour clock (e.g. 15.00).

Whether using words or numerals, dates should be expressed in the following order: day, month, year (except in the US where the order is month, day, year).

2 November 2006	(This is the preferred style in running text.)
02/11/06	(This is preferred in tables, etc.)

Ranges of dates can be expressed with a closed up en rule where this would replace the word *to*, but not after the preposition *from*. The en rule should not replace the word *and* after the preposition between.

> *the period 1999–2000* ✔
> *the years 2006–07* ✔
> *from 1999–2000* ✘
> *between 1999–2000* ✘

In general, centuries should be in words rather than numerals, for example the twenty-first century. Remember to add a hyphen when using it adjectivally, for example *twenty-first-century girl*.

BC and AD should be in small caps. BC comes after the year (e.g. 1003 BC) and AD comes before it (e.g. AD 55). CE (Common Era, e.g. 55 CE) and BCE (Before Common Era, e.g. 1003 BCE) can be used instead of the Christian eras AD and BC. From a marketing perspective this broadens your customer base by not excluding people of other religions or cultures.

Something to ponder...

If it wasn't for Old English, which dates back to the period between the invasion of the Angles, Saxons and Jutes up to around 1150, we wouldn't have words such as:

Pronouns: I, you, he, she, it, we, this, that, these, those
Nouns: friend, husband, anger, window, bull, cake, dirt, sun
Adjectives: happy, cold, black, tight, low, ill
Verbs: can, shall, get, give, want, call
Conjunctions: and, as, but, so, then
Prepositions: up, down, in, on, to, by
Adverbs: while, when, where.

Some final thoughts about punctuation

Here is a quotation from one of the most powerful men of the early twenty-first century (my guess is that he must have studied 'The Rotten Rules of Grammar', which follows the quote):

'I mean a child that doesn't have a parent to read to that child or that doesn't see that when the child is hurting to have a parent and help one or neither parent there enough to pick up the kid and dust him off and send him back into the game at school or whatever that kid has a disadvantage.'

(G.W. Bush, President of the United States of America)

The Rotten Rules of Grammar

Don't spel rongly
Don't never use no double negatives
Always use full stops they make sentences easier to read every sentence needs one
Always check your work to make you haven't any words out
Always a verb in every sentence
Always, word order important, is reading easier to make, remember
Don't use attenuated asseverations when uncomplicated vocabulary will suffice.

Looking towards the future of punctuation, here is verse by Fred Bremmer and Steve Kroese of Calvin College & Seminary of Grand Rapids, MI, USA. It was composed in response to a magazine's poll amongst its readership about computer punctuation marks. The readers established 'waka' as the appropriate pronunciation for the angle-bracket characters < and >, though some favoured 'norkies'

The poem:	It is best to read the poem aloud:
<>!*"#	= Waka waka bang splat tick tick hash,
^"`$$-	= Caret quote back-tick dollar dollar dash,
!*=@$_	= Bang splat equal at dollar under-score,
%*<>~#4	= Percent splat waka waka tilde number four,
&[].../	= Ampersand bracket bracket dot dot slash,
|{,,SYSTEM HALTED	= Vertical-bar curly-bracket comma comma CRASH.

Brains, pen, action!

I   Read this morning's newspapers. Make sure that one is a financial newspaper, one is a tabloid and one is a broadsheet.

2   Read the main news story in each, then divide every sentence into its component parts, such as: noun, verb, preposition, and so on.

3   Punctuate the following:

he said how much better it is to ride in a car and think how much better it is to ride in a car than it is to walk than it is to walk and to think how much better it is to ride in a car than it is to walk

Questions?
answers@gabaywords.com

Writers' words:

Denial ain't just another river in Egypt. Mark Twain

3. Why use ten words when one will do?

Without the right words, our language begins to sound rather comical;

"Losing the contract was a blue collar worker to swallow."

"I am going to have start all over again by going back to basics by shedding crocodile tears."

Aim to learn five new words a week (this tip isn't just for writers who use English as a second language). Just think, in a year you will have picked up 260 words.

Need more help?
www.gabaywords.com

Why use ten words when one will do?

Just as punctuation is an essential component of grammar, so too is vocabulary. After all, a word is of little or no value if it is not correctly inserted in a sentence.

According to the Oxford English Dictionary, 'vocabulary' first made an appearance around 1616. Since then, vocabulary has grown bigger and bigger in stature and presence. So much so that when it comes to showing off their vocabulary, according to the BBC, women speak around 15,000 words a day and men speak only 4,000 [*cough*! which of course reflects women's higher communication skills].

Recognising where to place a word in a sentence automatically increases the scope of your vocabulary. Early modern English had a vocabulary of around 100,000 words, compared to 500,000 words today. Shakespeare had a vocabulary of around 25,000 words – a quarter of the total vocabulary of English. To put this into context, that's like you or I having a vocabulary of around 150,000 words (today most people have a vocabulary of around 35,000).

Shakespeare's use of English teaches us the importance of choosing the appropriate words, rather than the number of words used.

Grace me no grace, nor uncle me no uncle.

(Richard II, act II, scene iii)

In the above example, Shakespeare uses a noun as a verb! In fact, whenever William wanted to express a concept for which there wasn't even a word, he simply invented one! He devised over 1700 of our everyday words: he changed nouns into verbs and verbs into adjectives; he linked previously unconnected words as well as adding prefixes and suffixes.

Brand origins:

Sellotape, 1937 – This is based on a trade name 'Cellophane', the film used in Sellotape.

Words accredited to Shakespeare

academe	dwindle	mimic
accused	elbow	monumental
addiction	epileptic	moonbeam
advertising	equivocal	mountaineer
amazement	excitement	negotiate
arouse	exposure	noiseless
assassination	eyeball	obscene
backing	fashionable	obsequiously
bandit	fixture	ode
barefaced	flawed	Olympian
blushing bet	frugal	outbreak
bump	generous	panders
beached	gloomy	pedant
besmirch	gossip	premeditated
birthplace	green-eyed	puking
blanket	gust	radiance
bedroom	hint	rant
bloodstained	hobnob	remorseless
buzzer	hurried	savagery
caked	impartial	scuffle
cater	impede	secure
champion	invulnerable	skim milk
circumstantial	jaded	submerge
cold-blooded	label	summit
compromise	lacklustre	swagger
courtship	laughable	torture
countless	lonely	tranquil
critic	lower	undress
dauntless	luggage	unreal
dawn	lustrous	varied
deafening	madcap	vaulting
discontent	majestic	worthless
dishearten	marketable	zany
drugged	metamorphose	

Loquacious language:

jugulation – the interruption of something by means of a dire measure, for example strangulation

Common phrases from Shakespeare

Brave new world (The Tempest, act V, scene i)

Miranda: *How beauteous mankind is! O brave new world,*
That has such people in 't!

Fair play (Troilus and Cressida, act V, scene iii)

Troilus: *When many times the captive Grecian falls*
Even in the fan and wind of your fair sword,
You bid them rise, and live.

Hector: *O, 'tis fair play.*

Foregone conclusion (Othello, act III, scene iii)

Iago: *Nay, this was but his dream.*

Othello: *But this denoted a foregone conclusion…*

Foul play (King Lear, act III, scene vii)

Gloucester: *Good my friends consider; you are my guests.*
Do me no foul play, friends.

Into thin air (The Tempest, act VI, scene i)

Prospero: *Our revels now are ended. These our actors,*
As I foretold you, were all spirits, and are melted into air,
into thin air.

It was Greek to me (Julius Caesar, act I, scene ii)

Casca: *But those that understood him smil'd at one another,*
and shook their heads;
But for mine own part, it was Greek to me.

The livelong day (Julius Caesar, act I, scene i)

Marullus: *Knew you not Pompey? Many a time and oft*
Have you climb'd up to walls and battlements,

Chiasmus:

He acts before he speaks, and afterwards speaks according to his actions. Confucius Analects--2.13.

> To towers and windows, yea, to chimney-tops,
> Your infants in your arms, and there have sat
> The livelong day, with patient expectation,
> To see great Pompey pass the streets of Rome.

One fell swoop (Macbeth, act IV, scene iii)

Macduff: Did you say all? — O Hell-kite! — All?
           What, all my pretty chickens, and their dam,
           At one fell swoop?

Rhyme and reason (Merry Wives of Windsor, act VI, scene vi)

Falstaff: And these are not fairies? I was three or four times in
            the thought they were not fairies; and yet the guiltiness
            of my mind, the sudden surprise of my powers, drove
            the grossness of the foppery into a received belief, in
            despite of the teeth of all rhyme and reason, that they
            were fairies.

Too much of a good thing (As You Like It, act IV, scene i)

Rosalind: Why then, can one desire too much of a good thing?
            Come sister, you shall be the priest and marry us.

Grammatical techniques: Shakespeare style

Don't worry too much about the strange sounding terms, instead think about using some of these techniques in your copy.

Alliteration – Repetition of the same initial consonant sound throughout a line of verse

> When to the sessions of sweet silent thought... (Sonnet 30)

Anadiplosis – Repetition of a word that ends one clause at the beginning of the next

> My conscience hath a thousand several tongues,
> And every tongue brings in a several tale,
> And every tale condemns me for a villain. (Richard III, act V, scene iii)

Twisted truths:

Exaggeration is a billion times worse than understatement.

Anaphora – Repetition of a word or phrase at the beginning of consecutive clauses

Mad world! Mad kings! Mad composition! (King John, act II, scene i)

Anthimeria – Substitution of one part of speech for another

I'll unhair thy head. (Antony and Cleoptra, act II, scene v)

Antithesis – Juxtaposition, or contrast of ideas or words in a balanced or parallel construction

Not that I loved Caesar less, but that I loved Rome more.

(Julius Caesar, act III, scene ii)

Assonance – Repetition or similarity of the same internal vowel sound in words of close proximity

Is crimson in thy lips and in thy cheeks. (Romeo and Juliet, act V, scene iii)

Asyndeton – Omission of conjunctions between coordinate phrases, clauses, or words

Are all thy conquests, glories, triumphs, spoils,
Shrunk to this little measure? (Julius Caesar, act III, scene i)

Chiasmus – Two matching pairs arranged in a parallel opposite order

Fair is foul, and foul is fair. (Macbeth, act I, scene i)

Diacope – Repetition broken up by one or more intervening words

Put out the light, and then put out the light. (Othello, act V, scene ii)

Ellipsis – Omission of one or more words, which are taken for granted by the listener or reader

And he to England shall along with you. (Hamlet, act III, scene iii)

Epanalepsis – Repetition at the end of a clause of the word that occurred at the beginning of the clause

Blood hath bought blood, and blows have answer'd blows.

(King John, act II, scene i)

Gabay at a glance:

A chiasmus is great for speech writing. 'Ask not what your country can do for you, but what you can do for your country.'

'A statesman is a politician who places himself at the service of the nation; a politician is a statesman who places the nation at his service.'

A diacope is also known as a tmesis (from Greek meaning, 'a cut'). It is ideal for writing advertising headlines featuring a product name: abso-Tango™-lutely.

In other words:

fireplace – a shooting range

Epimone – Frequent repetition of a phrase or question; dwelling on a point

> *Who is here so base that would be a bondman? If any, speak; for him I have offended. Who is here so rude that would not be a Roman? If any speak; for him have I offended.* (Julius Caesar, act III, scene ii)

Epistrophe – Repetition of a word or phrase at the end of successive clauses

> *I'll have my bond!*
> *Speak not against my bond!*
> *I have sworn an oath that I will have my bond.*
> (Merchant of Venice, act III, scene iii)

Hyperbaton – Altering word order, or separation of words belonging together, for emphasis

> *Some rise by sin, and some by virtue fall.* (Measure for Measure, act II, scene i)

Malapropism – Intentionally muddled use of words when an appropriate word is replaced by one with a similar sound but (often ludicrously) inappropriate meaning

> *I do lean upon justice, sir, and do bring in here before your good honour two notorious benefactors.*
> *Are they not malefactors?* (Measure for Measure, act II, scene i)

Also see
Metaphors
chapter 10

Metaphor – Implied comparison between two unlike things achieved through the figurative use of words

> *Now is the winter of our discontent*
> *Made glorious summer by this son of York.* (Richard III, act I, scene i)

Metonymy – Replacement of some attributive or suggestive word for what is meant (e.g. 'crown' for royalty)

> *Friends, Romans, countrymen, lend me your ears.*
> (Julius Caesar, act III, scene ii)

Onomatopoeia – Use of words to imitate natural sounds

> *There be moe wasps that buzz about his nose.* (Henry VIII, act III, scene ii)

Writers' words:

'It is possible to be a writer, but not to become one.' (Hermann Hesse)

Paralepsis – Emphasises a subject by seeming to overlook it, usually by such phrases as 'not to mention', 'to say nothing of'

> *Have patience, gentle friends, I must not read it.*
> *It is not meet you know how Caesar lov'd you.* (Julius Caesar, act III, scene ii)

Parallelism – Similarity of structure in a pair or series of related words, phrases, or clauses

> *And therefore, since I cannot prove a lover*
> *To entertain these fair well-spoken days,*
> *I am determined to prove a villain*
> *And hate the idle pleasures of these days.* (Richard III, act I, scene i)

Parenthesis – Insertion of some word or clause in a position that interrupts the normal flow of the sentence (asides are good examples)

> *...Then shall our names,*
> *Familiar in his mouth as household words—*
> *Harry the King, Bedford and Exeter,*
> *Warwick and Talbot, Salisbury and Gloucester—*
> *Be in their flowing cups freshly remembered.* (Henry V, act IV, scene iii)

Polysyndeton – The repetition of conjunctions in a series of coordinate words, phrases, or clauses

> *If there be cords, or knives,*
> *Poison, or fire, or suffocating streams,*
> *I'll not endure it.* (Othello, act III, scene iii)

Simile – Comparison between two things using 'like' or 'as'

> *My love is as a fever, longing still*
> *For that which longer nurseth the disease.* (Sonnet 147)

Synecdoche – A part of an object, relating to the entire thing

> *Take thy face hence.* (Macbeth, act V, scene iii)

In other words:

onward – the working environment for a nurse

Choose your words very carefully!

Consciously or unconsciously each of us is confronted, both in writing and speech, with two types of vocabulary: *active* and *passive*. Normally you wouldn't give a second thought as to whether active words are grammatically correct or not. On the other hand, passive vocabulary often includes words that get even the most accomplished copywriter running out of the office in search of a good stiff drink. The odd thing about all this is that, in practice, passive words are often featured more than the active ones!

A PIN number is required in order to use your cash card   *(passive)*

You need a PIN number to use your cash card   *(active)*

With this mind, it is important to be able to 'switch' your thinking from passive to active. The quickest way to achieve this is simply to read and listen. The more you read, the more you boost your vocabulary and store of alternative words. The more you listen – for example to the radio – the greater your ability to structure your message with appropriate words.

Now, all this isn't just about your capacity to be the equivalent of a 'walking thesaurus'. It's more to do with your understanding of how you can match words according to:

- their grammar

- their construction

- their relationships to words with similar meanings

- how they link with other words.

Delving a little deeper, this entails looking at the context of a word to understand its meaning. For example:

Also see
Euphemisms
chapter 12

- *Formal usage* – written or spoken language in a working or formal environment. Political correctness and good grammar are important.

- *Informal usage* – generally spoken language (although text and email are usually fairly informal – often missing out punctuation and superfluous words, even letters) aimed at people you know or understand.

Chiasmus:

'They have done what they like. Their difficulty is to like what they have done.' (Winston Churchill)

- Slang meanings – the use of 'street-cred' or industry-wide informal terminology.

Do you own a good dictionary? For copywriters it's an essential part of your arsenal, with which you can arm yourself with powerful words. I like to think of this as a record of historical dramas: explaining how words were used, are used and could be used. In one short entry you are given a word's meaning, usage, grammar, derivatives, etymology and pronunciation.

That said, dictionaries are out of date before they are even in print. Words, on the other hand, never stop evolving. At the time of writing, recent additions to Oxford English Dictionary included:

0898 number	*n.*	information fatigue	*n.*
Alawite	*n.* and *a.*	in octavo	*adv.*
anadama bread	*n.*	juku	*n.*
Anasazi	*n.* and *a.*	kegger	*n.*
Arkie	*n.* and *a.*	rap jumping	*n.*
arugula	*n.*	realo	*n.* and *a.*
Bahamian	*n.* and *a.*	ringgit	*n.*
BB	*n.*	rucola	*n.*
Bella Coola	*n.*	scratchie	*n.*
bilingualize	*v.*	second city	*n.*
bolete	*n.*	skoosh	*v.*
calicivirus	*n.*	sleazoid	*a.* and *n.*
Chewa	*n.* and *a.*	slice-and-dice	*a.*
chifforobe	*n.*	tadger	*n.*
fundie	*n.* and *a.*	Toronto blessing	*n.*
furo	*n.*	UK garage	*n.*
Ghuzz	*n.* and *a.*	vavavoom	*n.* and *a.*
herbologist	*n.*	weirded out	*a.*
home invader	*n.*	West Lothian question	*n.*
homestay	*n.*	XXXX	*n.*

No doubt there will be a many more new entries in the next edition.

Loquacious language:

longanimity – suffering in silence

Maintaining standards

There are two kinds of English language: *standard* and *non-standard*. Whilst 99 per cent of written English is in standard form, which is accessible to all English speakers, non-standard English helps individuals to express their identity but may be understood only by a certain group of people.

As people become more widely travelled in person and via the Internet (over 91,000,000 people use English on the Web – Source: Headcount.com) and other media, the traditional 'no-compromise' approach to standard English is steadily waning and so non-standard English is on the up. In response, stalwarts of grammatical standards often stock up on English style and grammar books to thwack over the heads of vocabulary vagabonds and grammatical grouches.

Driven by technological, military and cultural innovations, people's willingness to adopt a universal language has led to English becoming influenced by at least 350 other languages, which is why there are many kinds of world-English. These include, amongst others: South East Asian English (encompassing Philippines English, Hong Kong English, Pakistani English, etc.), African English, South African English, Caribbean English, Canadian Standard English, US English, Native American English, British and Irish English, and finally Australian and New Zealand English.

It is easy to see from the following examples how English words have been 'loaned' to other languages

Country	Expression	Meaning
France	alloman	telephone operator
Japan	rushawa	traffic
Germany	twens	twenties
Lithuania	muving piceras	movies
Spain	sueter	jumper
China	telefung	telephone
Ukraine	herkot	haircut

Writers' words:

'Outside of a dog, a book is man's best friend. Inside of a dog it's too dark to read.' (Groucho Marx)

The changing voice of vocabulary on the streets and in the stars

Some people may point an accusing finger at ramps who speak in strange tongues, ready to chuck a willy at any one who may suggest they a shakey*.

Even the most slapdash non-standard English has some kind of rationale to its structure.

Even though 'street' or dialect English is non-standard, there are some grammar rules that apply to it. (Here I offer a 'health warning' to readers of a nervous disposition. Unless you are a great fan of London-based soap operas, please skip the following non-standard English grammar section ... still here? ... well you have been warned!)

Typical non-standard English grammar affecting the noun phrase

- *Them* rather than *those* – **Them police make me sick.**

- Different comparative and superlative forms – **worser, bestest.**

- Possessive forms in the third person replace objective forms in this person *hisself/theirselves* rather than *himself/themselves*.

Typical non-standard English grammar affecting the verb phrase

- *Of* replaces auxiliary have after *should, would, etc.* – **He should of.**

- *Aint* and *innit* replace *am not, are not* and *is not.*

- Only one form is used for the present tense – **I wants, you wants, you be, I be**...

- Only one form is used for the past tense – **she was, we was, he was**...

  "I was fitted-up good and proper when we was up West."

Also see examples of rap p.443

(*Ramp, n. scruffy, smelly, obnoxious tramp. Chuck a willy. v. have a temper tantrum. Shakey, n. person whose intellect is markedly below normal standards.)

Medieval words:

brawl – an energetic dancing party

Typical non-standard English grammar affecting a clause

- *-ly* disappears from adverb endings – *he ran really quick, he ate real quick.*

- Multiple negation steps in – *I didn't expect no hassle at my time of life.*

- Relative pronouns suddenly change – *the film what I saw*

(Dearest, delicate reader, it is safe to resume.)

Even the most respected academics have been known to dabble in non-standard English for the purposes of fiction. J. R. R. Tolkien, the Oxford academic who wrote the Lord of the Rings, was an expert in ancient languages; he developed *two* forms of Elvish:

- **Sindarin** – based on the sounds of Welsh – is the more commonly used.

- **Quenya** – related to Finnish – is largely a ceremonial language.

Then there are the extra terrestrials, as featured in movies like Star Wars, who use non-standard English: English words but in a different word order. Take that little guy who looks like he could have been Kermit the Frog's wise old uncle – Yoda:

No! Try not. Do. Or do not. There is no try.

That place...is strong with the dark side of the Force. A domain of evil it is. In you must go.

No! No different! Only different in your mind. You must unlearn what you have learned.

Help you I can.

Decide you must how to serve them best. If you leave now, help them you could. But you would destroy all for which they have fought and suffered.

Away put your weapon.

(Yoda – Jedi Master)

Gabay at a glance:

Whenever writing colloquial language, check that you neither patronise nor belittle your audience. (Not you, of course, dear reader.)

Chiasmus:

'It is very much better . . . to have a panic feeling beforehand, and then be quite calm when things happen, than to be extremely calm before hand and go into panic when things happen.' (Winston Churchill)

The top common-use words

It is thought that just 1000 words make up ninety-nine per cent of all copywriting. Taking the 1000 most common word forms in UK English, based on 29 works of literature by 18 authors (4.6 million words), the top 100 list reads:

1. the	26. have	51. who	76. man
2. and	27. him	52. them	77. did
3. to	28. is	53. Mr	78. like
4. of	29. said	54. we	79. upon
5. a	30. me	55. now	80. such
6. I	31. which	56. more	81. never
7. in	32. by	57. out	82. only
8. was	33. so	58. do	83. good
9. he	34. this	59. are	84. how
10. that	35. all	60. up	85. before
11. it	36. from	61. their	86. other
12. his	37. they	62. your	87. see
13. her	38. no	63. will	88. must
14. you	39. were	64. little	89. am
15. as	40. if	65. than	90. own
16. had	41. would	66. then	91. come
17. with	42. or	67. some	92. down
18. for	43. when	68. into	93. say
19. she	44. what	69. any	94. after
20. not	45. there	70. well	95. think
21. at	46. been	71. much	96. made
22. but	47. one	72. about	97. might
23. be	48. could	73. time	98. being
24. my	49. very	74. know	99. Mrs
25. on	50. an	75. should	100. again

Brand origins:

Revlon, 1932 – from the founder of the company who added an 'L', in honour of one of his partners, Charles Lachman. (You can see why one of their products is called 'Charlie'.)

The website Ask.com lists the top 100 words used by writers of English as a second language.

Gabay at a glance:
The most curious aspect of this list is that no one seems to have mentioned sex!

1. the	26. from	51. which	76. more
2. of	27. or	52. do	77. day
3. to	28. had	53. their	78. could
4. and	29. by	54. time	79. go
5. a	30. hot	55. if	80. come
6. in	31. word	56. will	81. did
7. is	32. but	57. way	82. number
8. it	33. what	58. about	83. sound
9. you	34. some	59. many	84. no
10. that	35. we	60. then	85. most
11. he	36. can	61. them	86. people
12. was	37. out	62. write	87. my
13. for	38. other	63. would	88. over
14. on	39. were	64. like	89. know
15. are	40. all	65. so	90. water
16. with	41. there	66. these	91. than
17. as	42. when	67. her	92. call
18. I	43. up	68. long	93. first
19. his	44. use	69. make	94. who
20. they	45. your	70. thing	95. may
21. be	46. how	71. see	96. down
22. at	47. said	72. him	97. side
23. one	48. an	73. two	98. been
24. have	49. each	74. has	99. now
25. this	50. she	75. look	100. find

Loquacious language:

lypophrenia – the distant feeling of sadness without knowing why you are sad

Also see
top tips for
writing web
copy p.689

Speaking of words on the web, *www.andreas.com* took Usenet traffic for 1992 (343,945,617 words), removed personal names, plurals, contractions, computer words and other non-standard English words, and then sorted the words by frequency to arrive at the 250 most frequently used words in English as typed on the net.

the	to	of	a	I	and
is	in	that	it	for	you
as	was	but	at	in	from
about	would	can	one	my	will
there	me	out	your	what	which
who	any	up	get	am	if
people	know	only	their	than	this
been	time	had	were	and	note
also	good	how	could	way	very
these	see	may	as	even	you
many	well	such	really	first	same
work	being	used	too	anyone	here
still	need	said	find	off	him
us	going	they	might	since	never
long	someone	she	why	last	few
using	own	little	made	down	believe
both	around	another	through	for	thing
between	year	set	sure	probably	enough
put	lot	direct	each	information	part
real	course	anything	fact	when	best
demand	at	is	come	called	person
done	though	always	list	look	news

Etymology:

dentures (a set of artificial teeth) – this 1874 word comes from the French word 'denture' meaning 'a set of teeth'.

available	seen	quite	rather	to	less
found	tell	women	every	ever	against
mean	above	heard	thanks	doing	able
change	book	now	talk	well	new
man	following	send	example	several	computer
true	feel	wrong	type	let	stuff
show	power	remember	looking	why	until
car	are	actually	three	four	five
ten	yet	message	away	machine	interested
fifth	however	money	nothing	home	level
an	whether	given	test	user	big
area	include	write	mind	experience	memory
God	understand	matter	not	during	play
whole	do	human	interesting	just	cannot
maybe	these	nice	came	public	some
open	almost	full	buy	important	response
went	hope	told	tried	wanted	story
love	couple	law	answer	live	city
major	everyone	cost	care	word	usually
instead	job	written	size		

Gabay at a glance:

If you have to adapt a long section of copy for a website, first cut the words to no more than 100 per page. Next 'chunk' down your paragraph into headings such as:

· background · aim · project · results

Yinglish

From Yiddish... 'smendrek' to English... 'a jerk'

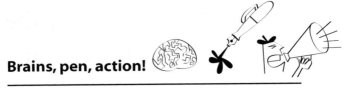

Brains, pen, action!

Whilst I am a strong advocate of simple 'tried and tested' words rather than convoluted claptrap, I still feel that learning new words is fun – and so sensuous. Imagine getting your tongue around the syllables of beauties like these:

ablation	miasma
bowdlerize	obloquy
conspectus	pullulate
dithyrambic	riparian
exiguous	soliton
factotum	transhumance
guerdon	urticating
incunabula	vatic
jejune	weltschmerz
lagniappe	xi
	zeitgeist

Have a go for yourself by making up sentences that include one or more of these words. (You may need to look them up in a dictionary first).

Questions?
answers@gabaywords.com

Writers' words:

'Every journalist has a novel in him, which is an excellent place for it.' (Russel Lynes)

4. Is it 'Its' or 'it's'? Choosing the right word for the right occasion

My grandfather loved English. So did his son, Maurice, and so does his grandson – me!

In 1918 my grandfather, who came from Gibraltar, bought a book called 'Commercial Correspondence and Commercial English'. The short guide offered *advice on composition for the commercial student and business man* (note the separation of 'business' and 'man'.)

I have the book at home. Whilst I agree with forty per cent of the advice given, I disagree with the rest; not because of any personal claims to being smarter than the book, but because English today has moved on. However, many questions regarding English remain if not the same, then certainly very similar.

So here are the new answers to the oldest questions in my grandfather's little red book.

bare or bear

Is it 'its' or 'it's'? – choosing the right word for the right occasion

Over the years I have found that certain questions of grammar and word usage crop up time after time. The questions are usually such that you've actually learnt the answer at some point to but can no longer put your finger on it.

Most of these issues deal with word endings, spelling confusions, word order and word aptness. The most common of such questions is where to place an apostrophe: a subject that I covered at great length in the grammar section on page 42. This chapter aims at providing a concise answer to many questions of word usage which you probably know yet can't quite get off the tip of your tongue and on to the tip of your pen. Hopefully then, this will help take the heat off some of our language's most hotly debated queries.

Note: Many of the following come with the apt 'health warning' from Isaac Bashevis Singer, Nobel Prize winner for Literature (1978):

I think the only reason languages disappear is when they lose any creative power.

Gabay at a glance:

Many linguists predict that just under half of the world's 6,000 languages will be extinct by the year 2050. Ninety per cent of 'living' languages are spoken by fewer than 100,000 people. Between 200 and 250 languages are spoken by more than one million people, with Chinese Mandarin, English and Spanish being the three most spoken languages.

In marketing, timing is vital:

It took 45 years after the invention of the tin can to invent the modern tin can opener.

A

Abbreviations

If an abbreviation (or rather an acronym) comprises individual capital letters, each representing a whole word, there is no need to place a full stop after each letter:

Bachelor of Arts ➜ BA   United States ➜ US

Also see
e.g.
page 91

If an abbreviation is made up of initial lower-case letters, you should place a full stop after each letter:

Latin for 'that is' (id est) ➜ i.e.

(although this is being lost in favour of ie in some contexts).

If an abbreviation starts with the first letter of a word and ends with its last letter you do not need to add any full stops:

Doctor ➜ Dr

On the other hand, if an abbreviation comprises the first part of a word, then end it with a full stop:

February ➜ Feb.

-able/-ible suffixes

In most cases, when the noun ends in -ation, you will be probably use -able to form the adjective (e.g. navigation ➜ navigable).

On the whole, when a word ends in -ion, use -ible (e.g. permission ➜ permissible).

If the root ends in a hard 'g' (e.g. navigation) use -able.

If the root ends in a hard 'c' (e.g. application) use -able.

If the root ends in a soft 'g' (e.g. negligent) use -ible.

If the root ends in a soft 'c' (e.g. force) use -ible.

Advice or advise?

Advice is a noun
Can you give me some advice?

Advise is a verb
What do you advise me to do about my grammar?

Affect or effect?

Affect is a verb
How does this book affect your thinking?

Effect is most commonly a noun
The effect was that I thought with greater clarity.

Effect can also be a verb
You can effect a change.

Loquacious language:

galactophagous – milk drinking

Ageing or aging?

Both are correct. However, if you wish to give emphasis to the word 'age', use ageing.

Agree to or agree with?

Your choice of preposition changes the meaning of the verb.

I agreed to do what Gabay advised.

I agreed to all the rules.

I agreed with everything he suggested.

Aim at, aim to or aim for?

As a verb, 'aim' can be written as 'aim at' as in 'aiming at something' (in the physical sense of the meaning) or 'aim at doing something'. In the UK, 'aim at' is preferable to 'aim for' or 'aim to'.

For American copy, write 'aim to'.

All most or almost?

almost = virtually or nearly

All ready or already?

already = 'by then'

All right or alright?

In formal writing I suggest you use the correct form, which is *all right*, although many copywriters get away with the less accepted *alright*.

All together or altogether?

altogether = totally

Allude, elude or illude?

allude = to refer to indirectly

elude = to avoid by dexterity or employment of tactics

illude = trick

All ways or always?

always = every time

all ways = each route

These are all ways to success.

Alternate or alternative?

alternate = every other

alternative = another option

Etymology:

the whole nine yards – this phrase, meaning 'everything is included', refers to cement contained in a rotating cement mixer. When emptied, a cement mixer truck should release 'the whole nine yards' of mix.

Amend or emend

Amend and emend are both used to refer to correcting text.
Amend can also mean change.
He amended his behaviour whilst in prison.
To make amends means make reparation for any injury or offence.

Among/amongst

You can use either. However, *among* is far more common.

Among or between?

Between means something shared by two people.
Among refers to something shared by three or more.

Amoral or immoral?

An *amoral* person does not appreciate the difference between right
and wrong.
An *immoral* person appreciates the difference but goes ahead anyway.
(Sounds like my relationship with eating too much chocolate cake!)

Ampersand (&)

This represents the word *and*. Only use it when citing the name of a
firm of which it forms an authorised part, such as Marks & Spencer.™

Amount or number?

Use *amount* with non-count nouns:
A large amount of the water is polluted.
Use *number* with plural nouns:
A number of items came to light.

Analyse

The US version is *analyze*, but this is not acceptable UK usage, even if
you opt to use *-ise* endings.

And or but?

Strictly speaking you should not begin a sentence with *and* or *but*.
But from a copywriting view it can be effective. But use it in moderation.
And remember you always have the alternative 'yet'.

Annex or Annexe?

annex (verb) = to take possession of a country or part of a country
annexe (noun) = a building added to the main building
My Granny flat is an annexe to my house.

Ante- or anti-?

ante- = before or previous
anti- = against

Oxymorons:

Enough time

Any more or anymore?

In formal writing this should be written as two words.

Anyone or any one?

anyone (pronoun) = anybody, any person
any one = any individual of a group

Anyplace

This is an Americanism for *anywhere*.

Anyway or any way?

Write as one word if you want to mean regardless, but two words if you want to mean 'any kind of method'.

Apostrophes

See Mind your Ps and Qs, p.43.

Apparently or evidently?

Apparently is a weaker version of *evidently*. With *evidently* there should be some evidence.

Artist or artiste?

An artist is skilled in the fine arts (e.g. drawing). Some use *artist* to mean an 'accomplished practitioner'.
An artiste is an entertainer.

As or like?

Like implies similarity.
As points to complete identity.
She is like a bird.
He went to the fancy dress party as a bird.
Smith looked like the thief, but Jones was later identified as the thief.

As of

Avoid this expression and replace it with *since* or *from*.

Assume or presume?

Both mean suppose.
Presume is based on evidence.
Assume takes something for granted without proof.

Assurance or insurance?

Assurance refers to things that are certain to happen, like death!
Insurance refers to things that may happen, like a house fire.

Foreign brand names:

Homo Sausage – Japanese beef jerky

Assure or ensure?

Assure and *ensure* both mean 'to guarantee'.

If you assure someone of something, it will definitely occur and so they can feel secure (peace of mind).

If 'success is ensured' it occurs because an action has been taken to make sure that it does.

At this moment in time

Try to avoid this phrase.

At your earliest convenience

Try to avoid this phrase.

Avenge or revenge?

Avenge (verb) means 'to deliver retribution'.

Revenge (noun) means 'getting even'.

Aural or oral?

Aural refers to the ears and hearing.

Oral refers to mouth and speaking.

B

Bail or bale?

Compare the following:

A bale (noun) of leaves.

He's out on bail (noun).

We bailed (verb) out of the boat.

Bath or bathe?

Compare the following:

I bathe (verb) in the bath (noun).

I bathe (verb) the wound.

Beside or besides?

beside = next to, by the side

besides = 'anyway'

Between you and I (✗)

Between you and me ✔

(See Mind your Ps and Qs, p.26)

Loquacious language:

Bi-

Prefix meaning 'two'
biannual = twice a year
biennial = every two years

Bible or bible?

Use a capital letter when referring to the Scriptures, but not when referring to any other authoritative work, for example:
Autotrader is the car buyer's bible.

Billion

These days it generally means a thousand million (1 000 000 000). Historically in the UK it meant a million million (1 000 000 000 000).

Biweekly

This confusing word can either mean fortnightly or twice a week.

Blond or blonde?

A man's hair is blond.
A woman's hair is blonde.

Bored by or bored with?

Both are correct. However, avoid *bored of.*

Borrow or lend?

Compare the following:
Yes, I will lend (allow you to use it) it to you.
May I borrow (use for a short period) a book from the library?

Both or and?

Compare the following:
She is both cute and bright ✔
She both is cute and bright ✘

You can use *both* by itself:
Both are correct and both of them have succeeded.

You should not combine *both* with *as well as*:
Both the New York Yankees as well as the Dallas Cowboys. ✘

When writing *both* followed by a preposition, you must repeat the preposition after *and*:
Both in London and in Detroit. ✔
Both in London and Detroit. ✘

Shakespearean insult:

'His brain is as dry as the remainder biscuit after a voyage.' (*As You Like It*, act II, scene viii)

Breath or breathe?

breathe (verb) – I can't breathe.
breath (noun) – I felt her breath on my lips.

Broach or brooch?

Compare the following:
I will broach the subject.   (verb)
That's a nice brooch. (noun)

Bulky modifiers

Tabloid headline writers sometimes feature bulky modifiers:
'English book shock sentence'

As you can appreciate from this example, they can be cumbersome.
Often they can be improved with hyphens:
Multi Pulitzer prize winning novelist Harry Peuneta's The Idiot is… ✗
Multi-Pulitzer prize-winning novelist Harry Peuneta's The Idiot is… ✔
Aim to avoid both of these breath-squeezing styles of sentence by
allowing the reader space to breathe:
'The Idiot' – by the multi-Pulitzer prize winning novelist Harry Peuneta – is…

C

Callous or callus?

callous = cruel, insensitive or uncaring
callus = a hard patch of skin

Can or may?

can = be able to
may = have permission to

Cannot or can not?

Both are fine, yet the former is much more widespread and so offers a far
greater chance of getting your readership's approval.

Capital letters

When to use them:
*   beginning of a sentence
*   in proper names, including titles attached to names
*   in the first word of a title
*   for individual historical periods, e.g. The Ice Age
*   for holidays, festivals and religious days
*   for many recognised religious names and terms,
    e.g. the Old Testament

Etymology:

Here's mud in your eye – this phrase used in a good-luck toast refers to a horse race. If the track is muddy, the rider of
a losing horse would get mud in his eye. So really, the good-luck wish is to oneself rather than another person!

- for brand names
- for names of countries
- for Roman numerals (apart from the front pages of a book or scenes in a play)
- for names of languages
- for nouns and adjectives referring to nationalities or ethnic groups, when these have their literal meanings, e.g. English history
- for days of the week or months of the year
- for the salutation of a letter, e.g. Dear Sir
- for each word of an address in a letter
- closing salutation of a letter, e.g. Yours truly
- to begin lines of poetry (although some poets prefer to avoid this style)
- for the pronoun 'I', irrespective of where it appears in a sentence
- for emphasis (use sparingly)
- for some acronyms and abbreviations (exceptions include acronyms that are now words in their own right, e.g. radar = radio detection and ranging).

Also see
Mind your Ps
and Qs
chapter 2

Cast or caste?

cast = a group of actors or performers
caste = a social Hindu group

Capital punishment or corporal punishment?

Capital punishment means death.
Corporal punishment refers to beating.

Category mistakes

Copywriters often mix their modifiers, for example:

cheap prices	✗	*low prices*	✔
fast speeds	✗	*high speeds*	✔

Equally, you could not write 'copywriters who write novels are few in number', because a number cannot be *few*, although it could be *small*. It's better to recast the sentence as 'a small number of copywriters write novels'.

Cater for or cater to?

UK – cater for
US – cater to

Censer, censor or censure?

censer = a vessel to burn incense
censor = an official who decides if a publication, play or film, etc. is appropriate for public viewing
to censure someone or something = to criticise harshly

Chiasmus:

'Study without thought is vain; thought without study is dangerous.' (Confucius Analects 2.15.)

Childish or childlike?

Childish refers to the qualities of a child. However, it is generally applied to mean an adult who acts irresponsibly – like a child.
Childlike means having the appealing traits of a child.

Children's

The possessive form of children is *children's*. There is no such word as childrens.

Check or cheque?

Compare the following:
Check (verb) your copy for accuracy.
May I write you a cheque (noun)? (US – May I write you a check?)

Circumlocutions

This means wordiness. Remember: less is more!

Circumstances (*under* or *in the*?)

You can use both. However, most purists would suggest that a state of affairs exists *in the circumstances*. On the other hand, an action is performed *under the circumstances*.

Coarse or course?

coarse = rough or crude
course = certainty, a series of lectures

Clichés

Also see
Clichés
chapter 9

Either avoid them like the plague or use to coin a phrase.

Commonsense or common sense?

Many write *commonsense*. However convention dictates to write it as *common sense*. If the word is used as a modifier hyphenate it:
A common-sense answer.
Oddly though, the derived adjective is *commonsensical*.

Comparatively or relatively?

Most copywriters mistakenly reach for one of these when they really need words like *somewhat, rather, quite, moderately, sort of, more or less* or *fairly*.
Why not drop *comparatively* or *relatively* and write what you mean instead? Only use *comparatively* or *relatively* if you are comparing two things.

Foreign brand names:

Super Piss – Finish solvent for unfreezing car locks

Communicate

One of those marketing expressions that, whilst being technically correct, can appear crass:

We need to communicate our copy better.

Complimentary or complementary?

complement = something that completes
compliment = term of flattery
complimentary = given free of charge
Her dentures complemented her smile.
She took his comments as a compliment (praise).

Comprise or compose?

Compare the following:
The brief is composed of (made up of) five sections
The brief comprises (contains) five sections

Complex or complicated?

Complex means having an elaborate structure.
Complicated means hard to comprehend or resolve.

Constitute or consist?

A whole consists of its parts: the alphabet consists of 26 letters.
Its parts constitute a whole: 26 letters constitute the alphabet.

Contagious or infectious?

contagious = disease passed on via bodily contact
infectious = disease passed on via air or water

Contemptible or contemptuous?

An action worthy of contempt is *contemptible.*
A person who shows contempt is *contemptuous.*

Continual or continuous?

continual = very frequent
continuous = uninterrupted

Continual showers = on-off-on-off
Continuous rain = non-stop

Contractions

These are words featuring apostrophes denoting missing letters:
I'd = I would
it isn't = it is not
I shan't = I shall not

Anagrams:

from WAITRESS to A STEW SIR?

Copywriters often draw on contradictions to show casual speech. This is fine, providing:

- such speech reflects a brand's tone of voice
- they are used consistently throughout a piece of copy.

Convince or persuade?

To convince is to make someone believe.
To persuade is to make someone act or do something.

Correspond to or correspond with?

If one thing corresponds to another, it matches up in an orderly way.
The receptionist's uniform corresponded to company guidelines.

If one thing or person corresponds with another, it means that one thing or person communicates with the other.
The nephew corresponded with his uncle.

Could of or could have?

This one is easy: there are absolutely no circumstances when you can write *could of.*

Credible or credulous?

credible = believable
credulous = gullible or easily led

Criticise, criticism and critique

Originally, *criticise* (verb) meant to evaluate the good and bad points of something. The activity was called *criticism* (noun). Today either word is taken as meaning to say something negative about something, which is why many copywriters believe that terms such as 'I want to offer some positive criticism of your copy' is nothing more than a crude oxymoron.

To critique someone's copy means to evaluate it (this is the modern form of *criticise*).

Crucial, vital and essential

There are no shades of crucial. Something either *is* or *isn't* crucial. Therefore you cannot use modifiers which suggest a degree of cruciality, e.g. very crucial, most crucial or highly crucial.
Equally, there is no higher form of urgency than something that is vital or something that is more essential than something else.

Medieval words:

baxter – a professional female baker

D

Dashes
See Mind your Ps and Qs, chapter 2.

Dangling modifier
This is a phrase without any grammatical connection to the rest of its sentence.
Sitting on the beach, the bird surprised us and started eating our lunch.
In this example, 'Sitting on the beach' is dangling. You're not sure who is doing the sitting: *us* or *the bird*.

There are two ways to put this right:
1. by adding something to which the modifier can affix itself (e.g. a pronoun):
Sitting on the beach, we were surprised when the bird started eating our lunch.

2. by rewriting the sentence entirely to clarify the meaning:
Whilst we were sitting on the beach, the bird surprised us and started eating our lunch.

Data
Strictly speaking, this is the plural of *datum*, although most copywriters would get away with writing *data* with a verb in the singular form.

Dates
See Mind your Ps and Qs, page 54.

Definite or definitive?
definite = certain, not vague
definitive = authoritative, final

Dependant or dependent?
For the adjective meaning 'reliant', use -ent.
For the noun meaning 'someone who relies on something or someone', use -ant.
(In the US both are acceptable.)

Derisive or derisory?
derisive = scoffing or mocking
derision = the act of deriding or laughing to scorn
Something derisory is worthy of derision.

Shakespearean insult:

'He has not so much a brain as ear-wax.' (*Troilus and Cressida*)

Descent or decent?

descent = a trip downwards
decent = an adjective meaning 'honest and upstanding'

Device or devise?

device (noun) = a piece of equipment
devise (verb) = to invent, to make
The wheel was a clever device.
I will devise a cunning plan to take over the world.

Different/dissimilar to or from?

Formal English would require *different from*. Casual copywriting can feature *different to*.

Be careful not to use *different* when it clearly doesn't make a difference:

I read three different books. Better to write: *I read three books.*

Also be careful not to use the phrase 'various different'. *Various* implies that they are different: both words are not necessary.

An item can be *dissimilar to* another but not *dissimilar from*.

Disassociate or dissociate?

You can use either. *Dissociate* is more widely used.

Disc or disk?

Use *disc* for everything except a computer disk.

Discreet or discrete?

discreet = careful or prudent (it comes from the noun *discretion*)
discrete = distinct or separate

Disinterested or uninterested?

disinterested = impartial, not acting for the benefit of others
uninterested = bored

So, whilst a judge may be *uninterested* by a case, he must always be seen to act *disinterested*.

It should be noted that, strictly speaking, *disinterested* should be written *disinterestedly*, as it is an adverb describing the verb 'act'. However, few copywriters follow this rule.

Dissatisfied or unsatisfied?

unsatisfied = unhappy because you lack, or have too little of, whatever you want
dissatisfied = angry or unhappy because what you have is not what you want

Which begs the question:

Are you unsatisfied or dissatisfied with your partner?

Doubling letters when adding a suffix

For US English, don't double a final letter unless the stress falls on the final syllable of the stem word.

US – canceled; UK – cancelled

US and UK – excelling

Double negatives

Avoid writing two negative words in a clause as it often leads to confusion.

Notable exceptions are:

When clearly both negatives are needed:

I can't not accept your offer.

When you combine *not* with a negative prefix like *dis-* or *un*:

Your attitude towards me has not gone entirely unnoticed.

Doubtless, no doubt or undoubtedly?

doubtless/no doubt = 'I have no cause to doubt' or 'I am too well-mannered to state my doubt'

undoubtedly/beyond any doubt/without doubt = beyond question

Draft or draught?

draft = preliminary version of a text

draught = cool air entering a room

Dream or dreamt?

You can use either, but in the UK it is more traditional to use the following constructions:

I have dreamed

I dreamt

Due to or owing to?

due to = caused by

owing to = because of

Owing to can generally replace *due* to but not vice versa. Avoid writing *due to the fact*, when you could write *because*.

Here's a good test:

Imagine you were announcing the late arrival of a train. The delay is caused by snow on the track. Would you announce 'due to snow …' or 'owing to snow …'?

Chiasmus:

'Mankind must put an end to war, or war will put an end to mankind.' John F. Kennedy

E

Each other or one another?

Each other is used for two only.
One another for more than two.
They killed each other = two dead
They killed one another = more than two dead
(Write *each other's work*, not *each others' work*.)

Economic or economical?

economic (adjective) = relating to the economy of a business or country
economical (adjective) = 'using the minimum amount of something'

-ed or ing?

Either is fine, however *-ing* can occasionally lead to uncertainty:
My ink needs to be changed. (This is more specific than -ing.)
My pen needs its ink changing.

-ed or -t?

Any of the following are fine:

dreamed	dreamt
learned	learnt
leaped	leapt
spelled	spelt
spilled	spilt
spoiled	spoilt

e.g.

This is an abbreviation of the Latin for 'for example'.
Always punctuate it: *e.g.* rather than *e.g* or *eg.*
In the body of your text use the words *for example*; *e.g.* can be used in brackets, notes, etc.
(Don't get *e.g.* confused with *i.e.*, which is the Latin abbreviation of *id est* and means 'that is to say'.)

ei/ie spelling rule

The rule is: 'i' before 'e' except after 'c', or when sounded like 'a' as in 'neighbour' and 'weigh'.
Some common exceptions: caffeine, either, foreign, forfeit, height, leisure, neither, protein, seize.

Did you know?

The second longest monosyllabic words in the English language are nine letters long each: 'scratched', 'scrunched', 'screeched', 'scrounged', 'squelched', 'straights' and 'strengths'.

Either ... or?

Is the verb singular or plural?

Either Bill or Ben was in the garden. (Bill singular + Ben singular = singular verb)

Either Helen or her cousins were in the garden. (cousins = plural verb)

Either her cousins or Ben was in the garden. (Ben (closest to the verb) = singular)

Also see
Split infinitives
page 135

Either comes before the description of what is being said:

I have either to write this advertisement or give-up ✔

I have to write either this advertisement or give-up. ✗

I have to either write this advertisement or give-up. ✗

Elicit or illicit?

elicit = to draw out

illicit = illegal

email, e-mail or E-mail?

During the summer of 2004, I conducted a Google™ search for the word 'email' and discovered 317 million listings. For 'e-mail', Google™ returned some 29 million listings.

The word 'email' first officially appeared on 5 July 1982 in the magazine 'Computerworld'.

The noun 'email' comes from 'electronic mail' and is predominantly written with a lower case 'e'. The same word has since been turned into a verb meaning to *communicate via electronic mail.*

Emigrant or immigrant?

An emigrant leaves his or her homeland to live in another country.

An immigrant moves into another country to live there permanently.

I was so taken by Israel that I became an emigrant. The experience was such a tremendous success that I became an immigrant.

Eminent or imminent?

eminent = distinguished

imminent = soon

Empathise or sympathise?

empathise = identify with someone

sympathise = feel sympathy for someone

Enrol or enroll?

UK – enrol; US – enroll

Twisted truths:

Go around the barn at high noon to avoid colloquialisms.

Enter (into)

Also see
etymology
page 142

You enter something tangible such as a place.
You enter into something abstract such as a contract.
*She entered the joint and then entered into a contract with
'The Big Cheese'.*

Equable or equitable?

equable = even-tempered, unchanging
equitable = fair and just

Equivalent or counterpart?

Two things are equivalent to (not of) each other when either can be
substituted for the other.
People holding similar positions should be referred to as counterparts
rather than equivalents.
My counterpart in Spain is Maria.

Especially or specially?

Especially refers to something in particular or for someone in particular.
Specially refers to a specific purpose.

Erupt or irrupt?

erupt = to blurt out violently
irrupt = to enter violently
Saddam Hussein irrupted into Kuwait.

etc.

This is an abbreviation of the Latin *et cetera*, meaning 'and other things'.
Never write it: e.t.c. or ect.
Avoid it wherever possible in formal copy. Instead introduce the list of
items with the terms '*for example*' and '*such as*' because these both
imply that the list is not complete.

Euphemism or euphuism?

Also see
Euphemisms
chapter 12

A euphemism is often used by copywriters to write something that will
not give any offence.
Euphuism is an absurdly bombastic style of writing. Someone who
writes in such a style is called a euphuist.

Every day or everyday?

Every day is an adverbial phrase.
My wife nags me every day.
Everyday is an adjective.
My wife's nagging is an everyday occurrence.

Brand origins:

Unilever, 1930 – from a merger of NV Margarine Unie, Margarine Union and Lever Brothers. William Heskith Lever, then
Viscount Leverhulme, and James Darcy Lever founded the English firm.

Gabay at a glance:

Here's a way to combine a chiasmus with advice for common word confusions 'To aim for her love he aimed at her heart'.
(Tip: When composing a chiasmus, write the central words first. For example 'aim at' – 'aim to' and then the rest of your message around them.)

Evoke or invoke?

evoke = to recollect in your mind
invoke = to call upon something for assistance or encouragement

Exceptional or exceptionable?

exceptionable = open to objection
exceptional = extraordinary

Explicit or implicit?

explicit = stated unambiguously
implicit = implied but not actually expressed

Extravert or extrovert?

Extravert is an obscure technical term.
An extrovert is an outgoing person

F

Factious or fractious?

factious = showing or caused by dissension
fractious = tired or irritable

Faint or feint?

faint = unclear or not strong, to lose consciousness
feint = an action or movement intended to distract or mislead

Farther or further?

Both can mean 'a greater distance'.
Further also means 'in addition/besides'.

Feel or think?

Thinking is on a higher plane than feeling.
Hooligans feel strongly and think weakly.

Female, feminine or feminist?

The adjective *female* refers to the sex of a person, animal or plant.
Feminine applies only to people, their attributes or words.
Feminist refers to people who hold the belief that women should enjoy equal opportunities and rights to men.

Also see
Category
mistakes
page 84

Fewer or less?

less = not as much
fewer = not as many

Loquacious language:

galoot – a clumsy oaf

Our car uses less petrol, so we make fewer stops for petrol.
Ten items or fewer.

Fictional or fictitious?

fictitious = not true
fictional = made up, i.e. a novel or story

Fill in or fill out?

What do you do with a form?
UK – fill in; US – fill out

(The verb *fill up* can occasionally be confused with *fill out* when referring to expansion).

First or firstly?

When writing a list, use *firstly* to introduce your first point. Follow this with *secondly, thirdly… finally.*

Fish or fishes?

The plural of *fish* is *fishes.* However, unless using the plural form in technical writing, you can usually get away with *fish.*

Fix or repair?

Both mean 'mend'.
Repair is more formal than *fix.* (The verb fix also means 'make firm or fasten'.)

Flaunt or flout?

flaunt = to show off
flout = to disregard or treat with contempt

Flier or flyer?

Provided you are referring to a something or a person that flies, you can write either.
(Note: a sales promotion leaflet is called a flier.)

Flounder or founder?

flounder = to struggle or move with difficulty
founder = to fall, collapse or break down

Foreign words

Take note of George Orwell's fifth rule:

Never use a foreign phrase, a scientific word or a jargon word if you can think of an everyday English equivalent.

Chiasmus:

'When we are happy we are always good, but when we are good we are not always happy.' (Oscar Wilde)

For ever or forever?

Traditionally in the UK this was written *for ever*. Nowadays many have succumbed to the US version *forever*.

Foreword or preface?

Both refer to remarks at the beginning of a book. A preface is written by the author. Someone other than the book's author often writes a foreword.

Forgo or forego?

forgo = to do without or concede
forego = go before or precede

Formally or formerly?

formally = in an official or formal style
formerly = previously

Formulae or formulas?

Mathematicians or scientists write *formulae* but in non-technical writing *formulas* is acceptable.

Forward or forwards?

If you are writing the word as an adjective, drop the final 's':
forward thinking

Often its adverbial sense includes the final 's' but many copywriters only use the adverb forwards when referring to a physical movement.

When writing idioms, such as *look forward to*, drop the final 's'.

Fuck or fuck it?

It must be stressed that the word *fuck* used as either a noun or verb is not recommended in general copywriting (although it has played an important role in AIDS awareness advertising).

On the whole, considering that there are in excess of six hundred thousand words in the Oxford English Dictionary, there must be more imaginative ways of expressing oneself than to say or write the F-word. (The F-word is both a noun and a verb. It was added to the OED in 2004.)

That said, I am asked so often about its use that, under duress, (things I have to do for my craft, eh…) I have assembled some notable answers on its rightful employment:
In the noun form, *fuck* can be used with the definite article as a pure expletive.

Quotations:

John Wannaker and Lord Leverhulme are amongst the many distinguished people attributed to have said that 'half my money spent on advertising is wasted, but I don't know which half'.

What the fuck are you doing, Sheila?
fuck (verb) = to have intercourse
Dave and Sheila are fucking.
Dave fucked Sheila

fuck around (verb) = do nothing important or nothing at all, to lie to someone
Dave's just fucking around.
Dave's fucking Sheila around all the time.

Fuck off! = expression in response to an unwanted and undesirable action done to the speaker
Fuck off, asshole!

fuck oneself (verb phrase) = get lost
Sheila told Dave to go fuck himself.

fuck up (verb) = make a mistake, to make a mess out of something, to cause someone to become psychologically unstable
Dave really fucked his copywriting up.
Dave's clients really fucked him up.

fucker (noun) = derogatory term (generally for a male person)
The little fucker copied my work.

Back in Shakespeare's day, compared to other obscenities, the F-word wasn't even that crude. Consider for instance, King Lear Act I Scene 1V
KING LEAR Do you bandy looks with me, you rascal?
OSWALD I'll not be struck, my lord.
KENT Nor tripped neither, you base football player.
So the ultimate insult in 1605 was to call someone a 'football player.' [They must have played for Mill Wall.]

For a Shakespearean reference to the actual 'F-word' itself, consider its usage as a pun, 'focative case'. in The Merry Wives Of Windsor. Or in Henry V (IV.iv), when the character Pistol threatens to 'firk' a French soldier, a word meaning 'to strike.'

An explanation to the origins of the word that has been 'doing the rounds' for years regards English archers, the Battle of Agincourt, and the phrase 'Pluck Yew'! This explanation is a play on modern

Brand origins:

Vauxhall, 1903 – the first car produced in Vauxhall, South London, where, in 1857, a Scottish engineer founded the Vauxhall Ironworks.

97

incorporation of the F-word into a confrontational phrase as exemplified in the movie 'Taxi Driver'.

'You talking to me? You talking to me? You talking to me? Then who the hell are you talking to? You talking to me? Well, I'm the only one here. Fuck you!'

Many suggest that early-recorded uses of the 'F word' originate from Scots. Take the Scottish poem by William Dunbar, entitled Ane [or A] Brash of Wowing or In Secreit Place. (1503).

His bony berd wes kemd and croppit.
Bot all with kaill it was bedroppit.
And he was townsyche, peirt and gukkit.
He clappit fast, he kist, he chukkit.
As with the glaikkis he were ourgane.
Yit be his feiris he wald haif fukkit: Ye brek my hairt, my bony ane.

Further suggested early uses of the word include the charge and consequent punishment met to a sailor for visiting a brothel *'Found Under Carnal Knowledge'*. Another more moot suggestion claims it referred to *'Fornication Under the King's Consent'*. The more likely origin is that the word comes from an Old English farming expression meaning *'to scatter seeds'*, which eventually had repercussions in Swedish and German (fiken').

Fulfil or fulfill?
UK – fulfil; US – fulfill

G

Gamble or gambol?
gamble = take a risk
gambol = run and jump playfully

General or generic?
general = overall, widespread, not specific
generic = an entire group or class; in marketing, a low-cost, unbranded product
a generic shampoo

Gipsy or gypsy?
Both are correct, however the original *gypsy* (wanderer) came from Egypt, so the 'y' version is more apt.

Writers' words:

98 'Thank you for sending me a copy of your book. I'll waste no time reading it.' Moses Hadas

Goodwill or good will?

If you mean a business's commercial trading value, use *goodwill*.
If you mean general feelings of consideration, use *good will*.

god, God or g-d?

God is written with a capital 'G' when referring to the 'supreme being' worshiped by a religion. It is written with a lower case 'g' when referring to a generic number of entities worshiped for their paranormal powers.

Compound nouns referring to a god are written as follows:

godlike, God-fearing, godforsaken

You can use g-d as written if you do not wish to cause offence through writing God's name in full.

Expressions such as 'For God's sake!' are written with a capital 'G'. However, as it is generally accepted that you should not take God's name in vain, why not write 'For pity's sake!'?

(Hopefully, that last comment should earn me an extra point when meeting my maker – or should that be Maker? Answers in an email to answers@gabaynet.com.)

Goods or freight?

Generally speaking, when referring to items transported by land write *goods* and use *freight* when referring to items transported by sea or air.

Gourmand or gourmet?

A gourmand is a person who enjoys eating, sometimes a little too much. A gourmet (noun) is a connoisseur of fine food. *Gourmet* can also be an adjective: gourmet meal.

Graceful or gracious?

Graceful refers to lovely actions, forms, shapes and movement.
Gracious refers to kind, courteous or compassionate.

Grand or great or grate?

Grand and great can refer to family relationships.

my great-uncle
my grandmother

Use the prefix *grand-* for the parents of your parents and the children of your children:

granddad or grandad
grandson

Use the prefix *great-* for the parents of your parents' parents and the children of your children's children:

great-granddaughter

Writer's words:

'I don't know the rules of grammar. If you're trying to persuade people to do something, or buy something, you should use their language.' David Oglivy.

Great can also refer to something being exceptional or large.
My great-grandfather was great: He had a great appetite for life.
Grate can either refer to a fireplace or a method of shredding food.
I toasted the grated cheese besides the great grate on the great fire that was in the great hall at my great-grandfather's mansion. It made me feel so grateful for having been part of that great family.

Grey or gray?

UK – grey; US – gray

Grill or grille?

A grill is used for cooking.
A grille is a grating over a window or door.

Grisly or grizzly?

grisly = gruesome
grizzly = having partly grey hair
That grizzly beard was grisly.

Guarantee, guaranty, or warranty?

A *guarantee* is a commitment to replace or repair goods. It is also an assurance that a certain agreement will take place.
Some copywriters use *guaranty* to refer to the piece of paper that features a guarantee.
A *warranty* is a pledge to the reliability that goods have been tested and checked before being marketed. It is also an undertaking given by one of the parties to a contract to the other, to be answerable for the truth of some statement incidental to the contract.

Both 'guarantee' and 'warranty' come from French. The Northern French term being 'warrantie' and the Southern being 'gurantie'.

Guerilla, guerrilla or gorilla?

Both *guerilla* and *guerrilla* refer to a fighter who belongs to an independent group.
A *gorilla* is a great big hairy ape (not to be confused with certain mother-in-laws or gruesome work colleagues).

Twisted truths:

Even if a mixed metaphor sings, it should be derailed.

H

Hail or hale?

hail (noun) = frozen rain
hail (verb) = to call for, e.g., a cab;
hail from means to be a native 'he hails from Zanzibar'.
You would describe a fit and healthy old person as *hale*.

Hanged or hung?

You hang your coat on a hanger. The past tense is *hung*. However, when referring to someone who was hanged by the neck, writing 'hung by the neck' would, for many sticklers of English, be considered as a hanging offence. *Hanged* can only be used when referring to the method of capital punishment.

His and hers

Neither requires an apostrophe.

He or she or they?

To be politically correct, instead of using the usual generic pronoun *he*, for example 'should he wish to, a customer can…', you could use *he or she* or even *she or he*. Or re-structure the sentence to use *they*:
Should they wish to, customers can…

Here-words: herein, hereof, herewith, hereby

Write simple twenty-first century English and abolish all the above to the 'hereafter' – except in legal writing where these are pretty standard terms.

Heritage or inheritance?

The noun *heritage* refers to cultural items, traditions or natural features passed down the generations.
The Western Wall is part of the Jewish heritage.
Acme bank has a proud heritage of customer service.

Inheritance refers to money or property bequeathed in a will.

High or tall?

Tall is an adjective meaning 'of greater than average size'. It can be used to describe people, animals, buildings and plants.
She's tall for her age.

Use *high* when referring to a distance something is above the ground.
The balloon is high in the sky.

Writers' words:

'From the moment I picked up your book until I laid it down, I was convulsed with laughter. Some day I intend reading it.' Groucho Marx

High-tech or hi-tec?

Both are spelt correctly. Commonly, *hi-tec* is preferred in the US. Although normally an adjective, it can also be written as a noun.
Step inside and open up a world of hi-tech opportunities.

Hindi, Hindu or Hindustani?

Hindi is one of the official languages of Northern India.
Hindustani is an old name for Hindi.
A Hindu follows the religion of Hinduism.

Historic or historical?

A past event is historical.
A historic event is exceptionally memorable.

Histrionic or hysterical?

Both are emotional outbursts.
Histrionic behaviour is a demonstration of artificiality or hypocrisy for melodramatic ends.
Hysterical behaviour comes about through losing control of oneself.
The 1966 World Cup football final was historical. For English football fans, it was an historic event. People became so emotional that they were hysterical. (Some accused them of histrionics.)

Honorary or honourable?

honorary = given as an honour
honourable = worthy of honour
My late father, Isaac Gabay MBE, was an honorary Member of the Order of the British Empire. He was an honourable gentleman.

Hypercritical or hypocritical?

hypercritical = excessively critical
hypocritical = two-faced

Horrible, horrid, horrific or horrendous?

Horrible and *horrid* are interchangeable. However, *horrid* smacks of an expression from a bygone era or something an overbearing school master would say to a pupil.
You, child, are horrid.
Horrific and *horrendous* suggest something even worst than *horrible* and *horrid*. (But enough of my attempts at telling a joke!)

Metaphors:

What will become of the sheep if a wolf is the judge? Anonymous

I

Idle, idol or idyll?

idle = not active

idol = an object of worship

idyll = a peaceful situation, a piece of work that describes such a situation

Idea or ideal?

Compare the following:

Her idea is ingenious!

Her ideals were questionable.

This is an ideal time to start up a copywriting agency.

If and when

If possible avoid writing *if and when*. Instead just write *if* or *when*.

Illegible or eligible?

eligible = qualified or suitable for a purpose

illegible = something that is hard to decipher

Illegible or unreadable?

Unreadable can mean the same as *illegible*, but can also mean something that is uninteresting or poorly worded.

Her handwriting was illegible and besides, the copy was unreadable. She'd better forget a career as a copywriter!

Imaginary or imaginative?

imaginary = something that only occurs in the imagination

imaginative = having a colourful imagination, creative

Immanent or imminent?

immanent = something inherent

imminent = about to occur

Important or importantly?

More important is an abbreviated form of 'what is more important'. Some copywriters treat it is an adverbial, so change the adjective *important* to *importantly*. Compare the following:

More important is the fact that our product…

More importantly, our product…

Did you know?

The shortest word in the English language featuring all five vowels is 'Eunoia' (a medical term referring to a state of normal mental health, from the Greek for 'well mind').

Imply or infer?
When you *imply* something (suggest or hint), I *infer* something (understand or draw a conclusion).

Impostor or imposter?
Neither spelling is the impostor – however some say that imposter is slightly suspect.

Impugn or impute?
To impugn is to question integrity or veracity.
'Are you daring to impugn my motives?' he asked. 'Well, your hands are doing the walking whilst you're doing the talking,' she replied.

To impute means to attribute, often without justification.
'That's damn unfair to impute blame on me – my fingers' actions are clearly out of my hands.'

Inapt or inept?
inapt = improper or inappropriate
inept = incompetent or clumsy

Indices or indexes?
Both are the plural of index, an alphabetical list.
Indices is also a mathematical term meaning the plural of an index, for example the superscript ^{2} which denotes 'squared'.

Indict or indite?
indict = accuse
indite = write down (this is an archaic term, rarely used these days)

Insofar as or inasmuch as?
They both mean 'to the extent that'.
Inasmuch as is most common. This can also be separate words: *in as much as*.
Insofar as is more popular in the US. This can also be separate words: *in so far as*.

In-depth
Always hyphenate.

Indiscriminate or undiscriminating?
indiscriminate = a lack of bias. It is often used to mean *random* as in 'indiscriminate layoffs at work'.
undiscriminating = lacking good judgement

Writers' words:

104

'If I had to give young writers advice, I would say don't listen to writers talking about writing or themselves.'
Lillian Hellman

Industrial or industrious?

industrial = relating to the manufacturing industry
industrious = hard-working

In fact or infact?

Use *in fact*. Note: as this is an aside, it should, in fact, always be separated from the rest of the sentence by a pair of commas.

Inflammable or inflammatory?

Inflammable bursts into flames.
Inflammatory gets people hot under the collar!

In front

Always write as two words.

Ingenious or ingenuous?

ingenious = intelligent, inventive
ingenuous = naive
The ingenuous professor was ingenious.

Inhuman or inhumane?

inhuman = lacking any human qualities
inhumane = lacking compassion and benevolence

Inoculate or vaccinate?

Both mean 'introduce a vaccine into the body'.
Inoculate can also refer to a wide sense of introducing a substance.
The British media inoculated the masses with their biased reporting of the Middle East.

Instal or install?

Both are correct, but *install* is the more common spelling.

Instantly or instantaneously?

Both mean 'without delay'. However, use *instantaneously* to give a sense of even greater immediacy.

Gabay at a glance:

When translating text for an overseas audience, use two interpreters, one to translate into the new language, another to translate back into English. This way you can be sure that your words have not lost their meaning. (Sure, it's expensive, but it is accurate!)

Did you know?

The longest known palindrome – a word which can be read the same backwards as forwards – in any language is the Finnish 19-letter word 'saippuakivikauppias'. It means someone who sells soap stone.

105

Intense or intensive?

intense = extreme

intensive = concentrated

After an intensive two days in each other's company,
our passion was intense.

–she spent a day in intensive care. [Maybe the passion was too intense!]

Inter- or intra-?

Use the prefix inter- to suggest between.

Use intra- to suggest within.

international = two or more nations

intranational = within one nation

Interment or internment?

interment = burial

internment = imprisonment

Internet, internet, intranet or extranet?

The Internet is a worldwide network of computer networks.
(Note: capital 'I')

An intranet is a local or controlled computer network.
(Note: lower case 'i')

An extranet is an intranet that can be accessed, via the Internet, by
a restricted group of sanctioned external users.

Interpreter or commentator?

An interpreter explains something.

A commentator writes historical 'commentaries', often by making
personal remarks on the events.

Intrinsic or extrinsic?

Intrinsic is an adjective meaning 'originating from within' or 'essential'.

Extrinsic relates to something on the outside.

Rooney's intrinsic football skills are of extrinsic interest.

Invent or discover?

invent = to form a new idea or make something new

discover = to find something that already exists

Ironic or sarcastic?

ironic = having the quality of being the subtle opposite of that
expressed by the words used.

Sarcastic overtly hurtful language, the opposite of that expressed by
the words used.

Chiasmus:

'Elections exist for the sake of the House of Commons and not the House of Commons for the sake of elections.'
Winston Churchill

-ise or -ize?

Americans insist on *-ize*. Traditionally UK usage prefers *-ise*, but the Oxford English Dictionary now also suggests *-ize*. To be honest, you can use either as long as you do so consistently. Bear in mind that if you are writing for the web, the *-ize* ending is the more globally accepted form.

Beware of the following words that *must* take the *-ise* ending: advertise, advise, chastise, clockwise, comprise, compromise, despise, devise, disguise, enterprise, excise, exercise, expertise, franchise, improvise, merchandise, otherwise, promise, revise, supervise and surprise. Also note that analyse, catalyse and paralyse retain the 's' (except in the US, where they take the *-yze* ending).

Its or it's?

It's is the contraction of *it is* or *it has*.
Its is a possessive pronoun; something belongs to it.
My kitten licked its whiskers as it ate its food. It's the sweetest site I have seen for a long time. In fact, it's really got to me, so I am going to cry, it's the least I can do, having seen its lapping.

(Copywriters often prefer writing advertisements with contractions such as *it's*, but for more formal documents, such as proposals, many prefer to write *it is*. Again, a general rule of consistency should apply throughout.)

Is when or is where?

If providing a specific definition, use neither.
A full stop is where punctuation completes a sentence   ✗
A comma is when a pause is required in a sentence   ✗

BOTH examples are not simply wrong, but gut wrenching!

J

Jail or gaol.

Use *jail*; *gaol* is archaic.

Jeopardise

The most common error is omitting the letter 'o'.

Jewellery or jewelry?

In the UK use *jewellery*; in the US use *jewelery*.
Similarly UK – *jeweller*; US – *jeweller*.

Jew, Jewish, Judaism or Judaic?

The Jewish religion is called Judaism.
A Jew is someone who's mother was born Jewish.
Only imbeciles use the word to mean 'tight-fisted'.
The adjective *Judaic* means 'pertaining to Jewish religion, culture or tradition'.

Also see
Mind your Ps
and Qs for a
more in-depth
discussion
page 43

Jones or Joneses?

For any surname ending with 'es' add 'es'.
But don't add an extra 's' to denote possession.
The Joneses' dog…

Judgement or judgment?

Both are correct, however the US prefers *judgment*.

Judicial or judicious?

Judicial means 'pertaining to judges or to the courts'.
Judicious means 'sensible or carefully considered'.

Jurist or juror?

A jurist is well-versed in issues relating to the law.
A juror is a member of a jury.

K

K

When writing the abbreviation of *kilo*, write *K* (capital letter).

Kneeled or knelt?

When writing the past tense and past participle of the verb to *kneel*, you can write either *kneeled* or *knelt*. The US prefers *knelt*.

Knit or knitted?

Most use *knitted* as the past tense and past participle of the verb *to knit*.

Knowledgable or knowledgeable?

Knowledgeable with the 'e' is preferable. However, an increasing number of copywriters drop the 'e'.

Koran or Qur'an?

For everyday purposes, write *Koran* (note the capital 'K').
However, for academic or more deferential purposes, write *Qur'an*. (Not *Quran* or *Qu'ran*).

Chiasmus:

'Nothing can cure the soul but the senses, just as nothing can cure the senses but the soul.' Oscar Wilde

L

Lama or llama

A lama is a Lamaist monk.
A llama is a South American animal related to the camel.

Larva or lava?

A larva is a an insect in the early stages of its life (plural *larvae*).
Lava is molten rock from a volcano.

Lath or lathe?

A lath is thin strip of wood.
A lathe is a machine for shaping wood.

Lawful, legal or legitimate?

All mean 'sanctioned by law'.
Lawful (allowed by law) should be used for set phrases such as a 'lawful practice'.
Legal (relating to law) should be used in contexts such as legal advice or legal action.
Legitimate means either 'genuinely lawful' or 'valid'. Its sense of authenticity can also be used in phrases such as 'these bargains are totally legitimate'.

Lay or lie?

Follow these examples:
It's my job to lay the table.
I am laying the table.
I have laid the table.
I was laying the table.
I laid the table last night.

I like to lie in bed to sleep.
I am lying in bed as we speak.
I have lain in bed every night.
I was lying in bed when I woke up this morning.
I lay in bed to sleep last night.

Lead or led?

Led is the past participle of the verb to *lead*.
You can lead a horse to water but you can't make it drink.
The horse was led to water but it did not drink.

Did you know?

The longest palindrome listed in the Oxford English Dictionary is the 12-letter word 'tattarrattat'. It is a nonce word (created for a specific event or circumstance). It means 'rat-a-tat'. James Joyce featured the word in *Ulysses* (1922): 'I knew his tattarrattat at the door.'

Leaned or leant?

Both spellings are correct and both can be used as the past tense and past participle form of the verb *to lean*.

Leaped or leapt?

Both spellings are right and both can be used as the past tense and past participle form of the verb *to leap*.

Learn or teach?

To learn is to gain knowledge.
To teach is to give knowledge.

Learned or learnt?

You can use either, but US copywriters are taught to learn *learned*.

Legend or legendary?

A legend is a whimsical tale.
A legendary person plays a role in such a tale or has earned legendary status thanks to his or her past achievements.

Lend or loan?

lend (verb) = to give someone money on the understanding that they return it
loan (verb) = to give someone money on the understanding that they return it
loan (noun) = money leant to someone

Lengthways or lengthwise?

UK – either; US – lengthwise

Liable or likely?

Both adjectives express probability.
He is liable to get angry.
I am likely (verb) to fall in love with my blind date.

Likely can also be an adverb meaning 'in a like or similar manner'
Liable also means 'legally obliged'.
He's liable for the money he owes.

Libel or slander?

libel = a written statement that can harm a person's character
slander = a spoken statement that can harm a person's character

Licence or license?

UK – license (noun) and license (verb); US – license (noun and verb)

Writers' words:

'I don't think anyone should write their autobiography until after they're dead.' Samuel Goldwyn

Licorice or liquorice?

US – licorice; UK – liquorice

Lighted or lit?

Use either as the past tense and past participle of the verb *to light*. When using these terms as adjectives there aren't any strict rules about which word to use, but the general trend is to use *lighted* where a flame is involved (e.g. a lighted match) and *lit* when light, in the sense of brightness, is involved (e.g. a romantically lit room).

Lightning or lightening?

lightning = thunderstorms, something happening very quickly
lightening = making something less heavy
Acme washing powder is lightning fast!
We'll lighten your load.

Likeable or likable?

Both are correct.

Liqueur or liquor?

A liqueur is an aperitif drink.
Liquor refers to any alcoholic drink.

Lineage or linage?

lineage = line of decent, ancestry
linage = the number of printed lines
She has class: She comes from a reputable lineage.
You are going to have to edit your work; the linage exceeds our requirements.

Liquidate or liquidize or liquefy?

Liquidize and *liquefy* (not liquefie) mean 'to make something liquid'.
Liquidate means to pay a company debt. It can also be a euphemism for killing.

Also see
Euphemisms
chapter 12

Literary or literate?

literary = relating to literature
literate = able to read and write

Lorry or truck?

UK – lorry; US – truck

Lose or loose?

lose (verb) = cease to have
loose (adjective) = untied or unfastened

Foreign brand names:

Shitto: spicy Ghanaian pepper sauce

'Lots of' or 'a lot of'?

You can write either, however, I'd rather you wrote neither. Instead use the following: *a great deal, much, many.*

Loath or loathe?

Loath and loth are adjectives meaning 'disinclined'.
Loathe is a verb meaning 'abhor'.
I am loath to remove my shirt in public in fear that people will loathe what they see.

Loud or loudly?

Loud is an adjective and an adverb, whereas loudly is just an adverb.
They shouted loudly (not loud) at the traffic.

Lunch, dinner or supper?

Lunch is eaten by the British middle-class at noon, with dinner around 6pm.
The British working-class eat dinner at noon, tea at 6 pm and supper after 8 pm.
The Scottish working-class eat high tea after 6 pm.

Lumbar or lumber?

lumbar (adjective) = the back between the lower ribs and the pelvis
lumber = timber, unwanted articles, to move gauchely
lumber with = to burden someone with something

Luxuriant or luxurious?

A fast growing plant is luxuriant (fertile).
A five star hotel is luxurious (opulent).

M

Macro- or micro-?

Macro- is larger than *micro-*.

Madam, Ma'am or Madame?

Madam is the polite way to address a lady.
Ma'am is the British way to refer to female royalty.
Ma'am is also the US way to address a lady.
Madame is the French equivalent.

Magic or magical?

The adjective *magic* is related to the art of magic.
Magical refers to something or somebody who is enchanting.

Chiasmus:

'Those whose lot it is to ramble can seldom write, and those who know how to write very seldom ramble.'
Dr Samuel Johnson

Magnate or magnet?

A magnate has lots of money.

A magnet is a piece of metal that attracts iron.

Majority or plurality?

A proof that the US and UK are divided on language is the difference in meaning between *majority* and *plurality*.

If a majority vote wins a British election, it may not have gained fifty per cent of the votes. If a party gains over fifty per cent of the votes, it is said to have won by an 'absolute majority'.

In the US and Canada, under fifty per cent gains a majority and over gains a plurality.

Male or masculine?

The adjective male refers to the sex of a person.

Masculine refers to characteristic male qualities. Such qualities can apply to either sex:

My first wife was so masculine that I didn't know whether to kiss her or shake her by the hand.

Martial or marital?

Martial relates to warfare.

Marital relates to marriage:

Our marital affairs were terrible: At times I felt I was living under martial law.

Marinade or marinate?

You marinate your chicken legs in the marinade.

Matt or matte?

Matt (or matte) is an adjective meaning 'not shiny'.

The US prefers *mat*. This can occasionally confuse British readers:

Matt's mate ordered a mat mat, because it mattered to Matt that the mat was non-slip.

May or might?

Both can be used in the present tense, but *may* tends to suggest greater confidence than *might*.

May I go to the ball?
Q. Might I be so bold as to ask if I can go to the ball?
A. No – sod off!

Might should be used as the past tense of *may*.

I might have been able to go to the ball if I had asked more confidently.

Shakespearean insult:

'It is certain that when he makes water, his urine is congealed ice.' (*Measure for Measure*, act III, scene v)

May have or might have?

Compare the following:
He may have had an affair with the White House Intern = I don't know for sure if he had the affair as I am unaware of the material facts.
I might have had an affair with the White House Intern = I didn't actually have an affair, but the circumstances were such that I could have had an affair.

May be or maybe

If you can replace the single word *maybe* with *perhaps* and still retain the sentence's sense of meaning, then you have the correct word.
The first cake may be better for me than the second
Maybe I'll eat the first.

Medieval or mediaeval?

Both are correct. However *medieval* is preferable.

Meet with, meet or meet up?

You meet or meet up with a colleague.
You meet your death.
When writing for a UK audience, only use *meet with* if referring to an experience or 'receiving something'.
Does it meet with your approval?
Has he met with an accident?

Mega-

This is used as an adjective in its own right meaning 'exceptional or big'.
It's a mega-deal!

Men's wear or menswear?

Menswear is the most common usage.

Meteor or meteorite?

A meteor is another name for a shooting star.
A meteorite is lump of stone or metal that has fallen to earth.

Metre or meter?

UK measurement is in metres; US measurement is in meters.

Mileage or milage?

The most common spelling is *mileage*.

Chiasmus:

'Each success brings with it the potential of failure and each failure brings with it the potential of success.'
John F. Kennedy

Miner or minor?

A miner works underground.
A minor is under age.

Missing preposition

Spot the mistake:

I have no knowledge or interest in Xitole. ✗

You don't have knowledge *in* something so you have to use the preposition *of* as well:

I have no knowledge of or interest in Xitole. ✔

A prize to the first reader who can tell me where Xitole is located.

Email: xitole@ gabaywords.com

Misuse or abuse

abuse = to use wrongly or badly (this has moral overtones)
He abused his authority as a marketing director.
misuse = to use for unsuitable purposes, e.g. fiddling the marketing budget

Modern or modernistic?

modern = contemporary
modernistic = characterised by modern trends

Morale or moral?

Compare the following:
I am feeling very sad: my morale is at an all-time low.
My moral is 'Always be happy!'

Muslim or Moslem?

A follower of the Islamic religion is a Muslim. Moslem is a more traditional spelling.
Never write *Mohammedan* or *Mohammedanism*.
Culture or traditions relating to Islam are called Islamic.

Mythical or mythological?

mythical = imaginary
mythological = of or relating to mythology

Etymology:

Spinster – this term for a mature, unmarried lady refers to the eighteenth century occupation of a spinster who spun yarn or thread. Because the spinster was unmarried, she had more time to devote to spinning!

N

Naked or nude?

They mean the same thing, but *naked* has more pornographic overtones.

The website showed pictures of naked women.

Nationalise or naturalise?

nationalise = to transfer ownership from private industry to state ownership

naturalise = to bestow full nationality on a foreigner

Naturalist or naturist?

A naturalist studies natural history.

A naturist is a nudist.

Naught or nought?

naught = nothing (is not used much these days), US spelling of nought

nought = the figure 0 (see 'zero')

Nauseated or nauseous?

Compare the following uses:

Her body was nauseous (adjective), it made me feel nauseated (verb, past).

Needless to say

An idiom meaning 'especially'.

Needless to say, it's needless to say it.

Neglectful , negligent or negligible?

Negligible means 'trivial or very small'.

Neglectful and *negligent* mean 'careless'.

Although the damage was negligible, the accident occurred through negligence.

Net or Web?

You can use either.

Web is the abbreviation of World Wide Web.

Net (capitalized or not) is sometimes used as a short form for Internet.

Nightime or night-time?

Write *night-time*.

Brand origins:

Typhoo, 1863 – a Birmingham (UK) grocer dreamt up the name for his tea because it sounded oriental, as in 'typhoon', and 'Tea' or 'Tips' made it alliterative.

No body or nobody?

Compare the following:

Inspector Morse knew Bob's death was a murder, even though no body had been found.

Nobody wanted to offer any evidence.

Non-

Use *non-* only as a prefix: never as a word in its own right.

No one or no-one?

Preferably *no one*. Never write it as *noone*.

None

The agreement between the noun and the verb is what is in question here. It has to do with whether you can count how many of the nouns there are.

With count nouns, such as apples (one apple, two apples, etc.), use the plural form of the verb.

None of the apples are rotten.

With non-count nouns, such as milk, use the singular form of the verb.

None of the milk is sour.

Be careful with personal pronouns: men, women, children are all non-count nouns even though they are plural.

None of the children liked school meals.

Notable or noteable?

Write *notable*. (*Notable* and *noteworthy* both mean 'worthy of notice'. *Noted* means 'famous'.)

His work is notable.

She was a noted copywriter.

Notwithstanding

This means 'despite'.

It can either precede or follow its object.

Notwithstanding the evidence, I am innocent.

The evidence notwithstanding, I am innocent.

Noxious or obnoxious?

A suicide bomber (a person) is obnoxious.

Suicide bombing is noxious (physically or morally harmful).

Writers' words:

'Yes there is a meaning; at least for me, there is one thing that matters – to set a chime of words tinkling in the minds of a few fastidious people.' Logan Pearsall Smith

Numbers

Number prefixes follow both Latin and Greek formats.

English	Latin	Greek
one	uni-	mono-
two	bi-	di-
three	tri-	tri-
four	quad-	tetra-
five	quin-	penta-
six	sex-	hexa-
seven	sept-	hepta-
eight	oct-	okta-
nine	nona-	ennea
ten	deca-	deka-
hundred	cent-	hector-
thousand	milli-	kilo-

Use words for the numbers one to ten and digits from 11 onwards. Alternatively, use words for the numbers one to ninety-nine and digits from 100 onwards. Just remember to be consistent.

Hyphenate the numbers twenty-one to ninety-nine.

If you are writing a whole number, don't exceed more than four digits, for example: *245 million* rather than *245 000 000*. If you must write numbers in full for the sake of accuracy, group the digits in threes on either side of the decimal point. This does not apply to numbers with four digits. For example:

> *2346*
>
> *2 346 876*
>
> *23 468.76*
>
> *2.346 876*

The international standard (ISO 31:1992) recommends using a slim space between each set of digits. This prevents large numbers being divided at line breaks. This practice is commonplace for mathematical and scientific texts. For more general use, you can use a comma instead of a space to separate the sets of digits before the decimal point; after the decimal point, run the digits together.

> *23,468.876*
>
> *2.346876*

For more on numbers see Mind your Ps and Qs page 53

Chiasmus:

'Most men begin to go to the theatre when they arrive at the stage of having . . . pocket money, but no family; and they leave off when they arrive at the stage of a family and (consequently) no pocket money.' George Bernard Shaw - From an article in The World, July 27 1893.

Nutritional or nutritious?

nutritional = of or relating to nutrition (the study of nutrients and their ingestion into the body)
nutritious = nourishing

O

O or Oh?

For religious or literary purposes use 'O' (always with a capital letter).
Hear O Israel, the Lord is our God, the Lord is one.
O sweet girl, how tender is your kiss…

Oh! is used as an exclamation ranging from astonishment to glee, from lament to disillusionment.

-o

When pluralizing nouns ending in -o, simply add an **s**.
avocados buffalos cargos fiascos flamingos frescos
ghettos halos mangos momentos mottos tornados

Exceptions include: echoes, heroes, tomatoes and potatoes.

Obliged to or obligated to?

Both refer to some kind of moral or legal obligation. They are interchangeable. *Obligated* is more common in US English.
The client is obliged to pay on time.
The agency is obligated to act professionally.

Occupied or preoccupied?

A person who is *occupied* is busy.
A person who is *preoccupied* is in a world of their own, engrossed in a train of thought.

Odious or odorous?

Something odious is extremely unpleasant.
Something odorous has a distinctive smell.

Of

Be careful not to write *of* instead of *have* or even more commonly, the contraction form *-ve*.
He should have (not 'of') told the truth.
The must've (not 'must 'of') eaten the entire bag of popcorn.

Loquacious language:

gongoozler – someone who stares redundantly at something

Official or officious?

official (noun) = something authorised
official (noun) = someone who holds office or who is in a position
of authority
A person who is *officious* is very hard to please and self-important.

OK

Use *OK* or *okay* rather than *Ok, o.k.,* or *ok*.

Omelette or omelet?

UK – omelette (from French); US – omelet

On to or onto?

Write the words separately if *to* is part of an infinitive such as
to write, to run.
He went on to eat another hamburger.
She went on to read another book.

Follow the same rule when you mean 'towards'.
We drove on to Madrid.

For the position 'on' you can use either two words or one word.
The newly weds jumped onto the bed.
The newly weds jumped on to the bed.

In this last sense the one-word form is more common in the US but is
still frowned upon in the UK.

Online or on-line?

Preferably *online*.

Onward or onwards?

As an adjective, **onward** is preferred in the UK.
onward motion

When using it as an adverb, use either *onwards* or *onward*.
A history of Australia from 2006 onwards.

Oppress, repress or suppress?

oppress = to overpower by cruel force
*Despite the CIA being mistaken about WMDs, everyone agreed
that Sadaam Hussein oppressed his people.*

Brand origins:

Toyota, 1930s – a Japanese inventor gave his son who was building a motorcar, a patent for an automatic lock
designed for a Lancashire weaving company (1929). Being superstitious the family changed the penultimate letter to T,
since the original TOYODA required ten Japanese letters and TOYOTA only eight. Eight is a lucky number in Japan.

repress = to keep an impulse or the actions of other people under control
I repressed my urge to throttle him.
The regime repressed the ideals of free speech.

repress = to keep hidden one's thoughts or feelings
He had repressed feelings of inadequacy

suppress = to put to an end
The soldiers tried to suppress the rebellion.
suppress = to subdue or not express a feeling or thought
He suppressed his feelings of lust for his secretary.

Optician or ophthalmologist?

For a person who tests eyes and prescribes glasses or contact lenses use *optician* or *optometrist*.
An **ophthalmologist** and an *oculist* deal with diseases of the eye and the medical treatment of such diseases.

Oral or verbal?

Both mean spoken rather than written.
Oral also means of or relating to the mouth: you don't have verbal sex!
Verbal also means of or related to words: you don't have oral diarrhoea!

Ordinance or ordnance?

An *ordinance* is a declaration.
The noun *ordnance* refers to military supplies and is used by Ordnance Survey, a UK government agency supplying mapping services and products.

Orient or orientate?

These words have an interesting etymology: they both derive from 'facing or turning to the East'.
So we orientate ourselves to find our bearings.
They are pretty much interchangeable.
They found it difficult to orient themselves. ✔
They found it difficult to orientate themselves. ✔

Note this exception:
The agency was client oriented.

Oscillate or osculate?

oscillate = move backwards and forwards
osculate = to kiss
We oscillated slowly to the last dance and then osculated gently.

Chiasmus:

'Words are also actions and actions are a kind of words.' Ralph Waldo Emerson

121

Outward or outwards?

outward (adjective) = of, on or from the outside, relating to the external appearance

The outward journey will last 20 minutes.

outwards (adverb) = towards the outside

Wear your jumper with the logo facing outwards.

Overall, total, or whole?

overall = end to end, taking everything into account

If you can replace the word *overall* with any of the following do so with: *altogether, average, comprehensive, general, inclusive, total* or *whole.*

Overlay or overlie?

overlay = to cover or superimpose, past tense of overlie

overlie = lie over or upon

P

Palate, palette or pallet?

palate = the roof of the mouth, a sense of taste

palette = the board an artist uses to mix paints

pallet = a platform for moving and storing goods

Partially or partly?

partially = not completely or fully

He is partially sighted.

partly = in part, not wholly

It's partly silicone and partly flesh.

Passed or past?

Compare the following:

Yesterday's past has passed.

I walk past the shops in the morning.

The parade passed through the streets.

Pate or pâté

The crown of your head is sometimes called the pate (highly noticeable on a bald person's head).

Pâté is French for 'paste'.

Writers' words:

'But words are things, and a small drop of ink, falling, like dew, upon a thought, produces that which makes thousands, perhaps millions, think.' Lord Byron

Peaceable or peaceful?

peaceable = disposed to peace
peaceful = something that is characterised as being calm
They were peaceable people who lived peace-loving lives in a peaceful town.

Pedal or peddle?

peddle = to sell
pedal = to cycle a foot-operated lever (as in ride a bike)

Pendant or pendent?

Follow this example:
The beautiful pendant (necklace) was pendent (hanging) around her neck.

Percent or per cent?

Also see
Mind your Ps
and Qs
chapter 2

UK – per cent; US – percent (though this is now common on both sides of the Atlantic)
In the plural, it can be spelt with an 's', but most writers would drop the final 's'.
Four percents

In text always opt for words *per cent* rather than the symbol (%).
Use the symbol in graphs, tables and diagrams.

Permissible or permissive?

permissible = permitted
permissive = tolerant or open-minded
It is permissible because we live in a permissive society.

Perpetrate or perpetuate?

perpetrate = carry out
perpetuate = cause to continue
He perpetrated a crime and in doing so perpetuated a long family tradition of thieving.

Persecute or prosecute?

persecute = harass
prosecute = take legal action
I felt persecuted so I prosecuted her.

Foreign brand names:

Ass Glue – a Chinese medicine

Perspective or prospective?

perspective (noun) = outlook, a way of looking at things
prospective (adjective) = likely
Looking at things in perspective, the prospective winner must be Mr Jones.

Phenomenon or phenomena?

Phenomena is the plural of *phenomenon*.
The unparalleled craze became a phenomenon that preceded all phenomena.

Piteous or pitiful?

Both mean 'deserving pity'.
Pitiful is often used scornfully.
It's a pitiful sight: it's pitiful that no one wants to help.

Plaintiff or plaintive?

If you start a legal action, you are called a *plaintiff*.
If you sing a melancholy song, it is a *plaintive* song.

The prisoner's blues
I got banged up,
'Coz I hit,
That mean ol' plaintiff.
Now all I can do
Is sing the blues
No more women
Not one more kiss
It's just me now and my
Plain plaintive.

(OK, I won't become a lyricist!)

Pleaded or pled?

UK – pleaded; US – pled
The UK has pleaded for justice.
The US has pled for justice.

Pleonasm or tautology?

This is a particularly important lesson for copywriters as great copy should be terse rather than torturous.
Pleonasm uses more words than are necessary to convey a meaning.

Shakespearean insult:

'(Your) food is such as hath been belch'd on by infected lungs.' (*Pericles*)

Pleonastic	Improved
true facts	*facts*
very widespread	*widespread*
let's see with our eyes	*let's see*
various different	*various*

Tautology is the unnecessary repetition of the same sense of something in different words.

Tautological	Improved
They arrived one after the other in succession.	*They arrived in succession.*
They were in close proximity of being near to the office.	*They were near the office.*
Let's revert back to where we were before.	*Let's go back.*

Practice or practise?
Practice is a noun (except in the US where it is both a verb and a noun).
Practice makes perfect. This is exemplified at my doctor's practice.

Practise is a verb.
My doctor had to practise his practical skills before starting up his practice.

Precedence or precedent?
The noun *precedence* means 'priority'.
Precedent refers to something serving as a model for future behaviours or practices.

Predict or predicate?
A fortune-teller predicts the future.
The actual events in the future predicate (verify) such predictions.

Prefixes?
Prefixes are attached to the beginnings of words. Depending on the circumstances, they may or may not be used with hyphens.
Suffixes are attached to the ends of words.

Also see
Mind your Ps
and Qs
chapter 2

See Suffixes
page 136

Chiasmus:

'The heroic cannot be the common, nor the common the heroic.' Ralph Waldo Emerson

Premier or premiere?

premiere (noun) = the official first performance of an event such as a movie

premier (noun) = meaning prime minister or other head of government

premier (adjective) = the first in order or importance

The English Premier Football League

Prerequisite or perquisite?

A *prerequisite* is required before something can go ahead.

A *perquisite* is a benefit, right or privilege.

Presumptuous or presumptive?

presumptuous = bold, brash

presumptive = based on probability, without having all the information

Preventive or preventative?

You can use either. However, in the UK preventive is more common.

preventive treatment

Principal or principle?

I would rank this question in the top ten of copywriting confusions.

principal (noun) = head of an organisation

principal (adjective) = most important

Our principal aim is to write great proposals.

principle (noun) = a general scientific law or fundamental or moral rule guiding one's actions

We must never abandon our marketing principles

Program or programme?

program = instructions input into a computer

programme = a list, broadcast, schedule, itinerary

In the US *program* is used for all of these meanings.

Proportional or proportionate?

With one notable exception, you can write either. Do not write *proportionate representation*; instead, use *proportional representation*.

Medieval words:

pandemayn – a daily bread

Proved or proven?

In Scotland, legal evidence that cannot be substantiated is said to be 'not proven'.

In England, writers would use proven in phrases such as:

proven track record
proven success.

Proved is the past tends of the verb to prove.

Albert proved his love to Victoria. (It is said that she approved but was not amused.)

Provided or providing?

Both mean 'on the condition that'.

Never write *provided/providing if.*

I will show you my copy provided/providing that you show me yours. ✔
I will show you my copy provided/providing if you show me yours. ✗

Psychologist, psychiatrist, psychoanalyst or psychotherapist?

A *psychologist* studies the human mind.

A *psychiatrist* is a doctor specialising in the medicines that treat mental illnesses.

A *psychoanalyst* is a qualified professional who treats patients with mental disorders through bringing repressed fears and conflicts into the conscious mind (psychoanalysis).

A *psychotherapist* treats people with mental, emotional or psychosomatic disorders using non-medical treatments.

Pupil or student?

A *pupil* studies at school.

A *student* studies at a higher education establishment.

(In US anyone who studies is called a 'student'.)

Q

Quality

This word should not be used without consideration. Too many copywriters feel obliged to write copy along the lines of 'a quality service'. Unless you can define 'quality', do not write it.

Quiet or quieten?

Both verbs mean 'to calm' or 'to relax'.

In the UK *quieten* is the more common.

Quieten the kids down.

In the US '*quiet*' is used for the same purpose.

Loquacious language:

Quit or quitted?

The official UK version is *quitted*. However, most have conceded to the US version *quit*.

R

Racism or racialism?

Racism is the preferred use on both sides of the Atlantic.

Racket or racquet?

Both spellings are acceptable, but *racket* is the most common. *Racket* can also means a loud noise.

Raise or rise?

You can use either of these verbs to mean 'move higher' or 'augment'.

Raise is transitive.
The competitors raised their prices.

Rise is transitive.
I watched the sun rise.

(In the US use *raise* to denote a salary increase.)

Also see
Mind your Ps
and Qs
page 23

Rateable or ratable?

Preferably *rateable*.

Re or re-?

Strictly speaking you do not have to write a compound verb with a hyphen. However, for clarity many copywriters do just that. The key thing to bear in mind is whether adding the hyphen actually changes the meaning of the word. Of course, in creative copywriting that very confusion may offer a headline an original interpretation of a subject.

Thanks to Acme home insurance everything's recovered including re-covering my settee.

Although strictly speaking the following do not agree with the OED, it may be better to use the hyphenated versions for clarity:

recount = to tell a tale
re-count = to count again

recreation = relaxation, leisure
re-creation = the act of creating something again

relay = to transfer a message, information, etc.
re-lay = to lay again

Metaphors:

Five thousand pounds stewing gently in its interest, making old age safe. – Marjorie Barnard, 'The Lottery'

Remember that if you are adding the prefix *re-* to a word beginning with an *e* you need the hyphen for clarity, for example *re-educate, re-engineer, re-examine*.

Recover or re-cover?
recover = reclaim
re-cover = place a new cover on something

Referee or umpire?
These nouns refer to a person who ensures sports are played according to official rules. A *referee* is also a person who provides a character reference on behalf of another person.
When referring to cricket, baseball, hockey and tennis, use *umpire*.
For football or boxing, use *referee*.

Reflective or reflexive?
Both words are adjectives.
reflective = meditative, capable of producing a reflection
reflexive = a grammatical term, e.g. a reflexive verb. This is a transitive verb in which the object and subject are the same.
He hid himself
I chastised myself

The pronouns *myself, ourselves, yourselves* and *themselves* are known as reflexive pronouns.

Also see
Mind your Ps
and Qs
page 28

Regretful or regrettable?
Follow this example:
Her slip of the tongue was regrettable. She is so regretful to have caused such great offence.

Relation or relationship?
Use *relation* for abstract associations.
Your argument bears no relation to my case.

Write *relationship* for human associations.
His relationship with the girl was a wild and beautiful thing.

Write *relations* when conveying common connections or dealings.
business relations, public relations

In other words:

tangent - a man with a suntan

Relation or relative?

If you are referring to a person connected by blood, marriage or adoption, use either (I prefer relative). However, in the figurative sense 'poor relation' you could not use relative.

Relative can also mean 'in comparison to something'.

Reliable or reliant?

Someone who is *reliable* is dependable.

Someone who is *reliant* depends on others.

Remedial or remediable?

Use *remediable* if you are referring to something that can be remedied. Use *remedial* if you are referring to something that is meant to be a remedy for slow learners.

a remedial English class

Repellent or repulsive?

Providing you are referring to something that is disgusting, you can use either. However, for something exceptionally horrid, use *repulsive*. *Repellent* is also used in the sense of repelling an unwanted entity.

cockroach repellent

Repetitious or repetitive?

Use *repetitious* if you want to criticise a repetitive act.

The programme is so repetitious.

Use *repetitive* when describing a task or activity.

I have repetitive strain injury from using a mouse.

Respective or respectively?

respective (adjective) = belonging or relating separately to each of two or more people or things

The men and their respective wives stepped onto the dance floor.

respectively (adjective) = separately or individually and in the order already mentioned

James and John and their wives (Penny and Poppy respectively) stepped onto the dance floor.

respectively (adverb) = Individually or seperately in the order previously mentioned in an earlier statement.

Jackie and I like apples and oranges respectively.

You shouldn't write *respectively* if doing so can lead to confusion or ambiguity.

The husband and wife loved each other respectively.

Loquacious language:

Groak – Someone who stands near a group of people, in anticipation that he will be invited to join them.

Résumé or curriculum vitae?

UK employers seek a CV (curriculum vitae) from candidates.
US employers seek résumés.

Reverend or reverent?

Compare the following uses.

The reverend John Smith was aptly titled The Revd. John Smith. As a reverent and respectful person, I showed him reverence.

Rigorous or vigorous?

rigorous = thorough, exhaustive, accurate
vigorous = full of energy or spirit

Nicki's love-making was rigorous: it required a great deal of vigour.

Rob or steal?

You *steal* valuables.
You *rob* a place or a person.

I stole the Crown Jewels when I robbed the Tower of London.

Robbing or robing?

robbing = stealing from a person
robing = dressing

The robber was robbing the robing department.

S

-s (adding as a suffix)

For second person singular ending

Most verbs in the present tense have the ending -s in the second person singular.

writes, loves, kills

For plural nouns

Virtually all nouns are pluralized by adding -s.
Add -es for nouns ending in 'o', 'y', 's', 'sh', 'ch', 'x' or 'z'.

matches, taxes, quizzes

Exceptions include *sheep, mice, shelves* and *wolves*, and the -ss examples below.

If a noun ends in 's' and has two or more syllables, add -es.

atlases, mattresses, surpluses

Twisted truths:

US and UK English differ when adding an plural -s to nouns of one syllable ending in an 's'.

Compare the following:

US	UK
busses	*buses*
gasses	*gases*

Sack or sac?
A sack is a large bag.
A sac is a bag-like part of an animal or mammal.

Saccharin or saccharine?
The sweetener is *saccharin*.
Something sweet can be said to be *saccharine*.

Saint, St or S.?
When writing the full name of a saint, write *Saint*.
If mentioning a saint incidentally as part of a larger text, you can write *St*.
When referring to a church featuring a saint's name, you can write *St*.
Geographical locations names after saints are also written *St*, except in French when personal and geographical names retain the word *Saint* (or *Sainte* – for the female counterpart).

Salary or wage?
Both nouns refer to regular payments made to employees.
A *salary* is often paid on a monthly basis.
A *wage* is usually paid on a weekly basis.

Saleable or salable?
Saleable is preferable.

Sank or sunk?
sunk = past tense *and* past participle of sink
sank = past tense of sink

All of the following are correct:
It has sunk beneath the waves.
(past participle – used with the auxiliary verb *to have)*
It sunk beneath the waves. (past tense)
It sank beneath the waves. (past tense)

Brand origins:

Sanyo – this Japanese word means 'three seas'; so called because the company's founder Toshio Iue set out to sell worldwide, across the Atlantic, Pacific and Indian Oceans.

Satiric or satirical?

Both adjectives mean 'using satire'.
In the UK 'satirical' is preferred.

Sari, saree or sarong?

A *sari* (or the less common form *saree*) is a long body covering worn by Hindu women.
A *sarong* is a long skirt worn in southeast Asia and the Pacific.

Scarves or scarfs?

You can use either.

Scarring or scaring?

Compare the following examples:
This horror movie is scaring me!
The operation left a lot of scarring on my leg.

Sceptic or septic?

Compare the following examples:
Many people are sceptical (US – skeptical) about marketing, as they believe it is often a dubious occupation.
The wound was left to fester; it turned septic.

Scots, Scottish or scotch?

Compare the following examples:
Robert has a very strong Scots (adjective) accent.
The Scottish (noun) are also known as the Scots (noun).
He has a strong Scottish (adjective) accent.

Scotch is an archaic term meaning Scottish – only refer to something as Scotch if the term has already been coined, for example Scotch whisky, Scotch pancake, Scotch egg.

Secret or secretive?

Compare the following examples:
I don't like telling too many people about my private business. That is why I am secretive (adjective).
The Da Vinci Code *by Dan Brown is all about secret (adjective) organisations operating in secrecy (noun).*
A secret (noun) can only be a secret (noun) if everyone has ensured it remains private.

Chiasmus:

'If a man owns land, the land owns him.' Ralph Waldo Emerson

Sensual or sensuous?

sensual = pleasing to the body, such as sex, food or drink
sensuous = affecting the senses (especially music, poetry and art) rather than the intellect
However, this distinction is being lost in modern language.

Sewed, sewn, sown, sowed or sowing?

Compare the following examples:
My son's suit was sewed by hand.
The tailor has sewn for twenty years.
The wheat is sown in Spring.
She sowed the seeds in autumn.
She is sowing the grass in time for summer.

Shall or will?

See Mind your Ps and Qs, page 24.

Should or would?

Follow the same rules as for *shall* and *will*.

Silicon or silicone?

The chemical element found on the earth and present in sand, glass and other minerals is known as *silicon*.
Silicone is a compound of *silicon*.

Smelled or smelt?

Both spellings are correct.

Sociable or social?

sociable = friendly
social = of society, promoting friendship
She was very sociable. In fact she joined the local social club.

Somebody or someone?

These are interchangeable.
Most writers on both sides of the Atlantic opt for *someone*.

Sometime or some time?

sometime (adverb) = at some point
sometime (adjective) = former
John Kerry, the sometime nominee for President…

Write *some time* when referring to a period of time.
She had meant to ditch her boyfriend for some time.

Shakespearean insult:

'You are as a candle; the better part burnt out.' (*Henry IV*, part II, act I, scene ii)

Sometimes or sometimes?

some times = on some occasions

sometimes = occasionally

There are some times when I want to run around dressed in a pantomime costume.

Sometimes I feel like drinking an orange juice.

Split infinitives

Q: What's the copywriting equivalent of a division of opinion?

A: A split infinitive.

The first thing is to establish exactly what an 'infinitive' is. An infinitive is a verb in its purest form (i.e. without any tense or pronoun being added to it, for example *to do, to make, to laugh)*. Instinctively you should know that the following are wrong: *we to laugh, we to sing*. (By the way, if this is your habit, may I suggest an alternative career to copywriting – something where accuracy isn't crucial… How about a politician?)

The problem occurs when you split the *to* and the verb and place another word or phrase in between them. Here's a famous example from Star Trek:

…to boldly go where no man has gone before.

Many copywriters use the split infinitive for emphasis; however, you should be made aware that if you follow this style you are in fact splitting the infinitive. The accepted rule is do not separate *to* from its infinitive.

That said, there are occasions when you simply cannot help splitting it:

Will Mary ask Jane to kindly tell the customer that she simply cannot help.

By putting *kindly* in front of *to* the entire meaning would change.

Will Mary ask Jane kindly to tell the customer that she simply cannot help.

To fiercely fight the Sudanese…

Here you have another example of a split infinitive, placing the adverb *fiercely* between the *to* and the verb *fight*. This could be avoided by moving the adverb to after Sudanese.

From a copywriting stance I suggest that if splitting an infinitive causes confusion, simply don't split it!

Here's a confusing example:

He failed to completely understand me.

Loquacious language:

henotheism – the belief that God is a hen

Swap it around to…

He completely failed to understand me.

…or *He failed to understand me completely.*

…and you have a sense of total rather than partial failure.

Stadiums or stadia?

You can use either. However, *stadiums* is more common.

Stationery or stationary?

Stationary means 'still'.

Stationery means 'writing materials'.

(A quick check: is someone who supplies stationery a stationer or stationar?)

Stratagem or strategy?

stratagem = a plan, trick or ploy intended to outwit an opponent

strategy = the skilful planning of a campaign

Both originally referred to military plans, coming from the Greek word for 'a general'.

Strategy or tactics?

Strategy relates to the broader plan or course of action to achieve a goal.

Tactics refers to the procedures required to achieve a strategy.

Stalactite or stalagmite?

Stalactites hang down; they hang on 'tite'.

Stalagmites stick up; they 'mite' get taller.

Such as or like?

Write *such as* to introduce an example.

Write *like* to introduce a comparison.

Suffixes

Suffixes often have a grammatical effect on the word to which they are added. Generally, there are two kinds:

inflectional: a suffix used to form an inflection

link + -s or -ed

light + -er or -est

derivational: a suffix used to form a derivative

Nouns: banker, booklet, softness

Adjectives: fearless, restrictive, tearful, workable

Verbs: characterise, shorten

Adverbs: happily

Medieval words:

beefeater – a servant paid in food and lodgings

Gabay at a Glance

A great packaging copy technique it to use '-able'
to describe a product.

-huggable -loveable -munchable

Or, why not try another type of suffix from this list.

Common suffixes:

Suffix	Meaning	Example
-able, -ible	able to be or do something	adaptable
-age	an action or condition	postage
-al	relating to	coastal
-al	an action or condition	postal
-an, -ian	a person coming from a country	Norwegian
-an; -ian	a professional or expert	mathematician
-ance, -ence, -ancy, -ency	a quality, state or action	persistence
-ant -ent	a person or thing that does something	student
-ar	belonging to	solar
-ary	a person doing something	emissary
-ary	connected with	luminary
-ary	a place for	seminary
-ate	a chemical compound	phosphate
-ate	possessing a quality	unfortunate
-ate	cause to have or become	perpetuate
-atic	used to create adjectives from nouns	bureaucratic
-ation	a state, condition or action	jubilation
-ation	an action	masturbation
-cide	killing	fratricide
-cy	a quality or state	tenancy
-dom	an area governed	kingdom
-dom	a state or condition	freedom
-dom	a group of people	officialdom

Writers' words:

'I'm all in favour of keeping dangerous weapons out of the hands of fools. Let's start with typewriters.' Solomon Short

-ed	used to form the past and past participles of verbs	mended
-ed	revealing or having a quality of state	mesmerised
-ee	someone in a specific condition or state	evacuee
-ee	a person to whom something is done or given	employee
-eer	a person who does or deals with something	mountaineer
-en	made of	wooden
-en	cause to become	soften
-er	used to form a noun from a verb	cooker
-er	used to form the comparative form of adjectives	neater
-er	a professional	copywriter
-er	someone who lives in a location	New Yorker
-er	a person or thing that has a certain attribute	teenager
-ery, -ry	a group of things	crockery
-ery, -ry	the practice of something	cookery
-ery, -ry	a condition	slavery
-ery, -ry	a place where something is done	fishery
-ese	a place or source of a nation and/ or its language	Taiwanese
-ess	used to form the feminine of nouns	baroness
-est	used to form the superlative of adjectives	shrewdest
-ette	used to form feminine nouns	usherette
-ette	a small or diminutive form of something	cigarette
-fold	the multiple of a part or the number of parts	six-fold
-ful	the quantity that something can carry or hold	cupful
-fu	having a quality	tearful
-fy, -ify	to make or become	liquefy
-gon	an angle	hexagon

Chiasmus:

'Nowadays, all the married men live like bachelors, and all the bachelors like married men.' Oscar Wilde

-hood	a period of being, a circumstance or condition	womanhood
-i	someone belonging to a religion or people	Hindi
-ic, -ical	related to	phantasmagorical
-ice	used to form abstract nouns	cowardice
-ics	a science or cluster of activities	meta-physics
-ide	a chemical compound	insecticide
-ine	made of something or connected with	crystalline
-ing	used to make the present participle of a verb	singing
-ing	a procedure, action or outcome	meeting
-ion	an action, process or state	retention
-ious	having a characteristic or trait	pious
-ise, -yse	used to form nouns of quality, state or function	exercise
-ise, - ize, -yse, -yze	used to create verbs	institutionalise
-ish	pertaining to a country or language	Finnish
-ish	having the undesirable traits of something	childish
-ish	to a degree	reddish
-ism	a trait, practice or deed	heroism
-ism	a system of political beliefs	communism
-ist	someone who follows a political, social or religious belief	communist
-ist	a person who does something in particular	motorist
-ite	a chemical substance	nitrite
-itis	a disease	appendicitis
-ity, -ty	a trait, circumstance or condition	sincerity
-ive	a cause giving rise to a quality	productive
-less	not having	careless
-let	something petite	eyelet
-like	akin to	monkeylike
-ling	someone or something small	duckling
-logy	a science or subject	sociology

Brand origins:

Hush Puppies – during a formal dinner, the sales manager for Wolverine Worldwide, Inc. was served small balls of fried corn dough called 'hush puppies'. He felt it was a great name for his company's range of pigskin shoes, which were marketed as having the ability to 'soothe a customer's aching feet' (aka their barking dogs).

-ly	used to form adverbs	costly
-ly	pertaining the qualities of something	sisterly
-ly	a regular timing of events	monthly
-man	someone who does something or lives in a place	Frenchman
-ment	a state, trait, condition, procedure or result	contentment
-most	the extreme	uppermost
-ness	a state, quality or circumstance	weakness
-oid	like	humanoid
-ory	having a quality	contributory
-ory	place	observatory
-ous	having a characteristic	illustrious
-phile	someone who particularly enjoys a subject or occupation	paedophile
-phobia	dread of something	xenophobia
-proof	able to resist something	showerproof
-ship	a skill	craftsmanship
-ship	a condition	hardship
-some	causing	irksome
-th	used to form adjectives from numbers (also known as ordinal numbers)	sixth
-th	a state	breadth
-tion	an action, procedure, condition or result	dedication
-ward, -wards	in a direction	forwards
-ways, -wise	a method	crosswise
-ways, -wise	concerning something	gardenwise
-y	having a quality	windy
-y	a tender name	mummy
-y	the act of conducting something; circumstance or situation	frenzy

Loquacious language:

hinny – the offspring of a female donkey and a male horse

When adding a suffix, follow one of these four rules:

The 1-1-1 rule

Does the stem word
have **one** syllable?
end in **one** consonant sound?
have **one** vowel?

If the answer to these questions is yes and the suffix starts with a consonant sound, you don't have to change the foundation word:

flat + ly ➔ *flatly*

If the suffix starts with a vowel, simply double the last letter of the stem word:

flat + est ➔ *flattest*
bet + ing ➔ *betting*
quit + ing ➔ *quitting*

Never double a final *w* or *x*:

flex + ing ➔ *flexing*
saw + ed ➔ *sawed*

The 'e' rule

If your ending starts with a consonant, keep the 'silent e':

hope + ful ➔ *hopeful*
appease + ment ➔ *appeasement*

Some exceptions are: argument, awful, duly, ninth, truly, whilst, wholly, wisdom. And do keep the 'e' with words ending in soft 'c' and soft 'g'.

If your ending starts with a vowel, leave out the 'e':

hope + ing ➔ *hoping*
appease + ed ➔ *appeased*
prepare + ation ➔ *preparation*

The 'y' rule

When adding an ending to a word finishing with a vowel + y
leave the 'y':

enjoy + ment   = *enjoyment*

If you are adding an ending to a word finishing with a consonant + 'y', change the 'y' to an 'i':

empty + er   = *emptier*
hazy + ness   = *haziness*

Writers' words:

'What is written without effort is read without pleasure.' Samuel Johnson

Exceptions include: daily – not dayly, laid – not layed, paid – not payed, etc. Also, when adding -*ing* to a consonant + 'y' stem keep the 'y' to avoid having to 'i's together (but the exception to the exception is skiing and taxiing – confused yet?).

The 2-1-1 rule:

Does the stem word	have **two** syllables?
	end with **one** consonant?
Is this consonant	preceded by **one** vowel?

In most cases, if the first syllable of your stem word is stressed you simply add your suffix without making any changes to the stem word.

target → *targeting*
question → *questioning*
slender → *slenderness*

Notable exceptions to this rule include doubling up the last letter in:

worship → *worshipping,*
kidnap → *kidnapping*
outfit → *outfitting.*

If the stem word is stressed on the second syllable, there is no change when adding a suffix that starts with a consonant:

regret + ful → *regretful*
displace + ment → *displacement*

If you want to add a suffix starting with a vowel to these kinds of words, simply double-up the final consonant:

regret + ing → *regretting*
begin + er → *beginner*

T

Tasteful or tasty?

tasteful = things which demonstrate fine aesthetic taste
tasty = things which have a good flavour

Temporal or temporary?

Temporal refers to something secular or ordinary rather than spiritual.
Temporary refers to something which only lasts a short time.

Terminal or terminus?

Both nouns refer to a finishing point. *Terminal* can be used for the arrival/departure point for any means of transport, whereas *terminus* only refers to railways.

Etymology:

the big cheese – this phrase, meaning 'very important person', comes from the Persian and Urdu word 'chiz', meaning 'thing'.

As an adjective *terminal*, means 'life-ending'.
a terminal illness

Testimonial or testimony?

testimonial = a formal open letter testifying to a person's character and qualifications
testimony = a formal written or spoken statement of evidence

Thank you or thank-you?

Never write *thank you* as one word.
Only hyphenate it when describing a noun.
She delivered her thank-you speech to the nation.
Thank you very much for your kind words.

That or this?

That refers to something in the past or at a distance.
I did that. I like that one over there.
This refers to something present or in close proximity.
I do this. I like this one here.

That or which?

Both can be used for defining clauses.
When writing incidental information, use *which* with commas acting as brackets.
The book, which Gabay wrote whilst on holiday in Outer Mongolia, sent a chill down my spine.

If it is not incidental information, use *that* without bracketing commas.
The book that is on the shelf is a really good read.

If you already have a lot of *thats* in the sentence you can use *which* instead.
That was the book that (which) he wrote that Sunday when that crate of boxes arrived.

There, they're or their?

there = that place
they're = they are
their = to something belonging to 'them'

Through or thru?

In the UK write *through*.
In the US – in informal writing – you can write *thru* when you mean 'from one end to the other'.
The sale is on Monday thru Friday.

Metaphors:

She came in looking flushed and fine, with diamonds of sleet in her hair. – Laurie Colwin, 'A Mythological Subject'

Till or until?

Both words mean *up to* (a point or limit), *as far as, so as to reach.*
Until is more formal and should be used at the beginning of a sentence rather than *till.*

Together with

This means 'in addition to'.
If you replace *together with* with *and,* the verb becomes plural:
The copywriter, together with the Account Director, presented the work.
The copywriter and the Account Director presented the work.

Tolerance or tolerate?

tolerance (noun) = the ability to put up with something
tolerate (verb) = to put up with something
My tolerance of pain is good.
I can't tolerate this kind of behaviour.

To, too or two?

To is a preposition denoting direction or position
To also makes up part of a finite verb, for example *to love.*
Too means 'also' or 'to a greater degree'.
Two is the number 2.
I was too full to eat two cakes.

Tortuous or torturous?

tortuous = something full of twists and turns, something complex
torturous = agonising and painful
The route was tortuous.
Her singing was torturous.

Toward or towards?

You can use either, although in the UK it is preferable to use *towards.*

Transient or transitory?

Both refer to something lasting for only a short time.
When referring to the quickness of passing by it is best to use *transient.* It is best to use *transitory* to refer to the lamentable passing of time or a change.

Transport or transportation?

UK – transport
US – transportation
I can get to Newcastle using my own transport.
Our airline is the fastest form of transportation.

Foreign brand names:

Zit! – a German brand of chocolate and fruit confectionery

Transverse or traverse

transverse (adjective) = lying or sitting across
traverse (verb) = to go across
traverse (noun) = way or path across

Treble or triple?

These are interchangeable, although there are some instances where the usage is set.

treble clef

to do a treble (in sport to win three contests)

triple jump

triple time (music)

Troop or troupe?

troop = an army or group of people or animals
troupe = a group of performers

Tsar, tzar or czar?

These are all versions of the same word meaning Russian emperor. *Tsar* is the most common.

In English politics members of Parliament assigned with special responsibilities for social issues are called – *tzar* (lowercase 't').

youth tzar, drugs tzar, music tzar, patients tzar.

U

Underfoot or under foot?

Write as one word (*underfoot*), except in the colloquial sense:
My kids are always getting under foot.

Underhand or underhanded?

You can use either.

Underlay or underlie?

underlay (verb) = to place something underneath
Underlay the carpet.

underlay (noun) = what is put under a carpet
underlie (also underlying) = the cause or basis of something
There was an underlying tension in his voice.

Unexceptionable or unexceptional?

Something or someone *unexceptionable* is inoffensive.
Something or someone *unexceptional* is ordinary.

Twisted truths:

Getting your words in the correct order makes a huge difference. Which is correct?
Fried fresh fish, fish fried fresh, fresh fried fish, fresh fish fried, or fish fresh fried?

145

Unique

Too many copywriters claim that a product or service is *unique*. Invariably such products or services are not unique.

You cannot describe something as *very, quite, nearly* or *almost* unique. It is either unique or not. Continuous misuse of the word only serves to 'dumb-down' English and devalue the merits of a products and services.

Upon or on?

You can write either, but *upon* is more formal and is not common in everyday language or spoken English.

Upward, upwards or upwards of?

upward (adjective) = towards a higher point

An upward development.

upward and upwards (adverb) = towards a higher point

Jack and Jill went upwards.

Let's move upward towards success.

The US prefers 'upward'.

Some, especially in the US, use *upwards* for 'more than'.

The agency has upwards of fifty employees.

My recommendation is to stick to 'more than'.

Used to or be used to?

Compare the following:

I used to play the guitar. ✔

I use to play the guitar. ✘

I didn't used to play the guitar. (casual)

I used not to play the guitar. (formal)

I am used to playing the guitar. ✔

I am used to play the guitar. ✘

Urbane or urban?

urban = of a city or town

urbane = debonair, well-mannered

Usage or use?

usage = established procedure

This chapter deals with word usage.

use = a purpose for which something should be used

I put the Internet to good use.

Etymology:

pet – originally a term of endearment for an indulged child. By 1539, the meaning was extended to include domestic animals. 'Pet' was used as a verb around 1515, when it meant to *break wind*, from the Italian *Petto*.

Usable or useable?

Preferably *usable*.

Utilise or use?

Use means simply 'to take, hold or deploy something to accomplish a particular goal'.
Utilise specifically means 'put to a useful and productive purpose'.
Conscientious nations utilise waste for recycling.

V

Vagary, vagaries or vague?

vague = something unclear
vagary (noun) = an unexpected and inexplicable change
vagaries = plural of vagary
The vagaries of politics give me a vague sense of helplessness.

Valiant, valorous or valorise?

valiant = showing courage and bravery
valorous = describes a person who is valiant
valorise = to raise or stabilise the value of a commodity, to give value to something
The management decided to reduce production and valorise prices.

Vegetarian or vegan?

Both follow a meat-free diet. Vegans avoid eating any animal produce including eggs and dairy products.

Vendor or vender?

UK – vendor; US – vender

Venturous or adventurous?

Both mean 'daring, or ready to take a risk'. *Adventurous* is more common.
US variations include: *adventuresome* and *venturesome*.

Veranda or verandah?

Both are acceptable, but *veranda* is more common.

Verbiage or verbose?

Both refer to an excess of words.
verbiage (noun) = written text that is overly long or technical
verbose (adjective) = using more words than is necessary
(can apply to both speech and writing)

Also see
Pleonasm
page 124-125

Loquacious language:

ignicolist – a fire worshiper

Very or most?

very = to a higher degree

This is a very attractive offer.

most = to the highest degree

This is the most attractive offer you will find.

Vice or vise?

UK writers write *vice* for all occasions.

US writers write *vise* when referring to a clamping tool.

Visible or visual?

visible = able to be seen, in the public eye

The visible side of poverty.

visual = of or relating to sight

It was vision of visual stimulation.

Versus, vs, or v?

With the exception of legal writing, you can abbreviate versus either as *vs* or *v*. A full point is not necessary.

W

Wait for, wait on or wait up?

To indicate being in expectation of something or someone, write *wait for*.

Wait on is used to refer to the action on serving someone.
Wait on can also be used in the intransitive sense of 'being patient'.
Wait up means to stay up late waiting for someone to return. In Canada it means 'slow down'.

Wangle or wrangle?

wangle = to extract something by manipulating people

wrangle = quarrel or dispute (often ongoing)

They wrangled over the marketing contract.

Webpage or web page?

The OED prefers *web page*. Most of my clients prefer 'webpage'.

Website or web site?

The OED prefers *web site*, but *website* is also very common.

Wed or wedded?

Most people use *wed* unless referring to something closely connected:

Etymology:

obtuse – originally an English synonym for dull, stupid or insensible. By 1570, it meant an angle greater than 90 degrees. (An angle less than 90 degrees is known as an acute angle.)

We were wed in September.
He was wedded to Rock n' Roll.

Wacky or whacky?

You can spell this either way. Most opt for *wacky*.

Whatever or what ever?

If you want to emphasise 'what' then you can write *what ever*.
What ever could you have been thinking of!

If you intend to mean 'no matter what' write *whatever*.
Whatever happens, I will still love you.

What or which?

Which refers to a specific range of alternatives.
What refers to a broad range of alternatives.
Which book do you like the most?
What books do you like?

While or whilst?

UK – either; US – while

Whisky or whiskey?

The Scots make *whisky*.
The Irish and Americans make *whiskey*.

Who's or whose?

Who's is short for 'who is' or 'who has'.
Whose means 'belonging to whom'?

Who or whom?

Use *who* when the person to whom you are referring is the subject of the verb.
Use *whom* when the person to whom you are referring is the object of the verb.
The girl who loves candy… (She does the loving.)
The boy whom I saw… (I do the seeing.)
The man to whom I owe everything… (I do the owing.)

When writing questions, most people drop *whom* and write *who*.
Who did you give it to?

However, if you want to be absolutely correct:
To whom did you give it?

Chiasmus:

'The Ideal man . . . should always say much more than he means, and always mean much more than he says.'
Oscar Wilde

Whom or that?

When *whom* is written as a relative direct object, I suggest changing it to *that*, for example:

She is the girl whom I wanted to kiss. ✗
She is the girl that I wanted to kiss. ✔

-wise or -ways?

These can often be interchanged. However, for precision, remember that *-wise* relates to a particular manner and *-way*s to a particular direction.

He gave her a sideways glance.
She looked at him likewise.

Worthwhile, worth-while or worth while?

Write as two words after a verb and one word before a noun.

It is worth while seeing the show.
It is a worthwhile show.

Many copywriters simply write it as one word for all occasions.

Wrong or wrongly?

Use *wrongly* as an adverb.

She was wrongly imprisoned.

Wrong can be an adjective, adverb or noun:

It was the wrong turning.
The relationship went wrong after three months.
A terrible wrong was committed in New York.

WWW (short for World Wide Web)

Use capital letters. Don't punctuate it or write it at the beginning of a sentence.

X-Y-Z

Xmas or Christmas?

The 'X' in *Xmas* denotes the Greek letter *chi*, used as the first letter in the Greek form of *Christ*.

Many copywriters in Canada and America feature *Xmas* in seasonal advertising. (Note the correct usage of the capital 'X'.)

X-ray or x-ray?

Most writers opt for *X-ray* with a capital letter.

Anagrams:

from SEMOLINA to IS NO MEAL

Xerox or photocopy?

If you are referring to the company using the trademarked noun, always write *Xerox*™ with a capital 'X'.

If you referring are to the verb meaning 'to copy on a Xerox machine', write *xerox*. For any other type of photocopy, write *photocopy*.

Yogurt, yoghurt, or yoghourt?

UK writers prefer to write either *yoghurt* or *yogurt*. In a sample of yogurts at my local supermarket, *yogurt* was far and away the most popular spelling in current use.

Yoghourt appears in www.dictionary.com which features US spellings.

Yoke or yolk or yokel?

A *yoke* is a connecting bar.

A *yolk* is the yellow part of an egg.

A *yokel* is a scornful term for a country bumpkin.

Your or you're?

Your means 'belonging to you'.

You're is a contraction of 'you are'.

Yo-yo or yo yo

Yo-yo is preferable.

Yours faithfully, Yours sincerely, or Yours?

The advent of email has meant that a growing number of people no longer bother with formal closures to everyday correspondence. For those who refuse to sign a letter or email with either simply name or initials, here are the rules:

Yours faithfully is used when addressing an unknown reader.

Yours sincerely is used when addressing a letter to a person whose name you know.

You can abbreviate this to simply *Yours*.

Note the capital letter.

Yuck or yuk?

Either is okay, but *yuck* (adjective *yucky*) is the most common.

Zero, naught or nought?

Write *nought* (or less frequently *naught*) for the digit 0.

In scientific contexts use *zero*.

In sporting contexts use *love* or *nil*.

In the US *zip* is also common.

Number crunchers:

novemdecillion = 1000 octodecillion (US).

Brains, pen, action!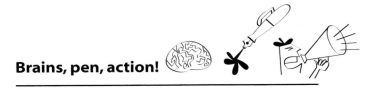

Something to ponder...

This chapter has dealt with pinpointing correct word structures. Precision is vital in copywriting.

- A hyponym is a word that is linked in meaning to, but is more specific than, another word. A hypernym is the more general term. For example:

Hypernyms	Hyponyms
flower	rose, tulip, carnation
music	hip hop, classical, pop
food	burger, chips, fruit

- A word that has more than one meaning is called a polysemic. For example:

  The verdict was clear.
  The road was clear.
  Water glass was clear.

1 Check your last piece of copy and ask yourself if it could be improved by adding more hyponyms than hypernyms, or perhaps vice versa.

2 Can you think of any more polysemes?

Brand origins:

When Pepsi entered the Chinese market, it's slogan 'Come alive with the Pepsi generation' translated as 'Pepsi brings back your dead ancestors'. In 1920, Coca-Cola's brand name in Chinese translated to 'Bite the wax tadpole'.

5. Spell well

It took me years to sort out my laundry. No matter how many times I was told, I simply could not remember how to spell words like 'necessary'. In the end, a simple notion of recalling the line 'one collar and two socks' did the trick. However, the thought of trying to remember such ditties for every difficult word in the English language begins to sound a little awkward – to say the least!

So, in addition to following some of the guidelines offered in this chapter, may I suggest you also invest in a dictionary. Ah! But not any old dictionary: a simple spelling dictionary as used in schools. They don't provide definitions but they do divide words into simple components.

Need more help?
www.gabaywords.com

Spell well

Spelling; a prelude

I have a spelling checker,
It came with my PC.
It plane lee marks four my revue
Miss steaks aye can knot sea.

Eye ran this poem threw it,
Your sure reel glad two no.
Its vary polished in it's weigh.
My checker tolled me sew.

A checker is a bless sing,
It freeze yew lodes of thyme.
It helps me right awl stiles two reed,
And aides me when eye rime.

Each frays come posed up on my screen
Eye trussed too bee a joule.
The checker pours o'er every word
To cheque sum spelling rule.

Bee fore a veiling checker's
Hour spelling mite decline,
And if we're lacks oar have a laps,
We wood bee maid too wine.

Butt now bee cause my spelling
Is checked with such grate flare,
Their are know fault's with in my cite,
Of nun eye am a wear.

Now spelling does knot phase me,
It does knot bring a tier.
My pay purrs awl due glad den
With wrapped word's fare as hear.

To rite with care is quite a feet
Of witch won should bee proud,
And wee mussed dew the best wee can,
Sew flaw's are knot aloud.

Sow ewe can sea why aye dew prays
Such soft wear four pea seas,
And why eye brake in two averse
Buy righting want too pleas.

(Source unknown)

Spelling: The curse of copywriters everywhere!

What with 'house-styles' urging us to spell email, 'e-mail', 'Email', 'eMail', and so on, spelling has become more confusing than ever!

Take heart. If you really are getting your vowels in a twist, follow the simple advice outlined here:

Choose your favourite authority on grammar, spelling and so forth, such as Oxford, Cambridge or Websters (I base my spelling on Oxford). Using this styling as your foundation, compile a list of the most common words used by your organisation.

In compiling the list, be sure to include a section on words with alternative spellings, especially if both spellings are in common use or altered according to which country your copy is aimed at. For example, US versus UK spellings on websites. If you are going to use a lot of US spelling, I recommend that you keep an American dictionary close to hand, such as, Random House's Dictionary of the American Language and Webster's New World Dictionary.

Also keep in mind that brand names are nouns, therefore spell them with a capital letter, unless the brand name was designed with a lower case letter.

Anagrams:

from CONTINUED to UNNOTICED

A general spelling list

Each of the words in the list below are spelled correctly. Some differ according to context, others can be spelled either way (for these words it is best to pick one and stick to it).

acknowledgment	acknowledgement
advise	advice
advisor	adviser
ageing	aging
appendixes	appendices
biased	biassed
by-law	bye-law
centring	centering
connection	connexion
disk (PC)	disc (recording)
dispatch	despatch
enyclopedia	encyclopaedia
fetus	foetus
focused	focussed
flyer	flier
gram	gramme
guerrilla	guerilla
gypsy	gipsy
inflexion	
('inflexion' in maths)	inflection
-ise	-ize
judgment	judgement
medieval	mediaeval
premiss	premise
programme	program (computer)
	– programmer has two 'm's in both cases
reflection	reflexion
storey	story

'History will be kind to me for I intend to write it.' Winston Churchill

British and American spelling guidelines

Some common mistakes

ae and oe	gynaecology, diarrhoea	gynecology, diarrhea
-ce or -se	(nouns) licence, defence, offence, pretence, practice	license (verb and noun), pretense, offense, pretense, practise (verb and noun)
Double letters	jeweller, marvellous, traveller, worshipped, woollen	jeweler, marvelous, traveler, worshiped, woolen
Silent e	axe, programme	ax, program
-f- or -ph-	sulphur	sulfur
-oul- or -ol-	mould, smoulder	mold, smolder
-our or –or	colour, favour, humour, neighbour	color, favor, humor, neighbor
-re or er	centre, theatre, calibre, sombre	center, theater, caliber, somber
-yse or -yze	analyse, paralyse	analyze, paralyze

Almost – but not quite the same

aeroplane	airplane
aluminium	aluminum
baby's bottle	baby bottle
crayfish	crawfish
doll's house	dollhouse
maths	math
railway	railroad
sanatorium	sanitarium
windscreen	windshield
waistcoat	vest
railway/bus station/bus garage	depot

Loquacious language:

moliminous – taking great effort over something

You say potatoe – I say potato!

adrenalin	epinephrine
bath	tub
biscuit	cookie
bonnet (car)	hood
boot (car)	trunk
bring up (children)	raise
curtains	drapes
deck chair	beach chair
draughts	checkers
dressing gown	bathrobe or robe
dustbin	trashcan or garbage can
flat (home)	apartment
jam	Jelly jello ™
lift	elevator
maize	corn
patience (game)	solitaire
pavement	sidewalk
petrol	gasoline or gas
rise (in pay)	raise or increase
rubbish or refuse	garbage
scone	biscuit
tap	faucet
terrace house	row house
trousers	pants

Brand origins:

Ribena, 1930s – this derives from the Latin botanical term for blackcurrants, 'Ribesnigrum'.

The comprehensive 'problem' list

The spellings given here are UK spellings taken from the Oxford English Dictionary. International readers would be advised to check their own version of the dictionary.

A

abattoir
aberration
abrogate
abscess
absence
abysmal
accelerate
accessory
accidentally
accommodate
accompany
accrue
accumulate
achievement
acknowledge
acquaintance
acquiesce
acquire
acquit
acquittal
acrylic
acumen
admissible
adrenalin
advertisement
advertising
aeon
aerial
aesthetic
affect
aggravate
aggressive
aghast

all right
allegiance
alliteration
already
ambience
amiable
amok (not amuck)
analyse
analysis
anemone
annex (verb), annexe (noun)
annihilate
apparatus
apparently
aqueduct
argument
artefact (also artifact)
asinine
asphalt
assistant
athlete
attendance
attorneys
avocado

B

baguette
balk (not baulk)
bandwagon
bankrupt
bargain
battalion
believe

beneficial
benefited
billeted
blond (man)
blonde (woman)
bogey (bogie is on a locomotive)
born (given birth to), borne (carried)
Brittany
broccoli
budgerigar
bureau
by-election
bylaw
bypass
by-product
by-word

C

caffeine
calendar
calypso
cannon (gun), canon (standard, criterion, clergyman)
canvass (seek opinion), canvas (cloth)
cappuccino
carcass
Caribbean
cash flow
caviar
cemetery

Metaphors:

I've heard it before. That joke has a long beard. – Yiddish proverb

census
changeable
channeled
chauvinism
cholesterol
choosy
chromosome
chrysanthemum
cipher
clientele
clubbable
coalesce
colloquial
colossal
combating
commemorate
commercial
committee
competent
complement (make complete)
complexion
compliment (praise)
concede
confident
congratulate
conscientious
consensus
convenient
coolly
coral (growth found in sea), corral (cattle pen)
corollary
correspond
correspondence
council (assembly)
counsel (give advice)
courteous
courtesy

criticism
criticise

D

dachshund
dahlia
defence
defendant
definite
definition
dependant (person), dependent (adjective)
depository (unless referring to American depositary accounts)
descendant
desiccated
desperate
detente (not détente)
deteriorate
development
dexterous (not dextrous)
diaphragm
difference
dignitary
dike (disparaging term for a lesbian)
dilapidate
disappear
disappoint
discreet (prudent)
discrepancy
discrete (separate)
dissociate (not disassociate)
distil
distiller
doesn't
doubt

douse (drench)
dowse (use a divining rod)
duly
dungeon
dyke
dysentery

E

ebullient
eccentric
economy
ecstasy
effervescence
efficiency
eighth
eligible
email
embarrass
ensure (make certain), insure (against risks)
envelop (verb)
envelope (noun)
epitome
erogenous
erroneous
exaggerate
exceed
exhilarate
existence
extension
extrovert
eyrie (eagle's nest), eerie (spooky)

Gabay at a glance:

Floccinaucinihilipilification (twenty-nine letters) means estimating something as worthless.

Etymology:

Yen (Japan) – This word was borrowed from the Chinese word yuan, which means round. The first yen was issued in 1870.

F

fahrenheit
fallible
familiar
fascinate
February
fiasco
fiery
flotation
forbear (abstain)
forbid (past tense: forbade)
forebear (ancestor)
foreclose
forefather
forego (precede)
foreign
forestall
foretell
forewarn
forgather
forgo (do without)
forsake
forty
fourth
freight
fuchsia
fuelled
fulfil, fulfilling
-ful, not -full (eyeful, earful, handful, etc)
fullness
fulsome
funnelling
further (additional, distance), farther (distance only)
fuselage

G

gauge
gazump
gherkin
ghoul
gigolo
glamour
glamorous
gnome
guillotine
government
grammar
gratitude
grey
grievous
grievance
guarantee
guidance
gymnasium

H

haemorrahage
haemorrhoids
hara-kiri
harangue
harass
hashish
height
heinous
hiccup
high-tech
hindrance
Hizbullah
honour
hotchpotch
hypochondria
hypocrisy
hysteria

I

icicle
idiosyncrasy
illustrate
imaginary
impatient
impeccable
impostor
impresario
impromptu
inadvertent
incandescent
incidentally
incompetent
incredible
incur
incurring
indispensable
inevitable
initial
innocence
innocuous
innovate
inoculate
inquire
install
intercede
interesting
intransigent
irrelevant
irresistible
its (possessive)
it's (it is)

J

jail (not gaol)
jamb (of door)
jeopardy

In other words:

jeweller
jewellery
judgement
juggernaut
juxtapose

K

kaleidoscope
khaki
kleptomania
Koran (Muslim noun, Qur'ān)

L

labelled
labelling
labyrinth
lackadaisical
lacquer
laissez-faire
lama (priest)
lambast
language
languid
languor
legitimate
leisure
length
lengthen
lenient
leukaemia
liability
liable
liaise
liaison
library
licence (noun)
license (verb)
lieutenant

lightening (making light)
lightning (weather)
linchpin
liquefy
liqueur (flavoured alcoholic drink)
liquor (alcohol or other liquid)
literal (exact, factual, etc)
llama (animal)
loath (reluctant)
loathe (to feel hatred)
loathsome
loneliness
longevity
loose (as opposed to tight)
loquacious
lose (as opposed to find)
losing
low-tech
Luxembourg

M

macabre
maelstrom
maintenance
malignant
mammoth
manoeuvre
manoeuvring
mantelpiece
manufacture
massacre
massive
mathematics
mayonnaise
meager
mediocre
Mediterranean

merely
meringue
meter (instrument for measuring)
metre (linear measurement)
mezzanine
migraine
mileage
millennium
minimum
minuscule
miscellaneous
mischief
Mishnah
misspell
mistakable
mnemonic
modelled
modelling
momentous
morose
mortgage
mould
moustache
Muslim (not Moslem)
mysterious
myxomatosis

N

naive
naivety
naturally
naught (nothing)
necessary
necessity
negate
negligible
negotiable
neurotic

Writers' words:

'Bright is the ring of words when the right man rings.' (RL Stevenson)

niggardly
nineteen
ninety
ninth
nominal
nonplussed
noticeable
nought (zero)
nullify

O

obligatory
oblivious
occasion
occur
occurred
occurrence
occurring
ominous
omitted
opaque
ophthalmic
ophthalmology
opponent
opposite
optimism
ornate
ostensible
outlandish
outspoken

P

pacific
pacify
painstaking
parallel
passionate
pastime
pedal (noun – foot lever)

peddle (deal in triviality)
pejorative
peninsula (noun)
peninsular (adj)
permissible
perpetual
perseverance
personnel
pessimistic
petty
phenomenon
phoney (not phony)
physician
piggyback (not pick-aback)
piquant
poky
Politburo
porous
possession
postpone
practically
practice (noun)
practise (verb)
praiseworthy
precede
predilection
preference
preferred
prejudice
prelude
presence
pretentious
prevalent
preventive (not preven-tative)
pricey
primary
principal (main)
principle (moral rule)

privilege
procedure
profane
professor
profited
proliferate
pronounce
pronunciation
protester
proximity
publicly
puerile
puny
pusillanimous
Pygmy
pzazz

Q

quarrelsome
questionable
questionnaire
queuing
quiescent (agitated)

R

rabble
racket
racquet (tennis)
rambling
rancid
rankle
rapt
rarefy
ratchet
raucous
razzmatazz
reassure
receipt
receive

Loquacious language:

morology – nonsense

recommend
recur
recurrent
recurring
reflective
regress
regretted
regretting
relevant
religious
remember
remembrance
remiss
remorseful
renege
renowned
repetition
repudiate
resemblance
resemble
reserved
respectfully
respectively
restaurant
restaurateur
resuscitate
rhythm
ropy
ruthless

S

sacred
sacrilegious
salutary (remedial)
salutatory (welcoming)
sanguine
savannah
sceptic
scissors
scurry

secondary
secretary
segregate
seize
sensual
shaky
sheath (noun)
sheathe (verb)
shenanigans
siege
similar
sincerely
skullduggery
slovenly
smidgen
smoky
smooth
soothe
sophomore
soyabean
speciality
specialty (referring to
medicine, steel and
chemicals)
sphinx
spoilt
stagnant
stockmarket
straight-faced
straitjacket
strait-laced
straits (narrow passage of
water, in a difficult
predicament)
stratagem
strategy
strength
stringent
subsequent
succeed
success

sufficient
superintendent
supersede
surplus
swap (not swop)
swathe
syllable
symptom
synonym
systematic

T

tacit
Talmud
tangible
teetotal
teetotaller
temporary
tendency
tentative
terse
their
theoretical
therefore
thief
thrifty
tired (sleepy)
titbits
titillate
tongue-tied
Torah
tormentor
tragedy
tranquil
transatlantic
transferred
transient
transpacific
transsexual
travelled (traveled – US)

Anyone around here speak English?

Sign in a Swiss café: 'Special today – no ice cream.'

travelling (traveling – US)
treacherous
treasurer
tricolour
trite
truly
tsar
Tuesday
tuneful
turbulent
tyre

U

unanimity
unanimous
unassuming
unbecoming
unbridled
uncouth
underhand
undoubtedly
unequivocal
ungainly
unity
unkempt
unparalleled
unruly
unsightly
untrammelled
useful
usually

V

vaccinate
vacuum
vague
vehemence
vehement
verbose

verify
vertical
veteran
vicious
vigorous
villain
voluble
voluntary
vulnerable

W

wagon (not waggon)
wane
warlike
watchful
weasel
weather (wind, rain, etc)
(the) Web
webcam
webcast
webpage (noun)
website (noun)
Wednesday
wether (castrated ram)
whether (expressing doubt)
wholly
whoopee
widescreen
widget
withhold
withholding
World Wide Web
world-class (adjective)
worldly-wise
world-ranking
worldwide
wreath (noun)
wreathe (verb)
wry

X

xenon
xenophobia
Xerox
Xmas
XML
X-ray
xylophone

Y

yield
yogurt
yolk
Yom Kippur
youthful
yo-yo
yuan (Chinese currency)

Z

zany
zeal
zeitgeist
zenith
zilch
zillion
zinc

Gabay at a glance:

When spelling a word, which indicates a grammatical unit e.g. medium-size, bear in mind that if the adjoining words are recognised nouns in their own right, you probably don't need to include the hyphen. Equally when words become common language, again drop the hyphen. For example 'to-day' is now spelt 'today'. 'Business class' does not need a hyphen to show that it is a unit of customers.

Business-class ✗
Business class ✔

Metaphors:

I shall try to get the honey from each moment. – Lucy Stone

Brains, pen, action!

Which of these is correct?

1 annoint *or* anoint

2 coolly *or* cooly

3 supersede *or* supercede

4 irresistible *or* irresistable

5 divlopment *or* development

6 alright *or* all right

7 seperate *or* separate

8 tyranny *or* tyrrany

9 harras *or* harass

10 desiccate *or* dessicate

11 indispensable *or* indispensible

12 receive *or* recieve

13 pursue *or* persue

14 reccomend *or* recommend

15 desperate *or* desparate

16 embarassment *or* embarrassment

17 accidently *or* accidentally

18 insistant *or* insistent

19 subpoena *or* subpena

20 definately *or* definitely

21 ocassion *or* occasion

22 consensus *or* concensus

23 sacreligious *or* sacrilegious

24 minuscule *or* miniscule

25 judgment *or* judgement

26 inoculate *or* innoculate

27 drunkenness *or* drunkeness

28 ocurrence *or* occurrence

29 dissipate *or* disippate

30 weird *or* wierd

Answers to
answers@gabaywords.com

In other words:

minimum - a short mother

6. Consonants divided by continents – UK v US language

I was attending a meeting, when an American gentleman told me that this woman he met 'blew him off the other day'. I blushed, explaining that although the meeting was about 'relationship marketing' I really didn't want to know that kind of detail about his personal relationships. At this, he looked at me oddly and said, 'I am referring to being ditched at the last moment from an important meeting!'

I coyly replied, 'But of course that's what I thought you meant.' Then I offered him another digestive biscuit…

Need more help?
www.gabaywords.com

US language

Brother can you spare a meaning

Two nations divided by a common language

Ever since 1607, when an Englishman picked up a shell on a beach in a delightful corner of the US called The Chesapeake Bay, the US and the UK have been divided by a common language. Back then, the first permanent English settlers set up home in the US. They named their settlement after King James 1, hence the name Jamestown. Thirteen years later the Mayflower brought over the first group of Puritan settlers, who landed at Cape Cod, Plymouth and Massachusetts. By 1640, they were joined by a further 25,000.

The Puritan settlers came mostly from around East Anglia. Their accents tended to lack an 'r' after vowels, whereas the original colonists who landed around Jamestown tended to come from the West Country, so 'imported' habits such as pronouncing 's' as a 'z', for example 'Zomerzet'.

Gabay at a glance:

Readers spend less than half a second at each component (headline, subhead, body copy and picture) of an advertisement.

It is hardly surprising that spoken English in the US varies so considerably from the UK version. For many years settlers lost touch with their families back in England. As more immigrants arrived in the US, so US English began to take on its own form. Many foreigners would read words as they thought they were pronounced, so 'broken English' became the norm.

In 1783 Noah Webster, an American lexicographer, suggested giving every letter in a syllable its own sound, particularly words ending with 'ary', 'ory' and 'ery'. By 1789, Webster went as far as to predict that eventually American English would become totally alien in sound and structure to UK English.

Each country's settlers left their mark on US English. The Dutch, for example, were responsible for giving New York its name (originally a Dutch settlement called New Amsterdam). Until the 1800s, German in particular became increasingly popular (many Germans settled around Pennsylvania and its locality), although English remained the primary language. Soon, French was also introduced (the French inhabited a vast area from Louisiana to the Gulf of Mexico).

Writers' words:

'Proper words in proper places make the true definition of style.' Jonathan Swift

The introduction of the American railways brought along a need for new words such as 'railroad' and 'grade crossing'; their English counterparts being 'railway' and 'level crossing'. Little literature was published at this time, so the differences weren't highlighted, and the void between the two dialects began to grow as wide as the Atlantic.

During the nineteenth century, immigration increased further. Europe was in turmoil. The Irish fled to the US in order to escape the potato famine of the 1840s. More Italians and Germans escaped the 1848 revolutions. By the 1880s, Jews from East and Central Europe fled bloody anti-Semitic pogroms. With such a rich salmagundi of languages to feast on, it is hardly surprising that today it is estimated that there are over 4000 words commonly used words which have different meanings in UK and US English.

Some words found in the US language can be directly traced back to other languages brought in by immigrants.

From Dutch	coleslaw, cookie, snoop
From French	cache, cent, chowder, poker, saloon
From German	cookbook, delicatessen, dumb, hoodlum, pretzel, sauerkraut
From Italian	espresso, pasta, spaghetti, zuchinni
From Spanish	canyon, lasso, marijuana, rodeo, ranch, tornado
From Yiddish	schmalz, schmuck, scram, Enjoy!, Get lost!

The Internet has played its own part in bridging the UK/US interpretation fissure. For copywriters dealing with web-copy, this alone has caused many to scratch their heads over local interpretation and usage. You need, therefore, to bear in mind that the closer you can get to a local market, the more sincere your copy will sound. To help you 'touch' either an English or American market, the following pages feature some popular terms listed by subject area.

Etymology:

postman – someone who delivers the mail. This word originated in the thirteenth century when Marco Polo described Kublai Khan's sophisticated network of relay stations. He gave them the Italian name of poste (meaning 'posts').

Food

US	UK
2% milk	semi-skimmed milk
beets	beetroot
biscuit	scone
candy apple	toffee apple
cookie	biscuit
corn	sweet corn
corned beef	salt beef
crawfish	crayfish
custard	baked custard
eggplant	aubergine
fava bean	broad bean
fish sticks	fish fingers
french fries/fries	chips
ground meat	minced meat
half and half	single cream
heavy/whipping cream	double cream
heel	crust
jelly	jam
layer cake	sandwich cake
oatmeal	porridge
popsicle	ice lolly
potato chips	crisps
pound cake	madeira cake
romaine lettuce	cos lettuce

Food cont

US	UK
rutabaga	swede
self rising flour	self raising flour
soda	fizzy drink
stick candy	rock (seaside)
sucker	lollipop
tollhouse cookie	chocolate chip biscuit
wiener	frankfurter
zuchinni	courgette

Clothing

US	UK
ascot	cravat
canvas sneakers	plimsolls/pumps
coveralls	boiler suit
crew neck	turtle neck
cuffs	turn ups
hose	stockings
made to order	bespoke
nightgown	nightdress
pant suit	trouser suit
pantyhose	tights
rubber boots	wellingtons
sneakers	trainers
suspenders	braces
sweater	woolly/jumper

Metaphors:

'A little sunburnt by the glare of life.' Elizabeth Barrett Browning, *Aurora Leigh*

Clothing cont

turtle neck	polo neck
undershirt	vest
undershorts	underpants
vest	waistcoat

Cars

accident spot	black spot
back up	reverse
blacktop	tarmac
automobile	car
dead battery	flat battery
detour	diversion
divided highway	dual carriageway
eighteen wheeler	juggernaut
fender	mudguard
gearshift	gear stick
guard rail	crash barrier
hood	bonnet
hub cap	wheel trim
jumper cables	jump leads
interstate/ freeway	motorway
parking/ emergency brake	hand brake
parking lot	car park

Cars cont

reflectors	cats eyes
sidewalk	pavement
station wagon	estate car
tag/license plate	number plate
tail pipe	exhaust pipe
tour bus	coach
traffic circle/rotary	roundabout
traffic diverter	bollard
trailer	caravan
truck	lorry
truck stop	transport café (aka greasy spoon)
trunk	boot
turn signal	indicator
wreck	accident

All tooled up

alligator clip	crocodile clip
blow torch	blow lamp
bone wrench	box spanner
boot	wheel clamp
jackhammer	pneumatic drill
monkey wrench	pipe wrench
wall anchor	Rawlplug
wrench	spanner

Brand origins:

Pepsi Cola, 1898 – originally marketed by Caleb D Bradham as an elixir to relieve dyspepsia.

Biz lingo

And for those who want to get the big *10-4* so that your market will *10 on that*, here are some of my favourite US-derived business terms.

10-4 – ok

10 on that – phrase used to agree strongly to a statement or affirm what has been said

100K – $100,000; K = 1000

A

a 180 – an about face, a total U-turn

'Assistant Attorney General Anne Bingaman will reveal an enforcement agenda that represents a 180-degree turn from the antitrust policy that has reigned for the past 15 years.'

(Business Week, 7 March 1994)

above board – transparently trustworthy

a-bomb – a ruinous bomb whose power results from nuclear fission

acculturate – adapt so that something or someone can be more like a surrounding or popular culture

acid test – definitive critical test, verification

administrivia – frivolous activities and reports required by administrators

agribusiness – the conglomerate industry comprising all aspects of the farming business from production to machinery

a lick and a promise – incomplete groundwork

aljazeerification – when your business is thrusted into the limelight due to adverse external events

all up in your shit – the act of exacting extreme prejudice on an adversary

If you continue your unchecked aggression I'll get 'all up in your shit'.

alpha geek – an organisation's technology specialist

antebellum – something relating to the era prior to the American Civil War

an old (China, Japan, etc.) hand – an experienced person

a rising tide that lifts all boats – something that benefits all

(attributed to President Kennedy)

at loggerheads – difference of opinion

Did you know?

The longest pencil in the world was manufactured in November 2002 by Faber-Castell of Selangor, Malaysia. Measurements: 19.75 m (64.79 ft) long, 80 cm (2.6 ft) diameter. Its lead is 15 cm (6 in) in diameter.

at the eleventh hour – at the final moment

Aunt Millie – derogatory term for an unsophisticated investor

B

back-door – introduction of something via an unconventional route

backwoods – a place located far from any urban centre and often frowned upon by 'city folk'

badonkadonk – a) the sound or image associated with an immensely large posterior, b) derogatory term for member of staff

bait and switch – an unethical sales promotion practice, promoting low priced items that turn out to be unavailable at the point of sale 'Sellers sometimes practice a form of false advertising known as bait and switch. A low-priced good is advertised but replaced by a different good at the showroom.'

(Journal of Political Economy, August 1995)

ballpark – approximate

bang for the buck – the greatest return on an investment

'Brown tries to get a lot of bang for the buck by not paying too much more than the market for a stock while finding companies with dramatically superior earnings growth and return on equity.'

(Fortune, 21 August 1995)

bangs – a section of hair that is cut across the forehead and above the eyebrows

base-tending – protecting one's assets

basket case – a) a person or situation doomed for failure,
 b) a person who is mentally incompetent or unfit

batting average – percentage of the time you are successful (baseball)

beatnik – nowadays an ageing follower of the so called 'Beat generation' whose vernacular included greetings such as 'Hey Daddy-o'

bebop – a post-Second World War style of jazz associated with artists such as Charlie Parker, Sarah Vaughan and Dizzy Gillespie

beef up – strengthening of a key proposition

begin on a shoestring – start off with restricted funds

bells and whistles – features and benefits

Betty – a pretty girl (refers to the Archie comic book character)

big board – popular name for the New York Stock Exchange, derived from its original large electronic board tracking stock activity

---

Metaphors:

'Victory finds a hundred fathers but defeat is an orphan'. Count Galeazzo Ciano

black knight – an unwelcome suitor who bids for a corporate takeover

blueshirts – IBM employees

boot camp – training facility or programme (military)

bootstrapped – build up without support

both sides of the aisle/table – each opposite party's views considered equally

brandalism – the practice of defacing art galleries, libraries and museums with logos from corporate sponsors

bring to the table – present an offer or proposal

C

can of worms – a set of problems

career limiting move (CLM) – an action adversely affecting your future

carve out a niche – establish a leading position in the market

catch 22 – a set of circumstances, which cause frustration, as one condition or outcome is dependent upon another, which is in turn reliant upon the first

cheapskate – a penny-pincher

Chinese wall – a self-imposed division of the same unit, enabling a company to work on two pieces of conflicting business simultaneously

click throughs – number of people who see and then open a banner or link on a website, usually expressed as a percentage compared to the number of people who saw the banner or link

comer – someone or something with renowned potential

cook the books (to) – falsify records

core business – fundamental business features

cradle to grave marketing – the practice of establishing lifelong brand loyalty

cross sabers – to confront an adversary

cube farm – sardonic reference to an office planned into cubicles

cybernate (to) – control by computer

D

dead wood – employees who don't contribute any tangible benefits

deep pockets – lots of money

devil's advocate (let me play) – ponder or predict negative criticism of a project as a means to improve the quality of the proposal

---

Loquacious language:

morosis – complete stupidity

Dilbert/Dilbert Principle – popular 1990s cartoon by Scott Adams, which finds humour in corporate absurdities

> 'The Dilbert Principle is adapted from the Peter Principle, a popular management aphorism of a few years ago. Mr. Adams observes that the most ineffective workers are systematically moved to the place where they can do the least damage: management.'
>
> (Wall Street Journal, 30 May 1996)

deja-moo – corporate 'bullshit' which you have heard before

dirty laundry – questionable or scandalous past activities

doctor/doctoring – alter through unscrupulous practices

dog-and-pony show – particularly simple presentation

Doh! – a derivative of 'Duh!' popularised by the American cartoon character Homer Simpson, 'Doh!' often refers to an act of stupidity carried out by oneself

don't make waves – don't disagree or contradict policy

down in the dumps – depressed

downtime – period when equipment isn't available to perform or person is unavailable for work

Do you read me? – Do you understand? (originally in military communications)

draw a line in the sand – make final undisputed conditions

Duh! – a sigh of frustration in response to someone acting stupidly (see 'doh')

dynamic scoring – political/economic forecasting technique that assumes budget reductions stimulate economic activity thereby further reducing budget deficits

E

eager-beaver – particularly energetic

> 'He had complained to the president that eager-beaver trustbusters were causing "damage [to] party contributions... 'There is a way we can trust-bust without doing in some of our best friends…'
>
> (Wall Street Journal)

ego surfing – typing in your own name in a search engine to see how famous you have become

elephant hunt – trying to locate a major corporation to move into your community and so fuel economic growth

> When Lancashire 'snared' Inc Corp to their county they had successful elephant hunts

Writers' words:

'You don't' write because you want to say something; you write because you've got something to say.'
F Scott Fitzgerald

emotional correctnesss – self imposed media censorship
following 9-11

empowerment – providing greater autonomy or individual
decision-making

F

face the music – accept all the consequences

fallen angels – precarious investments that were previously attractive

far out – unconventional

feather bedding – a superfluous job or added task

fence-mending – an act aimed at re-establishing good relationships

fishing expedition – an enquiry into an issue that has yet to be fully
formulated

'This type of unplanned search for interesting findings has been
called many things, from data sifting to a systematic fishing
expedition.'

(Marketing News)

five nines – 99.999 per cent precise

formica parachute – unemployment compensation; when US
corporations 'downsize' (reduce the size of the work force),
executives often receive 'golden parachutes' (attractive
compensation packages) while rank-and-file employees
receive only minimal unemployment compensation

foyerfication – the renovation of 70s, 80s and 90s office
reception areas

free ride – obtaining benefits, without having to do anything

from day one – from the outset of a project

from scratch – from the beginning

full court press – a) maximum pressure applied to a project,
b) an 'all hands to the deck' (recruit all available
workers) effort

fuzzword – business jargon

G

garage sale – bargain sale of redundant items

...gate – a political scandal (e.g. Iraqgate, Lewinskygate); derived
from the original Watergate crises during the Nixon presidency

get a kick out of (to) – feel excited by something or someone
(featured in the Frank Sinatra song 'I get a kick out of you')

Medieval words:

breeches – trousers which went from the ankle to the short trunks

give the nod (to) – offer permission to proceed with a task

'You'd have to give the nod to Delcor at this point.'

(Wall Street Journal, 17 May 1995)

globasm – a company or executive who becomes obsessed with expanding globally is said to be experiencing 'globasm'

glocal – global strategy with a local tactical bias

gofer/go-for – a) low ranking employee, b) errand boy

Go for it! – Go ahead! Get involved (originally an early twentieth century Australian term meaning 'I must have sex with you right here and now')

golden parachute – specially negotiated retirement benefits for valued company executives

grain of salt (with a) – not to be assumed as being totally truthful (US equivalent of 'a pinch of salt')

grapevine – community gossip (popularised in the Marvin Gaye song 'I heard it through the grapevine')

greasy spoon – a modest UK café often frequented by blue-collar workers looking for cheap, basic meals that are notoriously appetising, yet high in fat (grease) content

Also see
cars
page 171

guilt-free leave– company policy of not allowing employees to take work with them on holiday

H

happy hour – post office working hours promotional offers at bars or restaurants; in the US, happy hour usually is from 4 p.m. to 7 p.m.

hardball – to be uncompromising

hatchet man – junior executive delegated with the task of firing employees

hired guns – management consultants such as legal experts, accountants and strategy planners or specialists in change management who provide additional resources during what are often 'highly charged' projects

Also see
Betty
page 173

hodad – a would-be surfer who is more interested in posing than getting his feet wet (in business someone who 'acts the part' but is, in fact, a 'small-bit player'); typically a Hodad drives to the beach with a board on the car, sticks his board in the sand, tans and then picks up 'Betties'

hold feet to fire – bring pressure to a situation

Loquacious language:

mumblecrust – someone without any teeth or a beggar

holy grail – the ultimate positive result

'Cost-cutting has become the holy grail of corporate management... But what helps the financial statement up front can end up hurting it down the road.'

(Wall Street Journal)

hot-boxing – a hotmail account used at work to send and recieve pornographic email

hot-desking – the practice of workers sharing an available pool of desks rather than being allocated their own workspace

hot potato – a controversial issue

The President's foreign policy is a hot potato.

How does that play in Peoria? – What is the probable reaction of the average person (aka 'average Joe') at grass roots or the factory floor?

hush money – a bribe offered in exchange for a person's discretion and secrecy

I

iceberg principle – the notion that the first impression of any circumstance provides only a passing glimpse of what is, in actuality, a much deeper and so multifarious state of affairs

Imprinting– the belief that if your advertising is emotionally adopted by children at an early age they will become loyal to you for life

I need it yesterday – a late-twentieth-century expression, still in use, that alludes to false man-made deadlines that need to be met urgently

integrated marketing – marketing campaigns featuring both awareness and response media

interface the public – communicate with customers

intestinal fortitude – endurance and courage; aka 'guts'

in the bag – a completed task

in the black – profitable

After five years of red ink (deficit) we are finally in the black.

ironclad – solid, guaranteed, as in an ironclad promise

it's a jungle out there – a competitive market

it should be a two-way street – both parties should become involved and so equally gain from a project

Also see
Rap
page 441

Yinglish:

From Yiddish...'meshuge' to English... 'mad'

it will never fly – stated dubiousness for a project's likelihood
of success

J

Jerry-built – low-cost mass-produced goods (Jerry = Second World
War pejorative for German)

Job-depth – the amount of influence a person's role has over an
organisation's direction

John Hancock – signature
John Hancock, as President of the Continental Congress, was the
first to sign the Declaration of Independence. He did so with such
vigour that in the US his name has become synonymous with
'signature'.

jump ball – undecided (basketball)

jump the gun (to) – act too soon

Junior Leaguers/Junior League – affluent non-working women
typically under 40 years old

jury-rigged – a temporary solution
'The downside in Japan [after the Kobe earthquake] will have to
depend on these jury-rigged transport links for some time
to come.'

(Wall Street Journal, 17 March 1995)

jump through hoops – undertake a detailed or arduous process, often
to please a customer or manager

K

keep a low profile or lie low – assume an inconspicuous role

keep up with the Joneses (to) – live beyond your means to demonstrate that your household consumer goods are of the latest and most
prestigious standards

kicker – something added to a proposal to make it more attractive

killing (make a) – gain from a quick profit

knuckle down (to) – to focus on a particular project

kowtow (to) – to heed to an expectation

kudos (gain) – to earn respect from your peers

L

last straw – last ditch management attempt at a task

lay cards on the table – be perfectly honest

Twisted truths:

The longest word in the dictionary is similes – there's a mile between the two 's's.

lead balloon (go down like a) – a complete and utter failure or unwelcome piece of news

'Hong Kong Governor Chris Patten said that the colony's 3.2m (million) holders of British Dependent Territories Citizen passports should be given the right to live in Britain. The comment went over like a lead balloon in London.'

(Far Eastern Economic Review)

learning curve – speed at which one learns

lemon – a defective product, especially a car ('Lemon laws' in the US typically allow a manufacturer four attempts to fix a recurring problem)

less than zero – a customer who costs a company more to retain than the person spends

level playing field – equal treatment

lightning rod – person who initiates change, particularly dramatic and potentially dangerous changes in an organisation

like an Edsel – a fiasco or utter failure

The Ford Motor Company introduced the Edsel in a blaze of publicity during the 1950s. The car was designed on out-of-date research; the result was that it became a miserable disappointment. (It went down like a 'lead balloon'.)

lion's share – largest portion

lip service – agreeing with someone or to something for the sake of officialdom rather than conscience

lock, stock and barrel – in totality (US equivalent of 'everything but the kitchen sink')

Luddites – workers who feel their jobs are threatened by changing technology.
The original Luddites, early 1800s British craftsmen, were followers of the mythic figure 'Ned Ludd'. They rioted, destroying the textile machines that had replaced them.

'The original Luddites made bad choices in resorting to violence, but they were trying to protect their way of life.'

(Wall Street Journal, 22 April 1996)

M

Magalogs – direct mail catalogues disguised as genuine magazines

mailman – a person employed to deliver mail

'I would especially like to recourt the Muse of poetry, who ran off with the mailman four years ago, and drops me only a scribbled postcard from time to time.'

(John Updike, 1968)

Writers' words:

'Fiction is the truth inside the lie.' Stephen King

marching orders – instructions to leave (from the military)

mark – an unwitting 'victim'; either a person or company targeted to be roused into an unscrupulous business venture

max out (to) – peach the pinnacle

'Riskier applicants include not only those who had payback problems in the past but also those who tended to "max out" on their available credit.'

(Wall Street Journal, 15 March 1996)

McCarthyism – character assassination

In the 1950s, Joseph McCarthy was a Senator from Wisconsin who gained national attention by his claims that the State Department and other agencies of the US government were infiltrated by Communist sympathisers.

Mcjob – low-paid work in service industries; a disparaging reference to the McDonalds™ Company

meter maid – a traffic warden

Mickey Mouse – simple, a 'no-brainer', unsophisticated

'Jim Bartlett warns of the dangers of not knowing your audience. He tells of a software salesman who reassured Walt Disney executives that his was no "Mickey Mouse" system.'

(Wall Street Journal, 9 January 1996)

Mommy Track – career tracks which come to a dead end because of parental responsibilities

'But in practice, many women (and men too, though in smaller number) who need to use them [flexible schedules] resist for fear of being relegated to the Mommy Track.'

(Wall Street Journal, 13 December 1995)

mossback – a very old fashioned person

multislacking – do nothing much of many things, all at once

mushroom job – a tedious job that keeps employees 'in the dark'

mutt – a mixed-breed dog; mongrel (also refers to a muddled-up project)

N

nanny state – a social system whose politicians assume the rule of parenting a community, rather than representing it

nest-guarding – to protect one's interests

nutraceutical – a health product marketed to promote its taste as well as its health benefits

Loquacious language:

napiform – something shaped like a turnip

ninth inning – at the last moment (baseball)

'Even though Schwab, based in San Francisco, is getting into the 401(k) game in the ninth inning, its arrival is sure to ruffle some competitors, especially given Schwab's reputation for low-cost service.'

(Wall Street Journal, 3 April 1996)

no-brainer – a decision of action that is so straightforward, no thought at all is required

not to amount to a hill of beans – something of absolutely no value, and will never have any value either, in content or context

Noob – a) a person online who is new and/or unfamiliar with the environment, b) a person who acts like they know everything (from 'newbie')

number crunching – laborious and intensive accounting or financial analysis

O

odd-ball – a loner deemed to be beyond the realms of acceptable convention

off-the-books – payment, often made to illegal aliens or immigrants, that is undocumented

oil patch – localities in the US noted for oil production and refining, including Texas, Oklahoma, Louisiana, California and Alaska

on a roll – working so well that a task is being handled with ease and at a good pace

on board (to be) – a) someone recruited either permanently or temporarily to a team, b) someone who is happy to declare their alliance and/or allegiance to a concept (in the US, the phrase is often associated with jobs in government)

on the back burner – kept in reserve for later development

on the carpet (called) – accused of a misdemeanour

An executive that is called on the carpet should ask the accusers if there is a written policy on the accusation.

on the clock – working to a deadline or full capacity

on the lam – escape from the law (US criminal slang)

on the same wavelength – common agreement or understanding

on the table – an issue that is presented for open debate

Ozzie and Harriet (like) – traditional two-parent/two-child household

---

Anagrams:

From CHRISTIANITY to ITS IN CHARITY

P

pacesetter – person or product setting the standards, time to market, or trends for others to follow

paradigm shift – a noticeable shift of emphasis; this can be commercial, scientific or technical (either product, structure or service based). The term comes from Thomas Kuhn's 1962 book, 'The structure of scientific revolution'. (This is almost a complete opposite of a mathematical paradigm shift).

parallel economy – an informal, unregulated economy

partnering – the quest for mutually rewarding business opportunities

pedal pusher – trousers that fit between the ankle and knee, originally designed for women cyclists (in business it refers to a worker who 'flaps' about a lot but goes nowhere)

perfectionism – any principle maintaining that spiritual, personal or social fulfillment is viable

people-based channel – off-line learning

pick someone's brain – solicit novel thinking from someone

pierce the corporate veil – reveal the true 'inside' story

pig in a python – especially slow movement or progress (as in digestion)

pipe dream – non-viable state of affairs; utopia (derived from opium smoking)

plain vanilla – simple basic version

play-by-play – live broadcast commentary of sporting details (in business refers to a detailed account of a meeting)

play hardball – deal with a situation brusquely and with little if any compromise

politics makes strange bedfellows – a set of circumstances that bring together parties who would otherwise be at odds with each other

pooh-poohing – refusing an offer or proposal

power lunch – conducting serious business whilst eating lunch financed by a company expense account (especially popular during the 1980s and 1990s)

pushing the envelope – extending activities beyond current guidelines or conventions

put on the map – make well known, often through marketing

put the scotch to – to halt a person's intended actions

Brand origins:

The grandfather of Lana Turner (the 1940s Hollywood star) invested in Coca Cola. But he didn't think the name would ever catch on. So he withdrew his investment and instead choose what he felt would be a much shrewder option – *The Raspberry Cola Company*.

Q

quality circles – management and worker groups which focus on improving the substance and value of their products (the concept was originally a Japanese management technique)

quick and dirty – cheap, easy but often compromised solution to a problem

'The poverty researchers couldn't have known at the time that their quick and dirty index would guide social and economic policy in the US for decades to come.'

(Wall Street Journal, 22 April 1996)

R

raspberry (the big) – disapproval usually associated with a flatulence sound

'Japan has given Snapple™ the raspberry.'

(Wall Street Journal, 15 April 1996)

received over the transom – unsolicited approach (a traditional style of door featuring a window)

rec room – a room for recreational activities that is often used by workers to 'escape' the drudgery of everyday tasks

red flag – a clear forewarning

rent-a-quotes – experts who may not be the best in the field but are very good at providing quotations to the media

reinvent the wheel – improve something that already exists

right off the bat – immediately, without delay

rosy scenario – an especially optimistic prediction or state of affairs

Rube Goldberg – a less-than-professional repair job.

Rube Goldberg was an early-twentieth-century cartoonist whose works depicted complex machinery with improbable parts. The machines involved enormous effort but resulted in very little.

'These Rube Goldberg routes may sound costly and inefficient and they are!'

(Wall Street Journal, 17 March 1995)

rule-of-thumb – general method of measurement (it originally meant the size of an instrument with which one can beat a wife – no bigger than a thumb)

rumour mill – the general unspecified source of office rumours

run it up the flagpole (and see if it gets a salute) – test to see if an idea gains approval

Metaphors:

Prejudice – a vagrant opinion without visible means of support. Ambrose Bierce, *The Devil's Dictionary*

runway – a long, raised walkway featured in fashion parades or beauty pageants (US equivalent of a catwalk); often used to describe a medium upon which to present a proposal

RV – recreational vehicle (a trendy alternative to the standard corporate car)

S

sacred cow – something beyond question, doubt or impeachment

sarchasm – the gap between the writer of witty copy and the reader who doesn't appreciate the humour

safety net – a) government social welfare programmes designed to assist the poor, b) a contingency plan (the term is derived from the net protecting circus trapeze artists should they fall)

saguaro – a large upright cactus with vertical branches growing up to 70 feet; occasionally used to describe a person who feels he or she is the only one with fresh ideas (water), whilst all others have 'dried-up'

sandbag (to) – a) mislead, b) unanticipated assault, c) unethical practice of establishing an easily attainable bonus plan

save our bacon – save from danger or protect interests

savvy – smart, aware, knowledgeable

scalawag – a rogue (the terms heralds from the US Reconstruction period in the South)

scarlet letter – a symbol of shame (the term comes from Nathaniel Hawthorne's novel The Scarlet Letter)

'Executives at Wal-Mart Stores Inc. are wearing something new on their lapel these days: a quarter... – representing the retailer's dismal fourth quarter – is a sort of scarlet letter.'

(Wall Street Journal, 23 February 1996)

scuttlebutt – rumours, gossip (see rumour mill)

sea change – an extensive change of direction

sea legs (to get one's) – to gain stability or familiarity with a job

seat of the pants operation – to act intuitively (from flying without instruments)

set on its ear – disrupt

sex kitten – a flirty young woman who bedazzles clients and employees alike

shoot-the-bull (to) – exaggerate without substance

shotgun approach – strike out widely and brashly, as opposed to targeted rifle shot

sky marshal – a plainclothes federal agent stationed aboard airlines

'Following 9-11, US has said it may require sky marshals on some international routes. The International Association of Airlines (IATA), based in Geneva, says about 25 governments have used sky marshals at one time or another.'

(CNN news)

slam-dunk – something easily accomplished by a person who is especially skillful at his or her job (from basketball)

smoke and mirrors (all) – tricks of the trade or political manoeuvres to hide and manipulate the truth seen by a market or audience

snafu – a befuddled or nonfunctional state of affairs (from the Second World War military acronym for 'situation normal, all fucked up')

somewhere (sometime) down the pike – sometime later (pike is an old word for road)

square peg in a round hole – a person who doesn't 'fit' comfortably or act appropriately

step up to the plate – willingly assume responsibility (from baseball)

stickiness – the ability of a website to attract and retain surfers

strategic alliance – an essential joint venture

T

tab – the bill, final cost or cheque

tailspin – uncontrolled fall towards disaster

take no prisoners – sales or management resolve to fully exploit a market at a competitor's expense

talking heads – commercials or promotional videos featuring either a pitch man/woman extolling the virtues of a product or delighted customers

talk until blue in the face – an attempt to convince someone of a proposal that falls on deaf ears

tattletale – a person, usually a child or who has a child-like disposition, who abuses another's confidence

that dog won't hunt – prediction that a suggestion is unworkable (this is a Southern US term popularised by President Lyndon Johnson)

throw it against the wall and see if it sticks (to) – attempt a new idea and see if it is successful

toe to toe (to go) – compete directly and aggressively (US boxing term)

to grandfather something – allow an exception to a rule to preexisting status

tongue in cheek – tease or tell a half-truth

took a haircut (or a bath) on that one – suffered a loss

the bottom line – the final outcome or fundamental meaning (from accounting)

the flip side – the reverse view of an argument (from flipping over a phonograph record)

the Genie is out of the bottle – a change that can never be reversed or a revelation that alters previous conceptions

the name of the game (is...) – the premise of an idea

the proof of the pudding is in the eating – to actually do something in order to demonstrate its validity

the whole nine yards – the complete offer, product or service

tweaking – delicate final adjustment

Also see my etymology of this phrase on page 78

U

Uncle Sam – the United States government (during the War of 1812 a New York pork packer named Uncle Sam Wilson shipped so many barrels of pork to troops with his first two initials on each barrel that his name came to symbolise the US Government itself)

under the table/counter – clandestine deal (the phrase is associated with bribes passed under the table; the opposite being an above board agreement)

unwind a deal – disassemble and re-examine a proposition

up to par – complies with standards (an analogy to golf, where par is measured as the average number of strokes per hole)

upskill – to learn new skills in order to improve or enhance a career path

Brand origins:

Persil, 1907 (Germany); 1909 (UK) – this name comes from the French for 'parsley'. A Frenchman who added bleach to soap featured a sprig of parsley as a trademark. Also 'Perborate' and 'Silicate' were two ingredients originally included in the product.

V

veg out – relax

> 'Following the tests, Mr. Napoli likes to "veg out" by the pool or have his body painted in mud.'
> (Wall Street Journal, 19 January 1996)

vested/vesting – served the minimum amount of time required to qualify for various company benefits

visioning – forecasting

voodoo economics – critic's description of 'Reaganomics' (The Reagan political platform included increased defence spending, decreased taxes and a balanced budget. Critics suggested that these goals could only be simultaneously accomplished using voodoo.)

> '"It's voodoo economics all over again", Senate Minority Leader Thomas Daschle said in a statement Friday.'
> (Wall Street Journal, 16 October 1995)

vulture fund – an investment fund that speculates in companies or property that have been significantly devalued

W

wallpaper the meeting – involve people predisposed to your ideas

wardrobe malfunction – a lame excuse offered by a major television network after broadcasting nude images of a celebrity

warm fuzzies – spoken shallow-hearted compliments

> 'David Goodall, a Motorola compensation executive, tells managers "to think beyond cash" about the "warm fuzzies".'
> (Wall Street Journal, 27 September 1994)

watchdog – a person or group that pores over the dealings of business or government

watering hole – a bar often frequented by white-collar workers

W-cubed – whatever, wherever and whenever you want it; to emphasise the importance of customer service, managers will claim their mantra is W-cubed

> 'So instead of subscribing to some a la carte, 24-hour channel, you'll just get the show you want on demand, whenever you want it. It will be W-cubed, whatever, wherever, and whenever you want it.'
> (Wall Street Journal, 16 February 1995)

what can you bring to the party (or table)? – defining a person's likely contribution towards a project

what makes him tick? – what motivates him?

Anagrams:

from DORMITORY to DIRTY ROOM.

whistling past the graveyard – attempt to remain resolved and courageous

whose ox gets gored? – which party will become debilitated by the plan?

Willy Lomans – die-hard sales people (Willy Loman was the central character in Arthur Miller's play Death of a Salesman)

Woody – a stock market in a strong, thrusting upward motion

X

X-factor (the) – the indefinable feature which makes a proposition, person, product or service particularly attractive

Y

Yankee bond – a bond issued by non-US entities trading in the US stock market

'In the corporate market a total of $450 million of corporate debt was priced, including a $250 million, two-part issue for Darden Restaurants and a $200 million Yankee bond issue for Corporation Andina de Fomento, a Caracas, Venezuela, banking company.'

(Wall Street Journal)

yes man – an employee who always agrees with the employer (aka 'ass kisser')

You bet! – an affirmation meaning surely or certainly

Z

zero-sum game – if someone wins, someone must lose

zilch – zero

zillion – an exceptionally big undetermined figure

zinger – a quick and sharp response or retort

'Mr. Moyers' moralizing has sometimes given him a sanctimonious air, but surprisingly, now that he has his own bully pulpit, it's rarely in sight. Instead, he has sent sharp, crisp zingers flying in all directions.'

(Wall Street Journal, 13 March 1995)

zip – zero

zombie bonds – bonds that were thought to be valueless (dead) for which trading resumes (the term was first attributed to traders at Goldman Sachs, a large New York investment company)

'Highly speculative bonds called 'zombie bonds' have run up in recent weeks, though they pose a risk to investors.'

(Wall Street Journal, 27 February 1995)

Brand origins:

Sindy The Doll by Pedigree Dolls and Toys, was named as a result of a street survey. Three alternative names along with a photograph of the doll were shown to girls. Cindy, a common name, couldn't be trademarked, so the doll was named Sindy.

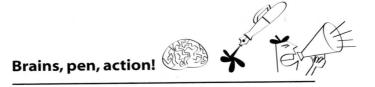

Brains, pen, action!

1   Think of six FMCG (Fast Moving Consumer Goods) products which could feature either one or more of these words in an advertising headline:

- holdup
- pedal pusher
- zillion.

2   You are writing a website for a German manufacturer. In which version of English should you write the copy: UK or US, and why?

3   You are addressing the management of a famous UK/US company. Write a two-minute speech (five hundred words) featuring at least twelve 'Biz Lingo' terms.

Answers to
answers@gabaywords.com

Metaphors:

The blind have eyes in their fingers. European proverb

7. Do you speak marketese?

Marketing has a list of technical terms as long as your arm. This chapter deals with some of the terms that have scratched on my eardrums over the years, with some explanations to help your own ears feel less stressed.

cashcow

Need more help?
www.gabaywords.com

Do you speak marketese?

Here are some of the most popular marketing terms that copywriters come across. I have listed them alphabetically, which hopefully will help you sort you're A/B splits from your zip envelopes (*also see 'Biz lingo' page 172*).

A–Z of marketing terminology

A

above-the-line-advertising	Advertising for which a payment is made and for which a commission is paid to the advertising agency, e.g. an advertisement in a magazine or a stand in a trade fair.
A/B split	The creative testing of two variations of one element in a direct mail package.
above-the-line	Originally referred to a form of agency remuneration. Nowadays it refers to advertising and marketing budget spent on TV, radio or published media. However this concept has been superseded by 'through-the-line' and 'integrated marketing', or 'media-neutral' advertising, which offers a combination of 'above-the-line' and 'below-the-line' advertising.
account	1. Client of an advertising agency or promotions/public relations agency. 2. General term given to describe a client's marketing affairs.
account executive	The person, usually at a middle management or junior management level, who liaises between the agency and client.
account group	Agency team that works on an account.
ACORN	*A Classification of Residential Neighbourhoods.* This is a consumer targeting system which provides a listed selection of residential property information.
activity sampling	Observation of tasks and their performances, carried out at random intervals.

Yinglish:

From Yiddish 'smok'...   to English ... either 'penis' or 'a dope'.

ad hoc research	Research carried out for a particular client or in a particular market.
ad view	Number of times an advertisement is downloaded from a webpage and assumed to have been seen by a potential customer.
adsterbation	Self gratifying advertising copy.
advertising	A planned and considered method of marketing that informs and persuades consumers to do something, or about something. Through doing so it establishes a sales or marketing communication link between a service or product provider, its distributors, users and advocates.
advertising agency	A company that produces advertising and organises advertising campaigns on behalf of its clients.
advertising platform	The main benefits of facts to be conveyed through a piece of advertising
advertising rate	The fee charged for time or advertising space in the media.
Advertising Standards Authority	The UK body responsible for overseeing public complaints of printed advertising. (The Independent Television Commission deals with complaints about TV.)
advertising wedge	A product or service's leading benefit or feature that is highlighted within an advertisement.
advertorial	A combination of advertising and editorial style of copy to give the appearance of a pure piece of editorial (often featuring the words ADVERTISING FEATURE).
advid	An advertising video tape often used by job applicants and US college applicants as an electronic CV (Now upgraded to a DVD).
advocacy advertising	*See issue advertising.*
advt.	Abbreviation for advertisement.
affiliate programme	Form of advertising on the web, in which a business persuades other businesses to put banners and buttons advertising products or services on their website and pays them a commission on any purchases made by their customers.
agency commission	The fee paid by the media to an agency for placing advertising.

Writers' words:

'Originality is the art of concealing your source.' Franklin Jones

AIDA	Model of stages in the effects of advertising on customers, i.e. you attract their **A**ttention, keep their **I**nterest, arouse a **D**esire and provoke **A**ction to purchase.

Gabay at a glance:

AIDA has had its day. Instead opt for AIDRA the 'R' representing 'reasoning'. Unless you can provide a logical reason for someone to do something, why should they bother to listen to follow your instructions?

alternative close	Closing a sales negotiation by asking the customer to choose something such as a method of payment.
ambush marketing	Linking of a promotion campaign to an event such as a sporting contest which is sponsored by another manufacturer without paying a fee.
animatic	Semi-finished TV commercial usually presented in a rough animated format. It is often used for research purposes.
answer print	Final print of a TV commercial for approval before broadcast.
art buyer	Person employed by an advertising agency to commission creative suppliers such as printers and photographers.
art director	Person responsible for the visual concept design and execution, including graphical or photographic management, of a creative advertising project. Often advertising agencies team art directors with copywriters, thereby creating macro units of creativity, supervised by a creative director. Generally, where such teamwork occurs, creative ideas are jointly conceived.
artwork	Final creative execution of a piece of advertising material ready for print.
atomistic test	Research testing of individual parts of a design or advertisement.
Aural branding	The notion that a company can lay claim to a sound. Not to be confused with 'sonic-branding' which uses a jingle to represent a corporate logo.
author's alteration	A proof reading correction made by a copywriter.
awareness	Measurable capacity for people to recall a specific advertisement when un-prompted.

Writers' words:

194 'The reality is more excellent than the report.' Ralph Waldo Emerson

B

B2B	Advertising or marketing that is aimed at other businesses rather than at consumers.
backgrounders	Public relations support material to aid journalists (this often includes short company, product or service summaries called 'notes to editor').
backload	To ensure that most of the costs of a promotional campaign come in the later stages. The campaign can be cut back if the response rate is inadequate. This is opposed to *frontloading*, where most of the costs are incurred in the early stages.
back-to-back	The broadcasting of commercials in a direct sequence.
backward integration	Process of expansion in which businesses deal with different stages in the production or sale of the same product joined together, i.e. a business becomes its own supplier.
bait and switch advertising	The now-outlawed process of advertising a low priced item in order to build customer traffic and then switch to selling a higher priced item.
bangtail	Envelope designed with an attached perforated 'tail' used as a coupon or order response device.
banker envelope	An envelope with a flap on the longest edge.
bastard size	Special size of paper.
Bayesian decision theory	Method for helping decision-making, often applied to new product development. The decision-maker is aware of alternatives, can work out the probable advantages or disadvantages of the alternatives, and makes up his or her mind according to the value of the best alternative
beauty shot	A close up shot of a TV or cinema advertised product (also known as a 'packshot').
behaviouristic segmentation	Segmentation of the market according to the customers' buying habits and usage of a product.
believability	The scale by which an advertisement is believed.
below-the-line	Advertising and marketing budget spent on promotions, including direct marketing and sales promotions as well as those areas not dealt with 'above-the-line'. (*See also* **above-the-line**.)
bill-me-later	Payment charged once the goods have been received.

Loquacious language:

lurdane – dull and lazy

bill-stuffer	*See statement stuffer.*
billboards	American term for poster sites.
billing	1. The fee charged to a client by an agency. 2. The net charge made by a media supplier to an agency; the gross charge less the discount given to the agency.
blanket branding	Giving a whole group or line of products the same brand name.
blind ad	A classified advertisement which does not reveal the identity of a client.
blitz	Marketing campaign which starts at full pressure, as opposed to a gradual build-up.
blow-in card	Loose reply card inserted into a magazine.
blurb	Basic product or service descriptive copy.
body copy	The main text of a piece of copy.
body type	The typeface used in the body copy.
border	The perimeter line that distinguishes one advertisement from another on the printed page.
Boston Box	System used to indicate a company's potential by analysing the relationship between its market share and its growth rate.
BRAD	*British Rates and Data.* A monthly reference source of media and advertising cost and circulation data.
brand	'A name, term, symbol or design (or a combination of them) which is intended to signify the goods or services of one seller or group of sellers and to differentiate them from those of competitors.' (As defined by the author of Marketing Management, Philip Kotler).
brand association	The mental link between a specific product or service and its general category.
brand attitude	A consumer's opinion of a product or service.

Gabay at a glance:

The modern name, 'brand' is based on the branding process carried out by American cowboys on their cattle. Using hot irons they branded their animals.

Anagrams:

from TEACHER to CHEATER

brand development index (BDI)	Index that compares the percentage of a brand's total sales in a given market to the percentage of the total population in the market
brand differentiation	The degree by which a product or service is perceived to be different from its competitors.
brand extension strategy	Application of an existing brand name to a new product
brand image	Emotive 'gut feelings' conjured up by advertising or marketing, felt by the consumer towards a product or service.
brand loyalty	The ultimate aim of a brand manager – to secure the continued custom and product or service endorsement from a client.
brand switching	The act of changing from choosing one brand to another.
BRE	Business Reply Envelope. A pre-addressed envelope from a mailer to be returned by a recipient.
broadsheet	Large sized newspaper as opposed to a small sized tabloid.
broadside	The traditional name given to paper printed on a single side only.
brochure	A printed bound pamphlet derived from the French word meaning to stitch - brocher.
bromide	A photographic print.

Gabay at a glance:

The Harrison Patent Knitting Machine Company of Portland Street, Manchester, placed the world's first photographically illustrated advertisement. It appeared 11 November 1887 and showed the company's attendant staff near a display stand.

buck slip	An American dollar-sized piece of paper that announces an offer for prompt reply.
business press	Specialist press aimed at the business community
by line	The name of a journalist responsible for a specific article or report.

Metaphors:

'The pen is the tongue of the mind'. Miguel de Cervantes, *Don Quixote*

C

campaign	A planned and co-ordinated sequence of advertising, marketing and promotional activities constructed to achieve a calculated result.
cannibalisation	An instance when a company launches a new product which sells well at the expense of another established product
CAP	*Code of Advertising Practice*
caption	Copy that describes or supports a specific illustration or photograph.
card deck	Series of small cards advertising different products or services, which are mailed as a pack in a plastic envelope to prospective customers.
cash cow	Product or subsidiary company that consistently generates good profits but does not provide growth.
category management	System where managers have responsibility for the marketing of a particular category or line of products.
Centre Européen des Relations Publiques (CERP)	European Federation of Public Relations Organisation.
centrefold spread	Centre spread of a publication which can be opened flat to show large headlines and pictures.
character count	The overall number of both type and spaces in a piece of copy.
Chartered Institute of Marketing	Europe's largest and most respected professional training body for marketing and sales practitioners (www.cim.co.uk).
Cheshire label	A name and address label used as an alternative to a window address envelope.
churn rate	Measurement of how often new customers try a product or service and then stop using it.
circular	A broadly distributed piece of advertising material.
classified display advertising	Advertising that, although it appears in a classified section, may also have individual features such as its own box border or the company logo.
clean copy	An error-free piece of copy.

Medieval words:

bulldoze – to threaten or overwhelm

clean proof	An error-free typeset proof.
clip	A short piece of film.
club line	The unsightly first line of a paragraph at the foot of a page with the rest of the paragraph printed on the next page or column (*also know as an* **orphan**).
cluster	A group of people sharing a common interest or feature.
cluster analysis	A statistical method for sorting samples of people into clusters.
cognitive dissonance	A consumer's disappointment when there is a vast perceived difference between what is expected from a product and what it actually delivers. The consumer then seeks justification to support the logic of their purchase. Cognitive dissonance can be avoided by stating clear product and service facts within copy and by featuring money back promises or guarantees if the consumer is not completely satisfied.
cognitive psychology	A general approach to psychology stressing the internal mental processes.
coin rub	See *scratch off.*
coined word	A word created for a specific purpose (also known as a 'nonce word').
cold lists	Lists of prospects which have never been previously contacted by an advertiser.
collectable	A one-off or series of objects sold as limited editions using direct marketing techniques.
column inch	The size of one standard newspaper or magazine column width x one inch deep.
column inch rate	The cost of a column inch.
concertina fold	A paper fold which opens out in the form of the bellows of a concertina (useful for direct mail formats).
contact report	A written account of a meeting between a creative supplier or agency and its client.

Gabay at a glance:

Always write a contact report as soon as possible following a creative meeting; never rely on the other party writing the report.

Etymology:

curfew – This word, meaning a time after which people must not leave a location, comes from the thirteenth century when bells were tolled to warn people to put out or cover fires at night. (A wise precaution as all the buildings were built of wood.) This time was called 'curfew' from the French word 'covrefeu' meaning 'cover the fire'.

contest	A sales promotion method that rewards prizes to consumers who perform tasks such as, 'Complete the following phrase…'
continuity writer	A person who writes programme publicity and information copy for commercial broadcasters.
control	The standard by which quality is gauged. Direct mailers feature a 'control package' that has proved the most effective of at least two mailings. All variations of a creative theme are measured against this 'control.' The term is also applied to the most successful creative interpretation of advertisement within a campaign.
controlled circulation	The free distribution of a publication to targeted addresses
conversion pack	A direct mail piece that is meant to convert an enquiry to sale.
copy approach	The main theme or creative thrust in a piece of copy.
copy chief (head)	Senior copywriter with management responsibilities.
copy editor	The journalist who approves and edits journalistic copy produced by reporters.
copy platform	Creative rationale and description based on an agreed advertising strategy.
corporate identity	Material representation through a logo, corporate colour scheme, uniform or livery of an organisation.
cost-per-thousand	The cost of an advertisement per 1000 viewers or readers. (Also known as CPM – Cost per Mille.)
	To calculate this, divide the cost of the advertisement by the circulation of the publication. (In the case of TV or radio you have to take into consideration the time at which the commercial is broadcast.)
cost plus	An advertising execution produced at production cost + agency expenses.
counter card	A point of sale notice highlighting a product name and price.
coverage	1. The geographic reach of a specific medium. 2. The declared parameters of a market. 3. The percentage of the audience within a market able to see an outdoor advertising poster. 4. The total number of people or households, irrespective of location that buy or receive a publication or see/hear a broadcast.

In other words:

kindred – a fear of relatives

CPE	*Cost per enquiry.* The total cost of a mailing divided by the number of inquiries that it produces.
CPO	*Cost per Order.* The total cost of a mailing divided by the number of orders that it produces.
creative director	Employee of an agency who is responsible for the output or creative work and overall supervision and co-ordination of creative staff (or teams).
creative strategy	A communications goal based on an intended result, product or service benefits and the data to support the marketing aim.
cut off	*See **deadline**.*

D

daily rate	The fee for advertising space charged for all editions of newspapers published during the normal working week.
database	A computerised pool of information from which selected data can be utilised.
deadline	The final time a completed advertisement or piece of copy can be accepted.
dealer listing	A list that is included in a piece of copy showing regional dealers who market a product or service.
dealer relations	PR directed at commercial distributors of products or services.
de-dupe	The method of eliminating and identifying duplicate names from mailing lists. Once completed, the information is referred to as 'de-duped data'. (*See also **merge** and **purge**.*)
demarketing	The method of discouraging consumers from buying or consuming.
demographics	The classification of an audience 'make-up' based on economic and social influences and conditions. Classifications can be segmented by age, sex, income, and working status.
desktop publishing	Computer generated advertising and publications including newsletters, leaflets and press advertisements.
die-cut	Paper or cardboard that has been cut to a specific shape.
direct mail	The targeted sending of advertising and promotional items direct to likely consumers.

Twisted truths:

Do not put statements in the negative form.

direct mail advertising	A term to describe advertising or promotional material sent or distributed via a mailing system.
direct marketing	A direct channel of distribution using any form of marketing communication that encourages a response and delivers a measurable result.
Direct Marketing Association (DMA)	British professional body for direct marketing practitioners.
dirty copy proof	Copy with handwritten comments and amendments. (*This is the opposite of* **clean copy proof**.)
display face	Typeface designed for display-sized advertisements.
donor list	List of people who have donated to a charity.
door-to-door	The direct marketing distribution of material by hand, usually to residential neighbourhoods.
double decker	An outdoor poster in two separate tiers.
double duty envelope	An envelope designed to be torn yet retain its return envelope features.
dummy	A mock-up sample of a communications piece.
dump bin	A point of sale item which carries products in a bin.

E

edit suites	Audio and video post-production facilities for editing purposes.
EDMA	European Direct Marketing Association.
electronic cottage	The term given to the residence of a freelance copywriter, designer or person who uses IT such as Broadband to link between home and office.
embargo	Request to withhold press information until a specified date and time.
English creep	The spread of English as an international language. Over 345 million people use English as their first language and an extra 400 million as a second.
envelope stuffer	Direct marketing material enclosed in a direct mail piece already containing a business letter, invoice or statement.
excess demand	Excecessive demand at the present price than sellers can satisfy.

Metaphors:

'Her enthusiasm was always on the boil'. Aldous Huxley, *Point Counter Point*

Gabay at a glance:

Avoid writing the word 'exclusive' on a press release unless the piece really is exclusive to a magazine or newspaper.

exclusive	A press release or other kind of information written for one medium (title).
experiential advertising	Advertising conveying the actual sensation of using the product.
experimental method	Controlled experiments to discover the influence of various variables in marketing such as types of promotion and sales training.
extension strategy	Marketing strategy aimed at extending the life of a product either by making small changes in it, finding new uses for it or finding new markets.
extensive marketing	Practice of using a wide network of distributors and a great variety of promotional activities to gain as large a section of the market as possible
extrapolation	Forecasting technique projecting past trends into the future.
eye camera	A special camera used to measure visual stimulation and record eye movements of research volunteers when reading copy. (See *eye-movement test*.)
eye-movement test	Advertising test which involves recording the movements of a person's eyes as they look at an advertisement to see which parts are of special interest.

F

face	1. A specified set of typefaces belonging to a 'family' of typefaces. 2. The bare frontage of an outdoor poster. 3. A page which when opened naturally faces the reader. 4. The opposite page to a piece of copy.
family life cycle	Life stages corresponding to different types of buying behaviour as consumers go through family life. These include: 1. young single people 2. young couples with no children 3. young couples with their youngest child under six 4. couples with dependant children 5. older couples with no children at home 6. older single people.

Does anyone around here speak English?

From a sign in a Benidorm hotel: 'We highly recommend the hotel tart.'

farm out	Sub-contract work.
fastmarketing	The concept of concentrating all promotions into a short space of time, so that customers cannot avoid being affected.
feedback	Data response from consumers that helps marketers to assess the overall performance of a product or service advertising and marketing campaign.
filler advertisement	An unreserved advertisement used to fill up blank publishing space.
filter question	A question in a questionnaire designed to separate respondents who are worth questioning further from those who are not.
flanker	Another term for a line-extension brand, referring to a spin-off companion product to a successful brand name.
flat animation	Two-dimensional animation.
flier	Simple one sheet of advertising material usually found in a mailing piece.
flush and hang	Text which features the first line of copy flushed with the left margin and subsequent lines indented.
FMCG	*Fast Moving Consumer Goods.* Products which are meant to have short retail shelf life and high stock requirement based on a fast repurchase demand, for example, soap, biscuits, butter.
fount	Alternative word for font, meaning a complete set of type of one style and size.
four colour process	Colour printing featuring primary colours separated by a filter.
frankly I'm puzzled	Traditional style of direct marketing copy which asks why the recipient has not as yet responded to an offer.
free-standing stuffer	A loose insert 'stuffed' into a publication.
free flier	An extra insert in a direct mail piece that offers a special gift for prompt reply.
free keeper	A low-cost item that the recipient of a mailing piece can keep at no obligation.
free newspapers	Typically weekly local newspapers delivered door to door.
free ride	A cost effective way to save mailing costs by including one specific offer within a different mailing.

Anagrams:

from MOTHER-IN-LAW to WOMAN HITLER

free trial	*See **sample**.*
freepost	A Royal Mail service whereby the mailer finances the cost of postage.
frequency	The average times that a prospect is exposed to a specific advertisement during a specified period of time.
fuzzword	A seemingly defined word that actually confuses a piece of communication. In other words, elegant gobbledegook.
fuzzy sets	Psychologist term for vague language that confuses the reader.

G

galley proof	The proofed copy text prior to being formatted into pages.
gatefold	1. Leaflet folded so that its two edges meet in the centre. 2. Multi- part insert or cover of a publication that has to be unfolded in order to be read.
generic advertising	An advertisement or commercial that highlights product or service benefits without mentioning a brand name or local outlets.
generic terms	Product descriptions such as cornflakes, which describe a product, yet are not registered trade names.
ghost writer	A person contracted to write in the name of someone else.
Greek	Also known as Latin. Garbled text on a 'rough layout' that represents the size and position where final copy will eventually sit.
group discussion	A survey method in which a focus group is brought together to discuss informally a market-research question.
growth share matrix	A model for a marketing strategy with various categories of product based on present performance and growth rate.
growth vector matrix	A model for a marketing strategy with various choices and combinations of strategy based on product and market development.
guaranteed circulation	The audited circulation of a magazine which is used as a basis for calculating advertising rates.
guardbook	Portfolio of a client account's creative work.

Writers' words:

'When fits of creativity run strong, more than one programmer or writer has been known to abandon the desktop for the more spacious floor.' Fred Brooks Jr

205

guerrilla marketing	A form of unconventional flexible marketing, adapted to the products or services sold, or to the type of customer targeted.
gutter	Space between columns of text without a vertical dividing rule, or pairs of pages.

H

hack	A hired writer who is probably willing to write about anything for any reasonable price.
hanging indent	The first line of the paragraph starts at the left margin, and subsequent paragraphs are indented.
headline	The largest display of text that sets a theme and agenda for the subsequent copy.
heart-stopper	A lottery card sales technique whereby a scratch card reveals all but one number in a sequence required to win a prize. This 'just missed' sequence of numbers usually encourages the purchaser to buy another card.
hidden persuaders	Research for advertising first described by V. Packard in the 1950s. Sometimes used to describe the role of PR professionals.
hoarding	*See **billboard**.*
horizontal industrial method	A market in which a product is used by many industries.
horizontal marketing system	Co-operation between or merger of two or more companies whose assets are complementary and who therefore all gain from coming together.
hotline	A specially promoted telephone response line which encourages sales, provides information or acts as a form of customer contact service. (The world's first telephone helpline was introduced by the Samaritans on 2 November 1953.)
house advertisement	An advertisement in a publication which is placed by the publication itself, e.g. one offering a readers' advice service or selling back issues of the publication.
house agency	An agency owned and/or managed by an advertiser.
house corrections	Type errors noted and marked on first proof before seen by a client.

Yinglish:

From Yiddish... 'shleper' to English... someone who carries heavy bags or is untidy.

huckster	A bygone insolent term for an account executive.
hunch marketing	Marketing decisions following a hunch, rather than relying on market research.
hype	Overstated publicity.

I

iconic medium	A medium such as TV or video in which images appear as reality.
idea bank	A pool of creative ideas that are logged and referred to when required.
ideogram	A graphic device that represents an idea or meaning.
illustrated letter	A letter that incorporates some kind of illustration or graphic.
imagery	Figurative language; the illustration and emphasis of an idea by parallels and analogies of different kinds to make it more concrete and objective.
impact	The tangible effect that advertising has on an audience.
impressions	The total number of exposures to a specific advertisement during a specified period of time.
in-ad coupon	A featured coupon within a press advertisement.
independents	Privately owned and managed media companies or publicity and advertising agencies.
in flight magazine	Magazine published by an airline and placed in the back of seats in an aircraft.
in-pack coupon	Redeemable coupon.
in-pack premium	A premium item offered free with a product.
inquiry response mailing	A mass targeted mailing designed to generate enquiries rather than orders.
insertion	An individual advertisement or commercial.
Institute of Direct Marketing	Trade organisation and educational body for direct marketing users, agencies and suppliers (www.theidm.co.uk).
International Public Relations Association	Senior professional body for PR practitioners around the world (www.ipra.org).
in the can	Completed radio, video or filmed commercial.

Loquacious language:

nescience – the lack of knowledge; total ignorance

island position	Advertisement surrounded by editorial.
issue advertising	When an organisation discusses its views on topical issues. (*Also known as **advocacy advertising**.*)

J

jingle track	Musical score for a commercial.
job sheet	Standard agency administration form describing expenditure and progress of a client project.
joint promotion	1. A promotion involving two companies; one features a product or service that support's another company's product or service. 2. One company endorses another.
judgement sampling	The choosing of a sample for a survey based on judgement of what criteria would be especially significant rather than applying any scientific techniques.
junk mail	Unsolicited, poorly targeted mail.

K

Key account	1. Important client of an agency. 2. Important retailer or distributor for a client.
key prospects	Potential customers
keyed advertisement	An advertisement which invites people to write to a coded address which points to where they saw the ad published.
KISS (keep it simple, stupid)	The need to make sure your advertising is clear and concise so as to improve its chances of getting a response.
knowledge capital	Specialist industry knowledge, that can be put to profitable use.
knowledge management	Co-ordinating the specialist knowledge possessed by employees so that it can be exploited to create benefits and competitive advantage for the organisation.

Gabay at a glance:

Alternatives to KISS include:

Clear Brief Concise
Keep Your Copy Simple
What's In It For Me?

Loquacious language:

nimiety – extravagance

L

launch	The introduction of a new service or product to a market.
layout	Sketch or blueprint showing the intended order of contents and visual styling of an advertisement mail piece, poster and so on.
lead	Opening section of copy.
lead time	The time gap between the creative concept and the final result.
LHE	*Left-hand edge.*
LHS	*Left-hand side.*
lifetime value	The entire term value of a consumer to an organisation. Typically the costs spent on acquiring a consumer are high. The longer the consumer remains loyal the less the investment costs and so the greater the overall lifetime value.
lift letter	A second letter within a direct mail piece designed to 'lift' response. (*Also known as a **publisher's letter**.*)
list ad	An advertisement listing more than one item, for example a series of records.
list broker	An agent who sells databases of sales prospects.
list cleaning	Removal of inaccurate data from a database.
list manager	An agent of database lists.
list segment	Section of list chosen against specific criteria such as sex and job title.
literal	Typesetting error by a printer.
live copy	Copy read 'live' on air.
live names	A term that describes active customers contacted through direct mail techniques.
live tag	'Live' message read 'on air' to provide additional local information relating to a pre-recorded national commercial.
logo	An abbreviation of logotype. A particular shape, design or trademark that distinguishes an organisation. Also known as a signature, sig, or sig cut.

Did you know?

In 1985, to increase awareness of postcodes, the UK Post Office promoted a quiz featuring just one question: 'What's your postcode'? Only a few responses were received – it was discovered that the Post Office had printed the wrong postcode!

loose insert	*See free-standing stuffer.*
lottery	A sales promotion prize contest based on chance.
lowercase	Small letters of the alphabet.

M

M2M	Market to market advertising. A viral marketing campaign which encourages macro markets to disseminate valuable information between communities.
media speak	Journalistic fad corruption of the British language. 'Stalking Horse' instead of opponent.
merge and purge	Assimilation of different databases that also removes duplicated or unwanted information. (*Also see* **de-dupe**.)
mf.	More Follows at the right hand foot of a press release when there is a continuation.
MGM	Member-get-Member advertising (*also known as* **recommend-a-friend** *or* **word-of-mouth advertising**). When a current customer recommends a product or service to a new prospect.
micromarketing	The study of the marketing strategy of an individual business.
mini catalogue	A shortened version of a larger catalogue, often featuring special seasonal offers.
mnemonic	Symbol or acronym to aid memory.
mock-up	A near-finished representation of a final creative execution.
monopolistic competition	A situation where there are only a few producers who control a market.
mood music	Musical track which helps establish a desired atmosphere.
morgue	Ready written obituaries for VIPs.
multi-mailer	One mailing containing several loose single promotional sheets.
multiple discriminant analysis	Assessing products by separating out their features, and estimating the relative values of these attributes to different market segments.
music bed	Musical background track.
musical logo	A melodic corporate signature.

Anagrams:

from SWEETHEART to THERE WE SAT

N

NABS (National Advertising Benevolent Society.)   Highly respected British charitable organisation for professionals working in the media.

network marketing   Marketing campaign carried out through a complete magazine network.

neuro marketing   The use of an MRI scanner to ascertain the effectiveness of a marketing campaign.

new entrant   A company which is going into a market for the first time.

news hole   The amount of news space in a publication after advertisements have been placed.

newsletter   Organisational journalistic style publication containing information of interest to members and associates of the organisation. They provide a sense of belonging as well as source of planned dissemination of management plans and member or employee developments.

Gabay at a glance:

The world's first recorded house journal was the British Mercury. In 1710 it was delivered three times a week to the homes of any client insurance policyholders who subscribed.

niche marketing   The promotion of a product aimed at one particular area of the market.

non-directive interview   An interview in which the questions are not set in advance and no fixed pattern is followed

non-durable goods   Goods which are used soon after they have been bought, e.g. food or newspapers.

non-price competition   An attempt to compete in a market through other means than price, such as quality of product and promotion.

non-store retailing   The selling of goods and services electronically without setting up a physical shop.

noting score   The percentage of total readers who note an advertisement.

novelty format   An unusually sized or shaped mailing piece.

nth name   A direct marketing database technique that divides the total number of names in a list by a required number of 'test' names to produce a sample. For example, 10,000 'test' names chosen from 100,000 names would result in every 10th name being selected for 'testing'.

Loquacious language:

noisime – a terrible smell

O

offer	The terms and conditions under which a direct mail item or service is promoted.
on camera narration	Narration delivered on screen by a presenter.
one-stage/step	A promotion in which a sales cycle is completed in one step without any need for further following up by letter or telephone. (The prospect reads an advertisement and, on its strength, places an order for a product or service.)
on-pack coupon	A coupon attached to the outside of a package.
on-pack premium	A free gift attached to the outside of a package.
open-rate	The most expensive chargeable media rate.
open end	1. Recorded commercial with allocated space for a tag. 2. Programme produced with time for commercials. 3. Programme with no set time to end.
opinion research	Research based on opinions rather than facts.
order card	A response card to complete and order by mail.
order form	A response form to complete and return by mail.
orphan	*See* **club line**.
outsourcing	The transfer of work previously done by employees of an organisation to another organisation, usually one that specialises in that type of work or offer a cheaper workforce.
own-brand goods	Products specially packed for a store with the store's name on them. (*Also known as* **own-label goods**.)

P

package insert	A promotional item inserted in a package.
package test	The evaluation of mailing elements individually or in their entirety.

Gabay at a glance:

Want to increase your direct mail response?

· *Handwrite the envelope.*
· *Use a real stamp.*
· *Avoid plastic clear envelopes - unless for sending catalogues.*
· *Check postcodes.*
· *Check spellings of names.*

Did you know?

Although it has become a visual cliché, you really can light up a bulb with every new idea: the brain runs at a power rating of 10 watts per minute and radiates 20% of body heat.

page impressions	The total number of customers who land on a webpage, e.g. in an ad view.
page proof	The printer's proof of a completed page.
paid circulation	A publication that is distributed to people who have paid a subscription.
pamphlet	A leaflet that contains four or more pages.
pantone	Colour matching system.
passive media	Media that requires the viewer or listener to do nothing more than watch or listen.
paste-up	A camera-ready layout.
peak time	Period which attracts the largest TV or radio audience figures.
peel-off label	A self-adhesive label that can be attached to an order form.
penetration	See reach.
penetration pricing	Competitively pricing a product to gain market penetration.
perceptual map	A diagram representing how consumers view various comparative products on the basis of specific factors or attributes.
permission marketing	Direct marketing requiring the seller to gain permission from each recipient before sending any promotional material.
personalisation	The inclusion of a recipient's personal address details within a mail piece. (Research proves that personalisation always increases response.)
personality advertising	Promotion drawing on a famous person to endorse a product.
piggyback	A secondary offer included within a mail piece.
pitch	A new business presentation.
planning	The activity of predicting future events and using those assumptions to develop strategies that will help achieve the ultimate goal.
poco	Brief for 'politically correct' sometimes used by feminists to refer to non-sexist language.
POPA	Point of purchase advertising.
pop-under ad	Web advertisement appearing in a distinctive browser window.

Loquacious language:

nullibiety – the state of being nowhere

portfolio	A case or folder of work examples.
portrait	Upright page. (*Opposite of* **landscape**.)
positioning	A strategy that 'positions' a product or idea according to how a consumer perceives that product or service relative to the competitive offerings from providers of similar goods or services.
post-purchase advertising	Advertising designed to minimise post-purchase anxiety.
PPI	*Printed Postage Impression.* The pre-printed Royal Mail licensed mark which typically appears on a direct mail envelope.
pradvertising	Cross between advertising and Public Relations.
premium	1. A free item or an item offered as an inducement to test trial and eventually purchase a product or service. 2. An extra charge for a special advertising position within a publication or as part of a broadcast.
presentation	Formal presentation of creative and strategic concepts and proposals.
press clipping	A published article of interest archived for future reference.
press officer	PR professional who specialises in press relations. Ivy Ledbetter Lee, a former New York financial journalist, was the first Public relations consultant. He opened for business in 1903 and his clients included a circus, bankers and politicians. The first PR company in Britain, Editorial Services Ltd, opened for business in 1924. The first Public Realtions Officer in Britain worked for Southern Railway and was appointed in 1925.
press pack	A portfolio of information relating to a specific press release or announcement.
price differential	The price difference between products in a range.
price fixing	An unlawful agreement between companies to charge the same price for competing products.
price-insensitive	Goods or services for which sales remain constant regardless of price.

Gabay at a glance:

Summarise who your product or service is meant to please:

It's for ... (two sentences). This includes an explanation of why it is attractive to a particular audience.

My product / service is ... (two sentences). This explains the nature of the product or service.

My market must have it because ... (write three sentences as well as bullet points with substantiation).

Brand origins:

Pretty Polly, 1920 – Hibbert and Buckland (manufacturers of PP) acquired the name from a wholesaler who originally took the name from a racing horse called Pretty Polly. The horse won him a fortune. His daughter told him that the name bought success.

price-off	A cut price strategy to encourage trial or increased usage of a product or service.
product portfolio analysis	A model for a marketing strategy with various categories of product based on present performance and growth rate, which can help a business to plan its product development and strategy.
production department	An advertising department that co-ordinates and supervises all aspects of technical creative production.
programming schedule	A notification of programme times and dates that aids a media buyer when selecting TV or radio commercial time.
promotion	A concerted marketing method to increase sales of a product or service, usually through using a sales promotion technique.
prompted recall	A test to see how well people can remember an advertisement. Respondents are given help such as a picture which they might associate with the advertisement.
prospect	A consumer who is likely to become a customer.
psychogalvanometer	An instrument used to measure emotional reactions to advertising. It checks sweat on hands.
psychographics	Classification of prospects according to lifestyle and personality traits.
publication date	The date a publication becomes available to the public.
publicity still	A photograph used for publicity purposes.
publisher's letter	See *lift letter*.
puffery	Advertising which praises the product or service being sold in an exaggerated way, without any specific factual data.
pull	Printer's proof.
pull quotes	The enlargement of text of key quotations to give added emphasis.
pull strategy	A method that invests in large advertising and marketing budgets to stimulate consumer demand and so encourage intermediaries to handle and promote a product or service.
push strategy	A method to encourage consumer demand and so stimulate intermediaries to stock a product.
PVR	Personal Video Recording is a major threat to advertisers as consumers can edit out all commercials when recording TV programmes to a hard disc (see page 422).

Loquacious language:

obambulate – to walk around aimlessly

Q

Q&A	Abbreviation for Question and Answer. This usually takes the form of a panel of questions and answers which relate to technical aspects of a product or service. Q&A panels typically appear towards the back of product or service brochure.
quantitative research	Research based sample quantities based on amount or degree rather than kind or condition. According to AGB Research in England, the key quantitative questions are:

- *Who are you?*
- *What do you buy?*
- *Where do you buy?*
- *How much?*
- *At what price?*
- *When?*
- *What else could you have purchase*d?
- *Where else could have purchased it?*

quarterly	Publication published on a three-monthly cycle, as opposed to bi-monthly (every other month) and anually.
questionnaire	A form featuring a sequence of closed or open questions to be completed and returned by a targeted respondent.

R

rate card	A form detailing specified media advertising costs and support information.
reach	The overall total percentage of targeted prospects in a specific area exposed to a specific advertisement during a specified duration. (*Also known as* **penetration**.)
reader ad	A copy-only advertisement that appears to be genuine news or editorial. (*Also see* **advertorial**.)
reader profile	A demographic classification of readers.
reader response	The response of readers to an article or piece of advertising.
readership	The total number of people reached by a publication.
redemption	1. The percentage of coupons or trading stamps that are cashed in. 2. The general cashing or trading in of coupons or trading stamps.
repeat mailing	A second mailing follow-up to the same list of names contacted by a first mailing.

Writers' words:

'How can I believe in God when just last week I got my tongue caught in the roller of an electric typewriter?'
Woody Allen

repositioning	A planned marketing attempt to reposition a product or service within a market by changing either features, price or distribution – or a combination of all three.
research director	Agency employee responsible for the purchase and analysis of information that influences a marketing strategy.
response	A planned reaction to a planned arousal.
response device	Any piece of communication which accommodates a response.
response list	List of individuals who have responded to a direct mail campaign.
retainer	A fee that secures the ongoing negotiated exclusive rights to call from time to time upon a person's professional services, such as copywriting.
rhetoric	The written and spoken language of persuasion. Also sometimes refers to a pompous style of language.
roll fold	A way of folding paper – usually a leaflet – whereby each printed section is rolled around the next at the paper's edge fold.
rough	A brush stroke layout indicating a general creative concept
round robin	Traditional name for direct mail letter.
run of book/paper	Advertising space and location determined by a publisher rather than advertiser.
run on	To continue copy on the same line rather than go to a new line.
rushes	Rough, unedited print of daily film footage.

S

sales promotion	'The range of techniques used to attain sales/marketing objectives in a cost effective manner by adding value to a product or service either to intermediaries or end users, normally but not exclusively within a defined time period.' (Institute of Sales Promotions.)
sample	1. Group of individuals representative of a larger percentage of the population. 2. Complementary portion or test quantity of a marketed product. (*Also known as a **trial offer**.*) 3. Quantity of data picked from a total direct mail data base.

Anagrams:

from CONVERSATION to VOICES RANT ON.

scratch-and-sniff	A method of incorporating scent onto paper. When scratched, an impregnated scent panel is activated.
scratch off	A direct mail device whereby a coin is used to scratch a coated paper to reveal a special message. (*Also known as coin rub.*)
selective demand advertising	Advertising aimed to create awareness and provide information about a particular brand.
self liquidator	1. Gift or premium, which is financed by its offered purchase. 2. Sales promotion display provided to a retailer for a fee to the supplier or manufacturer.
sharpening	A cognitive process in which the information retained becomes more vivid and important than the event itself.
shelf life	1. Amount of time that a product can remain on a retail shelf 2. Longevity of a product or service based on its popularity and demand.
shelf strip	A point of sale printed strip attached to the facing edge of a shelf.
shirt-board advertising	Advertising printed on the cardboard used to support laundered shirts. Popular in America.
sleeper	An unpublished 'seed' (designated recipien) who monitors a direct mailing campaign's postal progress.
spokesperson	A person who endorses an advertised product or service.
sponsored programme	1. TV or radio programme that is part financed by a named advertiser. 2. Any event which may be financially subsidised for marketing or advertising purposes.
statement stuffer	A small printed advertisement inserted in an envelope containing a bill. (*Also see **bill stuffer**.*)
stock	Music, art, graphics, mpegs or photographs available from specialist libraries.
style book	Manual of approved corporate styling ad design.
suit	Generic term referring to a non-creative employee of an advertising agency.
suspects	A consumer who may or may not become a customer.
sustaining advertising	Advertising that maintains consumer demand rather than increases it.

Medieval words:

cadence – a dance step

sweeps	The months of November, Feburary and May set by an American TV rating service to establish the ranking of TV network shows. This sets the level of advertising rates for local stations.
sweepstakes	A below-the-line technique in which prizes are offered to participants on a random chance; no skills are needed to win. An assumption is made that the technique will eventually encourage the consumer to buy a product (no immediate purchase required). Also the condition that a sweepstake or 'prize draw 'entry' is entered according to a defined set of published rules. (*See below-the-line.*)

T

take one	1. Leaflets or pamphlets freely distributed via a sales promotional desktop or mounted dispenser. 2. In America, a 'take one' is an attachment to a transit advertising vehicle card. The 'take one' is a coupon or information request sheet. It often incorporates an envelope or is part of a pad.
talking heads	A TV production featuring extreme head and shoulder close ups of subjects discussing a specific item or area of interest.
talking shelf strips	A point of sale printed strip or item attached or nearby the facing edge of a shelf which contains a movement sensitive electronic device. As the consumer passes, the device triggers a pre-recorded sound track which discusses the product. (Belgian advertisers found that such devices could increase sales by 500%.)
target audience	The ideal prospective audience which would be interested in a specific product or service.
tear sheet	A page torn from a publication sent to an advertiser as proof of publication.
teaser campaign	A series of brief announcement advertisements which stimulate curiosity.
telemarketing	The market prospecting, selling, servicing and informing via the telephone. (A function which is being increasingly outsourced to Asia.)
television director/producer	A person employed to manage and co-ordinate the production of TV commercials.
test marketing	(*See zone plan.*)

Anyone around here speak English?

A sign in a Moscow hotel: 'If this is your first visit to USSR, you are welcome to it.'

thank you letter	A direct mail copy technique in which a customer is thanked for making a purchase or enquiry.
The American Marketing	Founded in 1936, it is recognised as America's leading association of marketing managers and teachers Association (www.marketingpower.com).
threshold effect	The stage at which the effectiveness of an advertising campaign can be seen to be working.
thumbnail	A miniature, rough layout.
tie-in promotion	A promotion which markets more than one product or brand.
time-sheet	A standard form to record the amount of time spent working on a client project.
tip-in	A loosely placed publication insert. (*See also* **free-standing stuffer**.)
tip-on	A coupon reply card or sample glued by its edge for easy removal from a printed piece of advertising.
tombstone	Orignally an American Wall Street financial advertisement used, among other things, to announce new stock issues. So called because the copy only provides the bare-bones facts.
tone of voice	General attitude, expression or approach given to a message.
traffic building	An advertising piece of communications that can include sales promotion or direct marketing, designed to encourage retail store traffic.
traffic department	The department within an advertising agency which co-ordinates the work flow of projects between departments.
treatment	An overall styling or approach to a piece of advertising.
trial close	A copy technique whereby the reader is asked for an order at an early stage of a direct mail letter. The copy then directs the reader to the coupon. This technique can be repeated several times during one direct mail letter.
trial offer	A special marketing offer, meant to encourage future consumer purchase, made within a particular period of time. (*Also see* **sample**.)
TV shopping	TV programmes or channels that are likened to shopping catalogues. (*Also known as* **shop-at-home**.)

| two-stage/two-step | A promotion in which a letter or telephone call completes a sales cycle in two steps with a further follow-up. (The prospect reads an advertisement and, on its strength, applies for further details of a product or service.) It is the opposite of a one-stage/-step promotion. |

U

ultimate consumer	The person who actually uses the product.
umbrella advertising	The advertising of an organisation or an association of companies rather than a single product.
uncontrollable variable	A variable or factor in marketing that cannot be controlled, e.g. legislation or the state of the country's economy.
undifferentiated marketing strategy	A marketing strategy which seeks to present a product to the public without stressing any unique feature of the product, thus appealing to all segments of the market.
undifferentiated product	A product which has no unique feature to set it apart from others on the market.
unsolicited testimonial	A letter praising someone or a product, without the writer having been asked to write it.
usage pull	1. The power of advertising to encourage individuals to purchase an advertised service or product. 2. In the US: the degree to which those who see or hear advertisements for a product buy more of it than those who do not.
USP	*Unique Sellng Point.* The outstanding benefit or family of features which distinguish a product or service from its competition.

Gabay at a glance:

Rather than thinking of your product or service in terms of a 'USP' consider a 'POD' - Point of Difference.

To arrive at your POD list six attributes which a market would miss if they didn't purchase your product or service. Then summarise those attributes in a sentence of no longer than fourteen words; this is your POD.

| utility | The usefulness or satisfaction that a consumer gets from a product. |
| utility goods | Basic goods that are necessary for everyday life. |

Writers' words:

'A good novel tells us the truth about its hero; but a bad novel tells us the truth about its author.' GK Chesterton

V

VALS
A system of dividing people into segments according to their way of living. (*An abbreviation of **values and lifestyles**.*)

value analysis
Analysis by a producer of all aspects of a finished product to determine how it could be made at minimum cost.

value-added services
Services adding to a service or product being sold.

viral marketing
Marketing by word of mouth or electronically. (*Also see **M2M**.*)

voice-over
The voice of an unseen narrator or presenter.

volumetrics
Investigation of the relative influence of various media by considering the number of people who are exposed to them, and their importance as buyers.

voucher copy
A copy of an entire publication sent to an advertiser as proof of publication and advertising position as agreed.

W

web marketing
Marketing over the Internet.

wheel of retailing
Changes in the evolution of the retailing trade.

white mail
Letters sent to mail order firms, which result in more paper work, e.g. complaints and enquiries.

white space
Unprinted space, which gives greater emphasis to remaining, printed advertising space.

WIIFM
The fundamental motives affecting the decision taken by a prospective customer. (*An abbreviation of **What's in it for me?**) (Also see **KISS**.*)

window envelope
An opening or 'window' die cut into a direct mail envelope, which shows part of the contents of the mailing inside. The cut is usually covered by glassine, which is a type of transparent paper.

word spacing
The decrease or increase of space between words in a line of justified type.

wraparound
A cover/holder carrying a mail order catalogue and supporting material such as sales letters and order forms.

Etymology:

to cook your goose – this term meaning to destroy your chances comes from the sixteenth century Swedish legend of King Eric. The king had entered an enemy's town. The local community hung geese from towers, as if to say 'get out – what do you want with us?' The king's response was 'to cook your goose'.

X

x-factor
The undefinable aspect within a person or a company that can't be copied but equals success (*also see UK vs UK language page 189*).

Y

yes/no envelope
A response direct mail envelope which encourages readers to reply to an offer, irrespective of whether or not they intend to make a purchase.

yes/no stamp
Similar to the yes/no envelope response enhancement device. Instead either a YES or NO stamp is attached to a response device. This encourages customer involvement and gives a sense that the mailing is an 'active' item.

Gabay at a glance:

Rather than offer just a 'yes - no' option, also provide a 'maybe' option.
The more options, the higher the chances of a response, if not now, 'maybe' later.

Z

z fold
A method of folding paper such as a sales letter into three equal parts. The middle third forms the diagonal column of the letter 'Z'.

zip envelope
A direct mail envelope which is opened by pulling a tab.

zone plan
A strategy to test a new product or service using advertising in a highly targeted small geographic area. (*Also see **test marketing**.*)

Twisted truths:

Comparisons are as bad as colloquialisms.

Brains, pen, action!

Something to ponder...

Before you overwhelm people with marketing jargon think about these well-considered words:

"Short words are best and the old words when short are best of all."

Winston Churchill

"Words do two major things: they provide food for the mind and create light for understanding and awareness."

Jim Rohn

"Words mean more than what is set down on paper. It takes the human voice to infuse them with shades of deeper meaning."

Maya Angelou

Have you come across any marketing terms that are not in my list?

Send them to
jj@gabaywords.com

and they might appear in the next edition.

Chiasmus:

'Let us never negotiate out of fear; but let us never fear to negotiate.' John F. Kennedy

8. Idioms make the heart grow fonder

Closely related to clichés, idioms are common expressions whose meaning may not be fully understood at first glance.

As you will see in the following section, idioms have become as much a part of the living landscape of language as the people who use them locally and then take them into the hearts of neighbouring cultures and communities.

So, putting business before pleasure and trying not to cross the bridge before I come to it – after all, procrastination is the thief of time – enjoy these idioms, because if you look after the pennies, the pounds will look after themselves.

hold your horses

Modern idioms

Idioms are perennially popular with copywriters.

Most dictionaries describe an idiom along the lines of:

1   A speech form or expression of a given language peculiar to itself grammatically or cannot be understood from the individual meanings of its elements, as in 'keep tabs on'.

2   The specific grammatical, syntactic, and structural character of a given language.

3   Regional speech or dialect.

4   a) A specialised vocabulary used by a group of people; jargon: legal idiom.

   b) A style or manner of expression peculiar to a given people.

   'Also important is the uneasiness I've always felt at cutting myself off from my idiom, the American habits of speech and jest and reaction, all of them entirely different from the local variety'

   (SJ Perelman).

5   A style of artistic expression characteristic of a particular individual, school, period or medium: the idiom of the French impressionists; the punk rock idiom.

Still awake? Then there are four points about idioms that we need to look at individually:

1   Idioms are ideal for brochures, leaflets or direct mail letters and envelopes. They encourage readers either to open the brochure, read further into the leaflet or dip into an envelope – all so that they can complete the meaning of a sentence.

2   Idioms help copywriters to style their writing in such a way as to 'speak' specifically to a targeted audience. The only problem with this is that even if you know the correct words, unless your message is equally well targeted and 'street-cred', the entire exercise will turn out neither 'cool', 'wicked' or even 'straight-up' (more like, 'down the drain').

Brand origins:

Lucky Strike cigarettes – named after cigarettes given to miners who hoped to discover gold during the California Gold Rush of 1856.

3   As with point 2 above, idioms add realism to a message and often, at the same time, humour. For example, a poster for a London Trichologist, showing a balding man: *'Keep your hair on mate!'*

The problem with this is that if you venture too far into localised language, your wider audience may not be able to fully appreciate the nub of your proposition, or worst still, completely 'get the wrong end of the stick'. For example:

'Call a spade a spade' (to speak bluntly)

'He was calling a spade a spade when he began to criticise his equal opportunities employee for being lazy.'

4   On the other hand, it could be argued that regional dialect adds both a sense of curiosity from the wider public, as well as authenticity with your targeted community.

This usage of an idiom (remember, 'A style of artistic expression characteristic of a particular individual, school, period or medium') is useful if you want to evoke a sense of nostalgia or, perhaps, a deeper empathy with a targeted audience.

Example of rap dialect

Ayoo, I *'drop'* more rhymes, than a falling *'nursery-book'*

While you *'unlock you cell'* to anyone like an *'ursty-crook'*

ANY, your *'lines blow'*, so we know that your *'rhymes-suck'*, I throwing *'Gawd' 'clock's'* in *'heaven'* to show your *'times-up'*

This kid ain't hard, he soft as *'feathers'*, so you better *'duck-low'*,

You a fat kid playing *'tic-tac-toe'*, cuz your ass got *'stuck-in-the-row'*

Yo, your rhymes is like your *'appearance'*, a *'big-waste'*

Prewriting and posting *'quickly'*, ANY is trying to *'rig-haste'* (haste = speed)

You can beg for a *'tie'*, but the truth is *'knot'*, *'US'* victorious, a win *'Iraq'*, he couldn't be a *'soldier'*, if he packed a *'glock'*

Ma rhymes are *'right'*, cuz I *'left'* you *'clocked'*, like you *'inthamiddle-of-time'*, He likes *'playing with cocks'* like *'little-nines'*, but I'll *'cock'* my *'glock'* so don't fiddle-wit-mines

Have you parting with a *'broken spine'*, and lost respect, leaving with *'no-back'* – you, sum *'fake ass dealer'*, with a *'plumber'* is the only time he can *'show-crack'*

Writing landmarks:

1953 – French entrepreneur Marcel Bich bought the rights to Biró's patent and manufactured the first throw-away ballpoint pen.

227

Your mind is like a *'new document'* always *'blank', 'Dropping shit'* like a *'bird', 'depleting-your-mind'*, lyrics hitting me like a *'mindless'* prank, try-n compete-with-mines

ANY, couldn't *'cum pre-peared'* even if I *'busted'* in his *'fruit basket'* before the match ~ *'Dawg'*, I'm the *'pick of the litter'* while you ain't even in the batch

Truthfully, dawg, after a *'viagra kick'*, you'll still be on the *'short-end-of-the-stick'*

This kid's *'gay'*, so all I need is a *'pus$y'*, to *'fend-off-a-d!ck'*.

~holla~

(www.rapboard.com)

Did you spot the more common idioms in the above example?

The point that strikes me about the rap example is the use of punctuation – something that you, as a copywriter, need to keep in mind if you want to craft how, and precisely where, you wish to make an impact.

Regional dialects and idioms

Dialect examples from Liverpool, England

A dirty big plate of	A VERY large portion please
Ay ay	Hey!
Boogaroff	No thank you, please go away
Casey	Full-sized soccer ball
Ere, tatty 'ead!	Excuse me young woman
Gisalite	Could you oblige me with a match please?
I wanna	I want to
I wudden mind	Yes please
I'le mug yer	My treat!
La	I say, young man
Sarawak	Farewell, sir
Ta, Wack	Thanks, I am most grateful
Tanner-megge	Small football
T'sarrahwell	Farewell
Ullo dur!	Greetings! Pleased to make your acquaintance
Wack	Sir
We wuz playin'	We were playing

Writers' words:

'If my doctor told me I had only six minutes to live, I wouldn't brood. I'd type a little faster.' Isaac Asimov

Worrel?	What will?
Yer wanna	You ought to
Yer wha?	Do I hear you correctly?
Yerl get no bevvy 'ere	Not a licensed premises
Yis	Yes
Y'know like	Meaningless interjection

Dialect examples from Yorkshire, England

Aye	Yes
Brass	Money
In't it?	Isn't it?
Maardy	Moody
Missell	Myself
Neet	Night
Nowt	Nothing
Reyt	Right
Thinkon	Remember
Ye'sell	Yourself
Parky	Cold
Summat	Something

Dialect examples from Lancashire, England

Muck midden pride – a carriage weddin' an' a wheelbarrow flittin'.
The cost of being ostentatious

Beauty's only skin deep – but it's a bugger when tha 'ast use a pick ter ger at it.
There's ugliness – and then there's complete repulsiveness.

Tha met bi born but th'art not dee-erd yet.
You might be born but you're not dead yet, i.e. you might be proud of your achievements but things can still go wrong before your die, so don't be too confident.

Th'arl come to thi cake an' milk.
You'll get what's coming to you.

Loquacious language:

---

draffsack – rubbish bag

Dialect examples from Birmingham, England:

He's got a bob on hisself	He thinks a lot of himself.
A face as long as Livery Street	Fed-up
'Shiz inner oil tot'	She is in her element
Well, I'll go to the top of our stairs!	What a surprise!
When Nechells was a nice place	Long ago

Shakespearean idioms and expressions

Shakespeare's influence on English can never be overstated. Thanks to him, the following idioms were put into wide circulation:

A foregone conclusion	(Othello, III, iii)
A tower of strength	(Richard III, V, iii)
Beggars all description	(Anthony and Cleopatra, II, ii)
Cold comfort	(King John, V, viii)
Hoist with his own petard	(Hamlet, III, iv)
I must be cruel to be kind	(Hamlet, III, iv)
In my mind's eye	(Hamlet, I, iii)
It's Greek to me	(Julius Caesar, I, ii)
Salad days	(Anthony and Cleopatra, I, v)
To the manner born	(Hamlet, I, iv)

Biblical idioms and expressions

A lamb brought to the slaughter	(Jeremiah 11)
An eye for an eye	(Exodus 21)
Cast pearls before swine	(Matthew 7)
Eat sour grapes	(Ezekiel 24)
Go from strength to strength	(Psalm 84)
In sheep's clothing	(Matthew 7)
In the twinkling of an eye	(1 Corinthians 15)
Love thy neighbour	(Leviticus 19)
My brother's keeper	(Genesis 4)
Out of the mouths of babes	(Matthew 21)
Suffer fools gladly	(2 Corinthians 11)
The apple of his eye	(Deuteronomy 32)
The root of the matter	(Job 19)

Metaphors:

Cowardice... The jaundice of the soul. John Dryden, *The Hind and the Panther, VII*

The salt of the earth   (Matthew 5)

The signs of the times   (Matthew 16)

The skin of my teeth   (Job 19)

The straight and narrow   (Matthew 7)

A common issue with biblical idioms is appreciating their real meaning. Rabbis, for example, spend years debating the meaning of biblical idioms.

Take the following suggestions:

Idiom	Meaning	
Seed	Offspring	(Genesis 22:17)
Possess gates	Capture cities	(Genesis 24:60)
Said in heart	Thought to self	(Genesis 27:41)
The way of women	Menstruation	(Genesis 31:35)
Lift up your head	Restore to honor	(Genesis 40:13
Fruit of your loins	Descendants	(Exodus 1:5)
Flowing with milk and honey	Fertile	(Exodus 3:8)
Mighty hand	Force	(Exodus 3:19)
From the womb	From birth	(Judges 13:5)
Gave him another heart	Changed his attitude	(1 Samuel 10:9)
Open hand	Generosity	(Esther 1:7)
Saw his face	Had access to him	(Esther 1:14)

The contemporary lesson of all this? By all means feature idioms, but make sure that your copy remains clear (as punch!).

Idioms: Gabay's choice

Keeping in mind that you could be tackling a broad range of issues, I have chosen the following idioms as possible headlines for your next important wriring project. Many are straightforward directives – such as: 'Join the club'. These are particularly valuable in copy when you want someone to either act upon, or at least think about something. As with all similar expressions, don't overuse idioms, or your copy may end up sounding strained and crass.

On the other hand, feel free to use and play with my choice of idioms as sources of inspiration, not just for direct copy, but also as concepts, or perhaps to offer original interpretations of a subject matter. Another

Printing landmarks:

practical – as well as down right fun – use, is to change the spelling of one of the key words in the idiom, so as to give both the idiom itself and your elucidation of a message a novel twist.

For example:

A good job two?

(Picture of busy mother holding down a career and bringing up a baby.)

Ah yes. Don't forget to change singulars for plurals if it helps with the message; idioms are, after all, your *'flexible friends'*.

For example:

Can I help you? vs *Can we help you?* or *Can we help?*

Have fun!

A to Z of Gabay's favourites

A

All
All in all
All together now
All in a day's work
All the best
All well and good
All's well that ends well
Evening all

Anything
Anything doing?
Anything but
Anything like

As
As if
As if by magic
As it were
As you are

Ask
Ask a silly question
Ask for it
Ask me another
I ask you

Aunt
My giddy aunt

Away
Up, up and away
Away with you!
They're away!

B

Back
Back to square one
Back to the drawing board
Mind your backs!

Ball
The ball's in your court

Bang
Bang on
Flash, bang, wallop…!

Bark
His bark is worse than his bite

Barn
He (she, etc) must have been born in a barn

Bedpost
Between you, me and the bedpost

Brand origins:

Andrex, 1954. Originally manufactured in St Andrews Road, Walthamstow, London, and named after a local church.

Bee

He (she, etc) think he's (she's, etc) the bee's knees

Believe

Believe it or not
I believe you; thousands wouldn't
Would you believe?
I don't believe it!

Bell

That rings a bell
The bells of hell go ting-a-ling-a-ling
You can ring my bell
For whom the bell tolls

Belt

Belt up!

Best

All the best!
The best of luck
The best of British
Nothing but the best

Bet

You can bet your bottom dollar
Can't resist a bet
Bet your life
You can bet on it

Between

Between the two of us
Between you and me

Bird

A little bird told me
Watch the birdie!
Kill two birds with one stone
A bird in the hand…
Birds of a feather

Birthday

Birthday suit
Birthday wishes

Blame

Take the blame
I don't blame you
Blame it on…

Blaze

Go to blazes!
What (how, when, why, where, etc) the blazes?

Blind

It will make you go blind
Blind as a bat

Born

I wasn't born yesterday
Born with a silver spoon in his (her, their, etc) mouth(s)

Boy

(Oh) boy!
Old boy
That's my boy!

Breathe

As I live and breathe

Brother

Oh brother!
Like sister and brother
Brothers in arms

Business

Mind your own business
Business is business
That's my business
That's show business

Butter

Butter wouldn't melt in his (her) mouth

Buzz

Buzz off!

Metaphors:

Critics in general are venomous serpents that delight in hissing. WB Daniel, *Rural Sports*

C

Cake
A piece of cake
You can't have your cake and eat it

Carpet
Sweep something under the carpet

Cat
(Has the) cat got your tongue?
It's the cat's whiskers
Let the cat out of the bag
Who's she? The cat's mother?
Look what the cat's brought it
It's raining cats and dogs

Chalk
Not by a long chalk

Chance
(A) fat chance
Not a chance in hell
Give him (her, them, etc) a chance
Give peace a chance
Take a chance on me (us, him, her, etc)

Change
A change is as good as a rest
All change!
Change the record
Change the subject
It makes a change
Nothing much changes around here

Cheer
Cheer up!
Three cheers!

Cheese
Hard cheese!
Say 'cheese'!

Chin
Keep your chin up!

Chip
Chip off the old block
He's (she's, etc) got a chip on his (her, etc) shoulder

Clear
All clear!
Clear off!
Clear for landing
I can see clearly now…

Club
Join the club!

Come
As… as they come
Come again?
Come along
Come and get it!
Come back… all is forgiven!
Come, come!
Come off it!
Come on
Come to that
Coming up
How come?
If the worst comes to the worst
(Now) I come to think of it
What is… coming to?

Comment
No comment

Company
Just judge us by the company we keep
Two's company, three's a crowd
Present company excepted

Compliment
My (our) compliments to the chef
The compliments of the season

Cookie
That's the way the cookie crumbles

Writers' words:

234 'Any reviewer who expresses rage and loathing for a novel is preposterous. He or she is like a person who has put on full armor and attacked a hot fudge sundae.' Kurt Vonnegut Jr

Cool

Cool it
Keep your cool
Cool down
Stay cool
That's cool

Cotton

Bless his (little) cotton socks

Count

Count your blessings
Don't count your chickens (before they hatch)
Count to ten (before you lose your temper)!

Crack

Get cracking
You crack me up
You're crackers!
What's the crack?
(Come on) Get cracking
That's cracked it

Curiosity

Curiosity killed the cat

Customer

The customer is always right
The customer comes first

Cut

To cut a long story short
Cut it (or that) out!
Cut out the middle man
Let's cut to the chase

D

Dare

How dare you!
I dare say you won't…
Do you dare?
Don't you dare!

Yinglish:

Day

Any day of the week
Good day
In all my (his, etc) born days
The best days of your life
(It's) all in a day's work
It's not my (his, etc) day
One of these (fine) days
That'll be the day
Another day, another dollar
Those were the days
(In the) good old days

Devil

Be a devil
Go to the devil!
Talk (or speak) of the devil
The (or a) devil of a…
There'll be the devil to pay
Who (what, how, where, why) the devil?
You naughty devil
You little devil

Do

…and have (or be) done with it
Anything doing?
Been there, done that, got the T-shirt
Did you ever?
Do me (or us) a favour!
Don't do anything I wouldn't do
Easy does it
Fair dos
Have been and done it
How are you doing?
How do you do it?
Nothing doing
Sure do!
That does it!
That will do
That's done it!
Well done!
What can I (we, etc) do for you?
Why don't…
You know what you can do with…

Dog
Gone to the dogs
It's a dog's life

Dollar
You (can) bet your bottom dollar

Dozen
Six of one and half a dozen of the other

Dream
I wouldn't dream of it
Sweet dreams!

Duck
Lovely weather for ducks!
Take to (something or someone) like a duck to water

E

Ear

(Could I have) a word in your ear?
Play it by ear
Feel one's ears burning

Earth
Cost the earth
What (how, where, who, why) on earth?

Easy
Easy does it
Go easy (on)
I'm easy
Take it easy
Nice and easy

Eat
I'll eat my hat
What's eating you (him, etc)?

Enough
Enough is enough!
Enough of…
Enough said

Fair enough
Funnily enough
Curiously enough
Right enough
Sure enough
That's enough

Evening
Evening all!

Ever
Did you ever?
Ever so much
… For ever

Everything
Everything in the garden is lovely
Hold everything!
Stop everything!

Eye
Eyes down!
Here's mud in your eye!
You must have eyes in the back of your head

F

Face
Let's face it
Not just a pretty face
Shut your face
Face facts
Face up to the truth
About face!

Fact
As a matter of fact
For the fact
In actual fact
In fact
In point of fact
The fact is
The facts speak for themselves

Gabay tip:

One advertising technique which evolved from copywriting, is to use medial capitals. This refers to the practice of inserting a medial capital letter into the title of a process or product, for example CinemaScope.

Fail
Words fail me

Fancy
Fancy that!

Far
Far be it from me
Far from it
Far out!
So far, so good

First
First come first served
First off
First things first
Not have the first idea

Fish
Like a fish out of water
Plenty more fish in the sea

Fly
Go fly a kite!
Pigs might fly
There are no flies on him (her, etc)

Follow
Follow that!
Follow your leader
Follow that car!

Friend
Some of my (your, etc) best friends
are…
(To) absent friends!
We're just good friends
What's… between friends
Your friend and mine

G

Game
Game over
It's anyone's game

(So) that's your (his, etc) little game
That game is up
Two can play at that game
What's your game?

Get
Don't get me wrong
Get a load of this!
Get a move on!
Get along with you!
Get it?
Get knotted!
Get lost!
Get stuffed!
Get weaving!
Get you!
I get it
I've got it
You got me there

Girl
Old girl
Daddy's little girl
Who's the lucky girl then?
Thank Heaven for little girls

Give
Don't give me that
I don't give a damn
Give it a rest!
What gives?
Give over!
Give or take
I give up
Give in?

Go
As the saying goes
Go along with it
Go easy
Go man, go
Go to it
Go to the dogs
Going, going, gone

Loquacious language:

draisine – a kind of bicycle

Here goes!
Here we go again
How's it going?
(It's) no go
My heart goes out to you
Off we go
That's the way it goes
There you go again
Where do we go from here?
Who goes there

Good

A good one
(And a) good job too
Good afternoon
Good day
Good night
Good for you (him, etc)
Good gracious!
If you can't be good, be careful!
It's a good thing
So far, so good

Guess

Guess what
Guess who
I guess
It's anybody's guess
Your guess is as good as mine

H

Half

A… and a half
Half a moment
Half a tick
Not half
Not half bad
The half of it
Too… by half
There's always two halves to a story

Hand

A big hand for
All hands on deck!
All hands to the pump!
Hands off!
Hands up!
Put 'em up!
I've only one pair of hands
On one hand… and (or but) on the other…
Shake hands

Hang

Hang in there!
Hang it all!
Hang on
Hang about
I'll be hanged
Let it all hang out
Thereby hangs a tail

Hat

I'll eat my hat
My hat!

Head

Heads or tails?
Mind your head(s)!
Off with his (her) head!

Heart

Bless your (his, etc) heart
Cross my (your, etc) heart
Have a heart
You're breaking my heart
Put your (his, etc) heat and soul into…

Heaven

By heaven!
For heaven's sake!
Good heavens
Heaven forbid
Heaven help him
Heaven knows

Brand origins:

Aspirin, 1899 – derived from Greek by scientist C Witthauer. Full name Aceylirte Spirsäure (acetylated spiraeic acid + suffix 'in').

Heaven preserve us!
Heavens above
In heaven's name
Thank heavens!

Hell

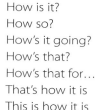

Go to hell!
Hell's bells!
Like hell
The hell he can (or can't)
To hell with…
What (how, where, who, why, etc) the hell?

Hello

Hello, hello, hello!
Hello stranger!
Hello there!

Help

Can I help you?
Not if I can help it
Here's a helping hand
Help, just when you need it most
Just ask for help
We are happy to help
Happy to help

Hold

Hold it!
Hold on!
Hold on tight!
Hold everything!
Hold your horses!

How

And how!
Here's how
How about…?
How about that (this)?
How are you?
How are you keeping?
How come…?
How do you do

How is it?
How so?
How's it going?
How's that?
How's that for…
That's how it is
This is how it is

Idea

Not have the foggiest (idea)
What's the (big) idea?
Not my (his, etc) idea of…
The very idea!

If

As if…
If I were you
If only…
If you could (or would)
What if…?

It

It's me
That's it
This is it
Who is it?

J

Job

(And a) good job too
(That's) just the job

Join

If you can't beat 'em, join 'em!
Join the club!

Joy

Full of the joys of spring
No joy

Number cruncher:

sexdecillion = 1000 quindecillion (US).

Just

Isn't (wasn't, etc) it (he, etc) just!
Just a moment
- Half a mo
- Half a moment
- Just a jiffy
- Just a tick
- Just a minute
- One moment
Just as well
Just so
Just the thing

K

Keep

How are you keeping?
Keep one's fingers crossed
Keep smiling!
Keep on taking the tablets!
Keep your shirt (or hair) on!
You (he, etc) can keep…
You can't keep a good man down
Am I my brother's keeper?

Kid

You're kidding!
(And) no kidding!
Just kidding around
Here's looking at you kid

Know

And I don't know who (or what)
As you know
Don't I know it
Don't you know
For all I (you) know
He didn't want to know
Heaven knows
Lord knows
Goodness knows
I didn't know you cared!

I don't know
I don't know about that
I don't know, I'm sure
I knew it
I know the feeling
I'd have you know
Knowing you (him, etc)
You know what he (it, etc) is
Not if I know it
That's all you need to know
On a need-to-know basis
There's no knowing (or telling)
Well, what do you know (about that)?
You don't know when you're well-off
You don't know you're alive (or born)
You know something (or what)?
You know what you can do with…
You never know
You never know your luck

L

Laugh

Don't make me laugh!
Have (or get) the last laugh
Look who's laughing now!
The last laugh is on you
You're (or you'll be) laughing!
You must be having a laugh!

Lay

Lay it on thick
Lay off!

Leave

Leave it at that
Leave off!
I must love you and leave you
Take it or leave it

Leg

Break a leg
Not have a leg to stand on

Writing landmarks:

1958 – the first disposable pen was sold in Britain.

Shake (or show) a leg

Less
Less of…
Less of that (or it)
We'll have none of that

Life
For dear life
For the life of me (him, etc)
It's a dog's life
Not (or never) on your life!
Not on your nelly!
Run for your life!
That's life!
This is the life!
To save his (her, etc) life
Upon my life!
What a life!
You (can) bet your life

Like
I (we, etc) should (or would) like to
I'd like to see…
If you like
That's more like it!
(Well) I like that!
A likely story
Not likely!

Load
Get a load of this!
What a load of (old) cobblers!
That's a load of my mind

Loaf
Use your loaf!

Long
As broad as it is long
So long
Long time no see

Look
Be looking for a fight (or trouble)
It's (or that's) your (his, etc) (own) look-out
Look after yourself (or No 1)!
Look here!
Look lively (or smart)
Look sharp!
Look what you've done!
Look who's talking!
Look you!

Love
For the love of God (or Mike)
I love you, too!
I must love you and leave you
What is this thing called love?
There's no (or little, or not much) love lost

Low
Lower the curtain
Lower the boom
Lower the tone
Lower one's sights
The lowest of the low

Luck
As luck would have it
Bad luck!
Better luck next time
Good luck
I should be so lucky
Just my (his, etc) luck
Make one's own luck
No such luck
One's luck is in (or out)
Some people have all the luck
The luck of the draw
Try one's luck
Worse luck
You'll (he'll, she'll, etc) be lucky
You never know your luck

Metaphors:

'Through the window he saw the long grey fingers of the dawn clutching at the fading stars'. Oscar Wilde, *The Young King*   **241**

Lunch

Do lunch
There's no such thing as a free lunch
Out to lunch
Ladies who lunch

M

Man

A man of letters
A man of the world
A man's man
Be one's own man
Every man for himself
Every man has his price
Go man, go!
I'm your man
Man for all seasons
Man of God
Man of straw
Man of the cloth
Man of the moment
Man to man
Man's best friend
My good man
Oh man!
The man in the moon
The man on the Clapham omnibus
The man on the street

Mean

And I don't mean maybe
Do you mean to say?
I see what you mean
By all means
By no means
I mean
What do you mean by…?

Mention

Don't mention it!
I hate to mention it
To be mentioned in dispatches
Not to mention

Mile

Go the extra mile
A mile a minute
Run a mile
See (or tell or spot) a mile off
Stand (or stick) out a mile
Be miles away

Milk

Cry over spilt (or US spilled) milk
Milk and honey
Milk and water
The milk in a coconut
Milk of human kindness
Get off and milk it
Milk it for all its worth

Mind

Be in (or North America 'of') two minds
Cast one's mind back
Close one's mind
Come (or spring) to mind
Don't mind me (him, etc)
Give someone a piece of one's mind
Have a good (or great or half a) mind
Have a mind of one's own
Have one's own mind
I don't mind if I do
I wouldn't mind
If you don't mind mentioning it
Make your mind up time
Mind how you go
Mind how you go
Mind one's Ps and Qs
Mind over matter
Mind the shop
Mind your back (or backs)
Mind your own business
Mind your step
Not pay someone any mind

Printing landmarks:

1796 – lithographic printing was invented in Germany.

On someone's mind
Open one's mind
Out of one's mind
Read someone's mind
The mind boggles

Minute

… in a minute
Just a minute
One minute to midnight
There's one born every minute
Wait a minute

Mistake

And no mistake
Make no mistake about it!
There's no mistake about it!
There's no mistaking something/some-one

Money

Be in the money
For my money
Have money to burn
I am not made of money
Money burns a hole in one's pocket (or purse)
Money for jam (or old rope)
Money-bags
On the money
Put money (or put one's) money on
Put one's money where one's mouth is
See the colour of one's money
Throw good money after bad
Throw money at something
You pays your money and takes your choice

N

Name

…is my middle name
…or my name's not

…who shall remain nameless
Call someone names
Drop names
Give one's name to
In all but name
In heaven's name
Name and shame
Name names
Put a name to
Someone's name is mud
Take my (your) name in vain
The name of the game
What name shall I say?
What's in a name?
You name it

Nature

Nature calls
The call of nature
One's better nature
Get (or go) back to nature
In the nature of things
In a state of nature
The nature of the beast
Completely natural

Neck

Break one's neck
Get (or catch) it in the neck
Have the (brass) neck to do something
Neck and neck
The same neck of the woods
Up to one's neck in
Win by a neck
Stick one's neck out

Nothing

All or nothing
It was (or it's) nothing
Nothing doing
Nothing like
Nothing ventured, nothing gained
Thanks for nothing

Brand origins:

Pall Mall cigarettes, named after a fashionable street in central London.

There's nothing for it
There's nothing in it
There's nothing to it
Think nothing of it!
Sweet nothings
Have nothing on someone/thing
You ain't seen nothing yet
Stop at nothing

Now

Now for…
Now, now
Now or never
Now and then

Number

By numbers
Come in number…
Do a number on
Have someone's name and number on it
I've got your number
Have someone's number
Make one's number
Number one
Someone's (or something's) days are numbered
Take care of number one
You know when your number's up

O

Odds

Ask no odds
By all odds
It makes no (or little) odds
Lay (or give) odds
Odd one (or man) out
Over the odds
What's the odds?

On

It's just not on!
On, on!

On with…
You're on!
Be on about
Be on at someone
Be on to someone (something)
It's not on
On it
On side
You're on

Open

For openers
In (or into) the open
Keep one's options open
Open book
Open sesame!
Open-and-shut
With one's eyes open

Out

Come out
Come out of the closet
Out to lunch
Out and about
Out and away
Out of bounds
Out of hand
Out of his (her, etc) box
Out of order
Out of pocket
Out of sorts
Out of the question
Out of this world
Out of your (his, her, etc) mind
Out with it
Out with the old, in with the new
Out you go!
The great outdoors
You're either in or your out

Gabay at a glance:

I once used a variation on a popular idiom to sell mobile phones for British Telecom: 'Now you can be in when you are out'.

Loquacious language:

drumble – moving in a slow or lazy way

P

Pack
Pack a punch
Pack it in
Pack it up (or in)
Pack one's bag(s)
Send someone packing

Pay
Pays the piper
Pay one's respects
Pay through the nose
Pay its (or one's) way
It pays to…
You pays your money and you takes your chance

Penny
A penny for your thoughts
A pretty penny
Earn an honest penny
Not to have a penny to bless oneself with
Penny wise and pound foolish
Spend a penny
The penny dropped
Two (or ten) a penny

Pick
I've a bone to pick with you
Pick 'n' mix
Pick and choose
Pick of the bunch
Pick someone's brains
Pick something clean
Pick up the pieces
Pick up the threads

Piece
A piece of ass (or tail)
A piece of cake
A piece (or slice) of the action
Give someone a piece of one's mind

Go to pieces
Pick (or tear, pull) to pieces
Save us a piece
Say one's piece

Play
Level playing field
Make a play for it
Not playing with a full deck
Play a blinder
Play a hunch
Play ball
Play both ends against the middle
Play by the rules
Play ducks and drakes with
Play fair
Play fast and loose
Play for time
Play havoc with
Play hell with
Play hookey
Play it cool
Play it safe
Play one's Ace (or Joker)
Play politics
Play possum
Play something by ear
Play the field
Play the fool
Play the market
Play to the gallery
Play your cards right

Price
A price on someone's head
Name your price
Price someone out of the market
The price is right (i.e. the game show)
What price?
What's that go to do with the price of eggs/fish?

Writers' words:

'My parents kept me from children who were rough, who threw words like stones.' Stephen Spender

Pull

Like pulling teeth
Pull (one's) punches
Pull a face
Pull a fast one
Pull one's socks up
Pull one's weight
Pull oneself together
Pull out all the stops
Pull rank
Pull someone's leg
Pull strings (or wires)
Pull the other one (it's got bells on!)
Pull the wool over someone's eyes
Pull together

Push

At a push
Get the push
Give someone the push
Push off!
Push one's luck
Push the boat out
Pushing up the daisies
When push comes to shove

Q

Question

Ask a silly question (and you get a silly answer)!
Never question my authority
Q&A
The question is…
The sixty-four thousand dollar question
There are more questions than answers

R

Race

Be in the race
It's anyone's race
Race against time
Race the devil
The rat race

Rag

From rags to riches
In one's glad rags
Lose one's rag
Red rag to a bull
Run someone ragged
Tag, rag and bobtail

Raise

Raise a dust
Raise a family
Raise hell
Raise one's eyebrows
Raise one's hat to someone
Raise the devil
Raise the roof
Raise the wind
Raise Cain

Rain

A rainy day
Come rain or shine
It never rains but it pours
Rain cats and dogs
Rain on someone's parade
Take a rain check

Read

Read 'em and weep
Read all about it
Read between the lines
Read my lips
Read someone like a book
Read the riot act
Take something as read

Number crunchers:

octodecillion = 1000 septendecillion (US)

Reason

It stands to reason
Ours (is) not to reason why
Reasons best known to himself

Record

For the record
Off the record
On the record
Put (or set) the record straight

Red

(As) red as a beetroot
A red herring
Better dead than red
In the red
Paint the town red
Red letter day
Red-light district
Reds under the bed
See red
Was my face red!

Rest

(May God) rest his soul
(You can) rest assured
A change is as good as a rest
Give it a rest
Rest on one's laurels
Rest one's case
The rest is history

Right

All right
I am all right
Right as rain
Right enough
Right on!
She's right
Somewhere to the right of Genghis Khan
Too right!

Ring

Don't ring us, we'll ring you
Make (or run) rings round (or around) someone
Ring in one's ear
Ring off the hook
Ring the changes
That rings a bell
Throw one's hat in the ring
You rang, sir?

Rise

Rise and shine
Rise to the bait
Rise with the ashes
Rise with the sun
Someone's star is rising
The rise and fall of…

Roll

A roll in the hay
A rolling stone
It's all rock and roll to me
On a roll
Roll of honour
Roll on
Roll on the floor laughing
Roll up one's sleeves
Roll with the punches
Rolled into one
Rolling in money
Rolling drunk

Rose

(There is) no rose without a thorn
A bed of roses
Come up roses
Come up smelling of roses
Everything's rosy
Smell the roses

Round

A square peg in a round hole
Do the rounds

Writing landmarks:

US firm Gillette invented the first erasable ballpoint pen.

Go round in circles
In the round
Round the bend

Run

(Go and) take a running jump
A close run thing
A running battle
Be run off one's feet
Do a runner
Feeling run down
Given them the run-around
In (or out of) the running
Make a run for it
Make the running
Run dry
Run for their money
Run foul of
Run high
Run into the sand
Run its course
Run of the mill
Run off at the mouth
Run oneself into the ground
Run someone out of town
Run someone/thing to earth
Run the gauntlet
Trying to run before one can walk

S

Same

(And) the same to you
(The) same again
All the same
One and the same
Same difference
Same here

Save

Save one's breath
Save one's life

Save one's skin (or neck or bacon)
Save the day
Saved by the bell

Say

(Do) you mean to say?
(Let's) say
And so say all of us
As the saying goes
As you say
Confucius, he say …
Don't say a word
How say you?
I can't say
I couldn't say
I dare say
I mean to say
I must say
I say
I say, I say, I say!
I wouldn't say
I wouldn't say no
I wouldn't say that
I'll say this much
I'll say!
Never say die
Say again
Say no more
Say what you like
Say when
Says (or sez) you (he, etc)!
That is (to say)
That's what you say!
To say the least
What can I (we, etc) say
What do you say
You can say that again!
You don't say

See

As far as I can see
As I see it

Metapropisms:

Good punctuation means not to be late.

Don't you see?
I see what you mean
I'd like to see?
I'll (or we'll) be seeing you
I'll (or we'll) see about that
Let's see
Long time no see
See a man about a dog
See someone coming
See someone right
See you later

Shake
He's (she's) no great shakes
Shake (or quake) in one's shoes (or boots)
Shake a leg!
Shake hands
Shake the dust off one's feet

Shape
Get into shape
Lick into shape
Shape up or ship out
The shape of things to come

Shoot/Shot
A shot across the bow
A shot in the arm
A shot in the dark
A shot in the locker
Big shot
Call the shots
Get a shot of
Give it one's best shot
Like a shot
Not by a long shot
Shoot a line
Shoot from the hip
Shoot it out
Shoot one's cuffs
Shoot one's mouth off
Shoot oneself in the foot

Shoot someone/thing down in flames
Shoot the breeze (or the bull)
Shoot up
Shot to pieces (or to hell)
The whole bang shoot
The whole shooting match

Sign
Sign of the times
Sign off
Sign on the dotted line
Sign, sealed and delivered

Sit
Sit (heavy) on the stomach
Sit at someone's feet
Sit loosely on
Sit on it
Sit on one's hands
Sit on someone's tail
Sit on the fence
Sit tight
Sit up (and take notice)

Size
Any size you like
Size counts
Size em up
Size up to…
That's about the size of it

So
Ever so
How so?
Is that so?
It's so!
Just so
So be it!
So there!
So what?

Something
Say something
Something or other

Writers' words:

'Arguments over grammar and style are often as fierce as those over IBM versus Mac, and as fruitless as Coke versus Pepsi and boxers versus briefs.' Jack Lynch

Something tells me
Thirty-something
You know something?

Stand

It stands to reason
Leave someone/thing standing
Make a stand
Stand alone
Stand on one's feet
Stand out a mile
Stand out like a sore thumb
Stand up and be counted
Stand up for your rights

Stop

Pull out all the stops
Put a (or the) stopper on
Put a stop to something
Stop a gap
Stop at nothing
Stop one's ears
Stop someone's mouth
Stop the show

Straight

A straight fight
Going straight
Keep a straight face
Keep it straight
Straight as an arrow
Straight from the shoulder
Straight off
Straight talking
Straight to the top
Straight up
Take it straight (up)
The straight and narrow

Sure

(And) that's for sure
As sure as…
For sure

I don't know, I'm sure
I'm not (so) sure
Sure do!
Sure enough
Sure thing!
To be sure

T

Take

Eat in, or take away?
For the taking
Have what it takes
I can't take it any more!
It takes one to know one
It takes two to tango
On the take
Point taken
Take (it) as read
Take apart
Take care
Take it away!
Take it easy
Take it into one's head
Take it lying down
Take it on the chin
Take it or leave it
Take no prisoners
Take someone to task
Take someone to the cleaners
Take someone's name in vain
Take stock
Take that grin (or smile) off your face
Take that!
Take the biscuit
Take the high road
Take the point
Take to heart
Take to one's heels

Printing landmarks:

1829 – Louis Braille of France produced the first globally profitable embossed typeface for the blind.

Talk

Now you're talking
Talk about…
Talk dirty
Talking shop
Talk nineteen to the dozen
Talk of the devil!
Talk shop
Talk the hind legs off a donkey
Talk the talk
Talk through one's hat (arse)
Talk turkey

Tell

A little bird told me
Do tell
I'll tell you what
Something tells me
Tell it like it is
Tell 'n' sell
Tell someone where to get off
Tell someone where to put it
Tell something a mile off
Tell tales (out of school)
Tell that to the marines
Tell the truth
That would be telling
There is no telling
You never can tell

Thank

I thank you
Many thanks

No thanks to…
Thank heavens!
Thank one's lucky stars
Thank you very much
Thanks for having me (us, etc)
Thanks for nothing

That

Been there, done that
How's that?
Is that so?
That does it!
That will do
That's all
That's all there is to it
That's it
That's more like it!
That's that

Thick

A bit thick
Give someone (or get) a thick ear
Have a thick skin
In (or into) the thick of something
Thick as thieves
Thick as two (short) planks
Thick on the ground
Through thick and thin

Thing

(And a) good thing too
All things to all men (or people)
First things first
For one thing
How are things?
It's a good thing
Just the thing
Old thing
Other things being equal
Sure thing!
That's the thing
The thing is
Things that go bump in the night

Loquacious language:

emacity – eagerness to buy things

Think

(Now I) come to think of it
Good thinking
If you think (he thinks, etc) that, you've (he's, etc) got another thing coming
I (we) thought as much
Just think of it!
Let me think
Put on one's thinking hat
That's what you (he, they, etc) think
Think nothing of it
Think on one's feet
Think the world of
Think twice
What do you think?
Who do you think you are?

This

Get this
This is how it works
This is it
What's all this?

Throw

Throw good money after bad
Throw in the towel
Throw one's hand in
Throw one's lot with
Throw one's weight about/around/behind
Throw someone to the dogs
Throw stones
Throw the baby out with the bath water

Time

(And) about time too
(Only) time will tell
Know the time of day
Nick of time
Passing the time of day
Time and tide wait for no man
Time, gentlemen please
Time immemorial
Time is money
Time out of mind
Time's up

Top

At the top of (his, her, etc) profession
At the top of the tree
Go topless
Go to the top of the class
Off the top of one's head
On top of that
On top of the world
Over the top
That tops it
Tip top
To top it all
Top and tail
Top of the bill
Top of the morning (to you)!
Top of the pops
You can't top that

Touch

A soft (or easy) touch
A touch of class
A touch of the son
Lose one's touch
Out of touch
The Midas touch
Touch and go
Touch base
Touch bottom
Touch wood
Touchy!
Wouldn't touch it with a bargepole

Trust/Truth

Economical with the truth
It's a matter of trust
The Gospel truth
The naked truth
The truth of the matter is…

Yinglish:

From Yiddish… 'pupik' to English… 'belly button'.

The whole truth and nothing but the truth
To tell you the truth
Trust (name) to…
Trust me on this
Truth is…

Turn

A turn up for the books
It's your turn
One good turn deserves another
The lady's not for turning
To a turn
Turn a deaf ear
Turn a trick
Turn coat
Turn in one's grave
Turn someone's head
Turn tables
Turn the other cheek
Turn turtle
Turn up one's nose

U

Up

Be all up
Have the upper hand
Instant upgrade
On the up and up
On your uppers
Something is up
The upper crust
Up against it
Up and about (or doing)
Up for it
Up hill and down dale
Up in arms
Up sticks
Up the ante
Up the spout
Up to no good

Up to one's tricks
Up to snuff
Up to the mark
Up with you!
Up with…!
Up yours!
What's up?

V

Variety

Variety is the spice of life

View

A different viewpoint
A room with a view
Points of view
Take a dim view
The view is beautiful

W

Wait

(Just) you wait
I can hardly wait
No waiting
Some things are worth waiting for
Wait a minute/moment/second
Wait and see
Wait for it!
Wait for me!
Wait your turn

Want

He (she, etc) didn't want to know
What you need and what you want
You want to…

Walk

Go walkabout
Go walkies
Run before one can walk
Walk all over

Etymology:

Bull in a china shop – This phrase 'referring to someone's clumsiness' originates from 1834 when China stopped trading with England (commonly known at the time as John Bull). Which is why 'John Bull was angry – he threatened to destroy a 'China' shop.

Walk of life
Walk off his (or her) feet (or legs)
Walk on air
Walk on eggs (or eggshells)
(A) walk-on roll
Walk one's talk
Walk the chalk
Walk the plank
Walk tall

Way

(Be) on your way!
By the way
Fall by the wayside
Go out of one's way
Have it both ways
No way
Step this way
That's the way it goes
That's the way the cookie crumbles
The way of the world
There's (or there are) no two ways about it
They do have their ways
Way over the top
Way to go
Ways and means
Yes/no way
You go your way, I'll go mine

Well

(All) well and good
All's well that ends well
It's all very well
Just as well
Oh well
Very well
Well done!
Well, I'll go to the top of our street
Well, I never did!
Well, well
Well, well, well

You don't know when you're well-off

What

And I don't know what
And what's more
For what it's worth
I know what
Know what?
What about that!
What about?
What can I (we) do you for?
What can I (we) do for you?
What ho!
What if…?
What on earth?
What's going on around here then?
What's going on?
What's next?
What's it to you?
What's up?
What's your excuse?
What's yours?
You know what you can do with…
You what?

Word

A man (or woman) of his (or her) word
A word to the wise
(By) word of mouth
(Could I have) a word in your ear?
Eat one's words
Famous last words
If a picture could paint a thousand words
In other words
Mum's the word
My word!
Not another word
Not in so many words
One more word out of….
Put words into one's mouth
Someone's word is law

Printing landmarks:

254   1841 – Britain's first regular newspaper, *The Jewish Chronicle*, was published.

Take someone at their word
Take someone's word for it
The word on the street
Winged words
Words fail me

World

A man (or woman) of the world
A world of difference
A world of…
Brave new world
Come up in the world
Go down in the world
He's (she's, etc) got the whole world in his (her) hands
It's a small world!
Not of this world
On top of the world
Out of this world
The best of both (or all possible) worlds
The world and his wife
The world's your oyster
The world to come
Think the world of

Wrong

Born on the wrong side of town
Don't get me wrong
Get (hold of) the wrong end of the stick
Get in wrong with
Get out on the wrong side of the bed
Get someone wrong
In the wrong
The wrong side of the tracks

Y

Year

For donkey's years
Happy New Year!
It's been years

Put years on (or take off) someone
The vale of years
The years have been kind

Yes

…like to say yes
It's a yes!
Yes and no
Yes man

You/Yours

How's yourself?
There's… for you
Up your (his, her, etc) own backside
Up yourself
You and your
You bet!
You there!
You're another
You're as young as the woman (man) you feel
You're as young as you feel
You're not as young as you used to be
You're not getting any younger
Your actual
Yours for the asking
Yours free

Z

Zs

Catch some (or a few) Zs
ZZZZZZZZZzzzzzzzzz

Zero

A big fat zero

Zoo

It's a zoo out there!
Life is a zoo
Were you born in a zoo?

Metaphors:

The world as they had taught it to us broke in pieces. Erich Maria Remarque, *All Quiet on the Western Front*

Brains, pen, action!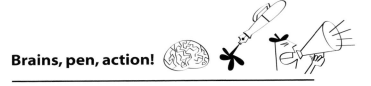

1 Write a five-minute presentation entitled 'The die is cast'.

2 Write a short commentary for a sporting event using as many sporting idioms a possible. To get you started:

- On the cards

- Two halves to every game

- Hedge one's bets

- On the ball

- Have a card up one's sleeve

- Loaded dice

- Have a good innings

- Off one's own bat

3 Attend a marketing meeting and note down how many idioms are said by the participants. Then write three sentences summarising your feelings about the meeting, featuring the same idioms.

4 Listen to the BBC Radio 4 daily play 'The Archers'. Count how many idioms are delivered in fifteen minutes. [I usually count around fifteen. Add clichés to this and the tally goes up to thirty!]

Yinglish:

From Yiddish... 'seykhl' to English... 'commonsense'

9. Clichés – they're playing our song again

As I write, I have just stepped away from a chat with a PR photographer. We were discussing how many press photographs produce little more than clichés. For example, business people outside tall buildings, families grinning as if they were on acid, and so on.

'What about you writers scribbling out those ridiculous headlines,' he said. 'Like one I saw the other day for gold credit card membership. It read Band of Gold. It was so cheesy.'

'That's a point,' I said. 'But, the thing to remember is that it's not what the cliché is, but what you do with it that matters.'

'That's just another example of a stupid cliché!' he replied. 'Look, at the end of day, a picture is going to be worth a thousand words.'

Ah well. To each his own…

egg on your face

Clichés – they're playing our song again

The trouble with clichés is that they have been in everyone's mouths.

Clichés are stereotyped phrases (and so closely related to idioms). They are often the first genre of words a novice copywriter reaches for; they are accessible, memorable, and tried and tested. However, they are certainly not original. By their nature, they are not actually meant to be novel. At best, they conjure up images that paint vivid snapshots from life, which most people can relate to in some way or other. Indeed, with a little crafty targeting through associating a cliché with a particular selling aspect of your product or service, you can ensure that your chosen cliché means different things to different sections of your market.

For example:

Weighing machine	*A balanced view*
Charity ad	*Desperate times call for desperate measures*
Valentine's day cards	*Heart and soul*
Good financial interest rate	*Outstanding figure*
Pickled gherkin	*Short and sweet*
Comfortable bed	*Rest in peace*
Pre-cut bread	*Thin end of the wedge*
Rambler's backpack	*He's got the whole world on his shoulders*

Rather like their 'first cousins' idioms, clichés are useful for headlines, especially those on posters, popular newspaper spreads, or headings in PowerPoint presentations.

ophelimity – the ability to please sexually

Yet like idioms clichés come with a strong health warning: if you have to use 'tired' clichés, only do so in moderation, and when absolutely appropriate. If not, copy starts to sound too much like a series of puns, or worse still, 'vanilla flavoured' – in other words, bland.

As metaphors, characterised by their overuse, many clichés were once as 'fresh as a daisy' (sometimes I just can't help myself!), yet through abuse they have wilted. Many clichés are elaborate generalisations that don't say much, but speak volumes. Which is why when it comes, for example, to copy within report writing or for press releases, clichés are often frowned upon.

On the other hand, like their ancestors aphorisms, clichés often summarise a complicated proposition in a few apt and impressive words. Why? Well, they sort of sound 'right' to the ear, which, in turn, makes them 'stick' in the mind. Some linguists even suggest that pithy clichés come easily to mind because they are stored, for quick access, in the right hemisphere of the brain – the creative part.

An advanced method of writing clichés is to use concatenation (linked thoughts). This offers a broader 'canvas' to draw a reader into the body of your copy. For example:

...this man is AHEAD OF HIS TIME IS ON MY SIDE...
(Once again, use sparingly.)

Related to concatenation of clichés is composing copy using clichés to tell a complete story. For example:

The doctor was *a man after my own heart*. This was a shame, because I really wanted someone to look at my *Achilles heel*. However, *all things considered* he wasn't shocked at my fear, and being an *outstanding figure*, he reassured me, *over and over again* that *seeing me overcome by emotion* was *all in a day's work*.

Concatenation tends to make one's mind wander, especially if you change the spelling of various words. For example:

Come to a head (cum to a head)
Come from behind (cum from behind)
Come and get it (cum and get it)

All amusing (if only in an naive, giggly, 'under the sheets' school-boy fashion).

As with similar expressions, some of the most effective clichés for copy deliver a directive, such as *go, give, take, make, get, have, do, win, ask,* and so on.

Medieval words:

fee – moveable property such as money or goods

A further technique is to adopt the emphatic full stop. Here each word of the cliché is given the opportunity to count for itself or as a unit with the other words in the expression.

For example:

New computer CPU	*Box. Clever.*
Clothes for the larger person	*Big. Deal.*
Precious diamond	*Clear. Cut*
Financial software	*Creative. Accounting.*
Helpline operative	*Call. Girl.*
Limited edition porcelain	*Cup. Final.*
Business website	*Business. Opportunity.*

An up-and-coming practice is to shorten a cliché for brand names. For example, there is an insurance company in the UK called More Than™. This technique is quite a clever use of clichés, as the audience can't help associating the words with the more familiar phrases: more than words can say or more than I could wish for.

All in all, to tell a few home truths, I am actually a secret cliché admirer. In fact, often when stuck for an idea, I'll switch on my I-pod™, bung in the headphones and look up a cliché. Then, depending on my mood, I'll flick on something like Mozart or Foo Fighters and see where, in terms of imagery, a cliché takes me.

So, certainly in terms of awareness and direct response copy, clichés are here to stay; for better or for worse, depending on your view.

Here are over 1300 of my favourite clichés, chosen for their popular usage in copy (although, at least try not to opt for 'old timers' like *Buy one get one free* or *Without obligation*).

For total flexibility, I have listed them in alphabetic, rather than topical, order.

Gabay at a glance:

When writing copy appealing to a market's emotions (the product or service's 'ESP' - Emotional Sales Point) feature specifics rather than generalisations. Equally remember that a POD (Point of Difference) is far more credible that a USP (Unique Sales Point.)

Anyone around here speak English?

260   A sign in a Israeli butcher: 'I slaughter myself twice daily.'

Gabay's favourite clichés

A

above and beyond the call of duty

above board

absence makes the heart grow fonder

absolute disgrace

absolutely marvellous

according to plan

acid test

across the board

act of faith

act the fool

after the break

against the grain

against the odds

ages ago

ahead of his time

aim high

alive and well

all for a good cause

all for one

all in one

all in the same boat

all men are created equal

all or nothing

all right then

all roads lead to Rome

all smoke and mirrors

all the tea in China

all the time

all to the good

all work, no play

all bets are off

all change

all clear

all's fair in love and war

almighty flop

an act of faith

and that's that

ankle deep

annoying habit

another day, another dollar

another way of saying it

appearances can be deceptive

Are you a man or a mouse?

armed to the teeth

around the clock

around the corner

artistic licence

arty farty

as if you cared

as soon as possible

as the crow flies

asking price

at arm's length

at short notice

at the drop of a hat

at the end of the day

at the end of the line

at the very least

attack of nerves

attempt on goal

attractive offer

audience ratings

B

back in the saddle

back of a fag packet

back of an envelope

back off

back to front

back-handed compliment

backed into a corner

backs to the wall

bad hair day

bad reputation

balance of payments

balanced view

balancing act

bald as a coot

ball breaker

ballpark figure

band of gold

band of hope

barely deserved

barking up the wrong tree

barrel of laughs

battle lines

be here now

be prepared

be the death of me

bearing a grudge

beat the rap

beating around the bush

beauty is only skin deep

beg the question

behave yourself

Etymology:

to bone up (to study) – this refers to a twentieth Century academic publisher named Bohn. It published a guide to help students with Latin and Greek. Students used to say they would 'bohn up' for their exams.

behind the scenes
below the belt
benefit of the doubt
best foot forward
best kept secret
best out of three
best things in life are free
better and better
better half
better late than never
better luck next time
beyond belief
beyond reasonable doubt
big deal
big girl's blouse
big shot
bird brained
bird in the hand
birthday boy
bit part player
bite the bullet
bite the dust
bite to eat
black and blue
black and white
black hole
black look
black magic
blanket approach
blast from the past
blind leading the blind
blood sweat and tears
blowing hot and cold
blown off course
blue moon
blue movie
body bags

bolt from the blue
both sides of the coin
bottom line
bottom of the barrel
bottom of the pile
bound and gagged
boundaries of science
bowled over
box clever
boy's own
brand spanking new
brass balls
brass necked
brave new world
break a leg
break in
break the bank
break the ice
break the news
bridge the gap
bridge too far
bring and buy
bringing home the bacon
broad church
brownie points
bull in a china shop

Gabay at a glance:

See my etymology for 'bull in a china shop' page 253

burn the candle at both ends
burn the midnight oil
bury the hatchet
business as usual
business end

business lunch
business opportunity
bust a gut
busy as a bee
busy doing nothing
button pusher
buy out
buzz words
by hook or by crook
by the book
by the same token
by the short and curlies
by the way

C

call girl
call out
call the shots
calm before the storm
camp followers
can't face it
can't judge a book by looking at the cover
can't put a finger on it
can't see the wood for the trees
cards on the table
carnival atmosphere
carpet bagger
case the joint
cash and carry
cash on the nail
catch the post
cat on a hot tin roof
caught out
cause and effect
cause for complaint
cause for concern
centre fold

Anagrams:

from THE DETECTIVES to DETECT THIEVES

chain is only as strong as its weakest link

chain reaction

champagne celebrations

chance would be a fine thing

chance of a lifetime

chance result

chance your arm

change of gear

change of heart

change of plan

change your mind

changing face

changing the face of

character assassination

charm offensive

charm the birds

chattering classes

cheer leader

cheque book journalism

chew the fat

chill out

chips are down

city slicker

clear agreement

clear as a bell

clear as crystal

clear as mud

clear cut

clear signs

clear targets

clear the air

clear the decks

clock watching

closed book

closer and closer

closing down

clothes make the man

coal face

cold as ice

come and get it

come back

come together

comedy of errors

comfort zone

coming across

coming back for more

coming out of the woodwork

coming to the boil

coming to the crunch

common enemy

common knowledge

common touch

common understanding

con artist

consenting adults

control freak

cool as a cucumber

cop out

core business

core values

cost cutting

cost reduction

could eat a horse

creative accountancy

credit rating

crime wave

criminal conspiracy

crisis point

crocodile tears

crunch time

cry for help

crying out

crystal clear

culture shock

cup final

cupboard love

current betting

curtain call

curtain raiser

curtain up

customer loyalty

customer service

cut and dried

cut and run

cut down

cut from the same cloth

cut inside

cut price

cutting edge

D

daft as a brush

daggers out

daily service

damage limitation

dark horse

dark secret

dark side of the moon

day by day

day in day out

daylight robbery

daylight saving

day one

dead eyed

dead from the neck up

dead heat

dead on target

dead on time

dead centre

death or glory

death sentence

deep down you know

deep end

Etymology:

Aha – from various sections of the Old testament. For example Isiaiah 44:16 'Aha I am warm, I have seen the fire'.

deeply concerned

delaying tactics

depths of despair

devil may care

devil to pay

diamond in the rough

dicey situation

difficult to know

dig deep

dig for victory

disaster zone

disorderly conduct

distant drums

divide and conquer

divide and rule

divide the spoils

divine inspiration

do away with

do or die

do without

do your best

do your bit

do/done a bunk

do/done a runner

does your head in

dog days

dog eat dog world

dog's breakfast

doing porridge

doing time

dolly bird

domino effect

don't ask

SPANIEL AND CHIPS

TERRIER TRIFLE

MENU

POOCH ON TOAST

FIDO SURPRISE

don't bank on it

don't do anything stupid

don't give up the day job

don't let the bastards grind you down

don't look a gift horse in the mouth

don't panic

don't read too much into it

don't rock the boat

don't want to be involved

don't worry

don't you dare

done all right

done and dusted

done over

doom and gloom

door stepping

door to door

door-to-door salesman

dot the Is and cross the Ts

double act

double dealing

double edged

double jeopardy

double or nothing

double standard

double take

double time

double whammy

down and out

down at heel

down in the dumps

down in the mouth

down market

down the hatch

down the middle

down to you

down town

drag artist

drama queen

draw the line at

dream weaver

drink up

drive a coach and horses through it

driving me crazy

drop dead

drop dead gorgeous

drop your guard

drug abuse

drumming up support

drunk as a skunk

dry out

duck the question

dummy run

E

eagle eyed

early bath

early retirement

early warning

earth shaking

ease off

easily led

easy answer

easy as pie

easy come easy go

easy going

easy touch

eat humble pie

eating crow

economic slump

egg on your face

eggs in one basket

element of doubt

Etymology:

to leave no stone unturned – this phrase, meaning to search everywhere, originates from 477 BC. Searching for Persian treasure, the Theban general Polycrates was told by the oracle at Delphi to look under the Persian general's tent and 'leave no stone unturned'.

emotional blackmail

empty gesture

empty promises

end game

end of a chapter

end of the road

environmentally friendly

equal footing

equal opportunities

equal partners

equal terms

escape clause

escape committee

escape hatch

every dog has its day

every last penny

everyone's favourite

everything in the garden is rosy

everything to play for

everything's all right

everything's hunky dory

evil eye

exact replica

exclusive opportunity

explore reforms

extra income

eye of the hurricane

eye of the tiger

eye witness

eye witness account

eyes like a hawk

F

face the music

face up to reality

fact is

fact of the matter

fact or fiction

fair deal

faith, hope and charity

fall guy

fall in the mire

false promises

false trail

familiarity breeds contempt

family values

famous for fifteen minutes

far from clear

far out

far out, man

far reaching

far right

fashion show

fast and loose

fast on your feet

fat of the land

feather in your cap

feather your own nest

feeble excuses

feel a need

feeling the pinch

few words of advice

fight night

figure of eight

figure of speech

final countdown

final curtain

final cut

final demand

final offer

fingers burnt

finish your drinks

firm favourite

first in line

fit as a fiddle

fit for anything

fits like a glove

fitted up

flare up

flash in the pan

flood of tears

flower people

fly by night

fly on the wall

fly the nest

flying by the seat of the pants

folding money

follower of fashion

fond farewell

footloose and fancy free

footing the bill

for all the tea in China

for better or worse

for future reference

for the record

for the love of God/Mike

forced landing

foregone conclusion

foreign aid

forgive and forget

forked tongue

formal agreement

formal complaint

fortune teller

forty winks

freak out

free advice

free as a bird

free for all

free love

free lunch

free offer

freedom of the press

freely given

Writers' words:

'Why do writers write? Because it isn't there.' Thomas Berger

friend in need is a friend indeed

friendly fire

frightened the life out of me

fringe group

frittering away

from here on in

from time to time

front runner

full range

full scale

full stop

full-time job

fully grown

fund raising

G

game for it

game on

game plan

game set and match

games people play

gang bang

gang up

geared up

genuine offer

get a grip

get a life

get even

get in the groove

get in top gear

get it right first time

get it together

get on with it

get stuck in

get to grips

giant killer

gilt edged

girl talk

give it a rest

give it up

give me a break

give up the ghost

give you the edge

glass ceiling

go a round or two

go ahead

go along for the ride

go down that road

go for it

go for the kill

go getter

go take a running jump

go through with it

going bananas

going down

going for a song

going through the hoop

going with the flow

gold standard

golden opportunity

good as new

good time girl

good vibrations

goody bag

got the message

grab what you can

grand final

grasp the nettle

grass roots

grave concerns

grave issues

grease monkey

grease paint

great divide

great tradition

green light

grudge match

guardian angel

guest of honour

gut feeling

H

half baked

half price

halfwit

hand made

hang 'em high

hang loose

happily married

hard as nails

hard case

hard faced

hard facts

hard liner

hat trick

head in the clouds

heart of the matter

heart to heart

help the police with their enquiries

here and now

here, there and every-where

hidden agenda

hide and seek

high and dry

high hopes

high on the agenda

high point

high profile

his and hers

hit man

hit the road

hit the sack

Medieval words:

capa – a short hooded cape worn by both men and women

hold up
holding the baby
hole in one
home front
home truths
hook, line and sinker
hot property
hot spot
hot stuff
hourglass figure
hue and cry
huge step
huge success
human rights
human shields

I

ideal solution
identity parade
if needs be
if the cap fits
if the price is right
image conscious
image is everything
image maker
in at the deep end
in case of emergency
infinitely better
in on the ground floor
inside information
inside out
inside track
insider dealing
instant payout
instant response
intellectual property
in the clear
in the nick of time

in the pink
in the red
in the thick of it
in this day and age
invisible man
in your dreams
iron curtain
iron will
irresistible force
it isn't over until the fat
lady sings
it's a small world
it's not over yet

J

Jack of all trades
jam it in
jam it open
job for life
job lot
jobs for all
jobs for the boys
joined up thinking
joint agreement
joint manoeuvres
joint negotiations
joint policy
joint statement
judgement day
jump on the bandwag-
on
just a minute
just desserts

K

keep fit
keeping up with the
Jones's
keep it under your hat

keep on taking the
tablets
keep the door open
keep your beak out
keep your hair on
keep your mouth shut
keep your nose out
kept in the dark
kept woman
key player
kick back
kick the bucket
kid glove treatment
king of the castle
kiss and tell
knock back
knock down
knock-on effect
knock on wood
knock out
knuckle under

L

ladies man
laid to rest
land of hope and glory
landmark decision
last chance saloon
last ditch
lasting love
last laugh
last minute nerves
last waltz
late arrival
laugh a minute
laughing all the way to
the bank
laughing boy
law and order

Writers' words:

'Talk is cheap. Poetry economical' Thomas S Thomas

laws of nature
lay down the law
leader of the pack
leading question
leading role
lean and mean
leave aside
leave it out
leave it to you
leave out in the cold
less and less
let it all hang out
let it go
let loose the dogs of war
life is what you make it
light as a feather
light fingered
light show
like a breath of fresh air
like it or lump it
like peas in a pod
line dancing
line up
live life to the full
live show
live wire
living hand to mouth
living in the past
living legend
lock, stock and barrel
log jam
lonely hearts club
long and short of it
long distance
long shot
long sighted
look at the evidence
look on the bright side

loop the loop
loud and clear
low down
low profile
low yield

M

made in heaven
made to measure
make my day
make a killing
make a meal of it
make an honest woman of her
make and mend
make ends meet
make hay while the sun shines
make it clear
make it work
make love
make love not war
make me an offer
make or break
make the grade
make tracks
make your eyes light up
make-your-mind-up time
makes (make) my day
man trap
man of the moment
man of all seasons
man of honour
man of the world
mark my words
mark of respect
mark time
marketing ploy

means to an end
message in a bottle
middle of the road
might is right
mind games
mind your language
mind your Ps and Qs
mind your step
missing link
mister nice guy
mixed blessing
money for nothing/old rope
money up front
more of the same
more and more
morning glory
move forward
move on
music to my ears

N

never too late
never again
never say die
new broom
new beginnings
new look
next time around
nice one
nice round number
nice try
nick of time
nip it in the bud
no worries
no argument
no chance
no choice
no comment

Brand origins:

Nabisco, 1898 (registered 1901) – the name is an abbreviation of the National Biscuit Company

no man's land
no offence
no oil painting
no option
no problem
no regrets
no rest for the wicked
no room at the inn
no time like the present
no turning back
not a problem
nothing to it
nothing to lose
now and again
now and then
now is the hour
now or never

O

off and on
off the back of a lorry
off the wall
oh no it isn't
oh what a tangled web we weave
older and wiser
on top of the world
on message
on the face of things
on the brink
on a wing and a prayer
on a plate
on a roll
on average
on budget
on firm ground
on bended knee
on the back burner
on the ball

on the cards
on the lookout
on the spot
on time
on your bike
once in a lifetime
once in a blue moon
one thing after another
one born every minute
one day at a time
one for the road
one in a million
one man woman
one night stand
one step at a time
only natural
open plan
open arms
open book
open door
opening moves
open it up
open minded
open up a can of worms

opinion forming
opportunity knocks
order now
out of hours
out and about

out of control
out of focus
out of his mind
out of it
over the moon

P

package deal
paint the town red
panic button
party girl
pass the buck
patch things up
pay as you go
pencil thin
penny for your thoughts
perfect harmony
perfect timing
pick-up joint
pick of the crop
picture of health
pie in the sky
pile 'em high
pipe dream
place your bets
plain sailing
play on words
play your cards right
playing around
poetic licence
pole position
power games
power play
practice makes perfect
practise what you preach
precious time
pregnant silence

Loquacious language:

opisthoporeira – involuntary walking backwards

prepare the ground
prepared for the worst
press gang
price war
price cut
pride and joy
problem child
problem area
problem solved
proof of the pudding is in the eating
property rights
prospective buyer
protest movement
public enemy number one
publicity seeker
public outcry
public scrutiny
puff of smoke
pull together
pull out all the stops
pushing the envelope
put your job on the line
put aside
put in a bid
put in a good word
put it behind
put it here
put it there
put the boot in
put the screws on
putting it about
put up a good show
put your back into it
put your feet up
put your house in order
put your mind at ease
put your money where

your mouth is
put yourself in my shoes

Q

quality of life
question of time
quick as a flash
quick turnaround

R

rain dance
raise the roof
read between the lines
ready and willing
reap what you sow
record breaking
red carpet treatment
as red as a beetroot
right as rain
right now
right on the money
right on target
rights and wrongs
ring of truth
rip off
rock bottom
rock and roll
roll with the punches
room at the top
room for improvement
root and branch
rose between two thorns
rose by any other name would smell as sweet
rough and ready
rough and tumble
rules of engagement

S

safe as houses
salad days
sales pitch
salt of the earth
satisfaction guaranteed
saturation point
saving grace
saving up for a rainy day
say it out loud
say what you mean
say what you like
seal of approval
second chance
security risk
self defence
sell out
sell yourself short
sense of belonging
sense of achievement
serious proposition
service with a smile
sexy thing
sharp end
shell out
ship shape
shock tactics
shop till you drop
short list
short and sharp
shot in the dark
show of hands
show who's boss
show your true colours
shuffle the pack
sick to the back teeth
side issues
side saddle

Brand origins:

Ovaltine, 1904 – originally called Ovolmaltine (Latin 'ovum' meaning 'egg' plus 'malt', and the suffix 'ine').

side by side

sign of the times

sign on the dotted line

silence is golden

silent minority

simple truth

sing along

sing for it

sitting pretty

sky's the limit

slow and easy

smash and grab

smooth operator

snakes and ladders

so far so good

soap opera

social call

society at large

soft soap

solid as rock

something to tell your grandchildren

song and dance

sooner than you think

sooner or later

sort it

sound advice

sound bite

special case

speech day

spell it out

spirit of the times

spit and polish

splash out

split vote

spot the difference

spot the ball

spread it about

spring in your step

spring is in the air

square the circle

square things up

square meal

square deal

squeaky clean

stamped out

stand by

stand easy

stand and deliver

stand on ceremony

stand by me

star performer

step on it

step up

step in

step too far

step by step

stepping stone

stick it out

stop gap

story board

straight up

straight as an arrow

straight and narrow

straight talking

stranger than fiction

straw poll

strings attached

stronger than ever

stuff it

suck it and see

suits me fine

sup with the devil

supply and demand

sure thing

surprise, surprise

swift and sure

swinging sixties

swings and round-abouts

T

tailor made

take a break

take a chance

take a dive

take a rain check

take a stand

take the rough with the smooth

take your time

take a walk

take two

take the gloves off

take the lead

take that

take the rise

take the biscuit

take out

take it or leave it

take my word

takeover bid

talk of the town

talk your way out of this one

talking shop

talking turkey

talk is cheap

tapping into

target practice

tattered and torn

team work

terms of endearment

thanks for the memory

theatre of dreams

the best money can buy

Brand origins:

Oxo, 1899 – from 'Ox' plus the suffix 'O'. The product was a refinement of Liebig's 'Extract of Meat'.

the bigger they come, the harder they fall

the bottom line

the buck stops here

the butt of his joke

the calm before the storm

the changing face

the coast is clear

the cold shoulder

the darkest hour is before the dawn

the easy way or the hard way

the eleventh hour

the end of the road

the finishing touches

the jury's still out

the middle way

the morning after

the one and only

the other woman

the perfect solution

the plot thickens

there is no doubt

there's hope yet

the right stuff

the right thing

the sands of time

the silent majority

the third degree

the truth is out there

the way the cookie crumbles

the world's your oyster

the writing on the wall

thick as a brick

thick as two short planks

thick as a brick

thin on the ground

think twice

think again

thinking cap

thinking time

third time lucky

three wishes

three of a kind

three in a row

throw in the towel

throw together

thumbs up

tie the knot

tight fisted

time after time

time and time again

time bomb

time capsule

time flies

time heals

time is running out

timeless classic

time of your life

time on my hands

time pressure

time will tell

tip of the iceberg

tip top

tomorrow never comes

tongue in cheek

too good to refuse

tooled up

top and tail

top of the bill

top of the class

top of the morning

top of the pile

top man

top secret

tough talk

tough nut

tough measures

tough policies

track record

trade gap

treatment room

trial and error

tricky situation

trouble at mill

true or false

truth of the matter

tuned in

turkey shoot

turn the other cheek

turn the tables

turn over a new leaf

turn up the pressure

turned down

turned on

two chances

two fingers

two of a kind

two peas in a pod

two sides to every story

two-way street

two wrongs don't make a right

type cast

U

ultimate objective

unceremoniously dumped

under pressure

under the skin

under the thumb

under the weather

Metaphors:

He had crossed over the gulf to her. – DH Lawrence, *The Horse Dealer's Daughter*

unemployment statistics

unfair advantage

unforeseeable circumstances

up and over

up and under

up front

upper hand

up market

up to you

up to the neck in it

up tight

use your head

usual suspects

V

value for money

variety is the spice of life

vital statistics

voice from the past

volume control

W

wait a minute

wait and see

waiting game

wake up to the fact

walk out

walk tall

walk the walk

walk a mile in my shoes

walk this way

walk on by

walking a tightrope

war footing

war games

war zone

war of words

warm as toast

warm blooded

warm feeling

warning shot

wasn't my fault

watch my lips

watch your mouth

watch your step

water under the bridge

way of life

we can work it out

wear your heart on your sleeve

weasel words

welcoming committee

what goes around comes around

what a drag

What can I get you?

What's new?

What's the score?

What's what?

whatever you want

when the chips are down

white as a sheet

Who cares?

who dares wins

Who knows?

Who's minding the shop?

Who's next?

whole new ball game

whole truth

Why not…?

Why are we waiting?

Why worry?

wide open

willing and able

wind up

window of opportunity

window dressing

window shopping

wine, women and song

wing and a prayer

wings of an angel

winning combination

winning ways

winning streak

wired up

wish you were here

wish list

wishful thinking

with a pinch of salt

woman's touch

women's intuition

word in private

words of wisdom

work closely

work cut out

working day and night

working together

work in progress

work it out

work of art

work on it

work out

work together

world class

world number one

world record attempt

worse than first thought

worse ways to make a living

worth more than

wrapped up

writing on the wall

Writers' words:

'It's a good thing for an uneducated man to read books of quotations.' Winston Churchill

wrong side of the law
wrong signals
wrong number

Y

year zero
yearn for
yellow bellied
yellow light
you can be sure
you can be sure of it

you can't be too careful
you couldn't be more
wrong
you get what you give
you get what you pay
for
you know exactly what
I'm saying
you know what I mean
you know what they say
you wouldn't dare

you're on
you've got a nerve
young blood

Z

zero tolerance

Brains, pen, action!

Something to ponder...

1   Write a short essay of no longer than 200 words
    detailing what you did at the weekend. Include at
    least ten clichés.

2   Your company sells words. Write an A4 product
    sheet explaining the virtues of your latest product:
    clichés.

3   Look through this chapter. Choose 30 clichés and
    write more direct, alternative descriptions.

3   As I have noted, there is a considerable crossover
    between idioms and clichés. Find six instances of
    such crossovers then feature each as either an idiom
    or cliché within a paragraph selling either:

    (a) Video-phone (b) Florist shop (c) Adult toys

In other words:

exporter – a person who used to carry bags

10. Metaphors – spot the resemblance

I mentioned in an earlier introduction a conversation between a photographer and me where he spoke of 'a picture painting a thousand words'. Well, a metaphor paints a million pictures. It is a word or phrase which provokes imagery in the mind. The more you can make readers 'picture' themselves in a situation, the easier it is to draw them into the heart of your proposition.

The roots of the device known as metaphor are in storytelling. As far back as AD 400 storytellers would explain news and events to villagers by way of stories, using words to inspire the imaginations of the people who rarely saw anything beyond their village.

Metaphor, one of the sharpest tools in the copywriter's toolbox, allows the reader to complete the tale on his or her own terms and – thanks to your writing skills – according to your rules.

all mouth and no trousers

Metaphors – spot the resemblance

What are metaphors?

Metaphors draw resemblances. For example:

a tiger = ferocious person

pussycat = gentle person

Metaphors paint pictures with words and so add vigour to a copywriter's range.

Metaphors which have become part of everyday language like *'The ball 'rocketed' into the back of the net'* are known as 'dead-metaphors'. This term may suggest lifelessness, but in practice, such metaphors, like a set of juggler's balls, remain in the air.

Mixed metaphors

Mixed metaphors 'fuse' two separate metaphors into one bold (often slightly bizarre) statement:

My pulse was a drum solo; in fact, it made anger a thorn in the heart.

This fusion of ideas even has its own unofficial name: a 'mixaphor'. Providing that each part of the 'mixaphor' relates to the other and you don't over do it, it's worth experimenting with the concept.

Also see
Portmanteau
chapter 13

'A leopard can't change his stripes.' – Al Gore

'Button your seat belts.' – Rush Limbaugh

'Dirty laundry is coming home to roost.' – Ray Romano

'Don't burn your bridges till you come to them.' – WWII US General.

Extended metapors

An extended metaphor occurs when writing a series of metaphors, one after the other, throughout a piece of copy. Poets tend to like them, as do lyricists. Here is an example from Christina Rossetti, where sleep is used as a metaphor for death:

Metaphors:

In this particular hive she was undoubtedly queen bee. Mary McCarthy, *Cruel and Barbarous Treatment*

Sleeping at Last

Sleeping at last, the trouble and tumult over,
Sleeping at last, the struggle and horror past,
Cold and white, out of sight of friend and of lover,
Sleeping at last.

No more a tired heart downcast or overcast,
No more pangs that wring or shifting fears that hover,
Sleeping at last in a dreamless sleep locked fast.

Fast asleep. Singing birds in their leafy cover
Cannot wake her, nor shake her the gusty blast.
Under the purple thyme and the purple clover
Sleeping at last.

Christina Georgina Rossetti (1830–1894)

Allegory

The next natural step from an extended metaphor is an allegory. This often gives a moral message by telling a story under the pretext of another subject. Many fairy tales and fables are examples of allegory; *The Ugly Duckling* by Hans Christian Andersen, for example.

The best way to feature a metaphor of any kind is in passing, rather than focusing too much on its explicit ingenuity. More often than not, the more you point the reader to an apparent metaphor, the greater the chance of it coming across as a pun or even parody of itself. So, like most techniques, use metaphors wisely and sparsely.

A

Ability	Skill and confidence are an unconquered army. George Herbert, Outlandish Proverbs
Absence	Absence… the pain without the peace of death. Thomas Campbell, 'Absence'
	Absence is death, or worse, to them that love. Sir Philip Sidney, 'A Country Song'
Abundance	Daddy was a fountain of money (to his young son reminiscing about a childhood family trip), Harold Broadkey, 'Verona: A young Woman Speaks', Esquire, 1977

Loquacious language:

emydosaurian – a crocodile

Achievement An achievement is bondage. It obliges one to a higher achievement
Albert Camus, Notebooks: 1942-1951

Acting/Actors She has made an acting style of postnasal drip
Pauline Kael, quoted in obituary for actress Sandy Dennis, The New York Times, 5 March 1992

Action/Inaction

I meant to see more of her. But I saw nothing. She was in the warehouse of intentions
Saul Bellow, The Bellarosa Connection

For months I had been living in a cave with my own small demons. Now I was ready to go out into the desert, which was my life.
Laurie Colwin, 'Saint Antony of the Desert', The Lone Pilgrim

Actions Our acts are an abridged edition of our possibilities.
Anonymous

Each act is an island in time, to be judged on its own.
Alan Lightman, Einstein's Dreams

Activeness/ inactiveness

There is a sort of dead-alive, hackneyed people about… and unless necessity lays about them with a stick, they will ever stand still.
Robert Louis Stevenson, 'An Apology for Idlers'

Gabay at a glance:

Quote metaphors directly in a speech, or adapt one to suit your own purposes.

Mr Bush is the Timex President: having taken a licking he is still ticking, with no clear indication of stopping anytime soon.
Michael Wines, The New York Times, 1 January 1993

Advice Advice is a stranger; if welcome he stays for the night; if not welcome, he returns home the same day.
Anonymous

Aerial views If you fly across the nation… the bones of the land are still apparent from ten thousand feet up.
John Keats, 'The Call of the Open Road'

Affection How wearily Ethel regarded Jim sometimes, as if she wondered why she had trained the vines of her affection on such a wind-shaken poplar.
F Scott Fitzgerald, 'Bernice Bobs Her Hair', Flappers and Philosophers

Printing landmarks:

1842 – *The Illustrated London News*, the first regularly published illustrated newspaper, was launched.

Affliction   He could not have said with certitude if he found this
blurry lady attractive. Near-sightedness is chaste.
Vladimir Nabokov, King, Queen, Knave

Age/Aging   Every woman after forty is a wasting asset.
Cyril Connolly, 'Covetousness', The Seven Deadly Sins

Living now in death's immediate neighbourhood, he
was developing a soldier's jaunty indifference.
John Updike, 'Playing with Dynamite', The New Yorker, 5 October 1992

The crown of old age is grand children.
Pirke Avot

Aggression   Her skill as an executive was sometimes overshadowed
by a reputation for an abrasive, take-no-prisoners style.
Bernard Weinraub, The New York Times, 30 August 1993

Agitation   Poisonville [town where novel is set] was beginning to
boil under the lid.
Dashiell Hammett, Red Harvest

Agreement/ disagreement
I talk cellar and he talks attic.
Yiddish proverb

My parents were, psychologically, at opposite poles from
one another.
Yevageny Yevtushenko, A Precocious Autobiography

Aimlessness   He had lost all sense of things; in the absence of air and
space, of light and sky, he circled aimlessly in the dense
core of a huge ball.
Peter Matthiessen, At Play in the Fields of the Lord

Ashley arrived at the Fonda at the moment when Mrs
Wickersham was losing control of her life's rudder.
Thornton Wilder, The Eighth Day

Alliances   'Very true', said the Duchess, 'flamingos and mustard
both bite. And the moral of that is – "Birds of a feather
flock together"'
Lewis Carroll, Alice's Adventures in Wonderland

Ambition   He who sacrifices his conscience to ambition burns a
picture to obtain the ashes.
Chinese proverb

Ambition is the mind's immodesty.
Sir William Davenant, Gondibert

Medieval words:

bastard – a sweet Spanish wine for drinking and cooking

Ambivalence   When I talk to my daughters about how they might achieve success, a dry crumb of ambivalence rises in my throat.

Michelle Gillett, 'Mothers to Daughters', The Berkshire Eagle, 5 July 1993

America/ Americans

America! half brother of the world!.

Philip James Bailey, 'The\Surface', Festus

Most Americans… have a sort of intoxication from within, a sort of invisible champagne.

GK Chesterton, The New York Times, 28 June 1931

Ancestry/ ancestors

To forget one's ancestors is to be a brook without a source, a tree without a root.

Chinese proverb

Anger   Anger is a thorn in the heart.

Yiddish proverb

Anger is a bow that will shoot sometimes when another feeling will not.

Henry Ward Beecher, Life Thoughts

Animation   The pleasures of living did more than percolate his chunky person. They boiled over.

John Mason Brown, The Portable Woollcott

Apathy   I'm just not up to this; I'm really running on empty.

Alice Adams, 'Earthquake Damage', The New Yorker, 1990

After Nora, my volcano seems more or less extinct.

Scott Turow, Pleading Guilty

Apology   Apology is only egotism wrong side out.

Oliver Wendell Holmes, Sr., The Professor at the Breakfast Table

Arousal/Rousers

When the cancer threatened my sexuality, my mind became immediately erect.

Anatole Broyard, Intoxicated By My Illness

My role is that of a grain of sand to the oyster. We've got to irritate Washington a little bit.

Ross Perot, Conference call with reporters, 19 March 1993

Writers' words:

'Prose: words in their best order. Poetry: the best words in their best order'. Samuel Taylor Coleridge

Arrogance/ humility

The State of New Jersey is a valley of humility between two peaks of conceit (New York and Philadelphia).
Anonymous, The New York Times, 3 May 1992

'One of the good things about this love affair', she said, 'is that it's shot my high horse right out from under me.'
Laurie Colwin, 'A Mythological Subject', The Lone Pilgrim

Arts and Entertainment

Public television… the green vegetables of video viewing.
Anna Quindlen, 'Public and Private', The New York Times, 30 November 1991

The classics may be the mountains of theatre, but you don't climb them just because they're there.
Frank Rich, 'Review/Theater', The New York Times, 9 December 1992

Attraction   Ah, she could feel the charm mounting over her again… could feel the snake biting her heart.
DH Lawrence, The Captain's Doll

Authority   Authority intoxicates,
And makes me sots of magistrates;
The fumes of it invade the brain,
And make men giddy, proud and vain.
Samuel Butler, Miscellaneous Thoughts

Awareness/unawareness

America can not be an ostrich with its head in the ground.
Woodrow Wilson, speech, 1 February 1916

B

Barriers   The fence that makes good neighbours needs a gate to make good friends.
Anonymous

Beauty   Beauty without virtue is a flower without perfume.
French proverb

For so many years
I was good enough to eat:
The world looked at me
And its mouth watered.
Randall Jarrell, 'Next Day'

Anagrams:

from ASTRONOMERS to NO MORE STARS

It was one of her moments of beauty – that fitful beauty which is so much more enchanting and perilous than the kind that gets up and lies down every day with its wearer.

Edith Wharton, The Children

Beliefs

We are all tattooed in our cradles with the beliefs of our tribe, the record may seem superficial, but it is indelible.

Oliver Wendell Holmes, Sr., The Poet of the Breakfast Table

Belonging/ outcast

I was ill at ease among them: a thistle in the rose garden, a mule at the racetrack, Cinderella at the fancy dress ball.

Lee Smith, 'The Bubba Stories', The Southern Review, 1991

Bigotry

Prejudice is a raft onto which the ship-wrecked mind clambers and paddles to safety.

Ben Hecht, A Guide for the Bedevilled

Biographies/ autobiographies

Biographies are but the clothes and buttons of the man – the biography of the man himself cannot be written.

Mark Twain, Autobiography

Our mothers' wombs the tiring houses be
Where we are dressed for this short comedy.

Sir Walter Raleigh, 'On the Life of Man'

Birthdays

At twenty man is a peacock, at thirty a lion, at forty a camel, at fifty a serpent, at sixty a dog, at seventy an ape, at eighty nothing at all.

Baltasar Gracian, Oracula Manual

Boasters/ boastfulness

He was not a youth to hide his light under a bushel.

Samuel Butler, The Way of All Flesh

Bodies/ the body

The healthy body, is a guest-chamber for the soul; a sick body is a prison.

Sir Francis Bacon, Advancement of Learning, Book 1

He watched her dress for dinner, her body flashing by in parts, a machine programmed with strategies to achieve goals.

Lynne Sharon Schwartz, 'The Two Portraits of Rembrandt'

Brand origins:

Wimpy, 1954 – named after the character in the Popeye cartoon called Wimpy who loved hamburgers.

Books   Food of the spirit .
             Anonymous, inscription on the Berlin Royal Library, 1780

             Some books are to be tasted, others to be swallowed,
             and some few to be chewed and digested.
             Sir Francis Bacon, 'Of Studies', Dedication to the Essay

Brain   The brain is a good stagehand. It gets on with its work
             while we're busy acting out our scenes.
             Diane Ackerman, A Natural History of the Senses

Breasts/ bosoms
             If I had the nerve, I swear I'd buy me some bigger
             breasts instead of walking around… with these little
             sunny-side-ups on my chest.
             Terry McMillan, Waiting to Exhale

Buildings and bridges
             Cathedrals, luxury liners laden with souls.
             WH Auden, 'On This Island'

Business descriptions
             Eighty percent of everything ever built in America has
             been built in the last 50 years and most of it is
             depressing… Potemkin village shopping plazas with
             their vast parking lagoons.
             James Howard Kunstler, The Geography of Nowhere

             Advertising tries to be a pyromaniac igniting
             conflagrations of desires for instant gratification.
             George Will, 'The Madison Legacy', Washington Post Syndicate, 7
             December 1981

C

Calmness/ volatility
             He was not a rushing river, boiling and tumbling over
             rocks, but the placid stream flowing through the quiet
             meadows.
             Ernest Longfellow, about his father, the poet, who died in 1882

Candour   Honesty… can become at times the moral equivalent of
             assault and battery. I don't think it hurts to cover hurts –
             the bandage principle of human intercourse.
             John Hersey, 'Fling', Grand Street

             But total candour can be the rape of hope.
             Martha Weinman Lear, 'Should Doctors Tell the Truth?'
             The New York Times Magazine, 24 January 1993

Twisted truths:

Be more specific. You can't be more or less specific, just specific.

Cause and effect

If you sow turkeys you will reap fools.
European proverb

The doctrine of karma teaches that what we reap accords with what we have sowed.
Philip Kapleau, The Wheel of Life and Death

Caution

We put a little toe in the water, but we didn't go all the way.
Anonymous, The New York Times, 26 August 1992

Chance

Luck never gives, it only lends.
Swedish proverb

Character

Character is a kettle that, once mended, always needs repairs.
Proverb

Characteristics

Modesty is the only sure bait when you angle for praise.
Earl of Chesterfield (Philip Dormer Stanhope), Letters to His Son, 8 May 1750

Charity

He who deserves to drink from the ocean of life deserves to fill his cup from your little stream.
Kahil Gibran, The Prophet

Childhood/ children

So this little worm is our daughter.
Shmuel Yosef Agnon, Shira

All of us once dwelt, half lost in a forest of Legs and Don'ts.
Clifton Fadiman, 'It's a Small World – and a Better One'

Choices and decisions

Seated at life's dining table, with the menu of morals before you, your eye wonders a bit over the entrees, the hors d'oeuvres, and the things a la though you know that roast beef, medium, is safe and sane, and sure.
Edna Ferber, Foreword, Roast Beef, Medium: The Adventures of Emma McChesney

As a metaphor for a difficult decision, it ['between a rock and a hard place'] has wrestled 'the horns of a dilemma' to the ground and inundated 'the devil and the deep blue sea'.
William Safire, On Language

Cities		Some cities are women and must be loved. Angela Carter, The War of Dreams

Dublin… a stock exchange for gossip, a casino of scandal.
Sean O'Faolain, 'The Faithless Wife'

Also see
Street scenes
page 316

Cityscapes The hot-blooded heartbeat of this passionate and mercurial city touches my soul… towering clouds under full sail, lightning that pirouettes across a limitless horizon.
Edna Buchanan, Never Let Them See you Cry

Civilisation Civilisation is the lamb's skin in which barbarism masquerades.
Thomas Bailey Aldrich, Ponkapog Papers

Clarity/ ambiguity
Everybody's… peering through the thick fog of dismal economic data.
Sylvia Nasar, The New York Times, 16 February 1992

Clinging She clung to Mary as though she were sinking but sometimes of her own accord Iris let go the boat.
Mavis Gallant, 'Careless Talk'

Coldness Still, she knew these two people by reputation, and was aware that they were not icebergs in their own waters.
Mark Twain, The Gilded Age

Colour Colours are the smiles of nature. When they are extremely smiling and break forth into other beauty besides, they are her laughs, as in the flowers.
Leigh Hunt, 'The Seer'

Commitment I love people who harness themselves, an ox to a heavy cart.
Marge Piercy, 'To be of use', To Be of Use

Communication/ non-communication
In reality they all lived in a kind of hieroglyphic world, where the real thing was never said or done or even thought, but only represented by a set of arbitrary signs.
Edith Wharton, The Age of Innocence

Competition/ competitors
Let everybody struggle to get their bucket in the stream and then do what they will with the water they fish out.
Scott Turow, Pleading Guilty

Oxymorons:

a new classic

Completeness/ incompleteness

When we speak of an individual we have likewise to speak of the age in which he lived. You disguise a portrait if you cut it out of its frame.

Henry Wadsworth Longfellow, Lecture on Moliere, c.1832

Complexion

His complexion is that of a corpse considerably advanced in corruption.

Germaine de Stael, letter, 1803

The beautiful children – red flags in their cheeks.

Eudora Welty, 'The Bride of the Innisfallen'

Compromise

The compromise our fathers made was a coffin of horror and the cradle of war.

Robert Green Ingersoll, Decoration Day address, 1870s

Confinement

A cat pent up becomes a lion.

Italian proverb

Conformity/ nonconformity

Much of private industry tends to follow the pack, seeking the surest returns and quickest profits.

Jeff Madrick, The New York Times, 19 January 1993

Confrontation

Hector: Do you think this is a conversation between enemies we are having?
Ulysses: I should say a duet before the full orchestra.

Jean Giraudoux, Tiger at the Gates, Act II

Connections

The drug companies have every intention of keeping Tomlinson's marriage to his prescription pad intact.

Elizabeth Stone, 'Off the Couch', The New York Times Magazine, 6 December 1992

Isn't the worthless rooster the poet's bird brother?

Jim Harrison, 'The Rooster'

Conscience

The worm of conscience keeps the same hours as the owl.

Johann Christoph Friedrich von Schiller, Kabala and Liebe, V

Gabay at a glance:

For some of the most intriguing metaphors you will ever come across, check out Pirke Avot (Sayings of the Jewish Fathers).

Brand origins:

Xerox – the process was invented in 1937. The name has Greek origins: it loosely means 'dry writing' as xerography doesn't use any liquids.

Consciousness

Consciousness is a poison when we apply it to ourselves.
Boris Pasternak, Doctor Zhivago

Consciousness is a light directed outward; it lights up the way ahead of us so that we don't stumble.
Boris Pasternak, Doctor Zhivago

Consistency/ inconsistency

Consistency is a paste jewel that only cheap men cherish.
William Allen White, Emporia Gazette, 17 November 1923

Contentment He drew the feet of contentment under the skirt of security.
Saadi (also know as Sadi), The Rose Garden (Gulistan)

Continuity All EC [European Community] states want the European train to keep rolling.
Chancellor Helmut Kohl, quoted in China Daily, 19 October 1992

The day that does not carry the seed of tomorrow in its womb is sterile.
Lewis Mumford, The Freeman

Control The teacher flogs with a stick and the rich man with a wallet.
Yiddish proverb

A mouth is not always a mouth, but a bit is always a bit, and it matters little what it bridles.
Colette, 'The Sick Child'

Commitee A committee is a cul-de-sac into which ideas are lured to be quietly strangled.
Anonymous, quoted by George F Will, Washington Post Writers Group, 16 August 1992

Conversation When a conversation becomes a monologue, poked along with tiny cattle-prod questions, it isn't a conversation anymore.
Barbara Walters, How to Talk with Practically Anybody about Practically Anything

So often a conversation is shipwrecked by the very eagerness of one member to contribute.
Christopher Morley, 'What Men Live By'

Writers' words:

'Pay no attention to what the critics say; there has never been set up a statue in honor of a critic.' Jean Sibelius

Corruption   Your silver has become dross, your choice wine is
diluted with water.
Isaiah 1:22

Countries, misc.
Yugoslavia, once a nation, now a scream of agony.
AM Rosenthal, 'On My Mind', The New York Times, 22 May 1992

Courage   Brave actions never want a trumpet.
Thomas Fuller, Gnomologia

We no longer need to clip the wings of our humanity.
It's time we flew again.
John Le Carre, speech to the Boston Bar Association, 3 May 1993

Cowardice   You miserable cowardly, wretched little caterpillar. Don't
you ever want to become a butterfly? Don't you want to
spread your wings and flap your way to glory?
Mel Brooks, The Producers

Craftiness   He had the instincts and timing of a cornered snake.
Ridley Pearson, Hard Fall

Creation   And the waves flourished at my prayer,
The rivers spawned their sand.
Geoffrey Hill, 'Genesis'

To realise one's high conception
On the night's canvas with a dot, just one.
Nikolai Morshen, 'Two Poems'

Creativity   After she left me and I quit my job and wept for a year
and all my poems were born dead, I decided I would
only fish and drink.
Jim Harrison, 'Drinking Song'

He is a tree that cannot produce good fruit; he only
bears crabs [small, sour fruit].
Samuel Johnson, quoted in Short Sayings of Great Men

Creativity comes from trust – trust your instincts.
Rita Mae Brown

Crime and punishment
Crime and punishment grow out of one stem.
Punishment is a fruit that unsuspected ripens within the
flower of pleasure which concealed it.
Ralph Waldo Emerson, 'Compensation', Essays: First Series

Twisted truths:

Understatement is always best.

Commit a crime and the earth is made of glass.
Robert Waldo Emerson, 'Compensation', Essays: First Series

Criticism/critics

Precisely what I predicted. The knives are flashing.
Truman Capote, telephone remark to John Malcom Brinnon, recorded in the latter's journal, 1947

My bait will not tempt the rats, they are too well fed.
Henry David Thoreau

I see critics as bus drivers. They ferry the visitors round the City of Invention and stop the bus here or there, at a whim, and act as guides.
Fay Weldon, Letters to Alice

Crowds

I love to dive into the bath of street life, the waves of the crowds flowing over me, to impregnate myself with the fluids of the people.
Isabelle Eberhardt, journal entry

Culture

When men die, they become History. When statues die, they become Art. This botany of death is what we refer to as culture.
Anonymous, description of short film Les Statues Meurent Aussi, bulletin: The Museum of Modern Art Department of Film, 16 April – 8 June 1993

For every culture is an island. It communicates with other islands but it is only familiar with itself.
Arthur Koestler, 'The Boredom of Fantasy'

Custom

Custom is a tyrant.
Latin maxim

Custom is the principal magistrate of man's life.
Sir Francis Bacon, 'Of Custom and Education'

D

Danger

The scary part is that everyone is flying blind.
Peter Passell, 'Economic Scene', The New York Times, 19 November 1992

Let the threatened thunders roll and the lightning flash through the sky.
William Lowndes Yancy, Southern rights speech, 1860

Darkness/light

Dead clods of sadness, or light squibs of mirth.
John Donne, 'Holy Sonnets: XV'

Oxymorons:

abundant poverty

Diversity	Variety's the spice of life, that gives it all its flavour. William Cowper, 'The Timepiece'
Divorce	Divorce is the sacrament of adultery. French proverb
Dominance	It is very difficult for a sapling to grow up in the shadow of a giant oak. Randolph Churchill
Doubt	Jane read this letter… with a slowly gathering doubt that seemed to materialise at last into a very dark cloud. Louis Auchincloss, 'The Stations of the Cross', Skinny Island
Dreams	Dreams are blind arrows that never leave the bow. Lewis Mumford, 'The Little Testament of Bernard Martin, Aet. 30' Luxuriously she floated on innocent visions of days after the morrow. Dorothy Parker, 'Glory in the Daytime'
Dullness	This is one of those rye-bread days, all dull and damp without. Margaret Fuller, diary entry, Life of Margaret Fuller-Ossoll

E

Earth	The earth is a beehive we all enter by the same door, but live in different cells. African proverb A country caught between the devil of tax increases and the deep blue sea of worker layoffs. Anonymous, The New York Times, 16 May 1992

Education and learning
Learning sleeps and snores in libraries, but wisdom is everywhere, wide awake, wide awake, on tiptoes.
Josh Billings

Effectiveness/ ineffectiveness
He was lashing with wet noodles. It didn't hurt that much.
Anonymous, public television broadcast of documentary on Armistead Maupin, author of Tales of the City, 24 June 1993

Ego/egotism	Socrates: Don't wrap your mind for ever round yourself. Aristophanes, The Clouds

Oxymorons:

ingeniously simple

Ego/ID	Everyone is a moon and has a dark side which he never shows to anybody. Mark Twain, Mark Twain's Notebooks and Journals
Embraces	Your arms a garland around my neck entwined. Gabriela Mistral, 'Poem of the Son'
	I am lost in you, wrapped in the folds of your caresses. Rabindranath Tagore, 'The Gardener, 47'
Emotions	She often felt she was nothing but a sponge sopped full of human emotions. Virginia Woolf, To the Lighthouse
	A rain of tears, a cloud of dark distain. Sir Thomas Wyatt the Elder, 'My Galley'
Endings	The sun of my political life sets in the deepest gloom. John Quincy Adams
Enemies	You don't get enemies for nothing. You pay for them. Yiddish proverb

Entanglements

Tangled I was in love's snare.
Sir Thomas Wyatt the Elder, 'Tangled I Was in Love's Snare'

Entrapment	He was caught in a skin that had gotten too tight. Jan Brenning McNamara, 'Most Likely to Succeed', quoted in The New York Times Magazine, by Alessandra Stanley, 22 November 1992
Envy	Then, as I watched you, Don Jeronimo, a gap of hunger opened in me. Jose Donoso, The Obscene Bird of Night
	He is still slipping on the skins of sour grapes. Dorrie Weiss
Epitaphs	Here lies one whose name was writ in water. John Keats, epitaph
	This model mother, sister, wife, believed, through all her joys and woes, that life is death, and death is life And now she knows. Kathleen Norris, her own epitaph, Vanity Fair, 1925
Ethics	What am I, a spiritual gigolo? Theodore Roethke, Straw for the Fire, Notebooks of Theodore Roethke

Loquacious language:

Evening   Evening wrapped about me the quickening moisture of its twilight sheets; evening laid a mother's hand upon my burning forehead.
Isaac Babel, 'My First Goose', Red Cavalry

Evil   Men... must have corrupted nature a little, for they were not born wolves, and they have become wolves.
Voltaire, Candide

Evil is unspectacular and always human,
And shares our bed and eats at our table.
WH Auden, 'Herman Melville'

Exactness/inexactness

Many a man strikes with his hammer here and there on the wall, and thinks he hits every time the nail on the head.
Johann Wolfgang von Goethe

Excess   They pumped the magazine full of steroids when they should have been making it leaner.
Anonymous, former New Yorker executive, quoted in The New York Times, 1 July 1992

Excitement   By this evening, effervescent as an Alka-Seltzer – which will surely be needed in the morning – Washington was a bubbly, carbonated city.
Patricia Leigh Brown, The New York Times, 21 January 1993

Expectations   That talented man just emerging from his chrysalis to breathe in the fragrant air of a rosy future.
Jose Donoso, The Obscene Bird of Night

He had drawn his cheque on the Bank of Expectation, and it had got to be cashed then and there.
Kenneth Grahame, 'The Magic Ring'

Experience   Experience is a good teacher, but she sends in terrific bills.
Minna Antrim, Naked Truth and Veiled Allusions

I have but one lamp by which my feet are guided, and that is the lamp of experience.
Patrick Henry, speech at the Virginia convention, 23 March 1775

Experience is a comb that nature gives to bald men.
Anonymous

Writers' words:

'Writing is a solitary occupation. Family, friends, and society are the natural enemies of the writer. He must be alone, uninterrupted, and slightly savage if he is to sustain and complete an undertaking.' Jessamyn West

Exploitation It would seem to me that I was nothing but a pit stop in the middle of a race.
Norman Mailer, Harlot's Ghost

Extravagance There was a hole in Mr Franklin's pocket that nothing would sew up.
Wilkie Collins, The Moonstone

Eyes Her eyes are candles in a burning shrine.
James Thurber, The Thirteen Clocks

Her eyes were great blue windows with timidities inside.
Jack Kerouac, 'The Mexicana Girl'

F

Faces Nature had carved him into a human monument, and he spent his life trying to live up to the importance of his face.
Anonymous, 'The Talk of the Town', The New Yorker, 5 July 1993

Facial Colour They are coffee-with-milk colour and the khaki they wear is the same colour as their skin, so they look all beige.
Julia Alvarez, How the Garcia Girls Lost Their Accents

Facts Facts are high explosives.
Hallie Flanagan, quoted in The New York Times, 4 March 1992

Facts are the air of science. Without them you can never fly.
Ivan Pavlov

Failure Quite soberly I am telling you that my ship is going down and that the water is already coming over the bridge.
Mikhail Bulgakov, letter to his brother, quoted in JAE Curtis's 1992 biography

The withered leaves of industrial enterprise lie on every side.
Franklin D Roosevelt, first inaugural address, 4 March 1933

Faith Faith builds a bridge across the gulf of death.
Edward Young, Night Thoughts, IV

Fame Fame is a food that dead men eat.
Henry Austin Dobson, 'Fame and Friendship'

Loquacious language:

faitour – a cheat

Families
The ungrateful son is a wart on his father's face; to leave it is a blemish, to cut it off a pain.
Afghanistan proverb

My expectation for my daughters has been that after I polish a few tarnished places, I can put down the cloth and they will continue to shine.
Michelle Gillett, 'Mothers to Daughters', The Berkshire Eagle, 5 July 1993

Fashion and Style
Her body jammed excruciatingly into her prison of a dress.
Wilfred Sheed, The New York Times Book Review, 4 October 1992

Fate
That's one of the few decent cards fate dealt us in the whole hand… unfortunately, that's not a card we can play except in the direst circumstances.
Donna Tartt, The Secret History

Fatness/thinness
I'm fat, but I'm thin inside. Has it ever occurred to you that there's a thin man inside every fat man, just as they say there's a statue inside every block of stone?
George Orwell, Coming Up for Air

Fear
Fear… is a carrion crow.
Ralph Waldo Emerson, 'Compensation', Essays: First Series

For weeks she had lived in a black sea of nausea and fear.
Mavis Gallant, 'Bernadette', The New Yorker, 1950–1960

Feelings
The tides of feeling round me rise and sink.
Donald Davie, 'The Evangelist'

Flattery
A flatterer carries water in one hand and fire in the other.
German proverb

He set my heart floating on the honey stream of his words.
Kshetrayya, 'Dancing-Girl's Song'

Flaws
Small faults indulged are little thieves that let in greater.
Thomas Fuller, Gnomologia

Flexibility/inflexibility
Max is liquid. He changes shape. He fills the container whatever the container is.
Martin Cruz Smith, Red Square

Oxymorons:

accurate rumours

Flowers   Blossoms are the clocks of the seasons.
Kara Ann Marling, The New York Times Book Review, 14 March 1993

Foreboding   A red flag at once began to flutter in her stomach.
Sean O'Faolain, 'The Faithless Wife'

Fortune/misfortune

Fortune is a god and rules men's life.
Aeschylus, 'Agamemnon'

Fragility   Our house is made of glass… and our lives are made of glass; and there's nothing we can do to protect ourselves.
Joyce Carol Oates, American Appetites

Freckles   There was a saddle of freckles across her small nose.
John Cheever, 'The Hartleys'

Freedom of expression

No man and no force can put thought in a concentration camp forever.
Franklin D Roosevelt, speech to American Booksellers Association, 23 April 1942

Freedom/restraint

Slavery… a weed that grows in every soil.
Edmund Burke, speech, 22 March 1775

Freedom is the open window through which pours the sunlight of the human spirit and of human dignity.
Herbert Hoover, on his ninetieth birthday, 10 August 1967

Freshness/staleness

Fish and visitors smell in three days.
Benjamin Franklin, Poor Richard's Almanack

Friendship   Through life's desert… the flower of friendship grows.
Oliver Wendell Holmes, Sr., 'A Song of Other Days'

Friendship is precious, not only in the shade, but in the sunshine of life; and thanks to a benevolent arrangement of things, the greater part of life is sunshine.
Thomas Jefferson, letter to Maria Cosway, 12 October 1786

Furniture   She saw the furniture as a circle of elderly judges, condemning her to death by smothering.
Sinclair Lewis, Main Street

Twisted truths:

One-word sentences? Eliminate.

G

God
A circle whose centre is everywhere and circumference nowhere.
Timaeus of Locris, quotation in Voltaire's Philosophical Dictionary

Good/evil
A man is born into this world with only a tiny spark of goodness in him. The spark is God, it is the soul: the rest is ugliness and evil, a shell.
Chaim Potok, The Chosen

Evil and good are God's right hand and left.
Philip James Bailey, 'Fetus'

Goodness
Turn his soul wrong side outwards and there is not a speck on it
Thomas Jefferson, letter, 20 January 1787

Gossip
Listening at closed doors, to the Wives, over tea and wine, spinning their webs.
Margaret Atwood, The Handmaid's Tale

The world rests on the tip of her tongue.
Yiddish proverb

Government
Congress is a swamp that must be cleared.
Pat Buchanan, speech during campaign for presidential nomination, 30 March 1992

Grammar and style
Nouns and Verbs are almost pure metal; adjectives are cheaper than ore.
Marie Gilchrist

Gratitude/ingratitude
If a small kindness is not forgotten it becomes a gnawing worm.
Friedrich Wilhelm Nietzsche, Thus Spake Zarathustra

Greed
A young child is a pig and a grown one is a wolf.
Yiddish proverb

Grief
My heart is turned into a wailing child.
Nahabed Kouchak, fifteenth-century poet

As I was letting myself in the empty apartment, grief sprang out of the dark hall and clubbed me.
Eileen Simpson, Orphans

Writers' words:

'Women do not always have to write about women, or gay men about gay men. Indeed, something good and new might happen if they did not.' Kathryn Hughes

H

Habits
Habits are cobwebs at first and cables at last.
Chinese proverb

Habit… a shirt made of iron.
Czechoslovakian proverb

Hair
The fair hair rippled in a shower of curls.
Honore de Balzac, 'The Firm of Nucungen'

Happiness/unhappiness
Bliss is happiness boiling over and running down both sides of the pot.
Josh Billings

Happiness is a rare plant, that seldom takes root on earth.
Lady Marguerite Blessington, The Victims of Society

Who is a happy man? He who is contented with his lot.
Pirke Avot

Hatred
The winds of hatred blow
Cold, cold across the flesh.
Theodore Roethke, 'Lull'

Heart
The heart is the best preacher.
Proverb

Her heart rolled slowly over, a wheel on which something is written.
Enid Bagnold, National Velvet

Heat
I walk without flinching through the burning cathedral of the summer.
Violette Leduc, Mad Pursuit

The whole world's a blazing pyre, especially the oven room.
Naguib Mahfouz, Palace of Desire

History
History is but the merest outline of the exceptional… A few mountain peaks are touched, while all the valleys of human life… are left in the eternal shadow.
Robert Green Ingersoll, decoration day address, 1870

Hope
The white bird of hope flew out the window.
Richard Selzer, 'A Pint of Blood', Letters to a Young Doctor

Printing landmarks:

Humanity/humankind

Man… a two-legged animal without feathers.
Thomas Carlyle, Past and Present, 1843

You are bows from which your children as living arrows are sent forth.
Kahill Gibran, The Prophet

Mankind are earthen jugs with spirits in them.
Nathaniel Hawthorne, American Notebooks

Humour

A sense of humour is the pole that adds balance to our steps as we walk the tightrope of life.
Anonymous

Hypocrisy

Out of the same mouth you blow hot and cold.
Aesop, Fables: The Man and the Satyr

I

Ignorance

Ignorance is a blank sheet, on which we may write.
Caleb Colton, Lacon

Illusion/reality

Illusion is the dust the devil throws in the eyes of the foolish.
Minna Antrim, Naked Truth and Veiled Allusions

Importance/unimportance

You're not the only pebble on the beach.
Harry Braisted, title and first line of nineteenth-century poem

Impossibility

We've been trying to make snowballs in the Mohave Desert.
Anonymous

Individuality

Nature made him – then broke the mold.
Ludovico Ariosto, Orlando Furioso

If a man does not keep pace with his companions, perhaps it is because he hears a different drummer. Let him step to the music which he hears.
Henry David Thoreau, Walden

Influence

Now and then an author comes along who rewires a part of our brains.
Gahan Wilson, The New York Times Book Review, 30 May 1993

Loquacious language:

fandangle – to fool around

Information   An ocean of data is sloshing around out there, and most
              of us are trying to sip it through a very narrow straw.
              James Gleick, The New York Times Magazine, 16 May 1993

Inheritance/inheritors
              The tears of an heir are laughter under a mask.
              Latin proverb

Innocence/inexperience
              To be left alone on the tightrope of youthful unknowing
              is to experience the excruciating beauty of full freedom
              and the threat of eternal indecision.
              Maya Angelou, I Know Why the Caged Bird Sings

Institutions Great libraries are temples of hope for the future.
              Stewart Brand, 'Immigration', educational video, broadcast on public
              television, 9 April 1990

Intelligence If a man empties his purse into his head, no one can
              take it from him.
              Benjamin Franklin

Intensity   The publicity campaign now reaching gale force cannot
              drown out some long sighs of disappointment.
              Calvin Tomkins, 'Madonna's Anticlimax', The New Yorker, 26 October 1992

Intoxication/intoxicants
              Brandy is as untrustworthy messenger. When you send it
              to the stomach, it goes to the head.
              Middle-European proverb

Isolation   Everything that has existed around me has disappeared,
              and I find myself in a desert.
              Gustave Flaubert, letter to George Sand, c. 1874

J

Jealousy   The jealous man poisons his own dinner and then
              eats it.
              Anonnymous

              Jealousy is a bitter root that we keep to gnaw on
              secretly.
              Josh Billings

Journal writing
              My journal keeps open house to every kind of
              happening in my soul.
              WNP Barbellion, diary entry, 22 January 1913

Oxymorons:

almost ready

Joy
I left the presence on the wings of elation.
Louis Auchincloss, 'Portrait of the Artist by Another', Skinny Island

Joy/sorrow
Joy and sorrow often wear the same clothing.
Anonymous

Sorrow and joy, two sisters coy.
Robert Bridges, 'Sorrow and Joy'

K

Kindness/unkindness
The humble virtue of simple kindness… is the one essential vitamin of the soul.
Joshua Loth Liebman, Peace of Mind

Knowledge
If we do not plant it [knowledge] when young, it will give us no shade when we are old.
Earl of Chesterfield (Phillip Dormer Stanhope), letters to his son, 11 December 1748

L

Landscapes
It is a dear little lullaby of a place sleeping between two small mountains.
Josh Billings

In that field, the sun lay hot on sheets of buttercups.
HE Bates, 'The Cowslip Field'

The vault of trees opened out above them, showing a river of sky in which stars twinkled.
Colette, 'Bella Vista'

Language
English is a stretch language: one size fits all.
William Safire, On Language

Laughter
Genuine laughing is the vent of the soul, the nostrils of the heart.
Josh Billings

Law/lawyers
Law is a bottomless pit.
John Arbuthnot, title of a pamphlet, 1712

Leaders/followers
It is better to have a lion at the head of an army of sheep, than a sheep at the head of an army of lions.
Daniel Defoe

History in the making:

When the Berlin Wall fell, top of the list of branded products to be imported by East Germany was the 'All American' McDonald's.

Leadership	A leader who has not his people's love is a very miserable little puppet. Vercors, The Silence of the Sea
Liberty	Liberty does not always have clean hands. Andre Malraux, Man's Hope
Lies	Falsehood… is a beautiful twilight that enhances every object. Albert Camus, The Fall

Life and death

I think of death as a fast approaching end of a journey.
George Eliot, letter, 22 November 1861

It is good to have an end to journey towards; but it is the journey that matters in the end.
Ursula K LeGuin, The Left Hand of Darkness

Life is…	Life is a jigsaw puzzle with most of the pieces missing. Anonymous

She could see now that an individual life is, in the end, nothing more than a stirring of air, a shifting of light.
Harriet Doerr, Consider This, Senora

Life… is full of steep stairs to go puffing up, and, later of shaky stairs to totter down.
Louis Kronenberger, The Cart and the Horse

Love	Love is the gold, but hate is the iron of that mine of emotions that lies within us. Honore de Balzac, Cousin Bette

love is like the measles; we all have to go through with it
Jerome K. Jerome

Love, defined Love is a rope, for it ties and holds us in its yoke.
Hadewijch, Dutch poet

Love – a temporary insanity curable by marriage.
Ambrose Bierce, The Devil's Dictionary

love is composed of a single soul inhabiting two bodies
Aristotle

Twisted truths:

Analogies in writing are like feathers on a snake.

M

Madness   He was a runaway train on a track of madness, picking up steam all the time, on and on and on.
Gerald Boyle, closing argument by the defence lawyer for mass murderer Jeffery Dahmer, 15 February 1992

Manipulation   To succeed in chaining the multitude, you must seem to wear the same fetters.
Voltaire, Philosophical Dictionary

Manners   Politeness is a guilt-edged investment that seldom misses a dividend.
Minna Antrim, Naked Truth and Veiled Allusions

Marriage   Marriage… a lottery in which men stake their liberty and women their happiness.
Renee de Chateauneuf Rieux

Mastery/subordination
A poor man who takes a rich wife has a ruler, not a wife.
Greek proverb

Maturation   This was a new bird taking wing. Jeannie was leaving the nest, testing her feathers.
Ed McBain, The Mugger

Memory/memories
In plucking the fruit of memory one runs the risk of spoiling its bloom.
Joseph Conrad, The Arrow of Gold

Old age begins when you open the trapdoor of memory.
Artur Lundkvist, Journeys in Dream and Imagination

Men and women
Man is fire; woman is firewood; the devil comes along and blows on them both.
Spanish proverb

The struggle of the sexes is the motor of history.
Alain Robbe-Grillet, Djinn

Middle age   And what is middle age if not the home office of tired blood?
Russell Baker, 'The Observer', The New York Times, 23 January 1993

Oxymorons:

Mind

The mind is but a barren soil – a soil which is soon exhausted, and will produce no crop, or only one, unless it be continually fertilised and enriched with foreign matter.
Joshua Reynolds, Discourses

Mistakes

The mistakes of a learned man are a shipwreck which wrecks many others as it goes down.
Arabian proverb

Mixture

My father was… a salad of racial genes.
Vladimir Nabokov, Lolita

Mobility/immobility

Her legs seem suddenly to have been hammered into the ground beneath her.
Julia Alvarez, How the Garcia Girls Lost Their Accents

Money

Money should be your servant, not your master.
Proverb

Money is a great soap – it removes almost any stain.
Yiddish proverb

Monotony

My life was one long yawn.
Mary Elizabeth Braddon, Dead Sea Fruit

Her life was a chain of routines that varied only with the seasons.
Isabel Allende, Of Love and Shadows

Moon

The thin gold shaving of the moon floating slowly downwards had lost itself on the darkened surface of the waters.
Joseph Conrad, Lord Jim

Morning

The morning is bleaching the edges of the sky.
Cristina Garcia, Dreaming in Cuban

Mountains

Mountains are earth's undecaying monuments.
Nathaniel Hawthorne, 'The Notch of the White Mountains', Sketches from Memory

Mouth

Watch her mouth… a mouth that clearly expects a spoonful of honey from life and gets a shot of vinegar every time.
David Richards, 'Sunday View', The New York Times, 26 April 1992

Movements

When she moved, it was swan moving.
Rosamond Lehmann, The Ballad and the Source

Writers' words:

'I find television very educating. Every time somebody turns on the set, I go into the other room and read a book.'
Groucho Marx

N

Nature

Forests are the ornaments of the earth.
Anton Chekhov, Uncle Vanya, Act 1

Nature is no temple but merely a workshop, and man is the craftsman.
Ivan Turgenev, Fathers and Sons

Night and day

Pillars of smoke… turned the metal of the night to rust.
Jorge Luis Borges, 'The Aleph'

O

Oblivion

Somebody has pushed the fast-forward button on history.
Anonymous, annual report of Control Data Corporation, quoted The New York Times, 1992

Occupations

Many a young dancer has drowned in the mirrors before which she spends her life.
Agnes DeMille, 'The Milk of Paradise'

Psychology… a consummate knowledge of human nature in general, of its secret springs, various windings, and perplexed mazes.
Henry Fielding

Old age

An old man is a bed full of bones.
Yiddish proverb

Soon the chill of old age began to creep about him, that keen north wind which penetrates and lowers the moral temperature.
Honore de Balzac, Cousin Pons

Openness

Mama… wore herself on the outside. Everything about her hung in view.
Fannie Hurst, Anatomy of Me

Opportunity

We have got to cheer and inspirit our people… with the vision of the open gates of opportunity for all.
Woodrow Wilson, 'The New Freedom'

Order/disorder

It was the clutter of a sunken ship, where every cloud of sea dust drifts away to reveal some new treasure.
Laurence Gonzales, 'Deep in with David Carradine'

Loquacious language:

flagitious – something which is incredibly wicked

Ordinariness   Liked? Liked is so margarine.
Margaret Atwood, 'Isis in Darkness', Wilderness Tips

P

Pain and suffering

Life is a bitter sea of suffering.
Chinese proverb

No matter what I do, it's as if my heart is wrapped around with barbed wire.
Sheila Bosworth, Slow Poison

Passion   Violent passions… will eat up your leaves, destroy your fruit and leave you a withered tree.
Ecclesiasticus (Catholic manuscript)

Past   The past is the only dead thing that smells sweet.
Edward Thomas, 'Early One Morning'

The past was a tunnel – a long, dark tunnel you strolled down on your own.
Laurie Colwin, 'Intimacy'

Peace   The wolf and the lamb shall feed together, and the lion will eat straw like the ox.
Isaiah 65:25

Perseverance

Hold on with a bulldog grip, and chew and choke as much as possible.
Abraham Lincoln, telegram to General Grant, 17 August 1864

Personality profiles

Lincoln is a cross between a sand-hill crane and an Andalusian jackass.
Anonymous, letter that appeared on the front page of The Louisville Daily Courier, 1 March 1861

Pessimism   A lot of journalists like to indulge in worst-case scenarios of civil war.
Yasushi Akashi, quoted in article headlined 'Chinese Support for Khmer Rouge Grows Cooler', New York Times, 9 May 1993

Philosophy   Philosophy… a filter turned upside down, where what goes in clear comes out cloudy.
Anonymous

Philosophy's the best medicine for the mind.
Marcus Tullius Cicero

Oxymorons:

terribly good

Physical appearance

He was a gentleman of sixty who seemed to be made out of highly durable leather.
Louis Auchincloss, 'The Wedding Guest', Skinny Island

Pity

The gilded sheath of pity conceals the dagger of envy.
Friedrich Wilhelm Nietzsche

Plagiarists

They lard their lean books with the fat of others' works.
Robert Burton, The Anatomy of Melancholy

Poetry/poets

If people need to exercise the spirit as well as the body, then poetry is gymnastics for the soul.
Dorothy L Hatch, quoted in The New York Times, 19 April 1992

He [the poet] unzips the veil from beauty, but does not remove it.
EB White, One Man's Meat

A Sonnet is a moment's monument.
Dante Gabriel Rossetti, 'The House of Life'

Poverty/prosperity

When it rains oatmeal, the poor man has no spoon to catch it with.
Swedish proverb

Power

Political power grows out of the barrel of a gun.
Mao Tse-tung

Praise

When angling for praise, modesty is the best bait.
Proverb

Problems and solutions

The way to stop financial joy-riding is to arrest the chauffeur, not the automobile.
Woodrow Wilson

We have the wolf by the ears, and we can neither hold him, nor safely let him go.
Thomas Jefferson, quoted in The Wall Street Journal, 2 December 1992

Progress

Human horizons altered with each new step in the evolutionary ladder.
Isaiah Berlin, 'The Pursuit of the Ideal', The Crooked Timber of Humanity

Protection/ protectors

I have a large umbrella. A lot of people stand under it.
Maya Angelou, quoted in The New York Times, 20 January 1993

Number crunchers:

vigintillion = 1000 novemdecillion (US)

Yet someone had loved him… But for her the race of the world would have trampled him under foot, a squashed boneless snail.

James Joyce, Ulysses

Q

Quarrels/ quarrelsomeness

His crackers don't sit well in my bowl of soup.

Bo Jackson

Quotations

A fine quotation is a diamond on the finger of a man of wit, and a pebble in the hand of a fool.

French Proverb

R

Rain

The rain came down in long knitting needles.

Enid Bagnold, National Velvet

Reading/readers

All his life he dunked himself each day in a sea of printer's ink.

John Mason Brown, The Portable Woollcott

Reading poetry is seeing a room lit by lightning – the details are jagged and sparse, but the illumination is stunning.

Dorrie Weiss

Reality/unreality

The skull of life suddenly showed through its smile.

Dorothy Canfield Fisher, The Deepening Stream

Wipe the dew off your spectacles, and see that the world is moving.

Elizabeth Cady Stanton, The Woman's Bible

Reform

A new broom sweeps clean.

John Heywood, Proverbs, Part 2

I'll turn over a new leaf.

Miguel de Cervantes, Don Quixote

Religion

Religion is a journey, not a destination.

Proverb

Brand origins:

Cutty Sark scotch was named after the clipper ship that won a precarious trans-Atlantic sailing race in the 1870s.

Renewal
There can be no purpose more enspiriting than to begin the age of restoration, reweaving the wonderous diversity of life that still surrounds us.
Edward O Wilson, The Diversity of Life

Reputation
Reputation is a bubble which a man bursts when he tries to blow it for himself.
Emma Carleton, The Philistine

Glass, china and reputations, are easily crack'd and never well mended.
Benjamin Franklin, Poor Richard's Almanack

Our names are labels, plainly printed on the bottled essence of our past behaviour.
Logan Piersall Smith

Rescue/ rescuers
He was so thrilled by the rope I had thrown him.
AB Yehoshua, Mr Mani

Restlessness
A wind's in the heart of me, a fire's in my heels.
John Masefield, 'A Wanderer's Song'

Retribution
God waits long and pays with interest.
Yiddish proverb

They say that Heaven's net, however big the meshes may be, is sure to catch the wicked.
Natsume Soseki, Botchan

Revolt
The man who serves a revolution plows the sea.
Gabriel Garcia Marquez, The General in His Labyrinth

Riches
Property, possessions and riches… were no longer a game and a toy: they had become a chain and a burden.
Hermann Hesse, Siddhartha

Insignificant thieves are hanged by the neck and important thieves are hanged by the purse.
Proverb

Risk-taking
He felt ready to cast the dice with death and glory.
Orhan Pamuk, The White Castle

Rooms
They're standing in the living room – or rather, on the narrow footpath between the canyons of furniture that obscure the walls.
T Coraghessan Boyle, 'Filthy With Things', The New Yorker, 15 February 1993

Printing landmarks:

1886 – *The New York Tribune* became the first newspaper to be printed using the Linotype method.

S

Sacrifice
: Death and sorrows will be the companions of our journey; hardship our garment.
Winston Churchill, speech, House of Commons, 8 October 1940

Sarcasm
: True sarcasm is in the point, not in the shaft, of the arrow.
Josh Billings

Satire
: Satire is a cruel weapon, but in malicious hands the handle is more dangerous than the blade.
Josh Billings

Science
: Science is a match that man has just got alight.
HG Wells, 1891

Scientific creativity is imagination in a straitjacket.
James Gleick, 'Part Showman, All Genius', The New York Times Magazine, 20 September 1992

Sea
: The waves on the shore stammered quietly, spreading softly on the sand.
Baptiste Racine, Andromaque

Seascapes
: The rested waters, the cold wet breath of the fog, are of a world in which man is an uneasy trespasser.
Rachel Carson, The Edge of the Sea

Seasons
: Spring is a virgin, Summer a mother, Autumn a widow, and Winter a stepmother.
Polish proverb

Here then was April… scalping them with a flexible blade of wind.
Kay Boyle, 'Wedding Day'

Secrecy
: An iron curtain is drawn down upon their front [the Russians].
Winston Churchill, telegram to President Harry S Truman, 12 May 1945

Self
: There is only one self; my day is to carve it.
Donald Hall, 'To Build a House'

Self-actualisation
: One day… the water-tight compartments in her will break down, and music and life will mingle.
EM Forster, A Room With a View

Etymology:

the die is cast – this phrase, meaning that something cannot be altered, is thought to refer to Julius Caesar's invasion of Italy in 49 BC. Upon crossing the River Rubicon he reportedly said 'Jacta alea est' (the dice have been thrown) meaning that there was no turning back.

Self-confidence

Nothing could dent his cast-iron assurance.

Stanley Elkin, 'The Moment of Decision'

Self-consciousness

She had spent her life trying to escape from the parlorlike jaws of self-consciousness.

Eudora Welty, 'June Recital'

Self-control

The passions may rage furiously… but judgement shall still have the last word in every argument, and the casting vote in every decision.

Charlotte Bronte, Jane Eyre

It was up to me to bring my nerves to heel.

Albert Camus, The Stranger

Self-destructiveness

Ireland is the old sow that eats her farrow.

James Joyce, Portrait of the Artist as a Young Man

Self-effacement

The person who makes a worm of himself will be stepped on.

Proverb

Self-expression

For the first time in his life he found himself talking freely, emptying out of his soul the dammed up waters of reflection.

Richard Wright, The Outsider

Self-images

I stood still and was a tree amid the wood.

Ezra Pound, 'The Tree'

I was a slow burning fuse… who could not fail to blow up the little gathering around the table.

Jane Smiley, Ordinary Love

Self-knowledge

There's a period of life when we swallow a knowledge of ourselves and it becomes either good or sour inside.

Pearl Bailey, The Raw Pearl

Self-pity

The hem of self-pity is showing.

Louis Begley, Wartime Lies

Self-reliance

I'm not afraid of storms for I'm learning to sail my ship.

Louisa May Alcott, 'Life in the Iron Mills', The Atlantic Monthly, April, 1861

Oxymorons:

bitter-sweet

Senses	As your senses awaken, all the inlets to the mind are set open. Cathleen Schine, Rameau's Niece
	My taste buds experienced a violent ecstasy. A whole opera of sensations rolled off my tongue. Henri Troyat, quoted in The New York Times by Dorie Greenspan, 22 July 1992
Separation	But a gulf of many years lay between them. Kawabata Yasunari, Beauty and Sadness
Sex/sexuality	She subscribes to feminism of her own vision, which seems to be inspired by piracy on the high seas, regarding it as an achievement to board every passing male ship. Scott Turow, Pleading Guilty
Shame	Shame is pride's cloak. William Blake, Proverbs of Hell
Shelter	The four-and-a-half mat room during those three and a half years was my castle… but now I had to part with the dear old nest which had given me shelter and protection so long. Natsume Soseki, Botchan

Significance/ insignificance

We are little better than straws upon the water.
Mary Wortley Montagu, letter to James Stewart, 19 July 1759

Sometimes I get the feeling that's all we are – ants.
Chaim Potok, The Chosen

Silence	Silence… the fence around wisdom. Greek expression
	Silence… a friend who will never betray. Confucius, Analects

Similarity/ dissimilarity

Everyone is kneaded out of the same dough, but not baked in the same oven.
Proverb

If the mother is a cow, the daughter is a calf.
Yiddish Proverb

Singing	I would rather sing one day as a lion than a hundred years as a sheep Cecilia Bartoli, quoted The New York Times Magazine, 14 March 1993

In other words:

intense – a dormitory for campers

Sin/Redemption

There are many people who think that Sunday is a sponge to wipe out all the sins of the week.
Henry Ward Beecher, Life Thoughts

To leave church by backdoor of sin and reenter through the skylight of repentance.
James Joyce, Portrait of the Artist as a Young Man

Sky

There was no sky – only a dark, ominous tent that draped in the tops of the streets and was in reality a vast army of snowflakes.
F Scott Fitzgerald, 'The Ice Palace', Flappers and Philosophers

The winter sun, poor ghost of itself, hung milky and wan behind layers of clouds.
Thomas Mann, 'Tonio Kroger'

Slander

Self-buzzing slander: silly moths that eat an honest name.
James Thomson, Liberty, IV

Sleep

Sleep's but a short death; death's but a longer sleep.
Phineas Fletcher, 'The Locusts'

Most people want to crash into sleep. Get knocked into it with a fist of fatigue.
Toni Morrison, Jazz

Sleeplessness

I lay awake at night flipping the channels of my attention.
Stanley Elkin, 'Out of One's Tree', Harper's, January 1933

Slowness

The hours went past on their rusty ankles.
Zora Neale Hurston, 'The Gilded Six-Bits'

Smallness

I was small once, hardly bigger than the laughter of a lemon.
Philip Levine, 'Burned'

Smiles

Smiles are the soul's kisses.
Minna Antrim, Naked Truth and Veiled Allusions

His grin was suddenly made of crumbling plaster.
Wilfrid Sheed, Office Politics

Snow

Snow was falling in earnest now – big silent petals drifting through the springtime woods, white bouquets segueing into snowy dark.
Donna Tartt, The Secret History

Foreign brand names:

Kowpis – Japanese fermented milk drink

From an invisible February sky a shimmering curtain of snowflakes fluttered down upon Chicago.
Richard Wright, The Outsider

Society

Society is a masked ball, where every man hides his real character, and reveals it in hiding.
Ralph Waldo Emerson, 'Worship', Conduct of Life

Sorrow

Sorrow… came in gusts, shaking the woman.
Marjorie Kinnan Rawlings, South Moon Under

Soul

My soul is a broken field
Ploughed by pain.
Sara Teasdale, 'The Broken Field'

The soul, fortunately, has an interpreter – often an unconscious, but still truthful interpreter – in the eye.
Charlotte Bronte, Jane Eyre

Sound

When there was a momentary calm in that tempestuous sea of sound, the leader gave the sign.
Nathaniel Hawthorne, 'My Kinsman, Major Molineux'

Speech

The polished pearls of impeccable speech.
Anonymous, Sir Gawain and the Green Knight

Speech is the mirror of the soul.
Publilius Syrus, Sententiae

Speeches

His speeches were beautiful songs, but all of them were sung pianissimo.
HL Mencken, in The Impossible HL Mencken

Speechlessness

There was a silence. Potter's mouth seemed to be merely a grave for his tongue.
Stephen Crane, 'The Bride Comes to Yellow Sky'

Sports

That may have been the respirator for this team.
Tim McCarvor, Broadcast of Mets v Phillies game, 13 April 1992

Spring

What a time of year it was – the freed earth suddenly breaking into life from every frozen seam!
Edith Wharton, Twilight Sleep

The hounds of spring are on winter's traces.
Algernon Charles Swinburne, chorus from 'Atlanta'

Stars

The stars are golden fruit upon a tree all out of reach.
George Eliot, Spanish Gypsy

Gabay at a glance:

Remember the 'three-ups' of speech writing and delivery:

Stand-up
Speak-up
Shut-up

Etymology:

Mind your Ps and Qs – this phrase, meaning 'to be on your best behaviour', is thought to originate from when the owner of a tavern would keep a record on a blackboard of how many pints and quarts a consumer, who would pay on credit, was drinking.

Stillness   The air was so quiet he could hear the broken pieces of the sun knocking in the water.
Flannery O'Connor, 'The River'

Stinginess   The husband is doing the death grip on his wallet.
Anonymous, 'Talk of the Town', The New Yorker, 15 May 1992

Storms   The wind spat hard raindrops against the window.
Allan Seager, 'The Street', Vanity Fair

Suddenly the black night showed its teeth, in a flash of lightning.
Rabindranath Tagore, Fruit-Gathering, 37

Strategies   Every day must have a plan, a track upon which to guide the restless colt of one's ambition.
Meg Pei, Salaryman

Street scenes   The long dusty ribbon of a long city street.
John Masefield, 'All Ye That Pass By'

The pavements of New York are filled with people escaping the prison sentence of personal history into the promise of an open destiny.
Vivian Gornick, The New Yorker, 17 October 1993

Strength/ weakness   She was the rock on which weaker natures broke.
Mavis Gallant, 'Careless Talk'

You're not seaworthy. You are cut away too much through the middle: you would go over in a good blow.
Joseph Hergesheimer, 'The Token'

In this business we are the sheep and you are the wolves.
Joseph Priestly, letter to the citizens of Birmingham

Stupidity   Either she knows something, or the inside of her head is so unfurnished that she can't remember what she ate for breakfast.
Rex Stout, Fer-de-Lance

Success is...   Success is a ladder you can't climb with your hands in your pockets.
American proverb

Success is a rare paint, hides all the ugliness.
Sir John Suckling, 'A Ballad upon a Wedding'

Printing landmarks:

1892 – The Weekly Summary became the first newspaper to be printed in Braille.

Success/failure

Success played hide-and-seek with Fielding.

JH Plumb, The Life of Mr. Jonathan Wild the Great

Summer

The summer days moved with the pace of a caged lion.

Claire McAllister, 'July In the Jardin Des Plantes'

Sun

The sun… that punctual servant of all work.

Charles Dickens, Pickwick Papers

Sunrise

The sun breaks on the hilltops, spilling its crimson yolk.

Julia Alvarez, How the Garcia Girls Lost Their Accents

The setting sun had left behind the redness of a heavenly slaughter.

Isaac Bashevis Singer, 'Brother Bettle'

Superstition

Superstition… the religion of feeble minds.

Edmund Burke, Letters on a Regicide Peace

Survival

We can't glance ahead with pleasure to the world our children will inhabit – they will have to swim for dear life.

Edward Hoagland, 'Home is Two Places', Commentary, April 1968

T

Tact

As she watched her cousin… that complaint long repressed, was on the point of breaking the frail envelope of discretion.

Honore de Balzac, Cousin Bette

Taste

Good taste is the flower of good sense.

Proverb

Tears

Between condolence and consolation there flows an ocean of tears.

Minna Antrim, Naked Truth and Veiled Allusions

Tears are summer showers to the soul.

Aldred Austin, Savonarola, IV

Technology

Technology is in the saddle and rides mankind.

Noel Brown, United Nations NGO Briefing, 4 November 1993

Temperament

The world has long realised he enjoys the central heating of temper.

John Mason Brown, 'The Trumans Leave the White House', The Saturday Review

Shakespearean insult:

'(Your) face is not worth sunbathing.' Henry V, act V

Temptation   The man who has tasted pleasure once will go to the well again.
Honore de Balzac, Cousin Bette

If you sup with the devil, use a long spoon.
Yiddish proverb

Thinking/thought
Thoughts are duty free.
Martin Luther

[The intellect] widens the horizon of the heart.
WH Auden, The Prolific and the Devourer

Thunder and lightning
The fierce lightning is scratching the sky with its nails.
Rabindranath Tagore, 'The Land of the Exile', The Crescent Moon

Time   Time is the best teacher.
Proverb

Time is the thief you cannot banish.
Phyllis McGinley, 'Ballads of Lost Objects'

Time passed. But time flows in many streams.
Kawabata Yasunari, Beauty and Sadness

Timeliness   Whoever hesitates for a second perhaps allows the bait to escape which during that exact second fortune held out to him.
Alexandre Dumas, The Three Musketeers

Toughness   An iron hand in a velvet glove.
Charles V

Towns   A town has a nervous system and a head and shoulders and feet.
John Steinbeck, The Pearl

Tradition   Tradition wears a snowy beard.
John Greenleaf Whittier, 'Mary Garvin'

Tranquillity   Nature seemed prim and staid that day, and the globe gave no hint that it was flying round in circus ring of its own.
Kenneth Grahame, 'The Magic Ring'

Transformation
You have put me here a cub, but I will go out a roaring lion, and I will make all hell howl.
Carrie Nation

Oxymoron:

boxing ring

He was a figure in a canvas, over which another had been painted.
Josephine Hart, Damage

Transience   Within a month his name would be a blown dust on the desert of centuries.
Morris L West, The Devil's Advocate

Travel   Travelling is a fool's paradise.
Ralph Waldo Emerson, 'Self-Reliance', Essays: First Series

Trees   The willow was winding the moon in her tresses.
Dorothy Parker, 'The Willow', Death and Taxes

Now in October, they [trees] had thinned into ghosts.
Phyllis Bottome, 'Found'

Troublemakers

They looked at him and saw a hand grenade with a bad haircut.
Peggy Noonan, Forbes Magazine, 14 September 1992

Trustworthiness

If his word was a bridge, we'd be afraid to cross.
Yiddish Proverb

Truth/lies   A lie is quick of tongue and nimble of foot, and gets a long start of the truth, but at the finish, truth comes jogging in always the winner of the race.
Josh Billings

Truth is a citizen of the world; it has no pedigree, and is the same in all languages.
Josh Billings

Honesty's an icicle: if it begins to melt, that's that!
American proverb

U

Uncertainty   They had entered the thorny wilderness, and the golden gates of their childhood had forever closed behind them.
George Eliot, The Mill on the Floss

Understanding

I remember distinctly the suddenness with which a key turned in a lock and I found I could read.
Graham Greene, 'The Lost Childhood', Collected Essays

Brand origins:

Virgin, 1970 – the name typified the Punk Culture of the 1970s. Plus, it entered a relatively 'virgin' type of approach to business. (It is thought that Virgin Records may have alternatively been called 'Slipped Disc'.)

A window in Merton's mind let in that strange light of surprise in which we see for the first time things we have known all along.

Gilbert Keith Chesterton, 'The Three Tools of Death'

Unity

A house divided against itself cannot stand.

Abraham Lincoln, speech at Republican State Convention, 16 June 1858

Uselessness

I tell you, I'm utterly incompetent. I'm the parasite on the British Oak, like the mistletoe.

DH Lawrence, 'Two Blue Birds'

V

Vanity

Vanity has a ravenous appetite and a remorseless digestion.

Josh Billings

The greatest magnifying glasses in the world are a man's own eyes when they look upon his own person.

Alexander Pope, letter, 1705

Victims

The boy seemed to have fallen
From shelf to shelf of someone's rage.

John Ashbery, 'A Boy'

Villainy/villains

Shakespeare, by making Shylock a Jew, gave him, as it were, an extra coat of Villainy, a coat of fresh poison.

Wilfred Sheed, 'Books', The New Yorker, 12 July 1993

Violence

A riot is the language of the unheard.

Martin Luther King Jr.

Visibility

I myself shall continue living in my glass house… where I sleep nights in a glass bed, under glass sheets, where who I am will sooner or later appear etched by a diamond.

Andre Breton, Nadja

Visitors

My evening visitors, if they cannot see the clock, should find the time in my face.

Ralph Waldo Emerson

Voices

Our voices, the endless ball of yarn that is our talk, crack with age.

Jose Donoso, The Obscene Bird of Night

The human voice is nothing but flogged air.

Seneca

Loquacious language:

fopdoodl – an insignificant fool

Vulnerability	There are strings… in the human heart that had better not be vibrated. Charles Dickens, Barnaby Rudge

W

War	In wartime, truth is so precious that she should always be attended by a bodyguard of lies. Winston Churchill
	For him the war was a disgusting disease which the people's body must overcome. Ilya Ehrenburg, The Storm
	When war is declared, Truth is the first casualty. Arthur Ponsonby, Falsehood in Wartime

Warriors and peacemakers
And in us we find the eagle and the dove .
John Donne, 'The Canonisation'

Watchfulness	She sat with her back to the books and facing the stairs, her dragon eye on the front door. Eudora Welty, One Winter's Beginnings
Weariness	I'm feeling wrung out hard and hung up wet. Katie Couric, interview, The New York Times, 9 April 1992
Wind	The wind was snarling in from the northeast with its teeth bared, chewing the tops off eight foot seas. John Hersey, 'The Captain', The Yacht
	Winds are the spirit of the sky's ocean Guy Murchie, Song of the Sky

Winning/losing
If this is a dream, then the Pittsfield players aren't interested in waking up.
Brian Sullivan, The Berkshire Eagle, 6 June 1993

Winter	Icicles filled the window with barbaric glass. Wallace Stevens, 'Thirteen Ways of Looking at a Blackbird'
Wisdom	The road of excess leads to the palace of wisdom. William Blake, 'Proverbs of Hell'
	The doors of wisdom are never shut. Benjamin Franklin, Poor Richard's Almanack

Twisted truths:

The passive voice is to be avoided.

Women

Women and God… the two rocks on which a man must either anchor or be wrecked.
Frederick William Robertson, Sermon

A woman is a bountiful table that one sees with different eyes before and after the meal.
French Proverb

Words

Our words have wings, but fly not where we would.
George Eliot, Spanish Gypsy

Short words are the best and the old words when short are the best of all.
Winston Churchill

Tart words make no friends; a spoonful of honey will catch more flies that a gallon of vinegar.
Benjamin Franklin, Poor Richard's Almanack

Words as weapons

Words are loaded pistols
Jean-Paul Satre

A sharp tongue is the only edged tool that grows keener with constant use.
Washington Irving, 'Rip Van Winkle'

A self-admitted physical coward… he was learning to jab with words.
Howard Teichmann, George S Kaufman

Work/workers

Living without working is entering a jewel-mine and coming out empty-handed.
Japanese proverb

World

The world is a wheel always turning. Those who are high go down low, and those who've been low go up higher.
Anzia Yezierska, 'The Fat of the Land'

The world is a dream and death is the interpreter.
Yiddish proverb

Worry

Anxiety is the rust of life, destroying its brightness and wakening its power.
Tryon Edwards

A spider of anxiety crawled up the back of my neck.
Donna Tartt, The Secret History

Oxymorons:

cold sweat

Wrinkles

Faint lines… beginning to make nets around her eyes.
Dashiell Hammett, Red Harvest

Behind her eyeglasses there was a fan of delicate lines, fine as paper cuts.
Sue Miller, For Love

Writing advice

All good writing is swimming underwater and holding your breath.
F Scott Fitzgerald, letter

Writing/writers

I think of a writer as a river: you reflect what passes before you.
Natalia Ginsburg, quoted in her obituary The New York Times, 7 October 1991

It is harder to put your foot in your mouth when you have a pen in your hand.
William Safire, On Language

Y

Youth

Youth is a very brief illness, one quickly gets over it.
Nathalie Sarraute, The Planetarium

Youth and Age

What the old chew, the young spit.
Yiddish proverb

We cannot at once enjoy the flowers of the Spring of life and the fruits of its Autumn.
Thomas Babbington Macaulay, John Dryden

Z

Zeal

That restless fever… zeal.
Aphra Behn, The Rover

Zenith

Her life was at its highest tide…
Margaret Widdemer, 'Changeling'

Brand origins:

Walls, 1922 – named after the founder whose clerk first suggested the concept of ice cream in 1913. Walls' brother Fred came up with the idea to sell ice creams from a trike ridden around the streets of West London. 'Stop me and buy one' became one of the 20th century's most enduring phrases.

Brains, pen, action!

Something to ponder...

I am sure you have your favourite parables, fables and fairy tales, all of which feature metaphors.

1   Look up some old fairy tales and see if you can spot the metaphors. Try Hans Christian Andersen or the Brothers Grimm.

2   Write a parable or fable about a copywriter who sets out on an adventure to find the source of all words.

Oxymorons:

Deliberate mistake

11. As thought-provoking as a well-placed simile

The craft of copywriting is not simply about written communications. It's how you share ideas in such a way that your audience feels involved with your message.

Similes, like other language techniques such as metaphors, alliteration, idioms, onomatopoeia, puns and collocation (the combination of two apparently unsuited words to make a new phrase eg. blueweekend) help to convey commonly understood messages through direct comparison: 'happy as the day is long', 'fits like a glove', and so on. With the added twist that the two things being compared are seemingly unconnected, similes serve to provide novel interpretations of what can otherwise appear as bland statements.

head like a bucket of wet sand

As thought-provoking as a well-placed simile

Similes

Similes remain one of the most powerful creative tools available to a copywriter. As with metaphors, they paint provocative pictures in the mind. Yet they go further still: providing humour and shrewd interpretation of a subject, as well as, more often than not, sharp headlines.

The fundamental key to writing a powerful simile is to feature the word 'as' or 'like'. The real 'trick', however, is to ensure that any comparisons are directly connected with either: the product or service; the visual; the audience's needs or emotions.

The following example is a great simile:

Business without advertising is like winking at a girl in the dark; you know what you're doing, but nobody else does.

This one allows the copywriter to demonstrate to the reader a real empathy about having a thumping headache:

Does your head feel like a bucket of wet sand?

Whilst the following two examples are technically similes, they simply don't 'feel' right. Firstly they are tired, and secondly they don't actually mean anything:

Are you as busy as ants at a picnic?
Is your copywriting as dull as cold tea?

So, when writing a simile, never forget to check the meaning, the connection to the audience and, of course, the subject, as well as ensuring that wherever possible it demonstrates a sense of originality.

Writing landmarks:

1871 – the Americans patented the first typewriter to have a QWERTY keyboard.

Some classic examples of similes to get you thinking

A

Abandoned
Abandoned as a ghost town
Abandoned like a one-pump gas station

Ablaze
Ablaze like poppies in the sun (Ouida)
Ablaze like a firebombed bamboo hut

Abrupt
Abrupt as a scissor cut (TC Boyle)
Abrupt as an axe chop

Absurd
Absurd as to expect a harvest in the dead of winter (Robert South)
Absurd as trying to put out a fire with applications of kerosene

Abundant
Abundant as dandelions
Abundant as the light of the sun (Thomas Carlyle)

Abysmal
Abysmal as death (Stephen R Donaldson)
Abysmal as deep depression

Ached
Ached like a freshly stubbed toe
Ached like a rotted tooth

Acted
Acted like a five-year old
Acted like a scared fool
Acted like scared rabbit

Active
Active as a Chinese fire drill
Active as a hornet's nest
About as active as a leftover fly in January

Adored
Adored him like an idol
Adored him like a schoolgirl with a crush

Advanced
Advanced like the shadow of death (John Ruskin)
Advanced like Sherman's army

Adventuresome
Adventuresome as a bee
Adventuresome as a puppy

Advice
Advice is like castor oil – easy enough to give, but dreadfully uneasy to take
Advice is like kissing; it costs nothing and is a pleasant thing to do

Ageless
Ageless as the mountains
Ageless as the sun (AC Swinburne)

Agile
Agile as a cat
About as agile as a walrus (Terry Ganey)

Alert
Alert as a child
Alert as a prowling cat

Printing landmarks:

1041 – the first movable type was invented in China. It did not catch on as Chinese pictograms are not really of much use outside China!

327

Alien
Alien as a cockroach in an anthill
(Hank Searles)
Alien as a whore in church

Alike
Alike as birds of a feather
Alike as two halves of an apple
Alike as if the same mule kicked the whole family

All over
All over him like a cheap suit
All over him like a rainstorm
All over him like scum on a pond

Alluring
Alluring as a ripe peach
(Guy De Maupassant)
Alluring as the apple of Eden

Alone
Alone as a leper
Alone as a scarecrow
(Truman Capote)

Aloof
Aloof as a lottery winner.
Aloof as Lady Nevershit.
(Arnold Wesker)

Ambitious
Ambitious as a Baltimore pimp
Ambitious as Lady Macbeth
(James G Huneker)

Ambled
Ambled like a lame beggar
Ambled like a man with the gout

American
American as the World Series
American as corn on the cob

Amiable
Amiable as a fruit merchant

Amiable as a tarantula with its belly full
(John Cosby)

Amorous
Amorous as a pair of lovebirds
Amorous as the first of May
(Alfred Tennyson)

Amusing
About as amusing as breaking your leg
About as amusing as a groin injury

Ankles
Ankles like Chianti bottles
(George Jean Nathan)
Ankles small and curved like axe handles and they looked as tough
(F Hopkinson Smith)

Anonymous
Anonymous as a railroad bum
Anonymous as the assistant purchasing agent of a one-saw sawmill

Anxious
Anxious as a hen with one chick
(Mary Stewart)
Anxious as an investor watching his stock go down

Appalling
Appalling as a great fat mother-in-law
(RS Surtees)
Appalling as a murder scene

Appealing
Appealing as apple pie à la mode
About as appealing as a hooded cobra
(George MacDonald Fraser)

Appetite
Appetite like a hungry bear
Appetite like a lumberjack

Writers' words:

'There was never a good biography of a good novelist. There couldn't be. He is too many people if he's any good.'
F Scott Fitzgerald

Arched
Arched like a cat's back at a dog show
Arched like a mule's back in a hailstorm

Arms
Arms as thin as pencils
Arms like legs of mutton
(W Somerset Maugham)
Arms like thighs

Arrogant
Arrogant as a sergeant major in the Foreign Legion (Charles Willeford)
Arrogant as Caesar (Stephen King)

Ascended
Ascended as the smoke of a furnace
(Old Testament)
Ascended like a gas-filled balloon

Ate
Ate like a bull (Robert Louis Stevenson)
Ate like a hog
Ate like he was going to the Chair

Attacked
Attacked like something gone mad
(Max Crawford)
Attacked like the Indians at Little Big Horn

Attracted
Attracted like a moth to a flame
Attracted like bees to honey
Attracted like flies to shit

Attractive
About as attractive as a dead toad
About as attractive as a truck-stuck weasel (TV show 'Bob Newhart')

Avoided it
Avoided it like a dead cow
(Owen Ulph)
Avoided it like a dog turd on the sidewalk

Awkward
Awkward as a bear
Awkward as a bull in a China shop
Awkward as a cow with a wooden leg

B

Babbled
Babbled like hyenas
Babbled like women at a bridge club

Back and forth
Back and forth like a shuttlecock
Back and forth like arguing fruit peddlers

Backbone
About as much backbone as a chocolate éclair (Theodore Roosevelt)
About as much backbone as a wet spaghetti

Bad
Bad as a jab in the arse with a sharp stick
Bad as a kick in the balls with a frozen boot
Bad as stepping on a rake

Bald
Bald as a balloon
Bald as a new marine
Bald as an egg
Bald as a coot

Bare
Bare as bones (JRR Tolkien)
Bare as the back of my hand
Bare like a carcass picked by crows
(Jonathan Swift)

Loquacious language:

bardolatry – the excessive admiration of William Shakespeare

Barren
Barren as a tavern after closing time
Barren as the ground around a cabin door (William Allen White)

Beamed
Beamed like a doting grandfather (TC Boyle)
Beamed like a new father

Beard
Beard like a matted buffalo robe (James Goldman)
Beard like Santa

Beat
Beat like a tom-tom
Beat like a borrowed mule
Beat like a slave

Beautiful
Beautiful as God's hand (John Ehle)
Beautiful as Mona Lisa
Beautiful as the face of a young Greek god

Begged
Begged like a cripple at a cross (Robert Whittingdon)
Begged like a dog for a bone.

Behaved
Behaved like an angry child
Behaved like sore loser

Behind
Always behind, like a donkey's tail (English proverb)
Always behind like the runt of the litter

Bellowed
Bellowed like a Mississippi towboat
Bellowed like an auctioneer

Belly
Belly like a barrel
Belly like a giant breast hanging over his belt

Bent
Bent like a bow (Robert Service)
Bent like a runover hat
Bent like a whip

Big
Big as a bus
Big as a palace
Big as Texas

Binding
Binding as a handshake
Binding as a wedding ring

Bitter
Bitter as bile
Bitter as quinine
Bitter as the guilt on your lips when you kiss your wife

Black
Black as a coal miner's neck
Black as a mineshaft
Black as a stove
Black as ebony (Alexandre Dumas)
Black as Satan

Blank
Blank as a wall.
Blank as death (Alfred Tennyson)

Blazed
Blazed up like dry kindling in a wood-stove (Stephen King)
Blazed like a barn afire

Bleated
Bleated like a ruptured choirboy (George MacDonald Fraser)
Bleated like a stuck pig

Oxymorons:

free credit

Bled

Bled like a fountain

Bled like stuck hog (Ferror Sams)

Blind

Blind as a bat

Blind as Mr McGoo

Blubbered

Blubbered like a crying drunk

Blubbered like a seal (CS Calverley)

Blue

Blue as azure

Blue as October skies

Blue as the Pacific

Blundered

Blundered about like a fly in a thunderstorm

Blundered into each other like two drunks on a dark night (Tom Wicker)

Blunt

Blunt as a mallet

Blunt as a hammer

Blushed

Blushed like a blue dog

Blushed like a schoolgirl (Harold Bell Wright)

Blushed like an opal

Bold

Bold as a blind horse (Greek proverb)

Bold as a life insurance salesman

Bold as barbed wire (Douglas C Jones)

Bolted

Bolted like a deer before hounds

Bolted like a rabbit

Bony

Bony as a skeleton key

Bony as a poor man's mule

Boomed

Boomed like a cannon

Boomed like loud speakers at a rock concert

Bored

Bored as an eel sorter in a fish market

Boring as the boss

Bounced

Bounced back like a billiard ball

Bounced like a paddle ball on a rubber string

Bounced up and down like the head of a rag doll (Richard Bachman)

Bountiful

Bountiful as a good harvest

Bountiful as April rains

Bowed

Bowed like a poppy in the breeze (Ogden Nash)

Bowed like a snow-covered sapling (TC Boyle)

Bowlegged

Bowlegged as a hockey goalie

Bowlegged as a pin setter in a bowling alley

Bragged

Bragged like a new boxing champ

Bragged like the father of twins

Brave

Brave as a bull

Brave as Lancelot

Brave as the voting public

Number crunchers:

octillion = 1000 septillion (US)

Brayed

Brayed like a jackass (Mark Twain)

Breasts

Breasts as firm as melons

Breasts drooped like an old woman's

Breasts like raspberry popovers

Breasts like two puppies fighting in a sack

Breath

Breath like stale cabbage
(Stephen King)

Breath smelled like a leper's armpit

Breath sour as a dragon's

Breathed

Breathed like a second-hand bicycle pump (O Henry)

Breathed like the bellows of a forge
(Lord De Tabley)

Bred

Bred like rabbits

Bred like rats on a grain ship
(Li Hung Chang)

Brief

Brief as the twinkling of an eye

Brief as the Z column in a pocket dictionary (Irvin S Cobb)

Bright

Bright as a bugle

Bright as a dozen suns

Bright as a new pin

About as bright as a small appliance bulb

Brilliant

Brilliant as a star (Ouida)

Brilliant as diamonds (Lee Smith)

Brisk

Brisk as a flea

Brisk as bottled ale (John Gay)

Bristled

Bristled like a gamecock (Margaret Mitchell)

Bristled like a panther (Victor Hugo)

Brittle

Brittle as an old bone

Brittle as glass

Broad

Broad as an aircraft carrier

Broad as the sea (Old Testament)

Broke (without money)

Broke as a sailor on his second day of shore leave

Broke as seven people

Brooded

Brooded like a dove for its mate

Brooded like an owl

Brown

Brown as a turd (TC Boyle)

Bruised

Bruised as a hockey goalie
(David Letterman, Late Night)

Bruised like a halfback in a football game (FW Crowninshield)

Bucked

Bucked like a colt

Bucked like a mule with a wasp on his nose (Tom Wicker)

Built (erected)

Built like a demented beaver
(Robert Adelman)

Built (strong physique)

Built like a brick outhouse

Built like a bull

Writing landmarks:

1883 – Lewis E Waterman (US) filed a patent for the first practical fountain pen.

Built like a truck
Built like the back end of an elephant

Bumbled
Bumbled like a bee
Bumbled like a bee in a tar tub

Burned
Burned like fire
Burned like molten jewels (WW Story)

Burrowed
Burrowed like a prairie dog
Burrowed like a weasel (RD Blackmore)

Burst
Burst like a firecracker
Burst like an overdone potato
(Arthur Conan Doyle)

Bustled
Bustled like a flea market
Bustled like a railway station
(Derek Robinson)

Busy
Busy as a beaver
Busy as dog with fleas
Busy as a one-legged ballerina

Buzzed
Buzzed like a fly
Buzzed like bees when they swarm
(Thomas Hood)
Buzzed like a spinster in her bed

C

Cackled
Cackled like a loon
Cackled like an overworked clock
(TC Boyle)

Calloused
Calloused as a shark's skin (Mark Twain)
Calloused as the sea
(Robert Louis Stevenson)

Calm
Calm as a child in its soft slumber lying
(EM Kelly)
Calm as a knitting party
Calm as a sister's kiss
Calm as night (Victor Hugo)

Came
Came and went like apparitions
(Jack Fuller)
Came and went like weather
(John Updike)

Came back
Came back like shooflies on a summer
day (Keith Korman)
Came back like swallows to Capistrano

Came down
Came down like a rock
Came down like a cat upon a mouse
(Robert Louis Stevenson)

Came down on him
Came down on him like a hammer on
an anvil (Mark Twain)
Came down on him like a shot
Came down on him like the wrath of
God (Derek Robinson)
Came down on him like a ton of bricks

Came in
Came in like a herd of elephants
Came in like a storm (Peter Dexter)

Came on
Came on like fury
Came on like Gangbusters

Loquacious language:

battologist – a person who repeats the same thing needlessly

Camp
Camp as a row of chiffon tents

Carefree
Carefree as children
Carefree as teenage lovers

Careful
Careful as a mule eating briars
Careful as mice in a house with a
hundred cats (Dean R Koontz)

Careless
Careless as the wind (William J Linton)
Careless and happy as children
(George Garrett)

Carried on
Carried on like they lost the twelve dis-
ciples (Mark Twain)
Carried on like wildcats (Mark Twain)

Casual
Casual as a hired gunslinger
(Stephen Longstreet)
Casual as a man waiting for eternity
(Ivan Doig)

Caught
Caught like a nut between two stones
(George MacDonald Fraser)
Caught like a possum in a poke

Cautious
Cautious as a burglar walking over a tin
roof in cowhide boots (Wallace Irwin)
Cautious as a squirrel (Robert Houston)

Certain
Certain as death and taxes
(Daniel Defoe)
Certain as night succeeds the day
(George Washington)

Chance
About as much chance as a cat in hell
without claws
About as much chance as a fart in
a windstorm
About as much chance as a snowball
in hell

Changeable
Changeable as the sea
Changeable as the wind (John Gay)

Charged
Charged like a mad steer on a
rampage (Zane Grey)
The angry rhino charged like a
demented express train

Charming
About as charming as a cobra
About as charming as a fox in a
hen house (Tom Wicker)

Chaste
Chaste as an Easter Lilly
Chaste as ice (William Shakespeare)

Chattered
Chattered like a mob of sparrows
(KK Jerome)
Chattered like bone castanets
(Lewis Carroll)

Cheap
Cheap as indifference
Cheap as water
Cheap as chips

Cheeks
Cheeks blazed like a maid's on the
marriage bed (Cecelia Holland)
Cheeks like a chipmunk

Cheerful
Cheerful as a carousel (Ferrol Sams)
Cheerful as tulips

Brand origins:

Brook Bond, 1869 – named after tea merchant Arthur Brook (alas, no Mr Bond)

Chin
Chin as sharp as a can opener
Chin like a rabbit

Choosy
Choosy as an alley cat

Circled
Circled like a vulture
Circled like buzzards waiting for a death

Clammy
Clammy as death (Owen Meredith)
Clammy as the grave (James Sherburn)
Clammy as an excuse

Clanged
Clanged like a boiler factory
(John Crosby)
Clanged like church bells

Clawed
Clawed like a frightened cat
Clawed like a parrot
(William Shakespeare)

Clean
Clean as a cat's ass
Clean as a pebble
Clean as a whistle (Lord Byron)
Clean as soap

Clear
Clear as a bell
Clear as air (F Hopkinson South)
Clear as creek water
Clear as reality
Clear as mud

Clever
Clever as a cat (Anthony Forrest)
Clever as the Indian rope trick

Close
Close as a clam
Close as kin
Close as the numbers on a dollar bill

Closed up
Closed up like a coffin
Closed up like a fist (TC Boyle)

Clumsy
Clumsy as a dancing bear
(Barry Cornwell)
Clumsy as an inebriated moose

Clung
Clung like a leech
Clung like barnacles
Clung like swarming bees (Lord Byron)

Clustered
Clustered like children afraid of the dark (Rosemary H Jarman)
Clustered like sheep when a wolf is near

Coarse
Coarse as a steel file
Coarse as horse hair (Eugene Sue)

Coiled
Coiled like a snake (WS Blunt)
Coiled up like the letter S
(Damon Runyon)

Cold
Cold as a dog's nose
Cold as a mackerel
Cold as a snake
Cold as an ice floe
(George MacDonald Fraser)
Cold as granite
Cold as the back coast of Ireland
(Norman Mailer)
Cold as yesterday's toast

Printing landmarks:

1450 – the German, Johannes Gensfleisch Gutenburg, invented the first useful moveable-type printing system.

Collapsed
Collapsed like a heart-shot deer
Collapsed like a paper bag (TC Boyle)

Comfortable
Comfortable as an old shoe
Comfortable as floating on a cloud
About as comfortable as a toothache
(Mark Twain)

Common
Common as a hedge
Common as coals from Newcastle
Common as white trash
(Margaret Mitchell)

Complex
Complex as a hill of ants
(James Goldman)
Complex as the Iliad (Victor Hugo)

Complexion
Complexion like a pizza
Complexion like peaches and cream

Composed
Composed as a statue (Ivan Doig)
Composed as heaven
(William Livingston)

Confident
Confident as a homing bird
(Doris Leslie)
Confident as four aces (Mark Twain)

Confused
Confused as a rabbit in a snare
(Stephen King)
Confused and stunned like a duck hit
on the head (Abraham Lincoln)

Conscientious
Conscientious as a dog
(Robert Louis Stevenson)

About as conscientious as a fox in a
poultry farm (George Bernard Shaw)

Constant
Constant as the flowing river
Constant as time passing

Consumed
Consumed like a flame
(Matthew Arnold)
Consumed like grasshoppers in a
bean field

Contagious
Contagious as a yawn
Contagious as wet paint

Contemporary
Contemporary as a man lounging in a
café (James A Michener)
Contemporary as a newspaper
(William Lyon Phelps)

Contented
Contented as a fat cat
Contended as a fox when the hounds
were drawn off and gone home
(Colley Cibber)
Contented as kittens before a fire

Contrary
Contrary as a handful of coat hangers
(Phyllis Born)
Contrary as a seventh-grader

Controlled
Controlled as a life-term prisoner
Controllable as putty in his hands

Convincing
Convincing as a gun
Convincing as the multiplication table

Cool
Cool as a cave
Cool as a cucumber

Writers' words:

'Everywhere I go, I'm asked if the universities stifle writers. My opinion is that they don't stifle enough of them.'
Flannery O'Connor

Cool as custard
Cool as well water (Tom Wicker)

Cordial
Cordial as a prostitute
Cordial as a welcome mat

Corrupt
Corrupt as a political boss
Corrupt as smugglers

Costly
Costly as eating money
Costly as termite damage

Coughed
Coughed like a smoker with pneumonia
Coughed and sneezed like a performing seal (Michael Carreck)

Countless
Countless as leaves on autumn's tempest shed (Percy B Shelley)
Countless as the desert sands
(Bayard Taylor)

Covert
Covert as the birth of thought
(James Montgomery)
About as covert as a Saint Patrick's Day parade

Cowered
Cowered like an often-kicked dog
Cowered like quail (Rex Beach)

Cosy
Cosy as a nest (Emile Zola)
About as cosy as standing on a bull's horns (Herman Melville)

Cracked
Cracked like a Brazil nut
(Nicholas Salaman)
Cracked like a whiplash

Crafty
Crafty as snake (John Keats)
Crafty as the sea (WB Yeats)

Crazy
Crazy as a coot
Crazy as a lord
Crazy as a shithouse rat
Crazy as a woodpecker drumming on a tin chimney (Owen Ulph)

Creaked
Creaked like an old house in a thunderstorm
Creaked like dry snow

Crept
Crept like a shadow
(William Shakespeare)
Crept like a thief in the night

Cried
Cried like a baby
Cried like blue murder

Crisp
Crisp as a November oak leaf
(Douglas C Jones)
Crisp as ancient paper
(Dean R Koontz)

Crooked
Crooked as a corkscrew
Crooked as a gaff
Crooked as an old man's teeth
(Stephen King)

Cross
Cross as a bulldog
Cross as tongs

Crouched
Crouched like a frightened animal
(Harold Bell Wright)
Crouched like a wild beast in its lair
(Henry W Longfellow)

Brand origins:

C&A Modes, 1841. Dutch Company, initially called Canada (still used) then Cyamodes, now C&A Co., founded by Clemens and August Brenninkmeyer.

Crowded

Crowded as chickens in a cluster
(John H Frere)
Crowded as herrings in a barrel
Crowded as shull on Yom Kippur

Cruel

Cruel as a switchblade (Michael Doane)
Cruel as loneliness (WL George)

Crumbled

Crumbled like a sand castle
(Dean R Koontz)
Crumbled like wet cardboard
(Derek Robinson)

Crushed

Crushed like an empty beer can
Crushed like old leather

Cunning

Cunning as a fox (George Garrett)
About as cunning as a dead pig

Curious

Curious as a fish (Johann Goethe)
Curious as a squirrel (Louis L'Amour)

Curled up

Curled up like a fishing worm
(Mark Twain)
Curled up like a writing worm
(Robert R McCammon)

Cut

Cut like soft butter
Cut like wire through cheese

Cut off

Cut off like carrot stems
Cut off like last year's hemline

Cute

Cute as a kitten
Cute as a spotted puppy

D

Dainty

Dainty as a doily
Dainty as thistledown
Dainty as your mum and dad at a disco

Danced

Danced like a man in a swarm of hornets
Danced like an Indian putting out a camp fire
Danced like he had two left feet

Dangerous

Dangerous as a kicking horse
(Robert Louis Stevenson)
Dangerous as a shark
Dangerous as walking under a ladder

Dark

Dark as a coalhole
Dark as a thief's pocket
Dark as the brooding thunderstorm
(John Greenleaf Whittier)
Dark as the inside of a tire

Darted

Darted like a bird (Victor Appleton)
Darted like a frightened hummingbird
(Margaret Mitchell)

Dazzling

Dazzling as a lightening storm
Dazzling as a pawnbroker's wife

Dead

Dead as a dodo
Dead as a nail in a coffin
Dead as Julius Caesar (Joseph Conrad)

Deaf

Deaf as a poker
Deaf as a post
Deaf as a white cat

Oxymorons:

found missing

Deceitful
Deceitful as a crow (Aeschylus)
Deceitful as a magician

Deep
Deep as despair
Deep as hell (William Shakespeare)
Deep as sullen quarry water
(Stephen King)

Delicate
Delicate as an eggshell
Delicate as old Chinese pots

Delicious
Delicious as forbidden fruit
Delicious as homemade ice cream

Delighted
Delighted as a child with a new toy
(Arthur Conan Doyle)
Delighted as a gutter puppy finding a
bone (Robert Adelman)

Demure
Demure as a nun
About as demure as an old whore at a
christening

Dense
Dense as falling leaves in October
Dense as London fog

Descended
Descended like a wolf on the fold
Descended like locusts

Desolate
Desolate as mausoleum
Desolate as death (Francis S Saltus)

Destructive
Destructive as a hurricane
Destructive as grasshoppers

Destructive as moths in a woollens
closet

Devoured
Devoured it like a hungry dog
Devoured it like a ravenous wolf that
had been starving a fortnight in the
snow (Daniel DeFoe)

Died
Died like a grown man
Died like a rat in a hole (Ranger Gull)

Different
Different as a yacht is to a coal barge
Different as day and night
Different as summer and winter

Dignified
Dignified as a dowager empress
concluding an audience (MM Kaye)
Dignified as Julius Caesar

Direct
Direct as a hammer (Tom Wicker)
Direct as the crow flies

Disappeared
Disappeared like a phantom
Disappeared like magic
Disappeared like the blues on a warm
spring day

Dishonest
Dishonest as a gas meter
Dishonest as local elections
(Amy Leslie)

Dismal
Dismal as a funeral chorus
(Robert Lewis Taylor)
Dismal as a wet Derby Day
(AE Housman)

Printing landmarks:

fifteenth century – block printing was introduced in Europe.

Dispersed

Dispersed like dandelion fluff on a brisk wind (Dean R Koontz)

Dispersed like smoke from a bonfire (Mary Stewart)

Disposition

Disposition as bright as a ten-cent shoe shine

Distant

Distant as death (Ivan Doig)

Distant as the horizon sail (George Meredith)

Dizzy

Dizzy as a drunk on St Patrick's Day

Dizzy as a moth that flutters round the flame (HH Boyesen)

Docile

Docile as a nun (D Giardina)

Drab

Drab as a February Day

Drab as unpolished pewter (Howard Spring)

Dragged

Dragged like a lamb to a slaughterhouse (Thomas Holcroft)

Dragged himself like a World War II prisoner on a death march (Peter Jenkins)

Drank

Drank like a fish

Drank like sieve

Drank like they were going to stop making it

Drawn

Drawn a crowd like a fistfight

Drawn like a magnet to a needle (TS Arthur)

Drawn like the moon draws the sea

Dressed

Dressed like a Christmas tree

Dressed like a used car salesman

Dressed like charity girls

Drifted

Drifted like an unanchored ship (Doris Leslie)

Drifted like flakes of snow

Dripped

Dripped like an old faucet (Lawrence Sanders)

Dripped like a kid's nose

Drooped

Drooped like a drunken dancing partner (H Allen Smith)

Drooped like an old man with a back problem (TC Boyle)

Dropped

Dropped like a full sack

Dropped like a stone

Dropped her like a prom queen with a dose of clap

Drowned

Drowned like a rat in a rain barrel (Stephen King)

Drowned like a mouse in a trap (George Bernard Shaw)

Drowsy

Drowsy as a yawn

Drowsy as the hum of a bagpipe

Drunk

Drunk as a bastard

Drunk as a fart

Drunk as a skunk in a trunk

Drunk as Zeus

Twisted truths:

One should never generalise.

Dry

Dry as a document (Thomas Harris)
Dry as a prune
Dry as a sponge
Dry as peanut shells

Dull

Dull as a dog biscuit
Dull as a post (John Gay)
Dull as books in a guest room

Dumb

Dumb as a box of rocks
Dumb as a milk cow
Dumb as an ox

E

Eager

Eager as a fine-nosed hound
(William Wordsworth)
Eager as understudy

Ears

Ears like a pickup truck with both
doors open
Ears like mangled doughnuts

Easy

Easy as a smile
Easy as biting a dentist
Easy as one, two, three
Easy as shooting birds on the ground
Easy as taking money from a child
About as easy as putting pants on a
bull (Ferrol Sams)

Edgy

Edgy as a man badly in need of a drink
Edgy as a terrier watching a rat hole
(Doris Leslie)

Effective

Effective as a blackjack
Effective as a bullet (Edgar Saltus)

Efficient

Efficient as a can opener
Efficient as furniture movers
(Sam Koperwas)

Elegant

Elegant as a five-star French restaurant
Elegant as poetry (Cecelia Holland)

Eloquent

Eloquent as a rattlesnake's tail
Eloquent as Cicero

Elusive

Elusive as a sunbeam
Elusive as an echo

Embarrassed

Embarrassed as a preacher's child
caught in a lie (Ridley Wills)
Embarrassed as a teen with new
braces

Embraced

Embraced like a lost lover (TC Boyle)
Embraced like old friends

Empty

Empty as church on Monday morning
Empty as a robbed room (John Ehle)
Empty as an old shoe (Doris Leslie)

Enduring

Enduring as eternity (Joseph Conrad)
Enduring as the stars

Energetic

Energetic as a convict on a one-day
pass (Norman Mailer)
Energetic as a tugboat
(Howard Jacobson)

Loquacious language:

bombilation – a humming sound

Enthusiastic

Enthusiastic as a kid in a toy store
(Tom Clancy)

About as enthusiastic as a guy going
to the chair (HC Witmer)

Enticing

Enticing as a riddle (PW Shedd)

Enticing as a summer's dip in the pool
(Robert Adelman)

Erect

Erect as a lightning rod (Mark Twain)

Erect as an aristocrat (Ferrol Sams)

Erection

Erection like a telephone pole

Erection like a tire iron (TC Boyle)

Erection like the Leaning Tower of Pisa

Erratic

Erratic as a dragonfly's flight
(John Masters)

Erratic as a woman's whims

Eternal

Eternal as mediocrity
(James G Huneker)

Eternal as the mountains

Even

Even as a row of telephone poles

Even as a row of West Point cadets
on parade

Evident

Evident as a light in the dark
(George Meredith)

Evident as the sun at noon
(Thomas Carlyle)

Exact

Exact as clockwork (Thomas Carlyle)

Exact as mathematics

Examined

Examined it like a pawnbroker's wife
(Derek Robinson)

Examined it like the owner of a
new car

Excited

Excited as a child on his first Christmas
(Peter Jenkins)

Excited as a dog with two tails
(Victor Canning)

Exciting

Exciting as uncovering a barrel of
snakes (Mark Childress)

About as exciting as watching grass
grow.

Exhilarating

Exhilarating as a cold shower

Exhilarating as love (Honore de Balzac)

Exotic

Exotic as fine perfume

Exotic as profanity from Mars
(Ivan Doig)

Exploded

Exploded like a clay pigeon

Exploded like a thirty-nine year old
virgin bachelor

Explosive

Explosive as a firecracker
(Peter Jenkins)

Expressionless

Expressionless as a lizard (Peter Straub)

Expressionless as a side of mutton
(Robert Lewis Taylor)

Extinct

Extinct as the bison (Finley P Dunne)

Extinct as the dodo

Eye-catching

Eye-catching as a mooner

Number crunchers:

nonillion = 1000 octillion (US)

Eye-catching as Joan of Arc at
the stake

Eyes

Eyes as big as buckeye seeds
(John Ehle)
Eyes as bright as a coin
Eyes as lidless as snakes
Eyes darted like newts
Eyes lit up like a kid's at Christmas

F

Face

Face as blank as a billiard table
Face like a bulldog chewing a nettle
Face as lined as a river delta (TC Boyle)
Face as white as a sheet
Face sweet and bland as a baby's smile
(Margaret Mitchell)

Faded

Faded like a dream of youth
(Oliver Wendell Holmes)
Faded away like a pound of soap in a
hard day's wash

Faint

Faint as a ghost
Faint as a rising star struggling in heavy
earthward mists (JRR Tolkien)

Fair

Fair as a virgin's vows
Fair as summer roses
Fair as youth

False

False as a harlot's tears
(Thomas D'Urfrey)
False as his teeth (Ferrel Sams)

Familiar

Familiar as the sun and moon
(Henry David Thoreau)

Familiar as turning a key
(Steve Callahan)

Far

Far as a country mile
About as far as one can throw a bull by
the tail

Farted

Farted like a marching band
(Tom Wicker)
Farted like a racehorse

Fascinating

Fascinating as a loose tooth
Fascinating as an ant farm

Fast

Fast as a derby winner in the last
furlong
Fast as a lottery winner making new
friends (Leda Silver)
Fast as a speeding bullet
Fast as wildfire

Fat

Fat as a cherub
Fat as a pig
Fat as lard

Fatal

Fatal as arsenic
Fatal as the scythe of death
(William Cowper)

Fearless

Fearless as a happy child too innocent
to fear (Robert Southey)
Fearless as an eagle

Feet

Feet like manhole covers
(James Herriot)
Feet like sled runners

Writing landmarks:

Fell

Fell like a load of bricks
Fell like an axed tree
Fell like tenpins

Fell apart

Fell apart as fast as a ten-dollar suit
Fell apart like a fifty-cent umbrella
in a gale

Felt

Felt like a half-dead goat the next
morning (Dean R Koontz)
Felt like a plugged nickel
Felt like the little boy the calf ran over
(Havilah Babcock)

Ferocious

Ferocious as a hungry bear
Ferocious as a wolf (Francoise Voltaire)

Fickle

Fickle as a weather vane
(Robert Baldwin)
Fickle as the wind (Horace)

Fidgeted

Fidgeted like a rabbit's nose
Fidgety as an old maid
(Honore de Balzac)

Fierce

Fierce as a famished wolf
(Robert Southey)
Fierce as a mother bird
Fierce as an eagle (Lee Smith)

Figure

Figure like a pillow
Figure like an hourglass

Final

Final as a chapter's end
Final as death

Fine

Fine as baby hair
Fine as gossamer
Fine as split silk

Firm

Firm as a rock
Firm as steel (Virginia W Johnston)
Firm as the Rock of Gibraltar

Fit

Fit like a banana skin
Fit like feathers on a duck
Fit like the paper on the wall
Fits like a glove

Fixed

Fixed as a star (William Wordsworth)
Fixed like a statue on a marble throne
(FW Faber)

Flamed

Flamed like a torch
Flamed like the jaws of hell

Flapped

Flapped like a torn flag (Keith Korman)
Flapped like wash in the wind
(TC Boyle)

Flashed

Flashed like a jewel (Robert Bridges)
Flashed like a meteor
Flashed like lightening

Flat

Flat as a flounder (John Gay)
Flat as a pancake
Flat as a plate
Flat as old cider

Fled

Fled like a passing thought
(Robert Burns)
Fled like a company was about to
go bankrupt

Loquacious language:

buffard – a fool

Fleeting

Fleeting as a greyhound

Fleeting as joy of youth (Edwin Arnold)

Flew

Flew like a dog that had burnt his paw
(Osmani proverb)

Flew about like a kite in the wind (Emma Marshall)

Flickered

Flickered like a lamp
(Sigmund Krasinski)

Flickered like fire

Flitted

Flitted like a June bug (Tom Wicker)

Flitted like bats at dusk
(Derek Robinson)

Floated

Floated about like a stone
(Alistair MacLean)

Floated around like milkweed in a strong breeze

Flopped

Flopped like a rag doll

Flopped around like a runover snake
(William Dieter)

Flourished

Flourished like weeds

Flourished like a young bay tree
(Jeffery Farnol)

Flowed

Flowed like a waterfall

Flowed like beer at a wedding

Flung

Flung aside like butcher's rags

Flung himself down like he'd just walked thirty miles

Flushed

Flushed like a zealot (Ferrol Sams)

Flushed and happy as a bride
(Victor Canning)

Fluttered

Fluttered like a moth assailing a lighted window (Own Ulph)

Fluttered like spent fire

Folded up

Folded up like a carpenter's ruler
(Stephen Longstreet)

Folded up like a parasol (TC Boyle)

Followed

Followed like a flock of sheep

Followed like a shadow

Fond

Fond as a miser is of his gold

Fond as hounds are of running after foxes (Thomas Hood)

Foolish

Foolish as to scratch one's head with a firebrand

Foolish as to talk of colour to a blind man

Forgotten

Forgotten like a dream
(Emma Marshall)

Forgotten like spilt wine
(AC Swinburne)

Forlorn

Forlorn as a lost and motherless child
(Margaret Mitchell)

Forlorn like autumn waiting for the snow (John Greenleaf Whittier)

Formal

Formal as a stockbroker
(George MacDonald Fraser)

Formal and stinted as Chinese theatre
(CL Skelton)

Twisted truths:

Avoid alliteration. Always.

Fornicated

Fornicated like rabbits

Fornicated like wild beasts
(Robert R McCammon)

Fought

Fought like a dog

Fought like demons

Fought like lions waiting for food
(William Shakespeare)

Fought like two old maids

Fragile

Fragile as a lily

Fragile as an egg

Fragrant

Fragrant as the breath of an angel
(Oliver Wendell Holmes)

Fragrant as the pants of a captured terrorist

About as fragrant as a cotton picker's armpit

Frail

Frail as a swallow (Wilbur Smith)

Frail as a young tree in a tornado
(Robert R McCammon)

Free

Free as a cloud (George Garrett)

Free as a lark

Free as water (W Levingston Comfort)

Fresh

Fresh as a crisp head of lettuce

Fresh as a daisy

Fresh as new paint

Fresh as wind-dried laundry

Friendless

Friendless as a leper

Friendless as Frankenstein

Friendly

Friendly as a Tenth Avenue whore

About as friendly as a shark with toothache

Frightened

Frightened as a rabbit caught in a trap

Frightened as though he had suddenly found himself at the end of a precipice
(Honor de Balzac)

Frigid

Frigid as a cave

Frigid as an iceberg

Frisky

Frisky as a colt (Geoffrey Chaucer)

Frisky as a kitten

Frugal

Frugal as a beggar's child
(Ralph Waldo Emerson)

Frugal as a poor farmer's wife
(George Garrett)

Frustrated

Frustrated as being between a dog and a fire hydrant

Frustrated as cleaning a window with a mud ball (William Pearson)

Full (often referring to a drunk)

Full as a fat bear cub (Peter Jenkins)

Full of money as a miser's stocking
(Augustus Mayhew)

Fumbled around

Fumbled around like a sleepwalker in a strange room

Fumbled around like a drunk in a dark bar

Fun

As much fun as a barrel of monkeys

As much fun as a hot fudge enema

About as much fun as kissing your sister

About as much fun as washing a dog

Number crunchers:

decillion = 1000 nonillion (US)

Funny
About as funny as a fart in a space suit
About as funny as gangrene

Furious
Furious as a hunt (George Garrett)
Furious as the wind (Thomas Otway)

Fussed
Fussed like a worried mother
Fussy as a nursery maid

Futile
Futile as curing crabs by setting your shorts on fire
Futile as turning back the hands of a clock

G

Game
Game as a lion
Game as a hornet (Alfred Henry Lewis)

Gaped
Gaped like a stuck pig (John Gray)
Gaped like an oyster

Garrulous
Garrulous as an old maid
Garrulous as parrots (Phoebe Gray)

Gasped
Gasped like a frog in a drought (Charles Kingsley)
Gasped like a netter fish (Stephen King)

Gathered
Gathered like ants
Gathered like wasps around a jam jar (Patrick McGinley)

Gaudy
Gaudy as a harlequin's jacket (William M Thackeray)

Oxymorons:

Alone together

Gaudy
Gaudy as an ape's rump (Cormac McCarthy)

Gaunt
Gaunt as a skeleton
Gaunt as icons of hunger

Gay
Gay as a butterfly (Charles Dickens)
Gay as a lark (La Fontaine)

Gazed
Gazed like a cow (George MacDonald Fraser)
Gazed like boxers before a bout

Gentle
Gentle as a fawn
Gentle as a lover's sighs (Claudian)
Gentle as sleep (Lord De Tabley)

Ghastly
Ghastly as a laugh in hell (Thomas Hardy)
Ghastly as a smile on a maniac's face

Giddy
Giddy as a drunken man (Charles Dickens)
Giddy as a schoolgirl

Giggled
Giggled like a housemaid (Doris Leslie)
Giggled like a schoolgirl (Margaret Truman)

Glad
Glad as children that come home from school (George Gascoigne)
Glad as the skylark's earliest song (Letitia E Landon)

Glared
Glared like a mad thing (George MacDonald Fraser)
Glared at each other like motorists with tangled cars (Stephen King)

Gleamed

Gleamed like a naked sword

Gleamed like gold
(Philander C Johnson)

Glistened

Glistened like a star (Emma Lazarus)

Glistened like the dews of morn
(Henry W Longfellow)

Gloomy

Gloomy as a graveyard on a wet
Sunday

Gloomy as a robbed tomb

Glossy

Glossy as a panther's pelt
(Wilbur Smith)

Glossy as wax (William Dieter)

Glowed

Glowed like a kiln

Glowed like a neon sign

Glum

Glum as an oyster

Glum as an undertaker
(William M Thackeray)

Go together

Go together like doughnuts and coffee

Go together like fish and chips
(Hugh McLeave)

Go together like salt and pepper

Gold

Gold as bread (Margaret Mitchell)

Gold as ripe wheat

Golden

Golden as the sun (Philip J. Bailey)

Golden as sunlight (Gustave Flaubert)

Gone

Gone like a morning dream, or like a
pile of clouds (William Wordsworth)

Gone like coins spilled in a gutter
(Anthony Forrest)

Gone like tenants that quit without
warning (Oliver Wendell Holmes)

Gone astray

Gone astray like a horny drunk in a
smoky tavern at midnight

Gone astray like a lost sheep
(Old Testament)

Good

Good as a pie

Good as snuff and not half as dusty

Gossip

Gossiped as freely as fishwives
(Anthony Forrest)

He told tall tales like a child
(Honore de Balzac)

Graceful

Graceful as a deer

About as graceful as an elephant on
roller skates

Grace

Grace as a mourning hearse

Grace as an eye dwelling on blood
(George Meredith)

Gracious

Gracious as a medieval queen
(Thomas Heywood)

Gracious as the morn (Victor Hugo)

Grand

Grand as a Greek statue
(Robert Browning)

Grand as the passion felt but never
spoken (Tracy Robinson)

Writers' words:

'Writing is the only thing that, when I do it, I don't feel I should be doing something else.' Gloria Steinem

Grating

Grating as a sawblade under the file
(Henrik Ibsen)

Grating as shards of broken crockery
(Stephen King)

Great

Great as an emperor (John Gray)

Great as God

Greedy

Greedy as a fox in a henhouse

Greedy as a hog

Greedy as a man in a sauna

Green

Green as an emerald

Greed as poison

Green as the Amazon (Ivan Doig)

Gregarious

Gregarious as a flock of geese

Gregarious as seals (Cecelia Holland)

Grew

Grew like the summer grass
(William Shakespeare)

Grew like weeds on a neglected tomb
(Percy B Shelley)

Grey

Grey as a dead lake (TC Boyle)

Grey as slate

Grim

Grim as a judge

Grim as death

Grim as peace in the Middle East

Grimaced

Grimaced like sow in labour

Grinned

Grinned like a baboon

Grinned like a cat eating paw paws

Grinned

Grinned like a Cheshire cat

Grinned like a well fed fox

Groaned

Groaned like a dying horse
(William Ward)

Groaned like an old man with arthritis

Growled

Growled like a dog at an intruder's
pant leg (TC Boyle)

Growled like a two-man saw (TC Boyle)

Grunted

Grunted like a hungry bear

Grunted like a startled warthog
(Stephen King)

Guilty

Guilty as a priest in a whorehouse
(Mario Puzo)

Guilty as homemade sin

H

Haggled

Haggled like a fishwife

Haggled like Merchants in a bazaar

Hair

Hair as white as snow (Lewis Carroll)

Hair like cornsilk (Joan Samson)

Hair like spun glass (Emma Marshall)

Hairy

Hairy as a highland cow
(George Garratt)

Hairy as an ape

Hand

Hand like a bird's claw
(George MacDonald Fraser)

Hand like a side of beef (Tristan Jones)

Hands as rough as nutmeg graters
(Howard Spring)

Writing landmarks:

1936 – The JiF-Waterman company of France patented the first ink cartridge.

Handshake

Handshake like a water pump

Handshake like it was a pump handle

Handsome

Handsome as a picture (Mark Twain)

Handsome as a set of solid gold teeth
(Rex Beach)

Handy

Handy as a pouch on a kangaroo

About as handy as a wooden ship in a
bottle

Happy

Happy as a boy at a baseball game

Happy as a clam

Happy as a dog with a bone

Happy as a lottery winner

Happy as a raccoon in a smokehouse

Hard

Hard as a barren stepmother's slap

Hard as nails

Hard as marble

Hard as the rocks of Dundee

Hard as making a silk purse out of a
sow's ear

Hard as riveting a nail into a
custard pie

Hard as teaching a pig to sing

Hard to lose as a flea on a hound dog

Hardy

Hardy as a mountain pine

Hardy as highland heather
(W Dudgeon)

Harmless

Harmless as a fly

Harmless as a strawberry festival

Harsh

Harsh as the bitterness of death
(AC Swinburne)

Harsh as truth (William L Garrison)

Hate

Hated like a cat and dog
(Thomas Carlyle)

Hate like poison (Rex Beach)

Head

Head like a peeled onion

Head was carried like a pagan prince
(Margaret Mitchell)

Healthy

Healthy as a horse

Healthy as a May morning

Heart

Heart beat like a drum

Heart beat like the wings of a caged
bird (Robert R McCammon)

Heart like a lion

Hearty

Hearty as a young dog
(Jack Matthews)

Hearty as an oak (Samuel Foote)

Heavy

Heavy as a dead elephant

Heavy as a rock

Heavy as lead (Thomas Hardy)

Held

Held on like a bulldog
(Margaret Mitchell)

Held on like summer cold
(George Ade)

Help

Helpful as the Salvation Army

About as much help as a high wind
in a prairie fire

Oxymorons:

Business ethics

Helpless

Helpless as a child (Robert Service)

Helpless as a lame beggar (Oudia)

Hesitated

Hesitated like a submissive voice of an inferior (Sir Walter Scott)

Hesitant as a recoiling groom (Douglas C Jones)

High

High as a giraffe's balls

High as a kite

High as a steeple

High as the first limb on a coconut tree

Hips

Hips as big as watermelons (Robert R McCammon)

Hips like the hills of sand (Arabian Nights)

Hissed

Hissed like a branding iron

Hissed like a snake (Victor Hugo)

Hit

Hit him like a locomotive

Hit him like a slap in the face

Hoarse

Hoarse as a crow (Robert Louis Stevenson)

Hoarse as a sidewalk hawker

Hollow

Hollow as a log

Hollow as the soul of an echo

Holy

Holy as a Baptist preacher (Douglas C Jones)

Holy as the Pope

Homely

Homely as a hedge

Homely as a stump

Honest

Honest as steel (Jack Fuller)

Honest as the skin between his brows (William Shakespeare)

Hooted

Hooted like butchers on a three-day drunk (TC Boyle)

Hooted and danced like pardoned criminals (TC Boyle)

Horny

Horny as a horned toad

Horny as a tomcat (TC Boyle)

Hot (high temperature, horny, or illegal)

Hot as a blast furnace

Hot as a firecracker

Hot as a scalded dog

Hot as a volcano

Hot as hell's kitchen

Hot as teenage love

Hovered

Hovered like a moth around a flame

Hovered like surgical student

Howled

Howled like a thousand demons (George Eliot)

Howled like a wolf (Charles Dickens)

Huddled together

Huddled together like sheep (Edward Eggleston)

Huddled together like survivors packed on a raft (Anthony Forrest)

Humble

Humble as a grateful almsman

Humble as a lamb (Alexander Barclay)

Loquacious language:

callipygian – someone having shapely buttocks

Hummed
Hummed like a cobbler
Hummed like a virgin in a choir

Hung
Hung like a tail (George Meredith)
Hung on like warts on a toad

Hung (anatomy)
Hung like a horse
Hung like a donkey

Hungry
Hungry as a bear
Hungry as a dog
Hungry as a polecat

Hunted
Hunted like a stag
Hunted like an escaped prisoner

Hurried
Hurried as if catching a train
(Frederick S Isham)
Hurried like one who had always a
multiplicity of tasks on hand
(Charlotte Bronte)

Hurt
Hurt like hose clamp on a
haemorrhoid
Hurt like a toothache

I

Idle
Idle as a summer noon (Omar Khayam)
Idleness is like a disease that must be
combated (Samuel Johnson)

Ignorant
Ignorant as a child
(Henry David Thoreau)
Ignorant as dirt (William Shakespeare)

Illusive
Illusive as a dream
Illusive as a shadow (Zane Grey)

Immaculate
Immaculate as a sheet of white paper
(Samuel Foote)
Immaculate as fresh snow (TN Page)

Immense
Immense as the oceans
Immense as the sea (AC Swinburne)

Immobile
Immobile as a sphinx's face
Immobile as stone (Douglas C Jones)
Immobile as my wifes nickers

Immoral
Immoral as the stars (Matilde Blind)

Immovable
Immovable as a setter at the scent
(O Henry)
Immovable as soldiers in a painting
(Tom Wicker)

Impartial
Impartial as a jury
Impartial as the grave (Rudyard Kipling)

Impassive
Impassive as a mannequin
(Charles McCarry)
Impassive as a weasel with a rat in
its mouth (TC Boyle)

Impatient
Impatient as a bull at a gate
Impatient as a hound waiting for the
hunt to begin (James Sherburn)

Impenetrable
Impenetrable as deaf ears
Impenetrable as granite (Ouida)

Writers' words:

'Anybody can make history. Only a great man can write it.' Oscar Wilde

Impersonal
Impersonal as a cyclone
Impersonal as doom (Charles Willeford)
Impersonal as an automated helpline

Impossible
Impossible as having your cake and eating it too
Impossible as scratching your ear with your elbow

Independent
Independent as a Gypsy in his caravan
Independent as the moon (Ivan Doig)

Indifferent
Indifferent as if he was ordering up eggs (Mark Twain)
Indifferent as thunder (Jack Fuller)

Individual
Individual as a fingerprint
(Stephen King)
Individual as a signature

Inert
Inert as a drowned rat
(Howard Jacobson)
Inert as stone

Inescapable
Inescapable as death
Inescapable as taxes

Inevitable
Inevitable as being born
Inevitable as predestination

Infamous
Infamous as Hitler
Infamous as hell (Earl of Rochester)

Infectious
Infectious as a spider poison
Infectious as the bite of an adder

Inflexible
Inflexible as granite block
Inflexible as an oak (Oliver Goldsmith)

Informal
Informal as a honky-tonk
Informal as a Polish wedding

Innocence
Innocent as a cloistered nun
Innocent as a newborn babe

Inoffensive
Inoffensive as a daisy
Inoffensive as a glass of water
(Victor Hugo)

Insecure
Insecure as a canary in a high wind
Insecure as a chicken in a cyclone

Insensitive
Insensitive as a wood tick
(Richard Bachman)
Insensitive as the IRS

Insignificant
Insignificant as a fart in a desert
Insignificant as a hill of beans

Insistent
Insistent as depression
Insistent as remorse (Victor Hugo)

Inspected
Inspected like a chimpanzee with fleas
Inspected like a mare at auction

Intangible
Intangible as smoke
(Robert R McCammon)
Intangible as a thought

Medieval words:

baptised – a person blessed by baptism

Intelligent
Intelligent as a Rhodes scholar
About as intelligent as a bundle of shawls (Henry James)

Intense
Intense as life (Theodore Winthrop)
Intense as a cat following a rolling ball of yarn (Ira Berkow, New York Times)

Intent
Intent as a camper
Intent as a cannibal at breakfast (TC Boyle)
Intent as a salesperson

Interest
About as much interest as a hog has in mutual funds (Stephen King)
About as much interest as a donkey has in a player piano

Intimate
Intimate as a stain on a bedsheet
Intimate as sardines in a can

Intricate
Intricate as the inside of a watch
Intricate as the rings around an onion (John Goldman)

Irish
Irish as Paddy's pig
Irish as whiskey in coffee (Hugh McLeave)

Irresistible
Irresistible as a rhumba
Irresistible as chocolate

Irrevocable
Irrevocable as a haircut (Readers Digest)
Irrevocable as paid taxes

Irritable
Irritable as a tired child
Irritable as red underwear to a bull (Gore Vidal)

Isolated
Isolated as an abandoned lighthouse (Ferrol Sams)
Isolated as shipwrecked mariners (Margaret Mitchell)

Itched
Itched like the pox
Itchy as poison ivy

J

Jabbed
Jabbed at his heart like a knife thrust (Margaret Mitchell)
Jabbed at his mind like a lightening bolt (Robert R McCammon)

Jabbered
Jabbered like crows
Jabbered like sparrows

Jaw
Jaw like a nutcracker
Jaw set like frozen yogurt (George MacDonald Fraser)

Jealous
Jealous as a couple of hairdressers (RC Trench)
Jealous as a Spanish miser (Charles Macklin)

Jerked
Jerked like a puppy on a leash
Jerked his head up and down like Punch (George MacDonald Fraser)

Jerky
Jerky as a ride on a buckboard

Oxymorons:

computer security

Jerky as a roller coaster ride

Jingled
Jingled like Christmas bells
Jingled like rattling handcuffs
(Ivan S Cobb)

Joy
Joy rises in me like a summer morn
(Samuel T Coleridge)
Joyful as a salvation (Tom Wicker)

Jumped
Jumped like frightened rabbit
(Erskine Caldwell)
Jumped like an old dog that had been
kicked (Stephen King)
Jumped at it like a trout at a mayfly
Jumped at it like a dog on a bone

Jumpy
Jumpy as a cricket
(George MacDonald Fraser)
Jumpy as a pea on a drum
Jumpy as a virgin at a prison rodeo
(Golden Girls)

K

Keen
Keen as a razor (John Gay)
Keen as a weasel on the scent of a
stricken bird (TC Boyle)
Keen as hate
Keen as mustard
Keen as steel (Ovid)

Kind
Kind as love (Richard L Sheil)
About as kind as Ivan the Terrible
(Donald McCaig)

Kinky
Kinky as a phone cord

Kinky as Hollywood sex

Kissed
Kissed like a volcano that's hot
(Elvis Presley and Otis Blackwell,
'All Shook Up')
Kissing a man without a beard is like
drinking soup without salt

Kneeled
Kneeled like a nymph
(George MacDonald Fraser)
Knelt like a graceful virgin at her altar
rites (Rex Beach)

Knew
Knew it like a book
Knew it like the back of his hand

Knocked
Knocked on the door like a storm
trooper
Knocked like a yellowhammer
(Ferrol Sams)

L

Laboured
Laboured like a galley slave
Laboured like a tramp freighter in a
heavy sea (ED Price)

Laid
Laid like a drunk in a gutter
Laid out like a rug

Large
Large as a log of maple
('Yankee Doodle')
Large as life (Zane Grey)

Laughed
Laughed like a drain
Laughed like he had feathers in
his shoes

Brand origins:

Bisto, 1910 – anagram of Browns Seasons and Thickens In One. Created by RHM Foods.

Lawless
Lawless as the town bull
Lawless as the storming wind

Lazy
Lazy as a fat cat
Lazy as a lobster
Lazy as the tinker who laid down his bag to fart

Leaks
Leaked like a mule pissing on granite
(Own Ulph)
Leaked like a sieve

Lean
Lean as dog in Lent
Lean as lance
Lean as a rake
Lean as a snake
Lean and thin as a fallen leaf
(George Garrett)

Leaned
Leaned like a man on a hillside
Leaned on him like a wounded man
(George Garrett)

Leaped
Leaped like a shot rabbit
(RD Blackmore)
Leaped like a stung whippet
(George MacDonald Fraser)
Leaped like a young rabbit
(Gary Jennings)

Lecherous
Lecherous as a ferret
Lecherous as a monkey
(William Shakespeare)

Leered
Leered at me with eyes askance like a seducer (Freidrich Nietzsche)

Leered like a satyr
(William M Thackeray)

Left
Left like a castaway on a rock
Left like rats deserting a sinking ship
(Doris Leslie)

Legs
Legs like Betty Grable
Legs like rubber
Legs like jelly
Legs numb as in a nightmare
(Margaret Mitchell)

Lengthy
Lengthy as a lord mayor's show
(Howard Spring)
Lengthy as a Fidel Castro speech

Liberal
Liberal as a man helping himself to strawberry jam (Anthony Forrest)
Liberal as the air (William Shakespeare)

Lied
Lied like a dog
Lied like a fortune teller
Lied like an auctioneer

Lifeless
Lifeless as a park bench bum
(John Irwin)
Lifeless as a wig (James Sherburn)
Lifeless as the grave

Light
Light as a cork (Henry James)
Light as a leaf
Light as dawn
Light as the singing bird that wings the air (Alfred Tennyson)
Light as whipped cream

Brand origins:

Bovril, first sales 1886–7. This name derives from the Latin 'Bos', short for 'bovis', meaning 'ox' and 'vril' from Lord Lytton's novel, *The Coming Race*. Bovril, aka Johnston's Fluid Beef, was created by John Lawson Johnston. (NB: 1930s brothels were also known as Bovrils.)

Limber

Limber as a watch chain
About as limber as a rail spike

Limp

Limp as a boned fish (JRR Tolkien)
Limp as a dishcloth
Limp as a rag doll

Limped

Limped like a man with the gout
Limped like a sore-footed soldier

Lingered

Lingered like a toothache
Lingered like an old melody
Lingered like hopeless love without
despair (Rufus Dawes)

Lips

Lips like maraschino cherries
Lips so warm and sweet like wine
(Andy Razaf)

Listened

Listened like a dove that listens to its
mate alone (CG Rossetti)
Listened like a turkey for the
mating call

Lit up

Lit up like a cathedral
Lit up like a Christmas tree
Lit up like a store window
Lit up like Broadway
Lit up like Times Square

Lived

Lived like a hermit in a cave
(Lee Smith)
Lived like a lord

Lively

Lively as a smiling day (Aaron Hill)

Loathsome

Loathsome as a nest of scorpions
(Rosemary H Jarman)
Loathsome as a toad
(William Shakespeare)

Locked

Locked up tight as a chastity best
Locked up tight as virgins in a
boarding school (Ferrol Sams)

Lonely

Lonely as a cloud
(William Wordsworth)
Lonely as a scarecrow in a field of
stubble
Lonesome as a dog in a pound
Lonesome as an abandoned dog
(Owen Ulph)

Long

Long as a snake's liver
Long as one's arm
Long as a dog's age
Long as a month of Sundays

Looked (appearance)

Looked like a Billy goat in stays
Looked like a chap who says his
prayers in a cold bath every day
(George MacDonald Fraser)
Looked like a guilty child
Looked like a man in the grip of a
deep migraine headache
(Stephen King)
Looked like death
Looked like death warmed up
Looked like he had just inspected God
on parade
Looked like something the cat
dragged in (Victor Appleton)
Looked just like a fly in a pan of milk
(Fannie Flagg)

Number crunchers:

undecillion = 1000 decillion (US)

Looked him/her over

Looked him over like he was a mare at auction (Tom Wicker)

Looked him up and down like a sergeant inspecting the ranks (George Garrett)

Loose

Loose as negligence (James Cawthorn)

Loose as wet string

Lost

Lost as an Easter egg

Lost like a river running into an unknown sea

Lost like a sea captain in a fog

Loud

Loud as a fart in church

Loud as the clappers of hell

Loud as the ocean when a tempest blows (William Wilkie)

Loud as thunder (Sydney Dobbell)

Lounged

Lounged like a boy of the South (Robert Browning)

Lounged like a haemophiliac prince (TC Boyle)

Lovely

Lovely as a prom queen

Lovely as a white Christmas

Low

Low as a flat frog in a dry well

Low as a snake in the grass

Low as the spats on a centipede

Loyal

Loyal as a dog

Loyal as a dove

Luminous

Luminous as a lit-up ballroom

(H DeVere Stacpole)

Luminous as a neon beer sign

Lumpy

Lumpy as a full diaper

Lumpy as a sackfull of door knobs

Lurked

Lurked like a carrion crow

Lurked like a vermin (John Davidson)

Lush

Lush as a rain forest

Lush as Eden (Steven Callahan)

Lustrous

Lustrous as laughter (AC Swinburne)

Lustrous as silk

Luxurious

Luxurious as a cluster of grapes (William M Ready)

Luxurious as an expensive fur coat

M

Mad

Mad as a buck

Mad as a hatter (Lewis Carroll)

Mad as a meat axe

Mad as a rat in a trap

Mad as a wet cat

Mad as a wet spider

Mad as the devil

Mad as an Al Qaeda sponsored diplomacy conference

Majestic

Majestic as Caesar

Majestic as the Alps

Malicious

Malicious as Satan (William M Thackeray)

Printing landmarks:

1476 – Englishman William Caxton introduced print to his homeland.

Malicious as Saul to David

Mean
Mean as a bear with a sore paw

Mean as a crab

Mean as a miser

Mean as a mule with shoulder galls
(Harold Bell Wright)

Mean as the devil

Mean as the man who told his children that Santa Claus was dead

Meandered
Meandered like drunk (TC Boyle)

Meandered like the river

Meek
Meek as a lamb

Meek as a saint (Alexander Hope)

Meek as May (Alexander Hope)

Meek as Moses

Melted
Melted like butter on a hot griddle
(Stephen Longstreet)

Merciless
Merciless as a male tiger

Merciless as chance (Tom Wicker)

Merciless as Othello (Ouida)

Merry
Merry as a cricket
(William Shakespeare.)

Merry as a magpie

Merry as a mouse in malt
(George Garrett)

Merry as flowers in May

Mild
Mild as a mother with her child
(Samuel T Coleridge)

Mild as cottage cheese
(Edna St Vincent Millay)

Mild as mother's milk (Frederic S Isham)

Mild and peaceful as Socrates

Mind
Mind like a sewer

Mind like a sieve

Mind like a steep trap

Mind about as open as a scared oyster
(Ferrol Sams)

Mischievous
Mischievous as a kitten

Mischievous as a wicked pixie

Miserable
Miserable like a wet hen
(Rosemary H Jarman)

Miserable as sin
(Francoise Chandernagor)

Moaned
Moaned like a dying hound
(Henry H Brownell)

Moaned like the voice of one who crieth in the wilderness alone
(Henry W Longfellow)

Modest
Modest as a violet

Modest and shy as a nun
(William Cullen Bryant)

Monotonous
Monotonous as mutton

Monotonous as the sea
(Richard M Milnes)

Moody
Moody as a reptile unable to shed its skin (Michael Doane)

Moody as an artist

Motionless
Motionless as a model (Thomas Hardy)

Motionless as an animal in a spotlight
(Joan Samson)

Oxymorons

diet ice cream

Mouth

Mouth hung open like an old hound
(Margaret Mitchell)

Mouth like a scarlet wound
(Graham Greene)

Mouth like the entrance to a fun house
(Stephen King)

Mouth opened like a trunk
(Mark Twain)

Mouth watered like a baby who's seen a nipple (John Ehle)

Moved

Moved like clockwork

Moved like his feet were on fire
(Stephen King)

Moved like rat in December

Moved like the Russian government

Muddy

Muddy as a sheepdog (Henri Murger)

Murmured

Murmured like a seashell

Murmured like bumblebees
(Tom Wicker)

Mute

Mute as a fish (John Gay)

Mute as a snail

Mute as snow (Elizabeth B Browning)

Mysterious

Mysterious as magic

Mysterious as voodoo

Mysterious as twilight

N

Naked

Naked as a shorn sheep

Naked as Adam (Thomas Ward)

Naked as the day you were born

Naked as the moon (George Sterling)

Naked as the point of a sword
(George Garrett)

Narrow

Narrow as a schoolgirl across the butt
(Robert Lewis Taylor)

Narrow as the gate to heaven
(Owen Ulph)

Natural

Natural as cherry pie

Natural as eating (Jeffery Farnol)

Natural as walking (Jeffery Fornal)

Near

Near as the bark to the tree
(William Camden)

Near as the end of one's nose

Neat

Neat as a nail

Neat as a pinky

Neat and bare like a GI's footlocker
(George Garrett)

Necessary

Necessary as breathing is to live

Necessary as water, air, and fire for man's life

Needed

Needed like a flower needs the sun
(Thelma Strabel)

Needed like snow for a skiing weekend

Needed like a drowning man needs a brick

Needed like a hole in the head

Needed like a tomcat needs a marriage licence

Nervous

Nervous as a bee with sore feet

Nervous as a mouse

Nervous as a wing bird in cat country

Loquacious language:

clavus – a sharp pain in the forehead

Nice
Nice as nip
Nice as pie

Nimble
Nimble as a boy
Nimble as a cow in a cage
Nimble as a hare
Nimble as a pig
Nimble as an eel

Nodded
Nodded his head like a puppet on a string (Raymond Paul)

Noise
Noise like a hammer striking a watermelon (Robert R McCammon)
Noise like an elephant breaking wind (Robert R McCammon)

Noiseless
Noiseless as a shadow
Noiseless as the fall of snow

Noisy
Noisy as a creditor's meeting
Noisy as an old sow leaving a corn patch with six hounds after it
Noisy as hell changing shifts (Ivan Doig)
Noisy as two skeletons wrestling on a tin roof

Nose
Nose hooked like a hen's beak (James Sherburn)
Nose like a garden implement (TC Boyle)

Nose like a sausage
He blew his nose like the falling of a tree (David Grayson.)

Nostrils
Nostrils like two hair cavern
Nostrils wiggled like a bunny rabbit

Numerous
Numerous as the bugs in a bed
Numerous as the hairs on his head (Paul Wiggins)
Numerous as the writings of ibid

Nutty
Nutty as a peanut bar
Nutty as a squirrel

O

Obedient
Obedient as a child
Obedient as a shadow (Jack D Bruce)

Obsolete
Obsolete as a mule
Obsolete as an Edsel
Obsolete as a scrivener

Obvious
Obvious as a lighthouse (Ferral Sams)
Obvious as a rat sign in a sugar bowl
Obvious as the nose on your face

Off
Off like a blue streak
Off like dirty shirt
Off like a flash (Victor Appleton)
Off like a shot
Off like a turpentined cat

Writing landmarks:

1938 – Laszlo Biró patented a prototype ballpoint pen.

Old

Old as Eve
Old as Methuselah
Old as my little finger (John Day)
Old as the hills
Old as the sphinx
Old as water

Ominous

Ominous as a raised fist (Tom Wicker)
Ominous as the still before the storm

Open

Open as the inn gates to receive
guests (George Gascoigne)
Open like an obscene cave

Oppressive

Oppressive as humidity
(Richard Brausch)
Oppressive as slavery

Orderly

Orderly as a corn crop (Peter Jenkins)
Orderly as the web of some
huge spider (JRR Tolkien)

Out

Out like a broken bulb
Out like a light
Out like a stunned boxer
Out as a gay carnival

Out of place

Out of place as a milk bucket
under a bull
Out of place as a white poodle on a
coal barge (Arthur Baer)
Out of place as three cheers at
a funeral

P

Paced

Paced like a dog on a chain
(Dudly Pope)
Paced back and forth like a new father

Packed

Packed like cigars in a box
Packed like puppies in a pregnant
poodle
Packed like salt cod in a barrel
(Tom Wicker)

Painful

Painful as a slap in the belly with a
wet fish
Painful as being kicked in your
stomach by a horse
Painful as stepping on a rake

Painless

Painless as floating on a cloud
Painless as a walk in the sun on an
autumn day

Pale

Pale as alabaster
Pale as dough
Pale as milk
Pale as paper (Cecelia Holland)
Pale as white wine (Kenelm Digby)

Panted

Panted like a climber
(Elizabeth B Browning)
Panted like a dog show in mid-July
(TC Boyle)
Panted like a spent dog

Parted

Parted like stone from a sling
(Charles Reade)
Parted like Moses parted the Red Sea

Number crunchers:

duodecillion = 1000 undecillion (US)

Passed

Passed like a dream
Passed like summer rain (Tom Wicker)
Passed swiftly like a dream
(Margaret Mitchell)

Passionate

Passionate as two minks in a sugar sack
Passionate as young love
About as passionate as shredded wheat

Passive

Passive as a cat
Passive as a monument

Pathetic

Pathetic as an autumn leaf
(George Moore)
Pathetic as an octogenarian messenger boy (Oscar Wilde)

Patient

Patient as a gentle stream
(William Shakespeare)
Patient as a spider weaving a broken web (Edward Bulwer-Lytton)
Patient as Job
Patient as the female dove
(William Shakespeare)

Peaceful

Peaceful as a closed shopping centre
(Robert Bausch)
Peaceful as old age (William M Raine)
Peaceful as Socrates

Penis

Penis as hard as a rock
Penis stiff as a lightening rod
Penis stood up like a tree
Penis as small as a shitake mushroom

Permanent

Permanent as marble (Bayard Taylor)
About as permanent as a pile of raked leaves (PF Kluge)

Persistent

Persistent as a mosquito
Persistent as an itch

Personal

Personal as a fingerprint
Personal as an autograph

Picked off

Picked off like ducks in a pond
Picked off like hunted coyotes
(William M Raine)

Piled

Piled like sacks of wheat in a granary
(Henry W Longfellow)
Piled up like fish on a slab
(George MacDonald Fraser)

Pink

Pink as a baby's bottom
Pink as coral (Doris Leslie)
Pink and tender as an unhealed scar
(Howard Jacobson)

Pious

Pious as a pope (Thomas Hood)
Pious as Deuteronomy recited backward

Pissed

Pissed as a fart
Pissed as a newt
Pissed as a rabbi on Purim

Pitiful

Pitiful as a dying duck in a thunderstorm
Pitiful as a crippled child standing in the rain

Oxymorons:

Pitiless
Pitiless as the grave (Gerarld Massey)

Placid
Placid as a duck pond
Placid as a mill pond
Placid as Socrates

Plain
Plain as a hat rack
Plain as a pool table
Plain as day
Plain as the sun in heaven
(Thomas B Macauley)
Plain as two and two make four

Played
Played like a kid
Played him like a poker hand from a stacked deck

Playful
Playful as a puppy
Playful as a rabbit (George P Morris)

Pleasant
Pleasant as good health
Pleasant as pie

Pleased
Pleased as a child (Harold Bell Wright)
Pleased as a hound with a dish of raw innards (Owen Ulph)
Pleased as punch

Plentiful
Plentiful as fleas on a dog
Plentiful as washing on a Monday morning line (Howard Spring)

Plump
Plump as a melon (Steven Callahan)
Plump as a pigeon (BQ Morgan)

Pointless
Pointless as a rubber ball
Pointless as scratching a wooden leg

Poised
Poised like a dancer (Mary Stewart)
Poised like a hummingbird hanging in air (FWH Myers)

Polished
Polished like a prize horse
(Stephen Longstreet)
Polished like a witch doctor's skull

Poor
Poor as a field mouse
Poor as a rat
Poor as gar broth
Poor as Lazarus

Popped
Popped like chestnuts in a fire
Popped like corn

Popped up
Popped up like mushrooms
Popped up like wildflowers
Popped like a toaster

Popular
Popular as a fire hydrant at a dog show
About as popular as pork in a synagogue

Populous
Populous as an anthill (Victor Hugo)
Populous as Hong Kong

Potent
Potent as a kick in the head (TC Boyle)
Potent as oblivion
(Stephen R Donaldson)

Printing landmarks:

1477 – the first book printed in England, *The Dictes, or Sayengis of the Philosophers*, was published.

Poured
Poured like hourglass sand
Poured like a fountain

Pouted
Pouted like a disappointed child
(Charlotte Bronte)
Pouted like a kicked pup (Ivan Doig)

Powerless
Powerless as an infant
Powerless as thistledown in a summer
storm (Doris Leslie)

Practical
Practical as a pocket on a shirt
Practical as a safety pin
Practical as taking your cat to obedi-
ence classes (Shelby Friedman)

Pranced
Pranced like a pair of cannibals about
to eat a victim (Honore de Balzac)
Pranced like a horse

Prated
Prated like a parrot
Prated like old women at a bridge
party

Prayed
Prayed like an angel afire
(Edward Eggleston)
Prayed like clockwork

Precise
Precise as guardsmen
(George MacDonald Fraser)
Precise as mathematics

Predictable
Predictable as a horse going back to its
barn (Richard Bachman)
Predictable as the sun will rise

Preened
Preened like a peacock
Preened like a teenager before his first
prom

Prepared
Prepared as a Boy Scout
Prepared as the United States Marines

Pretty
Pretty as a Georgia peach
Pretty as a little red wagon
Pretty as a picture (Mark Twain)
Pretty as a spotted horse in a daisy
pasture
About as pretty as a gargoyle
About as pretty as road kill

Prim
Prim as a peeled pine pole
Prim as an old maid substitute teacher

Privacy
About as much privacy as a statue
in a park
About as much privacy as Grand
Central Station

Profane
Profane as a drunken sailor
Profane as a teamster (Tom Wicker)

Profile
Profile like the blade of a knife; cold
and sharp (Honore de Balzac)
Profile like the edge of a key
(Dave Martin)

Protective
Protective as a hen with one chick
Protective as a smoke detector

Brand origins:

Proud

Proud as a cock on his own dunghill
(Turkish proverb)
Proud as a government mule
Proud as a lizard with two tails
Proud as Lucifer
Proud as Punch
Proud as a Jewish grandmother

Puffed

Puffed like a blacksmith's chimney
(George Garrett)
Puffed out like canvas in a sail
Puffed up like a toad-frog (Tom Wicker)

Punctual

Punctual as a cuckoo in a Swiss clock
(Edith Wharton)
Punctual as a tax collector
(Punch 1862)

Pure

Pure as a lily
Pure as heaven's snowflake
Pure as Ivory soap
Pure as the driven snow

Puzzled

Puzzled like man who's lost his glasses
Puzzled like a roach trying to crawl
downstairs on an escalator
(Arthur Baer)

Q

Quaked

Quaked like California
Quaked like mice when the cat is mentioned (Honore de Balzac)

Queer

Queer as a bug (Elvis Presley and Otis
Blackwell, 'All Shook Up')
Queer as soap in the officers' Mess

Quick

Quick as a cat
Quick as a flash
Quick as a mad cat
Quick as a panther (Zane Grey)
Quick as an arrow
Quick as you can bat your eye
Quick as a pig's whistle
Quick and wise as a goat
(George Garrett)

Quiet

Quiet as a cemetery (Peter Jenkins)
Quiet as a graveyard (Thomas Hardy)
Quiet as a mouse (Arsene Houssaye)
Quiet as the lighting of a fly on a feath-
er duster
About as quiet as two kittens

Quit

Quit like a sick cat (William M Raine)
Quit like an old car

Quivered

Quivered like a hunted beast
Quivered like a virgin's fan
(George MacDonald Fraser)
Quivered like jelly

R

Radiant

Radiant as a summer sun in morn
(James Whitcomb Riley)
Radiant as hope
(Stephen R Donaldson)

Rained

Rained like a cow pissing on a flat rock
Rained like bath time on Noah's ark
(Ivan Doig)

Loquacious language:

cumber-ground – a person who needlessly uses space

Raised hell

Raised hell like a weasel in a henhouse
(Ferroll Sams)

Ran

Ran as swift as a pudding would creep

Ran lightly as an Indian
(Margaret Mitchell)

Ran like a rabbit

Ran like hell

Ran like the village fire brigade
(George MacDonald Fraser)

Ran like the wind

Ran around like a lower primate with an itch in his testicles (TC Boyle)

Ran around and around like a weasel in a blender

Ran (operated)

Ran like fine Swiss watch

Ran like a Rolls

Ran like a sewing machine

Randy

Randy as a mink

Randy as a ferret

Randy as a dog on heat

Rare

Rare as a cat with wings

Rare as a flying pig

Rare as a unicorn (James Goldman)

Rare as Halley's comet

Rare as Sahara rain

Rare as walking on water

Rattled

Rattled like a loose bone in a goose's hind end

Rattled like the milkman

Rattled on like an amateur shrink
(Owen Ulph)

Raucous

Raucous as a Saturday night rodeo
(Robert R McCammon)

Raucous as a stag show

Read him

Read him like a book

Read his mind like an old tale he had learned by heart (George Garreett)

Readily

Readily as child takes sweetmeats at Mardi Gras (Ouida)

Readily as he would swat a fly
(George MacDonald Fraser)

Ready

Ready as a Boy scout

Ready as a primed cannon
(Thomas Carlyle)

Real

Real as death

Real as hunger

Rear end

Read end as wide as a bank president's desk (Stephen King)

Rear end like jelly on springs
(Michael Carreck)

Reassuring

Reassuring as a sheltering wing over a motherless bird (Louisa May Alcott)

About as reassuring as dentist with an instruction manual

Red

Red as a fire engine

Red as a radish

Red as a stop sign

Red as a vixen

Read as pure heart's blood
(Stephen R Donaldson)

Metaphors:

No man is an island entire of itself. John Donne, 'Devotions

Refreshing

Refreshing as a drink of cold water to a fever patient (Edward Eggleston)

Refreshing as an April shower

Regular

Regular as an almanac (Stephen King)

Regular as meals (Clyde Edgerton)

Regular as the tolling of a bell

Relaxed

Relaxed as an empty glove
(Bonne May Malody)

Relentless

Relentless as decay
(Joseph Wambaugh)

Relentless as fear (Rosemary H Jarman)

Reliable

Reliable as the swallows returning to Capistrano

About as reliable as a Pravda edition
(Joseph Wambaugh)

Reluctant

Reluctant as a child forced to dance for spinster aunts

Reluctant as the steps of a bridge to the altar (Donald G Mitchell)

Remote

Remote as time before birth
(CL Skelton)

Remote as the stars (Charles L Moore)

Resolute

Resolute as a drunken Irishman

Resolute as thunder (John Ford)

Responded

Responded like Pavlov's dog

Responded like soldiers to a trumpet's call to arms (William Pearson)

Rested

Rested like God on Sunday
(Patrick McGinley)

Rested peacefully as a night nurse on duty

Restless

Restless as a dog whose master is absent (Alexandre Dumas)

Restless as a gypsy

Restless as cattle in a pen

Restless as underfed lions in zoo cages
(Stephen King)

Returned

Returned like MacArthur

Returned like swallows to Capistrano

Rich

Rich as a lord

Rich as Midas

Rich as the mint

About as rich as a newborn sheep

Right

Right as a ram's horn

Right as rain

Right as the Church of England

Rigid

Rigid as a rock

Rigid as a statue

Rigid as stone

Risky

Risky as skating over thin ice

Risky as waving a red flag at a bull
(Victor Appleton)

Roamed

Roamed like a lost dog (Rikki Ducornet)

Roamed the country like a nomad
(Terry Ganey)

Brand origins:

Birds Eye, 1915 – Legend has it that the name referred to an ancestral court nobleman named Bird's Eye by a queen, after he shot a hawk though the eye with an arrow. Latterly, and more commonly accredited to Bob Birdseye, a New York fur trader who originated the frozen food process.

Roared

Roared like a beast
(Robert R McCammon)

Roared like a demon in torture

Roared like a lion

Roared like surf breaking on rocks

Rocked

Rocked like a ship at sea

Rocked like a mass of jelly that has
been visibly shaken

Rode a horse

Rode a horse like a Polish lancer
(George MacDonald Fraser)

Rode a horse like a sack of flour

Rode a horse like he was racing the
devil to the gates of hell
(Anthony Forrest)

Rolled

Rolled like a dog in a swift river

Rolled over like a tumblebug
(Erskine Caldwell)

Rolled up like a window shade
(Stephen King)

Romantic

About as romantic as a dead toad

About as romantic as the Chicago
stockyards (Will Irwin)

Rose

Rose like a kite (William Cowper)

Rose like an adder's head
(Robert R MacCammon)

Rose like smoke (George Garret)

Rotten

Rotten as a three-day-old dead fish

Rotten as the gills of an old mushroom

Rough

Rough as a badger's arse

Rough as a hedger (Thomas Hardy)

Rough as a rat-catcher's dog
(Norman Felton)

Rough as sandpaper (John Inzer)

Round

Round as a cannonball

Round as a hoop (Francois Rabelais)

Round as a pearl

Round as the globe (John Gay)

Roused

Roused like a huntsman to the chase
(AC Swinburne)

Roused as a bugle (Ouida)

Rude

Rude as a bear (Jonathan Swift)

Rude as rage

Runs

Runs like a Deere (John Deere slogan)

Runs like a Rolls (Rolls Royce slogan)

Rushed

Rushed like a torrid hurricane
(Thomas Hood)

Rushed around like a miniature whirlwind (Frederic S Isham)

Ruthless

Ruthless as Hitler

Ruthless as the sea (Maurice Hewlett)

S

Sacred

Sacred as churchyard turf (Eliza Cook)

Sacred as Hindu gods

Sad

Sad as a subpoena

Sad as night (William Shakespeare)

Sad as the Last Supper

Sad as the wheels of a train
standing still

Number crunchers:

tredecillion = 1000 duodecillion (US)

Safe

Safe as a child on its mother's breast
Safe as a crow in a gutter
Safe as houses
Safe as a mouse in a mill shop
Safe as sleep
Safe as a bank
About as safe as a cow in the stockyards

Sang

Sang like a bird
Sang like a siren (Francoise Voltaire)
Sang like she stepped in a bear trap

Sank

Sank like a rock/stone
Sank like a scuba diver (Sam Koperwas)
Sank like the Bismark/Titanic

Sat

Sat like a bump on a log
Sat like a man on thorns (Mary Stewart)
Sat like a wax dummy (Stephen King)

Satisfied

Satisfied as a breast-fed baby
Satisfied as a five-turd crap before breakfast (William Boyd)

Savage

Savage as a meat axe
Savage as the heart of a tiger chained (Edwin Arnold)

Scarce

Scarce as buttons on a goose (John Macdonald)
Scarce as hen's teeth
Scarce as snake hips
Scarce as white blackbirds

Scared

Scared as a fox caught in a trap (Thomas Thompson)
Scared as a nearsighted cat at a dog pound (Stephen King)
Scared enough to shit nickels (Stephen King)

Scattered

Scattered as a flock (Elizabeth B Browning)
Scattered like confetti (TC Boyle)
Scattered like monkey shit (Dan Jenkins)
Scattered like sheep
Scattered like wildflowers

Scooted

Scooted like a rodent (Charles McCarry)
Scooted like he was scalded (Douglas C Jones)

Screamed

Screamed like a fishwife
Screamed like a pig under a fence
Screamed like a steam whistle
Screamed like a tomcat caught in a hay baler (John Madson)

Screeched

Screeched like a hoot owl
Screeched like a wildcat

Searched

Searched like a bird dog sniffing game (Robert R McCammon)
Searched like a Hoover

Seared

Seared like a brand (JH Newman)
Seared like a hot iron

Oxymorons:

peace force

Secret

Secret as thought (Francis Fawkes)

Secret as Sicilian (Michael Mewshaw)

Secrets are like measles; they take easy and spread easy (Bartlett's)

Secure

Secure as a cradle

Secure as a mouse in China
(William Cowper)

Secure as the grave

Secure and surly as traffic court judge
(Stephen Kanfer)

Seedy

Seedy as pomegranate

Seedy as tangerine

Seedy as a Whitehouse restroom

Self-important

Self-important as a man with two car phones (J Richards)

Self-important as the German General of Staff (PF Kluge)

Selfish

Selfish as a hungry dog

Selfish as a spoiled child

Sensitive

Sensitive as a flower

Sensitive as a toilet seat

Separate

Separate them one from another as a shepherd divideth his sheep from the goats (New Testament)

Separate like oil from water
(Rex Beach)

Serene

Serene as a hermit (Ivan Doig)

Serene as waterfall

Serene as the dawn (Victor Hugo)

Serious

Serious as a philosopher
(Miles P Andrews)

Serious as a stroke

Serious as cancer

Serious as the fifth act of a tragedy
(Joseph Jefferson)

Serious as the Ten Commandments
(WB Yeats)

Sexy

About as sexy as Aunt Minnie's wallpaper

About as sexy as socks on a rooster

Sexless as an anaemic nun
(Sinclair Lewis)

Shallow

Shallow as pie pan

Shallow as teenage dreams

Shameless

Shameless as a nude statue
(Sydney Munden)

Shameless as a pregnant whore

Shapeless

Shapeless as a busted sofa

Shapeless as an old shoe

Sharp

Sharp as a pin

Sharp as a tiger's tooth

Sharp as filed steel
(William Shakespeare)

Sharp as mustard (Ogden Nash)

Sharp as the fangs of a rattler

Sharp as truth (Victor Hugo)

About as sharp as marble

Shattered

Shattered like wave against a rock
(Shelby Foote)

Shattered as an earthquake

Writing landmarks:

1943 – Biró patented the first practical ballpoint pen and sold the rights to Henry Martin in England.

371

Shifty
Shifty as a shithouse rat
Shifty as the sand

Shined
Shined like a new penny
Shined like burnished metal
Shined like spit on the sidewalk
(Gerald Duff)
Shined like the sun

Shivered
Shivered like an aspen leaf
(James Smith)
Shivered with fear like a thin dog in the
cold (Stephen Vincent Benet)

Shook
Shook like a dry palm in a high wind
Shook like a wet dishrag
Shook like the feeder on a thrashing
machine (Gene Stratton-Porter)
Shook her head like a dog coming out
of the water (Marge Piercy)

Shorn
Shorn as sheep
Shorn like a new marine

Short
Short as knee high to a duck
Short as the life of a wave
(Leonid Andreyev)
Short and sweet like an old woman's
dance (Abraham Lincoln)

Shot
Shot like a dog (Alfred Noyes)
Shot like a yellow dog
Shot out like a piston rod
(Richard Harding Davis)

Shrank
Shrank like a leaf in the fall
(Eugene Field)

Shrank like a puddle in the sun
(Cecelia Holland)
Shrank like a rabbit before a snake
(Rex Beach)

Shrewd
Shrewd as a goat (George Garrett)
Shrewd as a moneylender

Shrieked
Shrieked like a screech owl
(Patrick Smith)
Shrieked like a viola gone sour
(TC Boyle)
Shrieked like trapped birds

Shrivelled up
Shrivelled up like a worm on a hot
stove (HL Mencken)
Shrivelled up like the tongue of a
hanged man (Tom McEwen)

Shrunk
Shrunk like a naval (Rosemary H Jarman)
Shrunk like a walnut

Shuddered
Shuddered like a mule in fly time
(Ferrol Sams)
Shuddered like that of the deer when
he sees the hounds again upon his
track (Victor Hugo)

Shunned
Shunned as a mole shuns light
(O Henry)
Shunned like a viper (Matthew Carey)
Shunned like the plague
(Robert Brownwell)

Shy
Shy as a fawn (Ambrose Phillips)
Shy as a sheep
Shy as a squirrel (George Meredith)

Loquacious language:

dactylonomy – the science of counting on your fingers

Sick

Sick as a dog on grass
Sick as three dogs (Mark Childress)

Sighed

Sighed like a death rattle (Jack Fuller)
Sighed like zephyr (Mark Twain)

Silent

Silent as a catacomb
Silent as a corpse (Percy B Shelly)
Silent as a dream (Evan S Connell)
Silent as a mole
Silent as a stone
Silent as the sphinx
Silent as thieves
About as silent as schoolboys

Silly

Silly as a tipsy widow
(George MacDonald Fraser)
Silly as the pot calling the kettle black

Similar

Similar as two eggs
(William Shakespeare)
Similar as two peas in a pod

Similes

Similes are like songs of love / they much describe / they nothing prove.
(Matthew Prior)
Similes in each dull line, like glow-worms in the dark should shine.

Simple

Simple as a kiss under the mistletoe
Simple as a schoolboy's logic
Simple as earth

Sizzled

Sizzled like side meat (Tom Wicker)
Sizzled like strips of bacon

Skin

Skin as white and smooth as wax
(Lawrence Sanders)
Skin like silk (Arabian Nights)
Skin the colour of ripe grapefruit
(TC Boyle)

Skinny

Skinny as a greyhound
Skinny as a snake
Skinny as a worm

Skittered

Skittered like a water bug
(Douglas C Jones)
Skittered like bugs on the water
(Lee Smith)

Skulked

Skulked like a coyote
(Douglas C Jones)
Skulked like a shivering dog
(AC Swinburne)

Sky

Sky as clear as blue grass (Doris Leslie)
Sky pressed own like a weight
(TC Boyle)

Sleek

Sleek as a jet fighter plane
Sleek as a sports car
Sleek as an eel
Sleek and smug as a full-bellied shark
(TC Boyle)

Slender

Slender as a knife (Rosemary H Jarman)
Slender as reed

Slept

Slept like a baby
Slept like a dog
Slept like a drugged princess
(TC Boyle)

Writers' words:

'I take the view, and always have, that if you cannot say what you are going to say in twenty minutes you ought to go away and write a book about it.' Lord Brabazon

373

Slept like a log of wood
(Robert Louis Stevenson)
Slept like a night watchman
Slept like a top (John Gay)
Slept like wood, hollowed and fallen
over (Michael Doanne)

Slick
Slick as a greased pig
Slick as a snake
Slick as glass
Slick as goose grease (Ferrol Sams)
Slick as spit on a gold tooth
Slick as whale shit in an ice flow

Slimy
Slimy as a snail (Tabitha King)
Slimy as an eel

Slipped
Slipped away like steam from a kettle
(Keith Korman)
Slipped out of his grasp like a trout
(Charles McCarry)

Slippery
Slippery as a greased pig
Slippery as an eel dipped in lard
Slipper as ice (Theodore Watts-Dunton)

Slithered
Slithered like a rattler
(George MacDonald Fraser)
Slithered like a snake

Slow
Slow as a man in debt
(Elizabeth B Browning)
Slow as a river eroding rock
(Stephen King)
Slow as a postal worker on Valium
Slow as a snail with rheumatism
Slow as a swamp turtle
Slow as the days between Christmas
and the New Year (Robert Houston)

Slow as judgement (Robert Houston)
Slow as the last drops squeezed from a
lemon (Patrick McGinley)
Slow as the wrath as Christ (Ivan Doig)

Slurped
Slurped like an old man eating
chowder (Stephen King)
Slurped like grandpa sipping coffee
from a saucer

Sly
Sly as a fox
Sly as a submarine

Small
Small as a flea bite
Small as street sparrows

Smart
Smart as a cricket (Shelby Foote)
Smart as a steel trap
Smart as a whistle
Smart as forty crickets

Smelled
Smelled like a Chinese privy
(Stephen Longstreet)
Smelled like a dead camel
(George MacDonald Fraser)
Smelled like a French whore
Smelled like a rose
Smelled like Finnegan's goat
Smelled like something dead a week
(Lee Smith)
Smelled like old socks of a thousand
putrefied mummies (Tom McEwen)

Smile
Smile as sweet as flowers
(AC Swinburne)
Smile as wide and toothy as a death's-
head (Ferrol Sams)
Smile like a happy crocodile
Smile like a politician (Tom DeHaven)

Oxymorons:

religious tolerance

Smile like a skull
Smiled like the face of Buddha
(Lafcadio Hearn)

Smoked

Smoked like a furnace
(Erskine Caldwell)

Smoked like a kiln
(Robert Louis Stevenson)

Smoked like an Irish hut
(James Howell)

Smooth

Smooth like a dancer
Smooth as a poker table
Smooth as a spoon
Smooth as calm water
(Douglas C Jones)

Smooth as ice (Thomas Heywood)
Smooth as ivory (Jeffery Farnol)
Smooth as suede
Smooth as the palm of one's hand
Smooth and shiny as the face of a
spade (William Dieter)

Snapped

Snapped at it like a trout at a fly (George
MacDonald Fraser)

Snapped like a fiddle string
Snapped like a stick

Sneaked

Sneaked like a cat burglar
Sneaky as a snake in the grass
(MM Kaye)

Sneaky as an egg-sucking dog

Snored

Snored like a horse
Snored like a walrus
Snored like the rattle of autumn leaves
(Lee Smith)

Snorted

Snorted like a bull in heat
Snorted like an asthmatic horse
(William Pearson)

Snug

Snug as duck in a ditch
Snug as figures in a glass paperweight

Sober

Sober as a church
Sober as a coroner inspecting a corpse
(Amelie Rives)

Sober as a hangman (George Garrett)
Sober as a judge
Sober as a priest (Rosemary H Jarman)
Sober as an ice cream soda on a New
Year's Eve

Soft

Soft as a featherbed (TC Boyle)
Soft as a grape (Joan Samson)
Soft as baby clothes (Lee Smith)
Soft as dove's down
(William Shakespeare)

Soft as peach fuzz
Soft as Pillsbury Dough
Soft as pity (George D Sofatey)
Soft as pudding
Soft as the dawn (Samuel Lover)
Soft as young down
(William Shakespeare)

Sold

Sold like hotcakes
Sold like ice boxes in Alaska

Solemn

Solemn as a judge
Solemn as a soldier going to the front
(Norman Mailer)

Solemn as an owl

Number crunchers:

quattuordecillion = 1000 tredecillion (US)

Solemn as organ music
Solemn as the swearing in of an inspector of weights and measures

Solid

Solid as a gravestone
Solid as a sod house
(Alfred Henry Lewis)
Solid as a tank
Solid as a totem pole (Noel Behn)
Solemn as brass
Solid and squat as a Mayan temple
(Ferrol Sams)

Solitary

Solitary as a hermitage (CL Skelton)
Solitary as a tomb (Victor Hugo)

Soothing

Soothing as a massage
Soothing as a virgin's kiss
Soothing as a warm bath

Sore

Sore as a crab
Sore as a porcupine with ingrown quills (Arthur Baer)
Sore as a wet nurse's nipple

Sought after

Sought after like Bonnie and Clyde
Sought after like Jesse James
As Sought after as Bin Laden

Sounded

Sounded like a butter knife in a garbage disposal (H Allen Smith)
Sounded like a distressed cat
Sounded like a wet cloth slapped on stone (George MacDonald Fraser)

Sour

Sour as a pickle
Sour as rotten orange (John McCarthy)

Sparkled

Sparkled like a diamond
Sparkled like the morning dew

Sped

Sped like a house afire
Sped like a shot
Sped like greased lightening

Speechless

Speechless as a mummy
Speechless as a stone
(Elizabeth B Browning)

Speedy

About as speedy as a snail
About as speedy as a steamroller
(George Ade)

Spent money

Spent money like a drunken duke on his birthday
Spent money like it had been left to him (Rex Beach)
Spent money like pouring it down a rat hole (Margaret Mitchell)
Spent money like throwing it out the window (Thomas Hardy)

Spineless

Spineless as a chocolate éclair
Spineless as a jelly fish

Spit

Spit like a tobacco chewer
Spit like an angry cat
(Margaret Mitchell)

Spiteful

Spiteful as a monkey
(Honore de Balzac)
Spiteful as a middle aged housewife

Printing landmarks:

1605 – De Nieuwe, a bi-monthly, was published as the first newspaper in French and German.

Spoke

Spoke like a church elder to the town drunk

Spoke like a father to a hurt child (Margaret Mitchell)

Spotted

Spotted like a leopard

Spotted like a pair of dice

Sprang

Sprang like a switchblade

Sprang like Russian tumblers (TC Boyle)

Sprang upon like a tiger upon a lamb

Sprawled

Sprawled like a disregarded rag doll (Douglas C Jones)

Sprawled like a rolled drunk

Spread

Spread like a grassfire whipped by wind

Spread like cancer

Spread like fire broom sedge (Erskine Caldwell)

Spread like measles in a country school

Spread like wildfire

Sprouted

Sprouted like dandelions

Sprouted like weeds on a cow pie

Sprung up

Sprung up like Jack's beanstalk (Thomas Hardy)

Sprung up like wildflowers

Spry

Spry as a cricket

Spry as a goat (Mary Stewart)

Spry as an old yellow tomcat

Square

Square as a brick (F Hopkinson Smith)

Square as a chimney

Square as a die (Rex Beach)

Squeaked

Squeaked like a startled mouse (George MacDonald Fras)

Squeaked like a village of tree toads (Mary Stewart)

Squealed

Squealed like a drunken fishwife (Rex Beach)

Squealed like a sow farrowing a litter of broken glass (John Madson)

Squealed like a stuck pig

Squeezed

Squeezed like an orange

Squeezed like an accordion

Squirmed

Squirmed like a dog with fleas in its ass

Squirmed like a schoolboy undergoing maternal inspection

Stable

Stable as earth (Thomas Blackblock)

Stable as the hills (Lewis H Green)

Stacked

Stacked like a truckload of melons (Owen Ulph)

Stacked like canned goods in a super-market

Staggered

Staggered like child learning to walk

Staggered like a drunken man (Old Testament)

Stale

Stale as old beer

Stale as the butt of a dead cigar (Rudyard Kipling)

Oxymorons:

Stalked

Stalked like a heron
(H Jarman)
Stalked like a hunter

Stank

Stank like a city sewer (Jack Matthews)
Stank like a dead skunk in the road
Stank like a wet dog

Stared

Stared like a glass eye
Stared like a mad bull
Stared like an idiot
Stared like one dazed

Stately

Stately as a queen
(William M Thackeray)
Stately as a Victorian mansion

Steadfast

Steadfast as a sentry
Steadfast as the sun (Thomas Carlyle)

Steady

Steady as a clock
Steady as a rock
Steady as an old plough horse
Steady as an undertaker
(F Hopkinson Smith)
Steady and reliable as tested steel

Stern

Stern as a nun (Tom DeHaven)
Stern as stone (JRR Tolkien)

Sticky

Sticky as cockleburs
Sticky as fly paper

Stiff

Stiff as a dead body
(Jonathan Dickinson)

Stiff as a frozen statue
Stiff as a ramrod (Charles J Lever)
Stiff as a wax dummy
Stiff as frozen leather
(Bernard Cornwell)
Stiff as wood
Stiff as a dead gigalo

Still

Still as a monument
Still as a portrait
Still as a sunning crocodile
Still as lake water (Mary Stewart)
Still as the moment before creation
(Anita Mason)

Stirred up

Stirred up like a stepped-on anthill
(George Garrett)
Stirred up like the top of a drum (James Whitcomb Riles)

Stood

Stood as still as the angel of death
(Lee Smith)
Stood as straight and firm as a stone wall (Tom Wicker)
Stood like a lump
Stood like a watchful hawk

Stood out

Stood out like a snake in a bathtub
Stood out like matzo balls in chicken soup
Stood out like a salesman in a white suit (Ivan Doig)
Stood out like a sore thumb
Stood out like an unzipped fly

Stout

Stout as a mule
Stout as an oak (Peter Jenkins)

Loquacious language:

erotology – the 'science' of love

Straight

Straight as a beggar can spit
(Rudyard Kipling)
Straight as a die
Straight as a plank (F Hopkinson Smith)
Straight as a sapling (Doris Leslie)
Straight as a solider
Straight as a young tree
(Howard Spring)
Straight as the backbone of a herring
Straight as virtue (John Crosby)

Strange

Strange as a one-legged dance
(John Ehle)
Strange as a wedding without a bridegroom
Strange as snow in July

Stricken

Stricken like a child approached by a mean dog
Stricken like a rabbit confronted by a fox

Strong

Strong as Flanders mare
Strong as a horse
Strong as an ox
Strong as battery acid
Strong and solid as the biceps of Hercules (Robert R McCammon)

Struggled

Struggled like a fish on a line
Struggled like a flower toward heaven

Strutted

Strutted like a peacock
Strutted like a thespian

Stubborn

Stubborn as a mule
Stubborn as a stuck door

Stuck

Stuck like burr
Stuck like a fly in molasses
Stuck like a leech (RD Blackmore)
Stuck like a wet shirt
Stuck like glue
Stuck together like an Italian family

Stuck out

Stuck out like a sore thumb
Stuck out like a Thanksgiving turkey

Stuffed

Stuffed like a Christmas goose
(Anthony Forrest)
Stuffed like a roasting chicken

Stumbled

Stumbled around like a blind dog in a meat market
Stumbled around like a sleepwalker in a strange town (Jack Matthews)

Stung

Stung like a gall nipper
Stung like a scorpion
Stung like bees unhived
(Robert Browning)

Stunned

Stunned as if a good boxer had just caught him with a startling left hook and a stultifying right (Norman Mailer)
Stunned like a knocked-down boxer in the first round

Stupid

Stupid as a post (Clement Robinson)
Stupid as an excuse

Sturdy

Sturdy as an oak

Writers' words:

'All human beings have an innate need to hear and tell stories and to have a story to live by ... religion, whatever else it has done, has provided one of the main ways of meeting this abiding need.' Harvey Cox

Sure

Sure as eggs are eggs
Sure as preaching
Sure as the rising of the morning sun
Sure as the thorns in the beds of hell
(Owen Ulph)
Sure as you're alive
Sure as water will wet us, as surely as
fire will burn (Rudyard Kipling)

Surefooted

Surefooted as a goat (Ouida)
Surefooted as a Grand Canyon donkey

Surly

Surly as a butcher's dog
Surly as the night clerk at cheap hotel

Surprised

Surprised as a pregnant nun
Surprised as Dewey

Suspicious

Suspicious as a hairpin in a
bachelor's bed
Suspicious as a virgin nun
(Gerald Seymour)

Swaggered and strutted

Swaggered and strutted like a crow in
the gutter (George Garrett)
Swaggered and strutted like a peacock

Swam

Swam like an otter
Swam about like a stone
(Robert Louis Stevenson)

Swarmed

Swarmed like ants
Swarmed like bees (Lewis W Green)
Swarmed like Comanche's around a
wagon train (Robert R McCammon)
Swarmed like hornets

Swayed

Swayed like charmed cobra
(Jim Dodge)
Swayed like a snake about to strike
(TC Boyle)
Swayed like dancers (Wilbur Smith)

Sweated

Sweated like a horny sailor
(Derek Robinson)
Sweated like a pig (Stephen King)
Sweated like a trooper

Sweet

Sweet as a candy-dipper's handshake
Sweet as a church alto
(Thomas Thompson)
Sweet like a sugarplum
Sweet as first love
(Gerald Massey)
Sweet as the roses of May
Sweet as the sound of a bell
(Zane Grey)

Swelled up

Swelled up like a melon
Swelled up like a summer sausage
(Stephen King)
Swelled up like a turkey gobbler
Swelled up like the bosom of a man
set fire (William Wordsworth)

Swept

Swept like wildfire
Swept along like flecks of foam on a
river (Shelby Foote)
Swept the country like a plague
Swept up like roaches

Swift

Swift as a flash (Henry W Longfellow)
Swift as a thunderbolt
(Richard Lovelace)
Swift as an arrow (William Blake)
Swift as quicksilver (William Cowper)

Brand origins:

Abbey National, 1944 – merger between the Abbey Road building society (established 1894) and
the National Building Society.

Swore

Swore like a costermonger
Swore like a drunken tinker
(George Garrett)
Swore like a fish woman (Mark Twain)
Swore like a lord (T. Elyot)
Swore like a sailor
Swore like an imp (Victor Hugo)

Swung

Swung like a hanged man
Swung like a pendulum

Symmetrical

Symmetrical as a picture frame
Symmetrical as the handles on a vase
(John Updike)

T

Tacky

Tacky as poor manners
Tacky as turkey turds (Paul Hemphill)

Tactful

Tactful as a matured politician
Tactful as an ambassador

Talked

Talked like a soda-water bottle just uncorked (ASM Hutchinson)
Talked like he was vaccinated with a phonograph needle
Talked like an old man with a hernia
(George MacDonald Fraser)

Tall

Tall as a maypole
Tall as a steeple
Tall as nine axe handles
Tall and burly as a black oak
(Robert R McCammon)

Tantalizing

Tantalizing as a half-remembered tune
Tantalizing as the last piece of pie

Tapered

Tapered like a lizard's tail
(Oliver Wendell Holmes)
Tapered like an icicle

Tart

Tart as a sour pickle
Tart as a taste of juniper (TC Boyle)

Tasted

Tasted like a Summo wrestler's jock strap
Tasted like a wet dog
Tasted like dinosaur vomit
Tasted like panther piss
Tasted like the floor of a bird cage
Tasted like vulture spit (H Allen Smith)
Tasted like boiled piss

Tattered

Tattered as magazines in a dentist's office (Stephen King)
Tattered like an old quilt much used

Taunted

Taunted him like a bated badger
(Rex Beach)
Taunted him like his past

Taut

Taut as a fiddle
(Robert Louis Stevenson)
Taut as a guy wire
Taut as new-strung barbed wire
(Ferrol Sams)

Tedious

Tedious as a twice-told tale (Homer)
Tedious as eating a pomegranate

In other words:

sago – a word used to start a race

Temper
Temper as mild as milk (Thomas Hardy)
Temper like a firecracker
Temper like a wild dog's
(George MacDonald Fraser)

Temporary
Temporary as a sunset
Temporary as a wave
Temporary as a politician's promise

Tempting
Tempting as a box of chocolates
Tempting as Eve without a fig leaf

Tenacious
Tenacious as a recurring dream
Tenacious as a terrier (Vincent Bugliosi.)

Tender
Tender as a chick (John Gay)
Tender as a mother's heart
(Rick Roethler)

Tense
Tense as a cat (Clare Francis)
Tense as an 'E' string
(George MacDonald Fraser)
Tense as rigor mortis (Tom Wicker)

Terrible
Terrible as death
Terrible as the curse of a dead
man's eye

Thick (close-together)
Thick as peas in a pod
Thick as Egypt's locusts (John Dryden)
Thick as fleas on a yard dog
(Tom Wicker)
Thick as fog
Thick as huckleberries
Thick as mud

Thick as your aunt Nellie's gravy
(Peter DeVris)

Thick (dimension)
Thick as my arm
(George MacDonald Fraser)
Thick as your thigh

Thick (friendly)
Thick as thieves in bed
Thick as two peas in a pod
Thick as two pirates

Thick (stupid)
Thick as two short planks

Thin
Thin as a crane (Anita Mason)
Thin as a husband's alibi
Thin as a motel wall
Thin as a pencil
Thin as a shadow
Thin as a wafer
Thin as poorhouse gruel
Thin as Twiggy
Thin as boarding house soup
(Jack Buck)

Thirsty
Thirsty as a cross-country runner
Thirsty as a dry road (Cyril Harcourt)
Thirsty as a goat (Phoebe Gray)

Thorny
Thorny as a cactus
Thorny as a honey-locust
(Edward Eggleston)

Threatening
Threatening as a lawsuit
Threatening as legal jargon
Threatening as the flu

Oxymorons:

clearly missunderstood

Threw down

Threw down like candy bar wrapper

Threw down like a rag doll

Threw down like yesterday's newspaper

Thrived

Thrived like dandelions

Thrived like weeds (Andrew Mavell)

Throbbed

Throbbed like a swollen gum with an abscess in it (Stephen King)

Throbbed like an ancient refrigerator (Derek Robinson)

Throbbed like Robinson Crusoe's penis

Thud

Thud like a drunk on stairs (Tom DeHaven)

Thud like a drunk who fell off his bar stool

Thunder

Thunder like the devil bowling

Thunder like beer barrels tumbling down stairs (Ivan Doig)

Tidy

Tidy as an old maid's parlour

Tidy as spats on a rooster (Ivan Doig)

Tight

Tight as a bull's ass in fly time

Tight as a lid of a honey jar

Tight as a rat's ass

Tight as a size nine shoe on a size twelve foot

Tight as an eight day clock

Tight as lockjaw (Tom Wicker)

Tight as the bark on a tree

Tight as the skin on a sausage

Timid

Timid as a child deserted by its nurse

Timid as a doe (Robert Noel)

Timid as a sheep (Ouida)

Timid as an abused dog

Tired

Tired as a dog (Gene Stratton-Porter)

Tired as a tombstone (Robert Browning)

To and fro

To and fro like a Ping-Pong ball

To and fro like shuttlecocks

Tongue

Tongue like a filet of raw salmon (Owen Ulph)

Tongue tasted like a skid mark

Took it

Took it like Grant took Richmond

Took it like Sherman took Atlanta

Took off

Took off like a flock of vultures flushed from a kill (TC Boyle)

Took off like a three-year old at the start of a steeplechase (TC Boyle)

Took to it

Took to it like a duck to water

Took to it like a fox takes to chickens (Jack Matthews)

Took to it like a retriever to ducks (Ouida)

Toppled

Toppled like a lightning-struck pine (Gerald Duff)

Toppled like tenpins (Sidney Sheldon)

Tossed

Tossed like salad

Tossed around like a feather in a whirlwind

Tossed around like popcorn in a popper (Margaret Mitchell)

Loquacious language:

Touchy

Touchy as a new blister
(Mark Childress)

Touchy as the gout

Tough

Tough as a marine

Tough as an old field hand
(Mark Childress)

Tough as dog breath

Tough as iron

Tough as old boots

Tough as shoe leather

Tranquil

Tranquil as Christmas Eve

Tranquil as night

About as tranquil as a Texas cyclone

Transparent

Transparent as cellophane (Caryl Rivers)

Transparent as spring water

Trapped

Trapped like a bear in a trap

Trapped like a rabbit in its burrow
(Loup Durard)

Trapped like flies in a bottle

Trapped like flies on flypaper

Trembled

Trembled like a frightened deer seeking a place of refuge
(Lewis Carroll)

Trembled like a leaf (Victor Appleton)

Trembled like a man with palsy
(JM Barrie)

Trembled like a wet puppy
(James Sherburn)

Trembled like the last leaf of autumn
(Derek Robinson)

Tricky

Tricky as a concierge

Tricky as a magician

Trivial

Trivial as a parrot's prate
(William Cowper)

Trivial as the giggle of a housemaid
(Henry James)

Trotted

Trotted like a docile dog
(Thelma Strabel)

Trotted like a servile footman, all day long

Troublesome

Troublesome as a monkey
(Thomas Shadwell)

Troublesome as a she-bitch with crabs
(Stephen King)

True

True as a shepherd to his flock
(Lord Byron)

True as heaven is true (Robert Service)

True as the gospel (John Gay)

True as the light (Thomas Hardy)

Tucked away

Tucked away like a treasure
(Robert R MacCammon)

Tucked away money like a miser

Tumbled

Tumbled like a stuffed toy
(Stephen King)

Tumbled like bricks from a dump truck
(Derek Robinson)

Tuneless

Tuneless as a canary with strep throat

Tuneless as a guitar with old strings

Brand origins:

Adidas, 1920s – named after Adolf (Adi) Dassler, the company's founder.

Turned

Turned like a windmill sail
(John Greenleaf Whittier)

Turned like an ice skater

Turned down

Turned down like a bedspread

Turned down like a blind ate

Twanged

Twanged like a cheap guitar

Twanged like an ill-tuned fiddle
(Alain Paris)

Twirled

Twirled like a dervish

Twirled like a spinning top

Twirled like a whirligig

Twisted

Twisted like a nest of snakes
(Herman Melville)

Twisted like knotted snakes
(Charles Harpur)

Twisted like Pebble Beach pines

Twitched

Twitched like a landed trout
(Stephen King)

Twitched like a wagonload of old maids at a hayride (Ferrol Sams)

U

Ugly

Ugly as a buffalo's ass

Ugly as a rubber crutch

Ugly as an ape

Ugly as the devil (Henry Fielding)

Unappetising

Unappetising as the heel of a zookeeper's boot

Unappetising as the floor of a parrot's cage

Unblemished

Unblemished as a baby

Unblemished as the white-robed virgin choir (William Shakespeare)

Uncertain

Uncertain as the glory of an April day
(William Shakespeare)

Uncertain as the weather

Uncomfortable

Uncomfortable as a hard-backed oak chair

Uncomfortable as the Garden of Eden during mosquito season

Uneasy

Uneasy as a man at the ladies' bridge club meeting

Uneasy as a pit in a parlour

Unending

Unending as the changes in weather

Unending as the river and the stars
(WE Henley)

Unexpected

Unexpected as a clap of thunder on a clear day (Jack Matthews)

Unexpected as cuss words in a sermon
(Thomas Thompson)

Unexpected as winter thunder

Unhappy

Unhappy as a proctologist who's lost his rubber gloves

Unhappy as King Lear

Medieval words:

barber – from Latin *barba* meaning beard. A barber used a red and white striped vertical pole to announce their services of bloodletting.

Universal

Universal as children playing
Universal as seasickness
(George Bernard Shaw)

Unlikely

Unlikely as a mouse falling in love
with a cat
Unlikely as a pig laying eggs
Unlikely as teaching an alligator
to polka

Unlovely

Unlovely as leprosy
Unlovely as road kill

Unmanageable

Unmanageable as a fool
Unmanageable as an avalanche
(Stephen R Donaldson)

Unmistakable

Unmistakable as an accent
Unmistakable as foreign clothes
(Henry James)

Unpredictable

Unpredictable as a hen in a hurricane
(Ivan Doig)
Unpredictable as a storm at sea
Unpredictable as winter

Unravelled

Unravelled like a ball of yarn
Unravelled like a Singapore suit

Unrestricted

Unrestricted as a tornado
Unrestricted as the rain (Mark Twain)

Unruffled

Unruffled as a great horned owl
perched in a dead tree (Owen Ulph)
Unruffled as time (Edgar Saltas)

Unruly

Unruly as a riot
Unruly as a two-year-old child

Unseasonable

Unseasonable as snow in summer
Unseasonable as watermelons in
January

Unstable

Unstable as propane gas
(Jack Matthews)
Unstable as the waves of the sea
(George Bishop)

Untidy

Untidy as a Bohemian
(Alphonse Daudet)
Untidy like a bird of paradise that had
been out all night in the rain

Unwelcome

Unwelcome as water in a leaking ship
Unwelcome as water in your shoe

Unwieldy

Unwieldy as a sunken ship
Unwieldy as Noah's ark (Shelby Foote)

Unyielding

Unyielding as a rock
Unyielding as steel

Up and down

Up and down like a bucket in a well
Up and down like a drawbridge
Up and down like a yo-yo

Upright

Upright as a marble column
(Cecelia Holland)
Upright as a post
Upright as a stake

Oxymorons:

rap music

Useless

Useless as a broken feather
Useless as a chocolate fire-guard
Useless as a knitted condom
Useless as a lamp without a wick
Useless as a milk bucket under a bull
Useless as a trailer hitch on a Yugo
Useless as a wet gazette
Useless as Ex-lax in a dysentery ward
Useless as gasoline in a fire extinguisher
Useless as shouting down an empty well
Useless as tits on a boar hog
Useless as using a sieve to carry water
Useless as whispering in the ear of a dead corpse

V

Vain

Vain as a girl (William M Thackery)
Vain as an Etonian duke
(George MacDonald Fraser)

Valiant

Valiant as a lion (William Shakespeare)
Valiant as Hercules
(William Shakespeare)

Vanished

Vanished like a burst bubble
Vanished like a pebble in a pond
Vanished like a puff of smoke
(Frederic S Isham)
Vanished like vision (Charlotte Bronte)
Vanished like rats (Doris Leslie)

Vast

Vast as China (Lee Smith)
Vast as the Sahara

Veered

Veered like race cars at Indianapolis
Veered like water bugs (Normal Mailer)

Veined

Veined like a relief map of the moon
(TC Boyle)
Veined like grandma's legs
(Thomas Thompson)

Vibrated

Vibrated like a tuning fork
(Stephen King)
Vibrated like dishes during an earthquake

Vicious

Vicious as a hungry Doberman
Vicious as a pit bull

Virtuous

Virtuous as a reformed whore
(Rosemary H Jarman)
Virtuous as a saved soul

Visible

Visible as the stars
Visible as the sun in Montana

Vital

Vital as air
Vital as an elixir (Stephen R Donaldson)

Vivid

Vivid as a dream (William Wordsworth)
Vivid as a photograph
Vivid as language
(Stephen R Donaldson)

Voiceless

Voiceless as the funeral train (TB Reade)
Voiceless as the sphinx

Vomited

Vomited like a freshman
Vomited like a sailor (Tom DeHaven)

Writers' words:

'The difference between the right word and the almost right word is the difference between lightning and the lightning bug.' Mark Twain

Vulnerable

Vulnerable as a baby seal
(Patrick McGinley)

Vulnerable as a rabbit in the mown
field (Cecelia Holland)

W

Wailed

Wailed like a children's hospital ward
(John Irving)

Wailed like a midnight wind
(Aubrey De Vere)

Waist

Waist like a Vienna guardsman
(F Hopkinson Smith)

Waist like an hourglass

Wakeful

Wakeful as a man with three sparkin'-
age daughters (Louis L'Armour)

Wakeful as a sentry on guard

Walked

Walked like a gunslinger

Walked like a man who knew where he
was going

Walked like a mechanical toy

Walked like he was tiptoeing on eggs
(George MacDonald Fraser)

Walked like she had a feather up
her ass

Walked off like a madam bidding her
guests good night
(William Shakespeare)

Wandered

Wandered like a milkweed puff
(Gary Jennings)

Wandered like an unfettered stream
(Nathaniel Hawthorne)

Warm

Warm as a mouse in cotton

Warm as a wood cook stove

Warm as fresh milk in a pail

Warm as Indian summer

Warm as sunshine
(William Wordsworth)

Warm as wool (John Peele)

Warming

Warming as brandy on a bleak
November afternoon
(Lawrence Sanders)

Warming as a fireplace on a
winter's eve

Wary

Wary as a blind horse (Thomas Fuller)

Wary as a fox

Wary as a young thing that's been
caught (John Ehle)

Washed away

Washed away like duck decoys in a
winter flood

Washed away like makeup on a
widow's face (Thomas Thompson)

Watched

Watched like a hawk-bird
(Lee Smith)

Watched like a terrier at a rat's hole
(Charles Kingsley)

Watched him like a hen with chicks

Watchful

Watchful as a sentinel

Watchful as the eye of a bird

Waved

Waved like a red flag at a bull
(CL Skelton)

Waved like autumn corn
(Sir Walter Scott)

Weak

Weak as a cat

Weak as a drink of water

Writing landmarks:

The Miles-Martin Pen Co. manufactures Britain's first ballpoint pen to be used by the Royal Air Force.

Weak as a kitten
Weak as a moth
Weak as dishwater
Weak as yesterday's dreams
(Donald McCaig)

Weather-beaten
Weather-beaten as a fisherman's oar
(Thomas Wade)
Weather-beaten as an old barn

Welcome
Welcome as a long-awaited guest
(Margaret Mitchell)
Welcome as a raise
Welcome as four aces (Arthur Baer)
Welcome as the flowers of spring
About as welcome as a coal bill in
father's Christmas mail (Frank M O'Malley)
About as welcome as a turd in a
punch bowl
About as welcome as dog shit on a
new pair of shoes

Went
Went like a rat up a drainpipe
Went like goose shit through a tin
horn
Went like the devil
Went like wildfire

Went at it
Went at it like a weasel in a henhouse
(Jim Harrison)
Went at it like he was killing snakes
(Rex Breach)

Went down
Went down like a dead bird
(James Sherburn)
Went down like a shot rabbit
Went down like a sack of shit

Went for it
Went for it like a starving dog
(Phillip Kimball)
Went for it like a steer to salt
(Glendon Swarthout)

Went off
Went off like a firecracker
Went off like a pipe bomb

Went out
Went out like a light
Went out like a pissed-on campfire

Went over
Went over like a million bucks
Went over like a wet firecracker (Richard
Bachman)
Went over like a wet noodle

Went through it
Went through it like a dose of salts
through a widow woman
Went through it like a flash of lighten-
ing through a gooseberry bush
Went through it like a shot
(Mark Twain)
Went through it like the cannonball
express through Schenectady

Went up
Went up like a balloon
Went up like a rocket

Wept
Wept like a crocodile (Robert Burton)
Wept like a girl (Rex Beach)
Wept like a wench who has burned
her grandma (William Shakespeare)

Wet
Wet as a drowned rat
(Thomas Heywood)
Wet as a fish
Wet as Glasgow on Saturday night
(Clare Francis)

Oxymorons:

synthetic wool

Wheezed

Wheezed like an asthmatic adulterer

Wheezed like an old door (John Fuller)

Whimpered

Whimpered like a dog on a doorstep in the rain (Thelma Strabel)

Whimpered like a lowing cow
(John Gay)

Whirled

Whirled like a tornado (Doris Leslie)

Whirled like lightening
(George MacDonald Fraser)

White

White as a fang

White as a haunt

White as a marshmallow cream
(Jim Dodge)

White as a whale's tooth

White as an Easter lily

White as cotton

White as driven snow (John Lyly)

White as Italian marble

White as paper

White as terror

White as a winter mist
(Rosemary H Jarman)

White and secret like a virgin's dream
(Doris Leslie)

Wholesome

Wholesome as a big ripe apple
(Phoebe Gray)

Wholesome as the morning air
(George Chapman)

Wide

Wide as an axe handle

Wide as the whole state of Texas

Wide awake

Wide awake as a weasel
(Robert Lewis Taylor)

Wide awake as an owl with diarrhoea
(Stephen King)

Wild

Wild as a hawk

Wild as a tiger

Wild as the devil

Wilful

Wilful as a mule (Danish saying)

Wilful as a prince (Sir Walter Scott)

Willing

Willing as a prostitute on a slow Saturday night

Willing as a teenager on his first date

Wily

Wily as an old fox (Sir Walter Scott)

Wily as a collie

Winced

Winced like a nerve touched by a dentist's drill

Winced like a touched nerve
(Henry James)

Windy

Windy as a dog-day in Kansas
(O Henry)

Windy as Chicago

Wise

Wise as a hooty owl (Ivan Doig)

Wise as Shakespeare
(Henry David Thoreau)

Withered

Withered as an old stone (JRR Tolkien)

Withered like a rose without light

Wobbled

Wobbled like an elephant on ice skates

Wobbled like a sixty-five-year-old man on roller blades.

Printing landmarks:

1650 – The first daily newspaper, *Einkommenden Zeitungen*, was published in Germany.

Worked

Worked like a demon
Worked like a dog in a meat pot
(Edward Eggleson)
Worked like a galley slave
Worked like a madman
Worked like a slave (Thomas Hardy)
Worked like an ant on sugar

Worn

Worn as a carpet
Worn as the back seats of a cinema

Worthless

Worthless as a four-card flush
(Owen Ulph)
Worthless as crabgrass
(John McDonald)
Worthless as a Nira bill

Wound up

Wound up like a corkscrew
Wound up like a kid at Christmas
Wound up like atop

Wrinkled

Wrinkled as a baked pear
Wrinkled a professor's frown
Wrinkled as a fig

Writhed

Writhed like a nest of snakes
(Stephen King)
Writhed like a worm on a bed of chilli
peppers

Y

Yawned

Yawned like an English setter by the
fireplace
Yawned like a mouth of a tavern
(John Dennis)

Yelled

Yelled like a maniac (Alexander Dumas)
Yelled like a steam whistle
Yelled like the mate on a tramp
steamer (Joseph C Lincoln)

Yellow

Yellow as a cat's eye
Yellow as an old cur dog
Yellow as an old moulted bird
(Margaret Mitchell)
Yellow as corn in the sun (Ouida)
Yellow as jaundice (George Meredith)

Yelped

Yelped like a lost hound
(Margaret Mitchell)
Yelped like he was hornet-stung
(Robert R McCammon)

Z

Zigzagged

Zigzagged like a snipe
Zigzagged like lightening
(Robert Southey)

Zip

About as much zip as a wet potato
chip (Tim Rumsey)
About as much zip as road kill
About as much zip as an inarticulate
smile

Oxymorons:

plastic glasses

Brains, pen, action!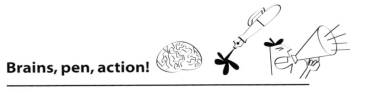

Something to ponder...

Many similes are as old as the oldest book of all –
The Bible.

The Kingdom of Heaven is like a mustard seed
planted in a field.

From Matthew 13

Think about your product or service.
Write a 200-word press release selling it to citizens
living during biblical times.
(Don't forget to use as many similes as possible).

12. Would you rather be cuddly or plump? It's all in the euphemism

It's so frustrating: you know what you want to say – even the word you need – yet you also know that you can't write what you need to say!

Never fear. There is a tool for the job: euphemisms; those politically correct examples of words that politely say what you would rather have said without the added airs and graces of political awareness. Advertising copy is full of them. Some brands like FCUK™ cleverly use euphemisms as part of their positioning to offer youth the chance to wear on their sleeve the thought that is in their mind.

Providing your euphemisms don't 'muffle' your message with insincerity, go ahead and fool around.

Need more help?
www.gabaywords.com

stir the porridge

Euphemisms

England is famous for many wonderful traditions. One in particular is the good old fish and chip shop. Like most Brits, during my youth I spent many an evening munching through a bag of freshly cooked chips (French Fries) sprinkled with a generous dusting of salt. (Ah, so wonderfully un-politically correct and yummy too!) To accompany this calorie-rich meal, I would tuck into a lovely order of rock salmon.

If I had known then what I know now, I am not sure that I would have had such a fondness for the food. Rock salmon turns out to be a euphemism for one of the most butt-ugly fish you would never want to pass your lips – the dogfish, a small sea-bottom-dwelling shark with a long tail.

I have a sneaky suspicion that a salesperson wishing to market the creature must have come up with the euphemism.

Speaking of predators, the sphere of warfare is always coming up with 'nice' ways to describe blood, death and destruction.

passed away	died
fatal injury	death
fatality	dead/killed person
casualties	deaths and injuries
caught in the line of fire	hit by bullet

Take that White House favourite 'collateral damage' meaning 'inadvertent casualties and destruction inflicted on civilians in the course of military operations'. In other words – 'bombs and bullets exploding in bodies rather than buildings'. Or travel further back in time to the Reagan Administration when the MX-Missile was renamed 'The Peacekeeper' or the 1940s when America changed the name of its War Department to the Department of Defense.

Anyone around here speak English?

A sign in a Lagos hairdresser: 'Gentleman's throats cut with nice sharp razors.'

Travel further still to the so-called, 'Great War' (the First World War) and you'll stumble across 'shell-shock': a sugary euphemism giving the impression of being 'in shock' through having endured terribly loud bangs. In reality the condition sent young men mad through having been physically as well as psychologically paralysed in the face of battle. Many generals considered the condition a sign of cowardice. Victims of the condition were treated with electric shocks; a few underwent psychotherapeutic treatment to restore courage. Some decades later, having learnt the error of their ways, the military renamed the condition 'combat fatigue', and thereby painted a quaint picture of soldiers feeling rather tired after a hard day at the front. After the Vietnam war, the condition was renamed as 'post-traumatic stress disorder'.

During the Iraq War launched in 2003 (later euphemistically called 'The War on Terrorism') the military came up with a reverse euphemism for shell-shock, this time relating to the 'shock' experienced by civilians rather than army personnel: 'shock and awe' suggested how the Iraqi people were meant to have feelings of reverential respect mixed with fear or wonder of the coalition blanket bombing. I believe the term makes a sneaky allusion to the Old Testament – in Exodus 20:18-20 it says, *'All the people, experiencing the thunder and lightning, the trumpet blast and the smoking mountain, were afraid – they pulled back and stood at a distance… Moses spoke to the people: "Don't be afraid. God has come to test you and instil a deep and reverent awe within you so that you won't sin."'*

Speaking of sin, in the Jewish Talmud, Eruvin 19, there are seven names – debatably euphemisms – for hell:

Nether world	Jonah 2:3
Annihilation/destruction	Psalm 88:12
(Pit) Well of destruction	Psalms 16:10
Tumultuous pit and miry clay	Psalms 40:3
Shadow of death	Psalms 107:10
Underworld	a name known by Jewish tradition

Add them all up and you get another euphemism: The seven gates of hell or seventh gate.

There is even a euphemism for 'euphemism'; the word 'doublespeak' originated in the early 1950s. Contrary to popular belief, it never appeared in George Orwell's novel 1984, but may be considered as a synonym for another word which certainly did make an appearance

Anagrams:

therein: 'newspeak' which means *'words deliberately constructed for political purposes intended to impose a positive mental attitude for the person using them'.* Along the same lines, Orwell referred to *'oldspeak'*, *'duckspeak'* (speaking from the throat without thinking 'like a duck') and 'doublethink' (maintaining a contradiction in mind as one speaks the opposite of one's own belief).

It is with little irony that in our world where TV dominates many living rooms, copywriters incessantly scratch about for euphemisms. Either they don't want to offend the target audience or seek a roundabout way to get around civil laws of decency (such as going into vivid descriptions for sanitary towels).

With so many commercials riddled with euphemisms it is hardly surprising that some products or services can come across as being described rather like a morning television chat show host would refer to a subject; in a puerile, middle-class, 'don't want to upset the neighbours' sort of way.

Take, for example, a diet plan. Would you rather be cuddled than cuddly? Or a visual euphemism such as showing blue liquid in a sanitary towel commercial.

Once a euphemism enters everyday vocabulary, it begins to slide towards becoming redundant, eventually to be replaced by yet another euphemism. By the time the euphemism reaches its third or fourth incarnation, it can often bear no resemblance whatsoever to its original meaning.

drunk ➜ *inebriated* ➜ *intoxicated* ➜ *half-cut* ➜ *basted* ➜ *boiled* ➜ *bug-eyed* ➜ *indisposed* ➜ *jolly* ➜ *nasty* ➜ *juiced* ➜ *loaded* ➜ *pruned* ➜ *stewed* ➜ *tanked up* ➜ *tipsy* ➜ *well away* ➜ *zonked*

Here's my thematic list of popular, often ludicrous and occasionally original euphemisms for your copywriting consideration.

Gabay at a glance:

I once worked for a financial client who was so worried about offending people with negative copy, that all unconstructive words such as, 'can't', 'cannot', 'won't', 'shouldn't'... were banned from internal communications such as newsletters. When asked for my opinion on this strategy, I replied, 'that's a great way to be positive about your negatives'.

Metaphors:

A quiet conscience sleeps in thunder. English proverb

Euphemisms by theme

Age
active
blue hair
blue rinse
certain age
crumbly
crown age
fail
get along
golden age
golden years (the)
mature
senior citizen
sunset years
third age (the)
young at heart

Alcohol
black stuff (the)
brew
dram
drop
Dutch cheer
French cream
freshen a drink
half a can
half and half
hard drink
hard stuff
hospitality
jar
juice (the)
little something
loaded
lush
mickey (finn)
mother's ruin
nightcap
one for the road
pick-me-up
pint (the)
public house
quick one
quickie
red-eye
sharpener
short
slug
snort
social glass
something for the thirst
something short
spirits
stiff-one
tipple
water of life
watering hole
wee dram
wee drop
wee half
wet goods
white satin

Animals
big animal
brute
drumstick
French pigeon
game
in season
man-cow
prairie oyster
roof-rabbit
rooster
stable horse
stunted hare
white meat

Auction and estate agencies (real estate)
agent
bijou
character
colonial
convenient
cosy
easy walking
eat-in kitchen
Georgian
handy
historic
immaculate
impressive
modern
much desired
negotiable
opportunity
prestigious
select
snug
walking distance

Banking
accumulate
adjustment
affordable
arrange
at risk
bait and switch
bean counter
bottom-line
bucket shop
budget
cherry pick
Chinese wall
churn
complimentary
consultant
convenient terms

Brand origins:

Velcro was invented as a direct consequence of a brainstorming session involving weeds with burrs in a jungle.

cost of living
dawn-raid
discount
do the books
downward adjustment
early-bird discount
easy payments
easy terms
energy release
expense account
family at large
fast buck
fiddle the books
good times and bad
gravy train
insider dealing
negative growth
nest egg
no obligation
no questions asked
non-profit
premium
put something aside
rainy day
spread the cost
technical adjustment
tidy sum
twenty-four hour
service
up as well as down
variable rate

Boasting

blow your own trumpet
bull
catch fish with a silver
hook
embroidery
fish story
give a line
log-rolling
Monday morning
quarterback
pay lip service

saddle soap
shoot the breeze
soft soap
swing the lamp
tall story

Body parts

back door
back passage
fleshy part of the thigh
heinie
dazzling smile (teeth)
latter end
lower limbs
rear end
between the legs
chopper
crown jewels
cupids arbour
cupids cave
endowed
family jewels
instrument
John Thomas
John Peter
love muscle
manhood
melons
nurse
organ
tackle
the intimate part
the lower stomach
the nether parts/regions
the private parts
the secret parts
thingy
tommy
vital statistics
wedding tackle
winkie

Brothels

abode of love

barrelhouse
bawdy house
call house
cat-house

chickie house
chicken ranck
common house
creep joint
escort agency
fish market
fleshpot
fun house
garden house
girlie bar
hot-house
house of sin
joy house
knocking-shop
loose house
make-out joint
massage parlour
meat-house
nanny-house
nunnery
parlour house
playhouse
rap studio
red-light district
rib joint
sauna
service station
snake-ranch
wang-house
zoo

Charity

aid
assistance
benefit

In other words:

barbecue – a queue of people waiting for haircuts

care
caring
entitlement
financial assistance
helping out
helping hand
in care
income support
living off the state
national assistance
on the dole
on the labour
public assistance
social security
welfare
welfare state

Cheating
catch a cold
chant
clip-artists
comic
con
con artist
cut
fix
horse-chanter
nickel and dime
operator
palm
plant the books
take to the cleaners
three-letter man
throw

Childbirth
bear
bundle of joy
drop
drop a bundle
facts of life
happy event
hatch

little handful
little stranger
mistake

Clothing
body shaper
booby trap
don't - name – 'em
enhanced contouring
falsies
flapper
flattering
flying-low
grow into them
generous
jock-strap
larger ladies
linen
lot of give
petite
room for growth
roomy
sensible
smalls
take in
take out
unmentionables
XYZ (Examine Your Zipper)

Contraception
armour
bareback rider
birth control
cardigan
collapsible container
Dutch cap
family planning
French letter
foggier
johnny
preventative
protected sex

marigold
on the pill
pill (the)
precautions
rubber
rubber glove
safe sex
sheath
something for the weekend
tickler
unprotected sex

Copulation
act of love
all the way
arouse
associate with
attentions
avail yourself
bareback
basket-making
bed and breakfast
bed-hopping
bedtime business
between the sheets
bit of the other
board the train
boom-boom
bouncy-bouncy
bring off
carnal knowledge
carnal act
carnal relations
carry on with
climb aboard
climb into bed (with)
close the bedroom door
cohabit
come together
congress
connect
connubial pleasures

Medieval words:

eschapins – light flat shoes

crack a Jane
crack your whip
deed (the)
deflower
dirty deed
drive thru
enjoy hospitality
free love
get a leg over
get it together
get laid
get off
get your rocks off
give a little
go all the way
have a bit
have it off
have relations
have your end away
horizontal acrobatics
hubada-hubada
hump
jig-a-jig
know the score
lay a leg over
lift a leg
make whoopee
night games
play around
play away
pork
rumpy-pumpy
screw
screw around
shag
sprain your ankle
stir the porridge
succumb
take advantage of
throw a leg over
upstairs
warm a bed
wicked way

yield to
you-know-what
zig-zig

Cosmetics
bikini wax
blue rinse
Brazilian
designer stubble
forehead challenged
high forehead
lift
homely
laughter lines
nose job
odorously challenged
receding
sensitive area
bikini line
rinse
touch up
war paint

Courtship and marriage
baby-snatcher
blind date
California widow
come to see
conjugal rights
cradle-snatcher
damaged goods
dance barefoot
date
do the right thing
feather your nest
free relationship
get off (with)
go out with
go steady
leave your pillow
unpressed
make a hit with
make an honest

woman of
on the peg
on the shelf
play gooseberry
pop the question
rob the cradle
single night
singles bar
singles joint
speak for
step out together
take down the aisle
take out

Dismissal
administrative leave
bounce
California kiss-off
career change
chop (the)
chuck (the)
cut numbers
dehire
delayering
demanning
downsize
drop-dead list
early release
early retirement
explore other
opportunities
flush down the drain
garden leave
get the p45
get the shaft
given notice
golden handshake
headcount reduction
kiss-off
make room
marching orders
negative employee situation
New York kiss-off

Metaphors:

The streets were filled with the rush hour flood of people. O Henry, 'An Unfinished Story', *The Four Million*

off the payroll
on health grounds
pink slip
push (the)
reduce your commitments
restructure
rightsize
sack (the)
send down the road
shove (the)
spend time with the family
stand down
streamline
take a hike
take a walk
terminate
walk the gangplank
written out of the script

Drugs

acid
base-head
blow
blow Charlie
blow snow
bombed out
candy man
chase the dragon
coke
cold turkey
crackhead
do a line
dope
feed your nose
grass
habit
heaven dust
hit the pipe
hot head
ice cream
jab a vain
jab off

joy rider
junked up
junkman
Magic mushrooms
Mexican brown
Mexican green
Mexican red
mood freshener
needle pusher
nose habit
on a cloud
on the needle
on the sniff
powder your nose
pusher
recreational drug
runny nose
shoot
smackhead

smashed
snort
spaced out
stoned
street drugs
sweet tooth
take needle
white powder
wrecked
zoned out
zonked

Employment

above your ceiling
between jobs
glass ceiling
golden hallo
golden handcuffs
headhunter
industrial action

moonlight
pull rank
resting
sellout
slowdown
team player
unofficial action
waiting for the right opportunity
walk out
working class

Entertainment

airport novel
best-seller
between shows
blockbuster
bonkbuster
doorstep
dumb down
early bath
instant best-seller
kiss-and-tell
overnight success
resting
say a few words
vanity publishing
words from our sponsor

Funerals

all-night man
bodybags
chapel of rest
cold box
Davy Jones's locker
floral tribute
garden of remembrance
lay out
lay to rest
memorial counsellor
memorial house
memorial park
put away
rest in peace

Anyone around here speak English?

A sign in a Spanish travel agency: 'Go away.'

room of meditation
slumber box
slumber cot
slumber robe
slumber room
stiff
vault
wooden box
wooden overcoat

Gambling
betting book
cross your fingers
debt of honour
have a flutter

Health
afflicted
aurally challenged
big C
buy it
C
cardiac incident
challenged
chuck up
cold deck
combat ineffective
condition
decline
delicate
dicky
differently abled
do in
done for
eating disorder
eliminate manhood
fly the yellow flag
funny tummy
groggy
hard of hearing
healthcare products
health clinic
health farm
heart condition

heart problem
impaired hearing
make comfortable
mobility impaired
nil by mouth
not feeling him/herself
off-colour
one foot in the grave
optically challenged
orally challenged
people with differing
abilities
person with AIDS
physically challenged
rather poorly
so-so
stone dead
surgical misadventure
temporarily abled
tender loving care
thick of hearing
throw up
under the weather
uniquely abled
unsighted
visually inconvenienced
weakness for horses
women's problems

Lovers
affair
bedfellow
better half
bit on the side
carry on with
companion
dirty weekend
familiar with
fancy bit
fancy piece
just good friends
kept woman
lady friend
liaison

live in (mortal) sin
live together
live with
live-in girlfriend
long-term friend
long-term relationship
love affair
love nest
more than a (good)
friend
on the side
open relationship
piece on the side
shack up (with)
significant other
sleeping partner
toy boy
warm up old porridge

Lying
cock-and-bull story
creative
credibility gap
deal from the bottom
of the deck
disinformation
eat the Bible
economical with the
truth
gild the facts
gild the lily
gild the truth
imaginative journalism
misspeak
need to know
news management
paint a picture
poetic truth
pork pie
story-teller
spin
swallow the Bible
terminological
inexactitude

Etymology:

to bring home the bacon – this phrase, meaning 'earn a wage or deliver a victory', derives from medieval England. If a married couple could prove to a mock jury that they had never regretted getting married or never quarrelled they were rewarded the Dunmow Flitch, which was a side of bacon. Which is why 'bacon' became synonymous with 'prize'.

to one side of truth

Mental illness
affected
bananas
barking
batty
both oars in the water
certifiable
crack pot
cracked
cuckoo
diminished responsibility
disturbed
dotty
eccentric
fruitcake
funny farm
half-deck
head case
loopy
loose in the head
lose your marbles
march to a different drummer
mentally challenged
nervous breakdown
nuts
nutter
nutty
off the rails
off your head
off your rocker
off your turnip
out of your head
out of your tree
out to lunch
potty
psycho
round the bend
screw loose
screwy
touched (in the head)

unbalanced
unglued
unhinged
unplugged
unwired
wired to the moon

Money problems
belly up
better manage
bounce
bust
cash flow problem
control
corporate recovery
do a runner
financial worries
fly-by night
go down the tubes
go to the wall
lose your pants
lose your shirt
lose your vest
money problems
need help
negative equity
over-indulge
pull the rug
set back
strapped for cash
up the creek
wiped out

Nakedness
birthday suit
buff
in his naturals
in the altogether
in the buff
in the raw
in the skin
skinny-dip
wear nothing but a smile

Obesity
a fuller figure
ample
battle of the bulge
big-boned
bit of stomach
chubby
couch potato
fond of food
heavily built
maturer figure
middle-age spread
people of size
pinch an inch
puppy fat
quantitatively challenged
reduce your contour
shorten the front line
spare tyre
weight problem
well-built
well-fleshed

Menstruation
come around
come on
domestic afflictions
female physiology
feminine hygiene
indisposed
irregular
monthly blues
personal hygiene
problem days
stomach cramps
time of the month
under the weather
women's things
wrong time of the month

Anagrams:

from SLOT MACHINES to CASH LOST IN EM.

Police
blue-and-white
bobby
cop
fuzz
man in blue
Mr plod
pigs
pull-in (for a chat)
smokey
special branch

Poverty
a moth in your wallet
assistance
benefit
depraved
down and out
economically abused
economically disadvan-
taged
economically exploited
economically margin-
alised
entitlement
financial assistance
financially constrained
hard up
in the red
negatively privileged
on a budget
on the labour
seen better days
socially excluded
the third world
tight-fisted
under privileged
underdeveloped
urban renewal
vulnerable

Pregnancy
accident
afterthought

an interesting condition
bump
bun in the oven
carry a child
delicate condition
eating for two
expectant
fall in the family way
how's your father
in the family way
in the pudding club
on the way
overdue

Race
a pigmentation
problem
affirmative action
African-American
African-descended
community relations
cultural deprivation
dark-complexion
dark-skinned
diversity
diversity training
ethnic minority
guest worker
multicultural
native American
new Australian
n-word (the)
person of/with colour
travelling people
visible community
visible minority ethnic
groups
visibly ethnic
west Briton

Religion
alternative
child of God
gentle people

give to God
good neighbours
holy wars
wise man
wise women

Sexual pursuit
ally-cat
bedroom eyes
beefcake
bird
bit of alright
bit of hot stuff
bit of how's your father
bit of jam
bit of skirt
bit of stuff
bit of you-know-what
bit on the side
carry a torch for her
cast sheep's eyes at
chase skirt
consensual relationship
defend your honour
designs on
dish
distracted by
doll
Don Juan
easy women
eye-candy
familiar with
fancy
fool around with
forget yourself
fun and games
get off with
get your feet under the
table
give the eye
hanky-panky
hot stuff
in the mood

Anyone around here speak English?

A sign in a Tokyo Bar: 'Special cocktails for the ladies with nuts.'

lady-killer
man about town
on the make
on the pull
popsy
roving eye
slap and tickle
stuck on
thing about
weakness for men /
women
womaniser

Smell
aroma
bouquet
fragrance
have the air of
hum
niff
nose
odour
perfume
pong
scent
whiff

Sweat
bedewed
BO
body odour
damp
glow
moist
odorously challenged
sticky
swelter
wetness

Toilets
ablutions
Aunt Jones
bathroom
bathroom paper

bathroom tissue
blue room
boys room
chamber pot
cloakroom
comfort station
commode
convenience
facility
gentlemen's conven-
ience
girl's room
going to go
house of commons
house of lords
hygienic facilities
karsey
ladies
convenience
lav
little boy's room
little girl's room
little house
loo
male
men's room
outhouse
powder room
private office
privy
public convenience
relief station
smallest room (the)
tearoom
upstairs
water closet
WC
what you may call it
whatsit
women
women's room
you-know-what

Urination
accident
call of nature
cleanliness training
dicky diddle
ease your bladder
ease yourself
freshen up
go upstairs
house-trained
leave the room
natural necessities
nature stop
number one(s)
pay a visit
powder your nose
relieve yourself
spend a penny
stretch your legs
tinkle
wash your hands

Etymology:

a sight for sore eyes – this phrase meaning welcome sight is thought to refer to an ancient superstition that disagreeable sights caused sore eyes, whilst agreeable sights reversed the process.(Today it has come to have negative connotations.)

Brains, pen, action!

Something to ponder...

Many words go through semantic changes, which alter their meaning. In addition to idioms, euphemisms and general political correctness there are many kinds of semantic change:

- Narrowing (or specialisation) – a word becomes more specific in meaning, for example:

  'Meat' used to mean any kind of food. Now it only refers to animal flesh.

- Broadening (or generalisation) – a word keeps its original meaning as well as added new meaning, for example:

  'Holiday' used to mean 'holy day'. Now it means leisure time off work.

- Amelioration – a word is given a more pleasant or positive meaning, for example:

  'Wicked' still means 'evil' but in slang it also means 'brilliant'.

- Weakening – a word loses it power, for example:

  'Soon' used to mean 'now'. Now it means 'in the near future'.

- Pejoration – a word becomes less favourable in meaning, for example:

  'Cowboy' can now mean a charlatan.

Also see
Metaphors
chapter 10

- Metaphor – words and expressions take on a new image and, therefore a new meaning, for example:

  'Her mind was a 'brick wall.'

Buy different magazines – each preferably dealing with a different business sector, such as finance, marketing, fashion, and so on. Underline as many euphemisms and examples of semantic change as possible.

Brand origins:

Max Factor, 1909 – the family business Max Factor & Co. was formed in 1909, although earlier, Max Factor Snr, a Polish make-up artist, opened a perfume, make-up and hair goods concession at the St Louis World Fair. His son Max created the first make-up for the film industry. By 1916 he broadened his market to the general public.

13. Portmanteau – copy blending

I returned home the other day to an argument among my young teenage son Joshua and his friends David and Max. They were working on an English homework assignment. Apparently they were searching for a word which described someone who was happy whilst being sad.

"Have you tried a portmanteau?" I asked.

They gave it a shot and combined 'happiness' with 'sorrow' coming up with 'sorriness'. Not the best portmanteau I had ever heard, but they were rewarded with a mark from their teacher. Mind you, he did deduct a further three marks for copying each other's work!

On the other hand it did serve to remind them – and me – that when all else fails in copywriting: plagiarise, plagiarise, plagiarise!

kangarooster

Portmanteau – copy blending

Recently I was packing my clothes in preparation for a short trip to deliver a copywriting lecture. As I placed my clothes into my portmanteau, I was reminded of the various meanings of the word.

Portmanteaus blend together shared characteristics of their component words. Often they blend the initial sounds or syllables of one word with the last sounds or syllables of another, for example *'guesstimate'*.

Also see
Clichés
page 173

Portmanteaus may combine elements from more than two words, as in *'entreporneur'* (a business person selling pornography). This variation of use often leads to puns, which, in themselves, can be counted amongst the outcasts of copywriting vocabulary (along with some clichés). However, their horridness is only skin deep. For where there are puns, there can also be imagery; take the portmanteau *'spoodle'* (a serving ladle) as an example.

Portmanteaus invariably have more than a fleeting relationship to onomatopoeia (also known by the terms 'phonaesthesia' and 'sound symbolism'). Onomatopoeia imitates a noise or action such as: 'The fly buzzed past'; or the frequently quoted *'murmuring of innumerable bees'*; or from *The Tempest* (III, ii): *'Sometimes a thousand twangling instruments will hum about mine ears'*.

In turn, the onomatopoeia is closely related to 'echoism', in which a word echoes a sound: for example *splash*, echoing a liquid striking something or something striking liquid; *crunch* suggesting the noise made when you eat something brittle.

The Japanese language is particularly adept at devising onomatopoeia which sound practically melodic. For example:

chika chika	Flickering light, light from stars
desu	To be extremely hungry, famished; to be weak from hunger
doki doki	Pounding heart; heart beating fast from excitement
gera gera	Ha ha
giri giri	Just barely; just in time, e.g. I just barely passed the test
gohhon!	Sound of someone sneezing
goro goro	To laze about, idleness; upset stomach; sound of lighting
hara hara	Heart going pit-a-pat; nervousness (see doki doki)
kira kira	Glitter and sparkle
kokekokko	Cock-a-doodle-doo
mecha mecha	Messed-up; illogical; incoherent; unreasonable; 'screwed-up'
mou-mou	The sound a cow makes, 'moo'
peko peko	To be extremely hungry, famished; to be weak from hunger
pera pera	Fluent in a language
pika pika	Glitter, twinkle, sparkle
pocha pocha	Splash water, dabble in water; plump, chubby
shitoshito	Sound of a light rain shower
sutaba	Starbucks coffee is so popular in Japan, its name is abbreviated (like Brad Pitt – 'burapi')
wan wan	Bark of a dog, 'bow-wow' (children sometimes call dogs 'Wan-Wan')
zaa zaa	The sound of pouring rain

In other words:

vice versa – pornographic Italian poetry

Many authorities suggest that the portmanteau word originates from the English author, Lewis Carroll, although in fact, examples of word blending have been found in 7th century Old English manuscripts.

Nevertheless, Mr Carroll certainly made the portmanteaus popular, and the greatest of all his portmanteau works is arguably the poem 'Jabberwocky', which was first published in 1872 as part of the classic book **Through the Looking Glass** (and as a passing point of interest, was later released as a Monty Python film under the same title). [Incidentally, **Jabberwocky** was the only movie that was so bad that I walked, if not ran out of the cinema within its first fifteen minutes.]

The word 'portmanteau' almost never made it the into the dictionary. Suggested alternatives included: *centaur words, amalgams, mongrel words, brunch words, fusions* and *telescope words*.

Yet 'portmanteau', latterly taken from a piece of luggage also known as a Gladstone – *a stiff leather case which opens down the middle like a book* – stuck. By the Victorian era, words like brunch, smug and electrocute were part of everyday English.

New portmanteaus appear almost daily. Copywriters are especially fond of them and use them to help devise new brand names – most of which seem to end up on daytime television and shopping channels. 'Can you afford not to buy the whizzomatic?'

One UK advertiser, Nissan, used the portmanteau technique to devise a series of 'nonce words' (these are words or expressions devised for specific occasions). For example, when Nissan wanted to explain that its Micra car was both spacious and safe, it described it as being 'spafe'.

Another major advertiser, Cadburys, used portmanteau words such as *'chocollect'* to promote a sales promotion offering prizes in exchange for chocolate wrappers.

Whilst remaining engagingly endearing, portmanteaus tend to also be 'very much of their time'. So, enjoy – whilst stocks last!

Gabay at a glance:

Also see my etymology for 'portmanteau'. (below)

Etymology:

Portmanteau – originally borrowed from French portmanteau, a compound formed from porter 'carry' and 'manteau' (cloak). A court official carried the King's cloak.

Jabberywocky

'Twas brillig, and the slithy toves
Did gyre and gimble in the wabe:
All mimsy were the borogoves,
And the mome raths outgrabe.

'Beware the Jabberwock, my son!
The jaws that bite, the claws that catch!
Beware the Jubjub bird, and shun
The frumious Bandersnatch!'

He took his vorpal sword in hand:
Long time the manxome foe he sought –
So rested he by the Tumtum tree,
And stood awhile in thought.

And, as in uffish thought he stood,
The Jabberwock, with eyes of flame,
Came whiffling through the tulgey wood,
And burbled as it came!

One, two! One, two! And through and through
The vorpal blade went snicker-snack!
He left it dead, and with its head
He went galumphing back.

'And, has thou slain the Jabberwock?
Come to my arms, my beamish boy!
O frabjous day! Callooh! Callay!'
He chortled in his joy.

'Twas brillig, and the slithy toves
Did gyre and gimble in the wabe;
All mimsy were the borogoves,
and the mome raths outgrabe.'

Lewis Carroll, Through the Looking Glass, 1872

Did you know?

The longest word in the English language in which each letter occurs at least twice is 'unprosperousness'. It comes from the word 'Sestettes', a musical term, meaning pieces of music for six voices.

Some useful examples of portmanteau

A

abhorrible	adj. (abhor + horrible)
abnormous	adj. (abnormal + enormous)
absolete	adj. (absolute + obsolete)
abusak	n. (abuse + muzak) A slang term for elevator music
adaptitude	n. (adapt + attitude)
advertique	n. (advertisement + antique)
advertorial	n. (advertisement + editorial)
alcoholiday	n. (alcohol + holiday)
anusurge	n. (answer + surge) An irresistible urge to answer a telephone
anticipointment	n. (anticipation + disappointment) A great sense of anticipation, quickly followed by an even greater disappointment

B

bacronym	n. (back + acronym) An acronym in which the word formed by the initial letters appears to have been deliberately selected to refer back to what is being abbreviated. For example, SLOSH a computer simulation used by the National Hurricane Centre to determine the potential effects of a hurricane tidal surge
badvertising	n. (bad + advertising)
bash	vb.(bash + smash) Onomatopoeic sound of a crushing blow
bastich	n. (bastard + son of a bitch)
blacketeer	n. (black market + racketeer)
blurb	n. (blurt + burble) A book description appearing on dust jacket of a book
boil	n. (boy + girl) A teenager whose sex is not immediately discernible
bomphlet	n. (bomb + pamphlet) A propaganda leaflet dropped from an aeroplane
brunch	n. (breakfast + lunch)
brutalitarian	n. (brutal + totalitarian)
bungersome	adj. (bungle + cumbersome)

Loquacious language:

orgulous – to be proud or a show off

C

cabrazy	adj. (cabaret + crazy)
calligram	n. (calligraphy + anagram) A word drawn to form a visually arresting picture
camelcade	n. (camel + cavalcade) A procession of camels
camouflanguage	
	n. (camouflage + language) Language that is used to disguise the truth
cangle	vb. (cajole + wangle) To quarrel or dispute
chipe	vb. (cheep + whine) Speaking in a high-pitched, persistent and complaining way
chortle	vb. (snort + chuckle) Joyful chuckling, coined by Lewis Carroll
confectionate	adj. (confection + affectionate)
copelessness	n. (cope + hopelessness) The inability to cope with life
croodle	vb. (crouch +cuddle) Act of a loving embrace

D

daffynition	n. (daffy + definition)
democrapic	adj. (democracy + crap) A form of political hypocrisy
deminology	n. (denim + technology)
depicture	vb. (depict + picture) To depict; to envisage
dripple	vb. (drip + dribble)
drunch	m. (drinks + lunch)
dumfusion	n. (dumb + confusion)
dipsy	adj. (tipsy + dippy)
ditsy	adj. (dizzy + dotty)
Dixican	adj. (Dixie + Republican)
docutainment	n. (documentary + entertainment)

E

Eastralia	n. (east + Australia)
echosultant	n. (echo + consultant) A consultant who reconfirms the findings of another consultant
entertrainment	n. (entertainment + training)
embargaining	vb. (embargo + bargaining) An agreement with a journalist who concurs not to release information until permitted by the source
euphobia	n. (euphoria + phobia) A neurotic fear of good news

Brand origins:

Nescafé, 1938 – this name is a combination of the manufacturer's name 'Nestlé' and the French word for coffee 'café'.

explaterate	vb. (explain + elaborate)
expugn	vb. (expunge + impugn) To erase or question
expunctuation	n. (expunction + punctuation) The removal of written copy during the editing process

F

faction	n. (fact + fiction) Book based on fact, but written as a novel
faddict	n. (fad + addict) Someone compelled to pander to a fashion craze
fagtory	n. (fag + factory)
fantabulous	adj. (fantastic + fabulous)
feep	n. (feeble + beep) Soft alarm featured in PCs
flabbergast	vb. (flap + aghast)
flamdoodle	n. (flam + flapdoodle) Boastful speech
flusticate	vb. (fluster + complicate)
fugly	adj. (fat + ugly)
fumorist	n. (female + humourist)

G

galimony	n. (gal + alimony) Recompense in lieu of alimony between alienated lesbians
geriatrickster	n. (geriatric + trickster) Elderly person who enjoys practical jokes
giverous	adj. (give + generous)
glob	n. (globe + blob)
goop	n., vb. (goo + drip)
grandacious	adj. (grand + gracious)
grasple	vb. (grasp + grapple)
grismal	adj. (grim + dismal)
gritch	vb. (gripe + bitch)
growsy	adj. (grumpy +drowsy)
guesstimate	n., vb. (guess + estimate)

H

habitude	n. (habit + attitude) An habitual approach to doing things
hain	n. (hail + rain)

Metaphors:

It is a bitter pill – but I shall have to swallow it. Ivan Turgenev, *Fathers and Sons*

hamateur	n. (ham + amateur)
hective	adj. (hectic + active)
hesh	pron. (he + she) A gender neutral pronoun
Hinglish	n. (Hindi + English) Hindi words or phrases derived from the English language
hintimation	n. (hint + intimation)
hoolivan	n. (hooligan + van) A police vehicle equipped with surveillance cameras to monitor mob behaviour
huggle	vb. (hug + snuggle)
humint	n. (human + intelligence)

I

ignostic	n. (ignorant + agnostic) A person who refuses to accept facts unless supported by empirical proof
imagineering	n. (imagine + engineering) Engineering and design utilising IT
impixolated	adj. (intoxicated + pixilated) Drunk
infomaniac	n. (information + maniac) Someone obsessed with trivial information
infomercial	n. (information + commercial)
infotainment	n. (information + entertainment)
innoventure	n. (innovative + venture) An unconventional business venture requiring finance
insinuedo	n. (insinuation + innuendo) A rumour discrediting a person's good name
Irhate	n. (Iraq + hate) American propaganda during Iraq war of 2003, encouraging xenophobia
itchitate	n. (itch + irritate) To irritate by causing an itch

J

jamocha	n. (java + mocha) Lingo for coffee
Japanazi	n. (Japaneze + Nazi) Military slang used in the Second World War referring to a combined Japanese and Nazi armed operation
jargantuan	adj. (jargon + gargantuan) The gargantuan task of interpreting the meaning of faddish professional jargon
jargoneer	n. (jargon + engineer) A person proficient at creating jargon; a jargonaut

Anyone around here speak English?

A sign in an Italian laundry: 'Ladies, leave your clothes here and spend the afternoon having a good time.'

jazzetry	n. (jazz + poetry) Poetry that accompanies jazz music
jeepney	n. (jeep + jitney) A popular vehicle in the Philippines
jocoserious	adj. (jocose + serious) Something simultaneously comical and serious
jollop	n. (jolly + dollop). A drink of spirits
jummix	n. (jumble and mix)
juvenescence	n. (juvenile + adolescence)

K

kangarooster	n. (kangaroo + rooster) Australian slang for an eccentric
Kanorado	n. (Kansas + Colorado) A city on the border of Kansas and Colorado
Kensee	n. (Kentucky + Tennessee)
kidult	n. (kid + adult) Television targeting term for viewers aged between 12 and 34
kissletoe	n. (kiss + mistletoe)

L

lamburger	n. (lamb + hamburger) Hamburger made of lamb
laspring	n. (last + spring) British dialect for young salmon
leerics	n. (leer + lyrics) Erotically provocative lyrics
lemoncholy	adj. (lemon + melancholy) A state of being in sour disposition or melancholia
leopon	n. (leopard + lion) The progeny of a leopard and lioness
lumbersome	adj. (lumber + cumbersome)
lupper	n. (lunch + supper) An afternoon meal

M

machodrama	n. (macho + melodrama) A movie celebrating male machismo
maddle	vb. (mad + addle) To incite a state of craziness
magnalium	n. (magnesium + aluminium) An aluminium-based alloy containing magnesium particles

Etymology:

ten gallon hat – this phrase referring to a large cowboy hat has nothing to do with size. It alludes to the Spanish for 'braided hat' – *sombrero gallon*.

malaphor	n. (malapropism + metaphor) A mixed metaphor
manglish	n. (man + English) Written or spoken sexist English favoured by young British males
manscape	n. (man + landscape) A 'sea' of faces in a crowd
mappen	interj. (may + happen)
maximin	adj. (maximum + minimum) The smallest gain that one can anticipate from a game plan or strategy
methodolatry	n. (method + idololatry) An gratuitous interest in methodologies
mizzle	n. (moan + grizzle)
Motown	n. (motor + town) Detroit (aka 'Motor City') *Motown* was a Detroit-based record company

N

namemanship	n. (names + gamesmanship) Someone adroit at name-dropping
Naussie	n. (new and Aussie) Australian term for newly arrived emigrant
needcessity	n. (need + necessity)
newelty	n. (new + novelty)
newszine	n. (news + magazine)
newzak	n. (news + Muzak) News whose impact has been lost through insistent repetition
Nickelodeon	n. (nickel + melodeon) Early 20th century theatre showing films for the price of a nickel; the performance was usually accompanied by live music from a keyboard instrument called a melodeon or melodion
noration	n. (narration + oration)
numberous	adj. (number + numerous)
nutarian	n. (nut + vegetarian)

O

obscureaucrat	n. (obscure + bureaucrat) A civil servant whose responsibilities are largely unknown
obstipation	n. (obstinate + constipation) Constipation that is hard to ease
opinionnaire	n. (opinion + questionnaire)
owdacious	adj. (audacious + outrageous)

Medieval words:

envoy – a short stanza to a ballad

Oxbridge	n. (Oxford + Cambridge) Collective term for twinned respected English universities

P

pajamboree	n. (pyjama + jamboree) A slumber party
palimony	n. (pal + alimony) Payments similar to alimony, which are demanded by unwed estranged lovers
pang	n. (pain + sting)
parlambling	n. (parlance + ambling) Rambling speech
pervertising	n. (perverted + advertising) Advertising which relies strongly on sexual innuendo
pessimal	adj. (pessimistic + optimal) The greatest possibility to produce the worst possible result
phallacy	(phallus + fallacy) A mistaken assumption about certain characteristics of male sexuality
piffle	vb. (piddle + trifle) To act or speak frivolously
piroot	vb. (pirouette + root) To meander idly
platiudinarian	n. (platitude + latitudinarian) Someone who relies on trite expressions
previnder	vb. (prevent + hinder)

Q

quaggy	adj. (boggy + quagmire)
querious	adj. (query + curious)
queerious	n. (queer and curious) A homosexual who is curious about heterosexual sensuality

R

racontage	n. (raconteur + anecdotage) A person who is adept at telling entertaining anecdotes
recomember	vb. (recollect + remember)
reversicon	n. (reverse + lexicon) A reverse dictionary
rockappella	n. (rock + a cappella) Rock music featuring unaccompanied singers
rollick	vb. (romp + frolic) Behave in a happy-go-lucky manner
routinary	adj. (routine + ordinary)
rubbage	n. (rubbish + garbage)

Anyone around here speak English?

A sign in a Hong Kong dentist: 'Teeth extracted by the latest Methodist.'

ruckus	n. (ruction + rumpus) A fracas
rumbumptious	adj. (rumbustious + bump) Raucous and rowdy
rurban	adj. (rural + urban) A city district which retains a rural character

S

sancatamoody	adj. (sanctimonious + moody) A person who acts in a piously gloomy manner
scance	vb. (scan + glance)
scriggle	vb. (squirm +wriggle)
scringe	vb. (shrink + cringe) To recoil in fear
sejole	vb. (seduce and cajole)
sexploitation	vb. (sex + exploitation) The commercial exploitation of sex
Shakesperience	n. (Shakespeare + experience) An advertising 'hook' to promote Shakespearean plays
skinjury	n. (skin + injury) A euphemistic advertising figure of speech referring to the treatment of small cuts and abrasions
slanguage	n. (slang + language) Slang used in everyday language
Spanglish	n. (Spanish + English) A hybrid dialect
squirk	vb. (squirm + twirl)

T

Tanzania	n. (Tanganyika + Zanzibar). East African country made up of the countries of Tanganyika and Zanzibar.
tearjerker	n. (tear + jerker) A film designed to educe an emotional response
televangelist	n. (television + evangelist) A preacher who evangelises on television
tenigue	n. (tension + fatigue) Physical and mental exhaustion caused through lack of physical exercise
testiculating	vb. (testicles + gesticulation) Behaving in a loutish manner (The expression comes from the notion that public loutish behaviour 'takes a lot of balls'.)
thwak	n. (thump + whack)
tizzy	n. (tipsy + dizzy)

Metaphors:

Scepticism is a good watchdog if you know when to take the leash off. Rex Stout, *Fer-de-Lance*

trainasium	n. (training + gymnasium)
trampede	n., vb. (trample + stampede)
tripewriter	n. (tripe + typewriter) A hack whose copy is untrustworthy
twee	adj. (tiny + wee) Northern English dialect to describe a very small object

U

ubookquitous	adj. (ubiquitous + book) A book which appears to be sold everywhere
uffish	adj. (uppish + selfish) Uppity; self-centred
uniquity	adj. (unique + iniquity) Singularly immoral
universanimous	adj. (universal and unanimous)
urbanality	n. (urbanity + banality) A self-conscious, sophistic kind of urbanity

V

vash	n. (volcanic + ash)
videotrocities	n. (video + atrocities) Offensive examples of banal television programmes, or commercials
vidiot	n. (video + idiot) A person infatuated with watching television
virangina	n. (virgin + angina) A first-time heart attack patient
vividity	n. (vivid + avidity) A state of being overly brazen and fervent
vulgularity	n. (vulgur + popularity) Something that despite, or because of its vulgarity, becomes popular

W

Wafrica	n. (West + Africa)
warmedy	n. (warm + comedy) A gushy, comedy designed to make the audience cry
warphan	n. (war + orphan)
weeny-bopper	n. (weeny + teeny bopper) A pre-adolescent who follows fads
whang	vb. (whack + bang)
whye	n. (wheat + rye) Hybrid crop
woggle	vb. (waggle + wobble)
womban	n. (womb + woman) A disparaging term for a woman

Writers' words:

'The last time somebody said, "I find I can write much better with a word processor," I replied, "They used to say the same thing about drugs."' Roy Blount Jr

Y

yabber	vb. (yack + jabber) To chat endlessly
yahoomanity	n. (yahoo + humanity) NOT an Internet search engine term, but a derisive name for humanity; the word 'Yahoo' was a contemptuous name for human beings, coined by Jonathan Swift in his novel Gulliver's Travels
yinglish	adj. (Yiddish + English)
yonks	n. (years + months + weeks) British slang for long period of time
yumptious	adj. (yummy + scrumptious)

Z

zebrass	n. (zebra + ass) The hybrid of a male zebra and female ass
zebrule	n. (zebra + mule)
zedonk	n. (zebra + donkey)
zonkey	n. (zebra + donkey)

Did you know?

The longest word featuring one vowel is 'strengths'.

Brains, pen, action!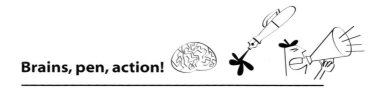

1 You are launching a new pen for left handed writers. Think of six product names using portmanteaus.

2 Watch tonight's news. Write portmanteaus to describe each of the politicians or celebrities discussed.

3 Read the first paragraph of a company brochure. Now combine the entire sentiments of its meaning into a portmanteau.

4 Write ten portmanteaus to describe having a headache.

5 Using the Jabberwocky poem as a guide, write your own version relating it to a tale of a powerful copywriter who rewrote every advertisement in the land.

(The best could be featured on www.gabaywords.com).

Answers to;
answers@gabaynet.com

osophagist – someone who is very picky about his or her food

14. All together now – collective nouns

What do you call a collection of collective nouns? There's no catch in the question. To find out, read this chapter.

Not fully appreciating the correct terminology for a group of people, professions, objects, classes, and so on can leave your copy sounding shallow. Hopefully this section will help your case gain deeper gravitas whilst keeping your message buoyant.

This chapter can also help you to devise your own versions such as:

• A mingling of broken vases • A tenet of palindromes • A rash of dermatologists A chain of lynx • A cast of orthopaedists • A bunch of florists • A column of architects • A great deal of used-car salesmen • A ring of jewellers

Need more help?
www.gabaywords.com

All together now – collective nouns

What do you call a room full of copywriters? It's not the lead-in to a joke. It's a genuine question. The problem with collective nouns is that choosing the correct noun causes more disputes than at a trade union congress. In fact, although many authorities list the proper collective nouns for a group of people, animals, objects or concepts, most are rarely used, and when a noun is agreed upon, the chances are that someone, somewhere will raise a questioning eyebrow.

It has often been said that many nouns originated from a 15th century English hunting tradition, which gave poetic names to prey. This accounts for so many collective nouns having descriptions that at best are quaint and at worst, well, quite barmy really. For example, a 'harass of horses'.

Collective nouns are part of our rich, ever-developing language. Neologists love nothing better than to post-up a new collective noun on the Internet. Most never quite make it into official dictionaries. Some enjoy a brief but busy life as slang-term, which through pronunciation of the words give them an extra shot of fame.

The rules of collective nouns

A prepositional phrase with a plural object often follows on from the collective noun.

> The *faculty of professors* was in total agreement.
> (prepositional phrase)

Usually, collective nouns are followed by singular verbs and pronouns.

> (singular verb)
> *The herd was reared by Old McDonald; it showed great promise for this year's cattle show.*
> (singular pronoun)

Did you know?

Copywriters really do let their hearts rule their heads: the heart produces at least twice as much electricity as the brain.

It is best to use the singular verb. Pronouns are also fine, unless the group in question refers to separate individuals. Compare the following:

> *The Board has issued a press release.*   (as a group)
>
> *The Board are tendering their resignations.*   (as individuals)

To check your verb form, try substituting the singular pronoun 'it' for the collective noun.

> *The faculty votes on Friday.*   (it votes)
>
> *The team works hard.*   (it works)

If you are qualifying the collective noun by a singular word, use the qualifiers 'the', 'this', 'that', 'every', etc.

> *The swarm is vast.*
>
> *Every battalion has its opportunity to attack.*

Any sentence related to a collective noun should either feature that/which + singular verb or who + plural verb:

> *It was not the company that cut the price.*
>
> (single verb)

> *The designers who are preparing the brochures*
>
> (plural verb)

A common mistake to keep in mind is mixing your singular and plural:

> *The team were now leaving. It formed groups.*

Refer to organisations as collective, even if the company name is plural. Be careful to always refer to a company as a single entity.

To help you pick the right collective noun, I have listed standard terms by type as well as kind and species.

From a copywriting perspective, I recommend that you have a go at devising your own collective nouns. Apart from being terrific fun, it offers you the opportunity to enliven your copy with piquant, as well as perceptive, descriptions relating the collective noun in question. To get you started, I have included some of my own which you will find listed after the standard entries.

Go out there you 'inspiration of copywriters' and neologise!

Metaphors:

Worry grows best in the soil of indecision. Anonymous

Collective nouns by species and kind

Birds

birds	dissimulation, volery, flock
bitterns	sedge, siege
bullfinches	bellowing
bustards	flock
buzzard	wake
capercaillies	tok
chickens	brood, peep
chicks	clutch
choughs	chattering, clattering
coots	cover, raft
cormorants	flight
cranes	sedge, siege
crows	murder, hover, storytelling
curlews	head
curs	cowardice
dotterel	trip
doves	dole, dule, flight, pitying, prettying
ducks	flush, raft, team (diving) dopping (in flight) team, plump (on water) paddling (brood) flush (pair) brace
dunlin	fling
eagles	convocation
falcons	cast
finches	charm, trimming, trembling
flamingoes	stand
geese	(at rest) gaggle, flock, nide (in flight) skein, wedge
goldfinches	charm, chattering, drum, glister, troubling
goshawks	flight
grouse	covey (single family) brood (large group) pack
guillemots	bazaar
gulls	colony, pack, screech
hawks	cast, leash, kettle
hens	brood
herons	sedge, siege
hummingbirds	shimmer, charm
jays	band, party
lapwings	desert, deceit
larks	exultation, bevy, ascension
magpies	tittering, tiding
mallards	sord (on land) flush, sute (on water) puddling
nightingales	match, watch
owls	parliament, stare
parrots	flock, company
partridges	covey, bew
peacocks	muster, ostentation, pride
penguins	raft (in water), waddle (on dry land)
pheasants	nye, bouquet
pigeons	flight, flock
plovers	congregation, leash, wing
poultry	run

Loquacious language:

ozostomia – terribly obnoxious bad breath

puffins	raft	
quail	bevy, covey	
ravens	unkindness, conspiracy	
rooks	parliament, building, clamour	
ruffs	hill	
sea fowl	cloud	
sheldrakes	dopping, doading	
snipe	(at rest) walk (in flight) wisp	
sparrows	host, quarrel, tribe	
starlings	murmuration	
storks	mustering	
swallows	flight	
swans	herd, bank, bevy, game, squadron, wedge, whiteness, drift	
swifts	flock	
teal	spring, coil, knob, raft	
thrushes	mutation	
turkeys	flock, dole, dule, raffle, raft, rafter	
turtledove	pitying	
vultures	wake	
waterfowl	plump	
widgeon	company, bunch, coil, knob	
wildfowl	trip	
woodcock	fall, covey, plump	
woodpeckers	descent	
wrens	herd	

Mammals

aardvarks	armory
antelopes	herd
apes	shrewdness, troop
asses	drove, herd, pace
baboons	congress, flange, troop
badgers	set
bats	colony
bears	sloth, sleuth
beavers	colony, lodge
boars	herd, singular, sounder
buffalo	herd, obstinacy
camels	caravan

caribou	herd
cats	clowder, cluster, glaring (kittens) kindle, litter (wild cats) destruction, dout
cattle	drove, herd, kine
chamois	herd
cheetahs	coalition
chinchillas	colony
colts	rake, rag
conies	bury
cows	herd, flink
coyotes	pack
deer	herd, leash, parcel

Did you know?

The only word in the English language with three consecutive sets of double letters is 'bookkeeper'.

dogs	pack, kennel
dolphins	pod, flock
donkeys	herd, drove
elephants	herd, parade
elk	gang
ferrets	business, cast, fesnying
foxes	skulk, lead, leash
giraffes	tower, corps
goats	trip, flock, herd, tribe
gorillas	band, woop
hares	drove, down, husk, leap, leash, trace, trip
hedgehogs	prickle, array
hippopotami	bloat, crash
hogs	drift
horses	drove, harass, herd, stable, team
hounds	cry, mute, pack
hyenas	clan
kangaroos	mob (only correct terminology)
leopards	leap, lepe
lions	pride, sault, sowse, troop
mares	stud
martens	richness
moles	labour, company, movement
monkeys	troop, cartload, tribe, mission
mice	nest
mules	barren, pack, rake
otters	family, bevy
oxen	team, yoke, span
pigs	drove, herd, sounder (piglets) farrow, litter

polecats	chine
ponies	string
porpoises	school
puppies	litter
rabbits	colony, bury, nest young rabbits) wrack
racehorses	field
rats	colony
rhinoceroses	crash
roe deer	bevy
seals	colony, harem, herd, pod, spring
sheep	flock, drove, fold
squirrels	dray
stoats	pack
swine	sounder
tigers	streak, ambush
walruses	herd
weasels	sneak, pack
wild cats	dout, destruction
wild pigs	sounder
whales	school, herd, gam, pod
wolves	pack
zebra	herd, zeal

Invertebrates

bacteria	culture
fungus	colony
jellyfish	stuck, smack, fluther
mushrooms	troop
worms	clew

Insects & arachnids

ants	colony, army
bees	swarm, grist, hive

Loquacious language:

palinoia – the repetition of an act over and over again until it is performed to perfection

butterflies	kaleidoscope, swarm, rabble
caterpillars	army
flies	swarm, business
gnats	swarm, cloud, horde
grasshoppers	cloud, cluster
locusts	plague
spiders	clutter

Molluscs

clams	bed
oysters	bed
snails	walk

Fish

archer fish	company
barracuda	battery
bass	shoal, fleet
butterfly fish	school
dogfish	troop
dragonet fish	swarm
eels	swarm
fish	draught, drift, scale, school, shoal
flying fish	glide
herrings	glean, army, shoal
minnows	stream
porcupine fish	cluster
rainbow fish	party
salmon	bind
sea horses	herd
sticklebacks	spread
swordfish	flotilla
trout	hover

Amphibians

frogs	army
toads	knot
turtles	dule, bale, nest, turn

Reptiles

crocodiles	bask
snakes	den, nest, pit
turtles	dule, bale, nest, turn
vipers	nest

Inanimate objects

aircraft	wing
arrows	quiver
asteroids	belt
bananas	bunch
beans	hill
bills	wad
bomblets	cluster
books	library, pile
bread	batch
brushwood	bavin
cards	deck
circles	crop
circuits	bank
collective nouns	catch
coins	roll, rouleau
computers	cluster, network
eggs	clutch
flowers	bed, patch, bouquet
grapes	bunch, cluster
hair	lock
homework	slew
information	wealth
islands	chain, archipelago

Twisted truths:

And don't start a sentence with a conjunction.

jewels	cache
keys	ring
lorries	convoy, fleet
money	rouleau
pearls or beads	
	string
peas	pod
poems	anthology
reeds	clump
satellites	constellation
ships	armada, flotilla
starlets	galaxy
stars	galaxy, constellation
tasks	agenda
trees	stand, clump, forest

People

academics	faculty
actors	cast, company
angels	chorus, host
arsonists	conflagration
athletes	team
barons	thought
bastards	shower
beauties	bevy
bureaucrats	shuffle
candidates	slate
car dealers	lot
car mechanics	
	clutch
cobblers	drunken ship
courtiers	threatening
directors	board
employees	staff
experts	panel

fairies	herd
friars	scull
gays	village
hackers	craft
harpists	melody
hoodlums	gang
horsemen	cavalcade
husbands	multiply
idiots	thicket
judges	bench
knights	banner
lawyers	huddle
mathematicians	
	number
men	band
Microsoft programmers	
	asylum, bloat
monks	abomination
mourners	cortege
natives	tribe
nudists	hangout
onlookers	crowd
performers	troupe
philosophers	ponder
relatives	descent
sailors	crew
senators	house
soldiers	squad
students	class
thieves	den
tourists	flock
troops	parel
widows	ambush
witches	coven
worshippers	congregation

Writers' words:

'Writing about music is like dancing about architecture.' Martin Mull

Gabay's neological collective nouns

an aria of sopranos
an abstinence of clergy
an apron of masons
an army of pacifists
an assemblage of jigsaw puzzlers
an autumn of leaves
a blush of virgins
a body of undertakers
a bond of spies
a brag of Texans
a brawl of freshman
a break of commercials
a bulb of luminaries
a calling of priests
a category of nouns
a chain of bicyclists
a change of traffic lights
a chanting of Buddhists
a chapter of writers
a chore of errands
a clutch of mechanics
a compass of maps
a core of apples
a coven of committees
a crack of yolks
a cranberry of turkeys
a crawl of tortoises
a cuddle of teddy bears
a culture of aristocrats
a cupful of breasts
a deal of salespeople
a detention of teachers
a doodle of designers
a dose of chemists
a drawer of toys
an error of software

an eyeful of beauties
an eyestrain of monitors
a finger of pedophiles
a fistful of gangsters
a flame of pyromaniacs
a flee of asylum seekers
a flee of cowards
a fatality of suicide bombers
a giggle of Prozac™
a gluttony of lawyers
a grief of parents
a grind of chores
a groan of elderly
a grope of prostitutes
a guilt of Catholics
a handful of wankers
a hope of virgins
a howling of vets
a hypothesis of scientists
an incompetence of managers
an inspiration of copywriters
a jewel of oysters
a jump of surprises
a launch of publicists
a leap of kangaroos
a lick of lesbians
a lie of politicians
a lipstick of gossip columnists
a mask of celebrities
a mess of garbage collectors
a mindset of philosophers

a mouthful of cabbies
a muscle of homosexuals
an opinion of consultants
an orbit of satellites
a passage of proctologists
a passing of clocks
a pelvis of Elvis impersonators
a pick of kleptomaniacs
a poke of whores
a pomposity of academics
a portfolio of artists
a Pot Noodle™ of geeks
a promise of marketers
a psychosis of dictators
a race of athletes
a rasher of pigs
a rebel of teenagers
a rest of chairs
a rumble of seismologists
a sack of postmen
a sacrifice of soldiers
a scare of headmasters
a scratching of nits
a sense of dictionaries
a sentiment of emotions
a share of communists
a sheath of condoms
a shrill of mobile phones
a signature of overnight couriers

Brand origins:

Marmite, 1902 – the name comes from the French name for stew pot (similar to the shape of the jar). The Oxford Dictionary of Modern English, c.1930s: 'An extract from fresh brewers' yeast, rich in vitamin B complex. Used for culinary purposes, e.g. making soups, and also medicinally.'

a slam of wrestlers
a smash of asteroids
a smattering of truths
a smirk of presidents
a smut of pornography
a snap of clams
a sneering of cynics
a snip of circumcisions
a sobbing of mourners
a spark of circuits
a spread of nymphomaniacs
a sting of wasps

a stocking of transvestites
a stretch of Viagra™
a stump of landmines
a surplus of economists
a sympathy of agony aunts
a synonym of thesauri
a ton of dieters
a touchdown of football players
a triplicate of bureaucrats

a truncheon of police
a trunk of elephants
a twitching of cockroaches
a verse of poets
a void of nihilists
a vomit of flies
a voyeur of onlookers
a waggle of tongues
a wheeze of smokers
a whisper of sycophants
a wisdom of rabbis
a wriggle of toddlers

Brains, pen, action!

Something to ponder...

1 What would you call a group of parlimentarians?

2 What would you call a group of clients?

3 What would you call a group of Hollywood actors?

4 What would you call a group of event organisers?

5 What would you call a group of glamour models?

6 What would you call a group of diplomats?

Metaphors:

Hope is a waking dream. Anonymous

15. Rhyme time

Writing verse requires quick access to rhyming words. You need the right rhyme ending and the right number of syllables. One example of this is when you give a company name a rhyming 'assonance': when the vowel sound in the middle two or more words is similar:

- Hot-Shot
- Nice Ice
- Quick Licks

This chapter provides a broad history of rhyme as well as over two thousand examples of the right word endings you need to 'seal the deal'.

Need more help?
www.gabaywords.com

Rhyme time

Rhymes and poetry have always played a major role in English, and current copywriting is continuing this trend.

Poetry's influence on our language is extensive and enthralling. Before the traditional alphabet, the Angles, Saxons and Jutes relied on the Rune alphabet. This comprised primarily straight lines (making the job of etching them onto stone much easier).

An 8th century example of rune poetry can be seen on the Ruthwell Cross near Dumfries in Scotland. This tells the story of the crucifixion, from the point of view of the cross on which Jesus was crucified.

Also, around the 8th century *Beowulf* was written. Many academics consider it to be the most important surviving example of Anglo-Saxon verse. *Beowulf* is 3182 lines long and is thought to be the fist major poem in a European vernacular language. The poem features newly created words which added to its charm and depth: '*ban-hus*' meaning bone-house and '*glee-wood*' meaning harp.

Beowulf chronicles the adventures of the Scandinavian hero Beowulf, who helps Hrothgar, the Danish king, battle a monster called Grendel. It is one of the longest and most complete examples of Anglo-Saxon verse, providing unrivalled insights into society at the time.

Throughout history, monarchs have relied on courtier-poets to praise great conquests or describe deep loves and so on. Queen Elizabeth I spoke six languages and translated French and Latin texts. She also loved to write her own poetry. For example:

> I grieve and dare not show my discontent;
> I love and yet and am forc'd to seem to hate;
> I do, yet dare not say I ever meant;
> I seem stark mute but inwardly do prate.
> I am and not, I freeze and yet am burned;
> Since from myself another self I turned.

(Queen Elizabeth I, from 'On Monsieur's Departure')

Gabay at a glance

Check out the poem, 'Beowulf at www.gabaywords.com

Brand origins:

Mars – Forrest E Mars emigrated to the UK in 1932 and introduced the Mars recipe. Originally made by hand, Mars bars sold for 2d each. Milky Way followed in 1935, and then Maltesers.

Poetry has long given a voice to doubt, warmth and passion. Queen Elizabeth's own courtier-poet was Sir Philip Sidney (1554–86). I mention him because his work had a tremendous influence on English. Sidney's elaborate romance Arcadia (1580) is the earliest example of poems used to depict an idyllic English country life. His love for Penelope Devereux inspired *Astrophel and Stella* (1591), the first English sonnet sequence (more on sonnets soon…).

An Apology for Poetry (1595) is the most important critical work of the Elizabethan era. In fact, it is thanks to Sir Phillip that we have expressions and words such as 'bugbear,' 'dumbstricken' and 'miniature'. His work also gave rise to ideas such as combining words like 'far-fetched'. He was also responsible for the expression 'my better half' for a spouse and even the word 'conversations' in terms of its meaning of having dealings with people through language rather than just of an open-ended type.

Sonnets

A sonnet is basically a poem of 14 lines, most often in iambic pentameter and usually employing Petrarchan or Shakespearean rhyme schemes. Just in case you thought, like me, that iambic pentameter sounds like a medical condition, let me put the record straight: it means *a metre in poetry, consisting of an unrhymed line with five 'iambs' or feet (hence pentameter)*. It is thought by many to be the most powerful of all metrical forms in English poetry.

Here is an example from Christopher Marlowe's *Dr Faustus*:

> Was this the face that launch'd a thousand ships
> And burnt the topless towers of Ilium?

(Christopher Marlowe, from Dr Faustus, ca. 1592–93)

The Italian sonnet form is commonly called the Petrarchan sonnet, based on a style introduced by Francesco Petrarca (1304–1374), and consists of an octet and a sextet, usually with an *a-b-b-a-a-b-b-a, c-d-e-c-d-e* rhyme scheme.

In its original form, the Italian sonnet was divided into an octave of eight lines and a sestet of six lines. The octave declared a proposition and the sestet its solution, with an obvious break between the two. The octave rhymed *a-b-b-a, a-b-b-a*. The sestet offered two different possibilities, *c-d-e-c-d-e* and *c-d-c-c-d-c*. Eventually, other alternatives were introduced.

Loquacious language:

pandiculation – to yawn and stretch

The octave usually presents an idea, raises an argument, makes a proposition, or poses a problem. A turning point ('volta') occurs between the octave and the sestet, and the sestet develops out of the octave by illustrating the idea in the octave, varying it, responding to it, or solving the problem it poses.

For example:

> O Earth, lie heavily upon her eyes;
> Seal her sweet eyes weary of watching, Earth;
> Lie close around her; leave no room for mirth
> With its harsh laughter, nor for sounds of sighs.
> She hath no questions, she hath no replies,
> Hushed in and curtained with a blessed dearth
> Of all that irked her from the hour of birth;
> With stillness that is almost paradise.
>
> Darkness more clear than noonday holdeth her,
> Silence more musical than any song;
> Even her very heart has ceased to stir;
> Until the morning of eternity
> Her rest shall not begin nor end, but be;
> And when she wakes she will not think it long.

(Christina Rossetti, 'Rest')

The Shakespearean sonnet consists of three quatrains of four lines and a couplet of two lines. The couplet generally introduced an unexpected sharp thematic or imagistic 'turn'. Usual rhyme schemes were *a-b-a-b, c-d-c-d, e-f-e-f, g-g* and a-*b-a-b, b-c-b-c, c-d-c-d, e-e*. Interestingly, Shakespeare didn't invent the English sonnet form, yet he was pretty good at writing them! So much so, we have the rendering *'Shakespearean sonnet'.*

The following example illustrates its classical structure:

> Let me not to the marriage of true minds
> Admit impediments. Love is not love
> Which alters when it alteration finds,
> Or bends with the remover to remove

Writers' words:

'Rock journalism is people who can't write interviewing people who can't talk for people who can't read.' Frank Zappa

O no, it is an ever fixed mark
That looks on tempests and is never shaken;
It is the star to every wand'ring barque,
Whose worth's unknown although his height be taken.

Love's not time's fool, though rosy lips and cheeks
Within his bending sickle's compass come;
Love alters not with his brief hours and weeks,
But bears it out even to the edge of doom.
If this be error and upon me proved,
I never writ, nor no man ever loved.

(William Shakespeare, 'Sonnet 116')

A variant on this form is the Spenserian sonnet, named after Edmund Spenser (c.1552–99), in which the rhyme scheme is *a-b-a-b, b-c-b-c, c-d-c-d, e-e*. For example:

Happy ye leaves! whenas those lily hands,
Which hold my life in their dead doing might,
Shall handle you, and hold in love's soft bands,
Like captives trembling at the victor's sight.

And happy lines! on which, with starry light,
Those lamping eyes will deign sometimes to look,
And read the sorrows of my dying sprite,
Written with tears in heart's close bleeding book.

And happy rhymes! bathed in the sacred brook
Of Helicon, whence she derived is,
When ye behold that angel's blessed look,
My soul's long lacked food, my heaven's bliss.

Leaves, lines, and rhymes seek her to please alone,
Whom if ye please, I care for other none.

(Edmund Spenser, from Amoretti, 1595)

Etymology:

clap-trap – this expression meaning 'to speak nonsense' comes from the theatrical profession. Playwrights occasionally insert dialogue that is badly written, but raises a laugh with the audience. (Probably a pun.)

During the First World War, poets like Wilfred Owen and Siegfried Sassoon captured the futility of battle so perfectly that their words continue to haunt us to this day:

> Bent double, like old beggars under sacks,
> Knock-kneed, coughing like hags, we cursed through sludge,
> Till on the haunting flares we turned our backs
> And towards our distant rest began to trudge.
> Men marched asleep. Many had lost their boots
> But limped on, blood-shod. All went lame; all blind;
> Drunk with fatigue; deaf even to the hoots
> Of disappointed shells that dropped behind.
>
> GAS! Gas! Quick, boys! – An ecstasy of fumbling,
> Fitting the clumsy helmets just in time;
> But someone still was yelling out and stumbling
> And floundering like a man in fire or lime. –
> Dim, through the misty panes and thick green light
> As under a green sea, I saw him drowning.
> In all my dreams, before my helpless sight,
> He plunges at me, guttering, choking, drowning.
>
> If in some smothering dreams you too could pace
> Behind the wagon that we flung him in,
> And watch the white eyes writhing in his face,
> His hanging face, like a devil's sick of sin;
> If you could hear, at every jolt, the blood
> Come gargling from the froth-corrupted lungs,
> Obscene as cancer, bitter as the cud
> Of vile, incurable sores on innocent tongues, –
> My friend, you would not tell with such high zest
> To children ardent for some desperate glory,
> The old Lie: Dulce et decorum est
> Pro patria mori.

(Wilfred Owen, 'Dulce et Decorum est', c. 1918)

Anyone around here speak English?

A sign in a Budapest zoo: 'Do not feed the animals. If you have any suitable food, give it to the guard on duty.'

Advertisers and marketers have long drawn on poetry to illustrate products or services. The poem, Night Mail by WH Auden (1907–73) was often featured to illustrate the role of a Royal Mail rolling sorting office, which remained in service until early 2004.

This is the Night Mail crossing the border,
Bringing the cheque and the postal order,
Letters for the rich, letters for the poor,
The shop at the corner and the girl next door.
Pulling up Beattock, a steady climb:
The gradient's against her, but she's on time.
Past cotton-grass and moorland boulder
Shovelling white steam over her shoulder,
Snorting noisily as she passes
Silent miles of wind-bent grasses.

Birds turn their heads as she approaches,
Stare from the bushes at her blank-faced coaches.
Sheep-dogs cannot turn her course;
They slumber on with paws across.
In the farm she passes no one wakes,
But a jug in the bedroom gently shakes.

Dawn freshens, the climb is done.
Down towards Glasgow she descends
Towards the steam tugs yelping down the glade of cranes,
Towards the fields of apparatus, the furnaces
Set on the dark plain like gigantic chessmen.
All Scotland waits for her:
In the dark glens, beside the pale-green sea lochs
Men long for news.

Letters of thanks, letters from banks,
Letters of joy from the girl and the boy,
Receipted bills and invitations
To inspect new stock or visit relations,
And applications for situations
And timid lovers' declarations
And gossip, gossip from all the nations,

Medieval words:

election – the astrological means to chose the perfect time for something to take place, such as travel, surgery or intercourse

News circumstantial, news financial,
Letters with holiday snaps to enlarge in,
Letters with faces scrawled in the margin,
Letters from uncles, cousins, and aunts,
Letters to Scotland, from the South of France,
Letters of condolence to Highlands and Lowlands
Notes from overseas to Hebrides
Written on paper of every hue,
The pink, the violet, the white and the blue,
The chatty, the catty, the boring, adoring,
The cold and official and the heart's outpouring,
Clever, stupid, short and long,
The typed and the printed and the spelt all wrong.

Thousands are still asleep
Dreaming of terrifying monsters,
Or of friendly tea beside the band at Cranston's or Crawford's:
Asleep in working Glasgow, asleep in well-set Edinburgh,
Asleep in granite Aberdeen,
They continue their dreams,
And shall wake soon and long for letters,
And none will hear the postman's knock
Without a quickening of the heart,
For who can bear to feel himself forgotten?

(WH Auden, 'The Night Mail', c. 1936)

Twisted truths:

If you reread your work, you can find on rereading a great deal of repetition can be avoided by rereading and editing.

Rap

In the same year Auden died, Rap was born. It was strongly prejudiced by African griots, who were travelling poets, musicians, and entertainers. They were famous for retelling tribal and family histories. Other influences included Chicago blues, bebop scat and wider influences such as the famed sayings of world heavyweight boxer, Mohammed Ali:'Float like a butterfly, sting like a bee.'

But Hip-hop, the subculture encompassing rap, graffiti art, and break-dancing, as well as distinctive codes of dress is accredited to Clive Campbell, aka DJ Kool Herc. DJ was soon joined by Grandmaster Flash and others. Until the release of 'Rapper's Delight' in October 1979, hip-hop (the music) was confined to the local neighbourhoods of New York. .

In 1982 Grandmaster Flash and MC Melle Mel released 'The Message' which featured a chorus that was to become the hip-hop positioning statement:

> It's like a jungle sometimes
> it makes me wonder
> how I keep from going under.

From there on, hip-hop's influence started to spread around the world. In fact, globally, hip-hop has given rise to words like 'bling-bling', which in turn has featured in many advertisements. It's also made the English language more dynamic, encouraging the young to express themselves through rhyme.

Gabay at a glance:

The trouble with featuring fads like hip-hop is that your copy can date and the message may alienate the very audience you are trying to attract.

Etymology:

I'll eat my hat – this phrase, meaning 'I'll be amazed if you can prove what you claim', comes from an old English meal called a 'hatte' featuring eggs, veal, dates, saffron and salt.

Max it – rap it

Ay yo trop	check this out
Ballin'	to have sex
Bama	a person with no fashion sense
Be geese	to leave
Biscuit	gun; behind or bottom
Bled	friend
Bling-bling	ostentatious jewelry
Boo	boyfriend/girlfriend
Cadillacing	relaxing
Cheeba	marijuana
Cutch	to chill; hang out
Flow	to rap
Fly	attractive
Janky	bad
Lunch	to act foolishly
Marinate	to chill; hang out
Max	to enjoy yourself
Nutt	good sex
Safe	cool person
Sik	good
Snow	cocaine
Smooth	stylish
Tagging	spray paint a gang's name on walls

Rhyme

Also see
Slogans
chapter 19

Slogans frequently incorporate rhyme. For example:

- Beanz Meanz Heinz™
- Best for less
- Don't be vague – ask for Haig™
- Drinka pinta milka day
- It's for you – hoo!
- Triumph has a bra for the way you are
- My goodness, my Guinness™

Loquacious language:

paronomasia – a pun

It is often thought that there are no rhymes for orange, purple and silver. Think again!

Orange   Blorenge (a hill near Abergavenny, Wales)

Purple   Hirple (to move with a gait between walking and crawling; to walk lamely, to drag a limb, to hobble)

            Curple (the rump, especially of a horse)

Silver   Chilver (a ewe lamb)

When using rhyme, the secret is in the syllables. Unless the final rhyming word has the same number of syllables as the word that it partners, the rhyme just doesn't work.

To get you started, here are over 2500 rhyming words – based on sound endings and the number of syllables.

-ar

are, ah, bar, car, scar, char, far, blah, bra, shah

Two syllables

drawbar, crowbar, towbar, rollbar, unbar, facebar, sidecar, streetcar, cha-cha, radar, shofar, Elgar, hoo-ha, dinar, faux pas, hurrah, Qatar, ta-ta, boudoir, memoir, Renoir, bourgeois

Three syllables

caviar, motorcar, la-di-da, Omaha, registrar, commissar, Parasha, tempura, baklava

-ay

day, gay, hey, hay, play, splay, slay, sleigh, may, neigh, nay, née, pay, ray, grey, tray, stray, weigh

Two syllables

ballet, foyer, sickbay, Bombay, rosebay ,okay, croquet, bouquet, risqué, heyday, Mayday, payday, bidet, Friday, workday, weekday, midday, half-day, someday, Monday, sundae, Sunday, washday, birthday, Thursday, Tuesday, doomsday, café, au fait, buffet, soufflé, inlay, replay, gourmet, foreplay, wordplay, parkway, Friday, hooray, passé, betray, portray, entrée, astray, x-ray, essay, cliché, crochet, pâté, convey, airway, fairway, midway, subway, doorway, halfway, gangway, slipway, outweigh, driveway, causeway

Writers' words:

'Books are never finished they are merely abandoned.' Oscar Wilde

Three syllables

holiday, everyday, teleplay, underplay, interplay, Hogmanay, consommé, résumé, divorcé, Kol Nidre, émigré, fiancé, ricochet, negligee, protégé, alleyway, anyway, expressway, motorway, Saturday, cabaret, attaché

err

fur, purr, stir, were, whirr

Two syllables

voyeur, recur, occur, incur, concur, coiffeur, defer, prefer, infer, confer, masseur, chasseur

Four syllables

entrepreneur

-air

air, heir, bare, bear, care, scare, chair, dare, fair, hair, lair, glare, snare, pear, pair, spare, tear, stair, stare, there, their, they're, wear, where, ware, swear

Two syllables

headsquare, neckware, hardware, firmware, elsewhere, sportswear, nightwear, footwear, software, menswear

Three syllables

overbear, aftercare, tableware, kitchenware, ironware, earthenware, premiere, thoroughfare, debonair, questionnaire, ladieswear

-eer

ear, beer, cheer, deer, dear, fear, sphere, gear, jeer, here, leer, clear, mere, smear, near, sneer, peer, pier, spear, queer, rear, sear, sere, sheer, shear, tear, tier, steer, we're, year

Two syllables

Zaire, reindeer, endear, headgear, footgear, Tangier, cohere, adhere, mishear, cashmere, Shakespeare, sincere, cashier, frontier, austere

Three syllables

bombardier, grenadier, commandeer, interfere, hemisphere, overhear, chandelier, gondolier, cavalier, musketeer, profiteer, gadgeteer, puppeteer, volunteer. atmosphere

In other words:

deceit – a place to sit

-ie

eye, buy, bye, sky, die, dye, guy, high, lie, fly, sly, my, nigh, pie, spy, wry, rye, cry, by, shy, tie, Thai, thy, why

Two syllables

Rabbi, thereby, whereby, hereby, nearby, flyby, bronchi, redeye, fungi, Shanghai, ally, mayfly, firefly, blowfly, gadfly, sandfly, housefly, Brunei, Sinai, porkpie, shuteye, necktie, pigsty

Three syllables

dissatisfy, preoccupy, decree nisi, edify, modify, magnify, unify, typify, specify, crucify, fortify, mortify, notify, sanctify, mystify, justify, vivify

Four syllables

syllabify, exemplify, personify, electrify, diversify, intensify, identify, solidify, humidify

-oor

moor, poor, sure, tour, you're , cure, lure, pure

Two syllables

amour, ensure, insure, liqueur, secure

Three syllables

reinsure, coinsure, manicure, insecure, premature, immature, overture, Troubadour, reassure

-oe

oh, beau, bow, dough, go, low, blow, flow, glow, slow, mow, know, row, roe, crow, grow, throw, sew, sow, so, show, toe, tow, stow, though, whoa

Two syllables

elbow, rainbow, longbow, crossbow, psycho, bronco, Moscow, gaucho, poncho, shadow, Bordeaux, dildo, nympho, ergo, forego, banjo, halo, deathblow, airflow, rhino, dunno, hippo, hypo, typo, tempo, burrow, scarecrow, also, fatso, narrow, zero, cargo, agro, gateaux, lotto, photo, blotto, motto, grotto, veto, cocoa, echo, rhino, sumo, wino, pesto, gusto, ouzo, window, aikido, judo, tango, bingo, lingo, barrow, arrow, marrow, tarot, panto, follow, hero, intro, ditto, yo-yo

Gabay at a glance:

Rhyme and alliteration can make great slogan partners. I used the partnership in an award-winning slogan for Woburn Safari Park in England 'Go Wild; go wow! Go Woburn'.

Loquacious language:

parisology – the pursuit of imprecision in language

Three syllables

radio, audio, rodeo, studio, cameo, stereo, embryo, video, piano, commando, overflow, volcano, fiasco, buffalo, Scorpio, patio, torpedo, indigo, flamingo, lumbago, potato, libretto, quid pro quo, cheerio, placebo, fiasco, alfresco, bravado, proviso, mistletoe, octavo, gazebo

Four syllables

portfolio, Orinoco, scenario, palomino, superego amoretto, amaretto, over-shadow

-oo

ooh, boo, chew, do, Jew, who, loo, blue, blew, clue, flu, flew, glue, moo, gnu, pooh, brew, crew, grew, drew, screw, true, shrew, stew, threw, too, to, two, woo, choux, few, dew, due, queue, lieu, new, view, zoo, shoe

Two syllables

bamboo, cuckoo, hairdo, redo, Urdu, voodoo, Hindu, undo, outdo, kung fu, shampoo, construe, Hebrew, untrue, lasso, thereto, onto, unto, into, rescue, fondue, nephew, preview, review, venue, ensue, pursue, argue, value, menu, issue, tissue, debut, tattoo

Three syllables

cockatoo, hereinto, revalue, impromptu, peek-a-boo, well-to-do, avenue, revenue, residue, kangaroo, interview, overdo

-y

Two syllables

baby, rugby, hardly, costly, homely, scarcely, chimney, angry, laundry, sundry, debris, pygmy, hungry, pastry, sultry, Nazi, envy, clumsy, filthy, paisley, empty, ivy, snowy, abbey, shabby, sixty, fifty, lively, flabby, crabby, shabby, hubby, sneaky, creaky, funky, junkie, lucky, silky, milky, cookie, rookie, catchy, crunchy, daddy, lady, monkey, sexy

Three syllables

industry, bankruptcy, dynasty, billowy, willowy, wallaby, landlady, cookery, unsteady, comedy, remedy, subsidy, tragedy, parody, custody

Four syllables

biography, chalcography, typography, geography, technology, philosophy, rockabilly, primarily, Christianly, accordingly, exceedingly, surprisingly

In other words:

melancholy – a sad sheep dog

-er

Two syllables

chamber, vodka, butcher, moisture, soldier, partner, gangster, monster, youngster, author, player, skier, flower, aqua, pecker, streaker, bicker, sliker, flicker, picker, snicker, nature, lecture, racer, tracer, actor, rector, drifter, smelter, delta, sticker, skier

Three syllables

ratepayer, soothsayer, purveyor, India, nuclear, barrier, carrier, warrior, Austria, media, Mafia, hosier, glazier, Haymaker, shoemaker, Jamaica, bookmaker, matchmaker, watchmaker, pacemaker, peacemaker, tiebreaker, dressmaker, lawbreaker, backbreaker, jawbreaker, caretaker, tearjerker, departure, professor, conductor

Four syllables

pizzeria, familiar, amplifier, magnifier, body-snatcher, legislature, architecture, manufacture, chipolata

Five syllables

paedophilia, anglophilia, haemophilia, unfamiliar, egomania, schizophrenia, qualifier, humidifier, Indonesia, manufacturer, xenophobia, agrophobia

-ack

back, black, flak, plaque, rack, crack, track, rack, shack, vac, whack, tack

Two syllables

sidetrack, wisecrack, racetrack, Slovak, rucksack, attack

Three syllables

stickleback, almanac, cardiac, maniac, leatherback

Four syllables

insomniac, celeriac

Five syllables

nymphomaniac, hypochondriac, aphrodisiac

Writers' words:

'The greatest writer cannot see through a brick wall but, unlike the rest of us, he does not build one.' WH Auden

447

-eck

Czech, check, cheque, deck, heck, fleck, neck, peck, speck

Two syllables

raincheck, crew-neck, roughneck, henpeck, shipwreck, Aztec

Three syllables

body-check, turtleneck, bottleneck

-ick

kick, chick, lick, click, flick, slick, brick, prick, trick, thick, wick, sick

Two syllables

garlic, Gaelic, bootlick, chromic, seismic, cosmic, Munich, beatnik, sputnik, toothpick, lovesick, non-stick, slapstick, pelvic, Gothic, comic, arsenic, logic

Three syllables

anarchic, heraldic, neuralgic, catholic, orgasmic, intrinsic, acoustic, frenetic, phonetic, sadistic, scholastic, logistic, agnostic, statistic, agnostic

Four syllables

diabetic, alphabetic, apathetic, empathetic, homophobic, journalistic, egoistic, realistic, euphemistic, pessimistic, optimistic, futuristic, Neolithic, sympathetic

-eech

each, beach, beech, leech, leach, bleach, peach, speech, breach, preach, teach

Two syllables

impeach

-ard

bard, card, chard, card, guard, lard, yard

Two syllables

placard, postcard, rearguard, fireguard, coastguard, die-hard, blowhard, mallard, dockyard, steelyard, farmyard, courtyard, graveyard

Three syllables

promenade, lumberyard, bodyguard

Loquacious language:

pedicular – lousy; rubbish

-eed

bead, deed, feed, heed, lead, bleed, plead, knead, speed, reed, creed, greed, Swede, swede

Two syllables

indeed, misdeed, handfeed, spoon-feed, nosebleed, mislead, groundspeed, inbreed, crossbreed, seaweed, fireweed, accede, exceed, succeed, proceed, Godspeed

Three syllables

underfeed, winterfeed, overfeed, millipede, tumbleweed

-id

bid, kid, hid, lid, quid, squid

Two syllables

outbid, naked, wicked, bearded, crowded, hooded, winded, dogged, rugged, timid, humid, learned, rapid, Cupid, stupid, liquid, varied, lurid, hurried, hybrid, Madrid, kindred, blessed, cursed, kilted, stilted, avid, livid, vivid, candid, splendid

Three syllables

half-naked, included, long-winded, unlearned, flat-footed, enchanted, unwanted, adopted, beloved, attended, unmounted, disjointed, demented, lamented, uncounted, acquainted

Four syllables

flabbergasted, unattended

Five syllables

uninterested, disinterested

-od

odd, bod, cod, hod, clod, plod, mod, nod, pod, quad, trod, sod, wad

Two syllables

bipod, tripod

Three syllables

demigod, unipod

Anyone around here speak English?

A sign in an Italian doctor's office: 'Specialist in women and other diseases.'

-d

Two syllables

chequered, drunkard, whiskered, steward, leopard, shepherd, backward, bastard, plastered, wayward, sideward, downward, upward, hazard, lizard, rumoured, myriad, treasured

Three syllables

good-natured, unstructured, self-centred, haphazard, uncovered

Four syllables

multicoloured, undiscovered

-and

band, canned, hand, land, bland, gland, brand, grand, strand, stand, slammed

Two syllables

headband, sideband, armband, rainband, disband, hatband, sweatband, waistband, forehand, backhand, expand, suntanned, handstand, withstand

Three syllables

second-hand, understand

Four syllables

misunderstand

-ainge

change, mange, range, grange

Two syllables

exchange, arrange, estrange, derange

-ell

bell, gel, hell, smell, spell, cell, sell, shell, tell, well, dwell, swell, yell

Two syllables

rebel, doorbell, cowbell, bluebell, handbell, dumbbell, lapel, propel, impel, compel, expel, inkwell, seashell, nutshell, cartel, speedwell, hotel, motel

---

Brand origins:

Lego – introduced as 'brick's in 1950s. Originally they were wooden toys made by Ole Kirk Christiansen, a carpenter. After World War II, his son Gotfred thought the idea of a connectable brick was worth marketing. The rest is history. 'Leg godt' in Danish means 'play well'.

-owl

owl, cowl, scowl, foul, fowl, jowl, howl, growl, prowl

-'l

Two syllables

babble, rabble, scrabble, pebble, treble, herbal, verbal, feeble, Bible, libel, tribal, cobble, bumble, jumble, humble, stumble, treacle, snorkel, ankle, rankle, rascal, fiscal, satchel, ladle, cradle, pedal, bundle, juggle, smuggle, signal, temple, dimple, pimple, crumble, viral, spiral, mongrel, pestle, wrestle, special, turtle, rectal, lintel, pastel, novel, marvel, navel, easel, diesel, weasel, chisel, muzzle, real, loyal, royal, mammal, opal, quarrel, martial

Three syllables

ensemble, triumphal, conjugal, archangel, caramel, deferral, cerebral, especial, interval, bilingual, embezzle, reprisal, ideal, surreal, bronchial, nominal, decimal, informal, criminal, regional, orchestral, apostle, credential

Four syllables

poroverbial, adverbial, perennial, industrial, memorial, pictorial, sartorial, phenomenal, universal, influential, residential, reverential, instrumental, oriental, arterial

-'m

Two syllables

album, welcome, boredom, condom, magnum, kingdom, slalom, bedlum, hoodlum, pogrom, tantrum, threesome, ransom, twosome, bottom, sanctum, rectum, quantum, system, anthem, fathom, phantom, buxom, ovum, darksome, irksome, bosom, Sweden, madam, tandem, chasm

Three syllables

popadom, martyrdom, maximum, minimum, quarrelsome, momentum, conundrum, cumbersome, stadium, tedium, medium, podium, premium, opium, platinum

Four syllables

candelabrum, American, Italian, officialdom, symbolism, euphemism, monarchism, masochism, criticism, atheism

Loquacious language:

pilgarlic – a bald headed man

-arn

barn, darn, tarn, yarn

Two syllables

maiden, Iran, Koran, Sudan, Teheran, Sawan, Japan

Three syllables

Indian, African, Pakistan, Turkistan

-een

been, bean, keen, dean, gene, lean, clean, mean, queen, screen, green, seen, scene, sheen, teen, wean, glean

Two syllables

has-been, sardine, praline, unclean, strychnine, serene, windscreen, latrine, gangrene, foreseen, thirteen, fourteen, fifteen, sixteen, protein, marine

Three syllables

Halloween, multiscreen, evergreen, seventeen, polythene, go-between, limousine, trampoline, submarine, contravene, intervene

-in

in, inn, skin, chin, spin, grin, sin, shin, tin, thin, win, twin

Two syllables

robin, cabin, bobbin, dustbin, gherkin, cooking, pumpkin, bearskin, foreskin, urchin, kitchen, coffin, dolphin, bargain, chaplain, hairpin, linchpin, tailspin, topspin, fountain, mountain, chicken, muffin, puffin, women, captain, toxin, begin

Three syllables

discipline, underpin, vitamin, assassin, heroin, heroine, masculine, examine, specimen, saccharin, medicine, bulletin, manikin

In other words:

copywriter – a person who corrects copy

-ine

dine, fine, line, spine, mine, pine, spine, brine, shrine, sign, wine, whine, swine, twine

Two syllables

define, refine, confine, hairline, beeline, feline, shoreline, neckline, guideline, sideline, touchline, deadline, headline, breadline, lifeline, tramline, hemline, streamline, coastline, clothesline, canine, equine, shoeshine, sunshine, moonshine, combine, decline, incline, recline, benign, assign, praline

Three syllables

concubine, calamine, auld lang syne, valentine, intertwine, underline, countersign

-'n

Two syllables

stubborn, Bourbon, Melbourne, Lisbon, Brisbane, slacken, beckon, blacken, liken, luncheon, drunken , shrunken, pardon, sudden, wooden, London, deafen, hyphen, often, orphan, roughen, vegan, slogan, Belgian, fallen, barman, lemon, German, sermon, fireman, Mormon, workman, linkman, churchman, Scotsman, watchman, madman, headman, fireman, legman, baseman, swagman, salesman, strongman, spaceman, batsman, statesman, yachtsman, sportsman, human, boatman, tribesman, sharpen, barren, baron, matron, patron, saffron, lectern, plankton, chieftain, lantern, python, cousin, dozen, crimson, crayon, iron, lion, Zion, golden, sultan, organ, region, villain, flatten, threaten, eaten, mitten, curtain, button, glutton, western, Britain, raisin, brazen, poison, chosen, frozen, olden, billion, million

Three syllables

rifleman, signalman, cattleman, gentleman, policeman, Englishman, half-open, reopen, distinction, extinction, revulsion, occasion, convulsion, abrasion, persuasion, dissuasion, simpleton, alien, Caucasian, downtrodden, embolden, cardigan, commotion, solution, production, allusion, collusion, illusion, transfusion, delusion, Manhattan, Egyptian, confusion, forgotten, pinion, Volkswagen, Moroccan, stableman, middleman, Malaysian, Hawaiian, subtraction

Loquacious language:

procellous – stormy or tempestuous, for example 'my mother-in-law was in a procellous mood.'

Four syllables

barbarian, Sicilian, reptilian, Albanian, Brazilian, Rumanian, Tasmanian, Iranian, Jordanian, Ukrainian Lithuanian, revolution, Darwinian, Hungarian, Bavarian, Mohammedan, shenanigan, reputation, evolution, institution, bellybutton, interwoven

Five syllables

vaudevillian, vegetarian, hallucinogen

-ing

king, cling, fling, sling, ping, ring, wring, bring, spring, string, sing, sting, thing, wing, swing

Two syllables

gnawing, drawing, dubbing, rubbing, backing, packing, cracking, working, sneaking, Peking, speaking, ducking, trucking, banking, catching, etching, teaching, breeching, poaching, scorching, touching, pudding, surfing, briefing, roofing, flagging, rigging, sterling, schooling, sealing, fiddling, crackling, weakling, branding, smuggling, grappling, dumpling, rattling, earthling, flaming, lemming, swimming, planning, mourning, morning, glazing, posing, lightning, evening, longing, ripping, whipping, shopping, sloping, fetching, searching, herring, piercing, lashing, fencing, hunting, smashing, cutting, fainting, painting, haunting, pointing, roasting, plaything, nothing, teething, soothing, starving, boxing, skiing, dying, flying, spying, baking, smocking, making, taking, licking, shading, fading, bedding, blessing, dressing, placing

Three syllables

disturbing, absorbing, bird-watching, demanding, scaffolding, travelling, performing, brainstorming, anything, everything, wellbeing, daydreaming, depressing, distressing, hairdressing, surprising, amazing, confusing, eye-catching

-ope

cope, scope, dope, hope, slope, mope, rope, pope, grope, soap

Two syllables

tightrope, elope

Three syllables

telescope, periscope, isotope, stroboscope, gyroscope, antelope

---

Brand origins:

Lucozade, 1930s – from glucose and 'ade' – as in cherryade, and lemonade. The drink was originally developed by a chemist whose daughter was jaundiced. To make it taste sweeter he added orange and lemon oils.

Four syllables

kaleidoscope

-ass

ass, bass, gas, lass

Two syllables

amass, groundmass, landmass

-arse

farce, class, glass, pass, sparse, grass

Two syllables

subclass, eyeglass, hourglass, surpass, bypass, impasse

Three syllables

underpass, overpass

-iss

kiss, hiss, bliss, diss, piss, this, Swiss

Two syllables

malice, palace, trellis, heirless, careless, hairless, tireless, wireless, lawless, fearless, flawless, jobless, speechless, needless, neckless, necklace, thankless, mindless, soundless, groundless, legless, ageless, harmless, nameless, shameless, homeless, seamless, gormless, painless, sinless, spineless, hapless, strapless, useless, voiceless, heartless, weightless, classless, baseless, spotless, guiltless, tasteless, dauntless, sexless, premise, weakness, weirdness, fondness, sharpness, auspice, hostess, witless, hospice, senseless

Three syllables

seductress, apprentice, armistice, cannabis, syphilis, penniless, merciless, pitiless, humourless, colourless, fatherless, motherless, passionless, motionless, senselessness, meaningless, limitless, spiritless, premises, happiness,

Four syllables

expressionless, mercilessness, pitilessness, powerlessness, meaninglessness, purposelessness, limitlessness, effortlessness, relentlessness, dubiousness

Loquacious language:

procerity – to stand tall

-'s

joyous, raucous, ruckus, porpoise, bronchus, fungus, compass, callous, campus, hummus, walrus, zealous, noxious, circus, focus, locus, terrace, gracious

Three syllables

alias, pancreas, gaseous, presumptuous, audacious, hazardous, contagious, embarrass, generous, cankerous, ambitious, grievous, atrocious, loquacious

Four syllables

rebellious, rumbustious, melodious, illustrious, hocus-pocus, advantageous, cantankerous, gratuitous

-nce

Two syllables

prudence, vengeance, parlance, sequence, entrance, fragrance, license, licence, patience, substance, brilliance, clearance, guidance

Three syllables

annoyance, clairvoyance, disturbance, elegance, ambulance, condolence, coherence, concordance, petulance, consequence, defiance, alliance, diligence, excellence, resemblance, impotence, assistance, existence, arrogance

Four syllables

experience, convenience, deliverance

-at

at, bat, cat, scat, chat fat, hat, splat, mat, gnat, rat, spat, twat

Two syllables

wombat, dingbat, cravat, hellcat, polecat, backchat, begat

Three syllables

diplomat, acrobat, Laundromat, automat, habitat, democrat, plutocrat, aristocrat

---

Pocket inspiration:

Too many people buy brands they don't need to impress people they don't even like.

-ait

eight, bait, skate, hate, late, plate, slate, crate, mate, great, freight, straight, state, weight

Two syllables

cheapskate, backdate, floodgate, inflate, nameplate, translate, checkmate, rotate, stalemate, shipmate, helpmate, classmate, flatmate, ornate, vibrate, mutate, dictate, estate, create, narrate, donate

Three syllables

permeate, deviate, mutilate, simulate, stipulate, decorate, terminate, violate, animate, intimate, paginate, generate, cogitate, vegetate, orchestrate, salivate, titivate, motivate, cultivate, activate

Four syllables

repatriate, exfoliate, humiliate, asphyxiate, negotiate, officiate, manipulate, annihilate, approximate, legitimate, coordinate, contaminate, orientate, consecrate

-it

it, bit, sit, kit, chit, slit, spit, quit, Brit, wit, twit

Two syllables

poet, debit, rarebit, cubit, blanket, casket, audit, bandit, target, toilet, eyelet, playlet, wallet, tablet, sonnet, gullet, booklet, anklet, omelette, ringlet, hermit, permit, admit, moppet, poppet, puppet, snippet, pirate, curate, turret, culprit, facet, tacit, whatsit, rivet, privet, private, halfwit, dimwit, nitwit, outwit, exit, habit, rabbit, circuit, wicket, limit, visit, comet, closet, whippet

Three syllables

albeit, advocate, counterfeit, hypocrite, aureate, laureate, cohabit, delicate, fortunate, aggregate, chocolate, explicit, illicit, solicit, implicit, exquisite, deposit, violet, opposite, vertebrate

Four syllables

inadequate, invertebrate, associate, appropriate, supermarket, Identikit, certificate

---

Etymology:

jock strap – this 1897 word comes from an invention by the BIKE manufacturing company. They invented the 'bicycle jockey strap' for cyclists who rode along bumpy roads. The garment was eventually known by its shortened name 'jock'.

-aint

ain't, paint, quaint, saint

Two syllables

complaint, repaint, greasepaint, acquaint, restraint, constraint

-ent

bent, dent, gent, meant, spent, rent, cent, scent, went, vent

Two syllables

hellbent, indent, relent, fragment, comment, torment, repent, well-spent, extent, accent, dement, cement

Three syllables

regiment, document, overspent, discontent, underwent, complement, compliment, represent

Four syllables

disorient, misrepresent

-'nt

Two syllables

vacant, hadn't, trident, sealant, silent, coolant, figment, pigment, judgement, vestment, pavement, stagnant, serpent, rampant, parent, fragrant, ancient, potent, constant, decent, recent, current, torrent, flippant, movement, shipment, latent, accent, patent, blatant, mutant, pleasant, distant, servant, peasant, pheasant, brilliant.

Three syllables

absorbent, recumbent, embankment, commandment, amendment, enlargement, alignment, inducement, government, department, excitement, assortment, recruitment, resentment, adjustment, investment, amazement, indignant, celebrant, apartment, enchantment, amazement, delinquent, occupant, adjacent, insolvent, radiant, gradient, salient, nutrient, sentiment, deviant, transient, indecent, attainment, battlement, displacement, pollutant, contestant, relaxant, penitent, competent, irritant

Four syllables

disagreement, advertisement, maladjustment, unimportant, disappointment, intermittent, omnipotent, decongestant

---

Did you know?

The first product to officially use the late Diana, Princess of Wales' logo was Flora margarine.

-eest

east, beast, feast, least, priest, yeast

-ist

fist, gist, list, mist, wrist, twist

Two syllables

cubist, stockist, sadist, modest, nudist, druggist, blacklist, enlist, stylist, demist, bassist, insist, fascist, greatest, rightist, flautist, harvest, Buddhist, palmist, dearest, forest, florist, jurist, tourist, purist, assist, persist, dentist

Three syllables

lobbyist, atheist, egoist, anarchist, monarchist, exorcist, activist, loyalist, royalist, fatalist, moralist, novelist, realist, analyst, catalyst, alarmist, bigamist, hedonist, pianist, humanist, therapist, guitarist, careerist, deforest, humorist, terrorist, satirist, motorist, lyricist, pharmacist, egotist, dramatist, pragmatist, hypnotist, optimist, pessimist

Four syllables

propagandist, motorcyclist, psychologist, apologist, tobacconist, perfectionist, polygamist

-ix

fix, mix, six, wicks, bricks

Two syllables

affix, prefix, suffix, transfix, helix, tropics, physics, onyx, tactics, antics, matrix, metrics

Three syllables

hydraulics, forensics, politics, logistics, ballistics, statistics, linguistics, acoustics, crucifix, dynamics, harmonics, hysterics, dramatics, dogmatics, athletics, genetics, phonetics, gymnastics, semantics

Four syllables

histrionics, electronics, atmospherics

Etymology:

atlas – the sixteenth century French geographer Gerhard Mercator published a book of maps which featured a picture of Atlas carrying the world on his back. Since then any collection of maps is commonly known as an atlas.

Brains, pen, action!

Something to ponder...

1   Write a jingle for your product or service

2   Write a jingle for your country's incumbent
    president or Prime minister.

3   Write a rap to advertise your local church,
    temple, mosque or synagogue.

Did you know?

The two longest words you can spell without repeating a letter are dermatoglyphics and uncopyrightable.

16. Get your tongue around this.... (tongue twisters)

It occurs to me that if I am to write a chapter on the upside down world of tongue twisters, I should make an effort not to write a preview, but first a summary…

…In conclusion, to write a quick and apt tongue twister, draw up a list of nouns, proper nouns, verbs and descriptive words (adjectives and adverbs) all starting with a particular letter (e.g. 'D').

nouns	names	verbs	adverbs
dream	David	dream	deeply
damsel	Daisy	dance	defectively

- Write down the first line of a story that makes sense.

- Add a second line, featuring words from your list, that develops the story.

- Next add a rhythm.

Go to the last page of the chapter to see how this particular one turned out...

Tongue twisters

Get your tongue around this...

Tongue twisters were particularly popular with purveyors of punchy English who pursued pronunciation problems by playing with the presence of parallel consonants interspersed with a multiplicity of vowels, as in:

Peter Piper picked a peck of pickled peppers.
A peck of pickled peppers Peter Piper picked.
If Peter Piper picked a peck of pickled pepper,
where's the peck of pickled peppers Peter Piper picked?

Classics like *Truly rural* and *She sells sea-shells* on the sea-shore have given rise to many memorable copywriting jargons and slogans.

Tongue twisters pose an interesting question to copywriters: should you use them because they are memorable – or is the act of remembering how to pronounce them simply too difficult to recollect the blighters in the first place?!

For example:

> *Chef's square shaped soups*
> *Show how a good soup should be.*

Or from BBC Radio 4's *Forty Nights in the Wilderbeast:*

> *It's time for, The Big Fact Hunt*

Allied to tongue twisters are slogans (see chapter 19) especially those featuring alliteration (repetition of a sound):

> *Britain's best business bank by far*
> *Discover the Dirvishire difference*
> *Don't dream it. Do it.*
> *Dream. Dare. Develop. Do.*
> *Functional... Fashionable... Formidable...*
> *Specialised staffing solutions*

Loquacious language:

quaintrelle – a women who is well dressed

The secret of writing tongue twisters is firstly to consider their pronunciation, and secondly how they sound through the effects of alliteration (repetition of a sound).

Often, words of similar but not identical sounds lead to making a Spoonerism where letters or syllables get swapped. This often happens accidentally in slips of the tongue.

These apparent mistakes can actually serve copywriters well, for they offer a completely different interpretation of an otherwise well known word or subject.

'Spoonerised' characters from Star Wars:

Varth Dader
San Holo
Sark Dide
Wobi On
Lincess Prea
Fie Tighter
Skuke Lywalker
Habba the Jut
Led Reader
Fillenium Malcon
Foba Bett

Tinglish errors and English terrors

Bad salad (Sad ballad)
Soap in your hole (Hope in your soul)
Mean as custard (Keen as mustard)
Plaster man (Master plan)
Pleating and humming (Heating and plumbing)
Trim your snow tail (Trim your toe nails)
Birthington's washday (Washington's Birthday)
Trail snacks (Snail tracks)
Bottle in front of me (Frontal Lobotomy)
Sale of two titties (Tale of two cities)
Rental Deceptionist (Dental Receptionist)
Flock of bats (Block of flats)
Chewing the doors (Doing the chores)

Did you know?

US baby food manufacturer Gerber featured a baby on its African food labels. Initial sales were low; they didn't realise that in Africa, labels were meant to indicate a product's ingredients.

In turn, spoonerisms have spawned their own progeny such as:

Diplograms
Words with every different letter appearing only twice.

Triplogram
Words with every different letter appearing only three times.

Quadrigram
Words with every different letter appearing only four times.

Pascal words
Words with one different letter once, another twice, another thrice... and so on.

The trouble with all these examples is they can all too easily lead (depending on your view) to the mark of a truly dire copywriter, stomach wrenching stand-up comedian or great sub-editor: the pun.

The Pun of the World headlines

Police Begin Campaign to Run Down Jaywalkers

Iraqi Head Seeks Arms

Is There a Ring of Debris around Uranus?

Teacher Strikes, Idle Kids

Miners Refuse to Work after Death

Juvenile Court to Try Shooting Defendant

War Dims Hope for Peace

If Strike Isn't Settled Quickly, It May Last Awhile

Red Tape Holds Up New Bridges

Typhoon Rips Through Cemetery; Hundreds Dead

Man Struck By Lightning Faces Battery Charge

New Study of Obesity Looks for Larger Test Group

Father Gordon inserted many plays on words in his sermon. So many that his congregation felt that these were: WORD PUNS OF MASS DISTRACTION.

Gabay at a glance:

None of the following have a 'singular' equivalent:

Agenda	*Clothes*
Cattle	*Pants*
Scissors	*Pliers*
Trousers	*Shorts*

Loquacious language:

qualtagh – the first person you meet after leaving your house on a special occasion

Further groans

Touchdown

Two American Football teams are on a tour of Europe and have a quiz to see which team can name most places in Holland. The game was won by a single word: Dutch Town.

Bad manners

A child was misbehaving by protesting loudly and rudely waving boards with crazy slogans on, while guests were visiting. He was punished for having mad banners.

William Tell the bowler

There is evidence that William Tell and his family were avid bowlers, but unfortunately all the league records were destroyed in a fire. Thus we'll sadly never know for whom the Tells bowled.

False steps

He said he'd not grown strong from all his dancing, but no one believed him. It was obvious to all that he was bearing waltz fitness.

Champagne to our friends

"Here's champagne to our real friends...

...and real pain to our sham friends."

That's quite enough of that!

Back to the serious stuff of tongue twisters (or the far more beautiful Italian word for it: 'scioglilingua'). The following examples are meant to inspire you to write your own. For simplicity, I have broken them down into the general resonance they produce when pursing lips and flexing tongues.

1. Sounds: b, p, m, wh

A monk's monkey mounted a monastery wall and munched melon and macaroni.

A plain pinewood police van, privately packed with protesting passengers, plies periodically to Plymouth prison.

A white witch watched a woe-begone walrus winding white wool.

The brisk brave brigadier brandished broad bright blades, blunderbusses and bludgeons.

Betty beat a bit of butter to make a better batter.

Mixed metaphors muddle middling minds.

Pragmatic politicians pontificate precociously.

Writers' words:

'Most writers need a wound, either physical or spiritual.' Martin Amis

"Big buns are better buttered," Billy muttered.

Truly rural, purely plural, truly rurally, purely plurally.

2. Sounds: t, d, l, n, r, s, z

A library littered with literary literature.

A purely rural duel truly plural is better than purely plural duel truly rural.

Lotty loves lollies when lolling in the lobby.

A rural ruler should be truly rural and recognise rural raillery.

A ship saleth south soon.

A tidy tiger tied a tie tighter to tidy her tiny tail.

If a doctor doctored another doctor, would the doctor doing the doctoring doctor the other doctor in the way the doctored doctor wanted to be doctored, or would the doctor doing the doctoring doctor the other doctor in his own way?

Twelve typological topographers typically translating types

Shy Sam Smith thought Sarah Short so sweet.

I want a dozen double damask dinner napkins.

Red leather, yellow leather, red leather, yellow leather.

Round and round the rugged rock the ragged rascal ran.

Seventeen slimy slugs in satin sunbonnets sat singing short sad songs.

Six steaming sheiks, sitting stitching sheets.

Thirty-six teasel tweezer trees.

3. Sounds: k g ng

Polly Cox's ox ate eight hollyhocks, now the eight hollyhocks eating ox lies in a great mahogany box.

A cup of creamy custard cooked for Cuthbert.

A canner, exceedingly canny, one day remarked to his granny, "A canner can can anything he can, but a canner can't can a can, can he?"

The conundrum constructed by the communist was catastrophical.

A wicked cricket critic.

A kiss is the anatomical juxtaposition of two orbicularis oris muscles in a state of contraction.

United States twin-screw steel cruisers.

Gabay at a glance

When rehearsing an important speech, use tongue twisters to improve your pronunciation and enunciation skills.

Loquacious language:

rampallion – a rampant woman

She stood on the balcony inexplicably mimicking him hiccupping and welcoming him in.

The gleaming green Glasgow glass gas-globe Grace gave Greta.

4. Sound: th

Freddy thrush flies through thick fog.

Where are the thick and thin thistles that Thornwick Thistledown pushed his thick thumb through?

If Timothy Theophyllis Thicklewade Thanckham thrusts his two thick thumbs through three hundred and thirty-three thousand three hundred and thirty-three thick and thin thistles, where are the three hundred and thirty-three thousand three hundred and thirty-three thick and thin thistles that Timothy Theorphylliss Thicklewade Thackham thrust his two thick thumbs through?

Miss Ruth's red roof thatch.

She is a thistle sifter, and she has a sieve of sifted thistles and a sieve of unsifted thistles, and the sieve of unsifted thistles she sieves into the sieve of sifted thistles, because she is a thistle sifter.

Six thick thistle sticks.

Ten tongue-tied tailors twisted tinted thistles with their teeth. If ten tongue-tied tailors twisted tinted thistles with their teeth, who tinted the tinted thistles that the ten tongue-tied tailors twisted?

Through ticket and bush, the thirty thrifty, thirsty Thracians thrust.

5. Sounds: f, v, s

Three free-flow thimble pipes.

A fat-thighed freak fries thick fish.

Five frantic fat frogs fled from fifty fierce fishes.

Five fine French frivolous friars fanning a fainted flea.

Frisky Freddy feeds on fresh fried fish.

My wife gave Mr Snipe's wife's knife a wipe.

Famous friezes figured fabulously.

Figs form fine fancy fare!

Four famous fishermen found four flounders (flippers flapping furiously) faithfully following four floppy female flat-fish.

I snuff shop snuff? Do you snuff shop snuff?

Francis fries fish fillets for Frederick. Frederick fillets first for Francis' fired fritters.

She saw thirty-four swift sloops swing shoreward, before she saw the forty-three spaceships soar.

Medieval words:

eisel – a sour wine

Where ignorance predominates, vulgarity invariably asserts itself.

Fred: You can have: Fried fresh fish; Fish fried fresh; Fresh fried fish; Fresh fish fried; Or fish fresh fried, Fred

And a potentially rude one. Be careful!

I'm not a pheasant plucker,

I'm the pheasant plucker's son;

And I'm only plucking pheasants

till the pheasant plucker comes.

6. Sounds ch, ge, sh, zh

Does this shop stock socks with spots on?

A soft shot-silk sash shop.

Cheryl's cheap chip shop sells cheap chips

Shiver and slither shovelling slushy squelchy snow.

If a shipshape ship shop stocks six shipshape shop-soiled ships, how many shipshape shop-soiled ships would six shipshape ship shops stock?

Chief Sheikh's sheep section is sure swell.

I wish I hadn't washed this wrist watch.

The Swiss witch which bewitched this switch, wished the switch bewitched.

She sells seashells on the seashore.

When does the wrist-watch strap shop shut?

Shy Sheila shakes soft shimmering silks

Shall Sarah Silling share her shining shilling? Sarah Silling shall share her shining shilling.

A selfish shellfish smelt a stale fish. If the stale fish was a smelt, then the selfish shellfish smelt a smelt.

Six Scotch soldiers shooting snipe.

The winkle ship shank; the shrimp ship swam.

Writers' words:

'Take care that you never spell a word wrong. Always before you write a word, consider how it is spelled, and, if you do not remember, turn to a dictionary. It produces great praise to a lady to spell well.' Thomas Jefferson

Finally, a tale to conclude…

Ned Nott was shot and Steve Shott was not. So it's better to be Shott than Nott. Some say Nott was not shot, but Shott swears he shot Nott. Either the shot Shott shot at Nott was not shot or Nott was shot. If the shot Shott shot shot Nott, Nott was shot. But if the shot Shott shot shot Shott himself, then shott would be shot and Not would not. However, the shot Shott shot shot not Shott but Nott. It's not easy to say who was shot and who was not, but we know who was Shott and who was not.

7. Sound: h

The horses' hard hoofs hit the hard high road. They were then hindered by the edge of the hedge.

He bade him eat his own hot ham, so his own hot ham he ate.

His hat hit Horace – Horace hollered.

The heir had hair that had an air about it, hadn't it.

Has Hugh heavily harnessed Helen's Harry hurriedly or has His Highness howled over the heads of all who have heard about Hugh's horrid hunting expeditions?

Last year I could not hear with either ear.

Etymology:

red-letter day – this phrase relates to a special occasion. It originates from the Middle Ages when religious dates on a calendar were printed in red rather than black.

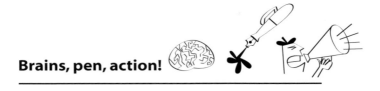

Brains, pen, action!

Back to where I ended (at the beginning)...

It goes a little something like this:

David dreamt a dream
Of damsel Daisy dancing defectively
David's damsel declined to dance
So David's dream was deeply derogatory

Choose some words and make up your own tongue twister.

Ta for taking time to tackle these tasty tongue twisters!

17. Words from the wise

In 400 BC Hippocrates published 'Aphorism'. It contained 'truths' which he felt would be apt and helpful for people who wished to study medicine. It included 'gems' like:

A woman does not become ambidextrous.

If the summer be dry and northerly and the autumn rainy and southerly, headaches occur in winter, with coughs, hoarsenesses, coryzae, and in some cases consumptions.

This chapter features slightly more apt aphorisms for today's needs, as well as proverbs and more besides – such as speech writing.

In all cases, keep in mind the words of one of my favourite essayists, Andre Gide:

Everything has been said before, but since nobody listens we have to keep going back and beginning all over again.

[Mind you, one does learn from one's mistakes.]

never ask a blind man for directions

Words from the wise

In this selection of useful quotes I have selected a mixture of aphorisms, proverbs and, quite simply, clever idea boosters. They deal with characteristics, emotions, people, human nature, morals, business, virtues and nature.

I suggest you consider using them as concept drivers, although many can also be used as either headlines or subheads. Also refer to my guidance on idioms (chapter 8).

As a wise man once said when asked the meaning of life –
'I am not sure but I know that right now, I would love a cold beer.'

Etymology:

America – This name was inspired by Amerigo Vespucci, a Florentine navigator who made four visits to the New World between 1497 and 1503. A German mapmaker named Martin Waldseemüller labelled the new land 'America'.

A

Ability

Everyone excels in something in which another fails.
Latin proverb

Any jackass can kick down a barn, but it takes a good carpenter to build one.
Sam Rayburn

Absence

Absence makes the heart grow fonder.
TH Bayly

Out of sight, out of mind.
Homer

Abstinence

It is easier to abstain than to restrain.
French proverb

Absurdity

There is nothing so absurd or ridiculous that has not at some time been said by some philosopher.
Oliver Goldsmith

Abundance

Abundance, like want, ruins man.
Benjamin Franklin

Abuse

There is more credit in being abused by fools than praised by rogues.
FE Smith

Academia

The average PhD thesis is nothing but the transference of bones from one graveyard to another.
J Frank Dobie

Accomplishment

Who begins too much accomplishes little.
German proverb

To accomplish great things, we must dream as well as act.
Anatole France

Achievement

Only those who dare to fail greatly can ever achieve greatly.
Robert F Kennedy

Don't let what you cannot do interfere with what you can do.
John Wooden

You can't build your reputation on what you're going to do.
Henry Ford

Action

Everything comes to him who hustles while he waits.
Thomas Edison

People forget how fast you did a job – but they remember how well you did it.
Howard W Newton

If a thing is worth doing, it is worth doing badly.
GK Chesterton

Activity

Lose no time; be always employed in something useful.
Benjamin Franklin

Activity is contagious
Ralph Waldo Emerson

Adaptability

The foolish and the dead alone never change their opinions.
James R Lowell

Medieval words:

Atarah – A Jewish torah crown

The bamboo which bends is stronger than the oak which resists.
Japanese proverb

Admiration

Admiration is the daughter of ignorance.
Benjamin Franklin

Adults

A boy becomes an adult three years before his parents think he does … and about two years after he thinks he does.
Lewis Hershey

Adventure

When you're safe at home you wish you were having an adventure; when you're having an adventure you wish you were safe at home.
Thornton Wilder

One does not discover new lands without consenting to lose sight of the shore for a very long time.
Andrew Gide

Adversity

When the going gets tough, the tough get going.
Robert Schuller

There is no education like adversity.
Benjamin Disraeli

Advertising

Give them quality. That's the best kind of advertising.
Milton S Hershey

Advice

Never trust the advice of a man in difficulties.
Aesop

Never put a sock in a toaster.
Eddie Izzard

Affliction

I thank God for my handicaps, for through them, I have found myself, my work and my God.
Helen Keller

Age

No one is so old as to think he cannot live one more year.
Cicero

Aggressiveness

Not only strike while the iron is hot, but make it hot by striking.
Oliver Cromwell

You can't achieve anything without getting in someone's way.
Abban Eban

Ageing

Few people know how to be old.
La Rochefoucauld

Age is a question of mind over matter. If you don't mind, it doesn't matter.
Satchel Paige

To me, old age is always fifteen years older than I am.
Bernard Baruch

Agriculture

Blessed be agriculture! If one does not have too much of it.
Charles Dudley

To the average British farmer, organic farming is about as relevant as caviar and a flight on Concorde.
Oliver Walston

Ambition

The ripest peach is highest on the tree.
James Whitcomb Riley

Writers' words:

'Just the omission of Jane Austen's books alone would make a fairly good library out of a library that hadn't a book in it.' (Mark Twain)

All ambitions are lawful except those which climb upward on the miseries or credulities of mankind.
Joseph Conrad

Amusement

I am a great friend to public amusements, for they keep people from vice.
Samuel Johnson

Ancestry

I would rather make my name than inherit it.
WM Thackeray

I don't know who my grandfather was; I am much more concerned to know who his grandson will be.
Abraham Lincoln

Anger

Never go to be bed mad. Stay up and fight.
Phyllis Diller

Anger is a better sign of the heart than of the head; it is a breaking out of the disease of honesty.
Marquess of Halifax

Animals

To his dog, every man is Napoleon; hence the constant popularity of dogs.
Aldous Huxley

A horse is dangerous at both ends and uncomfortable in the middle.
Ian Flemming

Answers

No answer is also an answer.
Danish proverb

Aphorists

Good things, when short, are twice as good.
Baltasar Gracian

Metaphors:

Whatever sentence will bear to be read twice, we may be sure was thought twice.
Henry David Thoreau

Appearance

How little do they see what is, who frame their hasty judgements upon that which seems.
Robert Southey

Appetite

Always rise from the table with an appetite, and you will never sit down without one.
William Penn

A stomach that is seldom empty despises common food.
Horace

Applause

The applause of the crowd makes the head giddy.
Richard Steele

Appreciation

We never know the worth of water till the well is dry.
English proverb

I now perceive one immense omission in my Psychology – the deepest principle of Human Nature is the craving to be appreciated.
William James

Architecture

Architecture is frozen music.
Johann Goethe

Arguing

I learned long ago never to wrestle with a pig. You get dirty, and besides, the pig likes it.
Cyrus Ching

There were several experienced verbal stunt pilots in the Glass family. – JD Salinger, *Franny and Zooey*

Aristocracy

A degenerate nobleman is like a turnip. There is nothing good of him but that which is underground.

English saying

Art

Art is poetry without words.

Horace

If my husband would ever meet a woman on the street who looked like the women in his paintings, he would fall over in a dead faint.

Mrs Pablo Picasso

Artists

An artist cannot speak about his art in anymore than a plant can discuss horticulture.

Jean Cocteau

Every artist dips his brush in his own soul, and paints his own nature into his pictures.

Henry Ward Beecher

Arts

Real books should be the offspring not of daylight and casual talk but of darkness and silence.

Marcel Proust

Aspiration

In the long run men hit only what they aim at. Therefore, though they should fail immediately, they had better aim at something high.

Henry David Thoreau

Atheism

The fool hath said in his heart, There is no God.

Psalms 14:1

By night an atheist half-believes in God.

Edward Young

Attitude

As long as a man imagines that he cannot do a certain thing, it is impossible for him to do it.

Benedit Spinoza

Whenever you are asked if you can do a job, tell 'em, Certainly, I can! – and get busy and find out how to do it.

Theodore Roosevelt

Auctions

At an auction keep your mouth shut.

Spanish proverb

Authors

It is as easy to dream a book as it is hard to write one.

Honore Balzac

There is no amount of praise which a man and an author cannot bear with equanimity. Some authors can even stand flattery.

Maurice Baring

B

Babies

A soiled baby, with a neglected nose, cannot conscientiously be regarded as a thing of beauty.

Mark Twain

A loud noise at one end and no sense of responsibility at the other.

Ronald Knox

Out of the mouths of babes comes a lot of what they should have swallowed.

Franklin P Jones

Shakespearean insult:

'(You) leather-jerkin, crystal-button, knot-pated, agate-ring, puke-stocking, caddis-garter, smooth-tongue, Spanish pouch!' (*Henry IV*, part 1, act II, scene iv)

Banks

It is easier to rob by setting up a bank than by holding up a bank clerk.

Bertolt Brecht

Bargains

Necessity never made a good bargain.

Benjamin Franklin

Beauty

Beauty without virtue is a flower without perfume.

French proverb

Beauty in distress is much the most affecting beauty.

Edmund Burke

Bedlam

Man has made his bedlam; let him lie in it.

Fred Allen

Begging

Better to beg than steal, but better to work than beg.

Russian proverb

Beginning

Once begun, a task is easy.

Horace

The beginning is the most important part of the work.

Plato

Gabay at a glance:

Once you feel you have the ideal beginning of your speech, the rest usually follows.

For example, Sir Bob Geldoff explained that once he had written the first lyrics for one of the last century's greatest Christmas songs, 'Do they know it's Christmas time', the rest of the words fell into place. 'It's Christmas time/there's no need to be afraid...'

Benefits

If you stop to think about it, there are very few benefits in your life for which you can take sole credit.

Gary Smalley

Bible

It is impossible to govern the world without God and the Bible.

George Washington

The whole inspiration of our civilisation springs from the teachings of Christ and the lessons of the prophets. To read the Bible for these fundamentals is a necessity of American life.

Herbert Hoover

Birth control

I want to tell you a terrific story about oral contraception. I asked this girl to sleep with me and she said no.

Woody Allen

Blame

He must be pure who would blame another.

Danish proverb

Blindness

Can the blind lead the blind? Shall they not both fall into the ditch?

Luke 6:39

Body

The body says what words cannot.

Martha Graham

The spirit indeed is willing, but the flesh is weak.

Matthew 26:41

Boldness

In difficult situations the boldest plans are safest.

Titus Livy

Writers' words:

Sommerset Maugham said there were three rules for writing – and nobody knows what they are. Joan Collins

When you cannot make up your
mind which of two evenly balanced
courses of action
you should take – choose
the bolder.
WJ Slim

Books

A drop of ink may make a million
think.
Lord Byron

That is a good book which is
opened with expectation, and
closed with profit.
A Bronson Alcott

Boredom

We often forgive those who bore
us, but can't forgive those whom
we bore.
La Rechefoucauld

A bore is a man who deprives you
of solitude without providing you
with company.
Gian Vincenzo Gravina

Borrowing

Borrowing is the mother of trouble.
Hebrew proverb

He who does not have to borrow
lives without cares.
Yiddish proverb

Boys

Boys will be boys, and so will a lot of
middle-aged men.
Kin Hubbard

Bravery

Courage is the first of human
qualities because it is the quality
which guarantees all others.
Winston Churchill

There is no such thing as bravery;
only degrees of fear.
John Wainwright

Breeding

Good breeding consists of
concealing how much we think of
ourselves and how little we think of
others.
Orson Wells

Budgeting

Budgeting: a method of worrying
before you spend instead of
afterward.
Anonymous

A budget is a numerical check of
your worst suspicions.
Anonymous

We didn't actually overspend our
budget. The Health Commission
allocation simply fell short of our
expenditure.
Keith Davis (Chairman, Wollongong Hospital),
Sydney Morning Herald, 'Sayings of the Week',
14 November 1981

Bureaucracy

Dealing with bureaucracy is like
trying to nail jelly to the wall.
John F Kennedy

Business

Whenever you see a successful
business, someone once made a
courageous decision.
Peter Drucker

Business is like riding a bicycle.
Either you keep moving or you fall
down.
John David Wright

Buying

The buyer needs a hundred eyes,
the seller not one.
Italian proverb

Brand origins:

Dr Martens, 1947 – they were the first air cushioned soles produced. UK production of Dr Martens – 1960. Following a
skiing accident Dr Maertens developed an air-cushioned sole to help to relieve discomfort.

A study of economics usually reveals that the best time to buy anything is last year.
Marty Allen

C

Capitalism

The capitalist system does not guarantee that everybody will become rich, but it guarantees that anybody can become rich.
Raul R de Sales

Cards

The cards are ill shuffled 'till I have a good hand.
Jonathan Swift

Career

To find out what one is fitted to do and to secure an opportunity to do it is the key to happiness.
John Dewey

Master a trade, and God will provide.
Midrash

Carelessness

Throw not the child out with the bath.
Danish proverb

Cars

When a man opens the car door for his wife, it's either a new car or a new wife.
Duke of Edinburgh, The Observer,' Sayings of the Week', 6 March 1988

Caution

Caution, though often wasted, is a good risk to take.
Josh Billings

Certainty

There is nothing certain in a man's life but that he must lose it.
Owen Meredith

Chance

Throw a lucky man into the sea, and he will come up with a fish in his mouth.
Arabian proverb

Challenges

Problems are only opportunities in work clothes.
Henry J Kaiser

Change

Change is not made without inconvenience, even from worse to better.
Richard Hooker

Don't ever take a fence down until you know the reason why it was put up.
GK Chesterton

Character

Character – the willingness to accept responsibility for one's own life – is the source from which self-respect springs.
Joan Didion

In matters of style, swim with the current; in matters of principle, stand like a rock.
Thomas Jefferson

Charity

As the purse is emptied, the heart is filled.
Victor Hugo

With malice toward none; with charity for all.
Abraham Lincoln

Writers' words:

The pen is mightier than the sword, and considerably easier to write with. Marty Feldman

Cheap

Cheap things are not good, good things are not cheap.
Chinese proverb

Cheerfulness

Cheerfulness, in most cheerful people, is the rich and satisfying result of strenuous discipline.
Edwin Percy Whipple

The sign of wisdom is continual cheerfulness.
French proverb

Children/ childhood

Childhood sometimes does pay a second visit to man; youth never.
Anna Jameson

The hardest job kids face today is learning good manners without seeing any.
Fred Astaire

The simplest toy, on which even the youngest child can operate, is called a grandparent.
Sam Levenson

Choice

Making a decision, even a bad one, is better than making no decision at all.
Jesse Aweida

Christianity

Christianity is a battle, not a dream.
Wendell Phillips

Circumstance

The circumstances of others seem good to us, while ours seem good to others.
Publilius Syrus

Circumstances! I make circumstances!
Napoleon Bonaparte

Citizenship

The first requisite of a good citizen in this republic of ours is that he should be able and willing to pull his weight.
Theodore Roosevelt

Civilisation

You can't say civilisation isn't advancing: in every war, they kill you in a new way.
Will Rogers

Committees

If you want to kill any idea in the world today, get a committee working on it.
Charles F Kettering

Common sense

A handful of common sense is worth a bushel of learning.
Spanish proverb

Common sense is the knack of seeing things as they are, and doing things as they ought to be done.
Calvin E Stowe

Common sense is not so common.
French proverb

Communication

Communication is depositing a part of yourself in another person.
Anonymous

Communism

The theory of Communism may be summed up in one sentence: Abolish all private property.
Karl Marx, Friedrich Engels

Writers' words:

Definition of a classic: a book everyone is assumed to have read and often thinks they have. Allan Bennet

Commuters

If God had meant us to travel in the rush hour, he would have made us much smaller.

Anonymous graffiti on the London Underground

Company

He that lies down with dogs will rise up with fleas.

Latin proverb

Competition

If you can't win, make the fellow ahead of you break the record.

Anonymous

Of all human powers operating on the affairs of mankind, none is greater than that of competition.

Henry Clay

Complaint

Complaint window: Fast feuds counter.

Daisy Brown

Compliment

A compliment is a gift, not to be thrown away carelessly unless you want to hurt the giver.

Eleanor Hamilton

You must not pay a person a compliment, and then straightaway follow it with a criticism.

Mark Twain

Computers

To err is human, but to really foul things up requires a computer.

Philip Howard, The Times, 25 February 1987

Man is still the most extraordinary computer of all.

John F Kennedy

Software is the part of a computer system which has no soul to be damned and no body to be kicked. Hardware is the bit you can kick.

Anonymous

Concentration

Concentration is my motto – first honesty, then industry, then concentration.

Andrew Carnegie

Conduct

Be swift to hear, slow to speak, slow to wrath.

James 1:19

Confession

Nothing spoils a confession like repentance.

Anatole France

The confession of evil works in the first beginning of good works.

St Augustine

Confidence

Doubt whom you will, but never yourself.

Christian Nestell Bovee

Conscience

Conscience does make cowards of us all

William Shakespeare

Conscience is the root of all true courage; if a man would be brave, let him obey his conscience.

George Washington

There is no hell like a bad conscience.

John Crowne

Writers' words:

'Anyone who believes you can't change history has never tried to write his memoirs.' David Ben Gurion

Consumers

The consumer, so it is said, is the king… each is a voter who uses his money as votes to get the thing done that he wants done.

Paul A Samuelson, Economics, 8th ed.

Contentedness

He who is content can never be ruined.

Chinese proverb

Contracts

Remember, in every lease the big print giveth and the small print taketh away.

Anonymous

Conversation

The less men think; the more they talk.

L de Montesquieu

Correspondence

As cold waters to a thirsty soul, so is good news from a far country.

Proverbs 25:25

Country

Indeed I tremble for my country when I reflect that God is just.

Thomas Jefferson

Court

The penalty for laughing in a courtroom is six months in jail; if it were not for this penalty, the jury would never hear the evidence.

HL Mencken

Cowards

To see what is right and not to do it is the part of a coward.

Chinese proverb

Cowards die many times before their deaths.

William Shakespeare

Creativity

The creative mind plays with the objects it loves.

Carl Jung

Credit

No man's credit is as good as his money.

Ed Howe

The surest way of establishing your credit is to work yourself into the position of not needing any.

Maurice Switzer

Crime

I have too great a soul to die like a criminal.

John Wilkes Booth

Set a thief to catch a thief.

Anonymous

Crisis

There can't be a crisis next week. My schedule is already full.

Henry Kissinger

Criticism

If you have no critics you likely have no successes.

Malcolm Forbes

He has a right to criticise, who has a heart to help.

Abraham Lincoln

Criticism comes easier than craftsmanship.

Zeuxis

Cross

Everyone thinks his own cross is heaviest.

Italian proverb

Cruelty

All cruelty springs from weakness.

Seneca

Loquacious language:

Angletwitch – a worm used for fishing

Curiosity

The important thing is not to stop questioning.
Albert Einstein

No man really becomes a fool until he stops asking questions.
Charles P Steinmetz

D

Dancing

Dancing is a wonderful training for girls: it's the first way you learn to guess what a man is going to do before he does it.
Christopher Morley

Danger

A timid person is frightened before a danger, a coward during the time, and a courageous person afterwards.
Jean Paul Richter

Fear the goat from the front, the horse from the rear, and man from all sides.
Russian proverb

Dawn

When God sends the dawn, he sends it for all.
Miguel de Cervantes

Death and life

I'm not afraid to die. I just don't want to be there when it happens.
Woody Allen

He who lives to live forever, never fears dying.
William Penn

Debt

Late payment is catching.
John Cope, The Independent, 21 July 1988

Decision

A decision delayed until it is too late is not a decision; it's an evasion.
Anonymous

Deeds

Great things are done when men and mountains meet.
William Blake

No need of words; trust deeds.
Ovid

Defeat

Defeat never comes to any man until he admits it.
Joseph Daniels

The man who wins may have been counted out several times, but he didn't hear the referee.
HE Jansen

Delegation

No man is able of himself to do all things.
Homer

Deliberation

If you think before you speak, the other fellow gets in his joke first.
Ed Howe

Democracy

Democracy is based upon the conviction that there are extraordinary possibilities in ordinary people.
Harry Emerson Fosdick

Desire

It is much easier to suppress a first desire than to satisfy those that follow.
La Rochefoucauld

Brand origins:

Disprin, 1944, by Roy Vickers of Liverpool – the name is a mixture of *dissolvable* and *aspirin*.

Destiny

What are the thoughts of the canvas on which a masterpiece is being painted? 'I am being soiled, brutally treated and concealed from view.' Thus men grumble at their destiny, however fair.
Jean Cocteau

One meets his destiny often in the road he takes to avoid it.
French proverb

Detail

Paying attention to simple little things that most men neglect makes a few men rich.
Henry Ford, Sr

Determination

Big shots are only little shots who kept on shooting.
Dale Carnegie

Devil

Resist the devil, and he will flee from you.
James 4:7

The devil's boots don't creak.
Scottish proverb

Difference

Honest differences are often a healthy sign of progress.
Mahatma Gandhi

Difficulty

A smooth sea never made a skilful mariner.
English proverb

Dignity

There is a healthful hardiness about real dignity that never dreads contact and communion with others, however humble.
Washington Irving

Dining

It isn't so much what's on the table that matters as what's on the chairs.
WS Gilbert

Disappointment

Too many people miss the silver lining because they're expecting gold.
Maurice Scitter

Disappointment is the nurse of wisdom.
Boyle Roche

Disasters

Calamities are of two kinds: misfortune to ourselves, and good fortune to others.
Ambrose Bierce

Disc jockeys

Radio news is bearable. This is due to the fact that while the news is being broadcast the disc jockey is not allowed to talk.
Fran Lebowitz

Discretion

It is not good to wake a sleeping lion.
Philip Sidney

Disease

Some remedies are worse than the diseases.
Pubililius Syrus

Disgrace

Better not live at all than live disgraced.
Greek proverb

Distrust

Never trust a man who speaks well of everybody.
John Churton Collins

Etymology:

abracadabra – originates from second century AD. The Roman Emperor, Caracalla, used the term as a charm to ward off toothache and fevers.

Doctors

The best doctor is the one you run for and can't find.
Denis Diderot

While the doctors consult, the patient dies.
English proverb

Dog

If you can't bite, don't show your teeth.
Yiddish proverb

A dog teaches a boy fidelity, perseverance, and to turn around three times before lying down.
Robert Benchley

Doing

What is done cannot be undone.
Italian proverb

Men are all alike in their promises. It is only in their deeds that they differ.
Moliere

Dreams

All men of action are dreamers.
James G Huneker

Daydreaming: wishcraft.
Bert Murray

Dress

It is an interesting question how far men would retain their relative rank if they were divested of their clothes.
Henry David Thoreau

Drink

A hot drink is as good as an overcoat.
Latin proverb

Alcohol is a good liquid for preserving almost everything except a secret.
Anonymous

One of the disadvantages of wine is that it makes a man mistake words for thoughts.
Samuel Johnson

What the sober man thinks the drunkard tells.
French proverb

Drowning

A drowning man will catch on to the edge of a sword.
Yiddish proverb

Dullness

Sir, he was dull in company, dull in his closet, dull everywhere. He was dull in a new way, and that made people think him great.
Samuel Johnson

He is not only dull in himself, but the cause of dullness in others.
Samuel Foote

E

Ears

The ear is the road to the heart.
French proverb

We have two ears and one mouth that we may listen the more and talk the less.
Greek proverb

Easy

The girl who is easy to get may be hard to take.
F Wisely

Writers' words:

There are books of which the backs and covers are by far the best parts. Charles Dickens

Eating

Better is a dinner of herbs where love is, than a stalled ox and hatred therewith.
Proverbs 15:17

Part of the secret of success in life is to eat what you like and let the food fight it out inside.
Mark Twain

There's no such thing as a free lunch.
Anonymous

A dinner lubricates business.
William Scott, Baron Stowell (1745-1836), quoted in Boswell's Life of Johnson, 1781

Education

The schools ain't what they used to be and never was.
Will Rogers

Education is an admirable thing, but it is well to remember from time to time that nothing that is worth knowing can be taught.
Oscar Wilde

Educate a man and you educate an individual – educate a woman and you educate a family.
Agnes Cripps

Effort

Any supervisor worth his salt would rather deal with people who attempt too much than with those who try too little.
Lee Iacocca

It is hard to fail, but it is worse never to have tried to succeed. In this life, we get nothing save by effort.
Theodore Roosevelt

Eggs

Put all your eggs in one basket – and watch the basket.
Mark Twain

He who treads on eggs must tread lightly.
German proverb

Emotion

It is easier to manufacture seven facts out of whole cloth than one emotion.
Mark Twain

Employee relations

Much outcry, little outcome.
Aesop

Respect a man, he will do the more.
James Howell

Encouragement/discouragement

Don't be discouraged; it may be the last key in the bunch that opens the door.
Stonsifer

Encouragement after censure is as the sun after a shower.
Goethe

Enthusiasm

Nothing great was ever achieved without enthusiasm.
Ralph Waldo Emerson

Envy

As rust corrupts iron, so envy corrupts man.
Greek proverb

Envy is a kind of praise.
John Gay

Equality

The only real equality is in the cemetery.
German proverb

Medieval words:

atrium – open entrance court before a church or house

Error

It takes less time to do a thing right than it does to explain why you did it wrong.
Henry W Longfellow

Escape

Oh, that I had wings like a dove! For then would I fly away, and be at rest.
Psalm 55:6

Ethics

It is easier to fight for one's principles than to live up to them.
Alfred Adler

Evidence

By their fruits ye shall know them.
Matthew 7:20

Evil

Woe unto them that call evil good, and good evil.
Isaiah 5:20

Evolution

All modern men are descended from a worm-like creature, but it shows more on some people.
Will Cuppy

Excellence

Excellence in any art or profession is attained only by hard and persistent work.
Theodore Martin

Excellence resides in quality, not in quantity. The best is always few and rare; much lowers value.
Gracian

Excuses

Two wrongs don't make a right, but they make a good excuse.
Thomas Szasz

Executives

The best executive is the one who has sense enough to pick good men to do what he wants done, and self-restraint enough to keep from meddling with them while they do it.
Theodore Roosevelt

Exercise

To exercise is human; not to is divine.
Robert Orben

I like long walks, especially when they are taken by people who annoy me.
Fred Allen

Expenses

Beware of little expenses; a small leak will sink a great ship.
Benjamin Franklin

Experience

Experience is not what happens to you, it is what you do with what happens to you.
Aldous Huxley

Experience is the name so many people give to their mistakes.
Oscar Wilde

Experts

Make three correct guesses consecutively and you will establish a reputation as an expert.
Lawrence Peter

Eye

An eye can threaten like a loaded and levelled gun, or it can insult like hissing or kicking; or, in its altered mood, by beams of kindness, it can make the heart dance for joy.
Ralph Waldo Emerson

Printing landmarks:

1700 BC – appearance of libraries in Chadea, Babylonia

F

Faces

Men's faces are not to be trusted.
Latin proverb

Facts

Let us keep our mouths shut and our pens dry until we know the facts.
Anton J Carlson

Facts do not cease to exist because they are ignored.
Aldous Huxley

Facts are stubborn things.
Tobias Smollen

Failure

Show me a thoroughly satisfied man – and I will show you a failure.
Thomas Edison

Fame

Fame usually comes to those who are thinking about something else.
Oliver Wendell Holmes, Jr

Famous remarks are very seldom quoted correctly.
Simeon Strunsky

Familiarity

Though familiarity may not breed contempt, it takes off the edge of admiration.
William Hazlitt

Family

God gives us relatives; thank God we can choose our friends.
A Mizner

A family is a unit composed not only of children but of men, women, an occasional animal, and the common cold.
Ogden Nash

The presidency is temporary, but the family is permanent.
Yvonne De Gaulle, Former First Lady of France

Farewells

Laughter is not all a bad beginning for a friendship, and it is far the best ending for one.
Oscar Wilde

It is amazing how nice people are to you when they know you are going away.
Michael Arlen

Father

What a father says to his children is not heard by the world, but it will be heard by posterity.
Jean Paul Richter

Children are a poor man's wealth.
Danish proverb

Fear

Fear is not an unknown emotion to us.
Neil Armstrong

Courage is often caused by fear.
French proverb

Fidelity

It is better to be faithful than famous.
Theodore Roosevelt

Drink waters out of thine own cistern.
Proverbs 5:15

Finance

Alexander Hamilton originated the put and take system in our national treasury: the taxpayers put it in, and the politicians take it out.
Will Rogers

Number crunchers:

quadrillion = 1000 trillion (US)

Fire

There is no smoke without fire.
Latin proverb

Firmness

The purpose firm is equal to the deed.
Edward Young

Flattery

It is easy to flatter; it is hard to praise.
Jean Paul Richter

Flirtation

It is the same in love as in war; a fortress that parleys is half taken.
Marguerite De Valois

Flowers

Where flowers degenerate man cannot live.
Napoleon Bonaparte

Flies

A shut mouth catches no flies.
Spanish proverb

Food

A hungry man is not a free man.
Adlai Stevenson

A smiling face is half the meal.
Latvian proverb

Fool

A learned fool is more foolish than an ignorant fool.
Moliere

A fool who can keep silent is counted among the wise.
Yiddish proverb

Force

Force and not opinion is the queen of the world; but it is opinion that uses the force.
Blaise Pascal

Forget

It is sometimes expedient to forget even what you know.
Latin proverb

Forgive

'I can forgive, but I cannot forget' is only another way of saying, 'I will not forgive.'
Henry Ward Beecher

He who cannot forgive breaks the bridge over which he himself must pass.
George Herbert

Fortune

Fortune makes him fool, whom she makes her darling.
Francis Bacon

Fortune truly helps those who are of good judgement.
Euripides

Freedom

Who has lost his freedom has nothing else to lose.
German proverb

Man is free at the moment he wishes to be.
Voltaire

Free speech

Some people's idea of free speech is that they are free to say what they like, but if anyone says anything back, that is an outrage.
Winston Churchill

The most stringent protection of free speech would not protect a man from falsely shouting fire in a theatre and causing a panic.
Oliver Wendell Holmes Jr

Brand origins:

The first UK company to adopt a distinctive brand name for a product line as opposed to generics, was Ricketts, Wills & Co of Bristol, which, in 1847, launched cut tobaccos called, 'Best birds eye' and 'Bishop blaze'.

Friends

To a friend's house the road is never long.
Dutch proverb

I am wealthy in my friends.
William Shakespeare

Friendship

If we were all given by magic the power to read each other's thoughts, I suppose the first effect would be to dissolve all friendships.
Bertrand Russell

Life is to be fortified by many friendships. To love, and to be loved, is the greatest happiness of existence.
Sydney Smith

Funerals

I did not attend his funeral; but I wrote a nice letter saying I approved of it.
Mark Twain

The only reason I might go to the funeral is to make absolutely sure that he's dead.
Anthony Sampson

Future

I never think of the future. It comes soon enough.
Albert Einstein

Light tomorrow with today!
Elizabeth R Browning

The trouble with our times is that the future is not what it used to be.
Paul Valery

G

Generosity

A small gift is better than a great promise.
German proverb

He who gives to me teaches me to give.
Dutch proverb

Genius

Genius is only great patience.
Count de Buffon

Adversity reveals genius, prosperity hides it.
Horace

Genocide

A single death is a tragedy, a million deaths is a statistic.
Josef Stalif

Gifts

A gift, though small, is welcome.
Greek proverb

Giving

He gives double who gives unasked.
Arabian proverb

The wise man does not lay up treasure.
The more he gives the more he has.
Chinese proverb

Gluttony

The mouth has a little hole, but it can swallow house and roof.
Yiddish proverb

Goals

Aim for the top. There is plenty of room there. There are so few at the top, it's almost lonely.
Samuel Insull

Metaphors:

My pulse was a drum solo. Scott Wentworth, *Gunmetal Blues*

The poor man is not he who is without a cent, but he who is without a dream.
Harry Kemp

Give me a stock clerk with a goal, and I will give you a man who will make history. Give me a man with no goals and I will give you a stock clerk.
James Cash Penney.

God

I could prove God statistically.
George Gallup

God moves in a mysterious way, His wonders to perform.
William Cowper

Golf

Golf is a good walk spoiled.
Mark Twain

Goodness

To a good man nothing that happens is evil.
Greek proverb

If you wish to be good, first believe that you are bad.
Greek proverb

Gossip

Gossip is the art of saying nothing in a way that leaves practically nothing unsaid.
Walter Winchell

Of every ten persons who talk about you, nine will say something bad, and the tenth will say something good in a bad way.
Antoine Rivarol

Government

The impersonal hand of government can never replace the helping hand of a neighbour.
Hubert Humphrey

Government is too big and too important to be left to the politicians.
Chester Bowles

Govern yourself and you can govern the world.
Chinese proverb

Gratitude

A thankful heart is the parent of all virtues.
Cicero

Nothing tires a man more than to be grateful all the time.
Ed Howe

Greatness

We are both great men, but I have succeeded better in keeping it a profound secret than he has.
Bill Nye

The great man is the man who does a thing for the first time.
Alexander Smith

Grief

Great souls suffer in silence.
F Von Schiller

Growth

There is no growth except in the fulfilment of obligations.
Anonymous

Guilt

He who flees from trial confesses his guilt.
Pubililius Syrus

The wicked flee when no man pursueth.
Proverbs 28:1

Loquacious language:

aprosexia – the inability to pay attention

H

Habit

Nothing so needs reforming as other people's habits.
Mark Twain

A nail is driven out by another nail; habit is overcome by habit.
Latin proverb

Hair

Gray hair is a sign of age, not of wisdom.
Greek proverb

Happiness

One is never as happy or as unhappy as he thinks.
La Rochefoucauld

Ask yourself whether you are happy, and you cease to be so.
John Stuart Mill

Happiness is not a station to arrive at, but a manner of travelling.
Margaret Lee Runbeck

Haste

Haste manages all things badly.
Latin proverb

Health

He who has health has hope, and he who has hope has everything.
Arabian proverb

Good health and good sense are two great blessings.
Latin proverb

Health food

Health food makes me sick.
Calvin Trillin

Heart

Believe it, you are a real find, a joy in someone's heart. You are a jewel, unique and priceless. God don't make no junk!
Herbert Barks

It is not by the grey of the hair that one knows the age of the heart.
Edward Bulwer-Lytton

A merry heart maketh a cheerful countenance.
Proverbs 15:13

Hell

Hell is truth seen too late.
Anonymous

The road to Hell is paved with good intentions.
Karl Marx

Heroes

The really great man is the man who makes everyman feel great.
GK Chesterton

The main thing about being a hero is to know when to die.
Will Rogers

History

History never looks like history when you are living through it. It always looks confusing and messy, and it always feels uncomfortable.
John W Gardner

Home

Be it ever so humble, there's no place like home.
JH Payne

Home is where you go when other places close.
Joseph Laurie

Writing landmarks:

1565 – the first description of a pencil

Home – the place where, when you
go there, they have to take you in.
Robert Frost

Honour

No revenge is more honourable
than the one not taken.
Spanish proverb

Hope

To the sick, while there is life there
is hope.
Cicero

What oxygen is to the lungs, such is
hope to the meaning of life.
Emil Brunner

Hospitality

Be not forgetful to entertain
strangers; for thereby some have
entertained angels unawares.
Hebrews 13:2

Human instinct

The strongest human instinct is to
impart information; the second
strongest is to resist it.
Kenneth Graham

Human relations

A sense of duty is useful in work,
but offensive in personal relations.
People wish to be liked, not be
endured with patient resignation.
Bertrand Russell

Humility

Humility is to make the right
estimate of yourself.
Charles Spurgeon

Don't be humble; you're not that
great.
Golda Meir

I believe the first test of a truly
great man is his humility.
John Ruskin

Humour

Everybody likes a kidder, but
nobody lends him money.
Arthur Miller

Good humour makes all things
tolerable.
Henry Ward Beecher

It is not enough to possess wit. One
must have enough of it to avoid
having too much.
Andre Maurois

Hypocrisy

Saint abroad, and a devil at home.
John Bunyon

For an idea ever to be fashionable
is ominous, since it must afterwards
be always old-fashioned.
Gorge Santayana

I

Ideas

If you want to get across an idea,
wrap it up in a person.
Ralph Bunche

Nothing is more dangerous than
an idea, when a man has only one
idea.
Alain

Idiot

Idiot, a member of a large and
powerful tribe whose influence in
human affairs has always been
dominant and controlling.
Ambrose Bierce

Ignorance

Where ignorance is bliss,
'Tis folly to be wise.
Thomas Gray

Etymology:

leotard – the suit worn by acrobats was named after the 1920s French trapeze artist, Jules Léotard.

Ignorance of one's misfortunes is clear gain.
Greek proverb

Illness

The sorrow which has no vent in tears may make other organs weep.
Henry Maudsley

If a man thinks about his physical or moral state, he usually discovers that he is ill.
Johann Goethe

Imagination

Man's mind once stretched by a new idea, never regains its original dimension.
Oliver Wendell Holmes

Imagination is more important than knowledge.
Albert Einstein

Immortality

The reward of great men is that, long after they have died, one is not quite sure that they are dead.
Jules Renard

If I have any belief about immortality, it is that certain dogs I have known will go to Heaven, and very, very few people.
James Thurber

Improvement

People seldom improve when they have no other model but themselves to copy after.
Oliver Goldsmith

Indecision

Through indecision opportunity is often lost.
Latin proverb

We know what happens to people who stay in the middle of the road. They get run over.
Aneurin Bevan

Independence

I would rather sit on a pumpkin and have it all to myself than be on a crowded velvet cushion.
Henry David Thoreau

Individuality

Dare to be what you are and to believe in your own individuality.
Henri Amiel

The shoe that fits one person pinches another; there is no recipe for living that suits all cases.
Carl Jung

Industry

Everything comes to him who hustles while he waits.
Thomas Edison

Like the bee, we should make our industry our amusement.
Oliver Goldsmith

Inequality

Some will always be above others. Destroy the inequality today and it will appear again tomorrow.
Ralph Waldo Emerson

Inferiority

We must interpret a bad temper as a sign of inferiority.
Alfred Adler

No two men can be half an hour together but one shall acquire an evident superiority over the other.
Samuel Johnson

Influence

Let him that would move the world, first move himself.
Socrates

Yinglish:

from Yiddish 'Bubby' to English 'Sweetie' (as in an intimate relative).

Information

Foolish are the generals who ignore the daily intelligence from the trenches.

Anonymous

Ingratitude

How sharper than a serpent's tooth it is to have a thankless child!

William Shakespeare

Ingratitude is the mother of every vice.

French proverb

Initiative

If there is no wind, row.

Latin proverb

He who seizes the right moment, Is the right man.

Johann Goethe

Injury

The injury we do and the one we suffer are not weighted in the same scales.

Aesop

No man is hurt but by himself.

Diogenes

Injustice

Those who commit injustice bear the greatest burden.

Hosea Ballou

He who commits injustice is ever made more wretched than he who suffers it.

Plato

Innocence

I used to be Snow White – but I drifted.

Mae West

Whoever blushes is already guilty; true innocence is ashamed of nothing.

Jean-Jacques Rousseau

Innovation

Even when I was young I suspected that much might be done in a better way.

Henry Ford, Sr

Insanity

When we remember we are all mad, the mysteries disappear and life stands explained.

Mark Twain

Instinct

Trust the instinct to the end, though you can render no reason.

Ralph Waldo Emerson

Instruction/ learning

They know enough who know how to learn.

Henry Adams

As long as you live, keep learning how to live.

Seneca

Insults

It is often better not to see an insult than to avenge it.

Seneca

If I have said something to hurt a man once, I shall not get the better of this by saying many things to please him.

Samuel Johnson

Fun is like life insurance; the older you get the more it costs.

Frank McKinney Hubbard (1868–1930), attributed

Metaphors:

Cars are whispering home from work. John Updike, *Rabbit, Run*

An insurance policy is like old underwear. The gaps in its cover are only shown by accident.
David Yates

Integrity

Integrity is the basis of all true-blue success.
BC Forbes

You cannot drive straight on a twisting lane.
Russian proverb

Intelligence

Intelligence is quickness in seeing things as they are.
George Santayana

An intelligent person often talks with his eyes; a shallow man often swallows with his ears.
Mr Tut-Tut

Intuition

Intuition is reason in a hurry.
Holbrook Jackson

Follow your hunches like the ancient navigators followed the stars. The voyage may be lonely, but the stars will take you where you want to go.
David J Mahoney

Invention

Great discoveries and improvements invariably involve the co-operation of many minds. I may be given credit for having blazed the trail but when I look at the subsequent developments I feel the credit is due to others rather than to myself.
Alexander Graham Bell

Investment

The best investment is in the tools of one's own trade.
Benjamin Franklin

Live on half of what you make and invest the rest in land.
Will Rogers

J

Jealousy

Jealousy is nourished by doubt.
French proverb

A jealous man always finds more than he is looking for.
Madeleine de Scudery

Jest

The worst jests are those which are true.
French proverb

Said in sport, meant in earnest.
German proverb

Jesus Christ

If you do not perceive that Jesus Christ is God, very well: then I did wrong to make you a general.
Napoleon Bonaparte

Jews

We Jews have a secret weapon in our struggle with the Arabs – we have no place to go.
Golda Meir

I determine who is a Jew.
Hermann Goering

Journalists

A journalist is a grumbler, a censurer, a giver of advice, a regent of sovereigns, a tutor of nations. Four hostile newspapers are more to be feared than a thousand bayonets.
Napoleon Bonaparte

Printing landmarks:

600 BC – The first known dictionary was published in Mesopotamia.

Joy

One can endure sorrow alone, but it takes two to be glad.

Elbert Hubbard

Judge

He who is a judge between two friends loses one of them.

French proverb

Judgment

I mistrust the judgment of every man in a case in which his own wishes are concerned.

First Duke of Wellington

At the day of judgment we shall not be asked what we have read but what we have done.

Thomas à Kempis

Justice

Delay of justice is injustice.

Walter S Landor

K

Keeping your word

Many promises impair confidence.

Latin proverb

Magnificent promises are always to be suspected.

Theodore Parker

Kindness

Let me be a little kinder, let me be a little blinder to the faults of those around me.

Edgar A Guest

Kindness has converted more sinners than zeal, eloquence or learning.

Frederick W Faber

Kindness consists in loving people more than they deserve.

Joseph Joubert

You cannot do a kindness too soon, for you never know how soon it will be too late.

Ralph Waldo Emerson

Kiss

A peculiar proposition. Of no use to one, yet absolute bliss to two. The small boy gets it for nothing, the young man has to lie for it, and the old man has to buy it. The baby's right, the lover's privilege, and the hypocrite's mask. To a young girl, faith; to a married woman, hope; and to an old maid, charity.

VPI Skipper

It is the passion that is in a kiss that gives to it its sweetness; it is the affection in a kiss that sanctifies it.

Christian Nestell Bovee

Knowledge

One cannot know everything.

Horace

A little knowledge is a dangerous thing.

Alexander Pope

As for me, all I know is that I know nothing.

Socrates

L

Labels

Don't rely too much on labels. For too often they are fables.

Charles H Spurgeon

Language

A language is a dialect that has an army and navy.

Max Weinreich

English heritage:

449 AD – Angles invaded Southern England and called it 'Angle-Land'.

Before using a fine word, make a place for it!
Joseph Joubert

Laughter

Ill-timed laughter is a dangerous evil.
Greek proverb

A merry heart doeth good like a medicine.
Proverbs 17:22

Of all days, the day on which one has not laughed is surely the most wasted.
S Chamfort

Laughter is the tranquiliser with no side effects.
Arnold Glasgow

Laughter is part of the human survival kit.
David Nathan

Law

Where law ends, there tyranny begins.
William Pitt

Laws too gentle are seldom obeyed;
Too severe, seldom executed.
Benjamin Franklin

I sometimes wish that people would put a little more emphasis on the observance of the law than they do on its enforcement.
Calvin Coolidge

Lawyers

The good lawyer is the great salesman.
Janet Rend

The lawyer with his briefcase can steal more than a hundred men with guns.
Mario Puzo

Laziness

Laziness is often mistaken for patience.
French proverb

A lazy boy and a warm bed are difficult to part.
Danish proverb

To do nothing is in every man's power.
Samuel Johnson

The habit of resting before fatigue sets in is laziness.
Jules Renard

Leader

A gifted leader is one who is capable of touching your heart.
JS Potofsky

Show me a country, a company, or an organisation that is doing well and I'll show you a good leader.
Joseph E Brooks

Leadership

The ability to recognise a problem before it becomes an emergency.
Arnold H Glasgow

Keep your fears to yourself, but share your courage with others.
Robert Louis Stevenson

A real leader faces the music when he doesn't like the tune.
Arnold H Glassgow

Leaders think. They think because they are leaders. They are leaders because they think.
Paul Parker

Metaphors:

Mutual interest, the greatest of all purposes, was the cement of this alliance. Henry Fielding, *The Life of Mr Jonathan Wild the Great*

Learning

The eagle never lost so much time as when he submitted to learn from the crow.
William Blake

It takes ten pounds of common sense to carry one pound of learning.
Persian proverb

Leisure

Leisure is the mother of philosophy.
Thomas Hobbes

He does not seem to me to be a free man who does not sometimes do nothing.
Cicero

Lend

He who lends to the poor gets his interest from God.
German proverb

You buy yourself an enemy when you lend a man money.
Yiddish proverb

Letter

I have made this letter longer than usual because I lack the time to make it shorter.
Blaise Pascal

One of the pleasures of reading old letters is the knowledge that they need no answer.
Lord Byron

Liar

A liar is not believed even though he tell the truth.
Cicero

Liberty

Liberty is the only thing you cannot have unless you are willing to give it to others.
William Allen White

When you have robbed a man of everything, he is no longer in your power. He is free again.
Alexander Solzhenitsyn

Lies/truth

No man has a good enough memory to make a successful liar.
Abraham Lincoln

I don't want any yes-men around me. I want everyone to tell me the truth – even though it costs him his job.
Samuel Goldwyn

Ask me no questions and I'll tell you no fibs.
Oliver Goldsmith

Sin has many tools, but a lie is a handle which fits them all.
Oliver Wendell Holmes

Life

Abortion is advocated only by persons who have themselves been born.
Ronald Reagan

In three words I can sum up everything I've learned about life. 'It goes on'.
Robert Frost

Limitations

One cannot manage too many affairs; like pumpkins in water, one pops up while you try to hold down the other.
Chinese proverb

Writers' words:

'You should never end a sentence with a preposition. You should find another word to end the sentence with.'
Winston Churchill

One cannot, as the Americans say, play every instrument in the band.
Elliot Paul

Listening

Give us grace to listen well.
John Keble

A good listener is not only popular everywhere, but after a while he knows something.
Wilson Mizner

One of the best ways to persuade others is by listening to them.
Dean Rusk

Literature

It has come to be practically a sort of rule in literature that a man, having once shown himself capable of original writings, is entitled thenceforth to steal from the writings of others at discretion.
Ralph Waldo Emerson

Loneliness

Loneliness is and always has been the central and inevitable experience of every man.
Thomas Wolfe

Man's loneliness is but his fear of life.
Eugene O'Neill

Losing

Victory has a hundred fathers but defeat is an orphan.
Galeazzo Ciano

Love

Scratch a lover and find a foe.
Dorothy Parker

What is irritating about love is that it is a crime that requires an accomplice.
C Baudelaire

Love is not only something you feel. It's something you do.
David Wilkerson

Loyalty

Loyalty is rare. It can only be proven under test.
Alfred Armand Montapert

We are all in the same boat in stormy sea, and we owe each other a terrible loyalty.
GK Chesterton

Luck

Shallow men believe in luck. Strong men believe in cause and effect.
Ralph Waldo Emerson

Depend on the rabbit's foot if you will, but remember it didn't work for the rabbit.
RE Shay

Lying

Lying lips are an abomination unto the Lord.
Proverbs 12:22

Large offers and sturdy rejections are among the most common topics of falsehood.
Samuel Johnson

M

Madness

We are all born mad. Some remain so.
Samuel Beckett

Though this be madness, yet there is method in it.
William Shakespeare

Majority

One, on God's side, is a majority.
Wendell Phillips

Brand origins:

Chrysler, 1923 – named after American engineer Walter Percy Chrysler. (WP Chrysler went on to head Chrysler Corp. and Buick Motor Co.)

The opinion of the majority is not the final proof of what is right.
Schiller

Management

If you command wisely, you'll be obeyed cheerfully.
Thomas Fuller

Lots of folks confuse bad management with destiny.
Kin Hubbard

To err is human. To forgive is not company policy.
Anonymous sign to company executives

Mankind

Man is equally incapable of seeing the nothingness from which he emerges and the infinity in which he is engulfed.
Blaise Pascal

It is easier to know man in general than to understand one man in particular.
La Rochefoucauld

Manners

The test of good manners is to be patient with bad ones.
Solomon Ibn Gabirol

When a man is positively rude, it is as if he had cast off all his clothes and stood before us naked. Of course, like most people in this condition, he cuts a poor figure.
Arthur Schopenhauer

Marriage

No labourer in the world is expected to work for room, board, and love – except the housewife.
Letty Cottin Pogrebin

Love is blind, but marriage restores its sight.
GC Lichtenberg

The husband who wants a happy marriage should learn to keep his mouth shut and his chequebook open.
Groucho Marx

My most brilliant achievement was my ability to be able to persuade my wife to marry me.
Winston Churchill

Masters

Masters' hints are commands.
Italian proverb

Not everyone who sits in the seat of honour is master.
Yiddish proverb

Matriarchy

America is the only matriarchy where women are fighting for equality.
A Roth

Maturity

I believe that the sign of maturity is accepting deferred gratification.
Peggy Cahn

Maturity is the capacity to endure uncertainty.
John Finley

Meanness

There are many things that we would throw away, if we were not afraid that others might pick them up.
Oscar Wilde

Measure

Better twice measured than once wrong.
Danish proverb

Loquacious language:

ascesis – the practice of being self-disciplined.

Just scales and full measure injure
no man.
Chinese proverb

Meddling
He who tastes every man's broth
sometimes burns his mouth.
Danish proverb

Medicine
It is part of the cure to wish to be
cured.
Latin proverb

Most things get better by
themselves.
Most things, in fact, are better by
morning.
Lewis Thomas

Melancholy
If there be a hell upon earth, it is to
be found in the melancholy man's
heart.
Robert Burton

Memory
The Right Honorable gentleman is
indebted to his memory for his jests
and to his imagination for his facts.
RB Sheridan

In plucking the fruit of memory one
runs the risk of spoiling its bloom.
Joseph Conrad

Mercy
Mercy to the criminal may be
cruelty to the people.
Arabian proverb

Blessed are the merciful: for they
shall obtain mercy.
Matthew 5:7

Miami beach
Miami Beach is where neon goes
to die.
Lenny Bruce

Metaphors:

Middle age
Patience makes a woman beautiful
in middle age.
Elliot Paul

The really frightening thing about
middle age is the knowledge that
you'll grow out of it.
Doris Day

Might
Where might is master, justice is
servant.
German proverb

Mind
A vacant mind is open to all
suggestions, as a hollow mountain
returns all sounds.
Chinese proverb

A noble mind is free to all men.
Latin proverb

Minorities
One dog barks at something, the
rest bark at him.
Chinese proverb

Mischief
He prepared evil for himself who
plots mischief for others.
Latin proverb

Misery
He that is down need fear no fall.
John Bunyan

Misery loves company but
company does not reciprocate.
Addison Mizner

Misfortune
By speaking of our misfortunes we
often relieve them.
French proverb

When misfortune sleeps, let no one
wake her.
Spanish proverb

She was a lamp for every moth that flew. – Wallace Stegner, *Angle of Repose*

Mistakes

Mistakes are often the best teachers. The shortest mistakes are always the best.
French proverb

The greatest mistake you can make in life is to be continually fearing you will make one.
Elbert Hubbard

Moderation

Even moderation ought not to be practised to excess.
Anonymous

The golden rule in life is moderation in all things.
Latin proverb

Modesty

Rare is agreement between beauty and modesty.
Latin proverb

Money

When money speaks the truth is silent.
Russian proverb

Those who despise money will eventually sponge on their friends.
Chinese proverb

Monument

I would rather have men ask why I have no statue than why I have one.
Greek proverb

Moralist

He who says there is no such thing as an honest man, you may be sure is himself a knave.
Bishop Berkeley

Wink at small faults; for thou hast great ones.
Thomas Fuller

Morality

To give a man full knowledge of true morality, I would send him to no other book than the New Testament.
John Locke

In any assembly the simplest way to stop transacting business and split the ranks is to appeal to a principle.
Jacques Barzun

Mother

A bustling mother makes a slothful daughter.
Latin proverb

What mother sings to the cradle goes all the way to the coffin.
H. W. Beecher

The mother-in-law remembers not that she was a daughter-in-law.
Spanish proverb

Motivation

Lord, grant that I may always desire more than I can accomplish.
Michelangelo

Men are not only bad from good motives, but also often good from bad motives.
GK Chesterton

One motivation is worth ten threats, two pressures and six reminders.
Paul Sweeney

Mouth

Mouth shut and eyes open.
Italian proverb

Brand origins:

Coca Cola, 1886 – invented by Dr John S Pemberton, but given its name by his bookkeeper, Frank Robinson; it contained cola nut and coca leaves. The Coca Cola trademark was registered in 1893. (Following his first advertisement, only 13 drinks were sold per day for eight months!)

Music

One cannot judge 'Lohengrin' from a first hearing, and I certainly do not intend to hear it a second time.
Gioacchino A Rossini

N

Names

The beginning of wisdom is to call things by their right names.
Chinese proverb

Nicknames stick to people, and the most ridiculous are the most adhesive.
Thomas Haliburton

Nature

Nature, to be commanded, must be obeyed.
Francis Bacon

Bees are not as busy as we think they are. They just can't buzz any slower.
Kin Hubbard

Necessity

Necessity makes even the timid brave.
Sallust

Negotiation

Don't ever slam the door; you might want to go back.
Don Herold

Enter into negotiations with the intention of creating an agreement that will allow both parties to achieve their essential goals.
Tom Hopkins

Neighbours

We make our friends; we make our enemies, but God makes our next-door neighbour.
GK Chesterton

A good neighbour doubles the value of a house.
German proverb

A neighbour is a person who can get to your house in less than a minute and takes two hours to go back home.
OA Battista

Neurosis

The psychotic person knows that two and two makes five and is perfectly happy about it; the neurotic person knows that two and two make four, but is terribly worried about it.
Radio Doctor

Neurosis is always a substitute for legitimate suffering.
Carl Jung

Work and love, these are the basics. Without them there is neurosis.
Theodor Reik.

News

As cold waters to a thirsty soul, so is good news from a far country.
Proverbs 25:25

Literature is news that stays news.
Ezra Pound

Newspaper

He had been kicked in the head by a mule when young, and believed everything he read in the Sunday papers.
George Ade

Medieval words:

badge – a heraldic identifying device, sewn or otherwise to a garment

Don't be afraid to make a mistake, your readers might like it.
William Randolph Hearst

Nobility

Send your noble blood to market and see what it will bring.
Thomas Fuller

Nose

Keep your nose out of another's mess.
Danish proverb

Let everyone pick his own nose.
Russian proverb

Nudity

I have seen three emperors in their nakedness, and the sight was not inspiring.
Prince Otto von Bismark

O

Oaths

A true word needs no oath.
Turkish proverb

Obedience

Obedience alone gives the right to command.
Ralph Waldo Emmerson

It is much safer to obey than to rule.
Thomas à Kempis

Obesity

He must have had a magnificent build before his stomach went in for a career of its own.
Margaret Halsey

That dark day when a man decides he must wear his belt under instead of over his cascading paunch.
Peter de Vries

Observation

Every man is a volume if you know how to read him.
William Channing

You can observe a lot just by watching.
Yogi Berra

Obstacles

If you want a place in the sun, you've got to expect a few blisters.
Anonymous

Obstinacy

The difference between perseverance and obstinacy is that perseverance means a strong will and obstinacy means a strong won't.
Lord Dundee

Occupation

The ugliest of trades have their moments of pleasure. Now, if I were a grave-digger, or even a hangman, there are some people I could work for with a great deal of enjoyment.
DW Jerrold

Old age

First you are young; then you are middle-aged; then you are old; then you are wonderful.
Lady Diana Cooper

I want to die young at a ripe old age.
Ashley Montagu

The great thing about old age is that you don't lose all the other ages you've been.
Madeleine L'Engle

Metaphors:

He was a cork that could not be kept under water many moments at a time. Mark Twain, *The Gilded Age*

Opinions

He thinks by infection, catching an opinion like a cold.
John Ruskin

The foolish and the dead never change their opinions.
James Russell Lowell

The trouble with letting people know where you stand is that you become a stationary target.
Marlys Huffman

Opportunity

Make hay while the sun shines.
English proverb

The sure way to miss success is to miss the opportunity.
Victor Charles

No great man ever complains of want of opportunity.
Ralph Waldo Emerson

In the middle of difficulty lies opportunity.
Albert Einstein

Optimism

Since the house is on fire let us warm ourselves.
Italian saying

A cheerful resignation is always heroic, but no phase of life is so pathetic as a forced optimism.
Elbert Hubbard

Originality

There is nothing new under the sun.
Ecclesiastes 1:9

Originality is simply a pair of fresh eyes.
Thomas W Higginson

P

Pain

Those who do not feel pain seldom think that it is felt.
Samuel Johnson

Paranoia

Even a paranoid can have enemies.
Henry Kissinger

Parenthood

Parents can give everything but common sense.
Yiddish proverb

To bring up a child in the way he should go, travel that way yourself once in a while.
Josh Billings

He who takes the child by the hand takes the mother by the heart.
German proverb

If discipline was practised in every home, juvenile delinquency would be reduced by 95 percent.
J Edgar Hoover

Partnership

When two friends have a common purse, one sings and the other weeps.
Anonymous

Two captains sink the ship.
Turkish proverb

Passion

Govern your passions, or they will govern you.
Latin proverb

It is difficult to overcome one's passions, and impossible to satisfy them.
Marguerite de La Sabliere

Number crunchers:

quintillion = 1000 quadrillion (US)

Past

Nothing is certain except the past.
Latin proverb

Patience

A handful of patience is worth more than a bushel of brains.
Dutch proverb

He that can have patience can have what he will.
Benjamin Franklin

Patriotism

A man who is good enough to shed his blood for his country is good enough to be given a square deal afterwards.
Theodore Roosevelt

Peace

Peace won by compromise is usually a short-lived achievement.
Winfield Scott

To be prepared for war is one of the most effectual means of preserving peace.
George Washington

All men desire peace, but very few desire those things that make for peace.
Thomas à Kempis

Peace, like charity, begins at home.
Franklin D Roosevelt

Pen

The pen is mightier than the sword.
Edward George Bulwer Lytton

People

When people don't want to come, nothing will stop them.
Sol Hurok

When people are free to do as the please, they usually imitate each other.
Eric Hoffer

Perseverance

It is a long road from conception to completion.
Moliere

Victory belongs to the most persevering.
Napoleon Bonaparte

It is my belief that talent is plentiful, and that what is lacking is staying power.
Doris Lessing

Pessimism

How happy are the pessimists! What joy is theirs when they have proved there is no joy.
Marie Eber-Eschenbach

In the long run, the pessimist may be proved right; but the optimist has a better time on the trip.
Daniel L Reardon

An optimist is a man who hasn't gotten around to reading the morning papers.
Earl Wilson

Philosophy

There was never yet philosopher that could endure a toothache patiently.
William Shakespeare

I've developed a new philosophy – I only dread one day at a time.
Charles M Schulz

Plagiarism

Whatever is well said by another, is mine.
Seneca

Writers' words:

'English usage is sometimes more than mere taste, judgment and education – sometimes it's sheer luck, like getting across the street.' (EB White)

Plagiarists have, at least, the merit of preservation.
Benjamin Disraeli

Planning

Act quickly, think slowly.
Greek proverb

Dig a well before you are thirsty.
Chinese proverb

In the long run you hit only what you aim at. Therefore, though you should fail immediately, you had better aim at something high.
Henry David Thoreau

Clear definition of goals is the key to success.
Edison Montgomery.

Pleasure

The great pleasure in life is doing what people say you cannot do.
Walter Bagehot

That man is richest whose pleasures are the cheapest.
Henry David Thoreau

Plenty

My cup runneth over.
Psalm 23:5

Politics

The essential ingredient of politics is timing.
Pierre Elliott Trudeau

Practical politics consists in ignoring facts.
Henry Adams

Popularity

Avoid popularity if you would have peace.
Abraham Lincoln

Positivism

A single sunbeam is enough to drive away many shadows.
Saint Francis of Assisi

Possession

Inanimate objects are classified scientifically into three major categories – those that don't work, those that break down, and those that get lost.
Russell Baker

Every increased possession loads us with a new weariness.
John Ruskin

Possibilities

Few men during their lifetime come anywhere near exhausting the resources dwelling within them. There are deep wells of strength that are never used.
Richard E Byrd

Poverty

I wasn't born in a log cabin, but my family moved into one as soon as they could afford it.
Malville D Landon

Power

Lust of power is the strongest of all passions.
Latin proverb

Practice

Practice makes perfect.
Latin proverb

Praise

The sweetest of all sounds is praise.
Xenophon

It is simpler and easier to flatter men than to praise them.
Jean Paul Richter

Writing landmarks:

1715 – the first English patent for a typewriter

Prayer

Prayer is the contemplation of the facts of life from the highest point of view.
Ralph Waldo Emerson

Prayer moves the hand which moves the world.
John Aikman Wallace

Do not have your concert first and tune your instruments afterward. Begin the day with God.
James H Taylor

The fewer the words, the better the prayer.
Martin Luther

Preach

Practise yourself what you preach.
Latin proverb

I preached as never sure to preach again, and as a dying man to dying men.
Richard Baxter

Prejudice

He hears but half who hears one party only.
Aeschylus

Everyone is a prisoner of his own experiences. No one can eliminate prejudices – just recognise them.
Edward R Murrow

Preparedness

In fair weather prepare for foul.
Thomas Fuller

Forewarned, forearmed; to be prepared is half the victory.
Spanish proverb

Make preparations in advance. You never have trouble if you are prepared for it.
Theodore Roosevelt

Presidency

No man will ever bring out of the Presidency the reputation which carries him into it.
Thomas Jefferson

The four most miserable years of my life.
John Adams

Press

In old days men had the rack. Now they have the press.
Oscar Wilde

Pretending

The only good in pretending is the fun we get out of fooling ourselves that we fool somebody.
Booth Tarkington

Pride

When a proud man hears another praised, he feels himself injured.
English proverb

There is a paradox in pride: it makes some men ridiculous, but prevents others from becoming so.
Charles Caleb Colton

When a man is wrapped up in himself, he makes a pretty small package.
John Ruskin

Pride is the never-failing vice of fools.
Alexander Pope

Principles

The difficulty is to know conscience from self-interest.
WD Howells

Loquacious language:

aspheterism – the ideology that there should be no private property.

Problems

Think as you work, for in the final analysis your worth to your company comes not only in solving problems but in anticipating them.
Herbert H Ross

I never take a problem to bed with me at night.
Harry S Truman

Taking first things first often reduces the most complex human problem to a manageable proportion.
Dwight D Eisenhower

Procrastination

Often greater risk is involved in postponement than in making a wrong decision.
Harry A Hopf

Procrastination is the thief of time.
Edward Young

Professionals

A professional is a person who tells you what you know already but in a way you cannot understand.
Anonymous

Profit

It is a socialist idea that making profits is a vice; I consider that the real vice is making losses.
Winston Churchill

Profit is a must. There can be no security for any employee in any business that doesn't make money. There can be no growth for that business. There can be no opportunity for the individual to achieve his personal ambitions unless his company makes money.
Duncan C Manzies

Progress

I will go anywhere provided it is forward.
David Livingstone

Always remember that the soundest way to progress in any organisation is to help the man ahead of you to get promoted.
LS Hamaker

It is hardly progress for a cannibal to use a knife and fork.
Sir Geoffrey Howe

Prohibition

Things forbidden have a secret charm.
Greek proverb

Promise

He loses his thanks who promises and delays.
Latin proverb

Promises may get friends, but it is performance that must nurse and keep them.
Owen Feltham

Promotion

Comrades, you have lost a good captain to make him an ill general.
Michel de Montaigne

Property

Property is the fruit of labour; property is desirable; it is a positive good in the world. That some should be rich shows that others may become rich and, hence, is just encouragement to industry and enterprise.
Abraham Lincoln

No man acquires property without acquiring with it a little arithmetic also.
Ralph Waldo Emerson

Twisted truths:

contradictions aren't necessary.

Prosperity

It requires a strong constitution to withstand repeated attacks of prosperity.
JL Basford

Prosperity is the surest breeder of insolence I know.
Mark Twain

Proverbs

A proverb is a short sentence based on long experience.
Spanish proverb

Providence

The longer I live, the more convincing proofs I see of this truth, that God governs in the affairs of man; and if a sparrow cannot fall to the ground without his notice, is it probable that an empire can rise without his aid?
Benjamin Franklin

Prudence

Don't count your chickens before they are hatched.
Aesop

A prudent man does not make the goat his gardener.
Hungarian proverb

Prying

Who is always prying has a dangerous life.
Spanish proverb

Psychiatry

Psychiatry enables us to correct our faults by confessing our parents' shortcomings.
Laurence J Peter

Psychoanalysis is confession without absolution.
GK Chesterton

Public

If it has to choose who is to be crucified, the crowd will always save Barabbas.
Jean Cocteau

Punctuality

Unfaithfulness in the keeping of an appointment is an act of clear dishonesty. You may as well borrow a person's money as his time.
Horace Mann

Punishment

He that spareth his rod hateth his son.
Proverbs 13:24

We are not punished for our sins, but by them.
Elbert Hubbard

Q

Quality

Conceal a flaw, and the world will imagine the worst.
Martial

I think there is only one quality worse than hardness of heart, and that is softness of head.
Theodore Roosevelt

Quarrels

In quarrelling, the truth is always lost.
Pubilius Syrus

It takes two to make a quarrel, but only one to end it.
Spanish proverb

Questions

A fool may ask more questions in an hour than a wise man can answer in seven years.
English proverb

Writers' words:

'Be careful about reading health books. You may die of a misprint.' Mark Twain

It is not every question that deserves an answer.
Pubilius Syrus

Quiet

Better is a dry morsel, and quietness therewith, than an house full of sacrifices with strife.
Proverbs 17:1

Quotation

It is a good thing for an uneducated man to read books of quotations.
Winston Churchill

Quotations when engraved upon the memory give you good thoughts.
Winston Churchill

R

Rain

After the rain cometh the fair weather.
Aesop

It never rains but it pours.
English proverb

Rainbow

The way I see it, if you want the rainbow, you gotta put up with the rain.
Dolly Parton

Reading

If we encountered a man of rare intellect, we should ask him what books he read.
Ralph Waldo Emerson

There is hardly any grief that an hour's reading will not dissipate.
L de Montesquieu

Rebellion

Inferiors revolt in order that they may be equal, and equals that they may be superior.
Aristotle

By gnawing through a dyke, even a rat may drown a nation.
Edmund Burke

Recruitment

When you hire people who are smarter that you are, you prove you are smarter than they are.
Robert H Grant

The first requisite in running a major corporation is the ability to pick good people.
Lee Iacocca

Reform

Reform must come from within, not from without.
James Gibbons

To reform a man, you must begin with his grandmother.
Victor Hugo

Regret

If you board the wrong train, it is no use running along the corridor in the other direction.
Dietrich Bonhoeffer

Regret is an appalling waste of energy; you can't build upon it; it's only good for wallowing in.
Katherine Mansfield

Relatives

The worst hatred is that of relatives.
Tacitus

Medieval words:

'Give someone the cold shoulder' dates back to medieval times when guests at French chateaus were at first served hot meat. However, if they outstayed their welcome, the host would offer them a cold shoulder of beef or mutton.

Religion

Every miracle can be explained – after the event. Not because the miracle is no miracle, but because explanation is explanation.
Franz Rosenzweig

Men never do evil so completely and cheerfully as when they do it from religious conviction.
Blaise Pascal

Remedy

If there be no remedy, why worry?
Spanish proverb

Remorse

Remorse is the pain of sin.
Theodore Parker

Repentance

The sinning is the best part of repentance.
Arabian proverb

Repentance costs dear.
French proverb

Reputation

A good name is better than precious ointment.
Ecclesiastes 7:1

A good name is rather to be chosen than great riches.
Proverbs 22:1

Judge a man by the reputation of his enemies.
Arabic proverb

Glass, china, and reputation are easily crack'd and never well mended.
Benjamin Franklin

Respect

There was no respect for youth when I was young, and now that I am old, there is no respect for age – I missed it coming and going.
JB Priestly

I don't know what a scoundrel is like, but I know what a respectable man is like, and it's enough to make one's flesh creep.
JM de Maistre

Responsibility

You can't escape the responsibility of tomorrow by evading it today.
Abraham Lincoln

The ability to accept responsibility is the measure of the man.
Roy L Smithy

The great developer is responsibility.
Louis D Brandeis

Responsibility is the price of greatness.
Winston Churchill

Rest

Come unto me, all ye that labour and are heavy laden, and I will give you rest.
Matthew 11:28

Too much rest itself becomes a pain.
Greek proverb

Results

By their fruits ye shall know them.
Matthew 7:20

Well done is better than well said.
Benjamin Franklin

Printing landmarks:

540 BC – the first public library opened in Athens.

Retail

Shopping has become a vital means of expression during a time of authoritarianism.
Neville Brody and Jon Wozencroft

Retirement

Two weeks is about the ideal length of time to retire.
Alex Comfort

You can put off being young until you retire.
Phillip Larkin

Few men of action have been able to make a graceful exit at the appropriate time.
Malcolm Muggeridge

Retribution

Whatsoever a man soweth, that shall he also reap.
Galatians 6:7

Men must reap the things they sow.
Percy B Shelley

Revenge

Living well is the best revenge.
George Herbert

Revenge is a confession of pain.
Latin proverb

Revolution

Every revolution was first a thought in one man's mind.
Ralph Waldo Emerson

Reward

No person was ever honoured for what he received. Honour has been the reward for what he gave.
Calvin Coolidge

Riches

A man is rich in proportion to the number of things he can afford to let alone.
Henry David Thoreau

Wealth lightens not the heart and care of man.
Latin proverb

Ridiculous

There is only one step from the sublime to the ridiculous.
Napoleon Bonaparte

Riding

He who knows the road can ride at full trot.
Italian proverb

Righteousness

If there is righteousness in the heart, there will be beauty in character. If there is beauty in character, there will be harmony in the home. If there is harmony in the home, there will be order in the nation. If there is order in the nation, there will be peace in the world.
Chinese proverb

Risk

Take calculated risks. That is quite different from being rash.
George S Patton

Great successes never come without risks.
Flavious Josephus

River

Where the river is deepest it makes least noise.
Italian proverb

Rose

He who plants thorns must never expect to gather roses.
Arabian proverb

Ruin

The road to ruin is always kept in good repair.
Anonymous

Rulers

He was a wise fellow that, being bid to ask what he would of the king, desired he might know none of his secrets.
William Shakespeare

However many people a tyrant slaughters, he cannot kill his successor.
Seneca

Rumour

What some invent the rest enlarge.
Jonathan Swift

I know nothing swifter in life than the voice of rumour.
Plautus

Rust

The tanned appearance of many Londoners is not sunburn – it is rust.
London Evening Standard

S

Safety

It is better to be safe than sorry.
American proverb

A ship in harbour is safe, but that is not what ships are built for.
John A Shedd

Sales

A man without a smiling face must not open a shop.
Chinese proverb

Every seller praises his wares.
Yiddish proverb

Salt

Salt is good, but if it loses its saltiness, how can you make it salty again?
Mark 9:50

Satisfaction

There's more credit and satisfaction in being a first-rate truck driver than a tenth-rate executive.
BC Forbes

Scandal

It is at home, not in public, one washes his dirty linen.
French proverb

Scandal dies sooner of itself than we could kill it.
Benjamin Rush

Scholars

He not only overflowed with learning, but stood in the slop.
Sydney Smith

Science

Enough research will tend to support your theory.
Anonymous

Secretaries

You can run the office without a boss, but you can't run an office without a secretary.
Jane Fonda, The Observer, 'Sayings of the Year', 3 January 1982

Loquacious language:

contranym - a word with two opposing meanings, for example cleave

Secrets

After nine months the secret comes out.
Yiddish proverb

Nothing is so burdensome as a secret.
French proverb

Security

Security is mostly a superstition. It does not exist in nature, nor do the children of men as a whole experience it. Avoiding danger is no safer in the long run than outright exposure. Life is either a daring adventure, or nothing.
Helen Keller

Self

We judge ourselves by our motives and others by their actions.
Dwight Morrow

Blessed are they who heal us of self-despisings. Of all services which can be done to man, I know of none more precious.
William Hale White

Self-centeredness

Talk to a man about himself and he will listen for hours.
Benjamin Disraeli

Conceit is the quicksand of success.
Arnold H Glassgow

Self-confidence

Be always sure you're right, then go ahead.
Davy Crockett

The history of the world is full of men who rose to leadership by sheer force of self-confidence, bravery, and tenacity.
Mahatma Gandhi

Self-control

He is strong who conquers others; he who conquers himself is mighty.
Lao-Tzu

Remember that there is always a limit to self-indulgence, but none to self-restraint.
MK Gandhi

Self-destructiveness

But I do nothing upon myself, and yet I am mine own executioner.
John Donne

Self-esteem

Every new adjustment is a crisis in self-esteem.
Eric Hoffer

Self-help

Nothing is more depressing than the conviction that one is not a hero.
George Moore

Self-improvement

There is no use whatever trying to help people who do no help themselves. You cannot push anyone up a ladder unless he be willing to climb himself.
Andrew Carnegie

Self-knowledge

Up to a certain point every man is what he thinks he is.
FH Bradley

Almost every man wastes part of his life in attempts to display qualities which he does not possess, and to gain applause which he cannot keep.
Samuel Johnson

Writers' words:

'The test of literature is, I suppose, whether we ourselves live more intensely for the reading of it.' Elizabeth Drew

Self-love

None so empty, as those who are full of themselves.

Benjamin Whichcote.

Self-praise

Let another man praise thee, and not thine own mouth.

Proverbs 27:2

Self-reliance

Chop your own wood, and it will warm you twice.

Henry Ford, Sr

Self-respect

He that respects himself is safe from others; he wears a coat of mail that none can pierce.

Henry W Longfellow

Self-sacrifice

Greater lover hath no man than this, that he lay down his life for his friends.

John 15:13

Present your bodies a living sacrifice, holy, acceptable unto God.

Romans 12:1

Selfishness

Everyone is eloquent in his own cause.

Latin proverb

Sensitivity

Exaggerated sensitiveness is an expression of the feeling of inferiority.

Alfred Adler

Servant

He that is the greatest among you shall be your servant.

Matthew 23:11

Few men have been admired by their servants.

Michel de Montaigne

Service

He profits most who serves best.

Arthur F Sheldon

Sex

Don't knock masterbation; It's sex with someone I love.

Woody Allen

The only time my wife and I had a simultaneous orgasm was when the judge signed the divorce papers.

Woody Allen

Shackles

Golden shackles are far worse than iron ones.

Mahatma Gandhi

Shame

Shame lasts longer than poverty.

Dutch proverb

Who has no shame for men, has no fear of God.

Yiddish proverb

Sheep

The sheep has no choice when in the jaws of the wolf.

Chinese proverb

Ships

Ships that pass in the night.

Henry W Longfellow

Shipwreck

Each man makes his own shipwreck.

Latin proverb

English heritage:

1150 – the beginnings of Middle English, a combination of Old English and French.

Sickness

Sickness is every man's master.
Danish proverb

How sickness enlarges the dimensions of a man's self to himself.
Charles Lamb

Sight

One man does not see everything.
Greek proverb

Seeing is believing.
Latin proverb

Silence

Better to remain silent and be thought a fool, than to speak out and remove all doubt.
Abraham Lincoln

He has the gift of quiet.
John Le Carre

In silence man can most readily preserve his integrity.
Meister Wickhart

True silence is the rest of the mind.
William Penn

Sin

Be sure your sin will find you out.
Numbers 32:23

For the wages of sin is death.
Romans 6:23

Sincerity

Be suspicious of your sincerity when you are the advocate of that upon which your livelihood depends.
John Lancaster Spalding

I want to see you shoot the way you shout.
Theodore Roosevelt

Slander

A slander is like a hornet; if you cannot kill it dead the first blow, better not strike at it.
HW Shaw

If slander be a snake, it is a winged one – it flies as well as creeps.
DW Jerrold

Slang

Slang is a language that rolls up its sleeves, spits on its hands and goes to work.
Carl Sandburg

Sleep

Sleep… knits up the ravell'd sleeve of care.
William Shakespeare

Sleep is the best cure for waking troubles.
Spanish proverb

Smile

What sunshine is to flowers, smiles are to humanity.
Joseph Addison

There are no language barriers when you are smiling.
Allen Klein

Snobbery

Laughter would be bereaved if snobbery died.
Peter Ustinov

Soldiers

An army, like a serpent, travels on its belly.
Frederick the Great

Solemnity

Nothing in the world annoys a man more than not being taken seriously.
Palacio Valdes

English Heritage:

1387 – Geoffrey Chaucer began to write his poem *The Canterbury Tales*.

Solidarity

We must indeed all hang together, or most assuredly we shall all hang separately.

Benjamin Franklin

Solitude

One can acquire everything in solitude but character.

Stendhal

Pray that your loneliness may spur you into finding something to live for, great enough to die for.

Dag Hammarskjold

Solution

There is always an easy solution to every human problem – *neat*, *plausible*, and *wrong*.

HL Mencken

Son

A wise son maketh a glad father; but a foolish son is the heaviness of his mother.

Proverbs 10:1

Song

Our sweetest songs are those that tell of saddest thought.

Percy B Shelley

These days, what isn't worth saying is sung.

Pierre de Beaumarchais

Sorrow

When sorrows come, they come not as single spies,
But in battalions!

William Shakespeare

A moment of time may make us unhappy forever.

John Gay

Soul

Be careless in your dress if you must, but keep a tidy soul.

Mark Twain

For what shall it profit a man, if he shall gain the whole world, and lose his own soul?

Mark 8:36

Spark

A little spark kindles a great fire.

Italian proverb

Speech/ speaker

When a man gets talking about himself, he seldom fails to be eloquent and often reaches the sublime.

Josh Billings

First learn the meaning of what you say, and then speak.

Epictetus

As a vessel is known by its sound whether it be cracked or not, so men are proved by their speeches whether they be wise or foolish.

Demosthenes

It usually takes me more than three weeks to prepare a good impromptu speech.

Mark Twain

Spending

He that spends more than he is worth spins a rope for his own neck.

French proverb

Spirit

There are only two forces in the world, the sword and the spirit. In the long run the sword will always be conquered by the spirit.

Napoleon Bonaparte

Printing landmarks:

868 AD – Diamond Sutra, the first known printed book, was published in China.

A wounded spirit who can bear?
Proverbs 18:14

Spit

Who spits against the wind, it fouls his beard.
Dutch proverb

Sports

Jogging is very beneficial. It's good for your legs and your feet. It's also very good for the ground. It makes it feel needed.
Charles M Schulz

Becoming number one is easier than remaining number one.
Bill Bradley

Spring

In the spring a young man's fancy lightly turns to thoughts of love.
Alfred, Lord Tennyson

Stomach

The stomach is easier filled than the eye.
German proverb

The way to a man's heart is through his stomach.
Spanish proverb

Strength

My strength is made perfect in weakness.
2 Corinthians 12:9

A threefold cord is not quickly broken.
Ecclesiastes 4:12

Study

If I had only three years to serve the Lord, I would spend two of them studying and preparing.
Donald Grey Barnhouse

Stupidity

Stupidity consists in wanting to reach conclusions. We are a thread, and we want to know the whole cloth.
Gustave Flaubert

If poverty is the mother of crime, stupidity is its father.
Jean de La Bruyere

Success

To climb steep hills requires slow pace at first.
William Shakespeare

Success is the child of audacity.
Benjamin Disraeli

It's not a successful climb unless you enjoy the journey.
Dan Benson

Suffering

The truth that many people never understand, until it is too late, is that the more you try to avoid suffering the more you suffer because smaller and more insignificant things begin to torture you in proportion to your fear of being hurt.
Thomas Merton

Superiority

Superiority is always detested.
Baltasar Gracian

Survival

To survive it is often necessary to fight, and to fight you have to dirty yourself.
George Orwell

Suspicion

The less we know the more we suspect.
HW Shaw

Loquacious language:

autophoby – the fear of referring to yourself: the reluctance to use the pronouns 'I' and 'me'.

A wise man will keep his suspicions muzzled, but he will keep them awake.
Marquess of Halifax

Sympathy

Rejoice with them that do rejoice, and weep with them that weep.
Romans 12:15

No one really understands the grief or joy of another.
Franz Schubert

T

Tact

Tact is the ability to describe others as they see themselves.
Abraham Lincoln

Silence is not always tact, and it is tact that is golden, not silence.
Samuel Butler

Tact comes as much from goodness of heart as from fineness of taste.
Enymion

Talk

Talk does not cook rice.
Chinese proverb

Two great talkers will not travel far together.
Spanish proverb

Taxes

Next to being shot and missed, nothing is quite as satisfying as an income tax refund.
FJ Raymond

The Eiffel Tower is the Empire State Building after taxes.
Anonymous

Tea

While there's tea there's hope.
Sir Arthur Pinero

Teaching

He who can, does. He who cannot, teaches.
George Bernard Shaw

Pure teaching, then, is not that which gives knowledge, but that which stimulates pupils to gain it.
Milton Gregory

Teamwork

No member of a crew is praised for the rugged individuality of his rowing.
Ralph Waldo Emerson

You cannot sink someone else's end of the boat and still keep your own afloat.
Charles Bower

Light is the task where many share the toil.
Homer

All your strength is in union. All your danger is in discord.
Henry Wadsworth Longfellow

Tears

Repentant tears wash out the stain of guilt.
Latin proverb

Technology

To err is human, but to really foul things up requires a computer.
Anonymous

Technology makes possible what good management knew but was formerly unable to achieve.
W Wriston

Brand origins:

Chase Manhattan, 1955 – this company is the result of a merger between Bank of Manhattan and Chase National Bank of the City of New York. 'Chase' is named after US lawyer and Statesman Salmon Portland Chase.

521

Television

Television is an invention that permits you to be entertained in your living room by people you wouldn't have in your home.
David Frost

Temptation

Temptation rarely comes in working hours. It is in their leisure time that men are made or marred.
WM Taylor

It is easier to stay out than get out.
Mark Twain

Theatre

All the movies used to be 'colossal'. Now they're all 'frank'. I think I liked 'colossal' better.
Beryl Pfizer

When the audience knows you know better, it's satire, but when they think you can't do any better, it's corn.
Spike Jones

Theology

Division has done more to hide Christ from the view of all men than all the infidelity that has ever been spoken.
George Macdonald

Thinking

When a man knows he is to be hanged in a fortnight, it concentrates his mind wonderfully.
Samuel Johnson

Curiosity is, in great and generous minds, the first passion and the last.
Oliver Wendell Holmes

Thirst

I am the bread of life: he that cometh to me shall never hunger; and he that believeth on me shall never thirst.
John 6:35

Time

Time wounds all heels.
Jane Ace

All the treasures of earth cannot bring back one lost moment.
French proverb

Time is a versatile performer. It flies, marches on, heals all wounds, runs out, and will tell.
Franklin P Jones

Tobacco

I have never smoked in my life and look forward to a time when the world will look back in amazement and disgust to a practice so unnatural and offensive.
George Bernard Shaw

Today

We are here today and gone tomorrow.
Anonymous

One today is worth two tomorrows.
Anonymous

Togetherness

Build for your team a feeling of oneness, of depending on one another and of strength to be derived by unity.
Vince Lombardi

My biggest thrill came the night Elgin Baylor and I combined for seventy-three points in Madison Square Garden, Elgin had seventy-one of them.
Rod Hundley

Loquacious language:

bablatrice – a talkative woman

Toil

He who toils with pain will eat with pleasure.
Chinese proverb

Tolerance

Why do you look at the speck of sawdust in your brother's eye and pay no attention to the plank of wood in your own eye?
Matthew 7:3

Judge not, and ye shall not be judged: condemn not, and ye shall not be condemned: forgive, and ye shall be forgiven.
Luke 6:37

Tomorrow

Tomorrow, tomorrow, not today,
Hear the lazy people say.
German proverb

Tongue

The tongue can no man tame; it is an unruly evil.
James 3:8

The tongue is a wild beast; once let it loose, it is difficult to chain.
Latin proverb

Torture

The healthy man does not torture others – generally it is the tortured who turn into torturers.
Carl Jung

Tourism

In the middle ages people were tourists because of their religion, whereas now they are tourists because tourism is their religion.
Dr Robert Runcie

Training

A man can seldom – very, very, seldom – fight a winning fight against his training: the odds are too heavy.
Mark Twain

Tree

The tree is known by its fruit.
Matthew 12:33

Trifle

Little drops of water, little grains of sand,
Make the mighty ocean and the pleasant land.
JF Carney

A trifle consoles us because a trifle upsets us.
Blaise Pascal

Troubles

When I go to bed, I leave my troubles in my clothes.
Dutch proverb

Troubles are tools by which God fashions us for better things.
Henry Ward Beecher

Forgetting trouble is the best way to cure it.
Latin proverb

Trust

Love all, trust a few.
William Shakespeare

To be trusted is a greater compliment than to be loved.
J Macdonald

Who mistrusts most should be trusted least.
Greek proverb

Brand origins:

Truth

A half truth, like half a brick, is always more forcible as an argument than a whole one. It carries better.
Stephen Leacock

Truth is such a rare thing, it is delightful to tell it.
Emily Dickinson

Tyranny

Any excuse will serve a tyrant.
Aesop

Tyranny is always better organised than freedom.
Charles Peguy

U

Understanding

Nothing can be loved or hated unless it is first known.
Leonardo da Vinci

I hear and I forget; I see and I remember; I do and I understand.
Chinese proverb

He who calls in the aid of an equal understanding doubles his own.
Edmund Burke

Unhappiness

The sole cause of man's unhappiness is that he does not know how to stay quietly in his room.
Blaise Pascal

Unity

United we stand, divided we fall.
Aesop

V

Vacation

No man needs a vacation so much as the man who has just had one.
Elbert Hubbard

A vacation is over when you begin to yearn for your work.
Morris Fishbein

Variety

With me a change of trouble is as good as a vacation.
David Lloyd George

Variety's the very spice of life; that gives it all its flavour.
William Cowper

Vengeance

The best manner of avenging ourselves is by not resembling him who has injured us.
Jane Porter

Vice

Great abilities produce great vices as well as virtues.
Greek proverb

To flee vice is the beginning of virtue.
Latin proverb

Vision

Vision is the art of seeing things invisible.
Jonathan Swift

Eyes that look are common. Eyes that see are rare.
J Oswald Sanders

The farther backward you can look, the farther forward you are likely to see.
Winston Churchill

Number crunchers:

septillion = 1000 sextillion (US)

Visit

Santa Claus has the right idea; visit people once a year.

Victor Borge

Vote

The future of this republic is in the hands of the American voter.

Dwight D Eisenhower

W

Wages

Be content with your wages.

Luke 3:14

War

War hath no fury like a non-combatant.

CE Montague

War does not determine who is right – only who is left.

Anonymous

Waste

Short as life is, we make it still shorter by the careless waste of time.

Victor Hugo

I wish I could stand on a busy street corner, hat in hand, and beg people to throw me all their wasted hours.

Bernard Berenson

Wealth

I'm opposed to millionaires, but it would be dangerous to offer me the position.

Mark Twain

All wealth is the product of labour.

John Locke

Men do not desire to be rich, but to be richer than other men.

John Stuart Mill (1806–1873),
Posthumous Essay on Social Freedom,
Oxford and Cambridge Review, January 1907

Weeds

Weeds never die.

German proverb

Weeping

Better the cottage where one is merry than the palace where one weeps.

Chinese proverb

Weeping makes the heart grow lighter.

Yiddish proverb

Welcome

He who brings is welcome.

German proverb

Who comes seldom is welcome.

Italian proverb

Whisper

What is whispered in your ear is often heard a hundred miles off.

Chinese proverb

Widowhood

Widows are divided into two classes – the bereaved and relieved.

Anonymous

Wife

A prudent wife is from the Lord.

Proverbs 19:14

A wife is a gift bestowed upon man to reconcile him to the loss of paradise.

Johann Goethe

Medieval words:

balm – a soothing ointment

Will

People do not lack strength;
they lack will.
Victor Hugo

Strength does not come from
physical capacity. It comes from the
indomitable will.
Mahatma Gandhi

Wine

There is a devil in every berry of the
grape.
The Koran

Winning

The last shot may give us the
victory.
Admiral Duchayla

The most difficult part of getting to
the top of the ladder is getting
through the crowd at the bottom.
Arch Ward

Missing is part of winning.
George Foreman

Wisdom

The price of wisdom is above
rubies.
Job 28:18

Through wisdom a house is built,
and by understanding it is
established.
Proverbs 24:3

From the errors of others a wise
man corrects his own.
Publius Syrus

The doors to wisdom are never
shut
Benjamin Franklin

Wise

Everybody is wise after the thing
has happened.
French proverb

A wise man's question contains half
the answer.
Solomon Ibn Gabirol

Wit

A man often runs the risk of
throwing away a witticism if he
admits that it is his own.
Jean de la Bruyere

Wit is the salt of conversation, not
the food.
William Hazlitt

Women

A beautiful lady is an accident of
nature. A beautiful old lady is a work
of art.
Louis Nizer

When the fine eyes of a woman are
veiled with tears it is the man who
no longer sees clearly.
Achille Tournier

Wonder

Wonder is the basis of worship.
Thomas Carlyle

Wooing

A man chases a woman until she
catches him.
American proverb

Word

Man does not live by words alone, despite the fact that sometimes he has to eat them.
Adlai Stevenson

He that hath knowledge spareth his words.
Proverbs 17:27

All words are pegs to hang ideas on.
Henry Ward Beecher

Words once spoken can never be recalled.
Wentworth Dillon

Work

All work and no play makes Jack a dull boy – and Jill a wealthy widow.
Evan Esar

Work expands so as to fill the time available for its completion.
C Northcote Parkinson

He who would eat the kernel must crack the shell.
Latin proverb

Leisure and I have parted company. I am resolved to be busy till I die.
John Wesley

What is a workman without tools?
Thomas Fuller (1654–1734)

World

All the world's a stage
And all the men and women merely players.
William Shakespeare

Worry

He'd give the devil ulcers.
Anonymous

It is not work that kills men; it is worry. Worry is rust upon the blade.
Henry Ward Beecher

Wounds

If you can't heal the wound, don't tear it open.
Danish proverb

Wrinkles

Wrinkles should merely indicate where smiles have been.
Mark Twain

Writer

Nothing gives an author so much pleasure as to find his works respectfully quoted by other learned authors.
Benjamin Franklin

Advice to young writers who want to get ahead without any annoying delays: don't write about Man, write about a man.
EB White

Writing

Writing is no trouble: you just jot down ideas as they occur to you. The jotting is simplicity itself – it is the occurring which is difficult.
Stephen Leacock

The greatest thing in style is to have a command of metaphor.
Aristotle

Wrong

We ought never to do wrong when people are looking.
Mark Twain

The man who says 'I may be wrong, but…' does not believe there can be any such possibility.
Kin Hubbard

Metaphors:

A book is a garden carried in the pocket. Arabian proverb

Y

Yesterday/ today/ tomorrow

The man who wastes today lamenting yesterday will waste tomorrow lamenting today.
Philip Baskin

A small decision now can change all your tomorrows.
Robert Schuller

Youth

Youth is a wonderful thing. What a crime to waste it on children.
George Bernard Shaw

One of the most difficult problems faced by a young man leaving home for the first time is giving up the fringe benefits.
Marguerite Whitley May

One stops being a child when one realises that telling one's trouble does not make it better.
Cesare Pavese

Youth is that period when a young boy knows everything but how to make a living.
Carey Williams

Z

Zeal

There is no greater sign of a general decay of virtue in a nation, than a want of zeal in its inhabitants for the good of their country.
Joseph Addison

Brains, pen, action!

Something to ponder...

Pep up your packaging copy by relating a quotation to a product's benefit. This also adds vitality to corporate material used at trade events and conferences.

Did you know?

The eighteenth century French typographer Pierre Fournier first proposed the standard typesetting unit: the point. Firmin Didot developed it into today's European standard. Until metric measures were universally adopted, standard sizes differed slightly from Anglo-American versions.

18. The business of quotes

'So much has been given to so many by so few.' So starts a presentation on brand monopolies. To arrive at the quote, I simply adapted a famous existing quotation. This simple technique may be just the sort of tonic you are looking for when offering a public relations quote for the press or perhaps an extra helping of spice for your annual conference speech.

You don't have to choose a quotation which 'sounds' worthy. In fact some of the best business quotes, like the products and services behind the company executives who deliver them, come out of adversity rather than triumph.

(Oooer! That little line may be picked up as a business quote one of these days.)

minds are like parachutes – they only function when they are open

The business of quotes

In this list of quotations, I have included witty and pertinent quotes about business. You shouldn't immediately copy them verbatim: instead, use them to inspire a creative concept or metaphor. Better still, adapt the quote to suit your specific needs.

So now, keeping in mind that 'time is money', 'let's get down to business...'

A

Accountants An accountant is a man hired to explain that you didn't make the money you did.
Anonymous

Everyone knew that as regards doing anything useful, accountants were very much like eunuchs; they knew how it was done, but they couldn't do it themselves.
James Leasor, The Sea Wolves

I never get the accountants in before I start up a new business. It's done on gut feeling, especially if I can see they are taking the Mickey out of the consumer.
Sir Richard Branston

Actuaries An actuary is someone who moved out of accountancy because he couldn't stand the excitement.
Anonymous

Actuaries have the reputation of being about as interesting as the footnotes to a pension plan.
George Pitcher, The Observer, 10 July 1988

Advertising If you call a spade a spade you won't last long in the advertising business.
Anonymous

Nothing works faster than Anadin… So get nothing!
Anonymous

Writers' words:

'Somebody said to me, "But the Beatles were anti-materialistic." That's a huge myth. John and I literally used to sit down and say "Now, let's write a swimming pool".' Sir Paul McCartney

If you've got nothing to say, sing it.
Anonoymous (quoted in Ken Hornsby, The Padded Sell)

If advertisers spent the same amount of money on improving their products as they do their advertising, then they wouldn't have to advertise
Will Rogers

Agriculture   A farmer is never satisfied; don't expect it.
E.W. Howe

Ambition   What seems to be generosity is often only disguised ambition – which despises small interests to gain great ones.
Francois, Duc de La Rochefoucauld

There is always room at the top.
Daniel Webster

Apprenticeship
There needs a long apprenticeship, to understand the mystery of the world's trade.
Thomas Fuller

Arts   Blessed are the pure in art.
Anonymous

All art is quite useless.
Oscar Wilde, The Picture of Dorian Gray

No artist retires: he can't.
Henry Moore

Auditors   Auditors are the troops who watch a battle from the safety of a hillside and when the battle is over come down to count the dead and bayonet the wounded.
Anonymous

I don't want to know when I am losing money three months after it has happened, so I've an auditor here almost full time.
Sir Freddie Laker

Aviation   The chopper has changed my life as conclusively as it did for Anne Boleyn.
Queen Elizabeth, the late Queen Mother

Loquacious language:

quiddity – the real meaning of something

B

Banks

I once wondered how the banks made their money, but when I procured a loan, I found out.
E.W. Howe

If you owe your bank a hundred pounds, you have a problem; if you owe it a million it has.
John Maynard Keynes

Bankruptcy

Poor bankrupt.
William Shakespeare, Romeo and Juliet, act II, scene ii

Capitalism without bankruptcy is like Christianity without hell.
Frank Borman

Boardroom

You ask what constitutes a crisis here. Well, if we ran out of white wine in the boardroom.
Patrick Cobbold

When an academic decries business for being so boring, you know he's never seen the thrills and spills of a boardroom.
Katherine Whitehor

Borrowing

An acquaintance is someone we know well enough to borrow from, but not well enough to lend to.
Anonymous

The habit of borrowing small sums of money – anticipating pay-day – is a pernicious practice and breaks many a friendship. It is no kindness to loan money to a professional borrower.
Elbert Hubbard

Budget

A budget is a numerical check of your worst suspicions.
Anonymous

We didn't actually overspend our budget. The Health Commission allocation simply fell short of our expenditure.
Keith Davis

Business

The nature of business is swindling.
August Babel

Anyone round here speak English?

The Big Mac™ originally retailed in France as 'Gros Mec', meaning 'big pimp' in French.

With an honest and good man, business is soon ended.

Thomas Fuller

A friendship founded on business is better than a business founded on friendship.

John D Rockeffeller

Businessmen Why do businessmen complain about bad business over expensive dinners?

Anonymous

Each [of my wives] was jealous and resentful of my preoccupation with business. Yet none showed any visible aversion to sharing in the proceeds.

J. Paul Getty

Businessman: One who gets the business and completes the transaction – all the rest are clerks and labourers.

Elbert Hubbard

C

Cartels Cartels are like babies: we tend to be against them until we have one of our own.

Lord Mancroft, attributed

Catering The aim of fast food marketing is to minimise the time and distance between a man and his meal.

Anonymous

In the past naval cooking at sea involved a choice between the lesser of two weevils.

Anonymous

British fish and chip shops deserve a battering.

Anonymous

Chairmen A tired chairman is a bad chairman. A dead one is usually worse.

Sir Nicholas Goodison

I can't bear being called Chair. Whatever I am, I am not a piece of furniture.

Baroness Seear

Medieval words:

climax – the number 63

Charity   Our charity begins at home, and mostly ends where it begins.
Horace Smith

In all the ages, three-fourths of the support of the great charities has been conscience money.
Mark Twain

The City   'Think the unthinkable but wear a dark suit' is a handy maxim for a city.
Katharine Whitehorn

When the city of London starts volunteering earnest homilies about 'social responsibility in investment', then something terrible must surely be afoot.
J.T. Winkler

Civil Service   Civil servants have many good qualities but when it comes to running businesses they tend, albeit for reasons largely outside their control, to be disastrous failures.
Leslie Chapman

You can cut any public expenditure except the Civil Service, those lads spent a hundred years learning to look after themselves.
Sir Richard Marsh

Britain has invented a new missile. It's called the civil servant- it doesn't work and it can't be fired.
Anonymous

Class   The poor and ignorant will continue to lie and steal as long as the rich and educated show them how.
Elbert Hubbard

The lower classes of men, though they do not think it worth while to record what they perceive, nevertheless perceive everything that is worth noting; the difference between them and a man of learning often consists in nothing more than the latter's facility for expression.
Georg Christoph Lichtenberg

Collective bargaining
Not a penny off the pay; not a minute on the day.
AJ Cook, slogan of the coal miners' strike of 1925

Loquacious language:

quidnunc – a gossip

Whatever may be the advantages of 'collective bargaining', it is not bargaining at all, in any just sense, unless it is voluntary on both sides.
Mahlon Pitney

Commerce

Men who have been very stingy and very grasping are usually men who have very strong commercial instincts.
George Bancroft

The commerce of the world is conducted by the strong; and usually it operates against the weak.
Henry Ward Beecher

Committees

A committee is something that keeps minutes but wastes hours.
Anonymous

A committee is a cul de sac down which ideas are lured and then quietly strangled.
Sir Barnett Cocks

What is a committee? A group of the unwilling, picked from the unfit, to do the unnecessary.
Richard Harkness

Communism

What is a communist? One who hath yearnings for equal division of unequal earnings, Idler or bungler, or both, he is willing, to fork out his copper and pocket your shilling.
Ebenezer Elliot

Communism is inequality, but not as property is. Property is the exploitation of the weak by the strong. Communism is the exploitation of the strong by the weak.
Pierre-Joseph Proudhon

Commuters

If God had meant us to travel in the rush hour, he would have made us much smaller.
Anonymous graffiti on the London Underground

Watch the genus commuter rush for his Dope (newspaper) when he reaches the station in the morning.
Elbert Hubbard

Etymology:

How now brown cow? – this phrase, meaning 'what's up?', derives from the eighteenth century term 'brown cow', meaning a barrel of beer. 'How now brown cow?' meant 'do you want another beer?'

Competence   And he was competent whose purse was so.
William Cowper

There are some electricians I would not allow in the toilet, and some plumbers I would not let flush it, and there are some fitters who could not fit a sausage.
Eddie Lynton

Competition   Every child of the Saxon race is educated to wish to be first. It is our system; and a man comes to measure his greatness by the regrets, envies and hatreds of his competitors.
Ralph Waldo Emerson

Competition brings out the best in products and the worst in people.
David Sarnoff

Computers   Man is still the most extraordinary computer of all.
John F Kennedy

Conferences   Conference: A gathering where the members can singly do nothing, but who together decide that nothing can be done.
Sir David Davenport-Handley

What with all their bits and bytes, the workings of todays's pc is more than most of us can chew.
JJ Gabay

Congress   If the present congress errs in too much talking, how can it be otherwise, in a body to which the people send one hundred and fifty lawyers, whose trade it is to question everything, yield nothing and talk by the hour? That one hundred and fifty lawyers should do business together, ought not to be expected.
Thomas Jefferson

With Congress, every time they make a joke it's a law, and every time they make a law it's a joke.
Will Rogers

Medieval words:

dump – an English dance

Consumers
The consumer, so it is said, is the king… each is a voter who uses his money as votes to get the thing done that he wants done.
Paul A Samuelson

The consumer is not a moron. She is your wife.
David Ogilvy

Consumption
Consumption never needs encouragement.
John Stuart Mill

If men ceased to consume, they would cease to produce.
David Ricardo

Contracts
A verbal contract isn't worth the paper it's written on.
Samuel Goldwyn

Contract: an agreement that is binding on the weaker party.
Frederick Sawyer

Men keep their agreements when it is an advantage to both parties not to break them.
Solon (c.630–c.555 BC)

Corporations
Corporation, n. An ingenious device for obtaining individual profit without individual responsibility.
Ambrose Bierce

(Corporations) cannot commit treason, nor be outlawed, nor excommunicate, for they have no souls.
Sir Edward Coke

A corporation cannot blush.
Howel Walshm (fl.1820)

Corruption
The first rule of business: do other men for what they would do for you.
Charles Dickens

Corruption is simply business without scruples.
Anonymous

Writers' words:

'The good writers touch life often. The mediocre ones run a quick hand over her. The bad ones rape her and leave her for the flies.' Ray Bradbury, *Fahrenheit 451*

Cosmetics	Most women are not as young as they are painted. Sir Max Beerbohm
	In the factory we make cosmetics, in the store we sell hope. Charles Revson
	There are no ugly women, only lazy ones. Helena Rubenstein
Costs	If the choice lies between the production or purchase of two commodities, the value of one is measured by the sacrifice of going without the other. HJ Davenport
	We first survey the plot, then draw the model; And then we see the figure of the house, Then we must rate the cost of the erection; Which, if we find outweighs ability, What do we then but draw anew the model. William Shakespeare, Henry IV, part II, act I, sc ene iii, 1597-98
Credit	Credit, like a looking glass, Broken once, is gone, alas! Anonymous
	As credit is a coy mistress, and will not easily be courted, so she is a mighty nice touchy lady, and is soon affronted; if she is ill used she flies at once, and 'tis a very doubtful thing whether ever you gain her favour again. Daniel Defoe (c.1660-1731)
	A credit card is an anaesthetic which simply delays the pain, and pain, after all, serves a function. Helen Mason
	In business one way to obtain credit is to create the impression that one already has it. Miguel Unamuno
Creditors	Creditors have no real affection for their debtors, but only a desire that they may be preserved that they may repay. Aristotle (384–322 BC)
	Creditors have better memories than debtors. James Howell

Did you know?

Brand management, as a marketing system, was introduced by Proctor and Gamble in the 1930s.

Customers   Passenger: You're one of the stupidest people I've met. Swissair employee: And you're one of the nicest gentlemen I've ever come across. But perhaps we're both wrong.
Swissair

Customs   Customs represent the experience of mankind; and in commerce, equity, fidelity, and integrity are simply customs. Experience is the mother of custom.
Henry Ward Beecher

D

Debt   Debt: 1. A rope to your foot, cockleburs in your hair, and a clothespin on your tongue.
2. The devil in disguise.
Frank McKinney Hubbard

Late payment is catching.
John Cope

Diplomacy   Diplomacy is the art of letting someone else have your way.
David Frost

Diplomacy is to do and say the nastiest things in the nicest way.
Isaac Goldberg

Division of Labour

Communion or community of labour would be a better term than division of labour.
JK Rodbertus

The greatest improvement in the productive powers of labour, and the greater part of the skill, dexterity and judgement with which it is any where directed, or applied, seem to have been the effects of the division of labour.
Adam Smith

Drink   Alcohol is a good liquid for preserving almost everything except a secret.
Anonymous

A hangover is the wrath of grapes.
Anonymous

Medieval words:

Wine: an infallible antidote to commonsense and seriousness.
Frank McKinney Hubbard

E

Economics

The purpose of studying economics is not to acquire a set of ready-made answers to economic questions, but to learn how to avoid being deceived by economists.
Joan Robinson

Those who have never seen the inhabitants of a nineteenth-century London slum can have no idea of the state to which dirt, drink and economics can reduce human beings.
Leonard Woolf

Economists

You can make even a parrot into a learned political economist- all he must learn are the two words 'supply' and 'demand'.
Anonymous

I found out where George Bush is today. He's visiting his economists. He's at Disneyland right now.
Lloyd Bentsen

An economist is a man who knows 100 ways of making love but doesn't know any women.
Art Buchwald

Economy

Economy is going without something you do want in case you should, some day, want something you probably won't want.
Anthony Hope

Economy, n. Purchasing the barrel of whisky that you do not need for the price of the cow that you cannot afford.
Ambrose Bierce

It is not economical to go to bed early to save the candles if the result is twins.
Chinese proverb

Education

There are obviously two educations. One should teach us how to make a living and the other how to live.
James Truslow Adams

Etymology:

touch and go – this saying, which means a risky situation, can be traced to the American wild west, when stage coaches raced against each other at high speed. If the vehicles wheels became entangled both would be smashed. However, if the wheels were simply to touch the coaches would still be able to 'go'.

The best education in the world is that got by struggling to get a living.
Wendell Phillips

Education is an admirable thing, but it is well to remember from time to time that nothing that is worth knowing can be taught.
Oscar Wilde

Efficiency

Do it now.
Anonymous

It is more than probable that the average man could, with no injury to his health, increase his efficiency fifty per cent.
Walter Dill Scott

It's pretty hard being efficient without being obnoxious.
Frank McKinney Hubbard

Employees

There is not one whom we employ who does not, like ourselves, desire recognition, praise, gentleness, forbearance, patience.
Henry Ward Beecher

Employees during working hours are the classic captive audience.
Earl Warre

Employers

The employer has a duty to perform, too, when a helper errs.
Elbert Hubbard

Forget the paternity leave; most bosses would look askance if (their male employees) asked to leave work early to take their children to the dentist. The immediate assumption would be that their wife must just have died.
Penelope Leach

Employment

To make a long story short, there is nothing like having the boss walking.
Doris Lily

Aim at employment and you head for disaster. Aim at prosperity and employment will be a by-product.
C. Northcote Parkinson

Loquacious language:

ranarium – a frog farm

Engineers
It has been said that an angineer is a man who can do for ten shillings what any fool can do for a pound.
Nevil Shute

Enterprise
Beware of all enterprises that require new clothes.
Henry David Thoreau

The successful conduct of an industrial enterprise requires two quite distinct qualifications: fidelity and zeal.
Anonymous

Entertainment
There's no such thing as a free lunch.
Anonymous

The mass production of distraction is now as much a part of the American way of life as the mass production of automobiles.
C Wright Mills

A dinner lubricates business.
William Scott, Baron Stowell

Entrepreneurs
I reckon one entrepreneur can recognise another at 300 yards on a misty day.
Sir Peter Parker

I wanted to be an editor or a journalist. I wasn't really interested in being an entrepreneur, but I soon found I had to become an entrepreneur to keep my magazine going.
Sir Richard Branston

Entrepreneurs come in all shapes and sizes. They straddle every class and every system of education. The common theme that links them is sound judgement, ambition, determination, capacity to assess and take risks, hard work, greed, fear and luck. The most dangerous entrepreneur is the self righteous one who preaches morality and pretends that he is doing it for the good of others. That kind of entrepreneur usually ends up bust, having dilapidated the savings of those who invested in him.
Sir James Goldsmith

Writers' words:

'Politics is not a bad profession. If you succeed there are many rewards, if you disgrace yourself you can always write a book.' Ronald Reagan

Equal Opportunities

When women ask for equality, men take them to be demanding domination.
Elizabeth Janeway

Whatever women do they must do twice as well as men to be thought half as good. Luckily this is not difficult.
Charlotte Whitton

Exchange

Each of us puts in what he has at one point of the circle of exchange and takes out what he wants at another.
PH Wicksteed

Nothing is to be had for nothing.
Epictetus, fl. AD 100, Discourses

F

Factories

The factory, for Taylor, was not only an instrument for the production of goods and profit, it was also a moral gymnasium for the exercise of the character.
Samuel Haber, Efficiency and Uplift, 1964

There is a disease known as factory melancholia. If there is a depression of spirit in the front office it goes out through the foreman, the superintendent, and reaches everybody in the employ of the institution
Elbert Hubbard

Fashion

We don't want to push our ideas onto customers, we simply want to make what they want.
Laura Ashley

A love of fashion makes the world go round.
Liz Tilberis

Finance

I would rather see Finance less proud and Industry more content.
Sir Winston Churchill

I'm old enough to know that to give financial advice is the quickest way of making enemies.
Hammond Innes

Forecasting

FORECAST: A pretence of knowing what would have happened if what does happen hadn't.
Ralph Harris

Loquacious language:

recusant – refusing to comply with a custom or rule

Forecast: To observe that which has passed, and guess it will happen again.
Frank McKinney Hubbard

Fraud

There are some frauds so well conducted, that it would be stupidity not to be deceived by them.
CC Colton

He that's cheated twice by the same man, is an accomplice with the cheater.
Thomas Fuller

Free Trade

In the long run, free trade benefits everyone; in the short run it is bound to produce much pain.
Henry Hobhouse

Free trade, one of the greatest blessings which a government can confer on a people, is in almost every country unpopular.
Lord Macaulay

Funeral directors

We're not the nicest people in town, but we're the last ones to let you down.
Anonymous funeral director at the undertakers' conference in Melbourne in March 1985

Gabay at a glance:

Here are some of my favourite business clichés (avoid them like the tax inspector):

Time is money.

Nice guys finish last.

Let's touch base.

Keep me in the loop.

They moved the goal post.

Wake up and smell the coffee.

Money talks; bullshit walks.

What is your blue-sky on this?

Give me a ballpark figure.

Let's fly it up the flagpole.

We offer a cutting edge, quality service.

This is a people business.

There is no 'I' in team.

Etymology:

to be above board – this saying, meaning 'to be honest', derives from card playing. Board is an old word for table. If you drop your hands below the table your opponent could believe you were cheating. However, if you played above board you clearly were a reputable player.

G

Gambling The gambling known as business looks with austere disfavour upon the business known as gambling.
Ambrose Bierce

A gambler knows when to play his luck and when not to, when to keep on and when to give up, and that is a good thing for a businessman.
Sir James Goldsmith

Gifts You cannot afford to have things given to you.
EW Howe

There are no free gifts in this world, only deferred payments.
Warren Tute

Gold Gold is good but may be dear bought.
James Kelly

When every blessed thing you hold is made of silver, or of gold, you long for simple pewter. When you have nothing else to wear but cloth of gold and satins rare, for cloth of gold you cease to care – up goes the price of shoddy.
WS Gilbert

Goodwill It is very difficult to gain good-will; but once you have it, it is easy to keep it.
Baltasar Gracian

Good will should be taken for part payment.
James Kelly

Government The Conservative Party has never believed that the business of government is the government of business.
Nigel Lawson

Though the people support the government, the government should not support the people.
Grover Cleveland

Democratic governments, by their nature, are pressure-responders rather than problem anticipators.
Walter W Heller

Did you know?

In 1996, a huge, collapsible Pepsi can was flown to the orbiting Russian Mir space station. The Russian Space Agency offered further advertising in space opportunities for any company willing to boldly go where no other competitor had gone before.

H

Health

Hard work never killed anybody but worrying about it did.

Anonymous

Executives should not worry about insomnia – it only keeps them awake.

Anonymous

In the health service itself, the fundamental fallacy is that the more efficient it becomes, the less money it will need. This is fantastic nonsense.

Edward Heath

Honesty

Honesty consists in never stealing but in knowing where to stop in stealing, and how to make good use of what one does steal.

Samuel Butler

'Tis my opinion every man cheats in his way, and he is only honest who is not discovered.

Susannah Centlivre

I

Incentives

If the condition of the industrious were not better than the condition of the idle, there would be no reason for being industrious.

Jeremy Bentham

If a man is producing nothing, nobody can be the worse for a reduction of his incentive to produce.

George Bernard Shaw

Income

A large income is the best recipe for happiness I ever heard of.

Jane Austen

All decent people live beyond their income nowadays, and those who aren't respectable live beyond other people's.

Saki

Writers' words:

'A short saying often contains much wisdom.' Sophocles

Industrial relations

Industrial relations are human relations.

Edward Heath, attributed

All of you who have read trade union literature know that there are not only trade unions in England, but also alliances between workers and capitalists in a particular industry for the purpose of raising prices and of robbing everybody else.

VI Lenin

Industrial Revolution

The Industrial Revolution was not indeed an episode with a beginning and an end… It is still going on.

EJ Hobsbawm

The elemental truth must be stressed that the characteristic of any country before its industrial revolution and modernisation is poverty.

Peter Mathias

Industry

The pursuit of alibis for poor industry performance is one of the great Australian art forms.

John Button

Industry must manage to keep wages high and prices low. Otherwise it will limit the number of its customers. One's own employees should be one's best customers.

Henry Ford

It takes more than industry to industrialise.

WW Rostow

Inflation

Inflation means that your money won't buy as much today as it did when you didn't have any.

Anonymous

Question: What sex is to the novelist, inflation is to the economist. Discuss.
Answer: I am not sure how I am supposed to answer this question but it may be said that both inflation and sex are characterised by a rising rate of interest.

Anonymous

Inflation is like sin; every government denounces it and every government practises it.

Sir Frederick Leith-Ross

Etymology:

---

cabbage – Alexander the Great introduced this vegetable to Europe in 325 BC. The name derived from the Latin 'caput', which means 'head'.

Imagine believing in the control of inflation by curbing the money supply! That is like deciding to stop your dog fouling the sidewalk by plugging up its rear end. It is highly unlikely to succeed, but if it does it kills the hound.

Michael D Stepthens

Inheritance   A good man leveth an inheritance to his children's children: and the wealth of the sinner is laid up for the just.

Bible

A son can bear with equanimity the loss of his father, but the loss of his inheritance may drive him to despair.

Niccolo Machiavelli

Innovation   We ought not to be over anxious to encourage innovation, in case of doubtful improvement, for an old system must ever have two advantages over a new one; it is established, and it is understood.

CC Colton

Every innovation has to fight for its life.

Elbert Hubbard

Insurance   How do you insure yourself against insurance premiums?

Peter Corris

Fun is like life insurance; the older you get the more it costs.

Frank McKinney Hubbard

An insurance policy is like old underwear. The gaps in its cover are only shown by accident.

David Yates

Interest   Interest works night and day, in fair weather and in foul. It knaws at a man's substance with invisible teeth. It binds industry with its film, as a fly is bound upon a spider's web.

Henry Ward Beecher

The rate of interest acts as a link between income-value and capital-value.

Irving Fisher

Medieval words:

548   cushion – the roasted haunch of a large animal

Inventions Edison, whose inventions did as much as any to add to our material convenience, wasn't what we would call a scientist at all, but a supreme 'do-it-yourself' man.
Sir Kenneth Clark

Anything that won't sell, I don't want to invent.
Thomas Edison

Inventions that are not made, like babies that are not born, are rarely missed.
John Kenneth Galbraith

Inventors If I have seen farther than others, it is because I am standing on the shoulders of giants.
Sir Isaac Newton

Investment To understand economics the rational investor would be wise to understand ethics.
Jason Alexander

Hell hath no fury like an investment analyst made to look foolish.
Robert Tyerman

L

Labour Labor disgraces no man; unfortunately you occasionally find men disgrace labor.
Ulysses S Grant

O God! That bread should be so dear and flesh and blood so cheap.
Thomas Hood

Laissez-Faire A considerable departure from laissez-faire is necessary in order to realise the theoretical results of laissez-faire.
Sir Hubert Henderson

The man who accepts the laissez-faire doctrine would allow his garden to run wild so that the roses might fight it out with the weeds and the fittest might survive.
John Ruskin

Land No land is bad, but land is worse. If a man owns land, the land owns him. Now let him leave home if he dare.
Ralph Waldo Emerson

Brand origins:

Jell-O – first patented in 1845. Mass-produced in 1897. Mary, wife of cough medicine manufacturer, John Wait, invented the term for her spouse's gelatine dessert.

Study how a society uses its land, and you can come to pretty reliable conclusions as to what its future will be.
EF Schumacher

Landlords
There is a disadvantage belonging to land, compared with money. A man is not so much afraid of being a hard creditor as of being a hard landlord.
Samuel Johnson

No one supposes, that the owner of urban land, performs qua owner, any function. He has a right of private taxation; that is all.
RH Tawney

Law
Lawful, adj. Compatible with the will of a judge having jurisdiction.
Ambrose Bierce

'The law supposes that your wife act under your direction.' 'If the law supposes that,' said Mr Bumble, squeezing his hat emphatically with both hands, 'the law is a ass- a idiot. If that's the eye of the law, the law is a bachelor; and the worst I wish the law is, that his eye may be opened by experience-by experience.'
Charles Dickens

Judge: A law student who marks his own papers.
HL Mencken (1880–1956), Sententiae

Lawyers
A lawyer starts life giving $500 worth of law for $5, and ends giving $5 worth for $500.
Benjamin H Brewster

That whether you're an honest man or whether you're a thief depends upon whose solicitor has given me my brief.
Sir WS Gilbert

A British Lawyer would like to think of himself as part of that mysterious entity called The Law; an American lawyer would like a swimming pool and two houses.
Simon Hoggart

Lending
If thou wilt lend this money, lend it not as to thy friends....But lend it rather to thine enemy, who if he break, thou mayest with better face exact the penalty.
William Shakespeare (1564–1616), Merchant of Venice

Loquacious language:

rhathymia – to be cheerful or optimistic

Lend less than thou owest.
William Shakespeare

Litigation   Fools and obstinate men make lawyers rich.
Thomas Fuller

Litigation: A form of hell whereby money is transferred from the pockets of the proletariat to that of lawyers.
Frank McKinney Hubbard 3

You never, but never, go to litigation if there is another way out…Litigation only makes lawyers fat.
Wilbur Smith

M

Management   Management is the art of getting other people to do all the work.
Anonymous

Managing a business requires a great deal of frankness and openness and you actually lead by being very honest with people.
Sir Michael Edwardes, The Observer, 'Sayings of the Week', 19 June 1983

Managing is the art of getting things done through and with people in formally organized groups. It is the art of creating an environment in which people can perform as individuals and yet co-operate towards the attainment of group goals. It is the art of removing blocks to such performance.
Harold Koontz

Good management is not just a bright tool-kit of techniques and specifications, although the professional skills are essential. It involves the arts of entrepreneurship and leadership, it means managing change, including change itself.
Sir Peter Parker

Management Consultancy
A management consultant is someone who tells management what it already knows but packages it differently.
Anonymous

Brand origins:

Johnson & Johnson, 1885 – Inspired by the eminent surgeon Sir Joseph Lister who identified airborne germs. Robert, brother of James Wood Johnson, decided to manufacture prepared sterile wrapped surgical dressings. In 1890 they applied Italian talc to a doctor's patient who complained of a skin rash. This was the start of their famous powdered product.

Simon: What's your husband do?
Jenny: He's a professional bullshit artist. A management consultant.

Anonymous

Marketing

Exports are becoming obsolete, because they are too slow. Marketers today must sell the latest product everywhere at once – and that means producing locally.

Carlo de Benedetti

Marketing is simply sales with a college education.

John Freund

The successful company is the one which is first to identify emerging consumer needs and to offer product improvements which satisfy those needs. The successful marketer spots a new trend early, and then leads it.

Edward G Harness

Pan Am takes good care of you. Marks and Spencer loves you. Securicor cares…At Amstrad:'We want your money'

Alan Sugar, The Observer, 'Sayings of the Week', 3 May 1987

Markets

In every market a dealer must conduct his business according to the custom of the market, or he will not be able to conduct it at all.

Walter Bagehot

The belief of the money market, which is mainly composed of grave people, is as imitative as any belief. You will find one day everyone enterprising, enthusiastic, vigorous, eager to buy, and eager to order: in a week or so you will find almost the whole society depressed, anxious, and wanting to sell.

Walter Bagehot

Market forces, like the sea, are powerful, bountiful but dangerous. And, as with the seas, the wise man treats the free market with the utmost respect, interfering only at the margin and after much thought.

Graham Searjeant

Marriage

(Marriage is) like signing a 356 page contract without knowing what's in it.

Mick Jagger

It is a woman's business to get married as soon as possible, and a man's to keep unmarried as long as he can.

George Bernard Shaw

Marriage is a bribe to make a housekeeper think she's a householder.

Thornton Wilder

Medicine

Commonly physicians, like beer, are best when they are old, and lawyers, like bread, when they are young and new.

Thomas Fuller

Doctors think a lot of patients are cured who have simply quit in disgust.

Don Herold

Let no one suppose that the words doctor and patient can disguise from the parties the fact that they are employer and employee.

George Bernard Shaw (1856–1950), The Doctor's Dilemma, 1913

Mining

There are three groups that no British Prime Minister should provoke: the Vatican, the Treasury and the miners.

Stanley Baldwin (1867–1947), attributed

Mining is the one-armed bandit of economic development: it is easy to pull the handle of the fruit machine, but difficult to anticipate the consequences.

Donald Denoon

Money

Money can't buy you friends; it can only rent them.

Anonymous

Money, it has been said, has two properties. It is flat so that it can be piled up. But it is also round so that it can circulate.

Sir Geoffrey Crowther

Money talks, they say. All it ever said to me was 'goodbye'.

Cary Grant

Etymology:

broccoli – this vegetable was developed over 2500 years ago in Cyprus. The Roman Emperor Tiberius once humiliated his son in public for eating the entire broccoli at an official banquet. The word derives from the Latin 'brachium', meaning 'branch'.

Monopoly

There is unfortunately no good solution for technical monopoly. There is only a choice among three evils: private unregulated monopoly, private monopoly regulated by the state, and government operation.

Milton Friedman

Private monopoly is absolutely indefensible and intolerable. If it is any monopoly, it must be a public monopoly and not a private monopoly.

Woodrow Wilson

Morality

Morality's not practical.

Robert Bolt

The bottom seems to have dropped out of morality.

Lord Hailsham

Motor Vehicles

When a man opens the car door for his wife, it's either a new car or a new wife.

Duke of Edinburgh

The automobile changed our dress, manners, social customs, vacation habits, the shape of our cities, consumer purchasing patterns, common tastes and positions in intercourse.

John Keats

N

Nationalization

If you want to show that crime doesn't pay, put it in the hands of the government.

Anonymous

Whatever may be thought as to be the respective merits of private and public ownership, it cannot be denied that private enterprise does take more risk than any government is likely to do except under pressure of military necessities.

Sir George Gibb

Negotiations

It's a well known proposition that you know who's going to win a negotiation: it's he who pauses the longest.

Robert Holmes à Court

Anyone round here speak English?

The Rolls-Royce Silver Myst in German means 'human waste'.

Let us never negotiate out of fear, but let us never fear to negotiate.
John F Kennedy, inaugural address, 20 January 1961

Newspapers   News is something someone, somewhere doesn't want you to print – the rest is advertising.
Anonymous

A newspaper consists of just the same number of words, whether there be any news in it or not.
Henry Fielding

We live under a government of men and morning newspapers.
Wendell Phillips

O

The Office   The organisation of many offices is rather like a septic tank – the really big chunks rise to the top.
'Epson's Compleat Office Companion'

I yield to no-one in my admiration for the office as a social centre, but it's no place to actually get any work done.
Katherine Whitehorn

Organisation (s)

The individual and the organisation are living organisms, each with its own strategy for survival and growth.
Chris Argyris

All organisations, nations, societies, and civilisations will prosper and advance only to the extent that they can encourage common men to perform uncommon deeds.
Courtney C Brown,

It might seem more efficient to have the front half of the cow in the pasture grazing and the rear half in the barn being milked all of the time, but this organic division would fail.
Luther Gulick

Nobody really likes large scale organisation; nobody likes to take orders from a superior who takes orders from a superior who takes orders…
EF Schumacher

Etymology:

Kiwi fruit – this Chinese fruit was imported to New Zealand at the beginning of the twentieth century. The Kiwis renamed it Chinese gooseberry. They were first imported to America in 1962 when a Los Angeles distributor named it after the New Zealand national bird 'the Kiwi'.

P

Parliament

Parliament itself would not exist in it's present form had people not defied the law.
Arthur Scargill

A Parliament is nothing less than a big meeting of more or less idle people.
Walter Bagehot

Anybody who enjoys being in the House of Commons probably needs psychiatric care.
Ken Livingstone

Partnerships

The partner of my partner is not my partner. (Socii mei socius, meus socius non est.)
Legal maxim

One of the most fruitful sources of ruin to men of the world is the recklessness or want of principle of partners, and it is one of the perils to which every man exposes himself who enters into partnership with another.
Sir R Malins VC (1805–1882), Mackay v Douglas (1872)

Payment

Alas! How deeply painful is all payment!
Lord Byron

He humbly prays your speedy payment.
William Shakespear , Timon of Athens, act II, scene ii

It is an axiom as old as the hills that goods and services can be paid for only with goods and services.
Albert J Nock

Pensions

I have considered the pension list of the republic a roll of honour.
Grover Cleveland

Pension never enriched young man.
George Herbert

People

Too bad all the people who know how to run the country are too busy driving taxi-cabs or cutting hair.
George Burns

Did you know?

There are only two common words with six consonants in row: catchphrase and latchstring.

There are three sorts of people in this world; those who make things happen, those who watch things happening, and those who don't know what is happening.

Sir David Nicholson

Personnel Management

To err is human. To forgive is not company policy.

Anonymous sign to company executives

Management and personnel administration are one and the same. They should never be separated. Management is personnel administration.

Lawrence A Appley

Piracy

He changes his flag, to conceal his being a pirate.

Thomas Fuller

Charity and piracy are things of the past. They are always closely akin, for pirates were very charitable, and ever in their train were troops of sturdy beggars.

Elbert Hubbard

Plain English

Gobbledygook is the methodology deployed by governmental bureaucracies, specifically designed to ensure that the simplest of instructions is encased in a plethora of treacherous sub-clauses, adverbial phrases and cross references with the result that the recipient is left baffled, bemused and confused.

Martin Cutts and Chrissie Maher

It is no exaggeration to describe plain English as a fundamental tool of government.

Margaret Thatcher

My mother pointed out that one could not say 'a green great dragon', but I had to say 'a great green dragon'. I wondered why, and still do.

J.R.R. Tolkien

Planning

He hath made a good progress in a business, that hath thought well of it before-hand.

Thomas Fuller (1654–1734), Gnomologia, 1732

Planning and competition can be combined only by planning for competition, but not by planning against competition.

FA Hayek, The Road to Serfdom, 1944

Brand origins:

Imperial Leather, 1938 – based on a perfume with the scent of leather (1780s). The perfume was called 'Eau de Cologne Imperial Leather Russe'.

Politics

The divine science of politics is the science of social happiness.
John Adams

Elections are like sex. The pleasure is momentary, the position ridiculous and the result can be damnably expensive.
Keith Hampson

The political problem of mankind is to combine three things: economic efficiency, social justice, and individual liberty.
John Maynard Keynes

You do not lead people by following them, but by saying what they want to follow.
Enoch Powell

Pornography

It'll be a sad day for sexual liberation when the pornography addict has to settle for the real thing.
Brendan Francis

Porn is an ideal Thatcherite industry. It provides a service, demands dedication and requires little in the way of start up capital. It would, in fact, be a prime candidate for the Business Expansion Scheme.
John Naughton

Poverty

The best way to help the poor is not to become one of them.
Lang Hancock

The greatest of our evils and the worst of our crimes is poverty, and…our first duty, to which every other consideration should be sacrificed, is not to be poor.
George Bernard Shaw

He will soon be a beggar, that cannot say nay.
James Kelly

Prices

What is a cynic?…A man who knows the price of everything and the value of nothing…And a sentimentalist…is a man who sees as absurd value in everything, and doesn't know the market price of any single thing.
Oscar Wilde, Lady Windermere's Fan

'Why don't you write books people can read?' Nora Joyce to husband, James Joyce

One person's price is another person's income.
Walter W Heller

Privatisation

Privatisation is now starkly revealed as a massive plunder of public property.
Michael Meacher

Everything that is most beautiful in Britain has always been in private hands.
Malcom Rifkind

Producers

The supposed conflict of labour with capital is a delusion. The real conflict is between producers and consumers.
W Stanley Jevons (1835–1882), attributed

Consumer's delusions result in producer's blunders.
John Bates Clark

Production

Man produces in order to consume.
Frederic Bastiat

The principles of saving, pushed to excess, would destroy the motive to production. If every person were satisfied with the simplest food, the poorest clothing, and the meanest houses, it is certain that no other sort of food, clothing, and lodging would be in existence.
Thomas Robert Malthus

Professions

A professional is a person who tells you what you know already but in a way you cannot understand.
Anonymous

The best augury of a man's success in his profession is that he thinks it the finest in the world.
George Eliot

Professionalisation is thus an attempt to translate one order of scarce resources – special knowledge and skills – into another – social and economic rewards.
MS Larson, The Rise of Professionalism, 1977, introduction

Profit

Profits are not due to risks, but to superior skill in taking risks. They are not subtracted from the grains of labour but are earned, in the same sense in which the wages of skilled labour are earned.
Frank A Fetter

Brand origins:

Jaguar, 1935 – originally appeared as SS Jaguar (Swallow Sidecar Co., owned by William Lyons). Mr Lyons felt a Jaguar mirrored his car's design and performance. SS was partially dropped because of the resemblance to the SS division of the Nazi party.

Nothing contributes so much to the prosperity and happiness of a country as high profits.
David Ricardo

It is a socialist idea that making profits is a vice; I consider the real vice is making losses.
Sir Winston Churchill

Profit Sharing The idea of making workers share in profits is a very attractive one and it would seem that it is from there that harmony as between Capital and Labour should come. But the practical formula for such sharing has not yet been found.
Henri Fayol

Progress It is hardly progress for a cannibal to use a knife and fork.
Sir Geoffrey Howe

Discontent is the first step in the progress of a man or a nation.
Oscar Wilde, A Woman of No Importance

Promotion To get on these days, it isn't what you know or even who you know that counts – it's usually what you know about who you know.
Epson's Compleat Office Companion

I would not risk spoiling my chances for a large promotion by asking for a small one.
Elbert Hubbard

Property Private property began the instant somebody had a mind of his own.
EE Cummings

Property is necessary, but it is not necessary that it should remain forever in the same hands.
Remy de Gourmont

Property is the most ambiguous of categories. It covers a multitude of rights which have nothing in common except that they are exercised by persons and enforced by the state.
RH Tawney

Medieval words:

chintz – fabric imported from Persia or India

Prosperity

Too much prosperity makes men greedy and desires are never controlled sufficiently to stop at the point of attainment.
Seneca

Few of us can stand prosperity. Another man's I mean.
Mark Twain

Protectionism

[Protectionism is] the sacrifice of the consumer to the producer, of the end to the means.
Frederic Bastiat

The protectionists are fond of flashing to the public eye the glittering delusion of great money-results from manufacturing, mines, artificial exports…But the really important point of all is, into whose pockets does this plunder really go?
Walt Whitman

Prostitution

Whether our reformers admit it or not, the economic and social inferiority of women is responsible for prostitution.
Emma Goldman

Prostitution gives her an opportunity to meet people. It provides fresh air and wholesome exercise, and it keeps her out of trouble.
Joseph Heller, Catch-22

Prostitutes believe in marriage. It provides them with most of their trade.
'Suzie', Knave,

Public Enterprise

A public utility thrives only as it is backed up by the best people in the town.
Elbert Hubbard

The common remark that public business is worse managed than all other business, is not altogether unfounded.
Herbert Spencer

Etymology:

snob – this word, meaning a supercilious person, originates from the early days of Oxford University in England. Students who were not from nobility added after their names the phrase *sine nobilitat*. This was abbreviated to *s.nob* which was the ideal definition for the common man who wished to mingle with the nobles.

Public Expenditure

Great nations are never impoverished by private, though they sometimes are by public prodigality and misconduct. The whole, or almost the whole public revenue is employed in maintaining unproductive hands.

Adam Smith

Thrift should be the guiding principle in our government expenditure.

Mao Tse-Tung

Public Relations

PR is like Christianity. If you don't believe in it, it won't work.

Alan Crompton-Batt

Facts influence. They are revered by people who cannot contradict them. Like statistics, they are extremely dangerous. They must be controlled and only revealed where essential.

Michael Shea

Publishing

The best part of every author is in general to be found in his book.

Samuel Johnson

The road that leads to publishers' counting houses is paved with the bones of artists and writers starved on the track.

Norman Lindsay

The assets of a publishing house are people – editors, the authors they attract, sales and publicity; all assets that are possessed of two feet and can walk away.

Hammond Innes

R

Radio

The ideal voice for radio may be defined as having no substance, no sex, no owner, and a message of importance for every housewife.

Harry V Wade

It's one-to-one dialogue. You open your mouth and you're talking to six million people.

Derek Jameson

Writers' words:

'A deadline is negative inspiration. Still, it's better than no inspiration at all.' Rita Mae Brown

Railways

No one – not even a railway manager – gives away money as a business transaction. The manager who reduces a rate on coal, or a third-class fare, does so hoping that traffic will be so stimulated that there will be a greater net profit on the larger traffic at the lower rate than there was on the smaller traffic at the higher rate… whatever railway critics may say, the Irish applewoman's principle, that you can afford to sell each apple at a loss if you only sell enough, is not universally true.

WM Acworth

Second-class carriages, though fairly full, are always reasonably quiet; first-class carriages are excessively noisy with their occupants all on expense accounts, boasting of their commercial ingenuity.

AJP Taylor

References

'As to being a reference,' said Pancks, 'you know in a general way, what being a reference means. It's all your eye, that is! Look at your tenants down the yard here. They'd all be references for one another, if you'd let 'em. What would be the good of letting 'em? It's no satisfaction to be done by two men instead of one. One's enough. A person who can't pay, gets another person who can't pay, to guarantee that he can pay.

Charles Dickins

Rent

Rent is an economical result as certain and as inevitable as the harvest is a natural result after the seed-time.

Benjamin Disraeli

As soon as the land of any country has all become private property, the landlords, like all other men, love to reap where they never sowed, and demand a rent even for it's natural produce.

Adam Smith

Reputation

A reputation for good judgment, for fair dealing, for truth, and for rectitude, is itself a fortune.

Henry Ward Beecher

Reputation, reputation, reputation! O, I have lost my reputation! I have lost the immortal part of myself, and what remains is bestial.

William Shakespeare, Othello, act II, scene ii

Writers' words:

'I don't expect executives to be creative but I do expect them to have courage.' Rita Mae Brown

Resignation	The Son of a bitch [General MacArthur] isn't going to resign on me. I want him fired. Harry S Truman
	It seems like nothin' ever gits t' goin' good till ther's a few resignations. Frank McKinney Hubbard)
Retailing	Shopping has become a vital means of expression during a time of authoritarianism. Neville Brody and Jon Wozencroft
	A unit trust which falls in value might detract from customers' confidence in the underwear, that intangible asset from which all the riches have flowed. Robert Peston
Retirement	The man who retires from business will shortly be retired by death. Elbert Hubbard
	You can put off being young until you retire. Phillip Larkin
	Two weeks ago I went into retirement. Am I glad that's over! I just didn't like it. Took all the fun out of Saturdays. Ronald Regan
Risk	Prudent business men in their dealings incur risk. Vice-Chancellor Bacon
	The ultimate risk is not taking risks. Sir James Goldsmith

S

Sales	The salesman knows nothing of what he is selling save that he is charging a great deal too much for it. Oscar Wilde
	The smoothest thing about a second-hand car is the salesman. Anonymous
Saving	The last dime that is earned is the first one that is saved. John Bates Clark

Etymology:

zany – this word meaning crazy originates from Italy in the sixteenth century. The 'zanni' was an idiot who was made fun of by clowns in the 'commedia dell'art'.

The power to save depends on excess of income over necessary expenditure.
Alfred Marshall

Science
If science has taught us anything, it is that the environment is full of uncertainties. It makes no sense to test it to destruction. While we wait for the doctor's diagnosis, the patient may easily die.
Prince Charles

The sciences are beneficent; they prevent man from thinking.
Anatole France

Scientists
If a scientist cannot explain to the woman scrubbing the lab floor what he is doing, he does not know what he is doing.
Lord Rutherford

Secretaries
If you want something done, give it to a busy man so he can get his secretary to do it.
Anonymous

Most secretaries can do their bosses' jobs, but their skills are generally not recognised.
M'lissa Dunn

You can run the office without a boss, but you can't run an office without a secretary.
Jane Fonda

Security
The borrower is a slave to the lender; the security to both.
Benjamin Franklin

Self-interest
The world will always be governed by self-interest. We should not try to stop this, we should try to make the self-interest of cads a little more coincident with that of decent people.
Samuel Butler

To feather one's own nest.
Thomas Fuller

Selling
Everyone lives by selling something.
Robert Louis Stevenson

Anagrams:

from WILLIAM SHAKESPEARE to I AM A PEAK WISH SELLER

To sell no matter what, no matter how, to no matter whom; behold in three words the whole diplomacy of the peasant at the fair.

Joseph Roux

He that sells wares for words, must live by the loss.

James Kelly

Service Industries

It is rare to find anywhere in the world a city of pleasure without an economically vital hinterland that supports and sustains the fun and games.

Henry Hobbhouse

They also serve who only stand and wait.

John Milton

If only Gilbert knew what would happen decades along the line!

Shareholders

The shares are a penny, and ever so many are taken by Rothschild and Baring. And just as a few are allotted to you, you awake with a shudder despairing.

WS Gilbert

The Annual Report was originally a dull, if respectable publication…For the modern stockholder the Company must provide, and does provide, a brightly coloured, smartly illustrated brochure, printed on art paper and bound in imitation vellum…The general effect is festive, innocent and gay, well suited to the more junior groups at kindergarten.

C Northcote Parkinson

Shipping

A shipbuilding industry is crucial to a shipping industry.

Lord Molloy

Life's like a shipping business you know; take a calculated risk with a stout heart and it almost always pays off.

Warren Tute, The Golden Greek, 1960

Show Business

I'm a businessman, I'm interested in the movie making money. I'm not hung up on being an actor's actor or doing what they call artistic movies.

Arnold Schwarzenegger

If it's a good script, I'll do it. And if it's a bad script, and they pay me enough, I'll do it.

George Burns

Writers' words:

'The difference between fiction and reality? Fiction has to make sense.' Tom Clancy

Socialism	Socialists make the mistake of confusing individual worth with success. They believe you cannot allow people to succeed in case those who fail feel worthless. Kenneth Baker
	Socialism:…A sincere, sentimental, beneficent theory, which has but one objection, and that is, it will not work. Frank McKinney Hubbard
	Socialism is about giving people what socialists think is good for them. Brian Walden
Speculation	Every transaction in which an individual buys produce in order to sell it again is, in fact, a speculation. JR McCulloch
	There are two times in man's life when he should not speculate: when he can't afford it, and when he can. Mark Twain
Spending	If it were not for holes in the pocket, we should all be rich. A pocket is like a cistern, a small leak at the bottom is worse than a large pump at the top. Henry Ward Beecher
	Know when to spend, and when to spare, and you need not be busy, and you'll never be bare. James Kelly
Sport	There is no business like show business – except sports business. William J. Baker
	When I was a director of Sheffield United for six months, the chairman told me normal business standards didn't apply in football. It was the most stupid advice I ever had. Mike Watterson
Statistics	Statistics are no substitute for judgement. Henry Clay
	Statistics are like a bikini. What they reveal is suggestive, but what they conceal is vital. Aaron Levenstein
Steel	Steel is Prince or Pauper. Andrew Carnegie

Brand origins:

Häagen Dazs – Ruben Mattus, a Polish immigrant in New York City, decided on the Scandinavian sounding name after the success of another of his food creations 'vichyssoises' a cold soup that he wanted to sound as if it came from France.

He found an America of wood and iron, and turned it into steel.

Burton J Hendrick

Stock Markets

Long-term investments are usually short-term investments which have gone wrong.

Anonymous

The freedom to make a fortune on the Stock Exchange has been made to sound more alluring than freedom of speech.

John Mortimer

Strikes

One of the main things that distinguishes democracies from dictatorships is the right to go on strike.

Len Murray

The general strike has taught the working classes more in four days than years of talking could have done.

AJ Balfour

Success

Be awful nice to 'em goin' up, because you're gonna meet 'em all comin' down.

Jimmy Durante

The great fault all over the world in business is that people over-complicate and forget that the main ingredients for success are commonsense and simplicity. I use lawyers and accountants as little as possible.

Peter de Savary

Big Companies are small companies that succeeded.

Robert Townsend

T

Takeovers

Takeovers are for the public good, but that's not why I do it. I do it to make money.

Sir James Goldsmith

You cannot buy a company merely by buying its shares.

Sir James Goldsmith

Tariffs

We've got so much taxation. I don't know of a single foreign product that enters this country untaxed except the answer to prayer.

Mark Twain

Writers' words:

'It is worth mentioning, for future reference, that the creative power which bubbles so pleasantly in beginning a new book quiets down after a time, and one goes on more steadily. Doubts creep in. Then one becomes resigned. Determination not to give in, and the sense of an impending shape keep one at it more than anything.' Virginia Woolf

For other countries to tax our exports to them is an injury to us and an obstacle to trade. For us to tax their exports to us is not a correction of that injury; it is just a separate additional obstacle to trade.
Sir William Beveridge

Taxation

I'm spending a year dead for tax reasons.
Douglas Adams

What an increase of rent is to the farmers, an increase of taxation is to the public… so long as it is confined within moderate limits, it acts as a powerful stimulus to industry and economy, and most commonly occasions the production of more wealth than it abstracts.
JR McCulloch

Our tax system is an outstanding example of complexity built upon complexity. I can't describe it as a house of cards because the damn thing certainly won't fall down.
EE Ray

All is fair in love, war and tax evasion.
Tom Sharpe, The Throwback

Tea

The occupation of a tea lady cannot by any stretch of the imagination be described as hazardous.
Mr Justice Comyn

While there's tea there's hope.
Sir Arthur Pinero

Technology

Technology makes possible what good management knew but was formerly unable to achieve.
W Wriston6

The imperatives of technology and organization, not the images of ideology, are what determine the shape of economic society.
John Kenneth Galbraith

Television

A stake in commercial television is the equivalent of having a licence to print money.
Lord Thompson of Fleet

Why should people go out and pay money to see bad films when they can stay at home and see bad television for nothing?
Samuel Goldwyn

Etymology:

taboo – this word, meaning something which is forbidden, originated from the Togan word 'tabu', meaning 'marked as holy'. The first taboos were against the use or mention of anything that would anger the gods.

Theft   It's much safer to steal from your employer than the tax man.
Dick Francis

Pick-pockets are sure traders; for they take ready money.
Thomas Fuller

Time   Time is of more importance than is generally imagined.
George Washington

To choose time is to save time.
Francis Bacon

Remember that time is money.
Benjamin Franklin

Timing   And one good lesson to this purpose I pike, From the Smith's forge, when th' iron is hot, strike.
John Heywood

Timing is the greatest single factor you're dealing with in art, people, or business.
Warren Tute

Tourism   In the middle ages people were tourists because of their religion, whereas now they are tourists because tourism is their religion.
Dr Robert Runcie

Trade   A handful of trade is worth a handful of gold.
James Kelly

After all the maxims and systems of trade and commerce, a stander-by would think the affairs of the world were most ridiculously contrived.
Jonathan Swift

Traders   It is the privilege of a trader in a free country, in all matters not contrary to the law, to regulate his own mode of carrying it on according to his own discretion and choice.
Baron Alderson

A merchant's happiness hangs upon chance, winds and waves.
Thomas Fuller

Etymology:

ambulance – this word, meaning a vehicle for transporting injured or sick people, originated from an invention of Napoleon Bonaparte 'l'hôpital ambulant' (walking hospital).

Trade Unions Had the employers of past generations dealt fairly with men, there would have been no trade unions.
Stanley Baldwin

It is one of the characteristics of a free and democratic modern nation that it have free and independent labour unions.
Franklin D Roosevelt

U

Unemployment

There must be something wrong with a system where it pays to be sacked.
Jo Grimond

It's a recession when your neighbour loses his job; it's a depression when you lose yours.
Harry S Truman

We believe that if men have the talent to invent new machines that put men out of work, they have the talent to put those men back to work.
John F Kennedy

Used cars Would you ever buy a used car from me?
John De Lorean

My greatest asset is that people would buy a used car from me.
Helmut Kohl

V

Vacation I find that a change of nuisances is as good as a vacation.
David Lloyd George

When some fellers take a vacation ever'buddy gits a rest.
Frank McKinney Hubbard

Anyone here speak English?

There are eight languages which spell taxi the same way: English, French, Danish, Swedish, German, Norwegian, Spanish and Portuguese.

Value

The value of all wares arise from their use; things of no use have no value, as the English phrase it, they are good for nothing.

Nicholas Barbon

Value depends entirely on utility.

W. Stanley Jevons

W

Wages

One man's wage rise is another man's price increase.

Sir Harold Wilson

Today's payslip has more deductions than a Sherlock Holmes novel.

Raymond Cuikota

All wages are based primarily on productive power. Anything else would be charity.

Elbert Hubbard

Wealth

The art of getting rich consists not in industry, much less in saving, but in a better order, in timeliness, in being at the right spot.

Ralph Waldo Emerson

He is not fit for riches, who is afraid to use them.

Thomas Fuller

If you can actually count your money, then you are not really a rich man.

John Paul Getty

Men do not desire to be rich, but to be richer than other men.

John Stuart Mill

Work

The best preparation for tomorrow's work is to do your work as well as you can today.

Elbert Hubbard

As I never tire of explaining, the English don't really like working and are not much good at it anyway.

Auberon Waugh

When a man says he wants to work, what he means is that he wants wages.

Richard Whateley

Loquacious language:

xenomania – a compulsion for foreign customs

Workers   The quality of the workers who leave the factory doors every evening is an even more important thing than the quality of the products which it delivers to the customers.
Samuel Courtauld

Not to oversee workmen, is to leave them your purse open.
Thomas Fuller

Brand origins:

Lee Jeans – Henry D Lee used to be a wholesaler of groceries, work clothes and other items. In 1911 he got fed up of waiting for late shipments of work clothes so he decided to manufacture his own. By 1924 he was making jeans for cowboys. By 1926 he introduced the first jeans with zips.

Brains, pen, action!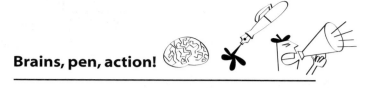

Something to ponder...

The term 'business as usual' first came into popular use when a copywriter called Herbert Morgan used it during World War I. It fell out of fashion because, quite simply, what with the terrible death toll and hardship endured throughout the war, the last thing anything wanted was 'usual'.

Look through the list of quotes with your product or service in mind. Can you adapt any of them to suit your needs?

Brand origins:

Hoover, 1908 – the original vacuum cleaner was built by J Murray Spangler. It was marketed by William Hoover. (The first Hoovers sold for $70.)

19. Is it a bird? Is it a plane?...
No it's a sloganeer!

As an adolescent, I grew up an in age of fear and panic. The British government's campaign warning against HIV contraction featured the powerful slogan 'Don't Die of Ignorance'. A picture of a tombstone accompanied this: all very chilling stuff.

I much prefer the British army's no-nonsense approach to safe-sex, as captured in a World War II slogan 'Whip it in, whip it out and wipe it'. This was the highlight in a film shown to the troops about venereal disease.

In the meantime, and on a much more sombre note, this chapter is dedicated to the late actor – died 11 October 2004 – Christopher Reeve, whose portrayal of Superman (the slogan 'Up, up and awa-a-a-ay!' was originally from Kellogg's Pep sponsored radio series) placed the notion of heroes in children's minds worldwide.

'Is it a bird? Is it a plane?... No, it's a sloganeer!'

Q: What's the last thing people see or hear in an advertisement yet the first they remember?

A: A slogan. These pithy summaries of a product or service are often derived from a company's mission statement or published set of 'values'.

- The UK advertising industry calls them end lines, endlines or straplines.
- In the USA, they are 'tags', 'tag lines', 'taglines' or 'theme lines'.
- The Germans refer to them as 'claims'.
- In Belgium, they are 'baselines'
- The French prefer to describe them as 'signatures'.
- In the Netherlands and Italy they are 'pay-offs' or 'payoffs'.

Slogans serve several purposes:
- They add continuity to a campaign.
- They instil public confidence in a company.
- They act as a surrogate logo (a company's trade mark) when logos are impractical (such as on radio commercials).

Slogans owe much to some of the oldest, yet most powerful English writing techniques, including:

Alliteration

Two or more syllable sounds, sound groups or letters at the beginning of words in a phrase, as in:

Perfect Print Produced to Perfection

Pun

A play on words, as in:

Hire cars at lower prices
The staple you can pin your hopes to

Loquacious language:

yaply – an adverb meaning eagerly, hungrily

Simile

A resemblance of one thing to another, using 'like' or 'as if', as in:

Wearing our scarves is like wearing a cuddle.

Allusion

Often connected to a well-known saying or proverb, as in:

Land of hope and glory (garden centre)

Metaphor

Never used literally, but always a certain likeness, as in:

A waterfall of freshness
A bucketful of love

Hyperbole

Extravagant statement not intended to be understood literally, as in:

Everything under the sun you could ever want

Comparison

Comparing similarities in two things, as in:

Serious work – child's play
A diamond is forever
Our cases are never closed books

Personification

Abstract ideas of lifeless objects named as a person, as in:

The Table family
Acme is business

Chiasmus

Reversal in the order of words in two otherwise parallel phrases, as in:

Our hard work means you don't work hard.
The first thing on our mind should be the last thing on yours (Will writing service).

Transferred epithet

Unusual use of an adjective with nouns, as in:

Sail a happy ship
Drive an honest car
Ride a careful train

Loquacious language:

yemeles – careless or negligent

Types of slogan

Essentially, there are around a dozen fundamental kinds of slogan:

Slogans are about you.

Directions
Your friendly Internet cafe

Acme Stores
We always sell lower

Slogans make promises

PCs 'R' us
Names you can trust

Acme Copywriting
Our word is your bond

Slogans call for action

Groceries Direct
We pick 'em, you click 'em

Books 'R' us
Always read the small print

Slogans create ideals

Acme portable swimming pools
*Now the sea is never further
than A–B*

Acme ice cream
*If it's Monday, it must be a
Sundae!*

Savings Inc.
We owe everything to you

Slogans may rhyme

Shopping City
Top for shops

Cellular phones
The home of phones

Slogans create utopias

Pens Direct
Enter a new world of writing.

**Slogans can be full of
alliteration**

Highland Salmon
Supremely Scottish: Salmon

Wholesalers Direct
Buy better. Buy bigger, by far.

Slogans can be direct

Watches 'R' US
Timeless watches

Gabay's Copywriters'
Compendium
The writer's choice.

 I think I'll buy one of those

**Slogans conveniently package
concepts**

PDAs Direct
*Affordable reliability in your
pocket*

MP3 players 'R' us
*Reach into your pocket and pull
out an orchestra*

**Slogans repeat key word
patterns**

Couriers 'R' us
Online, on price and on time.

Classic Pens Inc.
*The writing choice for the right
occasion.*

Brand origins:

Hovis, first in shops in 1890. S Fitton & Son of Macclesfield held a competition to name their bread. A student,
Herbert Grimes won the contest. The name was based on 'hominis vis' from Latin, meaning 'the strength of a man'/
'quantity of men'.

'The' slogan is king

The best.
The one.
The shape.
The answer.
The greatest.
The experience.
The genuine article.
The one you need.
The industry's choice.
The professional's choice.

Slogans are 'it'

Go for it.
It's here.
It's more.
It's forever.
Stick it.
You can't beat it.
It's hot.
Believe it
It's cool.
It's yours.
Try it, you'll like it.
Live it.

Buy it.
It's now.
It's less.
It's together.
You can't lick it.
You can't touch.
Click it.
It's tasty.
It's the best.
It's everything.
Be part of it.
Help it help you.

Remember these?

Used subtly yet consistently, slogans reinforce brand values. However, many advertisements that appear without slogans are still highly successful.

Looking through the following list of some of the world's most famous slogans – from advertising and far beyond – I believe that the best piece of advice is to keep them short and sweet.

(Or should that be: *slogans-short, sweet and neat*?)

Loquacious language:

transume – to make an official copy of a document

A

Ahh Bisto !

Bisto (gravy browning); UK, c. 1919. The product name is said to also feature a slogan. When the Cerebos company put in on the market in 1910, the product was nameless. The initial letters of the proposed slogan 'Browns, Seasons, Thickens in One' were rearranged to give the now familiar brand name. The endearing Bisto kids, illustrated by Will Owen, made their first appearance in 1919, smelling a whiff and whispering, 'Ahh Bisto!'

All for one, and one for all (Tous pour un, un pour tous)

Mythical motto of the Three Musketeers in the novel Les Trois Mousquetaires (1844–45) by Alexandre Dumas. Yet, did you now that three centuries earlier, in his poem, The Rape of Lucrece, 1. 141–4 (1594), Shakespeare wrote:

The aim of all is but nurse the life
With honour, wealth and ease, in waning age;
And in the aim there is much thwarting strife
The One for all, or all for one we gage

All talking! All singing! All dancing!

Originally from the movie 'Broadway Melody'; US, 1929. Hollywood's first musical – from MGM – was advertised with the slogan:

The New Wonder of the Screen!
ALL TALKING
ALL SINGING
ALL DANCING
Dramatic Sensation

And all because the lady loves milk tray

Cadbury's Milk Tray Chocolates; UK, 1968–76. This line alluded to the daring escapades of the secret agent, James Bond. It always appeared after a commercial showing a man negotiating difficult trails so he could deliver a box of yummy chocolates to a sultry looking woman.

Avon calling!

Avon cosmetics; US, 1886. The firm's founder D.H. McConnell used to sell cosmetics in the home. The first 'Avon Lady' was Mrs P.F.A. Allre. The line is still used in the twenty-first century.

Australians wouldn't give a XXXX for anything else

Castlemaine XXXX lager; UK, 1986. Very much like the FCUK (French Connection) style of advertising – playing on Australian friskiness and brashness.

Loquacious language:

tutoyant – to be intimate or affectionate

B

Back to basics

UK Conservative Government, 1993. John Major, the Prime Minister, delivered a keynote speech at the Conservative Party Conference:

> The message from this conference is clear and simple. We must go back to basics … The Conservative Party will lead the country back to these basics, right across the board: sound money, free trade; traditional teaching; respect for the family and the law.

As if on cue, the Conservatives were soon exposed to be associated with scandals which certainly weren't 'above board' and 'back to basics' in nature or content. Some years later John Major's extra marital affair with one of his Cabinet ministers was exposed. In the mid-1970s a US education movement also used to the slogan to highlight the importance of teaching of the fundamentals of reading, writing and mathematics.

Beanz Meanz Heinz

Heinz baked beans; UK, 1967. The copy was written by Maurice Drake, who explained:

> 'It was written – although after much thinking – over two pints of bitter in the Victoria pub in Mornington Crescent (London).'

Johnny Johnson wrote the music for the jingle, which in its entirety read:

> A million housewives every day
> Pick up a tin of beans and say
> Beanz Meanz Heinz

Best to you each morning, the

Kellogg's corn flakes and other breakfast cereals; US, from 1953.

Better red than dead

Nuclear disarmament slogan; UK, from c.1958. It was an era when the West was obsessed with Communist conspiracies and the possibility of a world nuclear war. Time Magazine (15 September 1961) offered 'I'd rather be Red than dead' as a slogan of Britain's Campaign for Nuclear Disarmament. The counter-cry 'Better dead than red' was a popular retort. (Hollywood's 'Love With a Proper Stranger' (US, 1964) saw the movie heart-throb, Steve McQueen, proposing to his leading lady, Natalie Wood, with a placard stating 'Better wed than dead'.)

Writers' words:

'Fill your paper with the breathings of your heart...' William Wordsworth

Big brother is watching you

From the novel by George Orwell, Nineteen Eighty-Four (1949). The book told of a totalitarian state where ordinary people were spied upon via a home TV set and reported to 'The Ministry of Truth'.

The slogan was turned on its head when TV programme makers devised 'Big Brother', in which viewers judged the antics of ordinary people living their lives on TV.

Buck stops here, the

Unofficial presidential motto of the 1940s US President Harry S. Truman. It is said that he had a desk sign with these words on it, signifying that the Oval Office was where the passing of the buck had to stop. When President Nixon published his memoirs, protestors wore badges reading: 'The book stops here'.

Burger King – Home of the Whopper

Burger King hamburger chain; US, since 1981. Burger King also used: 'It takes two hands to hold a Whopper'; UK, undated.

C

Castrol, liquid engineering

Castrol motor oil; UK, since 1977. Castrol also used: 'Oil is too small a word for it'. This line was devised by the Dorland Agency as an alternative for advertising the notion that the company was the brand leader in its field (a fact that couldn't be stated legally).

Cleanliness is next to godliness

Pears' Soap; UK/US, 1800s. The British advertising agent Thomas J. Barratt (1842–1914) sought a testimonial from a US person of note. He approached a preacher called Henry Ward Beecher (who wrote a popular pamphlet called Seven Lectures to Young Men). Beecher began his reply 'If cleanliness is next to Godliness…'

Crime Doesn't Pay

US, c. 1927. Adopted by the FBI and the comic strip character Dick Tracy.

Gabay at a glance:

Pay particular attention to slogans on the Internet. Do they actually make sense? Match the following slogans to their companies. (All were spotted on the Internet):

(a) Striving to make the world a better place.

(b) Makers of the world's finest products.

(c) A symbol of e-freedom.

(d) You've got a friend in the business.

1. South West Airlines.

2. Gateway Computers.

3. Ford Motor Company.

4. Philip Morris.

answers page 604

Loquacious language:

twitter-light – twilight

D

Does She ... Or Doesn't She ?

Clairol hair colourant; US, from 1955.

Don't die of ignorance

AIDS awareness slogan; UK, 1987. The main line from the British government's first and arguably most powerful AIDS awareness campaign. In no time, graffiti artists added this ending to the posters: *'Don't die of ignorance, Sun readers do'*. Also, in the autumn of that year 'It only takes one prick to give you AIDS' – aimed at drug addicts – also injected some dry humour to the proceedings.

Drink Coca-Cola

Coca-Cola; US, since the late 1880s. Coca-Cola claims to be the most widely advertised product in world – and probably it is.

Don't leave home without it

American Express credit card; US, since 1981. The late Bob Hope performed a spoof as the Pope carrying his Vatican Express card ('Don't leave Rome without it').

Dog is for life, not just for Christmas, a

National Canine Defence League; UK, probably from the late 1980s.

E

Elementary, my dear Watson!

Contrary to popular belief, the line does not appear in any of Sir Arthur Conan Doyle's stories. Holmes does say 'Elementary', as in 'The Crooked Man' (in The Memoirs of Sherlock Holmes, 1894), and 'my dear Watson' but never did the two together in any of the original 60 stories written by Conan Doyle. It was left to Hollywood to immortalise it in movies.

Exterminate! Exterminate!

Spoken by the Daleks in the BBC TV series Doctor Who (originally 1963–89), the world's longest running TV science fiction series. The Daleks, who were meant to be mutant creatures from the planet Skaro, were megalomaniacs, yet were limited in their powers to conquer civilisations because they could only move about on wheels. (Darn those steps!).

Writers' words:

'Writing ought either to be the manufacture of stories for which there is a market demand -- a business as safe and commendable as making soap or breakfast foods -- or it should be an art, which is always a search for something for which there is no market demand, something new and untried, where the values are intrinsic and have nothing to do with standardized values.' Willa Cather

F

For the person who has everything

General-use slogan; US; probably since the 1920s/30s. Promoting some odd luxury gift item, inessential and over priced. A salesman at the jewellery store in the film Breakfast at Tiffany's (US, 1961) produces something 'for the lady and gentleman who have everything'.

Fabulous sweetie!

From the cult BBC TV comedy series 'Absolutely Fabulous' (1992–96 in the UK; –97 in the US). Often uttered by Edina (Jennifer Saunders), the neurotic PR has-been and her insecure chum Patsy (Joanna Lumley). The series was said to have been loosely inspired by real-life PR guru – Lynne Franks.

Fly the friendly skies

Advertising slogan for United Airlines, introduced in 1965 to convey the airline's hospitality. From 1970, the airline promoted the slogan to underscore a powerful message of a sense of warmth in all its campaigns. The complete rendition was 'Fly the friendly skies of United'.

Famous for fifteen minutes

Phrase strongly linked to the artist Andy Warhol, who featured it in a 1968 exhibition catalogue. The full phrase was 'In the future everybody will be famous for fifteen minutes', and came from the era's tendency to make any aspiring 'nobody' a 'somebody' via television, the press or radio, albeit for a 'moment in time'. This concept eventually gave rise to self-publishing on the web and the proliferation of 'reality TV' show formats.

Frankie says Relax

A catchphrase of the early 1980s, when it appeared on T-shirts across Britain and then in the US after the song, 'Relax (Don't Do It)' by the British band Frankie Goes To Hollywood which made it big in 1983. The lyrics to the song was originally banned as it referred to a man ejaculating: 'Relax, don't do it when you want to cum.'

G

Greatest Show on Earth, The

Barnum & Bailey's circus; US, 1881. Name given by Phineas T. Barnum (1810–91) to the circus formed by the merger with his rival, Bailey. The Ringling Bros and Barnum & Bailey Circus still use it. Many remember it as the title of a Cecil B. De Mille circus movie 'The Greatest Show on Earth' (1952).

Loquacious language:

typocrate – a person who rules over others by controlling the press

H

Happiness is...

Used in US since 1960s as a panacea for many products wishing to convey an ideal. Adopted in the UK in the 1970s by Hamlet Cigars: Happiness is a cigar called Hamlet.

Have a break, have a Kit Kat

Rowntree's Kit Kat; UK, from c.1955.

Heineken refreshes the parts other beers cannot reach

Heineken Lager; UK, from 1975. Written by Terry Lovelock, who said:

> 'I wrote the slogan during December 1974 at 3 am at the Hotel Marmounia in Marrakech. After eight weeks in incubation with the agency (Collett, Dickenson, Pearce), it was really a brainstorm. No other lines were written. The trip was to refresh the creative's thinking. Expensive, but it worked!'

Hello boys

Wonderbra; UK, 1994. Posters featured the model Eva Herzigova glancing down at her ample bosom.

How to win friends and influence people

Dale Carnegie's self-improvement events were designed for the business community. In 1936, an ad campaign launched the best-selling book on self-improvement. As a result, a million copies were sold between December 1936 and November 1939 alone.

I

Inter-City makes the going easy, and the coming back

British Rail; UK, c. 1972 (London and South-East Region) and 1975 (Inter-City).

It could be YOU

National Lottery; UK, 1995. Original slogan for UK's first official national lottery.

I don't believe it!

Popularised by the fictional cantankerous pensioner Victor Meldrew, played by Richard Wilson, in the award-winning BBC TV series One Foot in the Grave (1990–2000).

Medieval words:

catch – an English chase or hunting song

I tawt I taw a puddy tat

Nervous observation referring to a devious cat called Sylvester, by cartoon character canary, Tweety Pie (characterised by Mel Blanc). Tweety would characteristically declare, 'I tawt I taw a puddy tat. I did! I did! I did taw a puddy tat!'

K

Keep 'regular' with Ex-Lax

Ex- Lax chocolate laxative; US, since 1934.

Keep Britain tidy

Anti-Litter slogan; UK, first appeared 1952 on a Central Office of Information sticker produced for the Ministry of Housing and Local Government.

L

Let the train take the strain

Written by the Brady and Marsh agency in 1970 for British Rail Away Day fares.

Lovely jubbly

Cockney turn of phrase meaning 'brilliant' or 'very nice' popularised by Derek 'Del Boy' Trotter (David Jason) in the BBC TV comedy 'Only Fools and Horses' (1987–2003).

Loadsamoney

Named after a rich, yet uncouth, character meant to epitomise the 'anyone can make it good' philosophy of Thatcherite Britain. Loadsamoney was created by British comedian Harry Enfield, who came into prominence in the BBC comedy series Saturday Night Live (1987–88).

Let yours fingers do the walking

Advertising slogan for the Yellow Pages (classified telephone directories) in the US and UK from 1961 to 1998.

Lucozade aids recovery

Lucozade (health drink); UK, up to c.1986. It had to be dropped by the manufacturer, SmithKline Beecham, as the AIDS epidemic made the word 'aids' something of a taboo. (The manufacturer suggested that the slogan was removed before the epidemic took hold.) Another product, Ayds – for slimming – was also 're-strategised'.

Etymology:

brand new – this tautological expression, meaning something recently purchased or produced, comes from the German word *'brand'*, which means fire. Horseshoes, which were produced 'fresh' from a blacksmith's forge, were known as *brandneu*. Branded goods first originated in the American Wild West, when cowboys *branded* their cattle with distinctive marks burnt onto their hides.

M

Man from Del Monte says 'Yes', the

Del Monte canned fruit and fresh fruit; UK, from 1985. TV ads showed a distinguished looking ambassador from Del Monte who would only give his official approval to the finest produce.

Man from The Pru, the

c.1940. Created in homage to local salesmen who visited homes to collect life insurance premiums on behalf of the Prudential Assurance Co.

Marlboro – come to where the flavour is. Come to Marlboro Country.

Marlboro cigarettes; US, since the mid-1950s. Originally devised by the Leo Burnett agency in Chicago to endear Marlboro cigarettes to men, rather than women. (Hence the 'macho' cowboy.)

This was the third time Philip Morris re-introduced Marlboro to the marketplace. The second was in 1924 with the slogan 'Mild as May', targeting 'decent, respectable' women. Copy from the 1924 advert read: *'Has smoking any more to do with a woman's morals than has the colour of her hair? Marlboros now ride in so many limousines, attend so many bridge parties, and repose in so many handbags.'*

The actual cigarette was introduced in 1902, the original Marlboro, and was positioned as the sophisticated ladies' cigarette, featuring a red tip to hide lipstick marks.

Martini is… the right one

In the 1970s the McCann-Erickson agency conjured up a sophisticated world of playboys (and girls) who had a taste for high adventure. The slogan was accompanied by a jingle composed by Chris Gunner:

> *Try a taste of Martini*
> *The most beautiful drink the world,*
> *It's the bright one, the right one.*
> *There's much more to the world than you guess,*
> *And you taste it the day you say 'yes'*
> *To the bright taste, the right taste*
> *Of Martini…*

Loquacious language:

sarcinarious – the ability to carry heavy loads

N

Naughty, but nice
The novelist Salmon Rushdie claimed to have originated this slogan for the UK National Dairy Council.

Next year in Jerusalem (Le shanah ha ba'ah yerushalalim)
A Jewish toast which has become a slogan expressing hope for a dispersed community to be reunited in their natural homeland – Israel.

Nice 'Ere, innit?
Campari; UK, 1976. Picture this: Venice; a chic, beautiful woman drinks Campari then cooly turns to the camera and says in a coarse Cockney accent, 'Nice 'ere, innit?' The line was penned by copywriter Terry Howard.

Nanoo nanoo
Catchphrase spoken by Robin Williams, then an up and coming comedian, as the alien Mork from Ork in the US TV sitcom Mork and Mindy (1978–82).

Nudge nudge, wink wink
A sexual insinuation popularized by a disreputable character played by the late Eric Idle in the cult BBC TV comedy series Monty Python's Flying Circus (1969–74).

O

Ooh matron!
A whimper linked with the late comedian Kenneth Williams, who would deliver this line in the British series of 'Carry On' movies when shocked. Hattie Jacques, who starred in 14 'Carry On' films, played the 'Matron' in question.

One down, a million to go
Unauthorised cruel racist slogan (on the death of a black man): UK, most likely 1950s. Attributed to John Kingsley, read by Salmon Rushdie in a 1982 televised lecture.

P

Probably the best lager in the world
Carlsberg; UK, from 1973. A clever use of the word 'probably', which was first understated brilliantly by the late Orson Welles in the original early 1970s TV ads.

Writers' words:

'When one reader reads of a witch being ducked, of a woman possessed by devils, of a wise woman selling herbs, or even a very remarkable man who had a mother, then I think we are on the track of a lost novelist, a suppressed poet … indeed, I would venture to guess that Anon, who wrote so many poems without signing them, was often a woman.' Virginia Woolf

Pure genius

Guinness; UK, from 1985. It remains one of the great slogans from one of the greatest purveyors of ingenious marketing campaigns.

Pure gold

Benson & Hedges cigarettes; UK, from 1964. Originally the slogan referred to the brand's gold packaging. Eventually the campaign dropped the slogan, yet alluded towards it with sumptuously captured imagery.

Pass!

From BBC TV's Mastermind, the quiz show which put even the most learned contestants on the 'hot-seat'. The questions were often so difficult that competitors simply mumbled 'pass'.

Phone home

Uttered by ET, the alien featured in Steven Spielberg's 1982 multi-million pound box office hit ET – The Extra-terrestrial. BT (British Telecom) later called on ET to use it on their call stimulation campaign. (Presumably they contacted him long-distance for the assignment.)

Q

Queen for a day

Just after the Second World War, rations were slowly withdrawn. So housewives were forced to be frugal with their spending and 'tied' to household chores. Jack Bailey, a US radio host, featured the slogan in a series which promised to offer lucky housewives the chance to be pampered for day.

R

Refreshes the parts that other beers cannot reach

Written by Terry Lovelock for Heineken beer (c.1975). Throughout the campaign's life, 'the parts' referred to a sense of complete contentment for the drinker.

Roses grow on you

Cadbury's Roses chocolates; UK, since mid-1960s. Double-entendre referring to the chocolates' appeal.

Loquacious language:

scamander – to wander around

S

Snap! Crackle! and Pop!

Originated in the US around 1928 an advertising slogan for Kellogg's Rice Krispies breakfast cereal. It referred to the cereal's onomatopoeia sound when drenched in milk.

Space – the final frontier

From the intro to the US TV series Star Trek: 'Space – the final frontier. These are the voyages of the star ship Enterprise'. 'The final frontier' alluded to mankind's last and most important quest to explore the Universe. From the same series came – 'to boldly go where no man has gone before'.

Soft, strong and very long

Andrex toilet tissue; UK – originally devised in the early 1980s and still going strong.

Splash it all over

Brut aftershave; UK, c.1974. From an enduring advertising campaign featuring the ex-British world heavyweight champion boxer, Henry Cooper, who converted an entire generation of young Brits to splash the aftershave on their tender cheeks at every possible occasion.

Sean Connery *is* James Bond

First spoken by a gruff voice-over artist to advertise the movie *You Only Live Twice*; UK, 1967 –The slogan '… *is* …' has become a formula of classic sloganeering. Other examples include: 'Michael Caine *is* Alfie' (1966); Paul Hogan *is* Crocodile Dundee (1987) and that lesser known classic uttered by my teenage son Joshua, 'Joshua Gabay *is* getting on Dad's nerves'.

Gabay at a glance:

UK copywriters should be conversant with The Financial Services Act, notably 'Section 3' as well as advertising regulations stipulated by the Advertising Standards Authority.

Check out:

www.fsa.gov.uk
www.asa.org.uk

T

Tell Sid

Devised to promote the privatisation of British Gas; UK, 1986. 'Sid' characterised the humble private investor who shouldn't miss out on making a profit by investing in the the stock market. (This was all before the Financial Services Association stepped in to ensure that advertisers did not overtly encourage investors to believe that shares were the equivalent of licences to 'print money'.) One year later the Dow Jones Industrial Average declined by almost one third, representing a loss in value of all outstanding United States stocks of approximately $1.0 trillion. (On reflection, perhaps Sid should have told everyone to 'mind their own business' and stick with his unassuming gardening.)

Twisted truths:

Avoid trendy locutions that sound effusive and portentous.

They're G-r-reat

Kellogg's sugar frosted flakes; US, since c.1951. The 'g-r' alludes to the sound of a tiger – characterised by the cartoon figure 'Tony the Tiger'.

Top breeders recommend it

Pedigree Chum dog food; UK, 1964

Thunderbirds are Go!

From one of the BBC's most popular children's science fiction series, Thunderbirds (1965-6). Each programme started with a dramatic countdown sequence accompanied by Barry Gray's dramatic music: 'Five! Four! Three! Two! One! Thunderbirds are Go!'

The programme featured wooden puppets but was resurrected in summer 2004 as a feature film with 'live' actors. (I refuse to comment of whether or not they had to recite 'wooden lines'.)

Typhoo puts the 'T' in Britain

Typhoo tea; UK, by 1969

U

Ultimate driving machine, the

BMW automobiles; US/UK, current 1981.

United Colours of Benetton

Benetton Clothing; UK, from the late 1980s onwards.

United we stand, divided we fall

Political slogan; US, from the late eighteenth century. Jonathan Dickinson wrote 'The Patriot's Appeal' (sometimes called 'The Liberty Song') in 1768: 'By uniting we stand; by dividing we fall'. It is now the axiom of Kentucky.

V

Very… very Sanderson

Sanderson furnishing fabrics and wall-coverings; UK. The company's original Central London store is now a very, very trendy hotel.

W

Was there a lion on your egg this morning?

British Egg Marketing Board; from 1987.

Wilkinson Sword – The World's finest blade

Wilkinson Sword razor blades; UK, since 1982

Loquacious language:

scleragogy – the harsh training of the body

World's Favourite Airline, The

British Airways from 1983. Saatchi and Saatchi, the 'pet' advertising agency of the then incumbent UK Tory party, based this slogan on usage and marketing surveys. BA justified its validity on the grounds that the airline flew more people to more destinations than any other airline.

World's Largest Store, The

Devised in 1981 and still true. Macy's in New York City, USA is an 11-story building occupying an entire block in Herald Square, covering an area of 198,500 sq.m. (2.15 million sq ft).

World's Greatest Entertainer, The

Featured on posters for the Russian-born 'all-round American' entertainer Al Jolson (1886–1950).

Y

Yes, we have no bananas today

Featured in the US 1923 song composed by Irving Cohn and Frank Silver, that opened: 'Yes, we have no bananas today'. I preferred the alternative song composed by Guy Marks – Loving you has made me bananas:

Oh, your red scarf matches your eyes,
You closed your cover before striking,
Father had the shipfitter blues,
Loving you has made me bananas,

Oh, you burnt your finger that evening,
While my back was turned,
I asked the waiter for iodine,
But I dined all alone,
Loving you has made me bananas.

Z

Zubes are good for your tubes

Zubes cough sweets; UK, 1960s.

Gabay at a glance:

Combine 'to boldly go …' as well as 'probably the best …' and you will get probably the most commonly split infinitive that man has ever boldly said!

Etymology:-

Red Herring: This word, which means a diversionary tactic, originates from the hunting fraternity. When a herring is smoked it turns red and gives off a strong smell. Hunters use red herring to train dogs to follow a scent. By dragging a red herring across a trail they can also throw a dog off a scent.

Some slogan-inspiring 'real life' wacky song titles to consider:

All I want for Christmas is my two front teeth

All the girls look prettier at closing time

C'mon down off the stove, granny, you're too old to ride the range

Don't cry on my shoulders cause your rustin' my spurs

Don't do anything 'til I hear from you

Don't run through the screen door honey. You'll only strain yourself.

Drop-kick me, Jesus, through the goal posts of life

Fido is a hot dog now

For better or worse, but not for long

Forget the night; help me make it through the door

From the Indies to the Andes in his undies

Get out the meatballs mama. We're coming to a fork in the road.

Get your biscuits in the oven and your buns in the bed

Get your tongue outta my mouth 'cause I'm kissing you goodbye

Heaven's just a sin away

Horses don't bet on people (and that's why they never go broke)

How could you believe me when I said I love you when you know I've been a liar all my life

I can't love your body if your heart's not in it

I didn't raise my dog to be a sausage

If fingerprints showed up on skin, wonder whose I'd find on you

If I can't sell it, I'll keep sitting on it

If I had shot you when I wanted to, I'd be out by now

If I said you had a beautiful body, would you hold it against me?

I flushed you from the toilets of my heart.

If money talks, it ain't on speaking terms with me

If my nose were full of nickels, I'd blow it all on you

If she puts lipstick on my dipstick, I'll fall in love

If you don't believe I love you, just ask my wife

If you leave me, can I come too?

If you really loved me you would have married somebody else

If you won't leave me alone I'll find someone who will

I hate every bone in your body except mine

I heard the voice of a pork chop

I just couldn't leave her behind alone

Brand origins:

Golden Wonder, 1947 – probably inspired by a variety of potato, although the 'spud' was unsuitable for making chips.

I just fell in something and I sure hope it's love

I kissed her on the lips, and left her behind for you

I'll marry you tomorrow but let's honeymoon tonight

I'll never get over you, so turn off the alarm it's your side of the bed

I'm just a bug on the windshield of life

I'm gettin' grey from being blue

I'm gonna build me a bar in the back of my car and drive myself to drink

I'm looking for a guy who plays alto and baritone and doubles on clarinet and wears a size 37 suit

I'm old enough to know better but still too young to care

I'm so miserable without you; it's like having you here

I'm sorry I made you cry, but at least your face is cleaner

I'm the guy that paid the rent for Mrs Rip van Winkle

I'm the only hell mama ever raised

I only have eyes for you, but look what I've got for your sister

In the good old days when times were bad

I ran over my dog in my pickup at the train station comin' back from my mother's funeral after I got out of jail, in the rain

I still miss you, baby, but my aim's gettin' better

I thought the acropolis was a ruin until I saw you

It's only the hair on a gooseberry (that stops it from being a grape)

I've been flushed from the bathroom of your heart

I've got Elgin movements in my hips (guaranteed a thousand hours)

I've got Ford engine movements in my hips (guaranteed a thousand miles)

I've got red eyes from your white lies and I'm blue all the time

I've got you on my conscience but at least you're off my back

I've got a funny feeling (I won't be feeling funny very long)

I've never seen a straight banana

I won't go huntin' with you Jake, but I'll go chasin' women

I wouldn't take you to a dog fight even if I thought you could win

In the footprints of time, I'm just a heel

Mama get the hammer (there's a fly on Papa's head)

My sweet tooth says I wanna, but my wisdom tooth says…

My wife ran off with my best friend, and I sure do miss him

Never hit your grandma with a shovel

Loquacious language:

zaftig – someone who is sexy by being plump and curvaceous

No matter how young a prune may be, it's always full of wrinkles

Noses run in my family

Not tonight, I have a heartache

Now I lay me down to cheat

Oh, I've got hair oil on my ears and my glasses are slipping down... But baby I can see through you

Pardon my southern movements, Miss Lou

Peekin' through the knothole in grandma's wooden leg

Poison ivories

Put on the soup Ma, Dad's rakin' the back yard with his false teeth

Run to the roundhouse, Sally. They can't corner you there.

She got the gold mine, I got the shaft

She made toothpicks of the timber of my heart

She was bred in Old Kentucky, but she's just a crumb out here

She's your cook, but she burns my bread sometimes

Since you bought the waterbed we've slowly drifted apart

Snore your blues away

Take me to the corn field honey and I'll kiss you between the ears

Take me to the quarry and I'll get a little bolder

The beer I had for breakfast is comin' back for lunch

The last word in lonesome is me

The pilot light has gone out on our oven of love

The pint of no return

These boots were meant for lickin'

Time wounds all heels

Velcro™ arms, Teflon heart

We used to just kiss on the lips but now it's all over

What kind of a noise annoys an oyster?

What made Milwaukee famous (has made a loser out of me)

When it's night time in Italy it's Wednesday over here

When it's oyster picking time in Chattanooga I'll muscle in on you

When we get back to the farm (that's when we really go to town)

When we were down to nothin' (nothin' sure looked good on you)

When you leave, walk out backwards, so I'll think you're walking in.

When your phone don't ring it'll be me

While she's raisin' cane in Texas, I'm pullin' weeds in Tennessee

Twisted truths:

Everyone should be careful to use a singular pronoun with singular nouns in their writing.

Whoop! Whoop!! Whoop!!! Make a noise like a hoop and roll away

Who put all my ex's in Texas?

Would a Manx cat wag its tail if it had one?

You blacked my blue eyes once too often

You called her up, now you call her off

You can't deal me all the aces and expect me not to play

You can't get many pimples on a pound of pickled pork

You can't have your Kate and Edith too

You done me wrong, but keep on doing it 'til you do it right

You may put me in prison, but you can't keep my face from breakin' out

You put me on my feet (when you took her off my hands)

You stole my wife, you horse thief

You were only a splinter as I slid down the banister of life

You're the reason our kids are so ugly

Some famous political slogans include:

54–40 or fight – US presidential election, 1844, democrats claim British Columbia for Oregon

Ein volk, ein reich, ein führer (one people, one country, one leader) – Nazi Germany

In your heart, you know he's right – Barry Goldwater, 1964 presidential campaign (and the alternative '**In your guts, you know he's nuts**' – an unofficial anti-Goldwater slogan)

Liberté, egalité, fraternité (liberty, equality, brotherhood) – the French Revolution

Labour isn't working – the British Conservative Party

Power to the people – socialism

Remember the Alamo – for Republic of Texas independence

Remember the Maine – the rallying cry by which William Randolph Hearst fomented the Spanish–American war

Rum, Romanism and rebellion – US presidential election, 1884, republicans strike against opponents on prohibition, membership by Catholic immigrants and southerners

War on terror – George W. Bush

Workers of the world, unite – socialist slogan written by Karl Marx

You ain't seen nothing' yet – a version of Al Jolson's 'You ain't heard nothin' yet', popularised by the late US president Ronald Reagan during his 1984 re-election campaign

Loquacious language:

zoanthropy – a person's belief that they are non-human

Finally, the slogans that changed brands

Drinks

After dark – Tia Maria

Australians wouldn't give a Castlemaine XXXX for anything else – Australian beer

Coffee at its best – Nescafe Gold Blend

Coke is it – Coca Cola

Get back your 'Oo' with Typhoo – Typhoo Tea

Good to the last drop – Maxwell House Coffee

Follow the bear – Hoffmeister Lager

Fosters – Australian for beer – Fosters Australian beer

I am Canadian – Molson Canadian beer

It's the real thing – Coca Cola

Like tea used to be – Yorkshire Tea

Lipsmackin' Thirstquenchin' Acetastin' Motivatin' Goodbuzzin' Cooltalkin' Highwalkin' Fastlivin' Evergivin' Coolfizzin' Pepsi – Pepsi Cola

Made in Scotland, from girders – Irn Bru

No nonsense – John Smith's beer

Probably the best lager in the world – Carlsberg

Pure life – Nestle Aberfoyle Natural Spring Water

Reassuringly expensive – Stella Artois

Refreshes the parts other beers cannot reach – Heineken

Same time tomorrow? – Diet Pepsi

Sch... You know who? – Schweppes

The beer that made Milwaukee famous – Schlitz

The champagne of bottled beer – Miller Beer

The pause that refreshes – Coca Cola

The real thing – Coca Cola

There's no taste like stones – Stones Bitter

What a refreshing change – Woodpecker Cider

What we want is Watney's – Watney's

Who's your soda? – Red Fusion soft drink, Dr Pepper

You know when you've been Tango'd – Tango Soft Drink

Your best bet for a fuller flavour – Carling Black Label lager

Loquacious language:

zoilist – a critic

Communications, broadcasting, and publishing

All the news that's fit to print – The New York Times

Fair and balanced – Fox News

Get more – T-mobile

If it's on, it's in – Radio Times

It's good to talk – British Telecom

Let your fingers do the walking – Yellow Pages

Nick is for kids – Nickelodeon TV channel

Seeing small business differently – SBC communications

The future's bright. The future's orange – Orange

The most trusted name in news – CNN

We never stop working for you – Verizon Wireless

Your friend in the digital age – Cox Communications

You give us 22 minutes, we'll give you the world – WINS Radio, New York

Electronics

Hello Tosh, gotta Toshiba? – Toshiba

Is it live, or is it Memorex? – Memorex video cassettes

Keeps going and going and going – Energizer batteries

Neighbour's envy, owner's pride – Onida TV (India)

IT

Acquire, manage and listen – Apple Mac computers

e-business solutions – IBM

GNU is not Unix – Free Software Foundation

Intel inside – Intel

It's so easy to use, no wonder it's number one – AOL

It's the Internet that logs onto you – SBC-yahoo dsl

Rip. Mix. Burn. – Apple Mac computers

Think different – Apple Mac computers

Think outside the box – Apple Mac computers

Welcome to the world wide wow – AOL (play on world wide web)

Where do you want to go today? – Microsoft

Wikipedia, the free encyclopedia – Wikipedia

Brand origins:

Gillette, 1903 – dull shaving blades needed expert sharpening and a new, more convenient method was needed. The razor blade was perfected by William E Nickerson. (I am not sure if this is where the term 'nick yourself shaving' derives from.)

Fashion

Children's shoes have far to go – Start-rite shoes

It takes a licking and keeps on ticking – Timex

Just do it – Nike, Inc (sportswear)

Lifts and separates – Playtex cross-your-heart bra

Maybe she's born with it. Maybe it's **Maybelline** – Maybelline

Finance

Because life's complicated enough – Abbey National

Merrill-Lynch is bullish on America – Merrill-Lynch

More human interest – Washington Mutual

The bank that likes to say yes – Trustee Savings Bank

The listening bank – Midland Bank

The world's local bank – HSBC

There are some things money can't buy. For everything else, there's Mastercard – Mastercard

Visa – it's everywhere you want to be – Visa (credit card)

When E.F. Hutton talks, people listen – E.F. Hutton

Food

57 varieties – H.J. Heinz company

A Mars a day helps you work rest and play – Mars Bar

A minty bit stronger – Trebor mints

Betcha can't eat just one – Lay's potato chips

Central heating for kids – Ready Brek porridge

Do you love anyone enough to give them your last Rolo? – Rolo confectionery

Do you eat the red ones last? – Smarties

For mash get Smash – Smash instant mashed potatoes

Full of Eastern promise – Fry's Turkish Delight

Gotta have my pops! – Corn Pops breakfast cereal

Have a break, have a Kit Kat – Kit Kat

How do you eat yours? – Cadbury Cream Eggs

I'd rather have a bowl of Coco Pops – Coco Pops breakfast cereal

If it doesn't get all over the place, it doesn't belong in your face – Carl's jr

It can only be Heineken – Heineken

Kid tested. Mother approved. – Kix breakfast cereal

Gabay at a glance: When choosing a URL, act with care, and aim to be 'first to market'. www.kit-kat.co.uk and www.whitehouse.com are two classic examples of online brand confusion.

Etymology:

right-hand man – this phrase, meaning a valuable assistant, comes from the seventeenth century, when soldiers who stood at the far right of the troops were given special responsibilities or commands.

Made to make your mouth water – Opal Fruits

Makes red blood! – Grape-nuts breakfast cereal

Nobody can say no to the honey nut Os in honey nut Cheerios – Cheerios breakfast cereal

Nowt taken out – Allinsons bread

One too many and you might turn Bertie – Bassett's Liquorice Allsorts

Only Smarties have the answer – Smarties confectionary

Only the best for the captain's table – Birdseye fish fingers

Shot from guns! – Quaker puffed rice

Shouldn't your baby be a Gerber baby? – Gerber

Tell them about the honey, Mummy – Sugar Puffs Breakfast Cereal

The lighter way to enjoy chocolate – Maltesers

The sweet you can eat between meals without losing your appetite – Milky Way

They're g-r-reat! – Kelloggs Frosties breakfast cereal

Too good to hurry mints – Murray Mints

You'll never put a better bit of butter on your knife – Country Life Butter

Fast food

Have it your way – Burger King

Have you had your break to day? – McDonald's

I'm lovin' it – McDonald's

It takes a tough man to make a tender chicken – Perdue

Jack's back – Jack in the Box fast food restaurant

Put a smile on, put a smile on. Everybody come on, put a smile on – McDonald's (aimed at children)

Put a smile on – McDonald's happy meal

Smile – McDonald's

Think outside the bun – Taco Bell

We love to see you smile – McDonald's

Where's the beef? – Wendy's restaurants

Yo-quiero Taco Bell – Taco Bell

You deserve a break today – McDonald's

You've always got time for Tim Hortons – Tim Hortons

Loquacious language:

ubiquarian – someone who goes everywhere

Household

Covers the earth – Sherwin Williams paint

For hands that do dishes… – Fairy Liquid

Kills bugs dead – Raid (an insecticide)

Kills germs dead – Domestos

It beats – as it sweeps – as it cleans – the Hoover vacuum cleaner

It's a lot less bovver than a hover – Qualcast Concord lawnmowers

Put the freshness back – Shake'n'vac

Quick, Henry, the Flit! – Flit insecticide

The appliance of science – Zanussi

Personal care

A totally organic experience – Clairol Herbal Essences

Because you're worth it – L'Oreal

For those who like the trade rough – Travis aftershave

Good morning! Have you used Pear's soap? – Pear's soap

I liked it so much I bought the company – Remington shavers

I never knew you had dandruff – Head & Shoulders shampoo

It floats! – Ivory soap

It won't let you down – Sure anti-perspirant

Maybe she's born with it. Maybe it's Maybelline – Maybelline (cosmetics)

Preparing to be a beautiful lady – Pear's soap

Raise your hand if you're sure – Sure

R-O-L-A-I-D-S spells relief – Rolaids (indigestion medicine)

The Lynx effect – Lynx deodorant

Which twin has the Toni? – Toni

You'll wonder where the yellow went when you brush your teeth with Pepsodent – Pepsodent

Recreation, entertainment, and travel

Don't just book it. Thomas Cook it – Thomas Cook

Get away – Thomas Cook holidays

Get out there – Royal Caribbean cruise lines

It's so bracing – Skegness

The happiest place on earth – Disneyland

We love having you here – Hampton Inn

Where wonders never cease – Alton Towers

Chiasmus:

'People who like this sort of thing will find this the sort of thing they like.' Abraham Lincoln

Tobacco

Camels soothe your t-zone – Camel cigarettes

Doctors recommend **Phillip Morris** – Phillip Morris tobacco products

I'd walk a mile for a Camel – Camel cigarettes

Just what the doctor ordered – L&M cigarettes

More doctors smoke Camels than any other cigarette – Camel cigarettes

Not a cough in a carload – Old Gold cigarettes

Reach for a Lucky instead of a sweet –Lucky Strike cigarettes

Taste me! Taste me! Come on and taste me! – Doral cigarettes

You're never alone with a Strand – Strand cigarettes

You've come a long way, baby – Virginia Slims cigarettes

Transport

Fly the friendly skies – United Airlines

Getting there is half the fun – Cunard line

See what brown can do for you – UPS

The world's favourite airline – British Airways

We're getting there – a much ridiculed British Rail slogan

We really move our tail for you – Continental Airlines

Gabay at a glance:

For the full story of British Airways' branding campaign read my book 'Teach Yourself Marketing' published by Hodder Headline.

Cars

Ask the man who owns one – Packard

Divers wanted – Volkswagen

If only everything in life was as reliable as a Volkswagen – Volkswagen

It's a Skoda. Honest. – Skoda

Like a rock – Chevrolet

Once driven, forever smitten – Vauxhall motors

Right service. Right price. – Meineke

Sheer driving pleasure – BMW

Sooner or later, you'll own Generals – General Tires Corp

The car in front is a Toyota – Toyota

The lion leaps from strength to strength – Peugeot

The real thing – Ford (Australia)

The ultimate driving machine – BMW

Think small – Volkswagen

Time to re-tire – Fisk Tires

We are professional grade – GMC Truck

Writers' words:

'The pen is mightier than the sword.' Richelieu

Vorsprung durch technik – Audi

You can with a Nissan – Nissan

Petroleum

Put a tiger in your tank – Esso

You can be sure of shell – Shell Oil

You can trust your car to the man who wears the star – Texaco service stations

Government

An army of one – US Army, 2001

Army soldier – Be the best – British Army

Be all you can be – US Army, 1981–2001

The army national guard, you can – US Army National Guard

(All rights and trademarks acknowledged.)

Gabay's slogan checklist

1. Make them memorable.
2. Sell benefits.
3. Make them make your brand distinctive.
4. Ensure they stress the positive
5. Let them reflect your brand's personality.
6. Make sure they are enduring.
7. Keep them simple.
8. Aim for originality.
9. Keep them short.
10. Make them specific.
11. Don't be ostentatious.
12. Never highlight negatives.
13. Ask if they sound believable.
14. Check they are not awkward to read.

Loquacious language:

ugsomeness – loathing or having the quality of being horrible

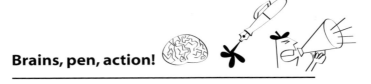

Brains, pen, action!

Write a slogan for each of the following:

- A high-security prison
- The Society of Stupid People
- The Nymphomaniacs' Club
- Your boss
- Your life
- Your partner
- Dog fleas
- Your journey to work
- Curried sweets
- Instead of Superman, 'Averageman'
- Your most hated food
- Your most loathed TV personality
- The advertising industry
- Atilah the Hun.

Answers to 'Gabay at a glance' page 582
a = 3   b = 4   c = 1   d = 2

Twisted truths:

Proofread ovary wood carefully.

20. Today's the day…

One of the most interesting and best–selling books from the end of the last century was 'A Brief History of Time' by Professor Stephen Hawking, published on 6 April 1987. The following brief section offers you a timely reminder of some historical dates. Knowing who died, what happened, and so forth on a particular date can add insight and intrigue to any presentation or piece of copy, especially when that copy relates to something like a product or service launch or an anniversary.

So here are some of the more interesting noteworthy dates, which I have managed to compile from the past couple of thousand years.

With a bit of luck, the date of your own next successful venture will be added in future editions.

Today's the day...

Knowing the significance of dates can provide vigour for press releases or presentations. Here are a selection of significant dates which you may want to refer to when next writing a speech or wanting to highlight the importance of a specific date.

January

1 1881   Postal Orders were first issued in Britain.

    1889   New York introduced the electric chair for capital punishment.

    1788   First edition of The Times, previously The Daily Universal Register, was published.

    2002   The Euro entered into circulation in the twelve participating Member States: Austria, Belgium, Finland, France, Germany, Greece, Ireland, Italy, Luxembourg, the Netherlands, Portugal and Spain.

    2005   Introduction of the English Freedom of Information Act

2 1938   Birth of David Bailey, British photographer.

    1987   Macdonald publishers surrendered to political correctness and announced that golliwogs would no longer be used in Enid Blyton's Noddy books; instead they would be replaced by gnomes.

    1968   Dr Christiaan Barnard performed the first successful heart transplant.

3 1795   Death of Josiah Wedgwood, English potter.

    1958   Sir Edmund Hillary reached the South Pole.

    1882   On arriving in New York, Oscar Wilde told customs officers, 'I have nothing to declare except my genius.'

4 1785   Birth of Jacob Grimm. He was the elder of two German brothers who became famous for fairy tales.

    1988   Karni Bheel, whose 7ft 10 in moustache was the longest in India, was found decapitated. It is believed that he was murdered by rivals for the title of the longest moustache.

    1847   Samuel Colt sells his first pistol in the United States.

5	1066	Death of Edward the Confessor.
	1855	King Camp Gillette, the razor-blade pioneer was born.
	1938	King Juan Carlos of Spain was born.
6	1759	George Washington married Martha Curtis.
	1945	George Bush (senior) married Barbara Pierce.
	1945	The 'Battle of the Bulge' ended.
7	1782	The first commercial American bank opened (Bank of North America).
	1785	The first balloon crossing of the English Channel took place by Jean-Pierre Blanchard and Jean Jefferies of Boston, Massachusetts.
	1953	President Harry Truman announced that the United States had developed a hydrogen bomb.
8	1880	Opening in London of the first soup kitchens for the poor.
	1935	Birth of Elvis Presley.
	1998	Cosmologists announced that the expansion rate of the universe is increasing.
	2004	Queen Elizabeth II names the Queen Mary II cruise liner.
9	1799	Introduction of Income Tax by William Pitt the Younger.
	1898	Birth of Gracie Fields, English singer.
	1951	United Nations headquarters officially opens in New York City.
10	1929	The first book of Tintin and his dog Snowy appeared.
	1945	Birth of Rod Steward, English singer.
	1990	Time Warner was formed from the merger of Time Inc. and Warner Communications Inc.
	1994	Lorena Bobbitt went on trial for severing the penis of her husband John (Manassas, Virginia).
	2000	America Online announced an agreement to buy Time Warner for $162 billion, the largest corporate merger in history.
11	1878	For the first time, milk was delivered in glass bottles, rather than from a churn into customers' own containers.
	1964	United States Surgeon General states that smoking may be dangerous to health. (First such statement from US government.)
	1972	East Pakistan becomes Bangladesh.

Writers' words:

'There is a Southern proverb: fine words butter no parsnips.' Sir Walter Scott

12 1893   Birth of Hermann Goering, German Nazi leader and also the founder of the Luftwaffe.

1976   Death of Agatha Christie.

1966   Batman debuted on ABC.

13 1929   Death of Wyatt Earp at the ripe old age of 80.

1969   Birth of Stephen Hendry, British snooker champion.

1957   Wham-O Company produces the first Frisbee.

14 1957   Death of Humphrey Bogart, star of such famous films as The African Queen, The Maltese Falcon and Casablanca.

1977   Death of Anthony Eden, British Prime Minister.

1690   The Clarinet was invented in Germany.

15 1558   Elizabeth I became Queen of England.

1797   Top hats first appeared in London.

1880   The first telephone directory in Britain was published with 255 names.

16 1547   Ivan the Terrible, the first Russian Tsar, was crowned.

1920   Prohibition came into force in the United States.

2002   The UN Security Council unanimously established an arms embargo and the freezing of assets of Osama bin Laden, Al-Qaida and the remaining Taliban.

17 1942   Cassius Marcellus Clay, later known as Muhammad Ali, was born

1944   Another famous boxer, Joe Frazier, shares this birthday.

1998   Paula Jones accused President Bill Clinton of sexual harassment.

2002   Eruption of Mount Nyiragongo in the Democratic Republic of the Congo, displacing approximately four hundred thousand people.

18 1882   World renowned children's author AA Milne, who wrote Winne-the-Pooh, was born.

1884   Another children's author Arthur Ransome, who wrote Swallows and Amazons, was born.

1934   And another… Raymond Briggs, who wrote Fungus the Bogeyman and The Snowman.

19 1946   Birth of Dolly Parton.

1920   The United States Senate voted against joining the League of Nations.

1935   Coopers Inc. sold the world's first men's briefs underwear.

Twisted truths:

Place pronouns as close as possible, especially in long sentences, for example of ten or more words, to their antecedents.

20 1975   England and France first abandoned the idea to go ahead with the Channel Tunnel.

     1986   England and France agree to build the Channel Tunnel.

     1999   The China News Service announces restrictions on Internet use, especially at Internet bars.

     2001   George W Bush is inaugurated as the 43rd President of the United States.

21 1924   Births of both Benny Hill and Telly Savalas.

     1950   Death of George Orwell.

     1968   Simon & Garfunkel released the original soundtrack to The Graduate.

22 1901   Death of Queen Victoria.

     1917   World War II: President Woodrow Wilson called for 'peace without victory' in Europe.

     1924   Ramsay MacDonald became the first Labour Prime Minister.

     1969   Death of Judy Garland.

23 1556   The worst ever earthquake, killing an estimated 830,000 people in Shensi province in China.

     1978   Sweden becomes the first nation to ban aerosol sprays that are thought to damage earth's protective ozone layer.

     2004   Death of Helmut Newton, photographer.

24 1899   The rubber heal was patented by Humphrey O'Sullivan.

     1924   St Petersburg, Russia is renamed Leningrad.

     1962   Brian Epstein signs to manage The Beatles.

25 1947   Death of Al Capone.

     1990   Death of Ava Gardner.

     2004   Opportunity (MER-B) landed on surface of Mars.

26 1962   Ranger 3 was launched to study the moon. The space probe missed the moon by 22,000 miles.

     1965   Hindi became the official language of India.

     1980   Israel and Egypt established diplomatic relations.

     1983   Lotus 1-2-3 was released.

27 1606   The trial of Guy Fawkes, who led the Gun Powder Plot, began. He and his conspirators were executed on 31 January.

     1880   Thomas Alva Edison filed a patent for his electric incandescent lamp.

Twisted truths:

If any word is improper at the end of a sentence, a linking verb is.

	1926	John Logie Bird gave the first public demonstration of television.
28	1807	Pall Mall in London became the first street in the world to be lit by gas lamps.
	1986	Space Shuttle Challenger exploded just after takeoff, killing the entire crew of seven astronauts.
	2004	September Dossier: Lord Hutton published his report into the death of UN weapons inspector Dr David Kelly.
29	1856	Queen Victoria institutes the Victoria Cross.
	1886	Karl Benz patented the first petrol-driven car.
	1916	Paris was bombed by German zeppellins for the first time.
30	1595	Shakespeare's Romeo and Juliet was performed in public for the first time.
	1649	Charles I was beheaded; the executioner was paid £30.
	1933	Adolf Hitler was sworn in as Chancellor of Germany.
	2005	First free elections held in Iraq following the defeat of Saddam Hussein.
31	1606	Guy Fawkes was hung, drawn and quartered.
	1945	Eddie Slovik was executed, the first American soldier since the Civil War to be executed for desertion.
	1950	President Harry S Truman announced a programme to develop the hydrogen bomb.
	1957	Liz Taylor's second divorce from Michael Wilding.

February

1	1852	Opening in London of the first men's public lavatory.
	1973	Vote in favour of allowing women on the floor of the London Stock Exchange.
	2019	Predicted date of possible collision of 2002 NT7 (a near-Earth object) with Earth.
2	1709	Alexander-Selkirk, on whom Robinson Crusoe was based, was rescued after four years and four months on Más a Tierra Island, where he had been shipwrecked.
	1940	Frank Sinatra debuted with the Tommy Dorsey orchestra.
	1943	World War II: The last Nazi forces surrendered to the Soviets following the Battle of Stalingrad.
	1962	For the first time in 400 years Neptune and Pluto align.
	1967	The American Basketball Association is formed.
3	1920	Birth of Dr Henry Heimlich, inventor of the 'Heimlich Manoeuvre' which was designed to prevent choking.

Writers' words:

'Those who write clearly have readers; those who write obscurely have commentators.' Albert Camus

	1917	World War I: The United States breaks off diplomatic relations with Germany a day after Germany announces a new policy of unrestricted submarine warfare.
	1918	The Californian Twin Peaks Tunnel begins service as the longest streetcar tunnel in the world (11,920 feet long).
	1945	World War II: Soviet Union entered the Pacific Theatre conflict against Japan.
	1959	Plane crash kills Buddy Holly, Richie Valens and The Big Bopper.
4		A bad day for earthquakes:
	1783	Estimated 50,000 dead in Calabria, Italy.
	1797	Estimated 40,000 dead in Quito, Ecuador.
	1796	Estimated 22,778 dead in Guatemala and Honduras.
5		Birth of three noteable actresses:
	1917	Zsa Zsa Gabor.
	1923	Melina Mercouri.
	1946	Charlotte Rampling.
6	1665	Birth of Queen Anne.
	1952	Death of King George VI.
	1933	The 20th Amendment to the United States Constitution goes into effect.
7	1938	Walt Disney's full-length cartoon Snow White and the Seven Dwarfs was given an 'A' certificate (children admitted only if accompanied by an adult) by the British film censors because the wicked witch was considered too frightening.
	1985	'New York, New York' became the official city anthem of New York City.
	1990	Collapse of the Soviet Union: The Central Committee of the Soviet Communist Party agrees to give up its monopoly of power.
	1992	The European Union was formed.
8	1977	Londoners felt a slight earthquake with a tremor measuring 5.0 on the Richter scale.
	1925	Birth of Jack Lemmon, actor and film director.
9	1962	I was born in Parsons Green, West London. The hospital was later demolished (any connection between my birth place and the demolition project is just hearsay).
10	1840	Queen Victoria married Prince Albert.
	1967	The 25th Amendment to the United States Constitution was ratified.

Loquacious language:

ustulat – sunburned

	1942	The first gold disc was awarded to Glenn Miller for his recording 'Chattanooga Choo Choo'.
11	1878	The British Meteorological Office started giving weekly weather forecasts.
	1978	China lifted a ban on works by Aristotle, Shakespeare and Dickens.
12	1809	Birth of Abraham Lincoln and Charles Darwin.
	1892	Former President Abraham Lincoln's birthday is declared a national holiday in the United States.
	1912	China adopted the Gregorian calendar.
	1915	In Washington DC, the first stone of the Lincoln Memorial is put into place.
	1924	Calvin Coolidge became the first President of the United States to deliver a political speech on radio.
13	1866	Jesse James robbed his first bank.
	1959	Barbie Dolls first went on sale.
	1955	Israel obtained four of the seven Dead Sea scrolls.
14	1779	Natives in Hawaii killed Captain James Cook.
15	1564	Birth of Galileo Galilei, the greatest physicist of the sixteenth century.
	1971	Britain changed to decimal currency after 1200 years of pounds, shillings and pence.
	2003	Global protests against war on Iraq in over 600 cities worldwide. Estimates of up to 15 million people make this the biggest day of protest in history.
16	1568	The Spanish Inquisition sentenced the whole of the Netherlands to death.
	1956	Britain abolished the death penalty.
	1987	The trial of John Demjanjuk, who was accused of being a Nazi guard dubbed 'Ivan the Terrible' in Treblinka extermination camp, began in Jerusalem.
17	1876	The first tin of sardines was produced in Eastport, Maine.
	1883	Mr A Ashwell of Herne Hill in London patented the Vacant/Engaged sign for lavatory doors.
	1933	The magazine Newsweek was launched.
18	1678	John Bunyan's The Pilgrim's Progress was published.
	1884	Mark Twain published The Adventures of Huckleberry Finn, 1884.
	1965	The Gambia gained independence from the United Kingdom.

Brand origins:

Gossard, 1901 – first office opened in 1921. The undergarments were originally inspired by the figure of Sarah Bernhardt, the actress.

19	1964	The Beatle look became so popular in the United States that half a ton of Beatle wigs were flown from the UK to the USA.
	1964	Paul Simon wrote 'The Sounds of Silence', the song which, in a year and a half, would catapult him and Art Garfunkel to stardom as Simon & Garfunkel.
	1986	Soviet Union launched the Mir space station.
	1986	The United States Senate approved a treaty outlawing genocide.
	2002	NASA's Mars Odyssey space probe began mapping the surface of Mars.
20	1944	First appearance of a Batman and Robin comic strip in newspapers.
	1966	Birth of Cindy Crawford, model.
	1967	Birth of Kurt Cobain, rock musician.
21	1947	The first instant camera (the Polaroid) was demonstrated by its inventor EH Land.
	1965	Malcolm X was assassinated at his mosque in New York City by black Muslims.
22	1732	Birth of George Washington.
	1988	Harvey Penson, when asked why he was celebrating his barmitzvah on the eve of his 93rd birthday, responded "Because I love all this Jewish stuff".
	1997	The adult sheep named Dolly was successfully cloned.
23	1885	John Lee survived three attempts to hang him at Exeter Prison when the trap door failed to open. Lee was released in 1917 and died in 1933.
	1917	The Russian Revolution began.
	1919	Benito Mussolini formed the Fascist Party in Italy.
	1940	The animated Disney movie Pinocchio was released.
24	1981	Prince Charles and Lady Diana Spencer announced their engagement.
	1938	The world's first tooth brush made with a nylon bristle was launched.
	1993	Death of Bobby Moore, English footballer and captain of the 1966 World Cup winning squad.
25	1570	Pope Pius V excommunicated Queen Elizabeth I of England.
	1793	George Washington held his first cabinet meeting.
	1946	The first post-war sale of bananas to the British public.

Etymology:

big wig – this word, meaning a very important person, originates from eighteenth century England. Lawyers used to wear short wigs, whereas judges wore long wigs, often down to their shoulders. So the judge was the most important person – a 'big wig'.

26 1797 The first pound note was issued by the Bank of England.

1995 United Kingdom's oldest investment banking firm Barings plc collapsed after a securities broker, Nick Leeson, gambled $1.4 billion of its money on the Singapore Monetary Exchange, Simex .

2001 The Taliban destroyed two giant buddhas in Bamiyan, Afghanistan.

27 1897 The first time a decorated wedding car was used by a wedding couple.

1932 Birth of Dame Elizabeth Taylor.

1996 Pokémon game introduced for Nintendo Game Boy.

2003 Rowan Williams was enthroned as the 104th Archbishop of Canterbury in the Anglican church.

28 1970 Cycling was first permitted across the Golden Gate Bridge in San Francisco.

1979 Death of Mr Ed, the 'talking horse' of the US TV show.

29 1784 John Wesley charters the Methodist Church.

1960 Hugh Hefner opened his first Playboy Club in Chicago.

March

1 1872 Yellowstone National Park is established as the world's first national park.

1873 E Remington and Sons in Ilion, New York, started production of the first practical typewriter.

1966 The Soviet space probe Venus III landed on Venus, the first craft to land on another planet.

2 1958 Gary Sobers scored 365 not out against Pakistan at Kingston, Jamaica, a record which lasted for over 35 years.

1995 Nick Leeson was arrested for his role in the collapse of Barings Bank.

1998 Data sent from the Galileo space probe suggested that Jupiter's moon Europa has a liquid ocean under a thick crust of ice.

2004 Al Qaeda carried out the Ashoura Massacre in Iraq, killing 170 and wounding over 500.

3 1802 Beethoven's 'Moonlight Sonata' was first performed.

1847 Birth of Alexander Graham Bell, regarded for a long time as the inventor of the telephone. In 2002 the US Congress officially recognised that the Italian inventor Antonio Meucci was the genuine inventor. (He initially called it the Teletrophone.)

Loquacious language:

scrippage – personal baggage and belongings

4 1801 Thomas Jefferson was inaugurated as the third President of the United States. States.

1825 John Quincy Adams was inaugurated as the sixth President of the United States.

1861 Abraham Lincoln was inaugurated as the sixteenth President of the United States.

1861 The 'Stars and Bars' was adopted as the flag of the Confederate States of America.

5 1953 Death of Joseph Stalin.

2004 A three-headed frog was found in Weston-super-Mare, England.

6 1899 Felix Hoffman patented Asprin.

1475 Birth of Michelangelo.

1619 Birth of Cyrano de Bergerac.

7 1933 Clarence Darrow modified the rules of a game called 'The Landlord's Game' to give us 'Monopoly'.

1996 The first democratically elected Palestinian parliament was formed.

1999 Death of Stanley Kubrick, film director.

8 1959 The Marx Brothers, Groucho, Chico and Harpo, made their last television appearance together.

1974 Charles de Gaulle Airport opened in Paris, France.

1983 President Reagan called the Soviet Union an 'evil empire'.

2004 A democratically-founded constitution was signed by Iraq's Governing Council.

9 1934 Birth of Yuri Gagarin, the first man in space.

10 1886 The first Crufts Dog Show opened in London.

1974 The last Japanese soldier of the Second World War surrendered. He was found on Luband Island in the Philippines, unaware that the war had ended.

11 1845 Henry Jones invented self-raising flour.

1985 Mikhail Gorbachev became Soviet leader.

1990 Lithuania declared itself independent from the Soviet Union.

1999 Infosys became the first Indian company to get listed on the Nasdaq stock exchange.

2003 The International Criminal Court was founded in The Hague.

2004 Terrorist bombs on rush hour trains in Madrid killed 191 people.

Writers' words:

'When the loo paper gets thicker and the writing paper thinner, it's always a bad sign at home.' Nancy Mitford

12 515BC Construction was completed on the Temple in Jerusalem.

1913 Canberra became the capital of Australia.

1918 Moscow became the capital of Russia.

1951 The Dennis the Menace comic strip appeared in newspapers across the US for the first time.

1968 Mauritius achieved independence.

1987 Les Misérables opened on Broadway.

1992 Mauritius became a republic while remaining a member of the British Commonwealth.

13 1943 German forces liquidated the Jewish ghetto in Kraków.

1996 Abelardo Cachique Rivera protested at being given a 12-year sentence for drug dealing in Peru, saying 'It's too low a sentence, given my status as a major drug trafficker.'

14 1879 Birth of Albert Einstein.

1933 Birth of Sir Michael Caine (born as Maurice Micklewhite).

1883 Death of Karl Marx.

15 44BC Julius Caesar assassinated by Brutus, Cassius and others in the Senate House in Rome.

1990 Mikhail Gorbachev was elected as the first executive president of the Soviet Union.

1991 Germany officially regained independence after the four post-World War II occupying powers (France, the United Kingdom, the United States and the Soviet Union) relinquished all remaining rights.

16 1849 Birth of the Reverend James E Smith, who went on to become a father at the age of 100 with a woman 64 years his junior.

2880 A 1/300 possibility prediction that Asteroid 1950DA will hit Earth, causing an extinction-level event.

17 1845 Stephen Perry of London patented the Rubber Band.

1931 Nevada legalised gambling.

1969 Golda Meir of Milwaukee, Wisconsin, USA, becomes Prime Minister of Israel.

18 1584 Death of Ivan the Terrible.

19 1848 Birth of Wyatt Earp.

2003 The invasion of Iraq began.

20 1917 Birth of Dame Vera Lynn.

2004 Millions worldwide protest the 2003 Iraq war.

Loquacious language:

shandygaff – the official name for shandy

21 1923 French scientists announced that smoking is good for one's health.

22 Births of two of the most well known men in stage musicals:

1930 Stephen Sondheim.

1948 Andrew Lloyd Webber.

1888 The Football League was formed.

1895 First private screening of motion pictures by Auguste and Louis Lumière.

1945 The Arab League is founded when a charter was adopted in Cairo, Egypt.

23 1923 First publication of the song 'Yes We Have No Bananas'.

1929 First telephone was installed in the White House.

24 Deaths of two Queens:

1953 Queen Mary, widow of King George V.

1603 Queen Elizabeth I.

1877 The only dead heat in the Oxford–Cambridge boat race.

25 AD31 The celebration of the first Easter, according to the six-century religious scholar and calendar-maker Dionysius Exiguus.

1969 During their honeymoon, John Lennon and Yoko Ono hold a bed-in for peace in the Amsterdam Hilton Hotel (until March 31).

1996 The EU's Veterinarian Committee bans the export of British beef and its by-products as a result of mad cow disease (BSE).

26 1845 Medicated adhesive plasters were patented.

1934 Introduction of driving tests in Britain.

1958 The first parking tickets were issued in Britain.

27 1968 Death of Yuri Gagarin, the first man in space.

1977 The world's worst air crash happened on the runway in Tenerife when two Jumbos collided, killing 574 people.

28 1947 The last episode of Buck Rogers in the 25th Century aired on radio.

1973 Marlon Brando refused to accept an Oscar for his role in the Godfather in protest against Hollywood's portrayal of Native Americans.

29 239BC Halley's comet came closest to the sun on its first recorded passage.

Twisted truths:

Writing carefully, dangling participles must be avoided.

	1827	Funeral of Beethoven at which some ten thousand people were present.
30	1842	An American surgeon Dr Crawford Long was the first surgeon to use ether as an anaesthetic when he removed a cyst from the neck of a student.
	1981	John Hinckley Jr shot and wounded President Reagan.
31	1918	Daylight Savings Time went into effect in the United States for the first time.
	1966	The Soviet Union launched Luna 10, which later becomes the first space probe to enter orbit around the Moon.
	1967	Jimi Hendrix burnt his guitar on stage for the first time.
	1991	The Warsaw Pact came to an end.
	1993	Actor Brandon Lee died during the filming of The Crow.

April

1	1998	The first red heifer calf was born after 5000 years in Dimona, a town in Southern Israel. The rare calf was first described in the Book of Numbers, Chapter 19, Verse 2 and relates to the coming of the new messianic age.
2	1805	Birth of Hans Christian Andersen.
	1962	Push-button panda crossings were introduced in London.
3	1882	Bob Ford shot Jesse James in the back of the head.
	1924	Births of Marlon Brando and Doris Day.
4	1964	The Beatles occupy all of the top five positions on the Billboard singles chart in the United States.
	1968	Assassination of Martin Luther King in Memphis.
	1969	Dr Denton Cooley implants the first temporary artificial heart.
5	1955	Winston Churchill resigned as British Prime Minister.
	1976	Harold Wilson resigned as Prime Minister.
	1982	Lord Carrington resigned as UK Foreign Secretary.
6	6BC	Biblical scholars claim that this date is the true birth day of Jesus Christ.
	610	The Koran was first revealed to Muhammad.
7	1853	Chloroform was given to Queen Victoria during the birth of her eighth child.
	1997	In Vietnam the first gay wedding took place.
8	563BC	Birth of Buddha, according to tradition.

Loquacious language:

slubberdegullion – a contemptible layabout.

	1986	Clint Eastwood was voted in as Mayor of Carmel, California.
9	1667	First public art exhibition held in Paris
	1838	Opening in London of the National Gallery.
10	1633	Bananas first went on sale in Britain.
	1849	Walter Hunt of New York patented the safety pin.
11	1855	The first pillar boxes appeared in London.
	1929	Popeye the sailor-man made his first appearance in a cartoon strip.
12	1911	Pierre Prier made the first non-stop flight from London to Paris taking just under 2 hours.
	1945	Harry S Truman was inaugurated as the thirty-third President of the United States.
	1946	Syria gained independence from France.
	1961	Yuri Gagarin became the first man to go in to space.
	1992	Euro Disney opened in Marne-la-Vallee, France
13	1963	Sidney Poitier became the first black actor to receive an Oscar.
14	1912	The Titanic struck an iceberg and sunk within a few hours.
	1983	The Cordless telephone was introduced in Britain.
15	1755	Samuel Johnson published his Dictionary of the English Language.
	1940	Birth of Jeffery Archer.

16 Births of three entertainers:

	1889	Charlie Chaplin.
	1918	Spike Milligan.
	1921	Peter Ustinov.
17	1932	Ethiopia abolished slavery.
18	1906	An earthquake in San Francisco took the lives of 450 people and destroyed about 28,000 buildings.
	1949	The Boy Scouts started their first 'bob-a-job week' when they would offer to do a job for people for a 'bob' (this was one shilling or five new pence).
19	1933	Birth of Jayne Mansfield.
	1956	The actress Grace Kelly became a princess by marrying Prince Rainier of Monaco.
20	1808	Birth of Napoleon III.
	1889	Birth of Adolf Hitler.

Brand origins:

Zippo lighters – these 'wind-proof lighters' were introduced in 1932 and named after the zipper.

21 1910 Death of Mark Twain.

22 1870 Birth of Vladimir Ilich Ulyanov, better known as Lenin.

23 1564 Birth of William Shakespeare. He died on the same day in 1616.

1850 Death of William Wordsworth.

1984 Discovery of the AIDS virus was announced.

24 1867 First report appeared of the founding of the Klu Klux Klan.

1934 Birth of Shirley Maclaine.

1942 Birth of Barbara Streisand.

25 1599 Birth of Oliver Cromwell.

1959 The first person now known to have AIDS admitted a hospital.

1961 Robert Noyce was granted the first patent for an integrated circuit.

26 1986 The world's worst nuclear disaster in peace time happened in Chernobyl in the Ukraine.

1989 Death of the comedienne Lucille Ball.

27 1959 Death of the inventor Gordon Armstrong, who invented the incubator for premature babies.

1954 White Christmas, starring Bing Crosby and Danny Kaye, premiered.

1960 Togo gained independence from French-administered UN trusteeship.

1981 Xerox PARC introduced the computer mouse.

28 1937 Birth of Saddam Hussein.

1945 Benito Mussolini, the Italian fascist leader, was captured, tried and shot then publicaly hanged, all within 24 hours.

29 Births of the following:

1769 Duke of Wellington.

1899 Duke Ellington pianist.

1901 Emperor Hirohito of Japan.

1935 Telephone link from England to Australia was established.

30 1808 First practical typewriter was made in Italy by Pelegrini Turri.

1901 New game launched called 'Ping-Pong', invented by James Gibb.

Etymology:

lady – this word, being a polite term for a woman, originated from the medieval name that was used by a woman who was proud to be a breadmaker or 'hlaefdige'. By the thirteenth century the word became 'levedi'. In the fourteenth century the word evolved into 'ladi' and finally by the sixteenth century it became 'lady'.

May

1 1751   The first cricket match was played in America.

  1927   The first cooked meals were served on a scheduled flight from London to Paris.

2 1933   The Inverness Courier reported a sighting of a 'strange spectacle on Loch Ness'.

  1997   Tony Blair became Prime Minister of the United Kingdom. At 44, he was the youngest prime minister for 185 years.

  1998   The European Central Bank was founded in Brussels in order to define and apply the EU's monetary policy.

  2000   Bill Clinton announced that GPS access equivalent to the US military would be available to the general public.

3 1494   Jamaica was sighted by Columbus. He named it 'St Iago'.

  1937   ' Gone With the Wind', by Margaret Mitchell, won the Pulitzer Prize.

4 1926   The General Strike in Britain began.

  1973   Female nudity appeared on network television in the USA for the first time.

  1979   Margaret Thatcher became Prime Minister of the United Kingdom.

5 1949   The Council of Europe was formed.

  1955   West Germany gained full sovereignty.

  1988   The Japanese transmitted the first live television pictures from the summit of Mount Everest.

6 Famous births of the following:

  1856   Sigmund Freud

  1895   Rudolph Valentino

  1915   Orson Wells

7 1824   Beethoven conducted the debut of his ninth symphony.

  1945   World War II: General Alfred Jodl signed unconditional surrender terms at Reims, France, ending Germany's participation in the war.

  1946   Tokyo Telecommunications Engineering (later renamed Sony) was founded with about 20 employees.

  1948   The Council of Europe was founded during the Hague Congress.

  1980   Paul Geidel was freed from Fishkill Correctional Facility in Beacon, New York, after serving an amazing 68 years and 8 months.

Did you know?

The only English word in which an 'f' is pronounced like a 'v' is 'of'.

8	1926	Birth of the naturalist Sir David Attenborough.
	1933	The gas chamber was first used to carry out a death sentence in the USA.
	1945	VE Day declared – the end of World War II.
9	1938	Scotland Yard announced its intention to use police dogs.
	1949	Britain's first launderette was opened.
10	1811	Paper money became legal tender in Britain.
	1907	The first Mother's Day was celebrated in Philadelphia.
	1924	J Edgar Hoover appointed head of the Federal Bureau of Investigation.
	1940	Winston Churchill appointed Prime Minister of the United Kingdom.
	1941	World War II: Rudolf Hess parachuted into Scotland claiming to be on a peace mission.
11	1812	The Waltz was introduced to Britain and immediately condemned as immoral.
	1939	Siam changed its name to Thailand.
12	1935	In Ohio William Wilson founded the famous organisation Alcoholics Anonymous.
	1960	Elvis Presley appeared on the Frank Sinatra special on television.
13	1888	Brazil abolished slavery.
	1981	Mehmet Ali Agca shot and wounded Pope John Paul II in St Peter's Square.
14	1908	First passenger flight in an aircraft took place.
	1948	Declaration of Israel as a sovereign state.
	1973	Skylab, the United States' first space station, was launched.
15	1930	Miss Ellen Church of Iowa became the very first air hostess in the world. Applicants for the position had to be aged under 25, weigh no more than 115 lb and be no taller than 5ft 4in.
	1948	Egypt, Transjordan, Lebanon, Syria, Iraq and Saudi Arabia attacked Israel.
	1957	Britain tested its first hydrogen bomb in Operation Grapple.
	1970	The Beatles' last LP, Let It Be, was released in the United States.
16	1955	Birth of Olga Korbut, Soviest gymnast.
	1970	Birth of Gabriela Sabatini, the Argentinian tennis player.

Brand origins:

Heineken beer – a Dutchman named GA Heineken wanted to start a business. Being broke, he knew the only person to finance such a venture would be his mother. She hated drunks. So he suggested that she should help him start a brewery; in this way people could drink beer all night long, rather than get drunk on spirits. Amazingly she agreed.

17 1861 First package holiday in Britain took place when Thomas Cook arranged for a party from a working men's club to go from London Bridge to Paris for six days.

1890 First weekly comic, Comic Cuts, began in London.

1900 Birth of Ayatollah Khomeini.

18 Births of famous tennis players:

1909 Birth of Fred Perry.

1960 Birth of Yannick Noah.

1996 The High Court in Rome ruled that parents must not smack their children, even for educational value.

19 1536 Anne Boleyn, Henry VIII's wife, was beheaded.

1892 Birth of Ho Chi Min.

1982 Sophia Loren, the actress, was jailed for tax evasion.

20 1917 Birth of the singer Vera Lynn.

1969 John Lennon married Yoko Ono.

21 1819 The first bicycles were seen in America, known as 'Swift Walkers' in New York City.

1979 Elton John was the first Western rock star to perform in the USSR.

22 1892 British dentist, Dr Sheffield, invented the first toothpaste tube.

1908 The Wright Brothers patent their aircraft.

1998 A federal judge ruled that United States Secret Service agents can be compelled to testify before a grand jury concerning the Lewinski and President Clinton scandal.

23 1934 Bonnie Parker and Clyde Barrow were killed in a police ambush in Louisiana.

1945 Heinrich Himmler committed suicide.

1960 Adolf Eichmann was kidnapped by Israeli agents in Argentina.

24 1956 The first ever Eurovision Song Contest which was won by Switzerland.

1991 Israel evacuated thousands of Ethiopian Jews from Ethiopia to Israel.

25 1850 Britons saw a hippopotamus for the first time on its way to the London Zoo.

1940 World War II: the Battle of Dunkirk started.

1961 Apollo program: President Kennedy announced his goal to put a 'man on the moon' before the end of the decade.

Loquacious language:

steatopygous – someone with fat buttocks

26 1868   Michael Barrett was the last person to be hanged in Britain in public.

1886   Birth of Al Jolson, American musician and singer.

1907   Birth of John Wayne (aka Marion Robet Morrison).

1887   Betting on horses at American race tracks became legal.

1988   The start of John Lennon and Yoko Ono's bed-in for world peace in room 1742 of the Queen Elizabeth Hotel in Montreal, Canada.

27 1863   In England, Broadmoor was set up (the first asylum for the criminally insane).

Births of two great horror film actors:

1911   Vincent Price.

1922   Christopher Lee.

28 1742   England's first indoor swimming pool opened in London.

1908   Birth of Ian Fleming, author and creator of the character 'James Bond'.

2003   Birth of Prometea, the world's first cloned horse.

29 1871   Britain's first official Bank Holiday commencing with Whit Monday.

1886   Chemist John Pemberton began to advertise Coca-Cola (ad in the Atlanta Journal).

1886   Putney Bridge opened in west London.

1942   Bing Crosby recorded the famous song 'White Christmas'.

30 1431   Joan of Arc was burnt at the stake.

1908   Birth of Mel Blanc, the voice of Bugs Bunny, Daffy Duck, Elmer Fudd, and many other cartoon characters.

31 1678   Lady Godiva rode naked through Coventry as a protest against taxation.

1923   Birth of Prince Rainier III of Monaco.

1930   Birth of Clint Eastwood.

June

1 1935   First ever driving tests in Britain.

1942   First television licence was introduced in Britain.

2 1953   Coronation of Queen Elizabeth II.

3 1865   Birth of King George V.

1969   The science fiction television series Star Trek broadcast its final new episode after three years of shows.

Writers' words:

'Write a wise saying and your name will live forever' Anonymous

4   1896   Henry Ford test-drove the first automobile he designed – the Quadricycle

      1937   The appearance in Oklahoma of the first supermarket trolley.

5   1973   Britain voted to enter into the Common Market.

      1977   The Apple II, the first practical personal computer, went on sale.

6   1882   Henry Seely of New York patented the first electric iron.

      1944   D-Day – Allied troops landed on the beaches of Normandy (the beginning of the end of World War II).

      2012   Transit of the planet Venus.

7   1939   George VI and HM Queen Elizabeth became the first King and Queen of Britain to visit the United States.

      1982   Priscilla Presley opened Graceland to the public.

8   1866   The Canadian Parliament met for the first time in Ottawa.

      1887   Herman Hollerith patented the punch card calculator.

      1978   Naomi James of New Zealand became the first women to sail around the world single-handed.

9   1790   The Philadelphia Spelling book became the first US copyrighted book.

      1934   Donald Duck debuted in The Wise Little Hen.

      1957   Sir Anthony Eden resigned as British Prime Minister.

10   1921   Birth of Prince Phillip, Duke of Edinburgh.

      1943   Laszlo Biro patented his ball-point pen.

11   1872   The last time the criminal stocks were used in Britain.

      2004   United States observed a National Day of Mourning for former president Ronald Reagan.

12   1964   South Africa sentenced Nelson Mandela to life in prison.

      1965   The Beatles were presented with MBEs.

13   1842   Queen Victoria was the first British Monarch to travel by train. She went from Slough to Paddington.

      2004   A 4 kg meteorite hit the house of Phil and Brenda Archer in Ellerslie, New Zealand, destroying the roof and a couch.

14   1967   The People's Republic of China tested its first hydrogen bomb.

      1982   Margaret Thatcher said 'Britain is great again' after the surrender of Argentina in the Falklands War.

Loquacious language:

stentorophonic – speaking in a very loud voice

15 1667 The first human blood transfusion was administered by Dr Jean Baptiste. He transfused 12 ounces of sheep blood to a 15-year-old boy (the boy later died and Baptiste was accused of murder).

1934 Hitler and Mussolini met for the first time.

16 1903 Pepsi-Cola trade name was registered.

1948 The first airline hijack took place. It was on a flight from Macao to Hong Kong.

1963 Valentina Tereshkova became the first woman in space.

17 1823 Charles Macintosh, a Scottish chemist, patented a method of waterproofing (the Macintosh).

1991 The South African Parliament repealed the Population Registration Act, which had required all racial classification of all South Africans at birth.

1994 OJ Simpson was arrested for the murders of his wife Nicole Brown Simpson and her friend Ronald Goldman. (He was later found 'not guilty'.)

18 1942 Birth of Sir Paul McCartney.

19 1910 In Spokane, Washington the first Father's Day was celebrated.

20 1909 Birth of the actor Errol Flynn.

1963 The Kremlin and White House agreed to set up a hotline.

21 1953 Birth of Benazir Bhutto, the first female leader of Pakistan.

1982 Birth of Prince William.

22 1951 Birth of the actress Meryl Streep.

1969 Death of Judy Garland

1987 Death of Fred Astaire.

23 1845 Adolophe Sax received a patent for the saxophone.

1989 The movie Batman was released in the United States.

1991 Sonic the Hedgehog released for the Sega Genesis in North America.

1993 Lorena Bobbitt sliced off the penis of her husband John Wayne Bobbitt.

24 1441 Founding of Eaton College by King Henry VI.

1916 Mary Pickford became the first movie star to receive a million dollar contract.

1918 The first airmail service in Canada from Montreal to Toronto.

1932 A military coup ended the unconditional power of the King of Siam (Thailand).

Writers' words:

'Nothing, not love, not greed, not passion or hatred, is stronger than a writer's need to change another writer's copy.' Arthur Evans

25 1876 Colonel George Armstrong Custer and 264 men of the 7th US Cavalry were killed by the men of Chief Crazy Horse at the Battle of the Little Bighorn.

1969 Pancho Gonzales and Charlie Pasarell played the longest continuous match in the history of Wimbledon Tennis Championships. It lasted 112 games; that's 5 hours and 12 minutes!

26 1819 The bicycle was patented.

1963 John F Kennedy made a great faux pas: he said 'Ich bin ein Berliner', which, literally translated, means 'I am a doughnut'. He was supposed to have said 'Ich bin Berliner' ('I am a Berliner').

1964 The Beatles released the album A Hard Day's Night.

1974 The first retail product (a pack of chewing gum) was sold using a barcode reader.

1977 Last concert of Elvis Presley.

1979 Muhammad Ali retired.

27 1871 The Japanese introduced the Yen.

1967 Barclays Bank in Enfield, North London, installed the first cash dispenser in Britain.

28 1682 Dom Pierre Perignon invented champagne.

2004 Full sovereign power was given to the interim government of Iraq by the Coalition Provisional Authority, ending the US-led rule of that nation.

29 1613 During a performance of Shakespeare's Henry VIII at the Globe Theatre in London, a cannon which was used to mark the king's entrance, set fire to the thatched roof.

30 1864 Abraham Lincoln granted Yosemite Valley to California for 'public use, resort and recreation'.

1966 Birth of Mike Tyson, the boxer.

1938 Superman appeared for the first time in Action Comics.

July

1 1930 Birth of Imelda Marcos' the former first lady of the Philippines.

1961 Birth of Lady Diana Spencer.

2 1938 Birth of Dr David Owen, youngest ever government minister.

Loquacious language:

susurrant – a soft whisper and rustling

3	1969	Brian Jones of the Rolling Stones drowned at the age of 27.
	1971	Jim Morrison of the band The Doors died of heart failure
	1964	President Lyndon B. Johnson signed the Civil Rights Act, which prohibited segregation in public places.
4	1826	Deaths of John Adams and Thomas Jefferson (both ex-US presidents).
	1984	In the UK all dog licences were abolished.
5	1853	Birth of Cecil Rhodes, the man who gave his name to Rhodesia (now Zimbabwe).
	1975	Arthur Ashe became the first black man to win the Wimbledon singles title.
6	1535	Sir Thomas Moore was executed for treason.
	1946	Birth of Sylvester Stallone.
7	1940	Birth of Ringo Star.
8	1918	Birth of Nelson Mandela.
	1975	Death of William Cadbury, the 'chocolate king'.
9	1947	Engagement of Princess Elizabeth and Lt Philip Mountbatten.
	1947	Birth of OJ Simpson.
10		Births of two great tennis stars:
	1932	Arthur Ashe.
	1945	Virginia Wade.
11	1533	King Henry VIII of England excommunicated.
	1740	Jews expelled from Little Russia.
	1848	The Waterloo railway station in London was opened to the public.
	1859	A Tale Of Two Cities by Charles Dickens was published.
	1962	US frogman Fred Baldasare became the first person to swim the English Channel under water.
12	1851	Death of pioneer photographer Louis Daguerre.
	1854	Birth of George Eastman, founder of Kodak.
13	1837	Queen Victoria moved into Buckingham Palace London. She was the first British monarch to live there.
	1944	Birth of Erno Rubik the inventor of the famous cube.
14	1868	AJ Fellows patented the tape measure in a circular case.
	1965	Mariner 4 flyby of Mars took the first close-up photos of another planet.

Etymology:

coat of arms – this term, meaning a design showing a family crest, originates from the Middle Ages, when knights wore special coats to protect their armour. The coat was often decorated with a family crest.

15 1606   Birth of Rembrandt.

      1922   The New York Zoo gave the American people their first look at a duck-billed platypus.

16 1661   Sweden became the first European country to issue banknotes.

      1911   Birth of Ginger Rogers the famous film star dancer.

17 1790   Thomas Saint of London patented the sewing machine.

      1955   Disneyland opens in Anaheim, California.

18 1827   Death of Jane Austen.

      1848   Birth of WG Grace (one of Britain's best ever cricketers).

19 1545   The flagship of Henry VIII, the Mary Rose, sank in the Solent.

      1814   Birth of Samuel Colt, inventor of the colt revolver.

20 1960   Two Russian dogs became the first animals to survive a trip in space.

      1969   The first men landed on the moon.

      1976   The US Viking 1 made the first unmanned landing on Mars.

21 1957   Death of Bernard Spooner the inventor of the bullet-proof jacket.

22 1894   The first motor-car race was run from Paris to Rouen.

      1983   Dick Smith completed the first solo flight around the world in a helicopter.

23 1946   Britain introduced bread rationing due to a poor harvest.

24 1701   Detroit, Michigan was founded.

      1851   The window tax (meant to be paid on a house of more than six windows) was finally abolished in Britain after being in force for over 150 years.

25 1978   Birth of first test tube baby, Louise Brown, at Oldham General Hospital.

26 1956   Unveiling of ERNIE, the electronic random number indicator equipment that was going to pick the winning numbers of Britain's premium bonds.

      1965   British post office switched to number-only phone dialling.

27 1586   Sir Walter Raleigh brought his first tobacco from Virginia to England.

      1964   Winston Churchill made his last appearance in the House of Commons.

Loquacious language:

visagiste – a make up artist

28 Deaths of two famous composers:

1741	Antonio Vivaldi.
1750	Johann Sebastian Bach.

29 1588   The Spanish Armada was defeated by the English under Sir Francis Drake.

Births of two infamous characters:

1872	Rasputin.
1883	Mussolini.

30 Births of the following:

1818	Emily Bronte.
1898	Henry Moore.
1947	Arnold Schwarzenegger.
1935	The first paperbacks were brought out by Penguin.
1938	The first ever issue of Beano, the comic.
1966	England won the World Cup.

31 1941   Holocaust: Under instructions from Adolf Hitler, Hermann Göring ordered SS general Reinhard Heydrich to 'submit to me as soon as possible a general plan of the administrative material and financial measures necessary for carrying out the desired final solution of the Jewish question'.

    1971   First lunar roving vehicle, known as the 'moon buggy', was driven on the moon by David Scott and Jim Irwin.

August

1

1774	Sir Joseph Priestly announced his discovery of oxygen.
1834	Slavery was abolished in the British Empire.
1838	Victoria crowned Queen of Britain.
1944	Anne Frank made the last entry in her diary.
1969	The British halfpenny currency ceased to be legal tender.

2

1955	Velcro was patented.
1990	Iraq invaded Kuwait.
2004	Death of Roquel Billy Davis, composer of the jingle – 'I'd like to buy the world a Coke'.

3

1492	Christopher Columbus set sail from Palos de la Frontera, a town in the Spanish province of Huelva, to discover the Americas.
1492	The Jews were expelled from Spain.
1926	The first electric traffic lights in England were set up in Piccadilly Circus.

Writers' words:

'When a thing has been said and well, have no scruple. Take it and copy it.' Anatole France

4 1900 Birth of Elizabeth Angela Marguerite Biwes-Lyon, later to become Queen Elizabeth, the Queen Mother.

  1966 John Lennon of the Beatles said that the Beatles were more popular than Christ.

5 1926 Harry Houdini stayed in a coffin under water for one and a half hours.

6 1623 Anne Hathaway, Shakespeare's wife, died.

  1991 Tim Berners-Lee released files describing his idea for the 'World Wide Web'.

7 1556 First unidentified flying object was seen over Basle in Switzerland.

  1998 Bombing of the United States embassies in Dar es Salaam, Tanzania and Nairobi, Kenya killed 224 people and injured over 4500.

8 1963 In England, a gang of 15 train robbers stole £2.6 million in bank notes.

  1974 President Nixon announced his resignation.

9 1945 The atomic bomb nicknamed 'Fat Man' was detonated over the city of Nagasaki, Japan at 11:02 am (local time) with an equivalent force of 22,000 tons of TNT. An estimated 60–80 thousand died and more then 60 thousand were injured.

  1979 Britain's first nudist beach was opened in Brighton.

10 1948 Candid Camera was first televised after being on radio as Candid Microphone.

  1981 The Richard Nixon Museum closed in San Clement.

11 1711 The first meeting of horse racing at Ascot.

  1966 John Lennon held a press conference in Chicago apologising for the 'Jesus comment'. (See 4 August.)

12 1851 Isaac Singer received a patent for his version of the sewing machine.

13 1899 Birth of Alfred Hitchcock.

  1991 Death of Jack Ryan, creator of the Barbie Doll.

14 1961 The East Germans started building the Berlin Wall.

15 1057 Death of Macbeth, King of Scotland. He was killed by Malcolm, son of King Duncan.

16 Deaths:

  1948 Babe Ruth at the age of 53.

  1977 Elvis Presley at the age of 42.

  1958 Birth of Madonna.

Loquacious language:

viscerontonic – having a sociable easy-going personality

17	1896	Miss Bridget Driscoll of Croydon in Surrey became the first pedestrian killed by a motor vehicle in Britain, despite there being a 4 mph speed limit.
18	1933	Birth of Roman Polanski, French film director.
	1960	The birth control pill was launched in America.
19	1883	Birth of Coco Channel, French fashion designer.
	1987	The Hungerford Massacre took place, when Michael Ryan shot dead 16 people in a Berkshire town in England and then shot himself.
20	1940	Winston Churchill declared 'Never in the field of human conflict was so much owed by so many to so few.'
21	1930	Birth of Princess Margaret.
22	1926	Birth of Honor Blackman, who was to become the first female lead in the television series The Avengers.
23	1754	Birth of Louis XVI of France.
	1944	Paris was liberated, having been occupied by German forces since June 1940.
24	1680	Death of Colonel Blood, who tried to steal the Crown Jewels from the Tower of London.
	1892	Goodison Park, the home of Everton Football Club, was opened.
25	1530	Birth of Ivan the Terrible.
	1930	Birth of Sean Connery, British film actor.
26	55BC	Julius Caesar's Roman forces invaded Britain.
27	1883	An eruption of Krakatoa blew up most of the island. The noise of the eruption was heard in Australia over 2000 miles away, and the resulting tidal waves killed thirty-six thousand people.
	2003	Mars made its nearest approach to Earth in 60,000 years, passing approximately 34 million miles (55 million kilometres) from Earth.
28	1933	The BBC made the first broadcast appeal on behalf of the police, for Stanley Hobaday, who was wanted for murder.
	1944	Birth of David Soul, the American actor best known for his character of Hutch in the cult programme Starsky & Hutch.
29	1915	Birth of Ingrid Bergman, film star.
	1911	Ishi, considered the last Stone Age Native American was discovered in California.
	1982	Death of Ingrid Bergman.

Writers' words:

'All of us learn to write in the second grade. Most of us go on to greater things.' Bobby Knight

30 30BC   Cleopatra VII committed suicide.

      1483   Death of Louis XI of France.

31 1900   Coca-Cola was first sold in Britain.

      1986   Death of Henry Moore, the English abstract sculptor.

      1997   Death of Diana, Princess of Wales.

September

1 1939   The BBC 'Home Service' began.

      1951   The first supermarket opened in Earl's Court in London.

2 1666   The Great Fire of London began in Pudding Lane.

      1969   The first automatic teller machine in the United States is installed in Rockville Centre, New York.

3 1189   Richard the Lion heart came to the throne.

      1658   Death of Oliver Cromwell.

      1939   Great Britain and France declared war on Germany.

      1967   Sweden switched from driving on the left to driving on the right.

      2004   Chechen separatists kept more than one thousand children and adults hostage in a school at Beslan in Russia. Over three hundred people – mostly children – eventually died.

4 1972   Mark Spitz of America became the first to win seven Olympic gold medals.

5 1885   In Indiana the first petrol pump was delivered to a garage-owner.

6 1852   Opening in Manchester of the first free lending library.

      1879   The first telephone exchange opened in London.

      1899   Carnation processed its first can of evaporated milk.

      1966   The first broadcast on television of Star Trek.

7 1921   Margaret Gorman, a 15-year-old blonde from Washington became the first Miss America.

8 1858   Abraham Lincoln quoted the following famous words in a speech 'you can fool all of the people some of the time, and some of the people all of the time, but you cannot fool all of the people all of the time'.

Births of two great British comedians (who both appeared in the Goon Show):

      1921   Sir Harry Secombe.

      1925   Peter Sellers.

Loquacious language:

volacious – suitable for flying

9	1087	Death of William the Conqueror.
	1754	Birth of William Bligh, captain of the Bounty.
10	1897	George Smith, a London taxi driver, became the first person to be convicted of drunken driving. He was fined £1.
	1977	Last ever execution took place in France.
	1990	Will Smith made his debut in the television show The Fresh Prince of Bel-Air.
	2003	Anna Lindh, the foreign minister of Sweden, was stabbed fatally.
11	1885	Birth of DH Lawrence, the writer.
	1917	Birth of Ferdinand Marcos, the Philippines dictator.
	2001	Deaths of 3021 people in terrorist attacks on the World Trade Centre in New York and the Pentagon in Washington DC caused by the world's worst ever terrorist attacks.
12	1960	The MOT test for cars was introduced in Britain.
	1910	Alice Wells of the Los Angeles Police Department became the first policewoman in America.
13	1788	New York became the federal capital of the United States.

Births of two of the children of the pop group The Beatles.

	1965	Zak Starkey, son of Ringo.
	1971	Stella McCartney, daughter of Paul.
14	1814	Lawyer, Francis Scott Key composed The Star-Spangled Banner.
	1886	Typewriter ribbon patented.
	1982	Death of Princess Grace of Monaco, killed in a car crash.
15	1620	The British pilgrim ship the Mayflower departed from Plymouth.
	1965	British Prime Minster Harold Wilson admitted that he enjoyed watching the TV soap Coronation Street.
16	1857	'Jingle Bells' was registered by Jane Pierpoint under the name 'One Horse Open Sleigh'.
	1955	Play-Doh™ was launched.
17	1394	Expulsion of Jews from France.
	1859	Joshua A Norton declared himself Emperor Norton I of the United States.
18	1949	Birth of Peter Shilton, former England goalkeeper.
	1970	Death of Jimi Hendrix, American singer and guitarist, due to a drug overdose.

Writers' words:

'Papa, potatoes, poultry, prunes and prism, are all very good words for the lips; especially prunes and prism.'
Charles Dickens

19 1893   New Zealand became the first country to give women the vote.

      1952   The US barred Charlie Chaplin from entering the country after a trip to England.

20 1934   Birth of Sophia Loren, the famous Italian actress.

      1946   The first Cannes Film Festival was opened.

21 1832   Death of Sir Walter Scott.

      1937   JRR Tolkien published The Hobbit.

Births of two famous authors:

      1866   HG Wells.

      1947   Stephen King.

      1986   Prince Charles admitted on television that he talks to plants.

22 1920   The Metropolitan Police 'Flying Squad' was formed.

      1955   The first television advertisement was shown in Britain. It advised viewers to brush their teeth with Gibbs SR toothpaste.

      1997   Death of Huan Huan, the giant panda. He was aged 25 and he was the only giant panda to father another panda in Japan.

23 1846   Johann Galle discovered Neptune.

      1939   Death of Sigmund Freud.

24 622   Muhammad completed his migration (or hegira) from Mecca to Medina.

      1975   Dougal Haston and Doug Scott became the first people to climb Everest by the South-West face.

25 1769   Honoretta Pratt was cremated; the first cremation in Britain.

      1818   Guy's Hospital in London was the first to use human blood for a transfusion.

26 1580   Sir Francis Drake circumnavigated the world.

      1955   Birds Eye Fish Fingers first went on sale.

27 1888   The nickname 'Jack the Ripper' was first used.

      1928   The Republic of China was recognised by the United States.

      1938   The ocean liner Queen Elizabeth was launched in Glasgow.

Loquacious language:

xanthippe – a bad-tempered wife

28 1745 At the Dury Lane Theatre in London the British national anthem 'God Save the King' was first sung in public.

1894 Michael Marks and Thomas Spencer opened their first Penny Bazaar in Manchester, later to establishing Marks & Spencer.

29 1758 Birth of Horatio Nelson, the English navel admiral.

30 1906 The first hot air balloon race took place in Paris.

1935 The Adventures of Dick Tracy was first aired on radio.

October

1 1928 Elastoplast dressings were first sold.

1971 Opening of Disneyworld in Florida.

1974 Opening of the first McDonalds in London.

2 1869 Birth of Mohandas K Gandhi, the founder of independent India.

1904 Birth of Shi Lal Bahadur Shastri, who became India's prime minister in 1964.

3 1906 The SOS signal replaced QDC as the international distress signal.

1952 The United Kingdom successfully tested a nuclear weapon.

4 1911 The first escalator in Britain was turned on at Earl's Court Underground station.

1957 Sputnik I, the first satellite to orbit Earth, was launched.

5 1974 The Guildford bombings occur in the UK.

6 1946 Birth of Tony Greig, English cricketer.

1973 The Yom Kippur War began.

7 1885 Birth of Desmond Tutu.

1922 The Prince of Wales made the first royal broadcast on the BBC.

1950 The first Frank Sinatra Show was broadcast on American television.

8 1967 The first breathalyser was used in Britain.

1991 The Croatian Parliament severed ties with Yugoslavia.

9 1963 Uganda became a republic.

1989 An official news agency in the Soviet Union reported the landing of a UFO in Voronezh.

Loquacious language:

xanthodontous – to have yellow teeth

	1996	The waterway code in Venice was changed to allow gondoliers to serenade their customers during the day as well as during the night.
10	1886	The first appearance of the dinner jacket at a place called Tuxedo Park Country Club in New York, hence the name.
	1985	Deaths of two famous actors: Orson Welles and Yul Brynner.
11	1899	The Boer war began in South Africa.
	1919	The first airline meal was served on a flight from London to Paris. This consisted of packed lunches costing three shillings each.
12	1822	Brazil became independent of Portugal.
	1859	Self-appointed 'Emperor of the United States' Joshua A. Norton ordered the United States Congress to dissolve.
	1986	Queen Elizabeth II became the first British monarch to visit China.
13	54	Emperor Claudius I died after being poisoned by his wife Agrippina.
	1792	The cornerstone of the White House was laid.
14	1066	Battle of Hastings.
	1922	Final turf was laid at the original Wembley Stadium.
15	1878	The Edison Electric Company opened.
	1839	Queen Victoria proposed to Prince Albert.
16	1793	Death of Marie Antoinette by guillotine.
	1854	Birth of Oscar Wilde.
	1922	Birth of Max Bygraves.
17	1849	Death of Frederic Chopin.
	1860	First professional golf championship was held at Prestwick in Scotland.
	1918	Birth of Rita Hayworth, American film star.
18	1826	Last state lottery in Britain until 1994.
19	1970	BP announced they had struck oil in the North Sea.
20	1822	The British newspaper the Sunday Times began publication.
	1973	The Sydney Opera House opened.
21	1824	Joseph Aspdin patented cement.
	1915	Women were allowed to become bus and tram conductors in London.

Etymology:

jeopardy – this word, meaning danger, can be traced back to ancient Rome, when the expression 'jocus paritus', meaning 'divided game', was given to a game that was tied. Later, the French changed it to 'jeu parti', which was applied to any game between evenly matched teams. To bet on such a game would be dangerous – hence 'jeopardy'.

22 1964 Jean-Paul Sartre was nominally awarded the Nobel Prize for Literature. (He turned it down.)

1997 The 2750 ton Gem Theatre in Chicago became the largest ever building to be moved on wheels to a new site.

23 1915 Death of WE Grace, famous English cricketer.

1950 Death of Al Jolson, American singer and entertainer.

24 1936 Birth of Bill Wyman of the Rolling Stones.

1957 Death of Christian Dior, French fashion designer.

25 1839 The first train timetable was published called 'Bradshaw's Railway Guide'.

1957 Britain's first nuclear attack defence manual was published. It recommended in the event of an attack to wear hats and gloves and to use lots of soapy water.

26 1881 Wyatt Earp defeated the Clanton gang at the gunfight at the OK Corral.

1929 It was announced that all London buses would be red.

27 1728 Birth of Captain James Cook, English explorer.

1939 Birth of John Cleese, English comedian.

28 1886 Unveiling of the Statue of Liberty by President Grovenor Cleveland.

1943 The Court of Appeal in London ruled that any money a housewife saves from her housekeeping belongs to her husband.

29 1618 Sir Walter Raleigh, English navigator and a favourite of Elizabeth I, was executed at Whitehall for treason.

1897 Birth of Nazi chief Paul Joseph Goebbels.

30 1905 Aspirin went on sale in Britain for the first time.

1974 Muhammad Ali knocked out George Foreman in round eight to regain the world heavyweight title.

31 1795 Birth of John Keats.

1926 Death of Harry Houdini, famous American escape artist. His real name was Erich Weiss.

November

1 1848 WH Smith opened their first railway station bookstall.

1959 The first stretch of the M1 motorway opened.

1982 Britain's fourth television station, Channel 4, transmitted for the first time.

Brand origins:

Fanta, World War II – the name comes for from the French 'fantasie'.

2	1896	The first motor insurance policies were issued.
	1913	Birth of Burt Lancaster, American film star.
	1924	The Sunday Express newspaper published the first crossword in a British newspaper.
	1950	Death of George Bernard Shaw.
3	1843	The 17 ft, 16 ton statute of Nelson was put on the top of a column in Trafalgar Square, London.
	1957	Laika, a stray dog from Moscow, became the first dog in space. It did not survive its trip.
4	1852	Completion of the House of Commons.
	1914	The first fashion show was held at the Ritz Carlton Hotel in New York.
5	1927	Britain's first automatic traffic lights came into operation in Wolverhampton.

Births of two famous singers:

	1931	Ike Turner of Ike and Tina.
	1942	Art Garfunkel of Simon and Garfunkel.
	1932	Gillespie Road Underground station changed its name to Arsenal in deference to the nearby football team.
6	1893	Death of Dracula in Bram Stoker's novel.
	1869	Opening of Blackfriars Bridge over the Thames in London.
7	1910	Death of Leo Tolstoy, the Russian novelist who wrote War and Peace and Anna Karenina.
	1974	Lord Lucan disappeared.
8	1927	Birth of Ken Dodd, English comedian.
	1974	After 300 years in Central London, Covent Garden market moved to a new site at Nine Elms.
9	1960	John F Kennedy was elected President of the USA.
	1989	The Berlin wall came down.
10	1925	Birth of Richard Burton, the British actor.
	1944	Birth of Tim Rice, the English song writer for musicals.
11	1830	Mail was first carried by railway on the newly opened Liverpool to Manchester line.
	1880	Ned Kelly, the notorious Australian bank robber, was hanged in Old Melbourne Gaol.
	1953	The BBC television programme Panorama was first shown.
	2004	Death of Palestinian Authority President Yasser Arafat.
12	1866	Birth of Sun Yat-Sen, Chinese nationalist and revolutionary leader.

Loquacious language:

sabaism – the worship of the stars

	1929	Birth of Grace Kelly, later to become Princess Grace of Monaco.
	1927	The first veteran car rally from London to Brighton sponsored by the Daily Sketch.
	1951	The first showing of the BBC television programme Come Dancing.
13	1850	Birth of Robert Louis Stevenson, author of Doctor Jekyll and Mr Hyde, Kidnapped and Treasure Island.
	1922	Birth of Charles Buchinsky, American actor later known as Charles Bronson.
	1851	The telegraph service between London and Paris was opened.
	1868	Death of Gioacchino Rossini, Italian composer of operas, he composed such operas such as The Barber of Seville and William Tell.
14	1840	Birth of Claude Monet, French impressionist painter.
	1935	Birth of King Hussein of Jordan.
	1948	Birth of Prince Charles, heir to the British throne.
	1952	Charts for single records were first published in Britain by New Musical Express.
	1969	The first colour programmes began on British TV.
	1973	Princess Anne married Captain Mark Phillips at Westminster Abbey.
	1983	The first cruise missiles arrived at the Greenham Common Base in Berkshire, England.
15	1837	Pitman's system of shorthand was published under the name of 'Stenographic Short-Hand'.
	1905	Birth of Mantovani, Italian conductor, in Venice.
	1934	Birth of Petula Clark, British singer.
16	1960	Death of Clarke Gable, American actor.
	1982	Death of Arthur Askey, British comedian.
	1961	Birth of Frank Bruno, British boxer.
17	1558	Death of Queen Mary I (aka Mary Tudor and Bloody Mary).
	1970	Russia's Luna 17 landed on the Sea of Rains on the moon and released the first moon-walker vehicle.
18	1626	St Peter's Church in Rome was consecrated.
	1852	Funeral of the Duke of Wellington in St Paul's Cathedral.
	1836	Birth of WS Gilbert (of Gilbert & Sullivan), English writer of comic operas.

Writers' words:

'All of the books in the world contain no more information than is broadcast as video in a single large American city in a single year. Not all bits have equal value.' Carl Sagan

	1983	In Liverpool Maternity Hospital Janet Walton gave birth to six girls named Hannah, Ruth, Sarah, Lucy, Kate and Jenny.
19	1943	Christopher Columbus discovered Puerto Rico.
	1917	Birth of Indira Gandhi, first woman Prime Minister of India.
20	1908	Birth of Alistair Cooke, the late English-American Journalist and Broadcaster.
	1945	Opening of the trials of 24 Nazi leaders at Nuremberg.
	1947	Queen Elizabeth II, as Princess Elizabeth, married Prince Philip in Westminster Abbey.
21	1936	Broadcast of the first gardening programme on the BBC, called 'In Your Garden' with Mr Middleton.
	1945	Birth of Goldie Hawn, American actress.
22	Births of the following:	
	1808	Thomas Cook, English travel agent pioneer.
	1890	Charles de Gaulle, who became French President.
	1943	Billie-Jean King, American tennis champion.
	1967	Boris Becker, German tennis champion.
	1963	Death of John F Kennedy, thirty-fifth President of the United States. He was assassinated in Dallas by Lee Harvey Oswald.
	1947	Vasco da Gama became the first person to round the Cape of Good Hope.
	1980	Death of Mae West, American actress.
	1986	Mike Tyson at 20 years old became the youngest ever heavyweight boxing champion when he defeated Trevor Berbick in Las Vegas.
23	1859	Birth of Billy the Kid, American outlaw and gunman.
	1887	Birth of Boris Karloff, American horror actor.
	1963	First broadcast of BBC television programme Dr Who, with William Hartnell playing 'the Doctor'.
24	1955	Birth of Ian Botham, English cricketer.
	1963	Lee Harvey Oswald, assassin of President Kennedy, was himself shot dead by nightclub owner Jack Ruby.
	1991	Death of Freddie Mercury, lead singer of the pop group Queen.
25	1941	Birth of Tina Turner, American rock singer.
	1952	Birth of Imran Khan, Pakistani test cricketer.
	1952	Opening of the longest running theatre play The Mousetrap by Agatha Christie at the Ambassador's Theatre. (It's still going!)

Loquacious language:

swasivious – agreeably persuasive

26 1922   Discovery of the tomb of king Tutankhamun by Howard Carter.

      1922   Birth of Charles Schulz, creator of the cartoon strip 'Peanuts'.

27 1852   William Shakespeare married Anne Hathaway at the age of 18.

      1941   Britain's first policewomen went on duty in Lincolnshire.

28 1905   Sinn Fein, the Irish political party, was founded in Dublin by Arthur Griffith.

      1934   'Baby Face' Nelson, American bank robber and a member of the John Dillinger gang, was gunned down.

      1968   Death of Enid Blyton, English writer of children's books.

29 1895   Birth of Busby Berkeley, US actor and choreographer

      1924   Death of Giacomo Puccini, Italian composer of such operas as La Boheme and Madame Butterfly.

      1975   Grahame Hill, British racing driver and father of Damon Hill, was killed in a plane crash.

30 Births of three great thinkers:

      1835   Mark Twain, American author.

      1874   Winston Churchill, British Prime Minister.

      1900   Birth of Oscar Wilde, Irish poet and dramatist.

      1944   Britain's largest ever and last battleship, HMS Vanguard, was launched in Clydebank, Scotland.

Also see Words from the wise chapter 17 for some famous quotations

December

1 1935   Birth of Allen Stewart Konigsberg, later known as Woody Allen, American comedian, writer and film director.

      1966   Britain's post officers issued the first special Christmas stamps.

      1973   Death of David Ben-Gurion, Israel's first Prime Minister.

2 1697   Opening of the rebuilt St Paul's Cathedral.

      1916   Lights of the Statue of Liberty were turned on by President Wilson.

      1966   British Prime Minister Harold Wilson met Ian Smith on HMS Tiger off Gibraltar for talks on the independence of Rhodesia (now called Zimbabwe).

3 1930   Birth of Andy Williams, American singer and entertainer.

      1980   Death of Sir Oswald Mosley, English politician and leader of the British Union of Fascists, who died in exile in Paris.

Writers' words:

  'Once a word has been allowed to escape, it cannot be recalled.' Horace

4 1791 First publication of The Observer the oldest Sunday news-paper in the United Kingdom.

1930 Birth of Ronnie Corbett, British comedian and actor.

5 1766 First sale held at Christie's, the famous auctioneers of London.

1901 Birth of Walt Disney, American cartoon film producer.

Deaths of the following:

1791 Wolfgang Amadeus Mozart, Austrian composer who died of Typhus.

1899 Sir Henry Tate, founder of the Tate Gallery in London.

1926 Claude Monet, French painter who was a recluse in Giverny.

1958 STD telephone service in Britain began in Bristol, by the Queen calling up Lord Provost of Edinburgh.

1958 Opening of the first motorway in Britain, the eight–mile Preston by-pass section of the M6.

6 1921 The Irish Free State was established after independence from the United Kingdom.

7 1732 Opening of the original Covent Garden Opera House in London.

1783 William Pitt the Younger became the youngest British Prime Minister, at the age of 24.

1817 Death of Captain Bligh, captain of the Bounty.

1941 Three hundred and sixty Japanese planes attacked the US Pacific Fleet anchored at Pearl Harbour in Hawaii.

8 1542 Birth of Mary Queen of Scots.

1925 Birth of Sammy Davis Jr, American singer and entertainer.

1934 The London to Australia airmail service began.

1978 Death of Golda Meir, Israeli Prime Minister from 1969 to 1974.

1981 Arthur Scargill was elected leader of the National Union of Mineworkers in Britain.

9 1918 Birth of Kirk Douglas, American actor.

1957 Birth of Donny Osmond, American singer and entertainer.

1960 First broadcast of the British soap Coronation Street.

1980 John Lennon, member of the pop group The Beatles, was murdered outside his Manhattan home by Mark David Chapman.

Loquacious language:

testudineous – to be as slow as a tortoise

10	1768	The Royal Academy of Arts was founded.
	1868	Publication of the first edition of Whitaker's Almanack.
	1898	Cuba became an independent state, Spain giving up all claims.
	1902	Opening of the Aswan Dam, a reservoir of over 1 billion cubic meters, which was built to control the Nile flood.
11	1894	Opening of the first Motor Show in the Champs-Elysees, Paris, with nine exhibitors.
12	1915	Birth of Frank Sinatra, American entertainer.
	1925	Opening of the first motel in California.
13	1577	Francis Drake began his voyage from Plymouth in the Golden Hind that was to take him around the world.
	1973	Three-day (working) week was ordered by the British Government due to the Arab oil embargo and the coalminers' slowdown.
14	1799	Death of George Washington, first President of the United States of America.
	1925	Iraq gained independence from the United Kingdom.
	2003	The news of the former Iraqi dictator Saddam Hussein's capture is announced. He was found at the bottom of a deep well.
15	1832	Birth of Gustave Eiffel, best known for his design of the Eiffel Tower.
	1890	Death of Sitting Bull, the Red Indian Chief of the Sioux, who was killed by police whilst resisting arrest.
	1966	Death of Walt Disney.
	1906	Opening of Piccadilly branch of the London Underground Railway system.
	1961	Adolph Eichmann, the Nazi official responsible for the execution of millions of Jews, was sentenced to death after a four month trial in Jerusalem.
	1982	Opening of Gibraltar's frontier with Spain after 13 years.
16	1653	Oliver Cromwell became Lord Protector of England. He ruled for over four years.
	1773	The 'Boston Tea Party' took place as a protest against British taxation.
	1775	Birth of Jane Austen, English novelist.
	1809	Marriage between Josephine and Napoleon Bonaparte came to an end after 13 years.
	1944	Death of Glenn Miller, American dance band leader, tragically killed in an aircraft crash.

Brand origins:

Heinz, 1876 – from HJ Heinz Company (established in 1888). The slogan '57 varieties' was inspired by an advert on New York railway which read '21 Styles of Shoes'. Heinz had over 60 products but liked the number 57.

17	1903	Orville Wright made the first successful controlled flight in a powered aircraft from Kill Devil Hill, North Carolina.
	1973	Birth of Paula Radcliffe, British athlete.
	1989	First half-hour length episode of The Simpsons was broadcast.
18	1865	Slavery was abolished in the United States of America.
	1916	Birth of Betty Grable, American film actress.
	1947	Birth of Steven Spielberg, American film maker.
	1980	Birth of Christina Aguilera, American singer.
	1969	Death penalty for murder was abolished in Britain.
	1970	Divorce became legal in Italy.
19	1848	Death of Emily Bronte, English novelist.
	1851	Death of Joseph Turner, English painter of landscapes.
20	1946	Birth of Uri Geller, Israeli psychic.
	1973	Death of Bobby Darin, American rock-and-roll singer.
	1999	Portugal returns Macau to China.
21	1620	The Pilgrim Fathers landed in Plymouth, Massachusetts aboard the Mayflower.
	1804	Birth of Benjamin Disraeli, British Tory Prime Minister.
	1879	Birth of Joseph Stalin, Soviet political leader.
	1937	Walt Disney's Snow White and the Seven Dwarfs was shown in Los Angeles and it was to become the first full length cartoon talking picture.
	1968	Launching of Apollo 8.
22	1880	Death of George Eliot, English novelist.
	1943	Death of Beatrix Potter, English writer of children's books such as Peter Rabbit.
	1965	Introduction of 70 mph speed limit in Britain.
	2001	Birth of CC the cat, the world's first cloned pet.
23	1888	Birth of J Arthur Rank, British film magnate.
	1913	Establishment of the central banking system of the United States, called 'The Federal Reserve'.
	1922	The BBC began daily news broadcasts.
	2012	According to one of the world's most accurate and ancient calendars – the Mayan Calendar – time runs out.
24	1906	The world's first radio programme is broadcast. It featured poetry and a violin solo.
	1914	First German bomb fell on Britain.
	1922	Birth of Ava Gardner, American film actress.

Loquacious language:

uxorilocal – to live with your wife's family

25	1066	Coronation of William the Conqueror at Westminster Abbey.
	1642	Birth of Sir Isaac Newton, English mathematician and scientist.
	1887	Birth of Conrad Hilton, hotel owner.
	1957	Queen Elizabeth II made her first Christmas broadcast on television, to the people of the Commonwealth.
	1977	Death of Charlie Chaplin, American film actor and director.
26	1893	Birth of Mao Tse-Tung, one of the founders of the Chinese Communist Party.
	1983	Death of Violet Carsen, English actress who played the part of Ena Sharples on British television's Coronation Street.
	2004	Over 250,000 people died and millions were left homeless across south and east Asia, as the direct result of a tsunami generated by a nine magnitude earthquake beneath the sea in Northern Indonesia.
27	1901	Birth of Louis Pasteur, French chemist and bacteriologist.
	1927	Leon Trotsky was expelled from the Communist Party.
	1975	The Sex Discrimination and Equal Pay Acts came into force in Britain.
28	1879	The Tay Railway Bridge collapsed carrying the Edinburgh to Dundee train. It fell into the water below, killing about ninety people.
	1950	The Peak District was designated as the first National Park in Britain.
29	1800	Birth of Charles Goodyear, inventor of vulcanising rubber.
	1809	Birth of William Ewart Gladstone, four times Prime Minister of Britain.
	1986	Death of Harold MacMillan, British Prime Minister.
30	1851	Birth of Asa Griggs Candler, the man who developed the formula for Coca-Cola.
	1961	Birth of Ben Johnson, Canadian athlete.
31	1923	First broadcast of the chimes of Big Ben.
	1935	'Monopoly' the most successful game ever was patented by Charles Darrow.
	1985	Death of Rick Nelson, American singer and songwriter, who died in a plane crash, aged 45.

This is by no means an exhaustive list. A quick search on the Internet may reveal other useful date facts.

Did you know?

The longest word in the English language (to date) allegedly has 1185 letters. It is the word meaning tobacco, mosaic virus of the dahlemense strain. However, *The Oxford English Dictionary*, which does not usually list technical words, suggests the 45-letter word 'pneumonoultramicroscopicsilicovolcanokoniosis'. This refers to a supposed lung-disease.

Brains, pen; action!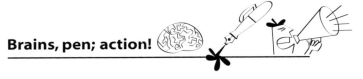

Something to ponder...

Interesting facts about the calendar

1 January 45 BC	Caesar changed date from the Roman to the Julian calendar
80 days	Time the old Roman calendar was misaligned with the solar year as designated by Caesar
AD 359	Date the Sanhedrin president Hillel II codified the Jewish calendar
1582	Date Pope Gregory XIII reformed the calendar to the one we use today
365 days, 5 hours, 49 minutes, 12 seconds	The length of a year according to Pope Gregory XIII (Gregorian calendar year)
10 minutes 48 seconds	Length of time the Julian calendar overestimates our calendar year per year
October 5–14 1582	Pope Gregory removed ten days to correct the calendar's drift.
1582–1584	Period during which most Catholic countries accepted the Gregorian calendar
1752	Date Great Britain (and the American colonies) accepted the Gregorian calendar
1784	Date Benjamin Franklin first proposed Daylight Saving Time

Loquacious language:

yerd-hunger – an uncontrollable desire for food

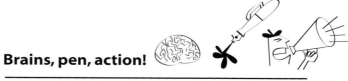

Brains, pen, action!

1873	Date Japan accepted the Gregorian calendar
1917 (and again in 1940)	Date Russia accepted the Gregorian calendar
1925	Date Daylight Saving Time was officially introduced into Britain
1949	Date China accepted the Gregorian calendar
1971	Date the Eastern Orthodox Church last voted to reject the Gregorian calendar and retain the Julian calendar
12	seconds per year (approx.) Length of time the Gregorian calendar is off from the average vernal equinox year
1972	Date Atomic Time replaced Earth Time as the world's official scientific time standard
86,400	seconds in a day

Writers' words:

'His words were smoother than butter.' Psalms 55:21

21. A world of facts

It's a fact: without the right information to hand, a copywriter is as useful as a pencil without a lead. The most important facts are covered in a brief. However, a close second place comes odds and ends of information that add substance to a creative proposition, such as when writing a report.

Over the years I have discovered that some facts are always needed. I used to keep scraps of paper with these miscellaneous tidbits scrawled all over them. Yet now I feel that for the sake of an orderly office and your sense of purpose it's time to note down the most commonly used ones.

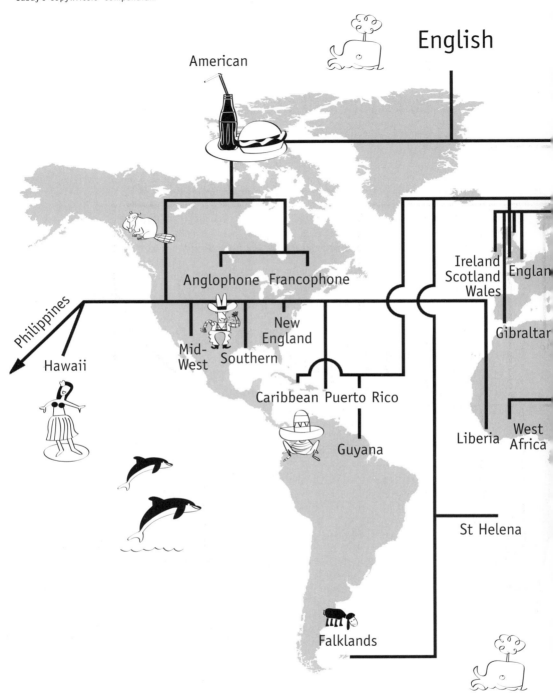

English

American

Anglophone   Francophone

Philippines

Hawaii

Mid-West   Southern

New England

Caribbean   Puerto Rico

Guyana

Ireland Scotland Wales   Englan

Gibraltar

Liberia   West Africa

St Helena

Falklands

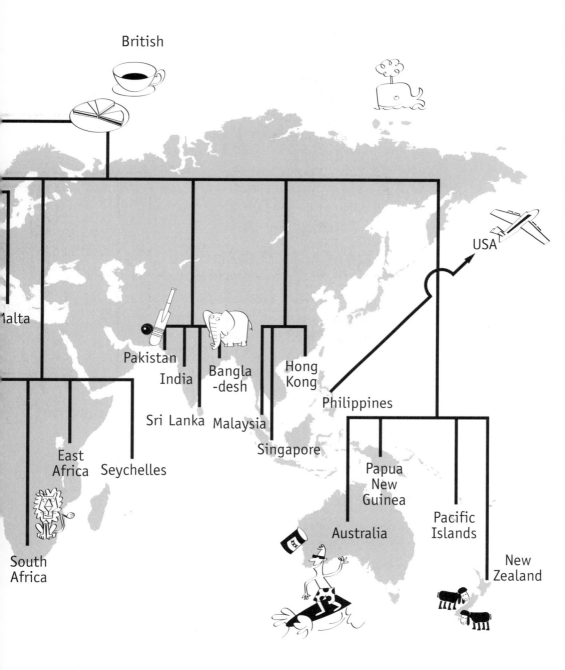

British

Malta

Pakistan

India

Bangla
-desh

Hong
Kong

Philippines

USA

Sri Lanka

Malaysia

Singapore

East
Africa

Seychelles

Papua
New
Guinea

Australia

Pacific
Islands

New
Zealand

South
Africa

A world of facts

As a copywriter, you often need quick access to useful data such as common measurements, notable religious dates and other general information about our planet and its make-up. The problem is having such information close to hand. Fret not: here are answers to some of the most commonly asked questions relating to your world in terms of geography, culture, history, weather and geology.

The Earth

Dimensions

Surface area = 510,069,120 km (196,938,800 miles), of which water makes up 70.92 per cent and land 29.08 per cent

Equatorial diameter = 12,756.27 km (7,926.38 miles)

Polar diameter = 12,713.50 km (7,899.80 miles)

Equatorial circumference = 40,075.01 km (24,901.46 miles)

Polar circumference = 40,007.86 km (24,859.73 miles)

Equator = 0-

North Pole = 90° N

South Pole = 90° S

Tropic of Cancer = 23° 26′ N

Tropic of Capricorn = 23° 26′ S

Arctic Circle = 66° 34′ N

Antarctic Circle = 66° 34′ S

The Tropics and the Arctic and Antarctic circles are affected by the slow decrease in obliquity of the ecliptic of about 0.5 arcseconds per year. The result is that the Arctic and Antarctic circles are presently moving towards their respective poles by about fourteen metres per year, while the Tropics move towards the Equator by the same amount.

Writers' words:

'It is of interest to note that while some dolphins are reported to have learned English – up to fifty words used in correct context – no human being has been reported to have learned dolphinese.' Carl Sagan

The Earth is divided by geologists into three layers:

- **Crust**: thin outer layer, with an average depth of 24 km (15 miles), although the depth varies widely depending on whether it is under land or sea
- **Mantle**: lies between the crust and the core and is about 2,865 km (1,780 miles) thick
- **Core**: extends from the mantle to the Earth's centre and is about 6,964 km (4,327) miles in diameter.

The atmosphere

The atmosphere is the air (a mixture of gases) enveloping the Earth. Various layers are identified by scientists, based on rate of temperature change, composition, etc. These are:

- **Ionosphere** (includes the thermosphere)
- **Mesopause**
- **Mesosphere**
- **Stratopause**
- **Stratosphere** (the upper atmosphere)
- **Tropopause**
- **Toposphere** (the lower atmosphere)
- (**Boundary layer** – up to 2 km)
- **Earth's surface**

Most weather conditions form in the troposphere, where most pollutants released into the atmosphere by human activity accumulate. The stratosphere is the layer in which most atmospheric ozone is found.

Loquacious language:

yirn – to whine

The component gases of the atmosphere are:

Gas % by volume

Nitrogen	78.10
Oxygen	20.95
Argon	0.934
Carbon dioxide	0.031
Neon	0.00182
Helium	0.00052
Methane	0.00020
Krypton	0.00011
Hydrogen	0.00005
Nitrous oxide	0.00005
Ozone	0.00004
Xenon	0.000009

Atmospheric pollution

The six main 'greenhouse' gases identified are:

- Carbon dioxide
- Methane
- Nitrous oxide
- hydrofluorocarbons (HFCs)
- perfluorocarbons (PFCs)
- Sulphur hexafluoride (SF6)

Brand origins:

654

Frisbee, 1957 – this name derives from baking tins thrown as a game at the Frisbie Bakery, Connecticut.

Earthquakes

The starting point of an earthquake is known as the hypocentre (often given in terms of latitude, longitude, and depth below the surface). The epicentre is the surface projection of the hypocentre.

Movements on or in the Earth generate seismic waves. There are a number of scales for comparing the relative size of earthquakes based on seismic waves, usually called seismic magnitudes. One earthquake can have many different seismic magnitudes. The Richter scale is one of the main magnitude scales for measuring earthquakes. It is named after Charles Richter, who invented seismic magnitude scales in the 1930s.

Richter scale magnitude intensity

1	Detectable only by instruments
2	Barely detectable, even near epicentre
3	Similar to vibrations from a heavy goods vehicle
4-5	Detectable within 32 km/20 miles of the epicentre; possible slight damage within a small area
6	Moderately destructive
7	Major earthquake
8	Great earthquake – total destruction

The highest magnitude that has ever been reached is 8.6. This was in Gansu, China, in 1920.

Each year the United Kingdom is struck by thousands of earthquakes. Most measure less than 2 on the Richter scale. However on 7th June 1931 the Dogger Bank (North Sea) earthquake measured 6.1 on the Richter scale.

Weather

World records

Air temperature

Maximum	57.8 °C/136 °F	
	San Louis, Mexico, 11/09/1933	
Minimum	–89.2 °C/–128.56 °F	
	Vostok, Antartica, 21/07/1983	

Etymology:

to get cold feet – this expression, meaning 'to back away from a commitment', originates from the early seventeenth century, when a person who had no money couldn't afford shoes (they had cold feet). By the eighteenth century the meaning referred to soldiers with frozen feet who were therefore likely to retreat from battle.

Rainfall

Greatest in a day

	1,870 mm/73.62 in	Cilaos, Isle de Reunion, 16/03/1952

Greatest in a calendar month

	9,300 mm/366.14 in	Cherrapunji, Assam, 06/1861

Wind speed

Fastest gust

	201 knots/231 mph	Mt Washington Observatory, USA, 12/04/1934

Cloud types

Clouds comprise suspended particles of water or ice, or both. The water is condensed from air, which rises into levels of lower atmospheric pressure. It expands and cools to form water drops. These can remain liquid to temperatures of –30 ºC but below this temperature start to freeze to ice crystals. Below –40 ºC clouds consist of ice crystals alone.

Four main types :

Latin Root	Translation	Example
cumulus	heap fair	weather cumulus
stratus	layer	altostratus
cirrus	curl of hair	cirrus
nimbus	rain	cumulonimbus

World geographical statistics

Oceans

	Area covered	
	Km2	Miles2
Pacific	166,240,000	64,186,300
Atlantic	86,550,000	33,420,000
Indian	73,427,000	28,350,500
Arctic	9,485,000	3,662,000

The division by the Equator of the Pacific into the North and South Pacific and the Atlantic into the North and South Atlantic makes a total of six oceans.

Loquacious language:

yisse – to desire or covet

Seas

	Area covered	
	Km2	Miles2
South China	2,974,600	1,148,500
Caribbean	2,515,900	971,400
Mediterranean	2,509,900	969,100
Bering	2,261,000	873,000
Gulf of Mexico	1,507,600	582,100
Okhotsk	1,392,000	537,500
Japan	1,012,900	391,100
Hudson Bay	730,100	281,900
East China	664,600	256,600
Andaman	564,880	218,100
Black Sea	507,900	194,100
Red Sea	453,000	174,900
North Sea	427,100	164,900
Baltic Sea	382,000	147,500
Yellow Sea	294,000	113,500
Persian Gulf	230,000	88,800

The continents

There are six geographic continents. However, America is often divided politically into North, Central and South America.

	Area covered	
	Km2	Miles2
Asia	43,998,000	16,988,000
America*	41,918,000	16,185,000
Africa	29,800,000	11,506,000
Antartica	13,209,000	5,100,000
Europe	9,699,000	3,745,000
Australia	7,618,493	2,941,526

North and Central America have a combined area of 24,255,000 km2 (9,365,000 miles2).

Writers' words:

'Poetry is an echo, asking a shadow to dance.' (Carl Sandburg)

Largest islands

	Area covered	
	Km2	Miles2
Greenland	2,175,000	840,000
New Guinea	821,030	317,000
Borneo	725,450	280,100
Madagascar	587,040	226,658
Baffin Island	507,451	195,928
Sumatra	427,350	165,000
Honshu	227,413	87,805
Great Britain*	218,077	84,200
Victoria Island	217,292	83,897
Ellesmere Island	196,236	75.767

Mainland only

Largest deserts

	Area covered (approx)	
	Km2	Miles2
Sahara	8,400,000	3,250,000
Australian	1,550,000	600,000
Arabian	1,200,000	470,000
Gobi	1,040,000	400,000
Kalahari	520,000	200,000
Takla Makan	320,000	125,000

Highest mountains

	Height	
	Metres	Feet
Mt Everest	8,850	29,035
K2 (Chogori)	8,607	28,238
Kangchenjunga	8,597	28,208
Lhotse	8,511	27,923
Makalu I	8,481	27,824
Lhotse Shar (II)	8,383	27,504

Loquacious language:

zabernism – the abuse of military rule or authority

The summits in the other major mountain ranges are:

By range or country

	Height	
	Metres	*Feet*
Pik Pobedy, Tien Shan	7.439	24,406
Cerro Aconcaua, Andes	6,960	22,834
Mt McKinley (S Peak), Alaska	6,194	20,320
Kilmanjaro, Tanzania	5,894	19,340

British Isles (by country)

	Height	
	Metres	*Feet*
Ben Nevis, Scotland	1,344	4,406
Snowdon, Wales	1,085	3,559
Carrantuohill, Rep of Ireland	1,050	3,414
Scafell Pike, England	977	3,210

Writers' words:

'Anyone who has got a book collection/library and a garden wants for nothing.' Cicero

The ancient world

The seven wonders of the world

1. The Pyramids of Egypt

From Gizeh, near Cairo, to a southern limit 96 km (60 miles) distant. The oldest is Zoser, at Saqqara, built c. 2650 BC.

The Great Pyramid of Cheops (built c. 2580 BC) covers 13.12 acres (230.4 x 230.4 m or 756 x 756 ft) at the base and was originally 146.6 m (481 ft) in height.

2. The Hanging Gardens of Babylon

These adjoined Nebuchadnezzar's palace, 96 km (60 miles) south of Baghdad. The terraced gardens, ranging from 25 m to 90 m (75 ft to 300 ft) above ground level, were watered from storage tanks on the highest terrace.

3. The Tomb of Mausolus

Built at Halicarnassus, in Asia Minor, by the widowed Queen Artemisia about 350 BC. The memorial originated the term mausoleum.

4. The Temple of Artemis at Ephesus

Erected around 356 BC as a tribute to the goddess and burned by the Goths in AD 262.

5. The Colossus of Rhodes

Bronze statue of Apollo, set up about 280 BC. Legend has it that it stood at the harbour entrance of the seaport of Rhodes.

6. The Statue of Zeus

Located at Olympia in the plain of Elis, and constructed of marble inlaid with ivory and gold by the sculptor Phidias, about 430 BC.

7. The Pharos of Alexandria

A marble watch tower and lighthouse on the island of Pharos in the harbour of Alexandria, built c. 270 BC.

Loquacious language:

zooerastia – sexual intercourse with an animal

Time measurement

Measurements of time are based on the time taken by:

- the Earth to rotate on its axis (day)
- the Moon to revolve around the Earth (month)
- the Earth to revolve around the Sun from equinox to equinox (year).

The orbits on which these timescales are based are not uniform, so average or mean periods have been adopted for everyday use.

Period	Actual length	Mean length
Day	23 hours, 56 mins, 4 secs	24 hours, each of 60 mins
Month (from New Moon to New Moon)	29 days, 12 hours, 44 mins	varies from 28 to 31 days
Year (tropical)	365 days, 5 hours, 48 mins, 45 secs	365 days (366 in leap year), each of 24 hours.

Etymology:

heard it through the grapevine – this expression, meaning 'heard news via gossip', originates from the American Civil War, when there were no telegraph lines to supply accurate information, the alternative was 'the grapevine telegraph' – literally grapevines.

Religious calendars

Christian

The Roman Catholic and Protestant Churches draw on the Gregorian calendar. The church year starts on the first Sunday in the season of Advent. Its main seasons are:

Advent	preparation for Christmas
Christmas	celebration of the birth of Jesus Christ
Epiphany	celebration of the manifestation of Jesus Christ
Lent	preparation for Easter
Easter	celebration of the death and resurrection of Jesus

The principal feasts and holy days in the Church of England are:

Christmas Day – 25 December

The Epiphany – 6 January

Presentation of Christ in the Temple – 2 February

Ash Wednesday – first day of Lent, 40 days before Easter Day

Annunciation to the Blessed Virgin Mary – 25 March

Maundy Thursday – Thursday before Easter Day

Good Friday – Friday before Easter Day

Ascension Day – 40 days after Easter Day

Pentecost (Whit Sunday) – nine days after Ascension Day

Trinity Sunday – Sunday after Pentecost

All Saints' Day – 1 November

The Eastern Orthodox Churches

Some of the Eastern Orthodox Churches use the Julian calendar and some a modified version of the Julian calendar. The Orthodox church year begins on 1 September. There are four periods of fasting and in addition to Pascha (Easter) 12 great feasts, as well as annual commemorations of the saints of the Old and New Testaments.

Etymology:

to drink a toast – this expression, meaning 'drink in honour of an event or a person', derives from the Middle Ages, when a piece of spiced toast was added to tankards of ale. This apparently improved the taste.

Hindu

The Hindu calendar is a luni-solar calendar of 12 months, each containing 29 days 12 hours. Each month is divided into a light fortnight (Shukla or Shuddha) and a dark fortnight (Krishna or Vadya) based on the waxing and waning of the Moon. A leap month occurs about every 32 lunar months, whenever the difference between the Hindu year of 360 lunar days (354 days 8 hours solar time) and the 365 days 6 hours of the solar year reaches the length of one Hindu lunar month (29 days 12 hours).

The names of the days of the week are derived from the Sanskrit names of the Sun, the Moon and the planets Mars, Mercury, Jupiter, Venus and Saturn: Raviwar, Somawar, Mangalwar, Budhawar, Guruwar, Shukrawar and Shaniwar. The months have Sanskrit names derived from 12 asterisms (constellations): Chaitra, Vaishakh, Jyeshtha, Ashadh, Shravan, Bhadrapha, Ashvin, Kartik, Margashirsh, Paush, Magh and Phalgun.

The major festivals are:

Chaitra – New Year
Dasara* – victory of Rama over the demon army
Diwali* – festival of lights
Durga-puja* – dedicated to the goddess Durga
Ganesh Chaturthi* – worship of Ganesh
Holi* – spring festival
Janmashtami* – birth festival of the god Krishna
Makara Sankranti – winter solstic festival
Navaratri* – nine-night festival dedicated to the goddess Parvati
Raksha-Bandhan* – renewal of kinship bond between brothers
           and sisters
Ramanavami* – birth festival of the god Rama
Sarasvati-puja* – dedicated to the goddess Sarasvati
Shivatatri – dedicated to the god Shiva

*The main festivals celebrated by Hindus in the UK

Loquacious language:

volpome – a devious schemer or miser

Jewish

The Jewish day begins between sunset and nightfall. The time used is that of the meridian of Jerusalem, which is 2 hours 21 minutes in advance of GMT.

A Jewish year is one of six types:

Minimal Common	365 days
Regular Common	354 days
Full Common	355 days
Minimal Leap	383 days
Regular Leap	384 days
Full Leap	385 days

Regular year = alternate months of 30 and 29 days
Full year = the second month has 30 instead of 29 days
Minimal year = the third month has 29 instead of 29 days
Leap year = an additional month of 30 days (Adar I) precedes the month of Adar, which in leap years also has 30 days

The months are:
Tishri (30 days), **Marcheshvan** (29/30), **Kislev** (30/29), **Tebet** (29), **Shebat** (30), **Adar** (29), **Nisan** (30), **Iyar** (29), **Sivan** (30), **Tammuz** (29), **Ab** (30) and **Elul** (29).

The mains festivals are:

Rosh Hashanah – New Year

Fast of Gedaliah

Yom Kippur – Day of Atonement

Succoth – Feast of Tabernacles

Hoshana Rabba

Shimini Atseret – Solemn Assembly

Simchat Torah – Rejoicing of the Law

Chanucah – Dedication of the Temple

Fast of Tebet

Fast of Esther

Purim – Festival of Lots

Shusham Purim

Pesach – Passover

Shavuot – Feast of Weeks

Fast of Tammuz

Fast of Ab

Loquacious language:

volpome – a devious schemer or miser

Muslim

The Muslim calendar is based on a lunar year of about 354 days, consisting of 12 months containing alternate months of 30 and 29 days. A leap day is added at the end of the twelfth month at stated intervals in each cycle of 30 years. The purpose of the leap day is to reconcile the date of the first day of the months with the date of the actual New Moon. In each cycle of 30 years, 19 years are common (354 days) and 11 years are leap (kabisah) years (355 days).

The months are:

Murarram (30 days), **Safar** (29), **Rabi'I** (30), **Rabi'II** (29), **Jumada I** (30), **Jumada II** (29), **Rajab** (30), **Sha'ban** (29), **Ramadan** (30), **Shawwal** (29), **Dhu-l-Qa'ada** (30) and **Dhu-l-Hijjah** (29).

The main festivals are:

Id al-Fitr – marks the end of Ramadan

Id al-Adha – celebrates the submission of the Prophet Ibrahim (Abraham) to God

Asshura – the day Prophet Noah left the Ark; Prophet Moses was saved from Pharoah (Sunni); Death of the Prophet's grandson Husan (Shi'ite)

Mawlid al-Nabi – birthday of the Prophet Muhammad

Laylat al-Isra'

Wa'l- Mi'raj – Night of Journey and Ascension

Laylat al-Qadr – Night of Power

Sikh

The Sikh calendar is a lunar calendar of 365 days divided into 12 months. The length of the months varies between 29 and 32 days.

Loquacious language:

voulu – something contrived or deliberate

Wedding anniversaries

1st	cotton		13th	lace
2nd	paper		14th	ivory
3rd	leather		15th	crystal
4th	fruit and flower		20th	china
5th	wood		25th	silver
6th	sugar or iron		30th	pearl
7th	wool		35th	coral
8th	bronze or electrical appliances		40th	ruby
			45th	sapphire
9th	copper or pottery		50th	gold
10th	tin		55th	emerald
11th	steel		60th	diamond
12th	silk and fine linen		70th	platinum

Birthstones

January	garnet		July	ruby
February	amethyst		August	sardonyx
March	bloodstone		September	sapphire
April	diamond		October	opal
May	emerald		November	topaz
June	pearl		December	turquoise

Signs of the Zodiac

♈	Aries	Mar 21–Apr 19	♎	Libra	Sept 23–Oct 22
♉	Taurus	Apr 20–May 20	♏	Scorpio	Oct 23–Nov 21
♊	Gemini	May 21–Jun 20	♐	Sagittarius	Nov 22–Dec 21
♋	Cancer	Jun 21–Jul 22	♑	Capricorn	Dec 22–Jan 19
♌	Leo	Jul 23–Aug 22	♒	Aquarius	Jan 20–Feb 18
♍	Virgo	Aug 23–Sept 22	♓	Pisces	Feb 19–Mar 20

Loquacious language:

weddinger – a wedding guest

Proofreading symbols

You may find the following proofreading symbols useful when marking up proofs to be corrected by designers or typesetters.

Instruction	Marginal mark	Textual mark
Delete	ℐ/	Strike through the ȼcharacters or words ~~words~~ you want deleting.
Delete and close up the space	⌐	Strike through the chaŗracter charaȼters and put a convex line above and below the deletion mark joining the two letters either side of the error.
Insert text	⋏where	Insert mark⋏text is missing.
Insert full stop	⊙⋏	Mark where full stop should go⋏
Insert comma	⋏ ⋏	Mark⋏of course⋏where commas should go.
Insert colon or semicolon	:⋏ ;⋏	Mark in the position where the punctuation should go⋏do you know where it should go?
Insert superscript text, such as an apostrophe or quotation marks	⋎́	Mark an apostropheˢ position as shown here.
Insert parentheses	(⋏)⋏	Marks⋏in the positions⋏where the parentheses start and finish.
Insert hyphen or en rule	⊢⊣⋏ or ⊢Ⓝ⊣⋏	Marks⋏in the positions⋏where insertion should go.
Leave it as it is	✓ or ⟨stet⟩	Dotted line under ~~characters~~ to remain.
Change to bold	∼∼∼/	Wavy line under word you want emboldened.
Change from bold to normal	∼/∼	Wavy line under or ⟨circle⟩round word to be unemboldened.
Change to italic	└┘	Line under word you want italicised.
Change from italic to upright	└┤┘	Line under or ⟨circle⟩round word you want unitalicised.

Writers' words:

'Times are bad. Children no longer obey their parents, and everyone is writing a book.' Cicero

667

Change to capitals capitals.	=/	triple line under characters to be in ≡
Change to lower case	≠/	Encircle characters to be (SET) in lower case.
Change to small capitals	=/	Double line under characters to be in small capitals.
Close up space	⌒/	Mark to link char⌒acters
Insert space (between words)	⊤/ or ✕/	Vertical line for space between words.
Insert space (between lines)	⊢/	Horizontal mark for space between lines.
Reduce space (between words or lines)	⊤ or ←	Upright mark for ⊤ space between words and horizontal ← space between lines.
Transpose (words, characters or lines)	⎣⌐ or ⊐	Mark under and over characters or words [be to] transposed
Indent	⊏	[Mark to the left side of the text.
Cancel indent	⊐	←[Mark to the left side of the text.
Move to the right	⊏	[Marks on the left and right.]→
Move to the left	⊐	←[Marks on the left and right.]
Take text on to the next line (but not starting a new paragraph)	⊏⊐	Mark surrounds the matter to be taken over. It [also extends in to] the margin.
Take text back to the previous line	⊐⊏	Mark surrounds the matter to be taken back. It also extends in to the [margin.]
New paragraph	⌐⌐	Mark goes after the closing full stop. [The new paragraph starts on the next line.
No new paragraph or new line	~	Mark the text that should [be run on.
Query	(?)	Encircle (text) being queried.

Chiasmus:

'No crime is vulgar, but all vulgarity is crime.' Oscar Wilde

Brains, pen, action!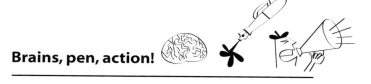

Something to ponder...

Here are some curious facts to get your creative juices flowing.

Ants	It is estimated that there are at least 1,000,000,000,000,000 living ants on earth.
	(There are 40,000 species of invertebrate in Britain.) Also refer to www.buglife.org.uk.
Brainwashing	The term 'brainwashing' was first used during the Korean War by the American journalist Edward Hunter as a translation of the Chinese 'his nao (wash brain).
Cocaine	Sigmund Freud bought his first sample of cocaine on credit for $1.29 a gram.
Divorce	According to ancient Jewish law you can divorce your wife if is she is a bad cook.
Earth	If you could speed up time so that each day contained one million years, every minute would be the equivalent of 695 years and each second 11 years and 7 months.
First words	All the the world's languages are thought by some anthropologists to have evolved from tribes wandering Central Europe twelve thousand years ago.
Gold	A cubic foot of gold weights half a ton.
Hip hip hooray!	
	This was cried by the Crusaders in the Middle Ages. 'Hep' was an acronym for 'Hierosylma est perdita' (Jerusalem has fallen).

Chiasmus:

'It is feeling that sets a man thinking and not thought that sets him feeling.' George Bernard Shaw- From a Fortnightly Review article, Feb., 1894.

continued

Ice	During the nineteenth century, Americans exported ice from ponds to India.
Intergalatic pets	
	The first fish in space was a group of South American guppies that spent forty-eight days on a Russian space station.
Jiffy	This is a length of time equal to one hundred thousand billion billionths of a second.
Kangaroo	Kangaroos are so named because when Captain Cook's crew asked what they were, an Aborigine replied, 'Kangaroo?' (What are you saying?)
Languages	There are fewer than 6,809 'living' languages in the world today.
Marriage	The patron saint of marriage is Sao Goncalo.
Measurement	The kilogram weight against which all the others in the world are measured, is known as 'K'. It is kept inside three glass domes in an underground chamber near Paris, France.
Money	On Manam Island in New Guinea, women wear necklaces made from dogs' teeth. Five teeth are worth around fifteen American cents.
Nudists	Nudists are highly unlikely to be chased by bulls, as the animals regards such undressed people as harmless creatures.

Can you fill in the rest of this A-Z of interesting facts?
Try searching on the Internet or in your trusty old encyclopedia
I'll publish the list as and when, entries come in.

Answers to
answers@gabaywords.com

Metaphors:

The dancing girls brought sunshine with them into the room. Natsume Soseki, *Botchan*

22. Top tips

As we approach the final pages of this book, here are some extra tips to help with your copywriting. They are based on the most common questions that I have been asked over the years. If you want any further tips, don't forget to check www.gabaywords.com where you can also send in your own tips as well as specific questions.

Need more help?
www.gabaywords.com

Top tips for direct mail copy

One of my first jobs in advertising was in direct marketing. There I learnt the classic styles of writing direct mail. These days, consumers are more 'advertising aware' and direct mail has evolved into something which many feel compelled to 'introduce' to their waste bins as soon as it hits the doormat.

So is all lost? Of course not! I believe that direct marketing creativity is stronger than ever. After all, it needs to be, just to escape the fate of the 'dreaded waste bin'!

Here are my recommendations for getting your letters opened, read and acted upon:

- Before you even consider writing one word of your letter, ensure your targeting is correct. Check your list of prospects. (You'll be amazed at how many companies, such as insurance organisations, write to people who are deceased!)

- The Royal Mail suggests that if you really want to ensure that your envelope gets opened you should: handwrite each address (if you have time!); use a real postage stamp; use a thick envelope or a Jiffy bag; never use a clear envelope; and check the recipient's details.

- Next consider the outline of your letter. What do you need to say? What is the proposition? Do you have at least three benefits to support that proposition? What do you want the reader to do in response?

- Bear in mind that people are sceptical – offer a believable message. People are lazy – make it easy to reply. People worry about making the wrong decision – use case histories, offer assurance. People avoid risk – give them a guarantee. Give your readers all they need to make a decision and not a word more. People say 'I didn't ask for this' – send your letter to an interested audience. People ask 'How will I benefit?' – tell them how. If you can, feature testimonials and provide references. People ask 'What's next?' – tell them what to do. People ask 'What If I'm dissatisfied?' – reassure them with your guarantee.

- Now it's time to write your real letter. Whilst many advocate the idea of long copy in letters, I recommend that in most cases you should try and keep your letter to one A4 page comprising: three paragraphs separated by pithy, suggestive, but not too revealing subheads; a proposition (headline); and (for consumer copy) a PS (research suggests that in the UK 60% of consumers read the 'PS' first, followed by the subheads and headline).

- Ensure your proposition addresses your reader's practical as well as emotive needs: 'If my reader only remembers one thing, what will it be?' Consider issues such as your reader's attitude towards the product or service or whether they prefer a technical or lifestyle approach. Then complete the following:

  My aim is to _____ so my reader will _____.

What are the key issues?

The top three points I want my reader to remember are: 1…, 2…, etc. In addition to helping you write your proposition, these three points can help structure the body copy of your letter.

- Remember to break up the copy with subheads (providing they don't 'give away' the entire contents of the paragraph).

- If you are writing to under 1000 people, rather than underline words in Word, use a pen and write it by hand. (The more personal your letter, the better).

- Always aim to include the words 'you', 'you'll' or 'yours' within the first paragraph of the letter.

- Try to make your sentences no longer than twelve words. Use simple words rather than wordy phrases:

- You are requested to…   =   Please…

- We'd like to draw your attention… =   Please see… or Please note…

- As a consequence of…   =   Because…

- Despite the fact that…   =   Though… or Although…

- Is of the opinion…   =   Thinks…

Brand origins:

Kellogg's – the wife of Seventh Day Adventist Church minister Dr John Harvey Kellogg suggested that a diet to aid 'right living' should be based on foods of vegetable and nuts origin. John and his brother William manufactured a toasted flake of maize to replace a heavy breakfast meal (1876). Battle Creek Toasted Corn Flake Company (1906) was founded. To distinguish his brand, William added his signature to each pack.

- Always ask yourself 'what's in this offer for my reader?' Then don't be afraid to sell your benefits, supported by examples, case studies and any other relevant information.

- Remember that your letter starts with the word 'dear' so make it conversational, personal and rewarding.

In conclusion:

- Know your aims.

- Write an outline of your letter before you start.

- Be specific.

- Get to know your reader.

- Talk about them – not you.

- Concentrate on benefits.

- Get to the point and keep it simple.

- Have a strong opening and theme.

- Be specific – not vague.

- Speak in their language/tone of voice.

- Offer believable arguments.

- Use testimonials.

- Offer reassurance.

- Consider a PS.

- Always check your copy.

- Make commonsense out-run objections.

- Don't use the first draft (I suggest three drafts.)

- Ask for action.

- Provide benefits for early response.

- Consider an incentive deadline for your reader.

Writers' words:

'It was a book to kill time for those who like it better dead.' Dame Rose Macaulay

Top tips for viral copy

Many marketers believe that viral marketing is something quite new. In fact it is over 5766 years old! (referring to the original date of creation according to the Old Testament)

The first known example of viral marketing must surely be the Old Testament. The 'Written Law' was given to Moses. However, the 'Aural Law' was passed on as follows: from Moses to Joshua to the Judges and prophets, right through to Jesus' time and beyond.

So why was the 'Aural Law' worthy of spreading? The answer: it's not the medium, which counts, but the message.

As with any direct marketing word-of-mouth campaign, the more beneficial the message is perceived to be to the reader, the better.

Some decades ago, New York City was notorious for rampant crime. Police increased their presence on the streets. Crime went down – but not enough. The use of illicit drugs was growing, confidence in the authorities was shrinking; something had to be done. The solution was to fix the broken windows in run-down tenements. You see, just as everything in life is connected in some way or other to the next, so it was that by having their windows repaired, people started to take pride in their own neighbourhoods. Likewise your viral marketing campaign must connect to the 'soul' of your community, rather than appease its generalised assumed traits.

So how did contemporary viral marketing become so popular? Well, the term was coined by a gentleman called Steve Jervertson, the venture capitalist behind Hotmail™. A few lines of copy at the foot of each Hotmail message changed the world of modern communications: *'Get Your Private, Free Email at http://www.hotmail.com'*. Within 18 months, Hotmail signed up 12 million users while spending just $500,000 on marketing.

Those simple words still echo the fundamental techniques, which ensure that your viral copy works – namely that your message is so beneficial that it is infectious.

Viral copy can be funny, providing that the joke demonstrates that the person sending the virus has a sharp sense of humour and wants to demonstrate that quick wit with others. It can also be serious, providing that it creates the feeling that the sender is going to be perceived as someone who will be respected for passing on the information.

Brand origins:

Kodak, 1888 – George Eastman wanted to simplify photography. Rather than target professionals, he developed a camera for the general public. He wrote, 'I knew a trade name must be short, vigorous, incapable of being misspelled... The letter K had been a favourite with me... It became a question of trying out a great number of combinations of letters that made words starting and ending with K... Kodak was the result.'

In other words, whatever your virus, it must be sufficiently provocative to encourage the person to whom you are sending the virus to feel that spreading the virus even further will enhance their own credibility.

Whatever your virus, unless it is viewed as coming from a source which is highly respected by a targeted community, it won't proliferate. Equally, it has to be embraced by that community to such an extent that the message can no longer be restricted to the community's own circle but must be allowed to break out to an even wider audience.

Your viral campaigns must be useful, clear, appropriately timed and easily accessible. For example, send your email in a 'plain-text' as well as HTML format. If sending multi-media formats, offer a range of choices, including Windows Media Player, Real Player and QuickTime.

In fact, the harder it is to access a virus (often through requesting Internet passwords or asking too many questions before the virus can continue its journey) the less chance it has of being a success.

Points to remember

- Ensure your viral copy, such as a regular 'mail blast' e-letter, is actually worth sending and reading!

- Make instructions easy.

- Craft memorable copy. A good lesson here is to remember how people used to pass on secret messages during World War II. Anytime the familiar 'da-da-da-dumm!' from Beethoven's 5th symphony was played on the BBC World Service, it was a secret prelude to an important message for partisans because of its familiarity and ease of use. This virus didn't just succeed, but in many instances, saved lives.

- There are many reasons why viral copy campaigns fail to take off:

  - The concept is not appropriate to the audience.

  - The campaign was not launched to the kind of audience respected by the next people 'along the line'.

  - The copy is neither fun nor easy to read.

  - Your copy doesn't offer an incentive based on personal prestige for an individual to pass on the virus.

Loquacious language:

word-grubber – someone who uses long and unusual words

- Your concept is too dependant on a topic, which may become passé by the time the virus is actually launched.

- The copy comes across as a company advert. (No one likes to be seen as a corporate envoy.)

In conclusion

- Work out in advance your viral campaign's key objectives.

- Write copy that reflects your audience's tone of voice, rather than your corporate doubletalk.

- Aim at keeping your creative work clear and simple.

- Don't rely on technical gizmos to gain credibility; the message is more important than the medium (providing that the medium is accessible and credible to your target audience).

- Consider whether the viral copy is actually appropriate for your brand or targeted consumer.

- Treat your viral campaign as part of an integrated campaign, rather than being a 'stand-alone' copy exercise.

Top tips for writing press releases

When I worked in Fleet Street, I was taught how to write a press release. To sum up the lessons of all those years in just one sentence I would advise: write the entire story in the first paragraph and any supplemental information in the following paragraphs, providing you try to keep the whole thing down to one side of A4 paper.

So that's it. Well, not quite…

Since those days, editors have become more cynical (if that is actually possible). Companies sending out press releases have become more savvy with their targeting methods and just about everyone wants to believe that one press release will lead to several 15 minutes worth of fame.

With so much at stake, including your reputation as the writer of newsworthy copy, I am going to take you through seven stages of writing the perfect press release:

Brand origins:

El Al, 1948 – created by Israel's first minister of transport David Remez, the name is taken from the Hebrew phrase in Hosea 11:7 – 'Through them to the most high.'

1. The outline

Before you commit your news story to paper, plan it. Write an outline of the key points that you wish to convey, followed by the key points, which you actually have to convey. Agree the outline with the person who has commissioned you. This includes special notes such as where you will find essential information and who will provide any quotations for the body of the copy.

2. The headline

This should be as short as you can make it. The whole essence of the headline is to capture an editor's attention. If you overlook these vital few lines, you may never get anyone to read any further. When appropriate, raise a giggle or a smirk, or even get their blood boiling a bit, with the exception of: hard news, something serious, life-threatening, or of worldly concern.

In terms of fonts, ensure that they are no larger than 16 point and no smaller than 12 point. Some suggest featuring a coloured font in the headline. Personally, I prefer to leave the headlines in good old fashioned black – perhaps emboldened.

3. Subhead or bullets

I like this innovation. It provides highlights of key points that are coming up in the press release. It sort of reminds me of an American TV programme before a commercial break urging the audience not to go away, 'because when we come back…'. (Tacky, I know, but at this stage your job is to keep the readers doing what they do best – reading.)

4. The first paragraph

Now we are back in familiar territory: the good old 'squeeze it all into the first paragraph'. Cram by all means, but don't cramp your style by giving every single important detail away. Be like an angler: throw in the bait, wait and then 'reel-in' the reader. With this analogy in mind, I suggest 'casting out' no more than three sentences for the first paragraph; your aim is to bond with the reader and 'tickle their fancy'.

Brand origins:

Quaker Oats, 1877 – two versions - you choose! A: The founder of an American Milling company wanted a name for his product. He chose Quaker from a dictionary as the religious order shared many qualities of oatmeal – strength, honesty, purity and manliness. B: The founder's partner William Heston, was inspired by a picture of William Penn, an English Quaker.

5. The body

The Institute of Public Relations recommends that the body of a press release should follow this structure:

Subject	This should also include the date of the release and any embargo notices (if applicable).
Organisation	Who you are.
Location	Where the event is taking place or location of a specific item.
Advantages	What are the advantages to the readership?
Applications	How can the readership use whatever it is?
Details	Any supporting evidence.
Source	Who sent the release and where can they be contacted? This should include emails, mobiles and out-of-office contacts.

6. The quotation

Unless the quotation is in itself the news item, be sure to feature at least one quotation from a named person. This could be a 'happy customer' or perhaps your MD. Either way, be sure that the quotation sounds genuine, and ask for permission from the named individuals to place words in their mouths!

7. The test drive

Read your press release aloud. Ask the key people involved if anything can be removed or added. Rewrite what sounds awkward or unclear.

Send any accompanying pictures as a laser-print with details on the back of who or what is in the picture, contact details and websites where hi-resolution JPEGs can be downloaded. Avoid standard pictures of management in boardrooms or – as is the case with marketing personnel – standing near fire-escapes. Instead, pose them at interesting locations, such as outside the Whitehouse.
(This is known as contextual endorsement.)

Writers' words:

'This is not a novel to be tossed aside lightly. It should be thrown with great force.' Dorothy Parker

Top tips for packaging copy

Think of an idea. Now pinpoint the soul of that idea in twenty-five words or less. If you can do that you are on your way to becoming a great packaging writer.

Writing copy for packaging is all about getting to the point in an alluring fashion. Copy on packaging has come a long way from its humble beginnings when all that was required was some kind of description as to what was inside the packet.

Today you have to consider your brand message, any legal requirements, such as wording relating to pharmaceutical products or cigarettes and still allow for details about ingredients, addresses and so on.

Branding on packing

Every brand has its own tone of voice. Aim to pin-point at least five 'action' words which would be used by your brand. For example, for bubble bath: 'luxurious', 'pampering', 'playful', 'delicate' and 'glamorous'.

Don't feel compelled to be literally descriptive with your copy. Allow imagery to also play its role in the communications process. Also consider emotive issues. A growing trend is to allow the emotive message to have an even greater dominance than the brand name itself. For example, you may consider writing headline copy for a family packet of yoghurts as follows:

Hmmm. dreamy, mellow, summer days…
(brand name)

Whichever approach you adopt, remember that if it is an international brand, the copy will have to be understood around the world. I was once involved with a project looking at international packaging copy for toothpaste. The packaging copy was in three languages – English, German and Polish. When sold outside the UK, using the English language translation alongside the Polish or German version encouraged the locals to feel that the product was glamorous.

However, in the UK, placing the non-English version first rather than giving prominence to the English version, often gave locals the impression that the product was mass-produced. (Yet another example of the importance of perceptions and copywriting.)

Legal requirements should be kept to the minimum. After all, space on packaging is at a premium. This said, if long caveats really are needed, simply add them to a small sheet of paper inside the packaging

'Beauty is only sin deep.' Saki (H. H. Munro)

(as with many drugs). Legal restrictions vary according to locality – always check with a legal professional.

Weights, quantities and general measures are also playing an increasingly important role in packaging copy. Around the world, consumers are becoming more and more concerned with what they are consuming and manufacturers are growing more and more concerned with being taken to court for breaking trade description rules. Such concerns can be turned into benefits. If your produce really is fresh – don't just add the word 'fresh' but think of alternatives like:

sparkling, clean, bright, newborn

These all help to shape your brand's character and personality.

Another proven technique is to allow the consumer to see the product using clear plastic packaging. In fact, use the entire package as your canvass of possibilities, remembering to take advantage of new thinking in materials and recycling.

Finally, with your packaging copy fighting for attention against similar products, aim for distinctiveness. Apart from the possible legal repercussions of your product looking and 'reading' the same as a competitor's, following the 'sheep' may leave your goods on the shelf and your bottom-line profits looking fleeced.

So, don't just 'buy me', 'try me', 'feel me', 'hold me', 'have me' – 'you know you want to…'

Top tips for great brochure copy

Writing a brochure is like writing a movie script: it all starts with planning your storyline. Too many copywriters resort to 'cut and pasting' existing copy from other associated brochures into a new brochure or leaflet. (This invariably doesn't work, as the project ends up the equivalent of trying to fit the proverbial 'square peg' into a 'round hole'.)

As with a movie-script, you need a concept to establish who or what you are writing about. This can be summed up in your proposition. The proposition is a combination of your theme, headline and visual.

Etymology:

fly in the ointment – this expression, meaning an imperfect detail which spoils an idealistic situation, comes from Ecclesiastes 10:1 – 'Dead flies make the perfumer's ointment given off an evil odour.'

When writing a short leaflet, consider the merits of featuring an idiom as a headline. (See Idioms, chapter 8).

Following the proposition, draw your reader into the next section: the 'set-up'. This takes the theme from your proposition and, in about a paragraph, introduces the reader to the main text.

The main text is where you provide substance to your proposition. Here you can offer information such as background, mechanics and so on. These usually feature 'bullet-points.'

Whenever showing graphs or product photographs, don't simply write captions which detail what is manifestly in the picture; instead explain implicit benefits of the picture's subject to the reader. Also be careful not to feature pictures which are little more than visual clichés for example:

• people around a boardroom table

• the girl with the headset

• the 'cheesy' shot of mum, dad and the cute little baby.

Aim for originality and relevance rather than 'quick-fix' solutions from photo library suppliers.

Finally, you need some kind of conclusion. Here you summarise the key benefits to your reader and include 'Call-to-Action' information such as website addresses and telephone numbers. (Keep in mind that every feature must have an application of how that feature is used, an advantage of that application and therefore a strong benefit statement for the reader.)

This flow of copy – proposition, set-up, main text and conclusion – can either be manifested across an entire brochure, section by section, or page by page.

To check that your brochure or leaflet is attractive, conduct the 'VIPS' test:

Visibility:	If you placed it amongst a pile of competitive brochures, does it stand out?
Identity:	Is your branding proposition recognisable from the copy style and design 'feel' of the brochure?
Promise:	Are your features clear and beneficial?
Simplicity:	Is the copy focused on one message (which can be supported by many benefits)?

Brand origins:

Kool-Aid – this was originally called Kool-Ade. However, the US Department of Foods forbade the term 'ade' as it meant 'a drink made from...' (which has always bewildered me, as the only thing it could have referred to was 'kool'). The drink's inventor changed the spelling to 'aid', meaning 'help'. (Kool move!)

The case study and product sheet

What about writing case studies or product sheets? My tip is to 'deliver the cream, rather than the entire bottle'. Let me explain: if you wanted to drink a bottle of milk and, in doing so, feel completely nourished, you would opt for a 'full-cream' milk version of the product rather than a skimmed or homogenised version. So it is when writing product summaries or case studies: aim to provide 'the cream' of your proposition, rather than a watered-down version.

Similarly, when it comes to writing case studies, firstly explain the issues that initially drove the project. Next elucidate on the specific needs of the client. The needs should be supported by at least three subheads, each describing a particular aspect that was addressed.

Now comes your solution. Try to keep this down to a paragraph, perhaps supported by some bullet points which highlight some features affecting various people involved with the project. This would be a good stage to add any quotations from named 'happy customers'. (If you can't name the person, at least note their job title.)

The implementation phase explains how you created your solution, including time schedules and any specific unusual aspects of the work with which your company was particularly adept.

Finally, add no more than six bullet points summarising the benefits.

Top tips for poster copy

Writing copy for posters is the purest form of creativity. It has to summarise your product benefits, brand statement, emotive proposition and be eye-catching (but not enough to cause an accident to a passing motorist!).

Posters are a unique copywriting media. Unlike radio or television, no one can turn off a poster. There is no editorial background. In fact in metropolitan areas, posters are an integral part of the community.

When it comes to considering copy for your posters:

- Be unsubtle.
- Don't mess with your logo – and make sure it can be seen.

Medieval words:

carol – an English song derived from a circle or round dance

- Feature dynamic graphics.

- Keep your headline to ten words or less.

- Only write long copy where appropriate (for example a poster appearing at a train station).

- Use the entire medium – including the shape of the poster, position of the poster and materials used in a poster (for example, you can place a poster on the corner of a wall and use the 'bend' to great creative effect).

- If you are writing copy for posters which will appear at trade events, never write more than thirty words of main body copy.

- If a motorist is approaching a poster 75 metres away whilst driving at 40 m.p.h., she has less than four seconds to 'take-in' your message.

- You should aim to make poster copy stimulate people to either rethink a concept, laugh, act or remember an issue.

Follow the tips above and you just may be able to achieve the ultimate accolade in poster writing – a sustained response rather than casual glances.

Top tips for great awareness (above the line) ads

During the first part of the twenty-first century, the West became obsessed with searching for WMDs (Weapons of Mass Destruction). They searched in Iraq, but couldn't find any. They searched in Afghanistan, but found nothing but rocks. If only they would have looked outside their own window: WMDs (Words of Marketing Distraction) are everywhere, especially in awareness advertising copy.

In fact, there are so many WMDs that the real issue is not uncovering them, but ensuring that they are sufficiently distinctive from each other. That's where your great awareness copywriting comes in.

Writing awareness ads is all about explaining your proposition. As I mentioned in other 'top tips', the proposition is your headline as well as

'Everyone has talent. What is rare is the courage to follow the talent to the dark places where it leads.' Erica Jong

your visual approach towards your piece of communication. The best kinds of written propositions are based on the readers' experiences. Of course, you can't possibly know all their experiences, but you can have a good 'shot' at making some presumptions. For example, if you were selling mouthwash, you could address the common need for a mouthwash which offers longer lasting fresh breath or easy-to-dispense packaging.

It's all a matter of balancing your product or service facts against their needs. In this way, you are able to provide the brand partnership, which people are seeking.

Of equal importance are your market's emotions. In my forthcoming book for Elsevier, The Truth About Marketing, I'll tell you more about the fascinating way your brain works when it comes to reading adverts. For now, be aware that when you 'receive' information, you simply cannot help but take your 'gut feelings' about that information into account. So, when it comes to awareness copy, never underestimate the power of the reader's emotive response to your advertisement or the humility of your message.

The most common reason that copy is forgotten is that it is not relevant. Relevance refers to both its practical significance as well as the copy having a sense of intrigue (especially in television copy, where you are battling to draw attention to your commercial).

As with the 'set-up' in writing brochures, the 'lead-in' paragraph of your copy takes up the story of your proposition and encourages your reader to delve deeper by exploring the MBs of your awareness ad. MBs refers to the 'main body' (or as I affectionately call it, the 'middle bits'). Here you offer fuller details, including, where applicable, bullet points.

Finally, wrap the whole thing up with a lead out section that also relates to the awareness statement in your proposition. If there are any 'calls to action' (CTAs) this is the place to include them.

Above all, when writing awareness copy, remember to feature your benefits and not your features. Do so and you'll stand at a distance from your competitors but always side-by-side with your market.

Brand origins:

Esso, 1973 – this name is abbreviation of Standard Oil company of New Jersey, preceded by 'es' from the French for petrol 'essence'.

Top tips for writing reports

I like to think of a report as written conversation. If the document doesn't 'speak' to the readers, nobody will listen.

From the first page, your readers should be encouraged to think 'I must… have it' or '…do it' or '…find out more', but above all, 'this has been worth reading'.

There is a big difference between writing a report and writing a proposal: a report is based on concrete facts and must be unbiased. A proposal should 'propose'; that is to say, it should express opinions as to why a reader should take up an offer or suggestion.

Most marketers write proposals but call them 'reports'. Whichever version you decide to write, the contents should be:

A ccurate

B rief

C ourteous

D ecisive

E nlightening

F actual

G alvanising

H elpful

I nteresting

J udicious (for reports)

K nowledgeable

L evel-headed

M indful

N eutral (for reports)

O rderly

as well as my four 'Ps' to be considered for any kind of proposal

Etymology:

Guinea pig – This term, which means someone who tests something for the first time, 'officially' originated from the South American rodent. It actually came from Guiana, but as a reference to slaves taken from Guinea in West Africa, the name was changed.

1. Position

You should begin any formal proposal with a clear positioning statement. What is your organisation's current position? What is the reader's current position?

This essential part of your proposal should:

- set the scene/topic/theme
- give your view on a subject
- establish your bias
- focus on relevant issues
- enforce your understanding/credibility
- set the tone/agenda.

2. Problem

Here you begin to explain specific problems which have been raised by the 'position' and so need addressing.

Write this section with the aim to:

- validate the 'position' with concrete facts and details
- develop interest
- ensure clarity
- provide the reader with a sense of urgency that something has to be done – but what?

Which leads to my next 'P'…

3. Possibilities

Now show the reader that you are professional enough to have considered the full range of available options. To be thorough, offer the pros and cons of each option.

This section should provide a clear indication of your intentions (you have nothing to hide) and any previews of what is still to come (in terms of detailed information).

You could consider using phrases such as 'timings','dates' and so on. It is important that you discuss all alternatives before narrowing down your suggestion. The trick is to sell, without being overtly 'pushy'.

Guinea pig continued - By the nineteenth century the term 'guinea pig became adopted as British slang for a well to do person who allowed his name to appear as company director (for a fee of course – paid in guineas). By the 20th century guinea pigs were used in scientific experiments.

4. Proposition

At last you reach the crux of the matter. You must be convincing, certain and conclusive.

To do that:

- explain in even greater detail what you specifically propose

- pre-consider answers to obvious questions or objections that may go through the reader's mind

- provide sufficient research to support your proposition

- draw to a suitable conclusion.

The only thing left is a Résumé of Contents (a short document of under six pages may not have a formal index) and detailed appendices (for examples of charts or bibliographies).

Be aware that many people take a sneaky look at the end of a proposal before looking at the beginning. This is why many writers like to include an executive summary at the end (although I still prefer to include one which is no longer than an A4 sheet of paper at the beginning).

In conclusion:

position	→	outline
problem	→	describe
possibilities	→	examine
proposal	→	recommend

Finally, make sure your presentation is packaged professionally. Consider suitable fonts, covers for your document and, of course, layouts. I prefer proposals to be left justified, rather than fully justified. It makes reading easier. Also consider the merits of including a wide left margin. This tends to draw the reader's eye to the body copy.

Metaphors:

She was hunched there tasting the bitterness at the bottom of her life. Ross Macdonald

Top tips for great web copy

Whenever I teach web writing, I am asked if there really is a difference between writing online and offline? Believe me, there is. The big change relates to control. A shrewd web-writer will craft copy to give the impression that the surfer is in control of how much copy is read, when it is read and even how it is read.

It's all to do with what web-writers call, 'chunking'. A 'chunk' is a paragraph of copy which has been crafted to be read quickly without losing any of its intrinsic meaning. Everything you write offline needs to be condensed to half its size for online. In this way you don't have to PDF everything onto a website. (After all, your website is not a 'grave' for lost 'soulless' PDFs!)

Remember these important points:

- Rather than present all of your information in one huge chunk, design it to be read in paragraphs of no longer than 60 words. (That's a big 'chunk'.)

- Be careful not to stifle the heart of your message with too much jargon or what I call 'marketing junk'. Get to the point.

- Observe the etiquette of web-styling. For example, use your homepage to explain the purpose of your site, what kind things can be found there and so on.

- Always ensure that your first paragraph (of fifty words or less) features important words that can be 'scanned' by the reader and 'picked-up by search engines.

- Never pepper your copy with hypertext links leading them offsite. Instead, place all relevant associated and supporting information into a clear sidebar navigational tool.

- Wherever possible, try and keep each subject on one page, rather than split it over two.

- Always use non-patronising and easily understandable language. Remember: your website potentially has a global audience.

- Whenever possible, incorporate testimonials from satisfied customers. If you can, include their personal names, or at least company names or titles.

Metaphors:

Of course you don't change a person's nature. You retouch it. Andre Maurois

- The more complex or involved your information, the more involved a surfer who is interested in the topic will feel and so will want to forage deeper to uncover it. In other words, think of your structure like a pyramid. The pinnacle has 'top line' information and the base has detailed information. Surfers must be allowed to decide for themselves how deeply they wish to surf.

- If you have to archive, use scrolls which are, on average, no wider than 12 words wide. Pay special attention to the first paragraph of your scroll. This should summarise the entire document. If the surfer wishes to find out more, they will scroll down the page.

- Help the surfer find what they are looking for in an archived scroll by including hypertext links within the scroll.

- If you are archiving documents such as press releases, be sure to include the document's title, date and short description of what it is about.

- Don't cut and paste documents between websites or from offline copy to online copy. Eight times out of ten, it will not work.

People are very attached to the web. Kids aged under ten have grown up with the Web and mobile communications. In fact, according to UK Government figures 75 per cent don't even know how to use a traditional phone book – instead they rely on search engines. So you must think in terms of bullet points – supported by strong substantiation messages.

Ensure that your site is 'user-friendly'. This includes considering accessibility for surfers with disabilities, such as the blind. To address this, your site must feature ALT text (text that can be interpreted by web-accessibility software).

Your site should also feature so called meta-tags which help search engines to find your pages and provide a useful description of the content on each page.

Writers' words:

'Deliver me from writers who say the way they live doesn't matter. I'm not sure a bad person can write a good book. If art doesn't make us better, then what on earth is it for?' (Alice Walker)

Top tips for radio ads

Whilst Sinatra got a kick from champagne, I get a 'tingle' from writing copy for radio. Given the right brief, it is so much fun. From an economic point of view, radio is more cost effective than its 'bigger brother' TV. You can target copy geographically. A commercial can be broadcast within hours of production being completed. And, best of all, a listener's mind will always see clearer than their eyes.

It's all about the power of imagination! For example, one great voice-over artist may conjure-up several voices. One brilliant sound effect may take your listener to places that no Hollywood special visual effect could ever hope to reach.

Many writers who have not fully explored radio's potential still believe that the medium is about a 'hard-sell'. In reality it can be far more subtle and convincing.

Once I have understood the benefits of a product or service, I like to eavesdrop on a target audience's conversations. By listening to the nuances of their language, I can often begin to write a commercial that doesn't just sell, but 'tells' a story in a style that the market will really appreciate. Believe me, this is not a case of my trying to boast about my own talents. It's an example to show you that writing for radio is as simple as listening to the everyday sounds of life.

So become a fly-on-the-wall. Write as people speak. For a thirty-second commercial, aim for no more than eighty words – any more and you'll drone on too much. Rather than rely on repeating a message, concentrate on writing a commercial that the listener will want to listen to again.

Be clever with the use of music; royalties can be expensive. Why not write a parody of your favourite tune?

If you are featuring a response mechanism, such as a telephone number, be sure to make it memorable, verging on unforgettable and in some cases, even irritating. (One commercial for a UK insurance company featuring an irritating ex-Hollywood movie director gained so much brand recognition that the company literally became the most successful insurance organisation of its genre in the UK.) Also consider jingles or a comedic technique such as Surrealism (see below).

Metaphors:

Patience is bitter, but its fruit is sweet. French proverb

Whatever response device you use, feature emotive 'action' words to encourage the listener to feel part of the 'audio picture'. Entice the listener to…

- feel something
- think something
- associate with something.

On the subject of memorable audio, turn your brand logo into a sonic brand trigger (SBT). SBTs work in the same way as visual reminders on television. For example, brand recognition can be triggered by a visual, such as the little red telephone used by Direct Line™ Insurance or a mug, as is the case with Nescafé™. Smell also works in the same Pavlovian way, such as fresh baked bread for a café.

SBTs can feature distinctive voices, music, or catchphrases and so on. If your commercial is part of a larger campaign featuring television as well, I recommend that you exploit the power of SBTs by also featuring some of the TV brand recognition sound track.

What about presenting your radio script? Remember the story of Mozart and his client: Mozart presents the score of The Blue Danube to the king, who studies it and says 'this is cool, but you see this note – page 8 – it's got a hole in the middle, shouldn't it be coloured in more?' Lesson: if you're presenting a radio commercial, let your client hear a CD version rather than just read it.

Always allow more time than you think for radio production. I suggest three hours: the first to record and the next two to perfect.

Make 'em laugh

Remain vigilant when writing humour for radio, television or, indeed, any media. There are seven kinds of comedy writing:

- Farce: this is rooted in Shakespearean plays. Farce occurs when you place an un-comical individual or group of people in an absurd situation.

- Irony: drawing on witty dialogue or asides. The best way to use irony is in a statement that sounds as if it was not meant to be ironic.

Brand origins:

Shell, 1897 – Marcus Samuel had an East End curio shop. His children used to stick seashells to empty lunch boxes. Each box was named after a resort. He sold the boxes and even offered customers imported, elaborate shell boxes. His shop was known as the Shell Shop.

- Parody: they say that imitation is the sincerest form of flattery. Its roots are in classic Greek literature. Parody (which should not be confused with pastiche or satire) remains vibrant in all forms of comedy writing. It works best when you 'write-in' small details about the person whom you are parodying.

- Pastiche: whilst parody is the scathing imitation of a genre of subjects, pastiche imitation intends to flatter a subject. The best writing approach is to keep pastiche subtle.

- Satire: what happens when you cross imitation with parody? You get satire. This style is meant to either hurt or correct a situation. Satire is dependant on something topical. So it is short lived.

- Slapstick: the old 'custard pie in the face' routine as as practiced by great comics like Lesley Crowther in BBC's Crackerjack. Slapstick is physical comedy: people walking into walls, each other, and so on. The original past masters of slapstick were Buster Keaton, Harold Lloyd, and Laurel and Hardy. Study any of their movies and you will learn not just about great comedic slapstick, but masterly timing. (Radio slapstick involves sound effects, music and double-entendre.)

- Surrealism: this is a tricky but effective type of comedy writing. You have to capture a situation which does not immediately make any logical sense, and then turn the context of that situation on its head. On radio, you can achieve this through wordplay such as the use of homophones, puns and homonyms.

Finally, in the UK most local radio stations will act on your behalf to get official clearance for broadcasting the commercial. However, if you are not sure, you should contact the Radio Advertising Clearance Centre (RACC) (see Useful contacts, page 694).

Gabay at a glance:

If you wanted to count more than once, twice, thrice, you couldn't - there is no such word.

Shell continued - By 1830 he had nurtured an international business in oriental curios. He eventually found a demand for barrelled kerosene at which stage (1897) the international business became Shell Transport and Trading Co. led by his son.

Useful contacts

UK

*Questions on copywriting to
the author*
answers@gabaywords.com
www.gabaywords.com

Advertising Association
www.adassoc.org.uk

Audit Bureau of Circulation
www.abc.org.uk

Advertising Standards
Authority
www.asa.org.uk

British Market Research
Association
(BMRA)
www.bmra.org.uk

Broadcasters' Audience
Research Board
Tel: (London) 0207 741 9110

Broadcasting Standards
Council
Tel: (London) 0207 233 0544

Broadcast Advertising
Clearance Centre,
www.bacc.com.uk

Radio Advertising
Clearance Centre
www.racc.co.uk

Management Centre Europe
www.mce.be

British Web Design and
Marketing Association
www.bwdma.com

Chartered Institute of
Marketing
www.cim.co.uk

Croner/Hawksmere training
www.hawksmere.co.uk

RACC Radio Copy Helpline
0207 727 2646

Communication, Advertising
and Marketing Foundation
(CAM) Ltd
www.cam.uk.com

Reed Training Ltd
www.reed.co.uk/training

Gabay Ltd
www.gabaynet.com

Grand Union Design
www.grandu.co.uk

Design Council
www.design-council.org.uk

Direct Marketing Association
www.dma.org.uk

Henley Centre
+44 171 878 3186

ICSTIS (The Independent
Committee for the Supervision of
Standards or Telephone
Information Services)
Tel: (0207) 240 5511 (Offers a
free checking service for copy
written for use over premium rate
telephone lines.)
(Complaints about premium rate
telephone lines, call 0800 500 212)
www.icstis.org.uk

Incorporated Society of British
Advertisers
www.isba.org.uk

Independent Television
Commission
www.itc.org.uk

Institute of Directors
www.iod.co.uk

Institute of Direct Marketing
www.theidm.co.uk

The Institute of Packaging
www.info@iop.co.uk

Institute of Practitioners in
Advertising (IPA)
www.ipa.co.uk
Institute of Public Relations
www.ipr.press.net

Institute of Sales Promotion
(ISP and SPCA)
www.isp.org.uk
Mailing Preference Service
www.dma.org.uk

Market Research Society
www.marketresearch.org.uk

The Marketing Society
email info@marketing-
society.org.uk

NABS
www.nabs.org.uk

The Newspaper Society
www.newspapersoc.org.uk

NOP Research Group
Tel (London) 0208 90 9439
email T.lees@nopres.co.uk
Oracle
www.oracle.com

Public Relations Consultants
Association
chris@prca.org.uk

Reed training
www.reed.co.uk/training

*To book Jonathan Gabay
as a public speaker in
Europe :*
email DanRix@aol.com
www.londonspeakerbureau.
co.uk

THE NETHERLANDS
Esomar
www.esomar.nl

AUSTRALIA
Council of Sale Promotional
Agencies
Tel: (203) 325 3911

Public Relations Institute of
Australia (New South Wales)
North Sydney
Tel: (02) 369 2029

Public Relations Institute of
Australia
Tel (02) 369 2029
PRIA (South Australia)
Marden South Australia 5070
Tel: 8 362 1559
PRIA (Victoria)
PO Box 21
Hawthorn Victoria 3122

PRIA (Queensland)
Tel: 7 368 3662
PRIA (Tasmania)
Tel: 0 233 4439

PRIA (Western Australia)
East Perth
Tel: 9 421 7555

Promotion Industry Club (Sales)
Naperville
Tel: (708) 369 3772

Australian Marketing Institute
Melbourne
Tel (03) 820 8788

Australian Association of
National Advertisers
Sydney
Tel: 61 2 9221 8088

Australian Federation of
Advertising,
North Sydney
Tel: (02) 957 3077

The Advertising Institute of
Australia
Adelaide
Fax: (8) 21 21 238

Australian Direct Marketing
Association Ltd,
Sydney
TEL: (02) 247 7744

CANADA

*To book Jonathan Gabay as a
public Speaker in USA or
Canada:*

www.thesweeneyagency.com
www.speakerbooking.com

Canadian Public Relations
Society Inc. (CPRS)
Ottawa Ontario
Tel: 613 232 122

Canadian Direct Marketing
Association,
Toronto, Ontario,
Tel: 416-391-2362

Institute of Canadian
Advertising,
Toronto Ontario
Tel: 416-482-1396

UNITED STATES OF AMERICA

Public Relations Society of
America (PRSA)
New York
Tel: 212 995 2230

Advertising Council Inc.,
New York
Tel: 212 - 922 -1500

American Advertising
Federation,
Washington DC
Tel: 202 - 898 0089

American Marketing
Association,
Chicago,
Tel: 312 - 648 -0536

American Association of
Advertising Agencies,
New York,
Tel: 212 -682 2500

Business Professional
Advertising Association,
Alexandria VA
Tel: 703 -683-2722

Direct Marketing Association,
NY   212 -768 -7277

International Advertising
Association,
New York
Tel: 212 -557-1133

Marketing Research
Association, Connecticut
Tel: 203-257-4008
Point - of - Purchase
Advertising Institute,
Englewood NJ
Tel: 201-894-8899
Public Relations Society of
America,
New York
Tel: 212 - 995-2230

HONG KONG

Public Relations Association of
Hong Kong Limited (PRAHK)
GPO Box 1264
Hong Kong

Further recommended reading:

Teach Yourself Copywriting for
Creative Advertising (Hodder
Headline)
ISBN 0-340-65477-5

Teach Yourself Marketing
(Hodder Headline)
ISBN – 0-340-85946-6

Successful Web Marketing in
a Week
ISBN - 0-340-84964-9

Reinvent Yourself (Pearson)
ISBN – 1 – 843 –04015 -8

Recommended Marketing
Courses:

The Chartered Institute of
Marketing
01628 427 500

Certificate in Advertising and
Marketing (CAM)
01628 427500

Institute of Direct Marketing
0208 9775705

Institute of Sales Promotion
0207 837 5340

Sources and recommended text books

I referred to the following great sources – I recommend
that you do too:

A Dictionary of Modern English Usage – Henry Fowler et al
The Oxford English Dictionary
The Oxford Style Manual – R. M. Ritter
www.askoxford.com
The Cambridge Guide to English Usage – Pam Peters
Teach Yourself Copywriting – J. Jonathan Gabay
Teach Yourself Marketing – J. Jonathan Gabay
Oxford Dictionary of Idioms
New Shell Book of Firsts
–The Internet
Contact the author: jj@gabaywords.com

Index

A

abbreviations 77
  full stops 37
  slashes 51
adjectives 28, 55
  see also nouns
  comparative 29
  compound 29
  hyphenated 46-7
  prefixes, common 137-40
  suffixes 30
adverbs 30, 55
  see also verbs
  prefixes, common 137-40
  and prepositions 31
  suffixes 30
advertising
  awareness 685
  portmanteau words 410
advertising poetry 439-40
air temperatures, records 655
allegories 277
alliteration 61, 576
  slogans 578
allusions 577
ampersands 79
anadiplosis 61
anaphora 62
ancient world, seven
wonders of 660
antimeria 62
antithesis 62
aphorisms
  Gabay's selection of
  business 530-73
  Gabay's selection of
  general 473-528
  uses of 472, 530
apostrophes 44-5
  contractions 42, 86
  history 35
  possessive 43
articles
  definite 26
  indefinite 26
assonance 62
asterisks 50
asyndeton 62

atmosphere
  gaseous components 654
  layers 653
  pollution 654
Auden, WH, *Night Mail*
439-40
awareness advertising
684-5

B

Biblical idioms 230-1
birthstones 666
bold type 52
brackets *see* parentheses
branding, packaging
copy 680
branding positioning,
copy briefs 17
briefs
  see also copy briefs
  full letter 12-13
  research 14
  short letter 13
brochures, copy briefs 18-19
bullet points 50
business terms, US English
172-89

C

calendars
  Christian
    Eastern Orthodox 662
    Roman and
    Protestant 662
  Hindu 663
  Jewish 664
  Muslim 665
  Sikh 665
capital letters 83-4
  headings 53
  proper nouns 53
  sentences 52
car slogans 602-3
Carroll, Lewis (pseudonym of
C.L.Dodgson), portmanteau
words 410, 411
chiasmus 62, 577
Christian festivals 662

clichés
  definitions 258
  Gabay's selection of 261-74
  to be avoided 544
  uses of 259-60
cloud formation 656
collective nouns 26, 424
  Gabay's neologism of
  431-2
  Gabay's selection of 426-30
  verbs and 424-5
colons 35, 40-1
comedy
  farce 692
  irony 692
  parody 693
  pastiche 693
  satire 693
  slapstick 693
  surrealism 693
commas 37, 39-40
  bracketing 37-8
  gapping 39
  joining 39
  listings 38-9
communications slogans
598
comparison 577
conjunctions 32, 55
consonants 22
continents, areas 657
contractions, apostrophes
42, 86
copy briefs 15-16
  brand positioning 17
  brochures 18-19
  leaflets 18-19
  websites 16

D

dangling modifiers 88
dashes
  see also hyphens
  en 45
  history 35
dates
  notable 606-48
  writing 54

deserts, largest 658
diacope 62
dialect
    Lancashire 229
    Liverpool 228-9
    rap 227-8
    Yorkshire 229
diplograms 464
direct mail
    targeting 672
    writing 672-4
double negatives 90
drink slogans 597

E

Earth
    atmosphere
        gaseous components
        654
        layers 653
        pollution 654
    dimensions 652
    layers of 653
earthquakes 655
    Richter scale 655
electronics slogans 598
ellipsis 51, 62
emboldening 52
English vocabulary 58
    changing 66, 68
    'loaned' 67, 67
epanalepsis 62
epimone 63
epistrophe 63
epithets, transferred 577
euphemisms 394-6
    Gabay's selection of
    397-405
exclamation marks 35, 49-50
extended metaphors 276-7

F

facts, curious 669-70
farce 692
fashion slogans 599
fast food slogans 600
finance slogans 599
food slogans 599-600
full stops 37

G

Gabay's selections
    aphorisms 473-528
    business aphorisms 530-73
    clichés 261-74
    collective nouns 426-30
    euphemisms 397-405
    idioms 232-55
    memorable slogans 580-92
    metaphors 277-323
    portmanteau words
    412-21
    proverbs 473-528
    similes 327-91
    slogans 580-92
government slogans 603
grammar, non-standard 68-9
grammatical techniques,
Shakespearean 61-4

H

Hindu festivals 663
household slogans 601
hyperbaton 63
hyperpole 577
hyphens 46
    compound modifiers 46
    history 35

I

idioms
    see also dialect
    Biblical 230-1
    definitions 226
    Gabay's selection of 232-55
    Shakespearean 230
    uses 226-7
inverted commas,
single/double 47-8
irony 692
-ise/-ize suffixes 107
islands, largest 658
IT slogans 598
Italian (Petrarchean) sonnets
435
italics 52

J

Japanese portmanteau
words 409
Jewish festivals 664

L

Lancashire dialect 229
language
    see also dialect; idioms;
    vocabulary
    English, 'loaned' 67, 67
    marketing terminology
    192-223
    US English, UK equivalents
    170-1
leaflets, copy briefs 18-19
listings, commas 38-9
Liverpool dialect 228-9
logos, poster copy 683

M

malapropisms 63
marketing terminology
192-223
metaphors 63, 577
    allegories 277
    definitions 276
    extended 276-7
    Gabay's selection of
    277-323
    mixed 276
metonymy 63
mixed metaphors 276
modifiers, dangling 88
mountains
    highest
        British Isles 659
        by range 659
        world 658
Muslim festivals 665

N

notable dates 606-48
nouns 55
    see also adjectives
    classification 25
    collective 26, 424
        Gabay's neologism of
        430-1

Gabay's selection of
426-30
verbs and 424-5
phrases 33
plural 131-2
prefixes, common 137-40
proper, capitalisation 53
numbers
dates 54
numerals, writing 118
ordinal 53
percentages 54
as prefixes 118
times 54
words/numerals 53, 54
numerals, writing 118

O

oceans, areas 656
onomatopoeia 63, 408
opportunities, zones of 14

P

packaging copy
branding 680
case study 683
cliches in 682
VIPS test 682
writing 681-2
paralepsis 64
parallelism 64
parentheses
history 35
round 48
square 48
parody 693
Pascal words 464
pastiche 693
percentages 54
personal care slogans 601
personification 577
Petrarchean (Italian) sonnets 435
petroleum slogans 603
phrases, common
Shakespearean 60-1
pleonasm 124-5
poetry
see also rhymes
advertising 439-40

history of 434-5
rap 441
sonnets 435-6
Petrarchean 435
Shakespearean 436-7
Spenserian 437
war 438
political slogans 596
pollution, atmospheric 654
polysyndeton 64
portmanteau words 408
in advertising 410
Gabay's selection of
412-21
Japanese 409
Lewis Carroll 410, 411
positioning statements,
report writing 687
possessives
apostrophes 43
determiners 42
double 44
pronouns 42
possibilities, report writing 677
poster copy
graphics in 683-4
logos 683
text 684
prefixes 125
numbers as 118
re- 128-9
prepositions 31, 55
and adverbs 31
press releases
length 677
planning 678
testing 679
text 678-9
problem statements, report
writing 687
products
SOSTAC analysis 14
SWOT analysis 12, 13
pronouns 28, 55
demonstrative 27
interrogative 28
personal 26-7
possessive 42
proofreading symbols 667-8
proper nouns,

capitalisation 53
propositions, report writing 688
proverbs, Gabay's selection 473-528
punctuation
see also punctuation marks
by name
importance of 36-7
mangled 55
medieval 34-5
origins 33
purposes 33
puns 464-5, 576

Q

quadrigrams 464
question marks 48-9
quotation marks 35, 47-8
see also inverted commas
quotations
Gabay's selection
business 530-74
general 473-528
uses of 472, 530

R

radio advertising
clearance 693
comedy in 692-3
construction 691
music 691
sonic brand triggers 692
Radio Advertising Clearance
Centre (RACC) 693
rainfall records 656
rap 441
dialect 227-8, 442
religious festivals
Christian 662
Hindu 663
Jewish 664
Muslim 665
report writing
key factors 686
positioning statements 687
possibilities 677
problem statements 687
propositions 688

research briefs 14
rhymes
-ack 447
-ainge 450
-aint 458
-air 444
-ait 457
-and 450
-ar 443
-ard 448
-arn 452
-arse 455
-ass 455
-at 456
-ay 443-4
-d 450
-eck 448
-eech 448
-eed 449
-een 452
-eer 444
-eest 459
-ell 450
-ent 458
-er 447
-err 444
-ick 448
-id 449
-ie 445
-in 452
-ine 453
-ing 454
-iss 455
-ist 459
-it 457
-ix 459
-'l 451
-'m 451
-'n 453-4
-nce 456
-'nt 458
-od 449
-oe 445-6
-oo 446
-oor 445
-ope 454-5
-owl 451
-'s 456
-y 446
difficult 443
slogans 442, 578

Richter scale, earthquakes
646, 655

S

satire 693
seas, areas 657
semicolons 41
sentences
    basic construction 32-3, 33
    capitalisation 52
services
    SOSTAC analysis 14
    SWOT analysis 12, 13
seven wonders of the world
(ancient) 660
Shakespeare, William
    common phrases 60-1
    grammatical techniques
    61-4
    idioms 230
    sonnets 436-7
    use of English 58
    words accredited to 59
Sidney, Sir Philip 435
signs of the zodiac 666
similes 64, 326, 577
    Gabay's selection of
    327-91
slapstick 693
slashes 51
slogans
    action and 578
    alliteration 578
    brands
        cars 602-3
        communications 598
        drinks 597
        electronics 598
        fashion 599
        fast food 600
        finance 599
        food 599-600
        government 603
        household 601
        IT 598
        personal care 601
        petroleum 603
        tobacco 602
        transport 602
        travel 601
    directed 578

effective words 579
Gabay's selection of
memorable 580-92
ideals 578
impact of 576
the 'it' word 579
packaged 578
personal 578
political 596
promises and 578
purposes of 576
repetition in 578
rhymes 442, 578
song titles 593-6
utopias 578
writing 603
song titles, slogans from
593-6
sonic brand triggers (SBT)
692
sonnets 435
    octave 436
    Petrarchean (Italian) 435
    Shakespearean 436-7
    Spenserian 437
SOSTAC analysis 14
speech marks see inverted
commas
spelling
    problem words 159-65
    sources 155
    UK English, and US English
    155-6
    US English 155
Spenser, Edmund, sonnets
437
split infinitives 135
Spoonerisms 463
suffixes 77, 136, 141
    adjectival 30
    adverbial 30
    common 137-40
    doubled letters 90
    -ise/-ize 107
    plural nouns 131-2
    US versions 90, 107
surrealism 693
SWOT analysis 12, 13
synecdoche 64

T

tautology 124-5
time measurement 661
times, writing 54
tobacco slogans 602
tongue twisters 462
  see also Spoonerisms
  b, p, m, wh sounds 465-6
  ch, ge, sh, zh sounds 468-9
  f, v, s sounds 467-8
  h sounds 469
  k, g, ng sounds 466-7
  slogans 462
  t, d, l, n, r, s, z sounds 466
  th sounds 467
transferred epithets 577
transport slogans 602
travel slogans 601
triplograms 464

U

underlining 52
  history 35
US English
  business terms 172-89
  development of 168-9
  language, UK equivalents
  170-1
  spelling 155, 157-8
  suffixes
    doubled letters 90
    -ise/-ize 107
  and UK spelling 157-8

V

verbs 22, 55
  see also adverbs
  and collective nouns
  424-5
  future tenses 24-5
  intransitive 23
  irregular 25
  past
    participles 23
    tenses 24, 91
  phrases 33
  prefixes, common
  137-40
  present
    participles 23
    tenses 24
  singular/plural 26
  split infinitives 135
  transitive 23
VIPS test, packaging copy
682
viral marketing
  effectiveness 675, 676
  failure 676-7
  formats 676
  humour in 675-6
vocabulary
  active 65
  changing 66, 68
  common-use 70-3
  English 58
  formal 65
  informal 65

  marketing terminology
  192-223
  new 66
  passive 65
  slang 66
vowels 22

W

war poetry 438
weather records
  air temperatures 655
  rainfall 656
wind speeds 656
web writing 689-90
websites, copy briefs 16
wedding anniversaries 666
wind speed records 656
words
  accredited to Shakespeare
  59
  common-use 70-3

Y

Yorkshire dialect 229

Z

zodiac, signs of the 666
zones of opportunity 14